SO-AAC-139

WHITE MOUNTAIN GUIDE

30TH EDITION

**AMC'S COMPREHENSIVE GUIDE TO HIKING TRAILS
IN THE WHITE MOUNTAIN NATIONAL FOREST**

Compiled and edited by
Steven D. Smith

Appalachian Mountain Club Books
Boston, Massachusetts

AMC is a nonprofit organization, and sales of AMC Books fund our mission of protecting the Northeast outdoors. If you appreciate our efforts and would like to become a member or make a donation to AMC, visit outdoors.org, call 800-372-1758, or contact us at Appalachian Mountain Club, 10 City Square, Boston, MA 02129.

outdoors.org/publications/books

Copyright © 2017 Appalachian Mountain Club. All rights reserved.

Distributed by National Book Network

Front cover photo of Mount Monroe © Paul Marinace/AMC Photo Contest
Back cover photo of Mount Crawford © Margaret Tomas/AMC Photo Contest
Cartography by Larry Garland © Appalachian Mountain Club
Cover design by Kim Thornton
Interior design by Abigail Coyle

Published by the Appalachian Mountain Club. No part of this publication may be reproduced or transmitted in any form or by any means, electronic or mechanical, including photocopying and recording, or by any information storage or retrieval system, except as may be expressly permitted by the 1976 Copyright Act or in writing from the publisher.

ISBN 978-1-934028-85-8

ISSN 2573-377X

The paper used in this publication meets the minimum requirements of the American National Standard for Information Sciences-Permanence of Paper for Printed Library Materials, ANSI Z39.48-1984. ∞

Outdoor recreation activities by their very nature are potentially hazardous. This book is not a substitute for good personal judgment and training in outdoor skills. Due to changes in conditions, use of the information in this book is at the sole risk of the user. The author and the Appalachian Mountain Club assume no liability for accidents happening to, or injuries sustained by, readers who engage in the activities described in this book.

Interior pages and cover are printed on responsibly
harvested paper stock certified by The Forest
Stewardship Council®, an independent auditor
of responsible forestry practices.
Printed in the United States of America,
using vegetable-based inks.
6 5 4 3 2 1   17 18 19 20 21 22

MIX
Paper from
responsible sources
FSC® C005010
www.fsc.org

EDITIONS OF THE WHITE MOUNTAIN GUIDE

First Edition	1907	Sixteenth Edition	1960
Second Edition	1916	Seventeenth Edition	1963
Third Edition	1917	Eighteenth Edition	1966
Fourth Edition	1920	Nineteenth Edition	1969
Fifth Edition	1922	Twentieth Edition	1972
Sixth Edition	1925	Twenty-First Edition	1976
Seventh Edition	1928	Twenty-Second Edition	1979
Eighth Edition	1931	Twenty-Third Edition	1983
Ninth Edition	1934	Twenty-Fourth Edition	1987
Tenth Edition	1936	Twenty-Fifth Edition	1992
Eleventh Edition	1940	Twenty-Sixth Edition	1998
Twelfth Edition	1946	Twenty-Seventh Edition	2003
Thirteenth Edition	1948	Twenty-Eighth Edition	2007
Fourteenth Edition	1952	Twenty-Ninth Edition	2012
Fifteenth Edition	1955	Thirtieth Edition	2017

KEY TO LOCATOR MAPS

The numbers in the boxes below and on the locator maps at the beginning of each section indicate which map or maps cover that section. Trail descriptions are sorted into sections according to where the trailhead is located; parts of a trail may lie in another section or sections.

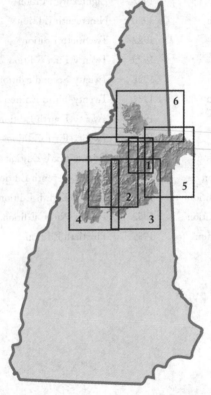

Map 1: Presidential Range

Map 2: Franconia–Pemigewasset

Map 3: Crawford Notch–Sandwich Range

Map 4: Moosilauke–Kinsman Ridge

Map 5: Carter Range–Evans Notch

Map 6: North Country–Mahoosuc Range

CONTENTS

ACKNOWLEDGMENTS

White Mountain Guide is the product of the efforts of many people. The current editor would first like to thank his wife, Carol Smith. Without her encouragement and support, as well as her companionship on many hikes, I would never have been able to give this book the time and energy it deserved. Therefore, I dedicate this edition to her, with love and gratitude.

I want to thank the dedicated staff of AMC Books, including Kevin Breunig, the former vice president of communications; Abigail Coyle, production manager; Shannon Smith, books editor; and Jennifer Wehunt, editorial director. Much gratitude is owed to AMC's cartographer, Larry Garland, whose trail maps are justly renowned for their clarity, accuracy, and ease of use. Larry and I frequently compared notes during the development of the 30th edition.

Many people from trail-maintaining agencies, organizations, and clubs provided invaluable information and advice. These included Dylan Alden, Cristin Bailey, Jenny Burnett, Tom Giles, Helon Hoffer, Brian Johnston, John Marunowski, and Justin Priesendorfer from the White Mountain National Forest; Alex DeLucia, Andrew Norkin, and Zack Urgese from the Appalachian Mountain Club; Judy Hudson and Randy Meiklejohn from the Randolph Mountain Club; Doug McVicar, Peter Smart, and Jack Waldron from the Wonalancet Out Door Club; Dan Newton from the Waterville Valley Athletic & Improvement Association; Brett Durham from the Squam Lakes Association; Kate Lanou, Howard Matthews, and Ken Smith from the Chocorua Mountain Club; Don Devine, Marvin Swartz, and Mike Zlogar from the Chatham Trails Association; John Oliver from the Lakes Region Conservation Trust; Sam Brakeley, Rory Gawler, and Sam Kernan from the Dartmouth Outing Club; Jason Berard from the Upper Valley Land Trust; Kim Nilsen and Ken Vallery from The Cohos Trail Association; Larry Ely and Dick Lussier from the Shelburne Trails Club; Dave Govatski from the Friends of Pondicherry; Andrew Zboray from the N.H. Division of Parks and Recreation; and John Dickerman from Crawford Notch State Park.

Many individual hikers provided comments, updates, and suggestions for the 30th edition. I would especially like to recognize the many contributions made by Dr. Peter Crane, Joanne and Kevin Jones, and Mike O'Brien. I also thank Steve Bailey, Summerset Banks, Bob Bulkeley, Jonathan Burroughs, Crawford Campbell, Mike Cherim, Jeremy Clark, Bruce Collins, John

Compton, Keith D'Alessandro, Thom Davis, Atha Demopoulos, Dennis Dixon, Erin Paul Donovan, Evan Dority, Roger Doucette, Ben English, Jr., Georg Feichtinger, Paul Gaitanis, Chris Garby, Cath Goodwin, Jason Greenberg, John Gutowski, Sue Johnston, Paul King, Michelle Kingsbury, Bob Kittredge, Mark and Marilyn Klim, Allen Koop, Ken MacGray, Raymond Merkh, Judy Michaels, Brian Milburn, Scott Monroe, Linda Moore, Steve Moore, Tim Muskat, Amy Patenaude, Jeff Perkins, Eric Rathbun, Bill Robichaud, June Rogier, Tom Ryan, Eric Savage, Dr. Carl Schildkraut, John Sobetzer, Ken and Ann Stampfer, Jim St. Cyr, J.R. Stockwell, Cathy Tarr, Gary Tompkins, Mark Tuckerman, Philip Werner, Lyn Whiston, and Bill White. The website newenglandtrailconditions.com provided much valuable information.

The current editor of the *White Mountain Guide* feels connected to a long and cherished tradition handed down by a century's worth of editors and committee members. There are far too many names to list here—for a comprehensive history of the guidebook, see *White Mountain Guide: A Centennial Retrospective,* published by AMC Books—but I would like to acknowledge a few individuals whose contributions were especially noteworthy. These include Harland Perkins, who guided the book through its first three editions; Ralph Larrabee, whose meticulous editing graced the fourth through ninth editions; Howard M. Goff, guidebook committee chairman for the 11th through 21st editions, covering a period of more than 35 years; Eugene S. Daniell III, editor or co-editor for the 23rd through 28th editions, a quarter-century of service; Jonathan Burroughs, co-editor for the 25th and 26th editions, who wheeled all the trails in the guide and—together with Eugene S. Daniell III and Vera Smith (also co-editor for the 23rd edition)—made many improvements and transitioned the guidebook's editing format from its former committee structure to its current stewardship under a single editor or two co-editors; and Mike Dickerman, co-editor for the 29th edition. It was an honor to work with Gene on the 27th and 28th editions and with Mike on the 29th edition. Louis Cutter, whose maps graced the book for many decades, deserves special mention, as well as Larry Garland, who has ushered AMC's mapmaking into a new era. Since its beginning in 1907, this beloved and trusted guidebook has been a truly collaborative effort, and the current editor is only building upon the outstanding body of work established by the many who have come before him.

Any errors of commission or omission are the sole responsibility of the editor.

HOW TO USE THIS BOOK

This book aims to provide complete coverage of hiking trails located in the White Mountain National Forest (WMNF) in New Hampshire and Maine. A number of trails outside the boundary of the forest—both in the Lakes region to the south and in northern New Hampshire and adjacent parts of Maine—have also been included in this work. For other regions in Maine, consult AMC's *Maine Mountain Guide*. *White Mountain Guide* also covers the Appalachian Trail (AT) and its side trails from the New Hampshire–Vermont boundary at the Connecticut River to Grafton Notch in Maine, just east of the Maine–New Hampshire boundary. New Hampshire's Route 25 (NH 25)—the highway that runs west to east across the state and separates the White Mountain region from the Lakes region and the Dartmouth–Sunapee region—is the southern boundary of the areas covered in the *White Mountain Guide;* however, the Middle Connecticut River region, which the AT crosses between Hanover and Glencliff, is included in this book to provide complete coverage of the section of the AT that runs through New Hampshire. Hikers interested in the area south of NH 25, including the Monadnock and Sunapee regions, should consult AMC's *Southern New Hampshire Trail Guide.*

For convenience of use, the trails are divided into twelve geographic regions. More than 500 trails are covered, totaling more than 1,400 mi. They range from easy waterfall strolls to strenuous ridge traverses, with many options available for every level of hiker. It is our hope that the user of this book will safely enjoy many days of outdoor pleasure and healthful exercise in the beautiful White Mountains.

TRAIL DESCRIPTIONS

Each trail in this book is described individually, usually in the ascending direction. Two pieces of information are included in the parenthetical following each trail name: the acronym of the organization responsible for maintaining that trail and a reference to the map or maps that correspond to the trail. A typical trail description first provides an overview of the trail, including its origin, destination, and, if notable, its general character (gradient, roughness, etc.). Trailhead driving directions are then given, where appropriate, followed by concise directions for following the trail. The description notes important features, such as trail junctions, stream crossings, viewpoints, and any significant difficulties.

In cases where a hike uses a combination of trails, the hiker will need to refer to several trail descriptions, in combination with the appropriate trail map. For example, if one wanted to climb Mt. Tom (a relatively easy 4,000-ft. mountain with partial views) from AMC's Macomber Family Information Center in Crawford Notch, the hiker would read and follow trail descriptions first for Avalon Trail, then A–Z Trail, and finally Mt. Tom Spur.

SUGGESTED HIKES

At the beginning of each section is a list of suggested hikes designed to supply readers with a number of options for easy, moderate, and strenuous hikes within a region. A short (easy) hike can be completed in about 2 hr. or less by an average hiker, a moderate hike in 3 to 4 hr., and a longer (strenuous) hike in 6 to 8 hr. The icons refer to features of note (see Key to Icons on p. xxxvi), and the numbers in the table underneath the icons indicate distance, elevation gain, and estimated time, calculated by the formula of 30 min. for each mile of distance or 1,000 ft. of elevation gain. The time allowances are merely a rough estimate; many parties will require more time and many will require less. The estimates do not include time for extensive stops for scenery appreciation or rest.

When choosing a hike, readers should consider distance, elevation gain, time required, and special factors, such as brook crossings or rough footing. A 6-mi. hike on easy terrain will require considerably less effort, though perhaps more time, than a 3-mi. hike over rocky trails with 1,500 ft. of elevation gain. A hike should be tailored to the amount of time and daylight available and to the experience, fitness, and ambition of the group. Larger groups will generally move at a slower pace.

DISTANCES, TIMES, AND ELEVATION GAINS

The distances, times, and elevation gains that appear in the tables above trail descriptions are cumulative from the starting point listed at the head of each table. Nearly all of the trails fully described in this book have been measured with a surveyor's wheel and in a few cases with GPS. Minor inconsistencies sometimes occur when measured distances are rounded, and the distances given often differ from those on trail signs. Elevation gains are given for the reverse direction only when these gains are 50 ft. or more; these gains are not cumulative and apply only to the interval between the current entry and the previous one. Reverse elevation gains are not given for trails that have summaries in both directions.

The following example shows users how to read the tables at the beginning of trail descriptions.

BOOT SPUR LINK (AMC; MAP 1: F9)			
From Tuckerman Ravine Trail (3,875 ft. [*elevation*]) to:	↕	↗	⟳
Boott Spur Trail (4,650 ft.)	0.6 mi.	850 ft. (rev. 50 ft.)	0:45
elevation	*distance*	*elevation gain (reverse elevation gain)*	*time*

Elevation gains are estimated and rounded to the nearest 50 ft.; in some places, such as where several minor ups and downs are traversed, they are only roughly accurate. The U.S. Geological Survey (USGS) maps are used as the basis for all such information, except for the area covered by Bradford Washburn's map of the Presidential Range, where that map supersedes the USGS maps.

There is no reliable method for predicting how much time a hiker or group of hikers will take to complete a particular hike on a particular day. The factors that influence the speed of an individual hiker or hiking group are simply too numerous and too complex. Most hikers will observe that individual speed varies from day to day, often by a significant amount, depending on a number of factors, many of which—such as fatigue, weight of pack, and weather conditions—are fairly easy to identify. Also, a given segment of trail will usually require more time at the end of a strenuous day compared with what it might have required if encountered at the start of the day.

To give hikers a rough basis for planning, however, estimated times have been calculated for this book by allowing 30 min. for each mile of distance or 1,000 ft. of climbing. These are known as "book times." No attempt has been made to adjust these times for the difficulties of specific trails. These times may be inadequate for steep or rough trails, for hikers with heavy packs, or for large groups, particularly those including inexperienced hikers.

Average descent times vary even more; agility and the condition of the hiker's knees are the principal factors. Times for descending are given in this book only for segments of ridge crest trails that have substantial descents in both directions. In winter, times are even less predictable: On a packed trail, travel may be faster than in summer, but with heavy packs or in deep snow it may take two or three times the summer estimate.

MAPS AND NAVIGATION

Hikers should always carry a map and compass and, if desired, a Global Positioning System (GPS) unit, and carefully keep track of their approximate location on the map. The six maps included with this guide are topographic maps (maps with the shape of the terrain represented by contour lines). Every mile of trail on these maps was hiked and electronically recorded with GPS technology. The resulting maps accurately depict trail locations. They provide complete coverage of the WMNF, with a contour interval of 100 ft. These maps (except map 1, Presidential Range) are designed at the same size and scale, allowing the user to easily read from one map to the next. Latitude and longitude and Universal Transverse Mercator (UTM) grid coordinates are included on the map sheets to facilitate the use of GPS units in the field. Waterproof Tyvek versions of these maps can be purchased through AMC's website (outdoors.org/amcstore), bookstores, many outdoor equipment stores, and AMC's information centers in Boston, Pinkham Notch, and Crawford Notch.

Maps with more topographic detail are available from the USGS for all of New Hampshire and Maine. These maps are published in rectangles of several standard sizes called quadrangles ("quads"). All areas in the regions covered in this guidebook are covered by detailed 7.5-min. quads, some of which are in metric format. Although topography on these maps is excellent (with 40- or 20-ft. contours), the locations of some trails are shown inaccurately, and many other trails are not shown at all. These maps can be obtained at a number of local outlets and from the USGS (888-ASK-USGS; usgs.gov). Index maps showing the available USGS quads in any state and an informative pamphlet titled Topographic Maps are available free upon request from the USGS. The USGS quads for all of New England are also available through a number of online sources. The WMNF is also covered by two National Geographic Trails Illustrated maps: WMNF West Half (#740) and WMNF East Half (#741), which were produced in partnership with AMC.

A baseplate compass (a circular, liquid-filled compass that turns on a rectangular base made of clear plastic) is well suited for use by hikers. Set such a compass to the bearing you want to follow, and then it is a simple matter of keeping the compass needle aligned to north and following the arrow on the base. Compass directions given in the text are based on true north instead of magnetic north, unless otherwise specified. There is a deviation (usually called declination) of 15 degrees to 16 degrees between true north and magnetic north in the White Mountains. This means true north will be about 16 degrees to the right of (clockwise from) the compass's north needle. If you take a bearing from a map, you should add 16 degrees to the bearing when you set your compass. On the maps included with this guide, the black lines that run from bottom to top are aligned with true north and south. For more instruction on how to use a compass and how to orient a compass to a map, refer to *AMC's Mountain Skills Manual* (AMC Books, 2017), available at outdoors.org/amcstore.

GPS units have become increasingly popular with hikers. These can be loaded with various versions of topographic maps. When used in conjunction with a printed map and a compass, a GPS unit can be a very useful tool in the woods, but it is not a satisfactory substitute for a map and a compass. GPS reception can be poor in deep valleys and under heavy foliage, and units may be subject to damage or battery failure. If you are going to use a GPS unit, we recommend preparing a list of coordinates for a number of useful landmarks before leaving for the trail and bringing a set of extra batteries. It is important to practice with a GPS unit to become familiar with its features before setting off on a trip.

INTRODUCTION

USE OF THE WHITE MOUNTAIN NATIONAL FOREST

Most of the higher peaks of the White Mountains are within the White Mountain National Forest (WMNF), which was authorized under the Weeks Act (1911) and now comprises about 796,000 acres, of which about 47,000 are in Maine and the rest in New Hampshire. This is not a national park, but, rather, a national forest; parks are established primarily for preservation and recreation, whereas national forests are managed for multiple uses. In the administration of national forests, the following objectives are considered: recreation management, timber production, watershed protection, and wildlife habitat management. About 45 percent of the WMNF is open to timber harvesting on a carefully controlled basis. The boundaries of the WMNF are usually marked wherever they cross roads or trails, typically by red-painted corner posts and blazes. Hunting and fishing are permitted in the WMNF under state laws; state licenses are required. Organized groups, including those sponsored by nonprofit organizations, must apply for an outfitter-guide permit if they conduct trips on WMNF land for which they charge a fee; contact any WMNF office for details. Much information has been published by the WMNF and is available free of charge at the forest supervisor's office in Campton, New Hampshire; at ranger district offices; and at other information centers.

Camping is restricted in many areas under the Forest Protection Area (FPA) program to protect vulnerable areas from damage. To preserve the rare alpine plants of the Presidential Range and other significant ecosystems within the entire WMNF, rules prohibit the removal of any tree, shrub, or plant without written permission. Federal law also protects cultural sites and artifacts (such as those found at old logging camp sites) on public lands. If you discover such remains, please leave them undisturbed; it is illegal to remove them from the WMNF.

Pets are allowed on WMNF trails; however, be sure to control your pet so it won't be a nuisance to other hikers and to clean up after your pet along the trail.

The Appalachian Mountain Club (AMC) earnestly requests that those who use trails, shelters, and campsites heed the rules (especially those having to do with camping) of the WMNF and the New Hampshire Department of Resources and Economic Development Division of Parks and Recreation (NHDP). New trails may not be cut in the WMNF without the approval of the forest supervisor or elsewhere without the consent of the landowners and definite formal provision for maintenance.

Some trails in this guide cross private land, and the same consideration and respect should be shown to private landowners; trails can be closed forever if a landowner objects to the way the public treats the land.

WILDERNESS AND SCENIC AREAS IN THE WMNF

The National Wilderness Preservation System, which included the Great Gulf Wilderness, was established in 1964 with passage of the Wilderness Act. Since then, the Presidential Range–Dry River, Pemigewasset, Sandwich Range, Caribou–Speckled Mtn., and Wild River Wilderness areas in the WMNF have been added to the system, bringing the WMNF's total Wilderness base to 149,500 acres, which is almost 19 percent of WMNF's total acreage. Regulations for these areas prohibit logging and road building, as well as the use of motorized equipment or mechanical transport, including bicycles. New Wilderness Areas are established by acts of Congress, with USFS recommendations providing critical input.

Management of these areas, in accordance with guidelines contained in the Wilderness Act, is entrusted to the USFS. Most important is the protection of the natural environment, but the USFS is also charged with preserving the opportunity for visitors to enjoy "solitude and challenge." For example, "structures for user convenience," such as shelters, are not permitted in Wilderness Areas. In general, visitors to Wilderness Areas should look forward to a rougher, wilder, more primitive experience than in other parts of the WMNF and should expect USFS regulations to emphasize the preservation of Wilderness qualities, even at substantial inconvenience to hikers. As a consequence, there are no mileages on signs and few, if any, blazes; "easy-over, easy-under" blown-down trees, or blowdowns, may be intentionally left in place to add to the wild character of the trail. Hiking and camping group size is limited to ten people in Wilderness Areas; specific camping and fire regulations vary by area. Wilderness regulations also prohibit storing equipment, personal property, or supplies, including geocaching and letter boxing.

The USFS has also established nine Scenic Areas in the WMNF to preserve lands of outstanding or unique natural beauty: Gibbs Brook, Greeley Ponds, Pinkham Notch, Lafayette Brook, Rocky Gorge, Lincoln Woods, Sawyer Pond, Mt. Chocorua, and Snyder Brook. Additionally, three Research Natural Areas—the Alpine Garden, the Bowl, and Nancy Brook—have been established as areas where "natural processes will predominate" and recreation use will be incidental.

PARKING FEES AND HIKER SHUTTLE

When parking at established WMNF trailhead parking sites with a posted fee sign, hikers must display a parking pass on their windshield or dashboard. Annual parking passes are available at WMNF ranger offices, information centers, and outdoor retail stores, as well as at AMC's information centers in Boston, Pinkham Notch, and Crawford Notch. Visit the WMNF website (www.fs.usda.gov/whitemountain) for details. Daily parking passes are available at some trailheads. Almost all of the proceeds from all passes go toward improvements to the WMNF.

Throughout the summer and on fall weekends, AMC offers a hiker shuttle service between Pinkham Notch Visitor Center, the Highland Center at Crawford Notch, and several major trailheads, including those serving popular routes to the AMC huts. (The shuttle route extends into Lincoln, New Hampshire, to connect with bus service from Boston.) For trips beginning and ending at different trailheads, many hikers leave their cars at the final trailhead and take the shuttle to their starting trailhead. Reservations are strongly recommended, and a fee is charged. For information, contact AMC's reservations office (603-466-2727) or visit AMC's website (outdoors.org/shuttle).

APPALACHIAN TRAIL

With the passage of the National Trails System Act by Congress on October 2, 1968, the AT became the first federally protected footpath in the country and was officially designated the Appalachian National Scenic Trail. Under this act, the AT is administered primarily as a footpath by the Department of the Interior in consultation with the Department of Agriculture and representatives of the states through which the AT passes.

The footpath runs more than 2,000 mi., from Springer Mtn. in Georgia to Katahdin in Maine. It traverses the White Mountains for about 175 mi. in a southwest to northeast direction, from Hanover, New Hampshire, on the New Hampshire–Vermont border in the Connecticut River Valley, to Grafton Notch, a short distance into Maine from the Maine–New Hampshire border. The AT's route traverses many of the major peaks and ranges of the White Mountains.

The trails that make up the AT in the White Mountains are all described in this book. In each section of this guide through which the AT passes, its route is described in a separate paragraph in the section introduction.

CLIMATE AND VEGETATION

The climate gets much cooler, windier, and wetter at higher elevations. For every 1,000-ft. rise in elevation, the average temperature decreases by about 3 degrees Fahrenheit, and the average annual precipitation increases by about 8 in. The summit of Mt. Washington is under cloud cover about 55 percent of the time. On an average summer afternoon, the high temperature on the summit is only about 52 degrees Fahrenheit; in winter, it's about 15 degrees Fahrenheit. The record-low temperature is −47 degrees Fahrenheit.

Average summit winds throughout the day and night are 26 MPH in summer and 44 MPH in winter. Winds have gusted to more than 100 MPH in every month of the year, setting a world record of 231 MPH on April 12, 1934. This record was surpassed by Typhoon Olivia in Barrow Island, Australia, where an unnamed instrument recorded wind speeds of 253 MPH in 1996. The 1934 record on Mt. Washington remains the highest recorded surface wind speed ever witnessed by humans. During the storm of February 24–26, 1969, the Mt. Washington Observatory recorded a snowfall of 97.8 in. Within a 24-hr. period during that storm, a total of 49.3 in. was recorded—at that time a record for the mountain and for all weather observation stations in the United States. Other mountains in the White Mountains also experience severe conditions in proportion to their height and exposure.

The forest in the White Mountains is of two major types: the northern hardwood forest (birch, beech, and maple), found at elevations of less than about 3,000 ft., and the boreal forest (spruce, fir, and birch), found from about 3,000 ft. to timberline. At low elevations, oaks and white pines may be seen, and hemlocks are found in some deep valleys; red pines may grow up to elevations of about 2,000 ft. in ledgy areas. Above timberline is krummholz, the gnarled and stunted trees that manage to survive wherever there is a bit of shelter from the violent winds, and tiny wildflowers, some of which are extremely rare. Hikers are encouraged to be particularly careful in their activities above treeline, as the plants that grow here have to cope with the severity of the environment, not to mention hiker trampling. For more information on the natural history of the area, see *Field Guide to the New England Alpine Summits*, by Nancy G. Slack and Allison W. Bell, and *Nature Guide to the Northern Forest*, by Peter J. Marchand, both published by AMC Books.

TRIP PLANNING, WEATHER, AND SAFETY

The typical hiking season runs approximately from Memorial Day to Columbus Day. In some years, ice or snowdrifts may remain at higher elevations until the early part of June and possibly later in some of the major ravines, on north-facing slopes, and in other sheltered places, such as Mahoosuc Notch. Such conditions vary greatly from year to year and place to place. See p. xxv for Winter Considerations.

Winter-like conditions can occur above treeline in any month of the year. Keep in mind that air temperature will drop about 3 degrees Fahrenheit with each 1,000 ft. of elevation gain, without factoring in the impact of windchill. As a result, even on sunny days in midsummer, hikers above treeline should always be prepared for cold weather with at least a wool or synthetic fleece jacket or sweater, a hat, gloves, and a wind parka, which will give comfort on sunny but cool days and protection against sudden storms. Spring and fall are particularly difficult seasons in the mountains because the weather may be pleasant in the valleys but brutal on the summits and ridges. Many serious incidents in the mountains occur in spring and fall, when hikers deceived by mild conditions at home or even at trailheads find themselves facing unanticipated and severe—perhaps even life-threatening—hazards once on the trail.

Plan your trip schedule with safety in mind. Consider the strength of your party and the general strenuousness of the trip: the overall distance, the amount of climbing, and the roughness of the terrain. Get a weather report but be aware that most forecasts are not intended to apply to the mountain region; a day that is sunny and pleasant in the lowlands may well be inclement in the mountains. The National Weather Service (NWS) in Gray, Maine, issues a recreational forecast for the White Mountain region's valleys and higher summits and broadcasts it on its shortwave radio station each morning (162.500 mhz for the Mt. Washington station; 162.550 mhz for the Holderness station). The forecast can be viewed on the NWS website (weather.gov/gyx); for the mountain forecast, choose "Recreational Forecast" from the menu. Both a Higher Summits Forecast and a Mt. Washington Valley Forecast from the Mt. Washington Observatory are posted at Pinkham Notch Visitor Center each morning. These are also available on the websites of both AMC (outdoors.org/outdoor-activities/backcountry-weather.cfm) and the Mt. Washington Observatory (mountwashington.org), and via the Observatory weather phone, at 603-356-2137, ext. 1. Another mountain weather resource is the Recreational Forecast from the Fairbanks Museum in St. Johnsbury, Vermont (fairbanksmuseum.org/eye-on-the-sky).

Plan to finish your hike with daylight to spare, and remember that days grow shorter rapidly in late summer and fall. Hiking after dark, even with flashlights or headlamps (which frequently fail), makes finding trails more difficult and crossing streams hazardous. Let someone else know where you will be hiking and make sure hikers, especially inexperienced ones, don't get separated from the group. Learn best practices for leaving your trip plans with a third party in *AMC's Mountain Skills Manual*.

Many unpaved roads are not passable until about Memorial Day, and from November to May, the WMNF locks the gates to many of its roads that are usually open during the summer season. (Current road conditions are listed on the WMNF website, www.fs.usda.gov/whitemountain). Many trips are much longer when the roads are not open.

2011 DAMAGE TO TRAILS AND ROADS

On August 28, 2011, Tropical Storm Irene brought as much as 10 in. of rain to the higher elevations of the White Mountains, causing sudden and extensive flooding in many areas. A number of trails and roads located along streams suffered severe damage in the form of washouts, eroded banks, altered stream locations, landslides, and fallen trees. Several trail bridges were washed away or badly damaged. In the wake of the storm, several trails were found to be impassable and were closed to all use by the USFS. Since the storm, a number of trails (and roads) have been repaired and, where necessary, relocated, and several bridges have been replaced. Some washed-out areas still require caution; these locations are mentioned in individual trail descriptions.

HIKESAFE HIKER RESPONSIBILITY CODE

You are responsible for yourself, so be prepared:

1. **With knowledge and gear.** Become self-reliant by learning about the terrain, conditions, local weather, and your equipment before you start.

2. **To leave your plans.** Tell someone where you are going, the trails you are hiking, when you will return, and your emergency plans.

3. **To stay together.** When you start as a group, you hike as a group and end as a group. Pace your hike to the slowest person.

4. **To turn back.** Weather changes quickly in the mountains. Fatigue and unexpected conditions can also affect your hike. Know your limitations and when to postpone your hike. The mountains will be there another day.

5. **For emergencies.** Even if you are headed out for only an hour, an injury, severe weather, or a wrong turn could become life threatening. Don't assume you will be rescued; know how to rescue yourself.

6. **To share the hiker code with others.** HikeSafe: It's Your Responsibility.

The Hiker Responsibility Code was developed and is endorsed by the WMNF and New Hampshire Fish and Game. For more information, visit hikesafe.com.

FOLLOWING TRAILS

In general, trails are maintained to provide a clear pathway while protecting the environment by minimizing erosion and other damage. Some trails may offer rough and difficult passage. Trails in officially designated Wilderness Areas, by policy, are managed to provide a more primitive experience. As a result, they are maintained to a lesser degree, are sparsely marked, and have few signs. Hikers entering Wilderness Areas must be prepared to make a greater effort to follow their chosen route.

Most hiking trails are marked by paint on trees or rocks, known as blazes, although a few have only ax notches cut into trees. The trails that compose the AT through the White Mountains are marked with vertical, rectangular, white-paint blazes. Side trails off the AT are usually marked with blue paint. Other trails are marked in other colors, the most popular being yellow, which is used on most trails in the WMNF that are not part of the AT system. Above timberline, cairns (piles of rocks) mark the trails.

Below treeline, the treadway is usually visible except when it is covered by snow or fallen leaves. In winter, trail blazes and signs at trailheads and intersections are often covered by snow. Trails following or crossing logging roads require special care at intersections to distinguish the trail from diverging roads, particularly because blazing is usually sparse where the trail follows the road. Around shelters or campsites, beaten paths may lead in all directions, so look for signs and paint blazes.

Hikers should be aware that some trails in this book (as noted in descriptions) are more difficult to follow than others: The presence of signs and blazes varies; some trails are too new to have a well-beaten treadway; others have received very little use. Trails may not be cleared of fallen trees and brush until late summer, and not all trails are cleared every year. Inexperienced hikers should avoid trails that are described as being difficult to follow, and all trail users should observe and follow trail markings carefully.

Although trails vary greatly in the amount of use they receive and the ease with which they usually can be followed, almost any trail might be closed unexpectedly or suddenly become obscure or hazardous under certain conditions. Trails can be rerouted, abandoned, or closed by landowners. Signs are stolen or fall from their posts. Storms may cause blowdowns or landslides, which can obliterate a trail for an entire hiking season or longer. Logging operations can cover trails with slash and add a bewildering network of new roads.

Momentary inattention to trail markers, particularly arrows at sharp turns or signs at junctions, or misinterpreting signs or guidebook descriptions can cause hikers to become separated from all but the most heavily traveled paths—or can lead them into what may be a much longer or more difficult route. Please remember that this book is an aid to planning, not a substitute for observation and judgment. All trail-maintaining organizations, including AMC, reserve the right to discontinue any trail without notice and expressly disclaim any legal responsibility for the condition of any trail.

IF YOU'RE LOST

If you lose a trail it is usually best to backtrack right away to the last marker seen and look again from there; this will be much easier if you keep track of where and how long ago you saw the most recent blaze. Many cases in which a person has become lost for any length of time involve panic and aimless wandering, so the proper order of operations is to stop and take a break, make an inventory of useful information, decide on a course of action, and stick to it. (The caution against allowing inexperienced persons to become separated from a group should be emphasized here because they are most likely to panic and wander aimlessly. Make sure that all party members are familiar with the route of the trip and the names of the trails to be used, so that if anyone does become separated, the lost member will have some prospect of rejoining the group.)

Even when the trail cannot be immediately found, it is a serious but not desperate situation. If you have carefully tracked your location on the map, you usually will be able to find a nearby stream, trail, or road to which a compass course may be followed. Most distances are short enough (except in the North Country, north of NH 110) that it is possible, in the absence of alternatives, to reach a highway in half a day, or at most in a whole day, simply by going downhill, carefully avoiding any dangerous cliffs, until you come upon a river or brook. The stream should then be followed downward.

WHAT TO CARRY AND WEAR

Good things to have in your pack for an ordinary summer day hike in the White Mountains include the following:

- guidebook and maps
- at least 2 quarts of water
- compass
- pocket knife
- rain/wind gear
- wool or synthetic jacket/sweater(s)
- long pants
- winter hat
- gloves or mittens
- extra shirt(s)
- watch
- lunch and high-energy snacks
- personal medications
- first-aid and repair kits
- nylon cord
- trash bag
- toilet paper
- sunscreen
- sunglasses
- whistle
- space blanket or bivy sack
- headlamp or flashlight
- extra batteries and spare bulb
- waterproof matches

Wear comfortable, broken-in hiking boots. Lightweight boots, which are sturdier than sneakers, provide ankle support on rough and rocky trails, of which there is an ample supply in the White Mountains. Two pairs of socks are recommended: a lightweight inner pair and a heavier outer pair that is at least partly wool. Adjustable trekking poles offer many advantages to hikers, especially on descents, traverses, and stream crossings.

Jeans, sweatshirts, and other cotton clothes are not recommended; once these become wet, they dry very slowly. In adverse weather conditions, they seriously drain a cold and tired hiker's heat reserves. Thus, the hiker's maxim "cotton kills." Synthetics and wool are superior materials for hiking apparel, especially for people who are planning to travel in adverse conditions, to remote places, or above treeline. Wool keeps much of its insulating value even when wet, and it (or one of several modern synthetic materials) is indispensable for hikers who want to visit places from which returning to civilization might require substantial time and effort if conditions turn bad. Hats, gloves, and other such gear provide safety in adverse conditions, and they allow one to enjoy the summits in comfort on crisp, clear days when the views are particularly fine. For more on essential clothing and gear, see *AMC's Mountain Skills Manual.*

HIKING WITH KIDS

Many trails in this book are suitable for hiking with kids. It is important to choose a hike that suits the age, fitness, and agility of your child and to bring adequate gear, food, and water. *AMC's Best Day Hikes in the White*

Mountains, Third Edition (AMC Books, 2016), by Robert N. Buchsbaum, is an excellent resource for hiking with kids in the White Mountains. A wealth of additional information on family hiking is available at outdoors.org/greatkids.

HIKING WITH DOGS

Many hikers enjoy the companionship of their dogs on the trail. Out of consideration for other hikers, please keep your dog under voice control at all times and on leash, if necessary. Carry out or bury dog waste. Choose a hike that matches your dog's fitness, age, and agility. Some trails—such as those with ladders or difficult boulder or ledge scrambling—are not suitable for dogs. The sharp rocks above treeline on the Presidential Range are extremely rough on a dog's paws. Be sure your dog has adequate water to drink, especially on hot summer days. For more information, see outdoors.org/doghikes. For more advice on hiking with kids and with dogs, see *AMC's Mountain Skills Manual.*

CAMPING

Those who camp overnight in the backcountry tend to have more of an impact on the land than day-hikers do. Backpacking hikers should take great care to minimize their effect on the mountains by practicing low-impact camping. If available on your chosen trip route, the best alternative is to use formally designated campsites to concentrate impact and minimize damage to vegetation. Many popular campsites and shelters have caretakers. In other areas, choose previously established campsites to minimize the impact caused by the creation and proliferation of new campsites.

When selecting an established campsite, choose ones that are farther from surface water to protect the water quality for future and downstream users. Several websites are devoted to Leave No Trace principles (see p. xxxiv).

More than 50 backcountry shelters and tentsites are located in the White Mountain area, open on a first-come, first-served basis. Some sites have summer caretakers who provide trail and shelter maintenance, educate hikers on low-impact camping methods, and oversee the environmentally sound disposal of human waste. An overnight fee is charged at these sites to help defray expenses. Some sites have shelters, others (called "tentsites") have only tent platforms or earthen pads, and some (called "campsites") have both. Shelters are intended as overnight accommodations for persons carrying their own bedding and cooking supplies. The more popular shelters are often full, so be prepared to camp at a legal site off-trail with tents or tarps. Make yourself aware of regulations and restrictions before your trip.

Each year, the fourteen AMC-managed backcountry sites host an average of 20,000 overnight visitors. Nine of the most popular sites see a combined average of 11,000 visitors in the summer months. More than one-third of those visitors are part of an organized group. The heavy use of these popular sites can lead to the improper disposal of human waste, erosion of heavily used trails, and trampling of vegetation—all of which have an impact on the forest. AMC requires pre-notification from large groups at least two weeks in advance concerning the sites they plan to use. If you are planning a group trip with six or more people during the summer or fall season, visit AMC's website for notification forms and updates on group availability at outdoors.org/group_notification.

If you camp away from established sites, look for a spot more than 200 ft. from the trail and from any surface water, and observe USFS camping regulations for the area. Bring all needed shelter, including whatever poles, stakes, ground insulation, and cord are required. Do not cut boughs or branches for bedding or firewood, or young trees for poles. Avoid clearing vegetation and never make a ditch around the tent. Wash your dishes and yourself 200 ft. away from streams, ponds, and springs. Bury human waste at least 200 ft. from the trail, the campsite, and any water sources. Heed the rules of neatness, sanitation, and fire prevention and carry out everything—food, paper, glass, cans—that you carry in. Food should not be kept in your tent; hang your food from a tree—at least 10 ft. off the ground from a high, sturdy branch and 4 ft. from the tree trunk—to protect it from raccoons and bears.

In some popular camping areas, a "human browse line," where people have gathered firewood over the years, is quite evident: Limbs are gone from trees; the ground is devoid of dead wood; and vegetation has been trampled. Please refrain from exacerbating this problem. The use of portable stoves is often mandatory in popular areas and is encouraged everywhere to prevent damage to vegetation. Wood campfires should not be made unless ample dead and downed wood is available near your site and you are certain that fires are legal in your particular camping area. Where fires are allowed, clear a space at least 5 ft. in radius of all flammable material, down to the mineral soil, before you begin to build your fire. Under no circumstances should a fire be left unattended. All fires must be completely extinguished with earth or water before you leave a campsite, even temporarily. Campers should restore the campfire site to as natural an appearance as possible (unless using a preexisting fire ring) before leaving the campsite.

CAMPING REGULATIONS

Trailside camping is feasible only within the WMNF, with a few limited exceptions, such as the established campsites on the AT. Camping and campfires are not permitted in New Hampshire state parks except in campgrounds. The state laws of Maine and New Hampshire require that permission be obtained from the owner to camp on private land and that permits be obtained to build campfires anywhere outside the WMNF in the region covered by this guide, except at officially designated campsites.

Overnight camping is permitted in almost all of the WMNF. The USFS has adopted regulations for a number of areas in the WMNF that are threatened by overuse and misuse. The objective of the Forest Protection Area program (FPA, formerly called the Restricted Use Area program) is to disperse use so that people can enjoy themselves in a clean and attractive environment without causing deterioration of natural resources. Because hikers and backpackers have cooperated with FPA rules, many areas once designated as FPAs have recovered and are no longer under formal restrictions; however, common sense and self-imposed restrictions are still necessary to prevent damage.

Stated briefly, the 2016 FPA rules prohibit camping (except on 2 ft. or more of snow, but not on frozen bodies of water) and wood or charcoal fires above timberline (where trees are less than 8 ft. in height); within 0.25 mi. of any trailhead, hut, shelter, developed tent site, cabin, picnic area, developed day-use site, or campground; within certain special areas; or within a specified distance of certain roads, trails, bodies of water, and other locations, except at designated sites.

These restrictions are in effect year-round. This guide provides information on FPAs as of 2016 in each relevant section. Signs are usually posted where trails enter and leave FPAs. Because the list of restricted areas may change from year to year, hikers should seek current information from the WMNF headquarters in Campton, New Hampshire, from AMC's Pinkham Notch Visitor Center, or from any ranger district office. A brochure outlining the current backcountry camping rules is available at WMNF ranger stations, information centers, and www.fs.usda.gov/whitemountain.

ROADSIDE CAMPGROUNDS

The WMNF operates a number of roadside campgrounds with limited facilities; fees are charged, and most of these campgrounds are managed by private concessionaires. Consult the WMNF offices for details or call the campground hotline at 877-444-6777. Many of these campgrounds are full on summer weekends. Reservations for sites at some WMNF campgrounds can be made through the National Recreation Reservation Service. Several New Hampshire state parks also have campgrounds located conveniently for hikers in the White Mountains, and reservations can be made at all of these. Literature on state parks and state and private campgrounds is available at New Hampshire highway rest areas. (*Note:* Visitors are not permitted to bring out-of-state firewood to any of the campgrounds, due to the risk of the spread of invasive insects. Violators are subject to warnings, tickets, and fines.) See Appendix A: Helpful Information and Contacts for websites and phone numbers for campground reservations in the WMNF and state parks.

FIRE REGULATIONS

Campfire permits are no longer required in the WMNF, but hikers who build fires are still legally responsible for any damage they cause. Fires are forbidden in FPAs, above treeline (where trees are less than 8 ft. tall), and in the Great Gulf Wilderness and Cutler River drainage. Fires are not permitted on state lands except at explicitly designated sites; on private land the owner's permission is required. During periods when there is a high risk of forest fires, the forest supervisor may temporarily close the entire WMNF against public entry. Such closures are given wide publicity so that local residents and visitors alike may realize the danger of fires in the woods.

WINTER CONSIDERATIONS

This book describes trails in the snowless season, which can vary considerably from year to year; higher elevations have much shorter snowless seasons. Snowshoeing and winter hiking on White Mountain trails and peaks have steadily become more popular, however, so a few general considerations are given here.

Although travel on the lower trails in average conditions can be relatively safe, much more experience is required to foresee and avoid dangerous situations in winter than in summer. Summer hiking boots are inadequate; flashlight batteries fail quickly (LED headlamps work much better, but may still fail); and drinking water freezes unless carried in an insulated container. The winter hiker needs good physical conditioning from regular exercise and must dress carefully to avoid overheating and excessive perspiration, which soaks clothing and soon leads to chilling. Cotton clothes should be avoided in winter; only some synthetic fabrics and wool retain their insulating values when wet. Fluid intake must increase, as dehydration can be a serious problem in the dry winter air. Larger packs are needed to carry the extra clothing and gear required in winter.

Snow, ice, and weather conditions are constantly changing, and a relatively trivial error of judgment may have grave, even fatal, consequences. Conditions can vary greatly from day to day and from trail to trail. Days are very short, particularly in early winter when darkness falls shortly after 4 P.M. Trails are frequently difficult or impossible to follow in deep snow, and navigation skills are hard to use (or learn) in adverse weather conditions. (Thus, out-and-back hikes—where one retraces one's tracks—are preferable to loop hikes, where unknown conditions ahead could make completion of the trip much more difficult than anticipated.) Brook crossings can be difficult and potentially dangerous if the brooks are not well frozen.

Deep snow requires snowshoes or skis and the skill to use them efficiently. Breaking trail on snowshoes through new snow can be strenuous and exhausting work. Trail courtesy suggests that winter hikers wear snowshoes when trails are not solidly packed out; "barebooting" in soft snow is unnecessarily tiring and creates unpleasant and potentially dangerous "postholes" in the trail for those who follow.

When ice is present on trails, as it often is in late fall, early spring, and after winter thaw-freeze cycles, there is particular danger on mountains with steep open slopes or ledges. If icy trail conditions are expected, hikers should bring traction footgear, such as MICROspikes (a popular brand of ice cleat), or if severe conditions prevail, full crampons, which require practice and care to use safely.

In spring, deep snowdrifts may remain on northern slopes and wooded ridge crests, even at lower elevations, after all snow is gone on southern exposures.

It is important to note that some trails go through areas that may pose a severe avalanche hazard. Gulfs, ravines, and open slopes are especially prone to avalanches, though slides can also occur below treeline. Information on avalanche danger for Tuckerman Ravine is posted daily at Pinkham Notch Visitor Center and on the AMC and Mt. Washington Observatory websites. These areas should be regarded as technical terrain and strictly avoided unless group leaders have been trained in avalanche safety; avalanches have caused a number of deaths and serious injuries in the White Mountains, often due to inexperienced, untrained hikers wandering into dangerous terrain.

Above timberline, conditions often require specialized equipment and skills, as well as experience of a different magnitude. The conditions on the

Presidential Range in winter are as severe as any in North America south of the great mountains of Alaska and the Yukon Territory. On the summit of Mt. Washington in winter, winds average 44 MPH, and daily high temperatures average 15 degrees Fahrenheit. The summit sees only a few calm days, and even on an average day, conditions will probably be too severe for any but the most experienced and well-equipped climbers. The Mt. Washington Observatory routinely records wind velocities in excess of 100 MPH, and temperatures are often far below zero. The combination of high wind and low temperature has such a cooling effect that the worst conditions on Mt. Washington are approximately equal to the worst reported from Antarctica, despite the much greater cold in the latter region. Severe storms can develop suddenly and unexpectedly. Winter weather in the White Mountains is extremely variable: It is not unusual for a cold, penetrating, wind-driven rain to be followed within a few hours by a cold front that brings below-zero temperatures and high winds.

Hikers who are interested in extending their activities into the winter season, especially at higher elevations, are strongly advised to seek organized parties with leaders who have extensive winter experience. AMC and several of its chapters sponsor numerous evening and weekend workshops, in addition to introductory winter hikes, through which participants can gain experience. Information on winter skills workshops are available at outdoors.org/activities; enter the keyword "instruction."

Obviously, obtaining a current mountain weather forecast is a critical component of trip planning in winter. The Mt. Washington Observatory posts both a Higher Summits Forecast and a Mt. Washington Valley Forecast early each morning at mountwashington.org. Both of these are also available via the observatory weather phone at 603-356-2137, ext. 1. Trail, snow, and weather conditions for AMC lodges and winter huts are posted daily on outdoors.org/outdoor-activities/backcountry-weather.cfm.

BACKCOUNTRY HAZARDS

Safe hiking means knowing how to avoid dangerous situations, as well as being prepared to deal with problems when they do occur. Courses that teach the principles of backcountry safety, wilderness first aid, and incident management are offered by AMC and many other outdoor organizations.

Dozens of books are available on such subjects. The following section outlines some common hazards encountered in the Northeast outdoors and discusses how to approach them.

Search and Rescue

In emergencies, call 911 or the toll-free New Hampshire State Police number (800-525-5555). Hikers should be aware that cell phone coverage in the backcountry can be very unreliable, particularly in deep valleys but also on some summits, and you have absolutely no assurance that a cell-phone call will get through to authorities in an emergency. Both phones and their batteries can fail, often at inconvenient times.

By state law, the New Hampshire Fish and Game Department is responsible for search-and-rescue operations in the New Hampshire outdoors, with assistance from several volunteer search-and-rescue groups and local fire departments. It takes a fair amount of time to organize rescue parties, which normally require a minimum of 18 people for litter carries. In addition, an unnecessary rescue mission may leave no resources to be called on if a real emergency occurs. Please make sure a situation is really an emergency before calling for help. All such operations are expensive, and they frequently put good people at risk. Also note that, under New Hampshire law, hikers who require rescue because of "reckless" behavior may be billed by the state for the cost of their rescue.

Hikers who wish to make monetary contributions in support of New Hampshire search and rescue organizations may purchase a voluntary hike-Safe Card from New Hampshire Fish and Game (wildlife.state.nh.us/safe/index.html) or by making a contribution to the New Hampshire Outdoor Council, PO Box 157, Kearsarge, NH 03847; nhoutdoorcouncil.org. Also see "HikeSafe Hiker Responsibility Code" on p. xviii.

Falls and Injuries

The remoteness of the backcountry makes any injury a potentially serious matter. Be alert for places where footing may be poor, especially in rainy weather and on steep, rough, or wet sections of trail. In autumn, wet leaves and hidden ice are particular hazards. Remember that carrying a heavy pack can affect your balance. Another potential cause of injury in certain areas is rockfall from ledges that rise above the trail.

In case of serious injury, apply first aid and keep the injured party warm and comfortable. Then take a minute to assess the situation before going or calling for help. Backcountry evacuation can take many hours, so don't rush. Write down your location, the condition of the injured person, and any other pertinent facts. If phone service is not available, at least one person should stay with the injured hiker while two others go for help. (Hence the maxim that it is safest to hike in the backcountry in groups of four or more.)

Hypothermia

Hypothermia, the most serious danger to hikers in the White Mountains, is the loss of ability to preserve body heat and can be caused by injury, exhaustion, lack of sufficient food, and inadequate or wet clothing. This often occurs on wet, windy days between 32 and 50 degrees Fahrenheit.

Symptoms of moderate hypothermia include shivering, impaired speech and movement, lowered body temperature, and drowsiness. Be on the lookout for what current hypothermia education programs refer to as the *umbles*—stumbles, mumbles, and bumbles—which amount to a loss of agility, an inability to speak clearly, difficulty with knots and zippers, and similar issues that indicate loss of control over normal muscular and mental functions. A victim should be given dry clothing and placed in a sleeping bag, if available, then given quick-energy food to eat and something warm (not hot) to drink.

In cases of severe hypothermia, which occurs when body temperature reaches a point below 90 degrees Fahrenheit, shivering ceases, but a victim becomes afflicted by an obvious lack of coordination to the point that walking becomes impossible. Sure indicators are slurred speech, mental confusion, irrational behavior, disorientation, and unconsciousness. Only prompt evacuation to a hospital offers reasonable hope for recovery. Extreme care must be used in attempting to transport such a person to a trailhead because even a slight jar can bring on heart failure. The victim should be protected from further heat loss as much as possible and handled with extreme gentleness; trained rescue personnel should be called for assistance.

Successful rescue of a profoundly hypothermic person from the backcountry is difficult, so prevention or early detection is essential. The advent of hypothermia is usually fairly slow, and in cold or wet weather, all members of a hiking group must be aware of the signs of developing hypothermia and pay constant attention to the first appearance of such signs—which may be fairly subtle—in all fellow party members.

Heat Exhaustion

Excessive heat can also be a serious problem in the mountains, particularly in midsummer on hot, humid days. Heat exhaustion, usually in a mild form, is quite common. The hiker feels tired, perhaps light-headed or nauseous, and may have cramps in large muscles. The principal cause is dehydration and loss of electrolytes (mostly salt) through perspiration, often combined with overexertion. On a hot day, a hiker can often be well along the way to serious dehydration before he or she even feels thirsty. To prevent heat exhaustion, hikers should carry plenty of water (or the means to treat water from natural sources en route) and drink copiously before thirst is evident. Wearing a hat to block sun is another preventive measure.

To treat heat exhaustion, provide adequate water and perhaps salt (salt without adequate water will make the situation worse), help the victim cool down (especially the head and torso), and minimize further exertion. Heat exhaustion must be taken seriously because it can proceed to life-threatening cardiac problems or heat stroke, a medical emergency where irreversible damage to the brain and other vital organs can quickly occur. This condition requires immediate cooling of the victim.

Lightning

Lightning is another serious potential hazard on any bare ridge or summit. Avoid these dangerous places when thunderstorms are likely. Look for shelter in thick woods as quickly as possible if an unexpected "thumper" is detected. Most thunderstorms occur when a cold front passes or on very warm days; storms produced by cold fronts are typically more sudden and violent. Weather forecasts that mention cold fronts or predict temperatures much above 80 degrees Fahrenheit in the lowlands and valleys should arouse concern.

Wildlife

In recent years, there have been hundreds of collisions between automobiles and moose, most occurring in spring and early summer, though the hazard exists year-round. Motorists need to be aware of the seriousness of the problem, particularly at night when these huge, dark-colored animals are both active and very difficult to see. Instinct often causes them to face an auto rather than run from it, and they are apt to cross the road unpredictably as a car approaches. Slower driving speeds and use of high beams are recommended at night. Moose normally constitute little threat to hikers on foot, although it would be wise to give a wide berth to a cow with young or to a bull during the fall mating season.

Bears are common but tend to keep well out of sight. Several recent serious incidents have been unnecessarily provoked by deliberate feeding of bears, or by harassment by a dog leading to an attack on people nearby. Bears are omnivorous opportunists, especially fond of nuts and berries. They have become a nuisance and even a hazard at some popular campsites; any bear that has lost its natural fear of humans and gotten used to living off us is extremely dangerous. Hikers confronted by a bear should attempt to appear neither threatened nor frightened, and should back off slowly—never run—but not abandon food unless the bear appears irresistibly aggressive. A loud noise, such as one made by a whistle or by banging metal pots, is often useful. Careful protection of food—and scented items such as toothpaste—at campsites is mandatory; these items must never be kept overnight in a tent but should be placed in a metal bear box (located at all AMC backcountry campsites) or a bear canister (available on a first-come, first-served basis at WMNF offices and visitor centers), or hung between trees well off the ground—at least 10 ft. high and 4 ft. away from the tree trunk.

There are no known poisonous snakes in the White Mountains.

Hunting Seasons

New Hampshire moose-hunting season runs from mid-October to late October; deer-hunting season (with rifles) is in November and early December, at which time you'll probably see many more hunters than deer. Seasons involving muzzle-loader and bow-and-arrow hunters extend from mid-September through mid-December. Most hunters usually stay fairly close to roads; in general, the harder it would be to haul a deer out of a given area, the lower the probability that a hiker will encounter hunters there. In any case, avoid wearing brown or anything that might give a hunter the impression of the white flash of a white-tailed deer running away.

Wearing bright-orange clothing, as is usually done by hunters, is strongly recommended. Hikers should also be aware of the wild turkey gobbler season in May, when authorities advise against wearing red, white, blue, or black clothing. For dates of New Hampshire hunting seasons, visit wildlife.state.nh.us or call 603-271-3211. For Maine, visit maine.gov/ifw or call 207-287-8000. Hunting is not allowed on Sundays in Maine.

Mosquitoes, Blackflies, and Ticks

Mosquitoes and blackflies are the woodland residents most frequently encountered by hikers. Mosquitoes are worst throughout the summer in low, wet areas, and blackflies are most bloodthirsty in late May, June, and early July. Head nets can be useful. The most effective repellents are based on the active ingredient N-Diethyl-meta-toluamide, generally known as DEET, but some have doubts about its safety. Recently, repellents with the active ingredient Picaridin have been found to be nearly or equally as effective. Hikers should apply repellents to clothing rather than skin where possible and avoid using DEET on small children.

Ticks have been an increasing problem, becoming common in woods and grassy or brushy areas at lower elevations, especially in oak forests. At present, the most feared tick—the tiny, easily overlooked deer tick, which can transmit Lyme disease—is not yet common in the White Mountains, although its range is steadily increasing. The common tick in the White Mountains is the larger wood tick (also known as the dog tick), which can also carry serious diseases, such as Rocky Mountain spotted fever.

Countermeasures include using insect repellent, wearing light-colored long pants tucked into your socks, and frequently checking clothing and skin. Ticks wander for several hours before settling on a spot to bite, so they can be removed easily if found promptly. Once a tick is embedded, care must be taken to remove it entirely; the head detaches easily and may remain in the skin, possibly producing infection.

Brook Crossings

Rivers and brooks are often crossable without bridges, and you can usually step from rock to rock; trekking poles, a hiking staff, or a stick can be a great aid to balance. Use caution: Several fatalities have resulted from hikers (particularly solo hikers) falling on slippery rocks and suffering an injury that rendered them unconscious, causing them to drown in relatively shallow streams. Often the safer course is to wade across a stream; if you do so, wearing boots without socks is recommended. If you suspect in advance that wading may be required, a good option is to bring lightweight sneakers or water footwear.

Many crossings that may only be nuisances in summer could be serious obstacles in cold weather when one's feet and boots must be kept dry. Another kind of hazard can occur in late fall, when cold nights may cause a treacherous thin layer of ice to coat exposed rocks. Higher waters, which can turn innocuous brooks into virtually uncrossable torrents, come in spring as snow melts or after heavy rainstorms, particularly in fall when trees drop their leaves and take up less water. Avoid trails with potentially dangerous stream crossings during these high-water periods. If you are cut off from roads by swollen streams, it is better to make a long detour, even if you need to wait and spend a night in the woods. Rushing current can make wading extremely hazardous, and several deaths have resulted.

Floodwaters may subside within a few hours, especially in small brooks. It is particularly important not to camp on the far side of a brook from your exit point if the crossing is difficult and heavy rain is predicted.

A useful website for assessing current streamflow conditions in the mountains is USGS Real-Time Water Data for New Hampshire, at waterdata.usgs.gov/nh/nwis/rt. This site provides streamflow data for the Androscoggin, Ammonoosuc, East Branch Pemigewasset, Pemigewasset, Saco, Swift, Upper Ammonoosuc, and Wild rivers.

Drinking Water

The presence of cysts of the intestinal parasite *Giardia lamblia* in water sources in the White Mountains is thought to be common, though difficult to prove. It is impossible to be sure whether a given source is safe, no matter how clear the water or how remote the location. The safest course is for day-hikers to carry their water; those who use sources in the woods should treat or filter the water before drinking it. If treating water, it should be brought to a rolling boil or disinfected with an iodine-based disinfectant. Allow extra contact time (and use twice as many tablets) if the water is very cold. Chlorine-based products are ineffective in water that contains organic impurities, and all water-purification chemicals tend to deteriorate quickly. Various kinds of filters are available; they also remove impurities from water, often making it look and taste better, so that sources that are unappealing in the untreated state can be made to produce drinkable water. For more on water treatment methods, see *AMC's Mountain Skills Manual*.

The symptoms of giardiasis are severe intestinal distress and diarrhea, but such discomforts can have many other causes, making the disease difficult to diagnose accurately. The principal cause of the spread of this noxious ailment in the woods is probably careless disposal of human waste. Keep it at least 200 ft. away from water sources. If no toilets are nearby, dig a hole 6 to 8 in. deep (but not below the organic layer of the soil) for a latrine and cover the hole completely after use. The bacteria in the organic layer of the soil will then decompose the waste naturally. It is advisable to be scrupulous about washing hands after answering calls of nature.

Break-Ins

Cars parked at trailheads are frequently targets of break-ins, so valuables or expensive equipment should never be left in cars while you are hiking, particularly overnight.

TRAIL MAINTENANCE

The trails that we use and enjoy are only in part the product of government agencies and nonprofit organizations. Many trails are cared for by one dedicated person or a small group. Funds for trail work are scarce, and unless hikers contribute both time and money to the maintenance of trails, the diversity of trails available to the public may well decline. Every hiker can make some contribution to the improvement of the trails, if nothing more than by pushing a fallen limb or tree off the trail rather than walking around it. Write to AMC Trails, Pinkham Notch Visitor Center, PO Box 298, Gorham, NH 03581, for more information regarding volunteer trail maintenance activities or see outdoors.org/volunteer. In addition to its own active Adopt-a-Trail program, AMC has worked cooperatively with both the WMNF and New Hampshire State Parks on Adopt-a-Trail programs in recent years. Other trail maintenance opportunities are available through the organizations and clubs listed in Appendix A: Helpful Information and Contacts. Another group that is very active in trail maintenance is Trailwrights, PO Box 1223, Concord, NH 03302; trailwrights.org; trailwrights@pobox.com.

LEAVE NO TRACE

AMC is a national educational partner of Leave No Trace, a nonprofit organization dedicated to promoting and inspiring responsible outdoor recreation through education, research, and partnerships. The Leave No Trace program develops wild land ethics, or guidelines for ways people should think and act in the outdoors to minimize their impact on the areas they visit and to protect our natural resources for future enjoyment. Leave No Trace unites four federal land management agencies—the USFS, National Park Service, Bureau of Land Management, and U.S. Fish and Wildlife Service—with manufacturers, outdoor retailers, user groups, educators, organizations such as AMC, and individuals. The Leave No Trace ethic is guided by these seven principles:

- Plan ahead and prepare.
- Travel and camp on durable surfaces.
- Dispose of waste properly.
- Leave what you find.
- Minimize campfire impacts.
- Respect wildlife.
- Be considerate of other visitors.

AMC is a national provider of the Leave No Trace Master Educator course. AMC offers this five-day course, designed especially for outdoor professionals and land managers, as well as the shorter two-day Leave No Trace Trainer course at locations throughout the Northeast.

For Leave No Trace information and materials, contact the Leave No Trace Center for Outdoor Ethics, PO Box 997, Boulder, CO 80306; 800-332-4100 or 302-442-8222; lnt.org. For a schedule of AMC Leave No Trace courses, see outdoors.org/education/lnt.

ABBREVIATIONS AND ACRONYMS

The following abbreviations are used in this book.

ACT Ammonoosuc Conservation Trust

AMC Appalachian Mountain Club

AT Appalachian Trail

ATC Appalachian Trail Conservancy

ATVs all-terrain vehicles

CMC Chocorua Mountain Club

CTA Chatham Trails Association

DOC Dartmouth Outing Club

est. estimated

FOP Friends of Pondicherry

FPA Forest Protection Area

FPRT Friends of the Presidential Rail Trail

FR Forest Road (WMNF)

ft. foot, feet

GPS Global Positioning System

HA Hutmen's Association

HC Horton Center

hr. hour(s)

in. inch(es)

jct. junction

LCC Littleton Conservation Commission

LP loop

LRCT Lakes Region Conservation Trust

MATC Maine Appalachian Trail Club

MBPL Maine Bureau of Parks and Lands

mi. mile(s)

min. minutes(s)

MPH miles per hour

Mt. Mount

Mtn. Mountain

NHA New Hampshire Audubon

NHDP New Hampshire Department of Resources and Economic Development Division of Parks and Recreation

NWSC North Woods Stewardship Center

OW one way

Rd. Road

rev. reverse elevation

RMC Randolph Mountain Club

RT round trip

RTA Rivendell Trails Association

SCC Sandwich Conservation Commission

SLA Squam Lakes Association

SPNHF Society for the Protection of New Hampshire Forests

SSOC Sub Sig Outing Club

St. Street

STC Shelburne Trails Club

TCTA The Cohos Trail Association

TNC The Nature Conservancy

USFS United States Forest Service

USFWS United States Fish and Wildlife Service

USGS United States Geological Survey

UTM Universal Transverse Mercator

UVLT Upper Valley Land Trust

WMNF White Mountain National Forest

WODC Wonalancet Out Door Club

WSPA Weeks State Park Association

WVAIA Waterville Valley Athletic and Improvement Association

X-C cross-country

yd. yard(s)

KEY TO ICONS

⇅ Distance

↗ Elevation gain

○ Time

≋ Waterfall

⬤ Pond, stream, spring, or other water feature

✽ Alpine zone (an ecological zone characterized by the lack of trees; ground cover and plants are typical of the Arctic Circle)

⚑ Exposed ledges (trail crosses an exposed ledge—a consideration in severe weather or in wet or icy conditions; hikes that end at a scenic ledge but do not cross an exposed ledge en route are not marked with this icon)

⚑ Steep or difficult terrain

⚑ Difficult brook crossings

◺ Shelter or hut

▲ Designated tentsite

🌲 Wilderness area (federally designated areas of restricted human activity, with specific rules and regulations)

🚶 Kid-friendly

🐕 Dog-friendly

♿ Wheelchair accessible

❅ Snowshoeing

⛷ Cross-country skiing

✹ Scenic views

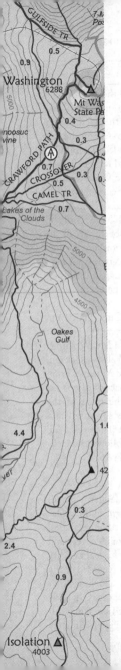

SECTION ONE

MT. WASHINGTON AND THE SOUTHERN RIDGES

SEC 1

INTRODUCTION

This section includes the summit of Mt. Washington and the major ridges that run south from it, which constitute the southern portion of the Presidential Range. The region is bounded approximately on the north by the Mt. Washington Cog Railway and Mt. Washington Auto Rd., on the east by NH 16, on the south by US 302, and on the west by US 302 and Cog Railway Base Rd. The northern portion of the Presidential Range, including Mts. Clay, Jefferson, Adams, and Madison, and the Great Gulf, is covered in Section Two. Many of the trails described in Section Two also provide routes to Mt. Washington. AMC's *White Mountains Trail Map 1: Presidential Range* covers this entire section except for Iron Mtn. Trail and several trails in the southern Montalban region, in the south part of the section. All these trails (and much of the rest of this section) are covered by AMC's *White Mountains Trail Map 3: Crawford Notch–Sandwich Range.* Davis Path is the only trail not completely covered by one map or the other; however, all but the southern end is on Map 1 and all but the northern end on Map 3.

In this section, the AT follows the entire Webster Cliff Trail from Crawford Notch to its intersection with Crawford Path, near the summit of Mt. Pierce, then follows Crawford Path to the summit of Mt. Washington. On the way, the AT also crosses the summits of mts. Webster, Jackson, and Pierce, and passes near mts. Eisenhower, Franklin, and Monroe. From Mt. Washington, the AT descends to Gulfside Trail (Section Two) via Trinity Heights Connector. Then, after passing over the ridge of the Northern Presidentials (although missing most of the summits) and through the Great Gulf—areas also covered in Section Two—the AT returns to Section One at Mt. Washington Auto Rd. and follows Old Jackson Rd. to AMC's Pinkham Notch Visitor Center and NH 16.

SAFETY ON MT. WASHINGTON

Mt. Washington has a well-earned reputation as the most dangerous small mountain in the world. As chronicled in *Not Without Peril,* by Nicholas Howe (AMC Books, 2009), more than 150 people have died on its slopes, many of them from exhaustion and exposure to the mountain's severe and rapidly changeable weather. Storms increase in violence with great rapidity toward the summit. The second-greatest wind velocity ever recorded at any surface weather station was attained on Mt. Washington, clocking in at 231 MPH on April 12, 1934 (the fastest being the 1996 Typhoon Olivia, as recorded in Barrow Island, Australia, at 253 MPH). Based on windchill temperatures, the worst conditions on Mt. Washington are approximately equal to the worst reported in Antarctica, although actual temperatures on Mt. Washington are not as low.

Winterlike storms of incredible violence occur frequently, even during summer months. Winds of hurricane force exhaust even the strongest hiker, and cold rain driven horizontally by the wind penetrates clothing and drains heat from the body. When a person's body temperature falls, brain function quickly deteriorates; this is one of the first, and most insidious, effects of excessive heat loss (hypothermia). For more information on this lethal condition, read the passage on hypothermia in the Backcountry Hazards section of this book's introduction; see p. xxix. If you begin to experience difficulty from weather conditions, remember that the worst is yet to come and turn back, without shame, before it is too late.

Hikers planning to ascend Mt. Washington should always check the weather forecast before setting out. The Mt. Washington Observatory issues a Higher Summits Forecast each day, early in the morning; it is available at mountwashington.org, outdoors.org, and by calling 603-356-2137, ext. 1. If the forecast is unfavorable, save the trip for a better day. When traveling above treeline, be sure to bring rain and wind gear, extra layers, and a hat and gloves; cotton clothes should be avoided.

Inexperienced hikers sometimes misjudge the difficulty of climbing Mt. Washington by placing too much emphasis on the relatively short distance from the trailheads to the summit. To people used to walking around their neighborhoods, the trail distance of 4 mi. or so sounds rather tame. But the most important factor in the difficulty of the trip is the altitude gain of about 4,000 ft. from base to summit, give or take a few hundred feet depending on the route chosen. To a person unused to mountain trails or in less-than-excellent physical condition, this unrelenting uphill grind can be grueling and intensely discouraging. If you are not an experienced hiker or a trained athlete, you will almost certainly enjoy the ascent of Mt. Washington a great deal more if you build up to it with easier climbs in areas with less exposure to potentially severe weather.

Visitors ascending the mountain on foot should carry a compass and a trail map and should take care to stay on the trails. If you are forced to travel in conditions of reduced visibility, favor the main trails with their large, readily visible cairns over the lesser-used connecting trails that are often far less clearly marked. It is a grave predicament when a hiker above treeline accidentally abandons a trail in dense fog or a whiteout, particularly if the weather is rapidly deteriorating. You have no completely satisfactory course of action in this situation because the objective is to get below treeline as quickly as possible—with or without a trail—but the weather exposure is generally worse to the west, and cliffs are more prevalent in the ravines to the east. If you know where the nearest major trail should be, then it is probably best to try to find it. If you have adequate clothing, it may be best to find a scrub patch and shelter yourself in it. In the absence of alternatives, take note that the Cog Railway on the western slope and Mt. Washington Auto Rd. on the eastern slope make a line, although a rather crooked one, from west to east. These landmarks are difficult to miss in even the darkest night or the thickest fog, except in winter conditions when snowdrifts may conceal them. Remember which side of the mountain you are on, and travel clockwise or counterclockwise, skirting the tops of the ravines; sooner or later you will reach either the Cog Railway or Mt. Washington Auto Rd. Given a choice, aim for the Auto Rd., as the railroad is on the side of the mountain that faces the prevailing winds.

Safe ascent of the mountain in winter requires much warm clothing; special equipment, such as crampons and an ice ax; considerable previous experience and training in winter hiking; and experienced leadership. The worst winter conditions are inconceivably brutal and can materialize with little warning. From Columbus Day to Memorial Day, no building is open to provide shelter or refuge to hikers. All water sources in this heavily used area should be considered unfit to drink; the safest course is to avoid drinking from trailside sources (see p. xxxiii). Water is available at the Sherman Adams summit building during the months in which it is open, roughly from Memorial Day to Columbus Day.

SUMMIT BUILDINGS

No hotel or overnight lodging for the public is available on the summit of Mt. Washington. The principal summit building serving tourists and hikers was named to honor Sherman Adams, a former New Hampshire governor, special assistant to President Eisenhower, legendary White Mountain woodsman, and, in his youth, trailmaster of AMC's trail crew. Operated by the New Hampshire Division of Parks and Recreation during the summer season (mid-May to mid-October), the building has food service, a pack room, a souvenir shop, public rest rooms, telephones, and a post office. The building houses the Mt. Washington Observatory, the Mt. Washington Museum, and facilities for park personnel.

The first Summit House on Mt. Washington was built in 1852. The oldest building still standing on the summit is the Tip Top House, a hotel built in 1853 and rebuilt after it burned in 1915. This stone building, now owned by the state of New Hampshire and a part of Mt. Washington State Park, has been restored and is open to the public as a historical site when the public summit facilities are in operation, but is not available for lodging or emergency shelter. The second Summit House, built in 1873, was destroyed by fire in 1908. The third Summit House was built in 1915 and razed in 1980 to make room for the Sherman Adams building.

Several other buildings are on the summit of Mt. Washington, none of them open to the general public.

MT. WASHINGTON OBSERVATORY

There has been a year-round weather observatory on Mt. Washington from 1870 to 1892, and from 1932 onward. The observatory maintains museum exhibits in the Sherman Adams summit building on Mt. Washington and at the Weather Discovery Center on NH 16 in North Conway. The Mt. Washington Observatory is operated by a nonprofit corporation, and individuals are invited to become members and contribute to the support of its important work. For details, visit mountwashington.org or call 603-356-2137.

MT. WASHINGTON AUTO RD.

This private road from the Glen House site on NH 16 to the summit, often called the Carriage Rd., was constructed from 1855 through 1861. Vehicles are charged a toll at the foot of the mountain. With long zigzags and an easy grade, the road climbs the prominent northeast ridge named for Benjamin Chandler, who died on the upper part from the effects of hypothermia in 1856. Hiking on the road is not forbidden, but despite easier grades and smoother footing than hiking trails, the distance is long and the competition with automobile traffic is annoying and potentially dangerous. After dark, however, its advantages increase markedly and its disadvantages decrease greatly, so this road may well be the best escape route for hikers faced with the onset of nightfall on the trails of Mt. Washington. In winter, severe icing and drifting, along with ruts from official snow-vehicle traffic, make the section above treeline a less pleasant and more difficult route than might be anticipated, particularly for skiers. The emergency shelters that were formerly located along the upper part of the road have been removed. The first 4.0 mi. of the road (below treeline), although still used by snow vehicles, are now officially maintained as a part of the Great Glen cross-country ski trail network (fee charged) and receive considerable use by skiers.

Limited parking is available at several trailheads for hikers who have paid the toll. Please park only in turnouts and make sure your vehicle is not blocking traffic. Check at the Toll House for the gate-closing schedule so you don't get locked in. Because of the continual theft and destruction of trail signs, they are often placed on the trails at some distance from the Auto Rd. The names of some trails are painted on rocks at the point where they leave the road.

The Auto Rd. leaves NH 16 opposite the Glen House site (elevation about 1,600 ft.), crosses the Peabody River, and starts the long climb. Just above the 2-mi. mark, after sharp curves right and then left, the AT crosses. To the south, the AT follows Old Jackson Rd. (now a foot trail) past jcts. with Nelson Crag Trail and Raymond Path to Pinkham Notch Visitor Center. To the north, the AT follows Madison Gulf Trail toward the Great Gulf and the Northern Presidentials. Low's Bald Spot, a fine viewpoint, can be reached by an easy walk of about 0.3 mi. from the road via Madison Gulf Trail and a short side path.

The Auto Rd. continues to treeline, passing to the left of the site of the Halfway House (3,840 ft.), and soon swings around the Horn, skirting a prominent shoulder known as the Ledge, where you have a fine view to the north. A short distance above the Ledge, Chandler Brook Trail descends into the Great Gulf on the right, and soon the route used by snow vehicles in winter diverges right.

Just above the 5-mi. mark, on the right, exactly at the sharp turn, are some remarkable folded strata in the rocks beside the road. Here, near Cragway Spring, Nelson Crag Trail comes close to the left side of the road. At about 5.5 mi., the road passes through the patch of high scrub in which Dr. B. L. Ball survived two nights in a winter storm in October 1855. (Dr. Ball's account of his ordeal, *Three Days on the White Mountains: The Perilous Adventure of Dr. B. L. Ball on Mount Washington,* published in 1856, is available in a reprint edition from Bondcliff Books.) A short distance above the 6.0-mi. mark, where the winter route rejoins, Wamsutta Trail descends on the right to the Great Gulf, and Alpine Garden Trail diverges left. The trenchlike structures near the road are the remains of the old Glen House Bridle Path, built in 1853. The road soon makes a hairpin turn and circles the left edge of a lawn sometimes called the Cow Pasture, where Huntington Ravine Trail enters on the left and the remains of an old corral are visible on the right a little farther along. Beyond the 7.0-mi. post, the Cog Railway approaches and runs above the road on the right; near the tracks, just below the summit, the Bourne monument stands at the spot where Lizzie Bourne perished in September 1855 at the age of 23, the second recorded death on the mountain. Soon, the road crosses Nelson Crag Trail, which enters on the left and climbs to the summit from the right side. Tuckerman Ravine Trail enters on the left just below the parking lot complex at about 8 mi.; from the parking lots, the summit buildings are reached by a wooden stairway. For information on schedules and fares for passenger vehicles, guided stage tours, and a limited hiker shuttle service, visit mtwashingtonautoroad.com or call 603-466-3988.

MT. WASHINGTON COG RAILWAY

The Mt. Washington Cog Railway, an unusual artifact of nineteenth-century engineering with a fascinating history, was completed in 1869. The railway roughly follows the route of Ethan Allen Crawford's second trail up the mountain, which he cut to provide a shorter and more direct route to Mt. Washington than Crawford Path over the Southern Presidentials. The railway's maximum grade, 13.5 in. to the yd., is equaled by only one other railroad in the world (excluding funicular roads), the railroad on Mt. Pilatus in the Alps. The location of the Base Station is called Marshfield, in honor of Sylvester Marsh, who was the chief promoter and builder of the railway, and Darby Field, the leader of the first recorded ascent of Mt. Washington. Hiker parking is available at the Base Station in a designated lower lot.

Walking on the Cog Railway track is not permitted. The Cog Railway ascends a minor westerly ridge in a nearly straight line to the treeline, which is reached near the trestle called Jacob's Ladder (4,800 ft.). This trestle, standing as much as 30 ft. above the mountainside, is the steepest part of the railroad. After crossing the shoulder that extends toward Mt. Clay, the line curves to the right and runs close to the edge of the Great Gulf; you have a fine view across the gulf toward the northern peaks above the crossing of Westside Trail (5,600 ft.). It is 3.0 mi. from Marshfield to the summit, and trains ascend in about 1 hr. The Cog Railway usually operates from spring through late fall; for a current schedule, visit thecog.com or call 603-278-5404.

ROAD ACCESS

Access to most of the trailheads in this section is from NH 16 or US 302, or from roads a short distance off these major highways. Other access roads include Cog Railway Base Rd. from US 302 at Bretton Woods; Mt. Clinton Rd. (not plowed in winter), which runs 3.6 mi. from Cog Railway Base Rd. opposite Jefferson Notch Rd. to US 302 just west of AMC's Highland Center at Crawford Notch; and Rocky Branch Rd. (FR 27), which starts as Jericho Rd. from US 302 in Bartlett and runs 4.4 mi. up Rocky Branch valley. The upper part of Rocky Branch Rd. is not plowed in winter. Other access roads are covered in individual trail descriptions.

GEOGRAPHY

Mt. Washington (6,288 ft.), the highest peak east of the Mississippi River and north of the Carolinas, was seen from the ocean as early as 1605. Its first recorded ascent was in June 1642 by Darby Field of Exeter, New Hampshire, and one or two Algonkian natives who may have reached the summit by way of the southern peaks—although no conclusive case can be made for any of the several reasonably practical routes because only two secondhand accounts of this expedition have survived. Field made a second ascent a month later, and several other ascents were made that year, including one by Thomas Gorges and Richard Vines of Maine. The discovery that the mountain's slopes were not strewn with precious stones led to a sharp decline in interest after this initial flurry, and it was almost two centuries before visits to Mt. Washington returned to this level. The mountain has a long and varied history of human activity, having been the site of several hotels; a road and a railway; a weather observatory; a daily newspaper; a radio station and a television station; and an assortment of auto, foot, and ski races. *The Story of Mount Washington,* by F. Allen Burt (Dartmouth Publications), covers the entertaining human history of the mountain in great detail, whereas Peter Randall's *Mount Washington* (Countryman Press) is a shorter and less detailed handbook of human and natural history; however, both of these books are currently out of print. *Not Without Peril,* by Nicholas Howe (AMC Books), provides a fascinating account of many of the accidents and other misadventures that have taken place on the Presidential Range.

In appearance, Mt. Washington is a broad, massive mountain, with great ravines cut deeply into its steep sides, leaving buttress ridges that reach up through timberline and support the great upper plateau. Timberline occurs at an elevation of 4,500 to 5,000 ft., depending on the degree of exposure to the mountain's fierce weather. The upper plateau, varying in elevation from 5,000 to 5,500 ft., bears comparatively gentle slopes interspersed with wide grassy areas strewn with rocks, which are called lawns. The summit cone, covered with fragments of rock and almost devoid of vegetation, rises steeply above this plateau.

The upper part of the mountain has a climate similar to that of northern Labrador, and its areas of alpine tundra support a fascinating variety of plant and animal life adapted to the extreme conditions of the alpine environment. Many of these species are found only on other high mountaintops or in the tundra many hundreds of miles farther north, and a few plants are found only or primarily on the Presidential Range. The alpine plants in particular have attracted many professional and amateur scientists (including, among the well-known amateurs, Henry David Thoreau), and many of the features of the mountain are named for early botanists, such as Manasseh Cutler, Jacob Bigelow, Francis Boott, William Oakes, and Edward Tuckerman. Great care should be exercised not to damage the plant life in these areas, as their struggle for survival is already severe. Hikers should avoid unnecessary excursions away from the trails and should step on rocks rather than vegetation wherever possible. AMC publishes the *AMC Field Guide to the New England Alpine Summits* (by Nancy Slack and Allison Bell), a handbook covering the ecological relations of the plants and animals found above treeline. The bedrock geology of the area is described in *The Presidential Range: Its Geologic History and Plate Tectonics,* by J. Dykstra Eusden (Durand Press), and the surficial geology is shown on a map, *Surficial Geology of Mount Washington and The Presidential Range, New Hampshire,* by Brian K. Fowler (Durand Press).

The slopes of Mt. Washington are drained by tributaries of three major rivers: the Androscoggin, the Connecticut, and the Saco. The tall, massive Northern Presidentials, or northern peaks (Section Two), continue the rocky alpine terrain of Mt. Washington to the north and northeast in an arc that encloses the Great Gulf, the largest glacial cirque in the White Mountains. (A glacial cirque is a landform that results when an alpine glacier, or a small local glacier in a mountain valley, excavates a typical V-shaped brook valley with a narrow floor and fairly uniform slopes, turning it into the classic U-shaped cirque with a broad, fairly flat floor and almost vertical walls.) The steep headwall of the Great Gulf is carved high into the northwestern flank of Mt. Washington.

Moving clockwise from the Great Gulf around the east side of the mountain, Chandler Ridge (by which the Mt. Washington Auto Rd. ascends the upper part of the mountain) passes over the small peak of Nelson Crag (5,635 ft.) before merging into the summit cone; this ridge divides the Great Gulf from the great ravines of the east face: Huntington Ravine, the Ravine of Raymond Cataract, Tuckerman Ravine (famed for spring skiing), and the Gulf of Slides. Huntington and Tuckerman ravines and the Ravine of Raymond Cataract are drained by branches of the Cutler River, and the New River flows down from the Gulf of Slides. Chandler Ridge also forms the north boundary of the lawn that is called the Alpine Garden for its colorful displays of alpine flowers in late June, which lies at the foot of the summit cone just above the eastern ravines. Lion Head, a pinnacled buttress named for its appearance when seen from points on NH 16 just north of Pinkham Notch Visitor Center, caps the north wall of Tuckerman Ravine. Slide Peak (4,806 ft.) encloses the Gulf of Slides on the south; on the ridge extending east from Slide Peak is the Glen Boulder, a huge glacial erratic that is a notable landmark in the Pinkham Notch area.

The steep eastern slopes of the mountain bear several notable waterfalls. Raymond Cataract falls through a series of wild and beautiful cascades in the Ravine of Raymond Cataract, but brush has covered a former footway, so this series of falls can be reached only by highly skilled bushwhackers. Crystal Cascade is easily reached from Pinkham Notch Visitor Center by a walk of about 0.3 mi. on Tuckerman Ravine Trail. Glen Ellis Falls, located deep in the Ellis River valley, can be easily reached from the parking area located on NH 16, 0.8 mi. south of Pinkham Notch Visitor Center, by a gravel path 0.3-mi. long, with rock steps and handrails, that passes under the highway through a tunnel then descends about 100 ft. The main fall is 70 ft. high, and below it are several pools and smaller falls. The WMNF plans significant improvements at this site in the near future.

Boott Spur (5,500 ft.), the great southeast shoulder of Mt. Washington, forms the south wall of Tuckerman Ravine and the north wall of the Gulf of Slides. The flat ridge connecting Boott Spur with the cone of Mt. Washington bears Bigelow Lawn, the largest of the Presidential Range lawns. Oakes Gulf, a glacial cirque at the headwaters of the Dry River, lies west of Boott Spur and east of Mt. Monroe.

Three major ridges run southwest or south from Mt. Washington, separated by deep river valleys from each other and from the ranges to the west and east: the Southern Presidentials, the Montalban Ridge, and the Rocky Branch Ridge. The Southern Presidentials, or southern peaks, form a great ridge—the second-most prominent in the range after the Northern Presidentials—that extends about 8 mi. southwest from the summit of Mt. Washington to the Webster Cliffs above Crawford Notch. To the northwest, the headwaters of the Ammonoosuc River (a tributary of the Connecticut River) flow across a broad, flat expanse, sometimes called the Fabyan Plain, that separates the Southern Presidentials from the much lower Cherry–Dartmouth Range.

The summits on the Southern Presidential ridge decrease steadily in elevation from northeast to southwest. The tallest of the southern peaks, Mt. Monroe (5,372 ft.), is a sharply pointed pyramid that rises abruptly from the flat area around the Lakes of the Clouds with a secondary summit, a small crag sometimes called Little Monroe (5,225 ft.), on its west ridge. The summit, crossed by Mt. Monroe Loop, is completely above treeline and affords fine views of the deep chasm of Oakes Gulf on the east, Lakes of the Clouds, and the nearby summit of Mt. Washington. Lakes of the Clouds are two small alpine tarns that lie in a small bowl on the northwest side of the ridge, near the low point between Mt. Washington and Mt. Monroe. The larger lake, often called Lower Lake, is at an elevation of 5,025 ft., and the much smaller Upper Lake lies to the north of Lower

Lake at an elevation of 5,050 ft. The flat region between Mt. Monroe and Lakes of the Clouds supports a bountiful number of alpine plants, including the extremely rare Robbins' cinquefoil (*Potentilla robbinsiana*), making this one of the most significant habitats in the White Mountains. Part of this area is closed to all public entry due to damage caused in the past by hikers coming to admire these plants, which can withstand the full violence of above-treeline weather but not the tread of hikers' boots.

Mt. Franklin (5,001 ft.) is a flat shoulder of Monroe that appears impressive only when seen from below, in the Eisenhower–Franklin col. The summit's exact location among a group of low, rolling ridges is not entirely obvious. The summit lies a short distance east of Crawford Path along an unmarked spur path and commands an excellent view straight down into Oakes Gulf.

Previously called Mt. Pleasant, Mt. Eisenhower (4,760 ft.) was renamed after the former president's death. Although a good deal of scrub is on the lower slopes of this dome-shaped mountain, the top is completely bald. Its summit is crossed by Mt. Eisenhower Loop.

The New Hampshire legislature named Mt. Pierce (4,312 ft.) for Franklin Pierce, the only U.S. president born in New Hampshire, in 1913. Although this name is officially recognized by the U.S. Board of Geographic Names and appears on all USGS maps, the name was not universally accepted, and the mountain's former name, Mt. Clinton, persists in Mt. Clinton Rd. and Mt. Clinton Trail, the path that ascends the southeast slope of the mountain. Mt. Pierce is wooded almost to the top of its flat summit on the west, but a broad open area on the east side affords fine views, and additional views can be seen from its southern shoulder. Its summit lies on Webster Cliff Trail just above its jct. with Crawford Path.

Named for Charles Jackson, a nineteenth-century New Hampshire state geologist and not (as many would suppose) for President Andrew Jackson, Mt. Jackson (4,052 ft.) has a square, ledgy summit with steep sides and a flat top, affording possibly the finest views among the southern peaks. Its summit is crossed by Webster Cliff Trail and is reached by the Jackson branch of Webster–Jackson Trail.

Once called Notch Mtn., Mt. Webster (3,910 ft.) was renamed for Daniel Webster, the great nineteenth-century orator, U.S. senator, secretary of state, and unsuccessful aspirant to the presidency, who once visited the summit of Mt. Washington with Ethan Allen Crawford as his guide. The ledgy summit of Mt. Webster is crossed by Webster Cliff Trail, which is intersected by the Webster branch of Webster–Jackson Trail not far from the top. The impressive Webster Cliffs form the eastern wall of Crawford Notch and afford many fine views.

To the southeast of the Southern Presidentials lies the Dry River, running down the central valley of the 27,000-acre Presidential Range–Dry River Wilderness. This river has also been called the Mt. Washington River, but "Dry River" has won the battle, possibly because of the ironic quality of the name. The Dry River runs from Oakes Gulf to the Saco River through a deep, narrow, steep-walled ravine. Although in a dry season the flow is meager, with many rocks lying uncovered in the streambed, its watershed has extremely rapid runoff, and its sudden floods are legendary: It has drowned unwary hikers. Access to the Dry River area has always been somewhat difficult, and ascents of the southern peaks from this side are relatively arduous. In the 1970s the WMNF made access somewhat easier (and safer) by eliminating many river crossings through trail relocations and by constructing a suspension footbridge at the first (and usually most difficult) remaining crossing. Several potentially dangerous crossings remain on the trails in the valley, however, and visitors need to keep a careful watch on the weather and consider any substantial rainfall in the previous few days. In accordance with USFS Wilderness policy, the trails in the Dry River/Montalban Ridge area are, in general, maintained to a lower standard than are trails outside Wilderness Areas, and considerable care may be required to follow them.

Montalban Ridge extends southward from Boott Spur, forming the longest subsidiary ridge in the Presidential Range, running for about 20 mi. between Rocky Branch on the east and Dry River and the Saco River on the west. At Mt. Resolution, the main ridge curves to the east along the Saco valley over several low peaks above the intervales of Bartlett and Glen, and the short Bemis Ridge carries the line of the upper ridge south to the great bend in the Saco. The peaks of Montalban Ridge, in order from the north, include a peak unofficially called North Isolation (4,293 ft.) and peaks named Mt. Isolation (4,003 ft.), Mt. Davis (3,819 ft.), Stairs Mtn. (3,463 ft.), Mt. Resolution (3,415 ft.), Mt. Parker (3,004 ft.), Mt. Langdon (2,390 ft.), Mt. Pickering (1,930 ft.), and Mt. Stanton (1,716 ft.). The peaks of the Bemis Ridge include Mt. Crawford (3,119 ft.), Mt. Hope (2,505 ft.), and Hart Ledge (2,020 ft.). Cave Mtn. (1,439 ft.), a low spur of the range near Bartlett village, is much better known for the cave on its south face than for its summit.

The views from the summits of mts. Isolation, Davis, and Crawford are among the finest in the White Mountains, and mts. Resolution and Parker also offer excellent outlooks. The Giant Stairs are a wild and picturesque feature of the region, offering a spectacular view from the top of the cliff that forms the upper stair. These two great steplike ledges at the south end of the ridge of Stairs Mtn. are quite regular in form and are visible from many points. A third and somewhat similar cliff, sometimes called the

Back Stair, lies east of the main summit but has no trail. Mt. Stanton and Mt. Pickering are wooded, but several open ledges near their summits afford interesting views in various directions. All these peaks are reached by well-maintained trails, except Mt. Hope and Hart Ledge. Mt. Hope is heavily wooded and very seldom climbed. The fine cliff of Hart Ledge rises more than 1,000 ft. above the meadows at the great bend in the Saco River, just above Bartlett, and affords views to the east, west, and south. The ledge is located on private land with no regular trail.

East of Montalban Ridge, beyond Rocky Branch but west of Ellis River valley, lies Rocky Branch Ridge. This heavily wooded ridge runs south from Slide Peak over a series of trailless peaks (3,921 ft., 3,633 ft., and 3,244 ft., the latter unofficially called South Engine Hill) then continues as a low, flat ridge to Maple Mtn. (2,601 ft.). Iron Mtn. (2,726 ft.) is an isolated small mountain rising southeast of Maple Mtn. and west of the village of Jackson. Iron Mtn. has a fine north outlook and a magnificent bare ledge at the top of its south cliff. Green Hill (2,181 ft.) is a shoulder of Iron Mtn. with an interesting view but no official path. To the east of Rocky Branch Ridge, Ellis River flows down from Pinkham Notch, with NH 16 running down through the valley, and the ridges of Wildcat Mtn. rising on the other side.

On the west face of Mt. Washington, an unnamed ridge that is ascended by the Cog Railway separates the two principal ravines on that side of the mountain: Ammonoosuc Ravine, which contains the headwaters of Ammonoosuc River, and Burt Ravine, which lies between Mt. Washington and Mt. Clay, the southernmost of the northern peaks. These ravines are less spectacular than are those on the east side of Mt. Washington but are still quite impressive.

HUTS AND LODGES

For current information on AMC's huts, Pinkham Notch Visitor Center, Joe Dodge Lodge, and the Highland Center at Crawford Notch, contact AMC's Reservation Office (603-466-2727) or visit outdoors.org/lodging.

Pinkham Notch Visitor Center and Joe Dodge Lodge (AMC)

Pinkham Notch Visitor Center is a unique mountain recreation facility in the heart of the WMNF. The center, originally built in 1920 and greatly enlarged since then, is located on NH 16, practically at the height-of-land in Pinkham Notch, about 20 mi. north of Conway and 11 mi. south of Gorham. The center is also 0.8 mi. north of Glen Ellis Falls and 0.9 mi. south of the base of Wildcat Mtn. Ski Area. Pinkham Notch Visitor Center offers food and lodging to the public throughout the year. Pets are not allowed inside any building of the visitor center. Concord Coach Lines offers daily bus service to and from Logan Airport and South Station in Boston, and AMC operates a hiker shuttle bus from the visitor center to many of the principal trailheads in the White Mountains during the summer.

Joe Dodge Lodge accommodates more than 100 guests in a variety of bunk, queen, and family rooms. It also offers a library that commands a spectacular view of nearby Wildcat Ridge, and a living room where accounts of the day's activities can be shared around an open fireplace. The center features a 65-seat conference room equipped with audiovisual facilities.

The Trading Post, a popular meeting place for hikers, has been a center of AMC's educational and recreational activities since 1920. Weekend workshops, seminars, and lectures are conducted throughout the year. The building houses a dining room and an information desk, where basic equipment, guidebooks, maps, and other AMC publications are available. The pack room downstairs is open 24 hr. a day for hikers to stop in, relax, use the coin-operated showers, and repack their gear.

Pinkham Notch Visitor Center is the most important trailhead on the east side of Mt. Washington. Free public parking is available, although sleeping in cars is not permitted. Additional parking is available in designated areas along NH 16 in both directions, but a USFS recreational permit is required. Although the permit is not legally required for parking at Pinkham Notch Visitor Center, AMC requests that hikers purchase one to support the USFS recreation program. Tuckerman Ravine Trail, Lost Pond Trail, and Old Jackson Rd. all start at the center, giving access to many more trails, and a number of walking trails have been constructed for shorter, easier trips in the Pinkham vicinity. Among these are Crew-Cut Trail, George's Gorge Trail, Liebeskind's Loop, and Square Ledge Trail.

Highland Center at Crawford Notch and Shapleigh Bunkhouse (AMC)

Located on 26 acres of AMC-owned land at the head of Crawford Notch, the Highland Center, opened in 2003, is a lodging and education center open to the public year-round. It is located at the site of the former Crawford House grand hotel on US 302, about 20 mi. west of North Conway and 8.7 mi. east of the traffic lights in Twin Mountain village. Highland Center is a stop on the AMC Hiker Shuttle routes during summer and on fall weekends.

The lodge contains 34 rooms, accommodating a total of 122 beds, including shared rooms with shared baths and private rooms with private baths. The adjacent Shapleigh Bunkhouse contains 16 beds in two bunkrooms, as well as a common room and pantry with a refrigerator and a microwave.

Reservations are encouraged. The center was constructed using energy-efficient materials and is designed to complement the landscape while paying tribute to the intriguing human history in Crawford Notch. Meals consisting of hearty mountain fare are served in a family-style setting.

A wide variety of educational programs and skills training for children, teens, and adults is offered at the Highland Center, helping participants increase their understanding of the natural environment and gain proficiency in outdoor skills, such as map and compass use or wilderness first aid. Day-hikers, backpackers, and other visitors can find trail and weather information at the center.

AMC's Macomber Family Information Center, open during summer and fall, is located in the historic Crawford Depot, a former train station renovated by AMC, and houses interpretive displays, an information desk, and a small store that stocks last-minute hiker supplies, guidebooks, AMC publications, and souvenir items. The center is also a major stop and transfer point for the AMC Hiker Shuttle, which operates throughout the summer and on fall weekends, and serves as a depot for the excursion trains that run on the Crawford Notch line during tourist season.

From AMC's Crawford Notch property, many trails described in Section One can be reached, including Crawford Path, Saco Lake Trail, and Webster–Jackson Trail. Parking for overnight guests is located on the Highland Center property near the main building. Parking for Crawford Path is available in the USFS lot (recreational permit required), located just off Mt. Clinton Rd. near its jct. with US 302.

Lakes of the Clouds Hut (AMC)

For more than 125 years, AMC's White Mountain hut system has offered hikers a bunk for the night in spectacular locations, with home-cooked dinners and breakfasts, cold running water, and composting or waterless toilets. Originally built in 1915 and greatly enlarged since then, Lakes of the Clouds Hut is open to the public from June to mid-September and closed at all other times. The hut is located on a shelf near the foot of Mt. Monroe, about 50 yd. west of the larger lake, at an elevation of 5,012 ft. The hut is reached by Crawford Path or Ammonoosuc Ravine Trail and has accommodations for 90 guests in bunkrooms for six, eight, twelve, and fifteen people. Pets are not permitted in the hut. Reservations are highly recommended (603-466-2727; outdoors.org/lodging/huts). Limited drinks, snacks, and gear are available for purchase by day visitors. A limited number of backpacker spaces are available at a significantly reduced rate for AT thru-hikers only, on a first-come, first-served basis. A refuge room in the cellar is left open in the winter for emergency use only.

SEC 1

Mizpah Spring Hut (AMC)

Completed in 1965, this hut is located at an elevation of 3,777 ft. on the site formerly occupied by the Mizpah Spring Shelter, at the jct. of Webster Cliff Trail and Mt. Clinton Trail, near Mizpah Cutoff. The hut accommodates 60 guests, with sleeping quarters in eight rooms containing from four to ten bunks. This hut is open to the public from mid-May to mid-October (caretaker basis in May). Lodging, with meals included, is available for a fee; reservations are highly recommended (603-466-2727; outdoors.org/lodging/huts). Limited drinks, snacks, and gear are available for purchase by day visitors. Pets are not permitted in the hut. Tentsites are nearby (caretaker; fee charged).

CAMPING

Presidential Range–Dry River Wilderness

In accordance with USFS Wilderness policy, hiking group size may not exceed ten people, and no more than ten people may occupy any designated or non-designated campsite. Camping and wood or charcoal fires are not allowed within 200 ft. of any trail except at designated campsites, which are marked with small wooden posts along several trails in the Wilderness Area. Several shelters have been removed, and the remaining one will be dismantled when major maintenance is required. See p. xiv for more information about Wilderness Area regulations.

Forest Protection Areas

The WMNF has established a number of FPAs, where camping and wood or charcoal fires are prohibited throughout the year. See p. xxiv for general FPA regulations.

In the area covered by Section One, no camping is permitted regardless of snow cover on the east face of Mt. Washington's summit cone, from Boott Spur to Nelson Crag (the area above Tuckerman and Huntington ravines, including the Alpine Garden area and East Snowfields).

No camping is permitted within 0.25 mi. of any trailhead, picnic area, or any facility for overnight accommodation, such as a hut, cabin, shelter, tentsite, or campground, except as designated at the facility itself. In the area covered by Section One, camping is also forbidden within 0.25 mi. of Glen Ellis Falls.

No camping is permitted within 200 ft. of certain trails. In 2016, designated trails included Ammonoosuc Ravine Trail.

No camping is permitted on WMNF land within 0.25 mi. of certain roads (camping on private roadside land is illegal except by permission of the landowner). In 2016, these roads included US 302, NH 16, Cog

Railway Base Rd. (FR 173), Jefferson Notch Rd. (FR 220) from Cog Railway Base Rd. to Caps Ridge Trail trailhead, and Rocky Branch Rd. (FR 27, a.k.a. Jericho Rd.).

In Tuckerman and Huntington ravines (Cutler River drainage, including the Alpine Garden and the east face of the Mt. Washington summit cone), camping is prohibited throughout the year; the only year-round exception is the Hermit Lake Shelters and adjoining tent platforms. Visitors in the ravine areas may not kindle charcoal or wood fires; people intending to cook must bring their own small stoves. Day visitors and shelter users alike are required to carry out all their own trash and garbage; no receptacles are provided. Updated information on these policies is available at Pinkham Notch Visitor Center or the Tuckerman Ravine caretaker's residence, or from WMNF offices. There is no warming room open to the public, and no refreshments are available.

Crawford Notch State Park
No camping is permitted in Crawford Notch State Park, except at the Dry River Campground (NHDP; fee charged; nhstateparks.org) on US 302.

Established Trailside Campsites
To reduce overcrowding during peak summer and fall periods, groups of six or more planning to use AMC-managed backcountry campsites are required to use AMC's group notification system. For more information, visit outdoors.org/group_notification.

Hermit Lake Campsite (AMC/WMNF), located in Tuckerman Ravine, consists of eight open-front shelters, with a total capacity of 86 persons, and three tent platforms open to the public. Tickets for shelter and tentsite space (nontransferable and nonrefundable) must be purchased for a fee at Pinkham Notch Visitor Center in person (first-come, first-served). Campers are limited to a maximum of seven consecutive nights, and pets are not allowed to stay overnight.

Nauman Tentsite (AMC) consists of seven tent platforms near Mizpah Spring Hut. In summer, there is a caretaker and a fee is charged.

Lakes of the Clouds Hut (AMC) has limited space available for AT thru-hikers at a substantially reduced cost.

Rocky Branch Shelter #1 and Tentsite (WMNF), with three tent platforms, is located near the jct. of Rocky Branch and Stairs Col trails, just outside the Presidential Range–Dry River Wilderness.

Rocky Branch Shelter #2 (WMNF), formerly located at the jct. of Rocky Branch Trail and Isolation Trail, has been removed and will be replaced with tent pads in the future.

**SEC
1**

Dry River Shelter #3 (WMNF) is located on Dry River Trail, 6.3 mi. from US 302, within the Presidential Range–Dry River Wilderness. This shelter will be removed when major maintenance is required.

Resolution Shelter (AMC), formerly located on a spur path off Davis Path at its jct. with Mt. Parker Trail, has been removed.

Mt. Langdon Shelter (WMNF) is located at the jct. of Mt. Langdon and Mt. Stanton trails, just outside the Presidential Range–Dry River Wilderness.

SUGGESTED HIKES

■ Easy Hikes

CRYSTAL CASCADE

RT via Tuckerman Ravine Trail	0.6 mi.	200 ft.	0:25

This short jaunt leads to a fine waterfall. See Tuckerman Ravine Trail, p. 23.

ELEPHANT HEAD

RT via Webster–Jackson and spur trails	0.6 mi.	150 ft.	0:25

An easy climb reaches this ledge with a view of Crawford Notch. See Webster–Jackson Trail, p. 46.

LIEBESKIND'S LOOP

LP via Old Jackson Road, Crew-Cut and George's Gorge trails, and Liebeskind's Loop	2.8 mi.	650 ft.	1:45

This interesting loop—including a short side trip to Lila's Ledge—delivers views of Pinkham Notch and Mt. Washington. See Liebeskind's Loop, p. 37.

IRON MTN.

RT via Iron Mtn. Trail	3.2 mi.	1,200 ft.	2:10

This small mountain, with one badly eroded section of trail, has a fine north outlook and a broad ledge with an excellent view from its south end. See Iron Mtn. Trail, p. 67.

■ Moderate Hikes

GLEN BOULDER

	⇅	⬈	↻
RT via Glen Boulder Trail	3.2 mi.	1,750 ft.	2:30

A fairly steep and rough, if short, route to treeline provides good views and passes a boulder perched on the mountainside. See Glen Boulder Trail, p. 30.

LOW'S BALD SPOT

	⇅	⬈	↻
RT via Old Jackson Road, Madison Gulf Trail (Section Two), and side path	4.4 mi.	1,050 ft.	2:45

This attractive and easy hike from Pinkham Notch Visitor Center leads to an outlook with interesting views of the Presidentials. To begin, see Old Jackson Road, p. 35.

HERMIT LAKE

	⇅	⬈	↻
RT via Tuckerman Ravine Trail	4.8 mi.	1,850 ft.	3:20

A steady climb is rewarded with views into the famed glacial cirque. See Tuckerman Ravine Trail, p. 23.

HARVARD ROCK

	⇅	⬈	↻
RT via Tuckerman Ravine and Boott Spur trails	4.2 mi.	2,000 ft.	3:05

This outlook offers a magnificent view into Tuckerman Ravine. See Boott Spur Trail, p. 29.

MT. CRAWFORD

	⇅	⬈	↻
RT via Davis Path and spur trail	5.0 mi.	2,100 ft.	3:35
RT to Crawford and Stairs via Davis Path and spur trails	9.8 mi.	3,150 ft.	6:30
RT to Crawford and Resolution via Davis Path, spur trail, and Mt. Parker Trail	9.0 mi.	3,000 ft.	6:00
RT to Crawford, Stairs, and Resolution via Davis Path, spur trails, and Mt. Parker Trail	10.8 mi.	3,500 ft.	7:10

The beautiful rock peak of Mt. Crawford offers extensive views. This is also part of an excellent longer trip that includes Stairs Mtn., Mt. Resolution via Mt. Parker Trail, or both of these excellent viewpoints. See Davis Path, p. 56.

MTS. JACKSON AND WEBSTER

	⮌	↗	○
RT to Jackson via Webster–Jackson Trail	5.2 mi.	2,250 ft.	3:45
RT to Webster via Webster–Jackson Trail	5.0 mi.	2,200 ft.	3:35
LP to both peaks via Webster Cliff Trail	6.5 mi.	2,550 ft.	4:30
LP to Webster via Webster-Jackson and Webster Cliff trails	5.8 mi.	2,200 ft.	4:00
RT to Webster via Webster Cliff Trail	6.6 mi.	2,850 ft.	4:45

The open summit of Mt. Jackson is reached by the Jackson branch of Webster–Jackson Trail; Mt. Webster, another fine viewpoint, is reached by the Webster branch of Webster–Jackson Trail. For both, see Webster–Jackson Trail, p. 46. A loop can be made over both summits via Webster Cliff Trail (p. 47). If spotting a car is available, another option is to ascend Mt. Webster by Webster–Jackson Trail and then make a leisurely descent of the magnificent Webster Cliff Trail down to the notch. Webster Cliff Trail can also be enjoyed as an out-and-back route to Mt. Webster.

MT. PIERCE AND MIZPAH SPRING HUT

	⮌	↗	○
LP via Crawford Connector, Crawford Path, Webster Cliff Trail, and Mizpah Cutoff	6.6 mi.	2,450 ft.	4:30

This interesting loop provides good views and a sampling of the alpine zone on Mt. Pierce, with a visit to a high-country hut on the return trip. See Crawford Path, p. 38.

MT. EISENHOWER

	⮌	↗	○
RT via Edmands Path and Mt. Eisenhower Loop	6.6 mi.	2,750 ft.	4:40

This moderate, graded route leads to a bald summit. See Edmands Path, p. 45.

■ Strenuous Hikes
MT. MONROE

	↻	↗	◔
RT via Ammonoosuc Ravine Trail, Crawford Path, and Mt. Monroe Loop	7.0 mi.	2,900 ft.	5:00
LP via Ammonoosuc Ravine Trail, Crawford Path, Mt. Monroe Loop, Crawford Path, and Edmands Path	8.2 mi.	3,000 ft.	5:35

This craggy peak is an excellent alternative to its more notorious neighbor, Mt. Washington, offering superb views. With a car spot, a magnificent open ridge walk can be enjoyed along Crawford Path with a descent via Edmands Path. To begin, see Ammonoosuc Ravine Trail, p. 43.

MT. WASHINGTON

	↻	↗	◔
RT via Jewell Trail–Gulfside Trail–Trinity Heights Connector	10.0 mi.	4,000 ft.	7:00
RT via Ammonoosuc Ravine Trail and Crawford Path	9.2 mi.	3,800 ft.	6:30
LP via Ammonoosuc Ravine Trail, Crawford Path, Trinity Heights Connector, Gulfside Trail, and Jewell Trail	9.6 mi.	3,900 ft.	6:45
OW via Tuckerman Ravine Trail	4.2 mi.	4,250 ft.	4:15
RT via Tuckerman Ravine Trail	8.4 mi.	4,250 ft.	6:20
LP via Boott Spur Trail, Davis Path, and Crawford Path	9.5 mi.	4,400 ft.	6:55
OW via Lion Head Trail and Tuckerman Ravine trails	4.3 mi.	4,250 ft.	4:15

The easiest way to climb Mt. Washington is probably the Jewell Trail–Gulfside Trail–Trinity Heights Connector combination on the west side, which begins at a parking lot on the road to the Cog Railway; this route is described in Section Two (to begin, see Jewell Trail, p. 135). Most hikers climbing from this side will be tempted to turn the hike into a loop by combining Jewell and Gulfside trails with Ammonoosuc Ravine Trail and Crawford Path, which begins at the same parking lot.

Ammonoosuc Ravine Trail and Crawford Path is a more interesting and beautiful route to Mt. Washington than Jewell Trail, but the section between Gem Pool and Lakes of the Clouds Hut can be extremely discouraging to a person in poor physical condition. On the descent, this section passes mostly over ledges and rocks, some of which are wet and slippery, and it can be tedious and tiring. On the whole, it is probably better to ascend

Ammonoosuc Ravine Trail and descend Jewell Trail, but if afternoon thunderstorms are threatening, the descent by Jewell Trail is more hazardous because it is far less sheltered; in rain without lightning, the steep, wet rocks on Ammonoosuc Ravine Trail may be more of a problem.

From the east side, Tuckerman Ravine Trail is the easiest and most popular route to the summit (see Tuckerman Ravine Trail, p. 23). Many other routes are available; although all of them are substantially less crowded, they are also either longer or more strenuous. In good weather, Boott Spur Trail offers better views, and though longer, it is not substantially more difficult. One can ascend by this trail and then descend through Tuckerman Ravine with the crowds or make the easier, faster ascent through Tuckerman Ravine and then a leisurely descent via Boott Spur (see Boott Spur Trail, p. 29). Lion Head Trail is about the same length as Tuckerman Ravine Trail and offers better views but has steeper sections and is generally rougher; for most people, it is probably a better route for the ascent than for the descent (see Lion Head Trail, p. 25).

TRAIL DESCRIPTIONS

MT. WASHINGTON FROM PINKHAM NOTCH

TUCKERMAN RAVINE TRAIL (WMNF; MAP 1: F9)

Cumulative from Pinkham Notch Visitor Center (2,032 ft.) to:	⇅	↗	↺
Boott Spur Trail (2,275 ft.)	0.4 mi.	250 ft.	0:20
Huntington Ravine Trail (3,031 ft.)	1.3 mi.	1,000 ft.	1:10
Huntington Ravine Fire Rd. (3,425 ft.)	1.7 mi.	1,400 ft.	1:35
Raymond Path (3,700 ft.)	2.1 mi.	1,650 ft.	1:55
Lion Head Trail (3,825 ft.)	2.3 mi.	1,800 ft.	2:05
Boott Spur Link and Hermit Lake shelters (3,875 ft.)	2.4 mi.	1,850 ft.	2:10
Snow Arch (4,525 ft.)	3.1 mi.	2,500 ft.	2:50
Alpine Garden Trail (5,150 ft.)	3.4 mi.	3,100 ft.	3:15
Tuckerman Junction (5,383 ft.)	3.6 mi.	3,350 ft.	3:30
Lion Head Trail, upper jct. (5,675 ft.)	3.8 mi.	3,650 ft.	3:45
Mt. Washington summit (6,288 ft.)	4.2 mi.	4,250 ft.	4:15

This trail to the summit of Mt. Washington from NH 16 at Pinkham Notch Visitor Center is probably the most popular route of ascent on the mountain. From Pinkham Notch Visitor Center, the trail follows a rocky tractor road up to the floor of Tuckerman Ravine. From there to the top of the headwall, the trail is a well-graded path, steady, but not excessively steep. The section on the headwall underwent major reconstruction by the AMC trail crew in 2011, including the placement of many new rock steps. Its final section ascends the cone of Mt. Washington steeply over fragments of rock. In spring and early summer, the WMNF often closes the section of trail on the ravine headwall due to snow and ice hazards, including dangerous crevasses, and notice is posted at Pinkham Notch Visitor Center. In these circumstances, Lion Head Trail is usually the most convenient alternative route. In winter conditions, the headwall is often impassable except by experienced and well-equipped technical snow and ice climbers, and it is frequently closed by the WMNF even to such climbers due to avalanche and icefall hazards. The winter route of Lion Head Trail, which begins on Huntington Ravine Fire Rd. 0.1 mi. from Tuckerman Ravine Trail, bypasses the headwall and usually provides the easiest and safest route for ascending Mt. Washington from the east in winter, though it is very steep.

Tuckerman Ravine Trail starts behind the Trading Post at Pinkham Notch Visitor Center; Old Jackson Rd. diverges right 50 yd. from here. Be careful to avoid numerous side paths, including Blanchard Ski Trail, in this area. In 0.3 mi., Tuckerman Ravine Trail crosses a bridge to the south bank of Cutler River, begins its moderate but relentless and rocky climb, and soon passes a side path leading 20 yd. right to the best viewpoint for Crystal Cascade. Boott Spur Trail diverges left at a sharp curve to the right, 0.4 mi. from Pinkham Notch Visitor Center, and at 1.3 mi., Huntington Ravine Trail diverges right. At 1.5 mi., Tuckerman Ravine Trail crosses a tributary then, at 1.6 mi., the main branch of Cutler River, both on bridges. At 1.7 mi., Huntington Ravine Fire Rd., which is the easiest route to Huntington Ravine in winter but offers very rough footing on some parts in summer, leaves on the right. The Lion Head winter route begins about 0.1 mi. up this road. At 2.1 mi., Raymond Path enters on the right where the Tuckerman trail turns sharply left, and at 2.3 mi., Lion Head Trail leaves on the right. In another 0.1 mi., Boott Spur Link leaves on the left, opposite the buildings located at the floor of Tuckerman Ravine, near Hermit Lake. Views from the floor of the ravine are impressive: The cliff on the right is Lion Head, and the more distant crags on the left are the Hanging Cliffs of Boott Spur.

The main trail keeps to the right (north) of the main stream and ascends a well-constructed footway into the upper floor of the ravine. At the foot of the headwall, the trail bears right and ascends a steep slope, where the Snow Arch can be seen on the left in spring and early summer of most years. In the early part of the hiking season, the snowfield above the Snow Arch usually extends across the trail, and the trail is often closed to hiking until this potentially hazardous snow slope has melted away. Some snow may persist in the ravine until late summer. The arch (which does not always form) is carved by a stream of snowmelt water that flows under the snowfield. (*Caution:* Do not approach or get too close to the arch, and under no circumstances cross over it or venture beneath it because sections weighing many tons may break off at any moment. One death and several narrow escapes have occurred as a result of falling ice. When ascending the headwall, be careful not to dislodge rocks and start them rolling; doing so would put hikers below you in serious danger. Several serious accidents in recent years have involved hikers who slipped off the side of the trail on the upper part of the headwall, often in adverse weather conditions, especially when the trail was slippery. Although the trail itself is relatively easy and quite safe, it passes within a very short distance of some extremely dangerous terrain, so a minor misstep off the side of the trail can have grave consequences.)

Turning sharply left at the top of the debris slope and traversing under a cliff, the trail emerges from the ravine and climbs almost straight west up a grassy, ledgy slope. At 3.4 mi., a short distance above the top of the head-wall, Alpine Garden Trail diverges right. At Tuckerman Junction, located on the lower edge of Bigelow Lawn at 3.6 mi., Tuckerman Crossover leads almost straight ahead (southwest) to Crawford Path near Lakes of the Clouds Hut; Southside Trail diverges from Tuckerman Crossover in 30 yd. and leads northwest, skirting the cone to Davis Path; and Lawn Cutoff leads left (south) toward Boott Spur. Tuckerman Ravine Trail turns sharply right (north) at this jct. and ascends the steep rocks, marked by cairns. At 3.8 mi., at Cloudwater Spring (unreliable) about a third of the way up the cone, Lion Head Trail reenters on the right. The Tuckerman trail continues to ascend to the Auto Rd. a few yards below the lower parking area, from which wooden stairways lead to the summit area.

Descending, Tuckerman Ravine Trail leaves the Auto Rd. at a sign a short distance below the lower parking area.

LION HEAD TRAIL (AMC; MAP 1: F9)

Cumulative from lower jct. with Tuckerman Ravine Trail (3,825 ft.) to:	⇅	↗	↻
Alpine Garden Trail (5,175 ft.)	1.1 mi.	1,350 ft.	1:15
Upper jct. with Tuckerman Ravine Trail (5,675 ft.)	1.6 mi.	1,850 ft.	1:45
From Pinkham Notch Visitor Center (2,032 ft.) to:			
Mt. Washington summit (6,288 ft.) via Lion Head Trail and Tuckerman Ravine Trail	4.3 mi.	4,250 ft.	4:15

Lion Head Trail follows the steep-ended ridge—aptly named for the appearance of its upper portion when viewed from points on NH 16 north of Pinkham Notch Visitor Center—that forms the north wall of Tucker-man Ravine. The trail begins and ends on Tuckerman Ravine Trail and thus provides an alternative, though much steeper, route to that heavily used trail. Lion Head Trail is especially important as an alternative when Tuckerman Ravine Trail over the headwall is closed during the spring or at other times when snow and ice create hazardous conditions on that trail. The winter route of Lion Head Trail is considered the least dangerous route for ascending Mt. Washington in winter conditions and is the most frequently used winter ascent route. An avalanche in 1995 destroyed the former winter route, and a new winter route was constructed; this route leaves Huntington Ravine Fire Rd. just past the crossing of Raymond Path, about 0.1 mi. from Tuckerman Ravine Trail, and rejoins the summer Lion Head

Trail at treeline. The signs and markings are changed by the USFS according to prevailing conditions at the beginning and end of the winter season (which on Mt. Washington extends from late fall through much of the spring in most years) to ensure that climbers take the proper route. The winter route is not open at times when it is not signed and marked as the currently open route.

Lion Head Trail diverges right from Tuckerman Ravine Trail 2.3 mi. from Pinkham Notch Visitor Center and 0.1 mi. below Hermit Lake. Running north, Lion Head Trail passes a side path on the left to one of the Hermit Lake shelters and crosses the outlet of Hermit Lake. The trail soon begins to climb the steep slope with rough footing then makes several switchbacks, scrambling up several small ledges and one ladder. The trail reaches treeline at 0.4 mi., where the winter route enters on the right as the main trail bears left. (Descending, the summer trail turns right and the winter route descends almost straight ahead.) The trail then ascends an open slope to lower Lion Head and continues to upper Lion Head at 0.9 mi., where the trail runs mostly level (with impressive views from the open spur), until it crosses Alpine Garden Trail at 1.1 mi. After passing through a belt of scrub, Lion Head Trail ascends steadily, then steeply, through an area of crags, with some short scrambles and a passage through a crack. The trail reaches its upper jct. with Tuckerman Ravine Trail at Cloudwater Spring (unreliable), about a third of the way up the cone of Mt. Washington, 0.4 mi. and 600 ft. below the summit.

HUNTINGTON RAVINE TRAIL (AMC; MAP 1: F9)

Cumulative from Tuckerman Ravine Trail (3,031 ft.) to:	⇅	↗	○
Raymond Path (3,425 ft.)	0.5 mi.	400 ft.	0:25
First-aid cache in ravine floor (4,075 ft.)	1.2 mi.	1,050 ft.	1:10
Alpine Garden Trail crossing (5,475 ft.)	2.1 mi.	2,450 ft.	2:15
Auto Rd. (5,725 ft.)	2.4 mi.	2,700 ft.	2:35
From Pinkham Notch Visitor Center (2,032 ft.) to:			
Mt. Washington summit (6,288 ft.) via Tuckerman Ravine, Huntington Ravine, and Nelson Crag trails	4.4 mi.	4,300 ft. (rev. 50 ft.)	4:20

Caution: This is the most difficult regular hiking trail in the White Mountains. Many of the ledges demand proper use of handholds for safe passage, and extreme caution must be exercised at all times. Although experienced hikers who are reasonably comfortable on steep rock will probably encounter little difficulty when conditions are good, the exposure on several of the steepest ledges is likely to prove extremely unnerving to novices and to those who are uncomfortable in steep places. Do not attempt this trail if you have difficulty on ledges on ordinary trails. Hikers encumbered with large or heavy packs may experience great difficulty in some places. This trail is very dangerous when wet or icy, and its use for descent at any time is strongly discouraged. Retreat under unfavorable conditions can be extremely difficult and hazardous, so one should never venture beyond the boulder slope known as the Fan in deteriorating conditions or when weather on the Alpine Garden is likely to be severe. During late fall, winter, and early spring, this trail (and any part of the ravine headwall) should be attempted only by those with full technical ice-climbing training and equipment. In particular, the ravine must not be regarded as a feasible escape route from the Alpine Garden in severe winter conditions.

This trail diverges right from Tuckerman Ravine Trail 1.3 mi. from Pinkham Notch Visitor Center. In 0.2 mi., Huntington Ravine Trail crosses Cutler River and, at 0.3 mi., the brook that drains Huntington Ravine. At 0.5 mi., Huntington Ravine Trail goes straight across Raymond Path. Huntington Ravine Trail crosses Huntington Ravine Fire Rd. and then climbs to meet the road again, turning left onto the road; at this jct., a fine view of the ravine can be obtained by following the road to a small rise about 100 yd. in the opposite direction. Above this point, the trail and road separate, rejoin, and cross several times; the junctions are not always well marked, but both routes lead to the same objective, and the major advantage of the trail is that it has somewhat better footing than the road. At 1.2 mi., the first-aid cache in the floor of the ravine is reached. Just beyond here are some boulders near the path whose tops afford good views of the ravine. Beyond the scrubby trees is a steep slope covered with broken rock, known as the Fan, whose tip lies at the foot of the deepest gully. To the left of this gully are precipices; the lower one is called the Pinnacle.

After passing through the boulders, with several scrambles, Huntington Ravine Trail ascends to the left side of the Fan and, marked by yellow blazes on the rocks, crosses the talus diagonally. The trail then turns left and ascends in scrub along the north (right) side of the Fan to its tip at 1.8 mi., crossing a small brook about two-thirds of the way up. The trail then recrosses the brooklet and immediately attacks the rocks to the right of the main gully, climbing about 650 ft. in 0.3 mi. The marked route up the headwall follows the line of least difficulty and should be followed carefully over the ledges, which are dangerous, especially when wet. The first pitch above the Fan—a large, fairly smooth, steeply sloping ledge—is probably the most difficult scramble on the trail. Above the first ledges, the trail climbs steeply through scrub and over short sections of rock, including some fairly difficult scrambles; one high rock chimney is particularly challenging. About two-thirds of the way up, the trail turns sharply left at a promontory with a good view then continues to the top of the headwall, where the trail crosses Alpine Garden Trail at 2.1 mi. From this point, Huntington Ravine Trail ascends moderately, and at 2.3 mi., the trail crosses Nelson Crag Trail; the summit can be reached in 0.8 mi. by turning left at this jct. Soon, Huntington Ravine Trail reaches Mt. Washington Auto Rd. just below the 7-mi. mark, 1.1 mi. below the summit.

NELSON CRAG TRAIL (AMC; MAP 1: F9)

Cumulative from Old Jackson Road (2,625 ft.) to:	↕	↗	↺
Closest approach to Auto Rd. near Cragway Spring (4,825 ft.)	1.7 mi.	2,200 ft.	1:55
Huntington Ravine Trail (5,725 ft.)	2.8 mi.	3,150 ft. (rev. 50 ft.)	3:00
Mt. Washington summit (6,288 ft.)	3.6 mi.	3,750 ft. (rev. 50 ft.)	3:40

This trail begins on Old Jackson Road, 1.7 mi. from Pinkham Notch Visitor Center and 0.2 mi. from the Auto Rd., and ascends to the summit of Mt. Washington. This is an attractive trail, relatively lightly used, fairly steep, rough in the lower part, and greatly exposed to weather in the upper part.

Leaving Old Jackson Road, this trail follows and soon crosses a small brook then climbs steadily, soon becoming quite steep. At about 1.1 mi., the trail rises out of the scrub, emerging on the crest of Chandler Ridge, from which you have an unusual view of Pinkham Notch in both directions. From this point, the trail is above treeline and very exposed to the northwest winds. It then bears northwest, climbs moderately over open ledges, and passes close by the Auto Rd. near Cragway Spring (unreliable) at the sharp turn about 0.3 mi. above the 5-mi. mark. The trail then climbs steeply to the crest of the ridge. The trail passes over Nelson Crag and crosses Alpine Garden Trail, swings left, skirts the south side of a rocky bump recently named Agiocochook Crag (5,735 ft.), and crosses Huntington Ravine Trail at 2.8 mi. Nelson Crag Trail climbs up the rocks to Ball Crag (6,112 ft.), descends briefly, runs across the Auto Rd. and the Cog Railway, and finally ascends to the summit. To descend on this trail, follow the walkway down along the lower (east) side of the Sherman Adams summit building.

BOOTT SPUR TRAIL (AMC; MAP 1: F9)

Cumulative from Tuckerman Ravine Trail (2,275 ft.) to:	⇅	↗	○
Harvard Rock (4,046 ft.)	1.7 mi.	1,750 ft.	1:45
Split Rock (4,337 ft.)	2.0 mi.	2,050 ft.	2:00
Boott Spur Link (4,650 ft.)	2.2 mi.	2,400 ft.	2:20
Davis Path jct. (5,450 ft.)	2.9 mi.	3,200 ft.	3:05
Cumulative from Pinkham Notch Visitor Center (2,032 ft.) to:			
Davis Path jct. (5,450 ft.)	3.3 mi.	3,400 ft.	3:20
Mt. Washington summit (6,288 ft.) via Davis and Crawford paths	5.3 mi.	4,400 ft. (rev. 150 ft.)	4:50

This trail runs from Tuckerman Ravine Trail, near Pinkham Notch Visitor Center, to Davis Path, near the summit of Boott Spur. Boott Spur Trail follows the long ridge that forms the south wall of Tuckerman Ravine and affords fine views. Grades are mostly moderate, but the trail has some rough footing. Much of this trail is above treeline and thus greatly exposed to any bad weather for a considerable distance.

This trail diverges left from Tuckerman Ravine Trail at a sharp right turn 0.4 mi. from Pinkham Notch Visitor Center, about 150 yd. above the side path to Crystal Cascade. Boott Spur Trail immediately crosses John Sherburne Ski Trail then climbs through a ledgy area, crosses a tiny brook, and climbs steeply up a ladder to the ridge crest. At 0.5 mi., Boott Spur Trail climbs over a ledge with a view of Huntington Ravine then turns sharply right, where a side trail (left) leads in 50 yd. to a very limited view east. Boott Spur Trail next crosses a level, muddy area and then ascends northwest up a steeper, rougher slope toward a craggy shoulder. Halfway up this section, an obscure side trail leads left 100 yd. to a small brook (last water). At the ridge crest, 1.0 mi. from Tuckerman Ravine Trail, the main trail turns left, and a side trail leads right (east) 25 yd. to an interesting though restricted outlook to Huntington Ravine. The main trail continues upward at moderate grades with several short scrambles, reaching a ledgy ridge crest that affords some views; at 1.7 mi., a side trail on the right leads in 30 yd. to Harvard Rock, which provides an excellent view of Tuckerman Ravine and of Lion Head directly in front of the summit of Mt. Washington.

Boott Spur Trail emerges from the scrub at 1.9 mi. then soon bears left and angles up the slope to Split Rock, which one can pass through or go around, at 2.0 mi. The trail then turns right, passes through a final patch of fairly high scrub, and rises steeply over two minor humps to a broad, flat ridge, where, at 2.2 mi., Boott Spur Link descends on the right to Tuckerman Ravine Trail near Hermit Lake. Above this point, Boott Spur Trail follows the broad, open ridge, which consists of a series of alternating step-like levels and steep slopes. After passing just to the right (north) of the summit of Boott Spur, the trail descends slightly and ends at Davis Path.

BOOTT SPUR LINK (AMC; MAP 1: F9)

From Tuckerman Ravine Trail (3,875 ft.) to:	⇅	↗	↻
Boott Spur Trail (4,650 ft.)	0.6 mi.	850 ft. (rev. 50 ft.)	0:45

This steep and rough but interesting trail climbs the south wall of Tuckerman Ravine, connecting the main floor of the ravine with the upper part of Boott Spur. The trail leaves the south side of Tuckerman Ravine Trail at the southeast corner of the clearing opposite the buildings at Hermit Lake, 2.4 mi. from Pinkham Notch Visitor Center. From this clearing, Boott Spur Link descends south-southeast and soon crosses the Cutler River on a bridge then crosses John Sherburne Ski Trail and swings to the left, descending to a jct. with a former route of the trail at 0.2 mi. Here, Boott Spur Link turns right and climbs straight up the slope very steeply through woods and scrub, with rapidly improving views back into the ravine. The trail then continues to climb steeply over open rocks to the crest of Boott Spur, where it meets Boott Spur Trail.

GLEN BOULDER TRAIL (AMC; MAP 1: G9)

Cumulative from Glen Ellis Falls parking area on NH 16 (1,975 ft.) to:	⇅	↗	↻
The Direttissima (2,300 ft.)	0.4 mi.	350 ft.	0:25
Avalanche Brook Ski Trail (2,600 ft.)	0.8 mi.	650 ft.	0:45
Glen Boulder (3,729 ft.)	1.6 mi.	1,750 ft.	1:40
Slide Peak (4,806 ft.)	2.6 mi.	2,850 ft.	2:45
Davis Path jct. (5,175 ft.)	3.2 mi.	3,200 ft.	3:10
Boott Spur Trail (5,450 ft.) via Davis Path	3.7 mi.	3,500 ft.	3:35
Mt. Washington summit (6,288 ft.) via Davis and Crawford paths	5.7 mi.	4,450 ft. (rev. 150 ft.)	5:05

This trail ascends past the famous Glen Boulder to Davis Path 0.5 mi. below Boott Spur. The trail begins on the west side of NH 16 at the Glen Ellis Falls parking area, 0.8 mi. south of Pinkham Notch Visitor Center. Parts of the trail are rather rough, but it reaches the treeline and views relatively quickly.

The trail leaves the parking area and ascends gradually for about 0.4 mi. to the base of a small cliff then climbs steeply around to the right of the cliff and meets the Direttissima, which enters from the right (north) coming from Pinkham Notch Visitor Center. At this jct., the trail turns sharply left (south) and soon passes a short branch trail that leads left to an outlook on the brink of a cliff, which commands a fine view of Wildcat Mtn. and Pinkham Notch. The main trail swings west, rises gradually, then becomes steeper. At 0.8 mi., the trail crosses Avalanche Brook Ski Trail, which is marked with blue plastic markers (but not maintained for hiking). Glen Boulder Trail soon reaches the north bank of a brook draining the minor ravine south of the Gulf of Slides. After following the brook, which soon divides, the trail turns southwest and crosses both branches. The trail is level for 200 yd. then rapidly climbs the northeast side of the spur through conifers, giving views of the minor ravine and spur south of the Gulf of Slides. Leaving the trees, the trail climbs over open rocks with one fairly difficult scramble and, at 1.6 mi., reaches Glen Boulder, an immense rock perched on the end of the spur that is a familiar landmark for travelers through Pinkham Notch. The view is wide, from Mt. Chocorua around to Mt. Washington, with the view of Wildcat Mtn. being particularly fine.

From the boulder, the trail climbs steeply up the open ridge crest to its top at 2.0 mi. then reenters high scrub and ascends moderately. At 2.3 mi., a side trail descends right about 60 yd. to a fine spring. The main trail continues to Slide Peak (also called Gulf Peak) at 2.6 mi.; this rather insignificant peak at the head of the Gulf of Slides offers fine views. The trail then turns north and descends slightly, leaving the scrub, and runs entirely above treeline—greatly exposed to the weather—and climbs moderately to Davis Path just below a minor crag.

THE DIRETTISSIMA (AMC; MAP 1: F9–G9)

From NH 16 near Cutler River bridge (2,025 ft.) to:	⇅	↗	↺
Glen Boulder Trail (2,300 ft.)	1.0 mi.	400 ft. (rev. 100 ft.)	0:40

For hikers desiring access to Glen Boulder Trail from Pinkham Notch Visitor Center, the Direttissima eliminates a road walk on NH 16. Although, in general, the trail is almost level, it is somewhat rough in places, with several significant ups and downs. The trail begins 0.15 mi. south of Pinkham Notch Visitor Center, at a parking area just south of the highway bridge over Cutler River, indicated by a sign at the north end of the parking area. Marked by paint blazes, the trail turns sharply left about 30 yd. into the woods and winds generally south, crossing a small brook. The trail skirts through the upper (west) end of a gorge and then crosses the gorge on a bridge at 0.5 mi. The trail continues past a viewpoint looking down Pinkham Notch, passes along the top of a cliff and then the bottom of another cliff, and ends at Glen Boulder Trail.

UPPER CONE OF MT. WASHINGTON

ALPINE GARDEN TRAIL (AMC; MAP 1: F9)

Cumulative from Tuckerman Ravine Trail (5,150 ft.) to:	⇅	↗	○
Lion Head Trail (5,175 ft.)	0.3 mi.	50 ft. (rev. 50 ft.)	0:10
Huntington Ravine Trail (5,475 ft.)	1.2 mi.	350 ft.	0:45
Nelson Crag Trail (5,575 ft.)	1.4 mi.	450 ft.	0:55
Auto Rd. jct. (5,305 ft.)	1.8 mi.	450 ft. (rev. 250 ft.)	1:10

This trail leads from Tuckerman Ravine Trail to Mt. Washington Auto Rd. through the grassy lawn called the Alpine Garden. Although Alpine Garden Trail's chief value is the beauty of the flowers (in season) and the views, it is also a convenient connecting link between the trails on the east side of the mountain, making up a part of various routes for those who do not wish to visit the summit. The trail is completely above treeline and exposed to bad weather, although it is on the mountain's east side, which usually bears somewhat less of the brunt of the mountain's worst weather.

The tiny alpine flowers that grow here are best seen in the middle to late part of June. Especially prominent in this area are the five-petaled white diapensia; the bell-shaped, pink-magenta Lapland rosebay; and the very small pink flowers of the alpine azalea. (See the *AMC Field Guide to the New England Alpine Summits*, AMC Books.) No plants should ever be picked or otherwise damaged. Hikers are urged to stay on trails or walk very carefully on rocks so as not to kill the fragile alpine vegetation.

The trail diverges right from Tuckerman Ravine Trail a short distance above the ravine headwall, 0.2 mi. below Tuckerman Junction. Alpine Garden Trail leads northeast, descending and then ascending and, bearing toward Lion Head, crosses Lion Head Trail at 0.3 mi. Beyond this jct., Alpine Garden Trail ascends gradually northward. The trail traverses the Alpine Garden and crosses a tiny stream that is the headwater of Raymond Cataract. (This water may be contaminated by drainage from the summit buildings.) The trail soon approaches the top of Huntington Ravine and crosses Huntington Ravine Trail at 1.2 mi. In winter and spring, take care not to approach too close to the icy gullies that drop precipitously from the edge of the Alpine Garden. Rising to the top of the ridge leading from Nelson Crag, the trail crosses Nelson Crag Trail at 1.4 mi. then descends and soon enters the old Glen House Bridle Path, constructed in 1853, whose course is still plain although it was abandoned more than 160 years ago. In a short distance, Alpine Garden Trail turns left and in a few yards enters the Auto Rd. a short distance above the 6-mi. mark, opposite the upper terminus of Wamsutta Trail.

SOUTHSIDE TRAIL (AMC; MAP 1: F9)

From Tuckerman Junction (5,383 ft.) to:	⇅	⤢	⟳
Davis Path (5,575 ft.)	0.3 mi.	200 ft.	0:15

This trail, which is completely above treeline, forms a direct link between Tuckerman Ravine and Crawford Path and Westside Trail. Southside Trail diverges right (northwest) from Tuckerman Crossover about 30 yd. southwest of Tuckerman Ravine Trail at Tuckerman Junction and climbs moderately. Southside Trail then skirts the southwest side of Mt. Washington's summit cone and enters Davis Path near its jct. with Crawford Path.

TUCKERMAN CROSSOVER (AMC; MAP 1: F9)

Cumulative from Tuckerman Junction (5,383 ft.) to:	⇅	⤢	⟳
Davis Path (5,475 ft.)	0.3 mi.	100 ft.	0:10
Crawford Path (5,100 ft.)	0.8 mi.	100 ft. (rev. 400 ft.)	0:25
Lakes of the Clouds Hut (5,012 ft.) via Crawford Path	1.0 mi.	100 ft. (rev. 100 ft.)	0:35

This trail connects Tuckerman Ravine with Lakes of the Clouds Hut. The trail is totally above treeline and crosses a high ridge where there is much exposure to westerly winds. The trail leaves Tuckerman Ravine Trail left (southwest) at Tuckerman Junction, where the latter trail turns sharply right to ascend the cone. In 30 yd., Southside Trail diverges right. Tuckerman Crossover then rises gradually across Bigelow Lawn, crosses Davis Path, and descends moderately to Crawford Path, which Tuckerman Crossover meets along with Camel Trail a short distance above the upper Lakes of the Clouds. After a left turn on Crawford Path, Lakes of the Clouds Hut is reached in 0.2 mi. In the reverse direction, Tuckerman Crossover is the left-hand of two trails that diverge to the right (east) from Crawford Path, 0.2 mi. above the hut; Camel Trail is the right-hand trail of the two.

LAWN CUTOFF (AMC; MAP 1: F9)

From Tuckerman Junction (5,383 ft.) to:	⇅	⤢	⟳
Davis Path (5,475 ft.)	0.4 mi.	100 ft.	0:15

This trail provides a direct route between Tuckerman Junction and Boott Spur, entirely above treeline. The trail leaves Tuckerman Ravine Trail at Tuckerman Junction and ascends gradually southward across Bigelow Lawn to Davis Path about 0.6 mi. north of Boott Spur.

CAMEL TRAIL (AMC; MAP 1: F9)

From Crawford Path (5,100 ft.) to:	⥮	↗	⟳
Davis Path (5,465 ft.)	0.7 mi.	350 ft.	0:30

This trail, connecting Boott Spur with Lakes of the Clouds Hut, is named for ledges on Boott Spur that resemble a kneeling camel when seen against the skyline. This is the right-hand trail of the two that diverge right (east) from Crawford Path 0.2 mi. northeast of Lakes of the Clouds Hut (Tuckerman Crossover is the other trail that diverges here). Camel Trail ascends easy grassy slopes, crosses the old location of Crawford Path, and continues in a practically straight line across the level stretch of Bigelow Lawn. Camel Trail aims directly toward the ledges that form the camel, passes under the camel's nose, and joins Davis Path about 250 yd. northwest of Lawn Cutoff.

WESTSIDE TRAIL (WMNF; MAP 1: F9)

From Crawford Path (5,625 ft.) to:	⥮	↗	⟳
Gulfside Trail (5,500 ft.)	0.9 mi.	100 ft. (rev. 200 ft.)	0:30

This trail was partly constructed by pioneer trail maker J. Rayner Edmands; as was Edmands's practice, many segments are paved with carefully placed stones. The trail is wholly above timberline, very much exposed to the prevailing west and northwest winds. As a shortcut between Gulfside Trail and Crawford Path that avoids the summit of Mt. Washington, it saves about 0.7 mi. in distance and 600 ft. in elevation between objectives in the Northern and Southern Presidentials. Westside Trail diverges left from Crawford Path at the point where the latter path begins to climb the steep part of the cone of Mt. Washington. Westside Trail skirts the cone, climbing for 0.6 mi. at an easy grade, then descends moderately, passes under the tracks of the Mt. Washington Cog Railway, and soon ends at Gulfside Trail.

TRINITY HEIGHTS CONNECTOR (AMC; MAP 1: F9)

From summit of Mt. Washington (6,288 ft.) to:	⥮	↗	⟳
Gulfside Trail (6,100 ft.)	0.2 mi.	0 ft. (rev. 200 ft.)	0:05

This trail was created to allow the AT to make a loop over the summit of Mt. Washington; formerly the true summit was a side trip, albeit a very short one, from the AT, so technically the AT did not pass over the summit. Trinity Heights is a name previously used for the summit region of Mt. Washington. From the true summit (a rock outcrop, marked by a sign, between the Tip Top House and Sherman Adams summit building), the path leaves at a sign to the right of the Tip Top House and runs northwest, descending moderately over the rocks to Gulfside Trail, less than 0.1 mi. to the north of its jct. with Crawford Path.

SEC 1

NORTH OF PINKHAM NOTCH VISITOR CENTER

RAYMOND PATH (AMC; MAP 1: F9)

Cumulative from Old Jackson Road (2,650 ft.) to:	↥↧	↗	○
Huntington Ravine Trail (3,425 ft.)	1.8 mi.	900 ft. (rev. 100 ft.)	1:20
Tuckerman Ravine Trail (3,700 ft.)	2.4 mi.	1,200 ft. (rev. 50 ft.)	1:50
Hermit Lake (3,850 ft.) via Tuckerman Ravine Trail	2.7 mi.	1,350 ft.	2:00

This trail, one of the older paths in the region, begins on Old Jackson Road 1.7 mi. from Pinkham Notch Visitor Center and 0.2 mi. from the Auto Rd., about 100 yd. south of the beginning of Nelson Crag Trail. Raymond Path ends at Tuckerman Ravine Trail about 0.3 mi. below Hermit Lake. Raymond Path grades are mostly easy to moderate.

After diverging from Old Jackson Road, the trail crosses several small branches of Peabody River, climbing moderately to the crest of a small ridge at 0.8 mi., where you have a restricted view of Lion Head and Boott Spur. The trail descends moderately for a short distance to a small mossy brook then begins to ascend easily, crossing Nelson Brook at 1.2 mi. and Huntington Ravine Trail at 1.8 mi. From here, the trail drops down a steep bank to cross the brook that drains Huntington Ravine on a ledge at the brink of Vesper Falls; one should use great care here in high-water or icy conditions, and perhaps consider a detour upstream. (This crossing can be avoided entirely by following Huntington Ravine Trail north 0.1 mi. to Huntington Ravine Fire Rd. then following Fire Rd. 0.3 mi. south until it crosses Raymond Path.) Soon the path crosses the brook coming from the Ravine of Raymond Cataract (sign) and then Huntington Ravine Fire Rd. before climbing 0.3 mi. at a moderate grade to Tuckerman Ravine Trail.

OLD JACKSON ROAD (AMC; MAP 1: F9)

From Pinkham Notch Visitor Center (2,032 ft.) to:	↥↧	↗	○
Mt. Washington Auto Rd. (2,675 ft.)	1.9 mi.	750 ft. (rev. 100 ft.)	1:20

This trail runs north from Pinkham Notch Visitor Center to Mt. Washington Auto Rd., providing access to a number of other trails, along with the most direct route from the visitor center to the Great Gulf. Old Jackson Road is part of the AT and is blazed in white. Because the trail is used as a cross-country ski trail in winter, it is usually also marked with blue diamonds year-round.

Old Jackson Road diverges right from Tuckerman Ravine Trail about 50 yd. from the trailhead at the rear of the Trading Post. After about 0.3 mi., Blanchard and Connie's Way ski trails cross, and at 0.4 mi., Link Ski Trail enters right, just before a bridge, and Crew-Cut Trail leaves right (east) just after the bridge. Soon, Old Jackson Road begins to ascend moderately and crosses a small brook that runs in an interesting gorge with a small waterfall just above the trail. At 0.9 mi., George's Gorge Trail enters on the right (east), and Old Jackson Road rises easily across the flat divide between the Saco and Androscoggin drainages and then descends gradually, crossing several small brooks. Just before reaching a larger brook, the trail makes a sharp left turn uphill then, after a short and steep climb, it turns right and runs nearly level. At 1.7 mi., Raymond Path leaves on the left, and in another 100 yd., just after a small brook is crossed, Nelson Crag Trail leaves on the left. Continuing north, Old Jackson Road climbs slightly up an interesting little rocky hogback, passes through an old gravel pit, and meets the Auto Rd. just above the 2-mi. mark, at a small parking area opposite the Madison Gulf Trail trailhead.

CREW-CUT TRAIL (AMC; MAP 1: F9–F10)

Cumulative from Old Jackson Road (2,075 ft.) to:	↑↓	↗	↻
Liebeskind's Loop (2,330 ft.)	0.5 mi.	250 ft.	0:25
NH 16 (1,960 ft.)	1.0 mi.	250 ft. (rev. 400 ft.)	0:40

Crew-Cut Trail, George's Gorge Trail, and Liebeskind's Loop, a small network of paths in the region north of Pinkham Notch Visitor Center, were originally located and cut by Bradford Swan. These trails provide pleasant walking at a modest expenditure of effort, passing through fine woods with small ravines and ledges.

Crew-Cut Trail leaves Old Jackson Road on the right 0.4 mi. from the visitor center, just after a bridged stream crossing and just before the point where Old Jackson Road starts to climb more steeply. After crossing a stony, dry brook bed, Crew-Cut Trail runs generally east-northeast, crossing two small brooks. On the east bank of the second brook, at 0.2 mi., George's Gorge Trail leaves left. Crew-Cut Trail continues generally northeast, rising moderately, and at times steeply, up the slope through open woods and crossing several gullies. It skirts southeast of the steeper rocky outcroppings until, at 0.5 mi. from Old Jackson Road, Liebeskind's Loop enters left, coming down from George's Gorge Trail. The spur path to Lila's Ledge, which affords fine views, leaves Liebeskind's Loop less than 0.1 mi.

from this jct. Crew-Cut Trail passes under the base of a cliff and turns right then descends steeply over a few small ledges and through open woods until it passes east of a small, high-level bog formed by an old beaver dam. Shortly thereafter, the trail crosses a small stream and Connie's Way Ski Trail, and goes through open woods again, emerging at the top of the grassy embankment on NH 16, 0.1 mi. south of the entrance to Wildcat Ski Area.

GEORGE'S GORGE TRAIL (AMC; MAP 1: F9)

From Crew-Cut Trail (2,065 ft.) to:	⬍	↗	↺
Old Jackson Road (2,525 ft.)	0.8 mi.	600 ft. (rev. 150 ft.)	0:40

This trail leaves Crew-Cut Trail on the left, 0.2 mi. from Old Jackson Road on the east bank of a small brook (the infant Peabody River). George's Gorge Trail leads up the brook, steeply in places, passing Chudacoff Falls (often dry) and crossing the brook twice, then swings sharply right away from the brook. Liebeskind's Loop leaves on the right at 0.5 mi., and George's Gorge Trail then climbs nearly to the top of a knob and descends west by switchbacks, crosses a small brook, and rises slightly to Old Jackson Road in the flat section near its halfway point, 0.9 mi. from Pinkham Notch Visitor Center.

LIEBESKIND'S LOOP (AMC; MAP 1: F9–F10)

From George's Gorge Trail (2,575 ft.) to:	⬍	↗	↺
Crew-Cut Trail (2,350 ft.)	0.6 mi.	50 ft. (rev. 250 ft.)	0:20
From Pinkham Notch Visitor Center (2,032 ft.):			
Complete loop via Old Jackson Road, Crew-Cut Trail, George's Gorge Trail, Liebeskind's Loop (including side trip to Lila's Ledge), Crew-Cut Trail, and Old Jackson Road	2.8 mi.	650 ft.	1:45

Liebeskind's Loop makes possible an interesting loop hike starting on Old Jackson Road 0.4 mi. from Pinkham Notch Visitor Center (using Crew-Cut, George's Gorge, Liebeskind's Loop, and Crew-Cut Trails). This loop hike is best made in the sequence noted above because George's Gorge is more interesting on the ascent, and Liebeskind's Loop is more interesting on the descent.

Liebeskind's Loop leaves right (east) near the high point of George's Gorge Trail, 0.3 mi. from Old Jackson Road, and descends to a swampy flat then rises through a spruce thicket to the top of a cliff and a fine lookout called Brad's Bluff, with a good view to the south down Pinkham Notch. Here, the trail turns left and runs along the edge of the cliff, finally descending by an easy zigzag in a gully to a beautiful open grove of birches. The trail continues east, descending through a small gorge and skirting the east end of several small swells, until it swings south and descends to a small notch in the ridge crest. Here, a spur trail leads left 0.1 mi. (50-ft. ascent) to Lila's Ledge (named by Brad Swan in memory of his wife), which affords excellent views of Pinkham Notch and the eastern slope of Mt. Washington; the lower ledge is reached by a short, steep descent that may be dangerous in wet or icy conditions. Liebeskind's Loop then descends on the other side of the ridge to join Crew-Cut Trail, which can then be followed back to the starting point by turning right (west-southwest).

MAIN RIDGE OF THE SOUTHERN PRESIDENTIALS

CRAWFORD PATH (WMNF; MAP 1: G8–F9)

Cumulative from Mt. Clinton Rd. parking area (1,900 ft.) via Crawford Connector to:	⇅	↗	↻
Mizpah Cutoff (3,490 ft.)	1.9 mi.	1,600 ft.	1:45
Webster Cliff Trail (4,250 ft.)	3.1 mi.	2,350 ft.	2:45
South end of Mt. Eisenhower Loop (4,425 ft.)	4.3 mi.	2,750 ft.	3:30
Mt. Eisenhower Trail (4,465 ft.)	5.0 mi.	2,900 ft.	3:55
South end of Mt. Monroe Loop (5,075 ft.)	6.2 mi.	3,550 ft.	4:55
Lakes of the Clouds Hut (5,012 ft.)	7.0 mi.	3,600 ft.	5:20
Westside Trail (5,625 ft.)	7.9 mi.	4,200 ft.	6:05
Gulfside Trail (6,150 ft.)	8.3 mi.	4,750 ft.	6:30
Mt. Washington summit (6,288 ft.)	8.5 mi.	4,900 ft.	6:40

CRAWFORD PATH, IN REVERSE (WMNF; MAP 1: G8–F9)

Cumulative from the summit of Mt. Washington (6,288 ft.) to:	⇅	↗	↻
Gulfside Trail (6,150 ft.)	0.2 mi.	0 ft.	0:05
Westside Trail (5,625 ft.)	0.6 mi.	0 ft.	0:20
Lakes of the Clouds Hut (5,012 ft.)	1.5 mi.	0 ft.	0:45
South end of Mt. Monroe Loop (5,075 ft.)	2.3 mi.	150 ft.	1:10
Mt. Eisenhower Trail (4,465 ft.)	3.5 mi.	200 ft.	1:50
South end of Mt. Eisenhower Loop (4,425 ft.)	4.2 mi.	300 ft.	2:15
Webster Cliff Trail (4,250 ft.)	5.4 mi.	500 ft.	2:55
Mizpah Cutoff (3,490 ft.)	6.6 mi.	500 ft.	3:35
Mt. Clinton Rd. parking area (1,900 ft.) via Crawford Connector	8.5 mi.	500 ft.	4:30

This trail is considered the oldest continuously maintained footpath in the United States. The first section, leading up Mt. Pierce (Mt. Clinton), was cut in 1819 by Abel Crawford and his son Ethan Allen Crawford. In 1840, Thomas J. Crawford, a younger son of Abel, converted the footpath into a bridle path, but more than a century has passed since it was used regularly for ascents on horseback. The trail still mostly follows the original path, except for the section between Mt. Monroe and Westside Trail, which was relocated to take Crawford Path off the windswept ridge and down past the shelter at Lakes of the Clouds. From the jct. just north of Mt. Pierce to the summit of Mt. Washington, Crawford Path is part of the AT and is blazed in white.

Caution: Parts of this trail are dangerous in bad weather. Several lives have been lost on Crawford Path because of failure to observe proper precautions. Below Mt. Eisenhower, a number of ledges are exposed to the weather, but they are scattered, and shelter is usually available in nearby scrub. From the Eisenhower–Franklin col, the trail runs completely above treeline, exposed to the full force of all storms. The most dangerous part of the path is the section on the cone of Mt. Washington, beyond Lakes of the Clouds Hut. Always carry a compass and study the map before starting. If trouble arises on or above Mt. Monroe, take refuge at Lakes of the Clouds Hut or go down Ammonoosuc Ravine Trail. Crawford Path is well marked above treeline with large cairns; in poor visibility, great care should be exercised to stay on the path because many of the other paths in the vicinity are much less clearly marked. If the path is lost in bad weather and cannot be found again after diligent effort, one should travel west, descending into the woods and following streams downhill to the roads. On the southeast side of the ridge, toward Dry River valley, nearly all the slopes are more precipitous, the river crossings are potentially dangerous, and the distance to a highway is much greater.

The main parking area at the south end of this trail is located on the west side of Mt. Clinton Rd., 0.1 mi. north of its jct. with US 302. The former parking lot on US 302 has been closed, and Crawford Path hikers are requested to use the Mt. Clinton Rd. lot because the parking spaces at other lots in the area are needed for the trails that originate from those lots. For historical reasons, the name Crawford Path continues to be attached to the old route of the trail that leads directly from US 302, and the short path that connects Crawford Path to the Mt. Clinton Rd. parking lot is called Crawford Connector. In the descriptions that follow, the main route will be described and distances given starting from Mt. Clinton Rd. via Crawford Connector, which is the route for most hikers using this trail.

The path is described in the northbound direction (toward Mt. Washington). Distances, elevation gains, and times are also given in the reverse direction.

Leaving the parking lot and soon crossing Mt. Clinton Rd., Crawford Connector climbs gradually for 0.4 mi. until it reaches the bridge over Gibbs Brook. Here, Crawford Cliff Spur diverges left.

Crawford Cliff Spur, a short side path, leaves Crawford Connector at the west end of the bridge over Gibbs Brook and follows the brook to a small flume and pool. Crawford Cliff Spur turns left and climbs steeply above the brook, then turns left again, becomes very rough, and reaches Crawford Cliff (2,400 ft.), a ledge with an outlook over Crawford Notch, the Willey Range, and the Highland Center, 0.4 mi. (350-ft. ascent, 20 min.) from Crawford Connector.

Crawford Connector continues across the bridge and ends at **Crawford Path**, 0.2 mi. from the latter trail's trailhead on US 302, opposite AMC's Highland Center at Crawford Notch. To continue ascending on Crawford Path, turn left here. Crawford Path follows the south bank of Gibbs Brook, and at 0.6 mi. from Mt. Clinton Rd., a side path leads 40 yd. left to Gibbs Falls. Soon the trail enters the Gibbs Brook Scenic Area then climbs moderately but steadily. At about 1.2 mi. from Mt. Clinton Rd., the trail begins to climb away from the brook, angling southeast up the side of the valley. At 1.9 mi., Mizpah Cutoff diverges right (east) for Mizpah Spring Hut. Crawford Path continues to ascend at easy to moderate grades, crossing several small brooks, then reaches its high point on the shoulder of Mt. Pierce and runs almost level through scrub, breaking into the open with fine views. At 3.1 mi., Crawford Path reaches the jct. with Webster Cliff Trail, which leads right (south) to the summit of Mt. Pierce in 0.1 mi. *Caution:* In winter, the trail can be very difficult to follow in the reverse direction where it enters the snow-packed scrub; in windy conditions, tracks may be quickly covered with snowdrifts.

From Mt. Pierce to Mt. Eisenhower, Crawford Path runs through patches of scrub and woods with many open ledges that allow for magnificent views in all directions. Cairns and the marks left by many feet on the rocks indicate the way. The path winds about, heading generally northeast, staying fairly near the poorly defined crest of the broad ridge, which is composed of several rounded humps. At 3.8 mi., the trail crosses a small stream in the col then ascends mostly on ledges to the jct. with Mt. Eisenhower Loop, which diverges left at 4.3 mi. The trip over this summit adds only 0.3 mi. and 300 ft. of climbing and provides excellent views in good weather. Crawford Path bears somewhat to the right at this jct. and runs nearly level with minor ups and downs—though with rough footing—through scrub on the steep southeast side of the mountain. Crawford Path is a better route in bad weather compared with Mt. Eisenhower Loop. Mt. Eisenhower Loop rejoins Crawford Path on the left at 4.8 mi., just above the sag between Mt. Eisenhower and Mt. Franklin, on a ledge that overlooks Red Pond, a small alpine tarn with little water. Edmands Path can be reached from this jct. by following Mt. Eisenhower Loop to the left for a short distance.

At 5.0 mi., Mt. Eisenhower Trail from Dry River valley enters right. Crawford Path then begins the ascent of the shoulder called Mt. Franklin, first moderately, passing ledges with excellent views back to Dry River valley and Mt. Eisenhower, then steeply for a short distance near the top. At 5.5 mi., the trail reaches the relatively level shoulder and continues, with minor descents and ascents, to a jct. at 6.0 mi. Here, an unmarked but well-worn path diverges sharply right and leads in 130 yd. to the barely noticeable summit of Mt. Franklin (cairn), from which there are excellent views, particularly into Oakes Gulf. (In the reverse direction, bear right and downhill at this jct., as the side path diverges left and uphill.) At 6.2 mi., Mt. Monroe Loop diverges left to cross both summits of Monroe, affording excellent views. The loop is about the same length as the parallel section of Crawford Path but requires about 350 ft. more climbing with rougher footing. Crawford Path is safer in inclement conditions because it is much less exposed to the weather. Crawford Path continues along the edge of the precipice that forms the northwest wall of Oakes Gulf then follows a relocated section, passing to the left of an area that has been closed to public entry to preserve the habitat of the dwarf cinquefoil, an endangered species of plant. (The area between the two ends of Mt. Monroe Loop is one of great fragility and botanical importance. To protect this area—probably the most significant tract of rare vegetation in the entire White Mountain region—hikers should take great care to stay on the defined trail.) At 6.9 mi., Mt. Monroe Loop rejoins on the left, and Crawford Path descends easily to Lakes of the Clouds Hut at 7.0 mi.

Ammonoosuc Ravine Trail enters on the left at the corner of the hut, and in another 30 yd., Dry River Trail enters on the right. Crawford Path crosses the outlet of the larger Lake of the Clouds and passes between it and the second lake, and in a short distance, at 7.2 mi., Camel Trail to Boott Spur and Tuckerman Crossover to Tuckerman Ravine diverge right at the same point. Crawford Path then ascends moderately on the northwest side of the ridge, always some distance below the crest. Davis Path, which has been following the original, less-sheltered location of Crawford

Path, enters on the right at 7.9 mi., at the foot of the cone of Mt. Washington. In another 50 yd., Westside Trail, a shortcut to the Northern Presidentials, diverges left. Crawford Path runs generally north, switching back and forth as it climbs the steep cone through a trench in the rocks. At the plateau west of the summit, Crawford Path meets Gulfside Trail at 8.3 mi. Now coinciding with Gulfside Trail, Crawford Path turns right and passes through the old corral (outlined by rock walls) in which saddle horses from the Glen House were kept. The combined trails then swing left (northeast) and lead between the Yankee Building and the Tip Top House on the left and the Stage Office and Cog Railway track on the right. Follow a sign, "Crawford Path to Summit." The summit, marked by a sign, is an outcrop between the Tip Top House and the Sherman Adams summit building.

Descending from the summit of Mt. Washington, the path is on the right (west) side of the Cog Railway track. The path leads southwest between the buildings then swings to the right (northwest) at a sign and large cairn; avoid random side paths to the south. After passing through the old corral, the path reaches a jct. where Gulfside Trail turns sharply right. Here, Crawford Path turns sharply left and zigzags downward through a trench in the rocks.

MT. EISENHOWER LOOP (AMC; MAP 1: G8)

Cumulative from south jct. with Crawford Path (4,425 ft.) to:	⇅	↗	⟳
Mt. Eisenhower summit (4,760 ft.)	0.4 mi.	350 ft.	0:25
North jct. with Crawford Path (4,475 ft.)	0.8 mi.	350 ft. (rev. 300 ft.)	0:35

This short trail parallels Crawford Path, climbing over the bare, flat summit of Mt. Eisenhower, which provides magnificent views. In 2009 the AMC trail crew installed new wooden steps and ladders on the trail. Mt. Eisenhower Loop diverges from Crawford Path 4.3 mi. from Mt. Clinton Rd. at the south edge of the summit dome, climbs easily for 0.1 mi., then turns sharply left in a flat area and ascends steadily to the summit at 0.4 mi. At the summit is a large cairn and a defined circular viewing area to protect surrounding alpine vegetation. From there, Mt. Eisenhower Loop descends moderately to a ledge overlooking Red Pond (more a bog than a pond) then drops steeply by switchbacks over ledges, passes through a grassy sag just to the left of Red Pond, and finally climbs briefly past a jct. on the left with Edmands Path to rejoin Crawford Path on a small, rocky knob.

MT. MONROE LOOP (AMC; MAP 1: F9)

Cumulative from south jct. with Crawford Path (5,075 ft.) to:	⇵	↗	○
Summit of Mt. Monroe (5,372 ft.)	0.4 mi.	350 ft. (rev. 50 ft.)	0:20
North jct. with Crawford Path (5,075 ft.)	0.7 mi.	350 ft. (rev. 300 ft.)	0:30

This short trail runs parallel to Crawford Path and passes over the summits of Little Monroe and Mt. Monroe. The views are fine, but parts of Mt. Monroe Loop are rough, and the summits are very exposed to the weather. The trail diverges from Crawford Path 6.2 mi. from Mt. Clinton Rd. and quickly ascends the minor crag called Little Monroe then descends into the shallow, grassy sag beyond. Mt. Monroe Loop climbs steeply over boulder fields to the summit of Mt. Monroe at 0.4 mi., follows the northeast ridge to the end of the shoulder, and drops sharply to Crawford Path 0.1 mi. south of Lakes of the Clouds Hut.

SOUTHERN PRESIDENTIALS FROM THE WEST AND SOUTH

AMMONOOSUC RAVINE TRAIL (WMNF; MAP 1: F8–F9)

Cumulative from Cog Railway Base Rd. parking lot (2,500 ft.) to:	⇵	↗	○
Gem Pool (3,450 ft.)	2.1 mi.	950 ft.	1:30
Brook crossing on flat ledges (4,175 ft.)	2.5 mi.	1,700 ft.	2:05
Lakes of the Clouds Hut (5,012 ft.)	3.1 mi.	2,500 ft.	2:50
Mt. Washington summit (6,288 ft.) via Crawford Path	4.6 mi.	3,800 ft.	4:10

Ammonoosuc Ravine Trail ascends to Lakes of the Clouds Hut from a parking lot on Cog Railway Base Rd., 1.1 mi. east of its jct. with Mt. Clinton Rd. and Jefferson Notch Rd. The parking area is a stop for the AMC Hiker Shuttle. The trail can also be reached on foot from Jefferson Notch Rd. via Boundary Line and Jewell trails (Section Two). Together with the upper section of Crawford Path, Ammonoosuc Ravine Trail provides the shortest route to Mt. Washington from the west. The trail follows the headwaters of Ammonoosuc River, with many fine falls, cascades, and pools, and affords excellent views from its upper section. This is the most direct route to Lakes of the Clouds Hut, and the best route to or from the hut in bad weather because the trail lies in woods or scrub except for the last 0.2 mi. to the hut. The section above Gem Pool is very steep and rough and is likely to prove arduous to many hikers, particularly those with limited trail-walking experience. Many hikers also find it somewhat unpleasant to

SEC 1

descend this section due to the steep, often slippery rocks and ledges. The trail must be followed with care on the ledges, where it is not always marked well. Leaving the parking lot, the trail follows a path through the woods, crossing Franklin Brook at 0.3 mi. then passing over a double pipeline as the trail skirts the Base Station area. The trail joins the old route of the trail at the edge of Ammonoosuc River at 1.0 mi., after a slight descent. Here a link trail from the Cog Railway joins from the left (sign: Cog R.R.). Descending, bear left here to return to the WMNF parking area.

Ammonoosuc Link. Ammonoosuc Ravine Trail can be accessed from the Cog Railway Base Station by this link path. Parking (fee charged) is available in a gravel lot on the right (south) side of the Base Road (sign: Hiker Parking), 0.4 mi. east of the WMNF trailhead parking area. Elevation is 2,640 ft. (The upper lots are reserved for Cog Railway customers.) Proceed on foot up the access loop road and through a parking lot to a sign for "Ammonoosuc Trail" behind the main Base Station building on the right. The route turns right on a paved driveway, passes between two cabins, and enters the woods at a trail sign to the right of a third cabin, 0.2 mi. from hiker parking (elevation 2,720 ft.). The link ascends moderately to meet Ammonooosuc Ravine Trail, 0.3 mi. from the Base Station, ascent 150 ft. (15 min.). From hiker parking: 0.5 mi., 250 ft., 25 min.

From this jct., **Ammonoosuc Ravine Trail** bears right along the attractive river. It ascends mostly by easy grades, though with some rough footing, crossing Monroe Brook at 1.7 mi. Soon the trail skirts an area that was severely damaged by a large avalanche in 2010; the avalanche track can be seen to the left of the trail. It then follows the main branch of the river away from the avalanche track, and at 2.1 mi., the trail crosses the outlet of Gem Pool, a beautiful emerald pool at the foot of a cascade.

Now the very steep, rough ascent begins, with many rock steps. At 2.3 mi., a side path (sign) descends right about 80 yd. to a spectacular viewpoint at the foot of the gorge. Above this point, the main brook falls about 600 ft. down a steep trough in the mountainside at an average angle of 45 degrees; another brook a short distance to the north does the same; and these two spectacular water slides meet in a pool at the foot of the gorge. The main trail continues its steep ascent, crossing a side stream and ascending steep, often slippery ledges, one by means of a short ladder. The trail passes an outlook over the cascades to the right and, at 2.5 mi., crosses the main brook on flat ledges at the head of the highest fall, a striking viewpoint. (Descending, turn left after crossing the brook and descend over ledges; avoid a beaten path leading ahead into the woods.) The grade now begins to ease, and the trail makes several more brook crossings; follow the trail with care where it crosses a brook and continues up ledges between that brook and another brook on the right. As the ascent continues, ledges become more frequent and the scrub becomes smaller and more sparse. At 3.0 mi., the trail emerges from the scrub and follows a line of cairns directly up some rock slabs (which are slippery when wet), passes through one last patch of scrub, and reaches Crawford Path at the south side of Lakes of the Clouds Hut.

SEC 1

EDMANDS PATH (WMNF; MAP 1: G8)

Cumulative from Mt. Clinton Rd. (2,025 ft.) to:	⇅	↗	⟳
Stone gateway (4,000 ft.)	2.2 mi.	2,000 ft.	2:05
Mt. Eisenhower Loop jct. (4,450 ft.)	2.9 mi.	2,450 ft.	2:40
Mt. Eisenhower summit (4,760 ft.) via Mt. Eisenhower Loop	3.3 mi.	2,750 ft.	3:00

Edmands Path climbs to Mt. Eisenhower Loop near its jct. with Crawford Path in the Eisenhower–Franklin col, starting from a parking lot on the east side of Mt. Clinton Rd., 2.3 mi. north of its jct. with US 302 and 1.3 mi. south of its jct. with Cog Railway Base Rd. and Jefferson Notch Rd. This trail provides the shortest route to the summit of Mt. Eisenhower and a relatively easy access to the middle portion of Crawford Path and the Southern Presidentials. The last 0.2-mi. segment before Edmands Path joins Mt. Eisenhower Loop and Crawford Path is very exposed to northwest winds and, though short, can create a serious problem in bad weather. The ledgy brook crossings in the upper part of the trail can be treacherous in icy conditions.

J. Rayner Edmands, the pioneer trail maker, relocated and reconstructed this trail in 1909. The rock cribbing and paving in the middle and upper sections of the trail testify to the diligent labor that Edmands devoted to constructing a trail with constant comfortable grades in difficult terrain. Erosion from the weather and foot traffic of many decades has made the footing significantly rougher in recent years. Still, the trail retains what is probably the most moderate grade of any comparable trail in the Presidential Range.

From its trailhead, the trail runs nearly level across two small brooks on log bridges. At 0.4 mi., the trail crosses Abenaki Brook on a bridge and turns sharply right onto an old logging road on the far bank. At 0.7 mi., the trail diverges left off the old road and crosses a wet area. Soon the trail begins to climb steadily with rougher footing, undulating up the west ridge of Mt. Eisenhower, carefully searching out the most comfortable grades. At 2.2 mi., the trail swings left and angles up the mountainside on a footway supported by extensive rock cribbing then passes through a tiny stone gateway. At 2.5 mi., the trail crosses a small brook running over a ledge and climbs a short, steep, rocky pitch. Soon the grade becomes almost level, even descending slightly, as the trail contours around the north slope of Mt. Eisenhower, affording excellent views out through a fringe of trees. At 2.8 mi., the trail breaks into the open, crosses the nose of a ridge on a talus slope with rough footing, and reaches Mt. Eisenhower Loop a few yards from Crawford Path.

WEBSTER–JACKSON TRAIL (AMC; MAP 1: G8)

Cumulative from US 302 (1,900 ft.) to:	⬆⬇	↗	⟳
Bugle Cliff (2,450 ft.)	0.6 mi.	550 ft.	0:35
Flume Cascade Brook (2,500 ft.)	0.9 mi.	650 ft. (rev. 50 ft.)	0:45
Mt. Webster–Mt. Jackson fork (2,800 ft.)	1.4 mi.	950 ft.	1:10
Webster Cliff Trail (3,800 ft.) via Webster branch	2.4 mi.	2,000 ft. (rev. 50 ft.)	2:10
Summit of Mt. Webster (3,910 ft.) via Webster Cliff Trail	2.5 mi.	2,100 ft.	2:20
Summit of Mt. Jackson (4,052 ft.) via Jackson branch	2.6 mi.	2,200 ft.	2:25
Loop trip over summits of Webster and Jackson (via Webster Cliff Trail)	6.5 mi.	2,550 ft.	4:30

This trail connects US 302 across from a parking area just south of AMC's Macomber Family Information Center (Crawford Depot) with the summits of both Mt. Webster and Mt. Jackson, providing the opportunity for an interesting loop trip, as the two summits are linked by Webster Cliff Trail. Sections of Webster–Jackson Trail are steep and rough.

The trail, blazed in blue, leaves the east side of US 302 0.1 mi. south of Crawford Depot and 0.1 mi. north of the Gate of the Notch. The trail runs through a clearing, enters the woods, and, at 0.1 mi. from US 302, passes the side path leading right to Elephant Head.

Elephant Head Spur. Elephant Head is an interesting ledge that forms the east side of the Gate of the Notch, a mass of gray rock striped with veins of white quartz that provides a remarkable likeness to an elephant's head and trunk. The path runs through the woods parallel to the highway at an easy grade then ascends across the summit of the knob and descends 40 yd. to the top of the ledge, which overlooks Crawford Notch and affords fine views; it is 0.2 mi. (100-ft. ascent, rev. 30 ft., 10 min.) from Webster–Jackson Trail.

Webster–Jackson Trail climbs along the south bank of Elephant Head Brook, well above the stream, then turns right, away from the brook, at

0.2 mi. The trail angles up the mountainside roughly parallel to the highway, nearly level stretches alternating with steep, rocky pitches. At 0.6 mi. from US 302, a side path leads right 60 yd. to Bugle Cliff. This is a massive ledge overlooking Crawford Notch, where the view is well worth the slight extra effort required; if ice is present, exercise extreme caution. The main trail continues climbing across the slope, with two short descents, then crosses Flume Cascade Brook at 0.9 mi. At 1.4 mi., after a mostly gradual ascent, the trail divides within sound of Silver Cascade Brook, the left branch for Mt. Jackson and the right for Mt. Webster.

Mt. Webster Branch

The Webster (right) branch immediately descends steeply to Silver Cascade Brook, crosses it just below a beautiful cascade and pool, then bears left and climbs steeply up the bank. The trail then climbs steadily south for 1.0 mi., often with wet, rough footing, meeting Webster Cliff Trail on the high plateau northwest of the summit of Mt. Webster, 2.4 mi. from US 302. The ledgy summit of Mt. Webster, with an excellent view of Crawford Notch and the mountains to the west and south, is 0.1 mi. right (south) via Webster Cliff Trail. For Mt. Jackson and Mizpah Spring Hut, turn left.

Mt. Jackson Branch

The Jackson (left) branch ascends gradually until it comes within sight of Silver Cascade Brook then begins to climb moderately, with rough, wet footing. About 0.5 mi. above the jct., the trail crosses three branches of the brook in quick succession. At 1.0 mi. from the jct., a short distance below the base of the rocky summit cone, the trail swings left and soon passes Tisdale Spring (unreliable, often scanty and muddy). The trail then swings right and ascends steep ledges, with several fairly difficult scrambles, to the open summit, 2.6 mi. from US 302, where the trail meets Webster Cliff Trail. Descending, the trail leads west down the right edge of a steep, open ledge slab.

WEBSTER CLIFF TRAIL (AMC; MAP 1: G8)

Cumulative from US 302 (1,275 ft.) to:	⇅	↗	⏲
First open ledge (3,025 ft.)	1.8 mi.	1,750 ft.	1:45
Summit of Mt. Webster (3,910 ft.)	3.3 mi.	2,750 ft. (rev. 100 ft.)	3:00
Summit of Mt. Jackson (4,052 ft.)	4.7 mi.	3,150 ft. (rev. 250 ft.)	3:55
Mizpah Spring Hut (3,777 ft.)	6.4 mi.	3,400 ft. (rev. 500 ft.)	4:55
Crawford Path (4,250 ft.)	7.3 mi.	3,950 ft. (rev. 100 ft.)	5:40

SEC 1

This trail, a part of the AT, leaves the east side of US 302 opposite Willey House Station Rd., 1.0 mi. south of the Willey House site. The parking area is a stop for the AMC Hiker Shuttle. The trail ascends along the edge of the spectacular cliffs that form the east wall of Crawford Notch, passing numerous viewpoints, then leads over mts. Webster, Jackson, and Pierce to Crawford Path, 0.1 mi. north of Mt. Pierce. The section of trail ascending to Mt. Webster is more difficult and tiring than the statistics would suggest, with a number of ledge scrambles interspersed through the ascent along the top of the cliffs.

From US 302, Webster Cliff Trail runs nearly east 0.1 mi. to a bridge (built in memory of Albert and Priscilla Robertson, founding members of the AMC Four Thousand Footer Club) on which the trail crosses the Saco River. Saco River Trail joins from the left at 0.2 mi. and departs on the right at 0.3 mi. Webster Cliff Trail climbs steadily up the south end of the ridge, winding up the steep slope, swinging more to the north and growing steeper as the trail approaches the cliffs. At 1.4 mi., the trail crosses a small landslide that fell in 2009 then makes a tricky scramble across the top of an older slide. At 1.8 mi. from US 302, the trail reaches the first open ledge (a good objective for a shorter hike). From here, as the trail ascends the ridge at easier grades with occasional sharp pitches, are frequent outlook ledges giving ever-changing perspectives of the notch and the mountains to the south and west. The trail passes through a small col, and at 2.4 mi., a ledge affords a view straight down to the state park buildings. After a scramble up open rock, you reach another ledge with a large cairn and an outlook to Mt. Washington; the trail turns left 15 yd. behind the cairn, where a false path leads to the right. Beyond another col, the trail crosses an outcrop with a view east to Montalban Ridge. The trail climbs at varying grades, scrambling up a few fairly difficult ledgy pitches and passing several more good outlooks, and reaches the jumbled, ledgy summit of Mt. Webster at 3.3 mi.

The trail then descends north, and in 0.1 mi., the Webster branch of Webster–Jackson Trail from US 302 at the top of Crawford Notch enters left. Webster Cliff Trail swings east along the ridge with a few ups and downs and occasional sharp scrambles, crossing several wet gullies. The final ascent up the ledgy cone of Mt. Jackson is quite steep with several scrambles, reaching the summit at 4.7 mi., where the Jackson branch of Webster–Jackson Trail enters left.

The trail leaves the summit of Mt. Jackson toward Mt. Pierce, following a line of cairns running north, and descends very steeply over the ledges at the north end of the cone into the scrub, where the grade eases. At 5.1 mi., the trail enters and winds through open alpine meadows with views of

SEC 1

Mt. Washington and Mt. Jackson then turns sharply left and drops into the woods. The trail continues up and down over a hump along the ridge toward Mt. Pierce then ascends gradually to the jct. at 6.3 mi. with Mizpah Cutoff, which leads left (west) to Crawford Path. At 6.4 mi., Mizpah Spring Hut (where a side path on the right leads 100 yd. south to Nauman Tentsite) is reached, and Mt. Clinton Trail to Dry River valley diverges right (southeast), heading diagonally down the hut clearing. Continuing past the hut, the trail soon ascends a steep, rough section with two ladders and reaches an open ledge with good views south and west at 6.6 mi. The grade lessens, and after a sharp right turn in a ledgy area, the trail reaches the summit of the southwest knob of Mt. Pierce, which affords a view of the summit of Mt. Washington. The trail descends into a sag and ascends easily through scrub to the summit of Mt. Pierce at 7.2 mi., where the trail comes into the open. It then descends moderately to the northeast over open terrain, ending in about 150 yd. at its jct. with Crawford Path.

MIZPAH CUTOFF (AMC; MAP 1: G8)

From Crawford Path (3,490 ft.) to:	⇅	↗	○
Mizpah Spring Hut (3,777 ft.)	0.7 mi.	350 ft. (rev. 50 ft.)	0:30
From Mt. Clinton Rd. parking area (1,900 ft.) to:			
Mizpah Spring Hut (3,777 ft.) via Crawford Connector, Crawford Path, Mizpah Cutoff, and Webster Cliff Trail	2.6 mi.	1,950 ft. (rev. 50 ft.)	2:15

This short trail provides a direct route from AMC's Macomber Family Information Center (Crawford Depot) area to Mizpah Spring Hut. Mizpah Cutoff diverges right (east) from Crawford Path 1.9 mi. from the Mt. Clinton Rd. parking area, climbs the ridge at a moderate grade, passes through a fairly level area, and descends slightly to join Webster Cliff Trail 100 yd. south of Mizpah Spring Hut.

SAM WILLEY TRAIL (NHDP; MAP 1: G8)

Cumulative from Willey House site (1,300 ft.) to:	⇅	↗	○
Saco River Trail (1,300 ft.)	0.5 mi.	0 ft.	0:15
Complete loop	1.0 mi.	0 ft.	0:30

This trail provides a short, easy walk at the base of the Webster Cliffs from the Willey House site on US 302, starting from the parking area on the east side of the road.

Leaving the parking area, the trail crosses the wooden dam over the Saco River. At a sign, Pond Loop Trail diverges left, providing a 0.2-mi. loop walk beside Willey Pond, with views up to the surrounding mountains. Sam Willey Trail continues 50 yd. ahead, where Pond Loop Trail rejoins from the left, then turns right and follows a graded path south. It turns sharply left at 0.2 mi., where a spur path leads 30 yd. right to a view of the Saco River. The main trail comes to a loop jct. at 0.4 mi. Going left (clockwise), the loop reaches the jct. at 0.5 mi., where Saco River Trail continues ahead (south). Sam Willey Trail swings around back to the north along the river, swings right past a fine view of the notch at the edge of a beaver swamp, and soon returns to the loop jct. To return to the Willey House site, turn left.

SACO RIVER TRAIL (NHDP; MAP 1: G8–H8)

Cumulative from Sam Willey Trail (1,300 ft.) to:	↥↧	↗	↺
Lower (west) jct. with Webster Cliff Trail (1,300 ft.)	0.7 mi.	50 ft. (rev. 50 ft.)	0:25
Dry River Trail (1,290 ft.)	2.4 mi.	300 ft. (rev. 250 ft.)	1:20

This trail, blazed in blue, provides easy walking through attractive forests along the floor of Crawford Notch, linking the Willey House site (via Sam Willey Trail) with Webster Cliff Trail, Maggie's Run, and Dry River Trail.

Leaving the most southerly point of the southern loop section of Sam Willey Trail, 0.5 mi. from the Willey House site, Saco River Trail runs briefly alongside the Saco River then bears left away from the river and traverses several minor ups and downs. At 0.5 mi., the trail dips to the edge of an open swamp, where there is a view of Mt. Willey. The trail swings left and ascends slightly, and at 0.7 mi., it meets Webster Cliff Trail (0.2 mi. from its trailhead on US 302) and turns left on it. The two trails coincide, climbing steadily eastward. At 0.8 mi., Saco River Trail turns right off Webster Cliff Trail and descends easily to the floor of the valley. At 1.2 mi., Saco River Trail crosses several channels of Webster Brook (often dry) and continues south through open hardwoods; in places, the footway must be followed with care. At 1.6 mi., the trail skirts a beaver swamp then ascends gently, though with some rocky footing, through an old-growth hardwood forest. It passes a connecting trail from Maggie's Run (Section Three) on the right at 2.0 mi., and ends at Dry River Trail, 0.5 mi. from that trail's trailhead on US 302 and directly across from the jct. with Dry River Connection, 0.4 mi. from Dry River Campground.

SACO LAKE TRAIL (AMC; MAP 1: G8)

From north jct. with US 302 (1,915 ft.) to:	↥	↗	↻
South jct. with US 302 (1,890 ft.)	0.3 mi.	0 ft. (rev. 25 ft.)	0:10

This short trail makes a loop around the east shore of Saco Lake, beginning and ending on the east side of US 302, with trailheads 0.2 mi. apart. Its north end starts 50 yd. north of the entrance to AMC's Highland Center at Crawford Notch. Parking is available by the northwest corner of the lake, 90 yd. south of the north trailhead. The trail passes a side path left to a pet cemetery at 0.1 mi. then runs along the shore to a short side path on the left (sign) that climbs steeply to a ledgy area with a metal railing. This ledge is called Idlewild, and offers a view of the lake and the Willey Range (use caution). The path continues along the shore, crosses an area of rocky rubble, and ends after crossing the dam at the south end of the lake.

DRY RIVER VALLEY

DRY RIVER TRAIL (WMNF; MAP 1: H8–F9)

Cumulative from US 302 (1,195 ft.) to:	↥	↗	↻
Dry River Connection and Saco River Trail (1,290 ft.)	0.5 mi.	100 ft.	0:20
Suspension bridge (1,560 ft.)	1.7 mi.	500 ft. (rev. 150 ft.)	1:05
Mt. Clinton Trail (1,900 ft.)	2.9 mi.	950 ft. (rev. 100 ft.)	2:00
Isolation Trail (2,600 ft.)	4.9 mi.	1,700 ft. (rev. 50 ft.)	3:20
Mt. Eisenhower Trail (2,675 ft.)	5.2 mi.	1,800 ft.	3:35
Dry River Shelter #3 (3,125 ft.)	6.3 mi.	2,250 ft.	4:20
Lakes of the Clouds Hut (5,012 ft.)	9.6 mi.	4,350 ft. (rev. 200 ft.)	7:00

Note: In 2011, Tropical Storm Irene caused extensive damage on Dry River Trail, with major washouts in multiple locations. The USFS closed the trail in fall 2011 and reopened it in 2014 with a number of rough relocations that must be followed with care. Expect a more primitive trail with a narrower, rougher tread requiring some route finding.

Dry River Trail is the main trail from US 302 up the valley of Dry River and through Oakes Gulf to Lakes of the Clouds Hut, giving access to Mt. Washington, the Southern Presidentials, and the upper portion of Montalban Ridge. This trail is almost entirely within the Presidential Range–Dry River Wilderness. Dry River Shelters #1 and #2 have been removed; Dry River Shelter #3 will be removed whenever major maintenance is required. This trail is, in general, rougher than most similar valley trails elsewhere in the White Mountains. The first 5.0 mi. follow fairly close to the route of an old logging railroad, although the river and its tributaries have eradicated much of the old roadbed, and the relocations that were cut in the 1970s to eliminate several potentially hazardous river crossings have bypassed much of the remaining grade. When water levels are high, the few Dry River crossings that remain on this trail—and on the trails that diverge from it—are at best difficult and at worst very dangerous. At such times, it is prudent not to descend into this valley if major stream crossings lie between you and your destination.

Dry River Trail leaves the east side of US 302 (sign, roadside parking) 0.3 mi. north of the entrance to Dry River Campground and 2.6 mi. south of the Willey House site. From the highway, the trail follows a wide woods road northeast for 0.5 mi. to its jct. on the right with the bed of the old logging railroad (sign: Dry River Connection), which reaches this point from Dry River Campground in 0.4 mi. At this jct., Saco River Trail enters on the left. From here, Dry River Trail follows the railroad bed, enters the Presidential Range–Dry River Wilderness at 0.7 mi., and leaves the railroad grade sharply left at 0.9 mi., staying on the west side of the river where the railroad formerly crossed it. Just downstream from this point is a pleasant pool. The trail climbs over a low bluff, rejoins the roadbed, leaves it again on a relocation around a washout, then climbs steeply on a narrow sidehill up a higher bluff to a restricted but beautiful outlook up Dry River to Mt. Washington, Mt. Monroe, and the headwall of Oakes Gulf. At 1.7 mi., after a short, steep, and rough descent, the trail crosses Dry River on a suspension bridge and continues up the east bank with several ups and downs then follows portions of the old railroad grade alternating with two rough up-and-down relocations to the right; at the end of the second relocation the trail angles left across a brookbed to regain the grade. At 2.9 mi., the trail turns sharply right off the railroad grade, where Mt. Clinton Trail diverges left to cross the river and ascends to Mizpah Spring Hut. Dry River Trail continues up the valley on a rougher section with many ups and downs, including four new relocations, crossing two brooks. At 4.2 mi., Dry River Trail makes a sharp turn away from the river then turns left and continues along the bank at a higher level. At 4.9 mi., the trail reaches Isolation Brook, turns right along the brook bank for 60 yd., turns left to cross the brook, turns right again, and in another 60 yd., Isolation Trail diverges right, heading up along the brook.

Dry River Trail bears left and continues along the high east bank of Dry River. At 5.2 mi., Mt. Eisenhower Trail diverges sharply left and descends the steep bank to cross the river and climb to Crawford Path. Dry River Trail continues along the east bank, passing at 5.4 mi. an unsigned, muddy, and rough side path on the left that leads 40 yd. down to the pool at the foot of Dry River Falls, a very attractive spot. The top of the falls, with an interesting pothole, can also be reached by an obscure path a short distance farther along the main trail. At 5.6 mi., the trail crosses the river to the west side; the crossing is normally fairly easy but could be a serious problem at high water. The trail continues up the valley, crossing an open washed-out slope with loose footing at 5.8 mi. (caution). At 6.3 mi., Dry River Shelter #3 is passed on the left. In another 60 yd., the trail crosses a major tributary of the Dry River just above the confluence (take care to avoid false paths in this area) and continues along the bank of the main stream, gradually rising higher above the river.

At 7.4 mi., the trail begins to swing away from the river and gradually climbs into Oakes Gulf, with wet and rough footing at times; this area is subject to frequent blowdown. After the trail crosses a small ridge and descends sharply on the other side, views begin to appear, although the trail remains well sheltered in the scrub. The trail climbs steadily up the headwall, with one ledge scramble, and at 8.7 mi. is a good outlook perch just to the right of the trail. The trail soon climbs out of the scrub, turns left, and crosses a small brook at a right angle. At 9.1 mi., the trail turns sharply right (northeast) from the gully it once ascended, where signs forbid public entry into the area formerly crossed by the trail. (The closed area is the habitat of the dwarf cinquefoil, an endangered plant species.) The trail continues to climb with excellent views down the gulf, passes the Presidential Range–Dry River Wilderness boundary sign in a patch of scrub, and reaches the height-of-land on the southwest ridge of Mt. Washington at 9.4 mi. The trail swings left (west) and descends to the larger of the two Lakes of the Clouds, follows its south edge, and ends at Crawford Path, at Lakes of the Clouds Hut.

MT. CLINTON TRAIL (WMNF; MAP 1: G8)

Cumulative from Dry River Trail (1,900 ft.) to:	⇅	↗	○
Dry River Cutoff (3,425 ft.)	2.5 mi.	1,550 ft.	2:00
Mizpah Spring Hut (3,777 ft.)	3.0 mi.	1,900 ft.	2:25

This trail connects the lower part of Dry River valley to Mizpah Spring Hut and the southern part of the Southern Presidentials, and lies almost entirely within the Presidential Range–Dry River Wilderness. This trail is lightly used, and parts of it, especially below Dry River Cutoff, are rough,

SEC
1

wet, and possibly overgrown. It requires considerable care to follow, especially at the many stream crossings. It is not recommended for inexperienced hikers. (*Caution:* The crossing of Dry River on this trail near its jct. with Dry River Trail can vary from an easy skip over the stones to a waist-high ford in a torrent, and there may be no safe way across. In high-water conditions, it is prudent not to descend from Mizpah Spring Hut by this trail because the only safe course to reach Dry River Trail might be a very rough bushwhack south along the riverbank for about 1.2 mi.)

The trail diverges left from Dry River Trail 2.9 mi. from US 302 and in 20 yd. makes the potentially hazardous crossing of Dry River. On the west side of the river, the trail, marked by small cairns, turns right and runs 120 yd. upstream (north) along the riverbed through an area of gravel and rock outwash. It then turns left, scrambles up a low washed-out bank, enters the woods, and follows an obscure, winding route 60 yd. to the right to meet the original trail route, where it turns left. Mt. Clinton Trail follows a short stretch of old railroad grade upstream then swings left up the bank of a major tributary, following an old logging road at a moderate grade much of the way. At 0.4 mi., it passes through a large cut blowdown and bears right. At 0.5 mi., the trail crosses the tributary brook for the first of seven times then scrambles up a washed-out area on the other bank and bears left onto an old logging road. The trail recrosses the brook, crosses a tributary, and crosses the main brook again. At 1.2 mi., the trail turns sharply left off the road and descends to the main brook, makes the fourth crossing at a ledgy spot with a small cascade and pool, and regains the road on the other side, soon skirting to the left of a wet area. The trail follows close to the brook, crossing two more tributaries as well as the main brook twice more, to the seventh crossing of the main brook at 1.8 mi. The trail soon climbs more steadily, and above an eroded section where a small brook has taken over the footway, walking on the old road becomes more pleasant. Dry River Cutoff enters on the right at 2.5 mi. From here, Mt. Clinton Trail crosses two small streams, ascends past a large boulder to the Presidential Range–Dry River Wilderness boundary at 2.9 mi., and soon enters the clearing of Mizpah Spring Hut, where the trail joins Webster Cliff Trail.

MT. EISENHOWER TRAIL (WMNF; MAP 1: G8)

Cumulative from Dry River Trail (2,675 ft.) to:	↥↧	↗	○
Dry River Cutoff (2,700 ft.)	0.3 mi.	150 ft. (rev. 100 ft.)	0:10
Crawford Path (4,465 ft.)	2.4 mi.	1,900 ft.	2:10

This lightly used trail connects the middle part of Dry River valley to Crawford Path at the Eisenhower–Franklin col and lies almost entirely within the Presidential Range–Dry River Wilderness. The trail's grades are mostly easy to moderate with good footing, and it runs above treeline for only a short distance at the ridge crest.

The trail diverges left from Dry River Trail 5.2 mi. from US 302 and descends rather steeply on a former route of Dry River Trail through an area with many side paths; care must be taken to stay on the proper trail. The trail turns right and crosses Dry River (may be difficult or impassable at high water) and follows the bank downstream. At 0.2 mi., the trail joins its former route and bears right up a rather steep logging road, and Dry River Cutoff diverges left at 0.3 mi. Soon the grade on Mt. Eisenhower Trail eases as it leads generally north, keeping a bit to the west of the crest of the long ridge that runs south from a point midway between mts. Franklin and Eisenhower. At 1.6 mi., the trail turns sharply right, then left, before ascending more steeply for a while. At 2.1 mi., the trail finally gains the crest of the ridge and winds up through scrub, passes the Presidential Range–Dry River Wilderness boundary sign, breaks into the open with fine views, and runs nearly level to Crawford Path in the Eisenhower–Franklin col, 0.2 mi. north of Crawford Path's northern jct. with Mt. Eisenhower Loop.

DRY RIVER CUTOFF (AMC; MAP 1: G8)

From Mt. Eisenhower Trail (2,700 ft.) to:	⇅	↗	○
Mt. Clinton Trail (3,425 ft.)	1.7 mi.	800 ft. (rev. 50 ft.)	1:15

This trail connects the middle part of Dry River valley to Mizpah Spring Hut and the southern section of the Southern Presidentials. Grades are mostly easy with some moderate sections. This trail is entirely within the Presidential Range–Dry River Wilderness.

Dry River Cutoff diverges left from Mt. Eisenhower Trail 0.3 mi. from the latter trail's jct. with Dry River Trail. In 0.1 mi., Dry River Cutoff crosses a substantial brook after a slight descent, turns sharply left and climbs the bank, crosses a tributary, then swings back and climbs above the bank of the tributary. The trail crosses the tributary at 0.6 mi. and again at 0.9 mi., where the trail swings left and climbs to the height-of-land on the southeast ridge of Mt. Pierce at 1.3 mi. Dry River Cutoff then runs almost on the level with wet and obscure footing in places and descends slightly to its jct. with Mt. Clinton Trail at 1.7 mi. Mizpah Spring Hut is 0.5 mi. to the right from this jct. via Mt. Clinton Trail.

MONTALBAN RIDGE

DAVIS PATH (AMC; MAPS 1 & 3: H8–F9)

Cumulative from parking area near US 302 (1,000 ft.) to:	⥮	↗	○
Mt. Crawford spur path (2,900 ft.)	2.2 mi.	1,900 ft.	2:05
Mt. Parker Trail (3,040 ft.)	3.7 mi.	2,250 ft. (rev. 200 ft.)	3:00
Stairs Col Trail (3,030 ft.)	4.0 mi.	2,300 ft. (rev. 50 ft.)	3:10
Giant Stairs spur path (3,450 ft.)	4.4 mi.	2,700 ft.	3:35
Mt. Davis spur path (3,600 ft.)	8.5 mi.	3,650 ft. (rev. 800 ft.)	6:05
Mt. Isolation spur path (3,950 ft.)	9.7 mi.	4,100 ft. (rev. 100 ft.)	6:55
Isolation Trail, east branch (3,850 ft.)	10.6 mi.	4,200 ft. (rev. 200 ft.)	7:25
Isolation Trail, west branch (4,140 ft.)	10.9 mi.	4,500 ft.	7:40
Glen Boulder Trail (5,175 ft.)	12.5 mi.	5,650 ft. (rev. 100 ft.)	9:05
Boott Spur Trail (5,450 ft.)	13.0 mi.	5,900 ft.	9:25
Lawn Cutoff (5,475 ft.)	13.6 mi.	6,000 ft. (rev. 100 ft.)	9:50
Crawford Path (5,625 ft.)	14.4 mi.	6,200 ft. (rev. 50 ft.)	10:20
Mt. Washington summit (6,288 ft.) via Crawford Path	15.0 mi.	6,850 ft.	10:55
From parking area near US 302 (1,000 ft.) to:			
Lakes of the Clouds Hut (5,012 ft.) via Camel Trail	14.6 mi.	6,000 ft. (rev. 450 ft.)	10:20

Davis Path, completed by Nathaniel T. P. Davis in 1845, was the third (and longest) bridle path constructed to the summit of Mt. Washington. The path was in use until 1853 or 1854 but became impassable soon afterward; it went entirely out of existence until it was reopened as a foot trail by AMC in 1910. At that time, the path was so overgrown that some sections could be located only by one of the original laborers, then a very old man, who relied on his memory of where the path had been built. The sections leading up the dauntingly steep southern slopes of Mt. Crawford and Stairs Mtn. give some idea of the magnitude of building a trail passable to horses along this ridge. The resolve that enabled Davis to push forward with this task was the inspiration for the naming of Mt. Resolution. This trail is almost entirely within the Presidential Range–Dry River Wilderness. The section of the trail between Stairs Mtn. and Mt. Isolation is lightly used, rough in places, and may be overgrown, requiring care to follow. Water is scarce along this ridge in dry seasons; you may have to go some distance down one of the trails that descend off the ridge.

The path leaves the east side of US 302 (on the west side of the Saco River) at a paved parking lot just north of Notchland Inn, 5.6 mi. south of the Willey House site in Crawford Notch State Park and 6.3 mi. north of the jct. with Bear Notch Rd. in Bartlett.

The path follows a gravel road (Crawford Valley Way) along the bank of the river about 200 yd. upstream (north) to a suspension footbridge (Bemis Bridge). Beyond the east end of the bridge, the trail passes through private land, continuing straight east across an overgrown field to the left of a house, then turns left through a brushy area and crosses a small brook on a log bridge. Davis Path then swings right and enters the woods and the WMNF. It soon joins and follows a logging road along the bed of a small brook (normally dry in summer), entering the Presidential Range–Dry River Wilderness. The trail crosses the brook bed where there may be running water upstream, crosses a tributary, and begins to climb away from the main brook. At 0.9 mi., the trail turns sharply right, soon enters the old and carefully graded bridle path, and begins to ascend the steep ridge between Mt. Crawford and Mt. Hope by zigzags, with many rock steps. Attaining the crest and the first outlook at 1.9 mi., Davis Path follows this ridge north, rising over bare ledges with more good outlooks, particularly to Mt. Carrigain and the Tripyramids; follow the trail with care in this ledgy section. At 2.2 mi. from US 302, at the foot of a large, sloping ledge, a side trail diverges left and climbs 0.3 mi. and 200 ft. (15 min.) to the bare, peaked summit of Mt. Crawford, from which you have a magnificent view of Crawford Notch, Dry River valley, and the surrounding ridges and peaks.

From this jct., Davis Path turns northeast, descends slightly to the col between the peak of Mt. Crawford and its ledgy, domelike east knob (sometimes called Crawford Dome), and resumes the ascent. The path soon passes over a ledgy shoulder of Crawford Dome, with good views back to the impressively precipitous face of the small peak of Mt. Crawford, and dips to the Crawford–Resolution col. Leaving this col, the path runs north, rises slightly, and keeps close to the same level along the steep west side of Mt. Resolution.

At 3.7 mi., Mt. Parker Trail diverges right (east) and in 0.5 mi. leads to open ledges near the summit of Mt. Resolution then continues to Mt. Langdon Trail and Bartlett village. Fine views can be obtained from open ledges by ascending this trail for little more than 0.1 mi. from the Davis Path jct. The spur trail that diverged left at this jct., opposite Mt. Parker Trail, and descended to the Resolution Shelter is no longer maintained, and the shelter has been removed. At 4.0 mi., Davis Path passes just west of Stairs Col—the small, wild pass between Mt. Resolution and Stairs Mtn. Here, Stairs Col Trail to Rocky Branch valley diverges right. Davis Path now veers northwest, passing west of the precipitous Giant Stairs, ascending gradually along a steep mountainside then zigzagging boldly northeast—with occasional steep scrambles on ledges—toward the flat top of Stairs Mtn. As the path turns sharply left shortly before reaching the top of the slope, a branch trail leads right a few steps to the Down-look, a good viewpoint at the brink of a cliff. (On the descent, where the main trail turns sharply right, take care not to follow this side path inadvertently because it ends at the dropoff very abruptly.) At the top of the climb, 4.4 mi. from US 302, a branch trail leads right (southeast) at easy grades for 0.2 mi., passing just south of the summit of Stairs Mtn., to the top of Giant Stairs and an inspiring view to the east and south.

Davis Path turns left and descends moderately along the north ridge of Stairs Mtn. for 1.0 mi. then turns right and runs east in a sag for about 0.1 mi. Turning north again and crossing a small brook (watch for this left turn), the path passes over a small rise and descends into another sag. The path next begins to ascend the long north and south ridge of Mt. Davis, keeping mostly to the west slopes, with several ups and downs. Grades are mostly easy along this wild, little-used section, but the footing is rough in places, and blowdown and overgrown sections may be encountered.

At 6.1 mi., a small spring is on the right, and at 6.5 mi., a small brook is crossed. At 8.5 mi., a side path diverges right (east) and climbs steeply 0.2 mi. and 200 ft. (10 min.) to the bare south summit of Mt. Davis, which commands perhaps the finest view on Montalban Ridge and one of the best in the mountains. The main path now descends to the col between Mt. Davis and Mt. Isolation, where it crosses a small brook before ascending Mt. Isolation. At 9.7 mi., a spur path (sign) diverges left at a ledgy spot, leading steeply in 125 yd. (swinging left to the high point at the top) to the open summit of Mt. Isolation, which provides magnificent views in most directions.

Davis Path descends moderately for 0.2 mi. then runs north along the ridge at easy grades. At 10.5 mi., the path leads past the site of the former Isolation Shelter, and at 10.6 mi., the east branch of Isolation Trail enters on the right from Rocky Branch valley. Water can be obtained by going down Isolation Trail to the right (east); decent-appearing water (which is nevertheless unsafe to drink without treatment) may be a considerable distance down. Davis Path now climbs steadily, and at 10.9 mi., as it reaches the top of the ridge and the grade decreases, the west branch of Isolation Trail diverges and descends left into Dry River valley. Davis Path passes over a hump and runs through a sag at 11.5 mi. then ascends steadily to treeline at 12.1 mi. From here, the trail is above treeline and completely exposed to the weather. At 12.5 mi., Glen Boulder Trail joins on the right just below a small crag; at 13.0 mi., Davis Path passes just west of the summit of Boott Spur, and Boott Spur Trail from AMC's Pinkham Notch Visitor Center enters on the right (east).

Turning northwest, Davis Path leads along the almost-level ridges of Boott Spur and crosses Bigelow Lawn. At 13.6 mi., Lawn Cutoff diverges right to Tuckerman Junction, and 200 yd. farther on, Camel Trail diverges left (west) to Lakes of the Clouds Hut. At 14.0 mi., Davis Path begins to follow the original location of Crawford Path and crosses Tuckerman Crossover, and in another 0.3 mi., Davis Path is joined on the right by Southside Trail. At 14.4 mi., Davis Path ends at the present Crawford Path, which climbs to the summit of Mt. Washington in another 0.6 mi.

STAIRS COL TRAIL (AMC; MAP 1: H9)

From Rocky Branch Trail (1,420 ft.) to:	⬍	↗	⏱
Davis Path (3,030 ft.)	1.8 mi.	1,650 ft. (rev. 50 ft.)	1:45

This trail connects Rocky Branch valley with Stairs Col on Davis Path, providing, in particular, the easiest route to Giant Stairs. Very little water is to be found along Davis Path, but water is usually available in small streams along the upper part of Stairs Col Trail. This trail is almost entirely within the Presidential Range–Dry River Wilderness.

Stairs Col Trail leaves Rocky Branch Trail opposite the side path to Rocky Branch Shelter #1 area and follows an old railroad siding for 50 yd. The trail then turns sharply left, crosses a swampy area, and climbs briefly to a logging road, where the trail enters the Presidential Range–Dry River Wilderness. From here nearly to Stairs Col, the trail follows old logging roads along the ravine of Lower Stairs Brook, becoming quite steep at 1.3 mi. and crossing the headwaters of the brook at about 1.5 mi., where the trail enters a birch glade. The trail becomes gradual as it approaches Stairs Col, with an impressive view up to the cliffs of Stairs Mtn. The trail crosses this small, ferny pass and continues down the west slope a short distance to meet Davis Path at 1.8 mi. For Giant Stairs, turn right at this jct.

ROCKY BRANCH TRAIL (WMNF; MAP 3: G10–H9)

Cumulative from parking lot off NH 16 (1,250 ft.) to:	⬍	↗	⏱
Height-of-land (3,100 ft.)	2.8 mi.	1,950 ft. (rev. 100 ft.)	2:20
Isolation Trail (2,800 ft.)	3.7 mi.	1,950 ft. (rev. 300 ft.)	2:50
Stairs Col Trail (1,420 ft.)	8.1 mi.	2,050 ft. (rev. 1,500 ft.)	5:05
Jericho Rd. (1,100 ft.)	10.1 mi.	2,050 ft. (rev. 300 ft.)	6:05

Note: In 2011, Tropical Storm Irene caused extensive damage on the southern section of Rocky Branch Trail, with major washouts in multiple locations. The section between Isolation Trail and Stairs Col Trail was closed by the USFS in fall 2011 and reopened in fall 2015 with numerous relocations, some of which require care to follow.

This trail provides access to the Saco River's Rocky Branch valley, which lies between the two longest subsidiary ridges of Mt. Washington: Montalban Ridge to the west and Rocky Branch Ridge to the east. In the upper part of the valley, the forest has largely recovered from fires that swept the slopes from 1912 to 1914. (*Caution:* Four river crossings between the jcts. with Isolation Trail and Stairs Col Trail, and one just east of the Isolation Trail jct., are wide, difficult, and possibly dangerous at high water.)

The northeast terminus of this trail is located at a paved parking lot on the west side of NH 16, about 5.3 mi. north of Jackson and just north of the highway bridge over the Ellis River. The Jericho (south) trailhead is reached by following Jericho Rd.—called Rocky Branch Rd. (FR 27) by the USFS—which leaves US 302 just east of the bridge over Rocky Branch, 1.0 mi. west of the jct. of US 302 and NH 16 in Glen; the road is paved for 1.6 mi. then is a good gravel road up to a parking area and gate at the beginning of the trail, 4.1 mi. from US 302; in winter it is gated at 2.5 mi.

At the northeast terminus, on NH 16 below Pinkham Notch, the trail leaves the north end of the parking lot (avoid a gravel road that branches left just below the parking lot) and climbs moderately by switchbacks on an old logging road. At about 0.5 mi., Avalanche Brook Ski Trail enters from the left then leaves on the right at 0.7 mi. At 1.3 mi., Rocky Branch Trail swings left, away from the bank of a small brook, and continues to ascend steadily then turns sharply left at 1.8 mi. and follows an old, very straight road on a slight downhill grade. After about 0.5 mi. on this road, the trail swings gradually right and climbs moderately, following a brook part of the way, and reaches the Presidential Range–Dry River Wilderness boundary just east of the ridge top. Passing the almost imperceptible height-of-land at 2.8 mi., the trail follows a short bypass to the left of a wet area and runs almost level then descends easily, with wet, rocky footing and small brooks running in and out of the trail.

At 3.5 mi., the trail begins to swing left, descends gradually to Rocky Branch and follows it downstream for a short distance before crossing it at 3.7 mi. This crossing may be very difficult, and the trail can be hard to follow from this crossing for travelers going toward NH 16, because the trail is poorly marked and there are well-beaten side paths to campsites. Heading for NH 16, the main trail first parallels the river going upstream and then swings gradually away from the river on a well-defined old road. On the west bank of the river at this crossing is the jct. with Isolation Trail, which turns right (north), following the riverbank upstream on the old railroad grade.

Rocky Branch Trail turns left downstream, also following the old railroad grade from this jct., and passes the former site of Rocky Branch Shelter #2 in 60 yd. (This shelter has been removed; the USFS plans to replace it with tent pads in the future.) The trail crosses a muddy spot and a rocky tributary below a cascade and runs generally south along the west bank, at times on the old railroad grade, crossing an open bank at 4.2 mi. The trail continues down the grade, crossing two tributaries (the first crossing is steep), then follows several relocated sections off and back onto the grade, crossing another tributary. At 6.2 mi., the trail makes the first of four crossings of the Rocky Branch. These crossings are difficult at high water and can only be avoided by a rough and difficult bushwhack along the west bank. Care must be taken to follow the trail at the crossings, particularly at the first one, where it angles to the right through a rocky area after crossing the river then swings left across a brookbed, between piles of uprooted trees, before turning right into the woods. The second crossing is at 6.3 mi., and the third at 6.5 mi. After the fourth crossing at 6.9 mi., the trail climbs by switchbacks on a relocation to a high bank, runs along the top of the bank, then descends back near the river. At 7.4 mi. it leaves the Presidential Range–Dry River Wilderness and immediately swings right across Upper Stairs Brook. It continues off and then on the railroad grade, passes to the right of a large log jam, and reaches a jct. at 8.1 mi. with Stairs Col Trail on the right. In another 20 yd. along Rocky Branch Trail, a spur path on the left leads 60 yd. to WMNF Rocky Branch Shelter #1; from the front of the shelter, a path leads 75 yd. ahead to the river, passing a spur on the right leading to three tent platforms. The main trail continues south along the railroad grade, loops out to the right on a relocation, and crosses Lower Stairs Brook at 8.7 mi. At 9.0 mi., it makes a bypass on the uphill (right) side of a boggy section of the grade, crossing another brook, rejoins the grade, and at 9.7 mi. enters a gravel logging road. It follows this road for another 0.4 mi. to Jericho Rd., crossing the river and Otis Brook on logging-road bridges just before reaching its south terminus.

In the reverse direction, where the logging road swings to the left 0.4 mi. from the Jericho Rd. (south) terminus, Rocky Branch Trail continues straight ahead into the woods at a kiosk on the old railroad grade, which looks like an old grassy road.

SEC 1

ISOLATION TRAIL (WMNF; MAP 1: G9–G8)

Cumulative from Rocky Branch Trail (2,800 ft.) to:	↑↓	↗	○
Fourth crossing of the Rocky Branch (3,423 ft.)	1.7 mi.	600 ft.	1:10
Davis Path, south jct. (3,850 ft.)	2.6 mi.	1,050 ft.	1:50
Davis Path, north jct. (4,140 ft.)	2.9 mi.	1,350 ft.	2:10
Isolation Brook (3,275 ft.)	4.3 mi.	1,400 ft. (rev. 900 ft.)	2:50
Dry River Trail (2,600 ft.)	5.3 mi.	1,400 ft. (rev. 700 ft.)	3:20

Cumulative from Rocky Branch Trail parking area on NH 16 (1,250 ft.) to:			
Isolation Trail (2,800 ft.) via Rocky Branch Trail	3.7 mi.	1,950 ft. (rev. 400 ft.)	2:50
Davis Path, south jct. (3,850 ft.)	6.3 mi.	3,000 ft.	4:40
Mt. Isolation summit (4,003 ft.) via Davis Path	7.3 mi.	3,250 ft. (rev. 100 ft.)	5:15

Note: In 2011, Tropical Storm Irene caused extensive damage on the lower western section of Isolation Trail. The USFS reopened the trail in 2014. Expect a more primitive trail with a narrower, rougher tread requiring some route finding.

This trail links Dry River valley (Dry River Trail), Montalban Ridge (Davis Path), and Rocky Branch valley (Rocky Branch Trail), crossing the ridge crest north of Mt. Isolation. Isolation Trail is entirely within the Presidential Range–Dry River Wilderness. The section west of Davis Path is lightly used, and parts may be rough, wet, and overgrown, although experienced hikers should be able to follow Isolation Trail fairly easily. East of Davis Path, Isolation Trail receives much more use but is still wet and rough in places and not marked well. The crossings of Rocky Branch are difficult in high water. This trail diverges from Rocky Branch Trail just north of the former site of Rocky Branch Shelter #2 on the west bank of the river, at the point where Rocky Branch Trail crosses the river, 3.7 mi. from its northeast terminus on NH 16. Isolation Trail follows the river north along the west bank on what is left of the old railroad grade, crossing the river at 0.4 mi. At 0.7 mi., the trail turns sharply right off the railroad grade, climbs briefly, then follows a logging road that at first runs high above the river. The trail crosses the river three more times; the next two crossings, at 1.4 mi., are only 70 yd. apart. The last crossing comes at 1.7 mi., after which the trail swings away from the main stream and climbs easily along a tributary with wet and rocky footing. Isolation Trail reaches Davis Path at 2.6 mi. after passing through an area of confusing side paths among bootleg campsites where the main trail must be followed with care.

Now, turning right and coinciding with Davis Path, Isolation Trail climbs steadily north for 0.3 mi. until it approaches the ridge crest. Here, the grade decreases, where the trail turns left off Davis Path. Isolation Trail runs at easy grades with minor ups and downs for 0.2 mi. then descends moderately southwest along the crest of a ridge into Dry River valley. The trail then descends fairly steeply to the left (south) off the ridge, and at 4.3 mi., reaches Isolation Brook, a branch of Dry River. The trail follows the northwest bank of the brook on an old logging road that has been disrupted by several small slides from the 2011 storm, where care is required to follow the footway on muddy side slopes. The trail continues down at moderate grades, crossing several small brooks, then crosses over and back through a rocky, debris-filled area along Isolation Brook (follow cairns with care) and in a short distance ends at Dry River Trail, 4.9 mi. from US 302.

MT. LANGDON TRAIL (WMNF; MAP 3: H9)

Cumulative from road on north bank of Saco River (700 ft.) to:	⮁	↗	⏱
Mt. Parker Trail (1,894 ft.)	2.5 mi.	1,450 ft. (rev. 250 ft.)	2:00
Mt. Langdon Shelter (1,760 ft.)	2.9 mi.	1,450 ft. (rev. 150 ft.)	2:10
High point on Mt. Langdon (2,380 ft.) via Mt. Stanton Trail	3.7 mi.	2,050 ft.	2:55

This trail runs to Mt. Langdon Shelter from the road on the north side of the Saco River near Bartlett village, meeting both Mt. Parker Trail and Mt. Stanton Trail, and thus gives access to both the higher and lower sections of Montalban Ridge. Despite its name, Mt. Langdon Trail does not get particularly close to the summit of Mt. Langdon, which is crossed by Mt. Stanton Trail. Most of Mt. Langdon Trail is either within or close to the boundary of the Presidential Range–Dry River Wilderness; Mt. Langdon Shelter is just outside the Wilderness Area. The first 1.0 mi. of this trail is located on private land.

From the four corners at the jct. of US 302 and Bear Notch Rd. in Bartlett village, follow River St. (the road that leads north) across a bridge over the Saco River to a T intersection at 0.4 mi. and bear left a short distance to the small trailhead parking area (sign) on the right. The trail follows a brushy logging road, continuing straight on the middle road at a three-way jct. in 75 yd., and climbs north at easy to moderate grades through an area of recent logging where there are intersections with numerous diverging logging roads. In general, the trail follows the main road straight ahead (north), and directional arrows and some blazes are found at the major intersections, but great care must be taken to follow the correct route. At

0.3 mi., the path to Cave Mtn. (marked by a small sign) diverges left. At 0.8 mi., Mt. Langdon Trail veers slightly right at an intersection of several roads, and at 0.9 mi., the trail bears left off the main road. The trail enters the Presidential Range–Dry River Wilderness just before crossing a brook at 1.0 mi. After recrossing the brook, the trail climbs more steadily with gravelly footing, bearing sharply right twice.

Mt. Langdon Trail crosses Oak Ridge at 2.2 mi. after passing through an unusual stand of red oak and descends, sharply at times, to the Oak Ridge–Mt. Parker col, where the trail bears right at 2.5 mi.; at this jct., Mt. Parker Trail continues ahead. Mt. Langdon Trail then descends gradually to the WMNF Mt. Langdon Shelter (capacity: eight), where this trail and Mt. Stanton Trail both end. Some care is required to follow the trail near the shelter. Water may be found in a brook 60 yd. from the shelter on Mt. Stanton Trail, although in dry weather the brook bed may have to be followed downhill for a distance.

MT. PARKER TRAIL (SSOC; MAP 3: H9)

Cumulative from Mt. Langdon Trail (1,894 ft.) to:	⇅	↗	⟳
Summit of Mt. Parker (3,004 ft.)	1.4 mi.	1,100 ft.	1:15
Branch trail to open southerly knob (3,200 ft.)	3.2 mi.	1,650 ft. (rev. 350 ft.)	2:25
High point on Mt. Resolution (3,400 ft.)	3.8 mi.	1,850 ft.	2:45
Davis Path (3,040 ft.)	4.3 mi.	1,850 ft. (rev. 350 ft.)	3:05

This pleasant, rugged, lightly used trail passes several excellent viewpoints and provides access from Bartlett to Mt. Parker, Mt. Resolution, the Stairs Col area, and the upper Montalban Ridge. The trail runs almost entirely within or close to the boundary of the Presidential Range–Dry River Wilderness. Parts of the trail may require care to follow due to blowdown and encroaching brush, although experienced hikers should have little problem. No reliable water is available on this trail.

This trail begins in the Oak Ridge–Mt. Parker col 2.5 mi. from Bartlett, continuing straight ahead to the north, where Mt. Langdon Trail turns right (east). Mt. Parker Trail climbs moderately with many switchbacks through brushy beech and oak woods, descends briefly to the right, and then swings left and continues its winding ascent to the open summit of Mt. Parker at 1.4 mi., where there are excellent views, especially north up Rocky Branch valley to Mt. Washington.

The trail now descends and follows the long ridge between Mt. Parker and Mt. Resolution, passing over three bumps and remaining in spruce woods nearly all the way. Some blowdown may be encountered in this area. The trail then runs along the west and south slopes of the remainder of the ridge (swinging inside the Presidential Range–Dry River Wilderness for the rest of its length) until reaching the southeast corner of Mt. Resolution. Here, the trail turns sharply right and zigzags up to the flat, scrubby col between the main summit ridge and a southerly knob at 3.2 mi. An unmarked and overgrown branch trail leads left 0.1 mi. to the top of this knob, which is a large, flat, open ledge with excellent views; the beginning of this obscure side path is along a flat section of the trail. Beyond this jct., Mt. Parker Trail climbs moderately then winds along the flat top of Mt. Resolution until it reaches a large cairn on an open ledge with excellent views at 3.8 mi. One summit knob is just above this cairn; another knob of almost equal elevation is about 0.1 mi. east-northeast and affords excellent views north, but no path leads to this knob through the dense scrub. From the cairn, the trail descends into a gully where it crosses a small, sluggish brook (unreliable water), then heads down (northwest) over fine open ledges and finally drops steeply to Davis Path; the former branch trail to Resolution Shelter that left Davis Path opposite Mt. Parker Trail has been closed, and the shelter has been removed.

MT. STANTON TRAIL (SSOC; MAP 3: H10–H9)

Cumulative from trailhead off Covered Bridge Lane (630 ft.) to:	⇅	↗	⟳
High point on Mt. Stanton (1,710 ft.)	1.4 mi.	1,100 ft.	1:15
High point on Mt. Pickering (1,920 ft.)	2.2 mi.	1,550 ft. (rev. 250 ft.)	1:55
Fourth Crippie (1,888 ft.)	3.4 mi.	1,900 ft. (rev. 400 ft.)	2:40
High point on Mt. Langdon (2,380 ft.)	4.6 mi.	2,600 ft. (rev. 200 ft.)	3:35
Mt. Langdon Trail at Mt. Langdon Shelter (1,760 ft.)	5.4 mi.	2,600 ft. (rev. 600 ft.)	4:00

This trail passes over the low eastern summits of Montalban Ridge and affords many views from scattered ledges. To reach the east trailhead (the west trailhead is at Mt. Langdon Shelter), leave the north side of US 302, 1.8 mi. west of its jct. with NH 16 in Glen and a short distance east of the bridge over Saco River. Follow a paved road (Covered Bridge Lane) west, bearing left at 0.2 mi. The road swings right (north), and at 0.9 mi., the trailhead (sign) is on the left where the road swings right again to head east as Hemlock Drive. Park on the roadside, taking care not to block any driveways. The yellow-blazed trail follows the left edge of a driveway for 80 yd. and enters the woods. The trail swings right, entering the WMNF and passing around a house, and climbs, turning left onto the older route of the trail at 0.3 mi. At 0.4 mi., Mt. Stanton Trail turns sharply left where the red-blazed WMNF boundary continues straight ahead. The trail climbs moderately, levels briefly, then ascends a steep gravelly section with poor footing. At the top of this pitch, the trail turns left and ascends at an easier grade, and the first of several outlooks from White's Ledge is passed at 0.9 mi. The trail climbs steeply again, with gravelly, slippery footing, after passing a large boulder on the right of the trail. At 1.3 mi., the trail turns sharply right on a ledge, where you have a good viewpoint just to the left of the trail, and climbing becomes easier. At 1.4 mi., the trail passes about 15 yd. to the right of the true summit of Mt. Stanton. The summit area is covered with a fine stand of red pines and provides good views from nearby scattered ledges.

The trail descends past a north outlook to the Stanton–Pickering col then ascends steadily, crosses a ledgy ridge, descends slightly, then climbs steeply and passes 30 yd. to the right of the true summit of Mt. Pickering at 2.2 mi. The trail then leads to ledges on a slightly lower knob, where you have excellent views north. The trail descends to a minor col then crosses several interesting small humps sometimes called the Crippies (the origin of this peculiar name is one of the mysteries of White Mountain nomenclature). These humps have scattered outlook ledges, and the best views are from several ledges on the fourth and last Crippie, which is crossed at 3.4 mi.

After crossing the last Crippie, the trail may be less well cleared and harder to follow. It descends somewhat along the north side of the ridge toward Mt. Langdon then climbs north moderately with a few steep pitches, passing a restricted outlook to Carter Dome, Carter Notch, and Wildcat Mtn. The trail swings left (south), and at 4.6 mi., it passes about 35 yd. to the right of the summit of Mt. Langdon, which is wooded and viewless. It then descends easily to a gravel slope, turns right, and continues downward to a brook that is crossed 60 yd. east of Mt. Langdon Shelter, where Mt. Stanton Trail ends.

CAVE MTN. PATH (MAP 3: H9)

Cumulative from Mt. Langdon Trail (840 ft.) to:	⇅	↗	↻
Cave (1,200 ft.)	0.3 mi.	350 ft.	0:20
Outlook (1,300 ft.)	0.4 mi.	450 ft.	0:25

Cave Mtn. (located on private property) is remarkable for the shallow cave on its south slope. The path is reached from Bartlett by following Mt. Langdon Trail for 0.3 mi. to a well-worn branch path that diverges left (watch for it carefully; marked by a small wooden sign). Cave Mtn. Path follows blue blazes through a recently logged area and skirts the east side of Cave Mtn. After 0.3 mi., this path passes a large prow-shaped boulder, swings right, and leads up a steep gravel slope with very poor footing (especially difficult on the descent) to the cave. A rough, red-blazed trail to the right of the cave leads to the top of the cliff, after a short scramble, where you have a view of Bartlett and mountains to the south.

SEC 1

JACKSON AREA

WINNIWETA FALLS TRAIL (WMNF; MAP 3: G10)

From NH 16 (970 ft.) to:	⇅	◢	◔
Winniweta Falls (1,300 ft.)	0.9 mi.	350 ft.	0:40

This trail provides access to an attractive waterfall. Its trailhead (sign, limited parking) is located on the west side of NH 16, 3.0 mi. north of the bridge over Ellis River in Jackson. Hikers using this trail must ford the wide bed of Ellis River, which is often a rather shallow stream, but which, in crossing, can require wading in even moderate flow and may be dangerous or impassable at high water. In winter, the crossing is even more treacherous because there is often considerable running water under a seemingly stable pack of snow and ice. This trail makes use of several cross-country ski trails maintained by Jackson Ski Touring Foundation. During winter, hikers should avoid walking on ski tracks and should yield to skiers, who have the right of way.

After reaching the far bank of Ellis River, Winniweta Falls Trail bears right and skirts the north side of an overgrown field, crossing Ellis River Ski Trail at 0.2 mi. After crossing another ski trail, the path joins and follows Winniweta Falls Ski Trail (sign) and climbs easily as the path approaches the north bank of Miles Brook on an old logging road. The trail temporarily steers away from the brook, passing through several muddy sections. After a moderate ascent, the trail again nears the bank of Miles Brook, and a short, unsigned path leads 20 yd. left to the top of the falls. To reach the base of the falls, head into the woods just below the unmarked path mentioned and continue downhill 75 yd. to the edge of the stream. The ski trail, meanwhile, continues uphill along the logging road.

IRON MTN. TRAIL (WMNF; MAP 3: H10)

Cumulative from Hayes Farm (1,920 ft.) to:	⇅	◢	◔
Summit of Iron Mtn. (2,726 ft.)	0.9 mi.	800 ft.	0:50
South cliffs (2,430 ft.)	1.6 mi.	850 ft. (rev. 350 ft.)	1:15

The summit of this mountain is wooded with restricted views, but an outlook on the north side and the fine south cliffs provide very attractive views for relatively little effort. Somewhat down the slope to the east of the cliffs are abandoned iron mines. A prominent easterly ridge, on which there was once a trail, descends over the open summit of Green Hill to the cliff called Duck's Head, named for its shape when seen from a point on NH 16 just north of the Jackson covered bridge. Iron Mtn. Trail is reached by leaving NH 16 in Jackson, next to the golf course and 0.3 mi. north of the red covered bridge that leads to Jackson village, and following Green Hill Rd. (sign) to the west. At 1.2 mi., the pavement ends (from here, the road is called Iron Mtn. Rd.), and at 1.4 mi., the road (FR 119) bears left at a fork where FR 325 bears right. The road now becomes fairly steep, a bit rough, and very narrow (be prepared to back up if required for other cars to pass); above the fork, the road is not passable in mud season and winter. At 2.6 mi. from NH 16, where the road ahead soon becomes very poor, park in a designated area generously provided by the landowner on either side of the road just before reaching the house of the former Hayes Farm (now a summer residence).

Iron Mtn. Trail starts at a sign on the left, 10 yd. up the road. The trail crosses a field with fine views, traverses a smaller field, passes through a band of trees, and emerges at the base of a brushy slope. Marked with wooden stakes and small cairns, the trail ascends through an old clear-cut grown to small trees, swings left then right, and enters mature woods at the top edge after 0.2 mi. The path climbs up a badly eroded footway, steeply at times, entering the WMNF at 0.3 mi. At 0.6 mi. is a side path to the right leading 20 yd. to a fine outlook up Rocky Branch valley to Mt. Washington, with the Southern Presidentials visible over Montalban Ridge; at 0.7 mi., a ledge on the left affords a restricted view to the east. The main trail continues to the summit at 0.9 mi., where you see remains of the former fire tower. The trail descends steadily along a rocky ridge, dropping about 300 ft., and crosses several small humps in thick woods; follow cairns and blazes carefully. At 1.5 mi., a faintly marked side path descends left 0.2 mi. and 250 ft. to the old mines (tailings, water-filled shaft, tunnel), and the main trail ascends in a short distance to ledges and the edge of the cliffs, where wide views to the south and west can be enjoyed; swing right to reach the best viewpoint. On the return, the trail leaves the northeast corner of the ledge area behind the cliffs and soon makes a right turn.

SECTION TWO

NORTHERN PRESIDENTIALS AND THE GREAT GULF

Map 1: Presidential Range

INTRODUCTION

This section covers the high peaks of Mt. Washington's massive northern ridge, which curves north and then northeast as a great arm embracing the magnificent glacial cirque called the Great Gulf. This ridge runs for 5.0 mi. with only slight dips below the 5,000-ft. level, and each of the three main peaks rises at least 500 ft. above the cols. AMC's *White Mountains Trail Map 1: Presidential Range* covers the entire area except for Pine Mtn. Trail, which is covered by AMC's *White Mountains Trail Map 5: Carter Range–Evans Notch*. RMC publishes a map of the Randolph Valley and Northern Presidentials, printed on Tyvek, and a guidebook, *Randolph Paths* (9th ed., 2016). The map covers the dense trail network on the northern slope of this region, and it is useful for people who want to explore some of the attractive, less crowded paths in this section. RMC maintains a considerable number of paths on the northern peaks; some of these paths are very lightly used and are wilder and rougher than many trails in the WMNF. Adventurous hikers will find them a delightful alternative to the heavily used principal routes in the range. This network of paths also provides opportunities for less strenuous, varied walks to the many waterfalls and other interesting places on the lower slopes of the range.

Caution: The peaks and higher ridges of this range are nearly as exposed to the elements as Mt. Washington and should be treated with the same degree of respect and caution. Severe winterlike storms can occur at any time of the year, and many lives have been lost in this area from failure to observe the basic principles of safety. In addition, all of the major peaks are strenuous climbs by even the easiest routes. The distances quoted may not seem long to a novice, but only one route to a major peak, Caps Ridge Trail to Mt. Jefferson, involves less than 3,000 ft. of climbing, and that trail is challenging. Although Caps Ridge Trail is relatively short, it is also quite steep, with numerous scrambles on ledges that a person unfamiliar with mountain trails might find daunting. Most other routes to the summits involve 4,000 to 4,500 ft. of climbing due to lower-elevation trailheads, thus making these ascents roughly equivalent in strenuousness to the ascent of Mt. Washington. Another consideration is the very rough, rocky footing on the upper slopes, which can slow travel times considerably. The substantial amount of effort required to climb these peaks, together with the threat of sudden and violent storms, should make the need to avoid overextending oneself quite apparent.

The Northern Presidentials were observed by Thomas Gorges and Richard Vines from the summit of Mt. Washington in 1642, but the men evidently considered these peaks to be part of Mt. Washington, for after their trip, the explorers wrote, with considerable geographic confusion, "The mountain runs E. and W. 30 mi., but the peak is above all the rest." In the early summer of 1820, a party led by Ethan Allen Crawford visited Mt. Washington, and from that summit named mts. Jefferson, Adams, and Madison but did not explore them. Later that summer, two members of a second party spent part of a day on the Northern Presidentials and were probably the first persons of European extraction to visit these summits. Dr. J. W. Robbins, who spent considerable time collecting botanical and other specimens there, made a more thorough exploration in 1829.

The first trail on the northern peaks was probably Stillings Path, which was cut around 1852, primarily for transporting building materials from Randolph to the summit of Mt. Washington, and did not cross any of the summits. In 1860 or 1861, a partial trail was made over the peaks to Mt. Washington; some sections still exist as parts of current trails. Lowe's Path on Mt. Adams was cut between 1875 and 1876; the branch path through King Ravine was made in 1876; and Osgood Path on Mt. Madison was opened in 1878. Many trails were constructed between 1878 and 1902, but this network was greatly damaged by timber cutting, which began in 1903 and continued for several years. Many trails were temporarily obliterated. The more important ones were restored after the most intensive period of lumbering ceased.

In Randolph Valley, where the Link crosses Cold Brook just below scenic Cold Brook Fall, Memorial Bridge stands in honor of J. Rayner Edmands, Eugene B. Cook, and other pioneer path makers who helped construct the superb trail network in the Presidential Range, including Thomas Starr King, James Gordon, Charles E. Lowe, Laban M. Watson, William H. Peek, Hubbard Hunt, William G. Nowell, and William Sargent.

In this section, the AT follows Gulfside Trail from its jct. with the Trinity Heights Connector near the summit of Mt. Washington to Madison Spring Hut. The AT then follows Osgood Trail over Mt. Madison and down into the Great Gulf, proceeding to the Auto Rd. via Osgood Cutoff, Great Gulf Trail (for a very short distance), and Madison Gulf Trail.

ROAD ACCESS

The highest points from which to climb the Northern Presidentials, not including the summit of Mt. Washington, are Jefferson Notch Rd. at Caps Ridge Trail (3,008 ft.); the parking lot on Cog Railway Base Rd., 1.1 mi. east of Jefferson Notch Rd., for Jewell Trail (2,500 ft.); AMC's Pinkham Notch Visitor Center (2,032 ft.); and Pinkham B Rd. (Dolly Copp Rd.) at Pine Link (1,650 ft.). Other important parking areas are the Great Gulf trailhead located 1.9 mi. south of Dolly Copp Campground on NH 16; Randolph East, on Pinkham B Rd. (Dolly Copp Rd.) near its jct. with US 2; Appalachia, on US 2, 0.8 mi. west of Pinkham B Rd. (a stop for the AMC Hiker Shuttle); Lowe's Store on US 2 (nominal fee charged by owner); and Bowman, on US 2, 0.9 mi. west of Lowe's Store. Several of the trailheads in the region, such as Randolph East, Appalachia, and Bowman, owe their names and locations to their former status as stations on the Boston & Maine railroad line, whose tracks were removed in 1997; the railroad grade is now the Presidential Rail Trail and is available for hiking. Pinkham B Rd. (Dolly Copp Rd.)—partly paved, partly gravel, and rough in places—runs 4.3 mi. from US 2, 0.8 mi. east of Appalachia at the foot of the long hill leading up to Randolph Hill, to NH 16, 4.5 mi. south of Gorham, where it serves as the access road for Dolly Copp Campground. The gravel-surface Jefferson Notch Rd. runs 8.9 mi. between Cog Railway Base Rd. and Valley Rd. in Jefferson; see the Caps Ridge Trail description for more information. Both Pinkham B Rd. and Jefferson Notch Rd. are closed in winter.

GEOGRAPHY

The upper part of the mass of the Northern Presidentials is covered with rock fragments; above 5,000 ft., there are no trees and little scrub. The southeast side of the range is dominated by the Great Gulf and the two smaller cirques that branch off from it, Jefferson Ravine and Madison Gulf. Many ridges and valleys radiate from this range on the north and west sides, the most important being, from north to south: on Mt. Madison, Osgood Ridge, Howker Ridge, Bumpus Basin, Gordon Ridge, and the ravine of Snyder Brook, which is shared with Mt. Adams; on Mt. Adams, Durand Ridge, King Ravine, Nowell Ridge, Cascade Ravine, Israel Ridge, and Castle Ravine, which is shared with Mt. Jefferson; on Mt. Jefferson, Castellated Ridge and Ridge of the Caps; and on Mt. Clay, an unnamed but conspicuous ridge extending westerly. The Great Gulf, Bumpus Basin, King Ravine, and Castle Ravine are glacial cirques, or landforms that result when an alpine glacier (a small local glacier in a mountain valley) excavates a typical V-shaped brook valley with a narrow floor and fairly uniform slopes, turning it into the classic U-shaped cirque with a broad, fairly flat floor and almost vertical walls.

The Great Gulf is the largest cirque in the White Mountains, lying between Mt. Washington and the Northern Presidentials and drained by the West Branch of the Peabody River. The headwall, bounded on the south by the slopes of Mt. Washington and on the west by the summit ridge of Mt. Clay, rises about 1,100 to 1,600 ft. above a bowl-shaped valley enclosed by steep walls that extend east for about 3.5 mi. The gulf then continues as a more open valley about 1.5 mi. farther east. The glacial action that formed the Great Gulf and its tributary gulfs is believed to have occurred mainly before the most recent ice age. The views from its walls and from points on its floor are among the best in New England, and steep slopes and abundant water result in a great number of cascades. The first recorded observation of the Great Gulf was by Darby Field (while making the first recorded ascent of Mt. Washington in 1642), and the name probably has its origin in a casual statement made in 1823 by Ethan Allen Crawford, who, having lost his way in cloudy weather, came to "the edge of a great gulf." It was once also called the "Gulf of Mexico," but this name is no longer used. J. W. Robbins, a botanist, visited the region in 1829, but even then, little was known about the area until Benjamin F. Osgood blazed the first trail through the gulf, from Osgood Trail to the headwall, in 1881. The 5,552-acre Great Gulf Wilderness was designated by Congress in 1964. In accordance with USFS Wilderness policy, the trails in the Great Gulf Wilderness are generally maintained to a lower standard than are trails outside Wilderness Areas. Considerable care may be required to follow them.

The first peak on the ridge north of Mt. Washington is Mt. Clay (5,533 ft.). Strictly speaking, it is only a shoulder, comparable to Boott Spur on the southeast ridge of its great neighbor, because Mt. Clay rises barely 150 ft. above the connecting ridge. But Mt. Clay offers superb views from the cliffs that drop away practically at the summit to form the west side of the Great Gulf headwall.

Mt. Jefferson (5,716 ft.) has three summits a short distance apart, in line northwest and southeast, with the tallest in the middle. Perhaps the most striking view is down the Great Gulf with the Carter Range beyond (better views of the gulf itself are obtained from points on Gulfside Trail to the north of the summit). The peak has other fine views, most notably those to Mt. Washington and the other northern peaks, to Bretton Woods on the southwest, and down the broad valley of the Israel River on the northwest. Castellated Ridge, the sharpest and most salient of the White Mountain ridges, extends northwest, forming the southwest wall of Castle Ravine; the view of the Castles from US 2 near the hamlet of Bowman is unforgettable. Ridge of the Caps, similar in formation but less striking, extends to the west from the base of the summit cone. Jefferson's Knees, the two eastern ridges that are cut off abruptly by the Great Gulf, have precipitous wooded slopes and gently sloping tops. South of the peak of Mt. Jefferson is a smooth, grassy plateau called Monticello Lawn (about 5,400 ft.). In addition to its share of the Great Gulf proper, Jefferson's slopes are cut by two other prominent glacial cirques: Jefferson Ravine, a branch of the Great Gulf northeast of the mountain, and Castle Ravine, drained by a branch of the Israel River, on the north. The boundary between these two cirques is the narrow section of the main Northern Presidential ridge that runs from Mt. Jefferson through Edmands Col to Mt. Adams.

The second highest of the New England summits, Mt. Adams (5,799 ft.) has a greater variety of interesting features than any other New England mountain except Katahdin: the sharp, clean-cut profile; its large area above treeline; its inspiring views, the finest being across the Great Gulf to mts. Washington, Jefferson, and Clay; its great northern ridges (sharp, narrow Durand Ridge and massive, broad-spreading Nowell Ridge); and its five glacial cirques. These consist of King Ravine and the four that Mt. Adams shares with its neighbors: the Great Gulf, Jefferson Ravine, Madison Gulf, and Castle Ravine. The two most prominent of the several lesser summits and crags of Mt. Adams are Mt. Sam Adams (5,585 ft.), a rather flat mass to the west, and Mt. Quincy Adams or J. Q. Adams (5,410 ft.), a sharp, narrow shark-fin ridge to the north. A northwestern spur of Mt. Adams, formerly called Adams 4, has recently been renamed Mt. Abigail Adams (5,355 ft.).

The farthest northeast of the high peaks of the Presidential Range, Mt. Madison (5,366 ft.) is remarkable for the great drop of more than 4,000 ft. to the river valleys east and northeast from its summit. The drop to the Androscoggin River at Gorham (4,580 ft. in about 6.5 mi.) is probably the closest approach in New England, except at Katahdin, of a major river to a tall mountain. The views south and southwest to the neighboring Presidential peaks and into the Great Gulf are very fine; the distant view is excellent in all other directions. Its two northern ridges, Gordon Ridge and Howker Ridge, enclose Bumpus Basin, a trailless glacial cirque, and Osgood Ridge extends southeast toward the lower Great Gulf.

Edmands Col (4,938 ft.), named for the pioneer trail maker J. Rayner Edmands, lies between Mt. Adams and Mt. Jefferson; Sphinx Col (4,959 ft.) lies between Mt. Jefferson and Mt. Clay. The col between Mt. Adams and Mt. Madison has an elevation of about 4,890 ft., which means a range of only about 70 ft. between the lowest and highest of the three major cols on this ridge. In the unnamed Adams–Madison col lies Star Lake, a small, shallow body of water among jagged rocks, with impressive views, particularly up to Mt. Madison and Mt. Quincy Adams. Nearby is the Parapet, a small crag that offers magnificent views into the Great Gulf.

Pine Mtn. (2,405 ft.) is a small peak lying to the northeast, between Mt. Madison and the great bend of the Androscoggin River at Gorham. Although low compared with its lofty neighbors, Pine Mtn. is a rugged mountain with a fine cliff on the southeast side that offers magnificent, easily attained views of its Northern Presidential neighbors and of the mountains and river valleys to the north and east.

HUTS
Madison Spring Hut (AMC)

For more than 125 years, AMC's White Mountain hut system has offered hikers a bunk for the night in spectacular locations, with home-cooked dinners and breakfasts, cold running water, and composting or waterless toilets. In 1888 at Madison Spring (4,800 ft.), a little north of the Adams–Madison col, AMC built a stone hut. The present hut, rebuilt and improved after a fire in 1940, and reconstructed in 2010 and 2011, accommodates 52 guests in two bunkrooms. Lodging, with meals included, is available for a fee; reservations are highly recommended (603-466-2727; outdoors.org/lodging/huts). Limited drinks, snacks, and gear are available for purchase by day visitors. The hut is open to the public from early June to mid-September. Pets are not permitted in the hut. It is located 6.0 mi. from the summit of Mt. Washington via Gulfside Trail and 6.8 mi. from Lakes of the Clouds Hut via Gulfside Trail, Westside Trail, and Crawford Path. In bad weather, the best approach (or exit) is via Valley Way, which is sheltered to within a short distance of the hut. Nearby points of interest include Star Lake and the Parapet, a crag overlooking Madison Gulf.

CAMPING
Great Gulf Wilderness

No camping is allowed within 200 ft. of any trail except at designated campsites, of which several are marked by tentsite symbols between the Bluff and the jct. with Sphinx Trail. Wood or charcoal fires are not permitted at any place in the Great Gulf Wilderness. Camping is prohibited within 0.25 mi. of Great Gulf Trail south of its jct. with Sphinx Trail, including Spaulding Lake and its vicinity. Camping and fires are also prohibited above treeline (where trees are less than 8 ft. tall), except in winter, when camping is permitted above treeline in places where snow cover is at least 2 ft. deep and not on any frozen body of water. All former shelters have been removed.

Forest Protection Areas

The WMNF has established a number of FPAs, where camping and wood or charcoal fires are prohibited throughout the year. See p. xxiv for general FPA regulations.

In the area covered by Section Two, no camping is permitted within 200 ft. of certain trails. In 2016, designated trails included Valley Way from its jct. with Scar Trail up to Madison Spring Hut.

SEC
2

No camping is permitted in the WMNF within 0.25 mi. of certain roads (camping on private roadside land is illegal except by permission of the landowner). In 2016, these roads included NH 16, Cog Railway Base Rd., Jefferson Notch Rd. from Cog Railway Base Rd. to Caps Ridge Trail trail-head, and Pinkham B Rd. (Dolly Copp Rd.).

Established Trailside Campsites

The Log Cabin (RMC), first built in 1889 and rebuilt in 1985, is located at a spring at 3,263 ft. elevation, beside Lowe's Path at the jct. with Cabin–Cascades Trail. The cabin is partly enclosed and has room for about 10 guests. A fee is charged. There is no stove, and no wood fires are permitted in the area. Guests are requested to leave the cabin clean and are required to carry out all trash.

The Perch (RMC) is an open log shelter (rebuilt in 2010) located at 4,313 ft. on Perch Path between Randolph Path and Israel Ridge Path, but much closer to the former. It accommodates eight, and four tent platforms are at the site. The caretaker at Gray Knob often visits to collect the over-night fee. Wood fires are not allowed in the area, and all trash must be carried out.

Crag Camp (RMC) is situated at the edge of King Ravine on Spur Trail at 4,247 ft. This is an enclosed cabin with room for about 20 guests. A fee is charged throughout the year. During July and August, it is maintained by a caretaker. Hikers are required to limit groups to ten people. Wood fires are not allowed in the area, and all trash must be carried out.

Gray Knob (RMC) is an enclosed, winterized cabin on Gray Knob Trail at its jct. with Hincks Trail, near Lowe's Path, at about 4,400 ft. The cabin is staffed by a caretaker year-round, and a fee is charged throughout the year. Gray Knob has room for about 15 guests and is supplied with cooking utensils. Hikers are required to limit groups to ten people. Wood fires are not allowed in the area, and all trash must be carried out.

These RMC shelters are all in FPAs, and no camping is allowed within 0.25 mi. of them, except in the shelters and on the tent platforms them-selves. Fees should be mailed to RMC (PO Box 279, Gorham, NH 03581) if not collected by the caretakers. Any infraction of rules or acts of vandal-ism should be reported to the same address.

Osgood Tentsite (WMNF), consisting of five tent platforms, is located near the jct. of Osgood Trail and Osgood Cutoff (which is on the AT).

Valley Way Tentsite (WMNF), consisting of two tent pads and a desig-nated overflow camping area, is located on a spur path off Valley Way, 3.2 mi. from the Appalachia parking area.

SUGGESTED HIKES

■ Easy Hikes

TRIPLE FALLS

	⌃⌄	↗	⏱
RT via Town Line Brook Trail	0.4 mi.	250 ft.	0:20

These cascades on Town Line Brook can be visited in a very short, if fairly steep, trip; use caution where the trail follows the edge of a gorge. See Town Line Brook Trail, p. 139.

GORDON, SALROC, AND TAMA FALLS

	⌃⌄	↗	⏱
LP via Fallsway and Brookbank	1.5 mi.	400 ft.	0:55

Pass three sets of falls on an easy loop. See Fallsway, p. 140.

STAIRS AND HITCHCOCK FALLS

	⌃⌄	↗	⏱
RT via Howker Ridge Trail	2.0 mi.	650 ft.	1:20

The lower part of Howker Ridge Trail passes these two waterfalls, as well as some smaller cascades and the interesting little gorge called Devil's Kitchen. See p. 109.

■ Moderate Hikes

PINE MTN.

	⌃⌄	↗	⏱
RT via Pine Mtn. Rd., Pine Mtn. Loop, Pine Mtn. Trail, and Ledge Trail	4.2 mi.	900 ft.	2:35
LP via Pine Mtn. Rd., Ledge Trail, Pine Mtn. Trail, Pine Mtn. Loop, and Pine Mtn. Rd.	3.5 mi.	850 ft.	2:10

This small, ledgy peak at the northeast end of the Presidential Range offers perhaps the best views in the region for the effort required. The main, round-trip route follows Pine Mtn. Rd., a good gravel road closed to public vehicular use but open to hiking, before picking up the trails above (see Pine Mtn. Rd. and Pine Mtn. Loop Trail, p. 138). From the viewless summit, one should continue on Ledge Trail 0.1 mi. to the south cliff outlooks.

This route is an asset for people looking for smooth footing. Still, many hikers will prefer a shorter and sportier ascent on Ledge Trail to the south ledges and a descent by the main route (see Ledge Trail, p. 139). By either route, add 0.4 mi. and 150 ft. for the out-and-back side trip to the rocky pinnacle of Chapel Rock (see Pine Mtn. Trail, p. 136).

SEC 2

THE BLUFF

	↺↻	↗	○
RT via Great Gulf Trail	5.4 mi.	950 ft.	3:10

This fairly easy trip follows the attractive West Branch of the Peabody River to a viewpoint in the lower gulf. See Great Gulf Trail, p. 94.

DOME ROCK

	↺↻	↗	○
LP via trails below	4.0 mi.	1,450 ft.	2:45

This fairly rugged trip from the Appalachia parking area offers good views from Dome Rock and several other open ledges. Follow Valley Way, Maple Walk, and Sylvan Way to Howker Ridge Trail near Coosauk Fall; ascend Kelton Trail; and descend Inlook Trail past Dome Rock (to begin, see Valley Way, p. 113). Return via Brookside, Valley Way, and either Fallsway or Brookbank trails (to begin, see Brookside, p. 111). Kelton and Inlook trails both have fairly steep sections with rough footing.

WATERFALLS

	↺↻	↗	○
RT via Link, Amphibrach, Monaway extension, and Cliffway	4.8 mi.	1,300 ft.	3:05
LP extension via Amphibrach, Randolph Path, Valley Way, and Fallsway or Brookbank	5.5 mi.	1,700 ft.	3:35
RT via Castle Trail, Israel Ridge Path, and Link	5.4 mi.	1,450 ft.	3:25

A good trip involving many waterfalls can be made by taking the Link and Amphibrach past Cold Brook Fall then making one side trip to the pleasant, broad Coldspur Ledges via the short eastern extension of Monaway and another to Spur Brook Falls via Cliffway (to begin, see the Link, p. 92). One can return by the same route or lengthen the trip by continuing to the end of the Amphibrach at the jct. called the Pentadoi then following Randolph Path down to Valley Way and soon diverging onto either

Fallsway or Brookbank. Another good trip follows Castle Trail and Israel Ridge Path (with a short side trip on the Link) to the First and Second Cascades on Cascade Brook (to begin, see Castle Trail, p. 131).

KING RAVINE

RT via Air Line, Short Line, and King Ravine Trail	6.2 mi.	2,400 ft.	4:20
LP via Air Line, Link, Amphibrach, King Ravine Trail, Short Line, Randolph Path, Valley Way, and Fallsway or Brookbank	7.0 mi.	2,500 ft.	4:45

SEC 2

Although usually regarded as a route to the summit of Mt. Adams, this wild ravine, with its rugged scenery and its fascinating boulders and boulder caves, is a completely worthy objective in its own right. The shortest, easiest route to the ravine floor is via Air Line, Short Line, and King Ravine Trail. It is also feasible to visit King Ravine as an extension of the 5.5-mi. waterfalls trip described above, following Amphibrach to the Pentadoi, King Ravine Trail from there to the floor of the ravine, and descending on Short Line to Randolph Path, Valley Way, and Fallsway or Brookbank. To begin either route, see Air Line, p. 115.

THE HOWKS

RT via Pine Link and Howker Ridge Trail	5.6 mi.	2,900 ft.	4:15

This rugged trip affords excellent views from several ledges on the northern ridges of Mt. Madison. On Howker Ridge Trail, continue to the open summit of the highest Howk. See Pine Link, p. 107.

MT. JEFFERSON

RT via Caps Ridge Trail	5.0 mi.	2,700 ft.	3:50

This route has some very steep, rough sections, but the relatively short distance and elevation gain make it most hikers' choice to Mt. Jefferson. See Caps Ridge Trail, p. 133.

■ Strenuous Hikes

Note: On ascents of the Northern Presidentials, one should never underestimate the potential severity of above-treeline weather or the strenuousness of the typical elevation gain of more than 4,000 ft. Possible routes of ascent are nearly limitless, considering all of the side trails and the variations and linkings they permit.

MT. MADISON

❄️ 🎿 🏃 🐾

	↻↑	↗	⏱
RT via Valley Way and Osgood Trail	8.6 mi.	4,050 ft.	6:20
RT via Daniel Webster–Scout and Osgood trails	8.0 mi.	4,100 ft.	6:05
RT via Great Gulf and Osgood trails	10.2 mi.	4,000 ft.	7:05
RT via Howker Ridge and Osgood trails	8.8 mi.	4,750 ft.	6:45

The easiest way to Mt. Madison is probably via Madison Spring Hut, using the first route above (see Valley Way, p. 113). The second and third routes offer greater difficulty and are rougher and much more exposed to weather (See Daniel Webster–Scout Trail, p. 105, and Great Gulf Trail, p. 94). The final route is beautiful and wild but is much rougher, requiring some care to follow, particularly above treeline (see Howker Ridge Trail, p. 108).

MT. ADAMS

❄️ 🎿 🏃 🐾

	↻↑	↗	⏱
OW via Lowe's Path	4.7 mi.	4,450 ft.	4:35
OW via Air Line	4.3 mi.	4,500 ft.	4:25
OW via Valley Way, Gulfside Trail, and Lowe's Path	5.0 mi.	4,500 ft.	4:45
OW via Air Line, Short Line, King Ravine Trail, and Air Line	4.6 mi.	4,500 ft.	4:35
OW via Valley Way, Scar Trail and Loop, and Air Line	5.0 mi.	4,500 ft.	4:45
OW via Link, Amphibrach, Randolph Path, Spur Trail, and Lowes Path	5.1 mi.	4,500 ft.	4:50

There are numerous direct routes to Mt. Adams, such as Lowe's Path and Air Line, not to mention the routes via Madison Spring Hut; the most popular route via the hut combines Valley Way, Gulfside Trail, and Lowe's Path (see Valley Way, p. 113). King Ravine Trail—including the variations afforded by the Great Gully Trail–Lowe's Path and Chemin des Dames–Air Line combinations—provides what are possibly the most scenic routes to the summit, but these are all extremely strenuous. One attractive route that is no more strenuous than the direct trails follows Valley Way, Scar Trail and Loop, and Air Line, thereby including the fine ledge outlook called Durand Scar and the long, open, knife-edged section of Durand

Ridge. Another route, perhaps a bit steeper and rougher than the direct routes, follows Link, Amphibrach, Randolph Path, and Spur Trail to Thunderstorm Jct., passing the Knight's Castle—an unusual and spectacular viewpoint on the brink of King Ravine's cliffs.

MT. JEFFERSON
❄️ 🥾 🏠 🥾 🦅

	↕️	↗️	⏱️
RT via Castle Trail	10.0 mi.	4,200 ft.	7:05
LP via Caps Ridge Trail, Castle Trail, and Link	6.8 mi.	2,850 ft.	4:50

Castle Trail is a beautiful but strenuous route requiring some fairly difficult ledge scrambling on the spectacular Castles (see Castle Trail, p. 131). The loop involving the Caps Ridge and Castle trails and the Link is scenic and very entertaining, but one must consider the roughness of the Link, with its numerous ankle-twisting holes between rocks and roots (see Caps Ridge Trail, p. 133). For this route, you'll need an adequate supply of energy and daylight.

SPAULDING LAKE
🌊 💧 🥾 🏕️ 🦅

	↕️	↗️	⏱️
RT via Great Gulf Trail	13.0 mi.	3,000 ft.	8:00

This trip passes cascades and pools en route to a tiny pond enclosed by high mountain walls. See Great Gulf Trail, p. 94.

TRAIL DESCRIPTIONS

MAIN RIDGE
GULFSIDE TRAIL (RMC/WMNF; MAP 1: F9)

Cumulative from Madison Spring Hut (4,800 ft.) to:	⇅	↗	↻
Air Line (5,125 ft.)	0.3 mi.	300 ft.	0:20
Thunderstorm Junction (5,490 ft.)	0.9 mi.	700 ft.	0:50
Israel Ridge Path, north jct. (5,475 ft.)	1.0 mi.	700 ft.	0:50
Israel Ridge Path, south jct. (5,250 ft.)	1.5 mi.	750 ft.	1:10
Edmands Col (4,938 ft.)	2.2 mi.	750 ft.	1:30
Mt. Jefferson Loop, north end (5,200 ft.)	2.4 mi.	1,000 ft.	1:40
Six Husbands Trail (5,325 ft.)	2.7 mi.	1,150 ft.	1:55
Mt. Jefferson Loop, south end (5,375 ft.)	3.1 mi.	1,200 ft.	2:10
The Cornice (5,275 ft.)	3.2 mi.	1,200 ft.	2:10
Sphinx Trail (4,975 ft.)	3.7 mi.	1,200 ft.	2:25
Mt. Clay Loop, north end (5,025 ft.)	3.8 mi.	1,250 ft.	2:30
Jewell Trail (5,400 ft.)	4.6 mi.	1,600 ft.	3:05
Mt. Clay Loop, south end (5,400 ft.)	4.9 mi.	1,650 ft.	3:15
Westside Trail (5,500 ft.)	5.0 mi.	1,750 ft.	3:25
Great Gulf Trail (5,925 ft.)	5.5 mi.	2,200 ft.	3:50
Trinity Heights Connector (6,100 ft.)	5.7 mi.	2,350 ft.	4:00
Crawford Path (6,150 ft.)	5.8 mi.	2,400 ft.	4:05
Mt. Washington summit (6,288 ft.) via Crawford Path	6.0 mi.	2,550 ft.	4:15
From Madison Spring Hut (4,800 ft.) to:			
Lakes of the Clouds Hut (5,012 ft.) via Westside Trail and Crawford Path	6.8 mi.	1,950 ft.	4:20

GULFSIDE TRAIL, IN REVERSE (RMC/WMNF; MAP 1: F9)

Cumulative from the summit of Mt. Washington (6,288 ft.) to:	⇅	⬈	⟳
Crawford Path jct. (6,150 ft.)	0.2 mi.	0 ft.	0:05
Trinity Heights Connector (6,100 ft.)	0.3 mi.	0 ft.	0:10
Great Gulf Trail (5,925 ft.)	0.5 mi.	0 ft.	0:15
Westside Trail (5,500 ft.)	1.0 mi.	0 ft.	0:30
Mt. Clay Loop, south end (5,400 ft.)	1.1 mi.	0 ft.	0:35
Jewell Trail (5,400 ft.)	1.4 mi.	50 ft.	0:45
Mt. Clay Loop, north end (5,025 ft.)	2.2 mi.	50 ft.	1:05
Sphinx Trail (4,975 ft.)	2.3 mi.	50 ft.	1:10
The Cornice (5,275 ft.)	2.8 mi.	350 ft.	1:35
Mt. Jefferson Loop, south end (5,375 ft.)	2.9 mi.	450 ft.	1:40
Six Husbands Trail (5,325 ft.)	3.3 mi.	450 ft.	1:55
Mt. Jefferson Loop, north end (5,200 ft.)	3.6 mi.	450 ft.	2:00
Edmands Col (4,938 ft.)	3.8 mi.	450 ft.	2:10
Israel Ridge Path, south jct. (5,250 ft.)	4.5 mi.	750 ft.	2:40
Israel Ridge Path, north jct. (5,475 ft.)	5.0 mi.	1,050 ft.	3:00
Thunderstorm Junction (5,490 ft.)	5.1 mi.	1,050 ft.	3:05
Air Line (5,125 ft.)	5.7 mi.	1,050 ft.	3:20
Madison Spring Hut (4,800 ft.)	6.0 mi.	1,050 ft.	3:30
From Lakes of the Clouds Hut (5,012 ft.) to:			
Madison Spring Hut (4,800 ft.) via Crawford Path, Westside Trail, and Gulfside Trail	6.8 mi.	1,750 ft.	4:15

This trail, the main route along the Northern Presidential ridge crest, leads from Madison Spring Hut to the summit of Mt. Washington. The trail threads its way through the principal cols, avoiding the summits of the Northern Presidentials, and offers extensive, ever-changing views. Elevations range from about 4,800 ft. close to the hut to 6,288 ft. on the summit of Mt. Washington. The name Gulfside was given by J. Rayner Edmands, who, starting in 1892, located and constructed the greater part of the trail, sometimes following trails that had existed before. All but about 0.8 mi. of the trail was once a graded path, and parts were paved with carefully placed stones—a work cut short by Edmands's death in 1910. Gulfside Trail is part of the AT, except for a very short segment at the south end. For its entire distance, Gulfside Trail forms the northwestern boundary of the Great Gulf Wilderness, although the path itself is not within the Wilderness. The trail is well marked with large cairns, many topped with a yellow-painted stone, and while care must be used, Gulfside can often be followed even in dense fog. Always carry a compass and study the map before starting so you will be aware of your alternatives if a storm strikes suddenly. The trail is continuously exposed to the weather; dangerously high winds and low temperatures may occur with little warning at any season of the year. If such storms threaten serious trouble on Gulfside Trail, do not attempt to ascend the summit cone of Mt. Washington, where conditions are usually far worse. If you are not close to either of the huts (Madison Spring or Lakes of the Clouds), descend below treeline to shelter in the woods, by trail if possible, or without trail if necessary. A night of discomfort in the woods is better than exposure to the weather on the heights, which may prove fatal. Slopes on the Great Gulf (east and southeast) side are more sheltered from the wind but are generally much steeper, with numerous dangerous cliffs, and are much farther from highways than slopes on the west side. It is particularly important not to head toward Edmands Col in deteriorating conditions: There is no easy trail out of this isolated mountain pass (which often acts like a natural wind tunnel) in bad weather, and hikers have sometimes been trapped in this desolate and isolated place by a storm. The emergency refuge shelter once located here was removed in 1982 after years of misuse and abuse (including illegal camping) by thoughtless visitors. To enjoy a safe trip through this spectacular but often dangerous area, there is no substitute for studying the map carefully, checking the weather forecast, and understanding the hazards and options before setting out on the ridge.

The trail is described in the southbound direction (toward Mt. Washington). Distances, elevation gains, and times are also given for the reverse (northbound) direction.

Part I. Madison Spring Hut–Edmands Col

The trail begins on the northwest side of Madison Spring Hut and runs 35 yd. northwest to a jct., where Valley Way diverges right. Here Gulfside Trail swings left and leads southwest through a patch of scrub. The trail then aims to the right (north) of Mt. Quincy Adams and ascends its steep, open north slope. At the top of this slope, on the high plateau between King Ravine and Mt. Quincy Adams, Gulfside Trail is joined from the right by Air Line, which in turn was just joined by King Ravine Trail. Here, you have striking views back to Mt. Madison and into King Ravine at the Gateway, a short distance down on the right. Gulfside Trail and Air Line coincide for 70 yd., before Air Line branches left toward the summit of Mt. Adams. Much of Gulfside Trail for about the next 0.5 mi. is paved with carefully placed stones. It rises moderately southwest, then becomes steeper, and at

0.9 mi. from the hut, reaches a grassy lawn in the saddle (5,490 ft.) between Mt. Adams and Mt. Sam Adams. Here, several trails intersect at a spot called Thunderstorm Junction, marked by a large and prominent cairn. Entering the jct. on the right is Great Gully Trail, coming up across the slope from the southwest corner of King Ravine. Here, also, Gulfside Trail is crossed by Lowe's Path, ascending from Lowe's Store on US 2 to the summit of Mt. Adams. About 100 yd. down Lowe's Path, Spur Trail branches right for Crag Camp. The summit of Mt. Adams is 0.3 mi. from the jct. (left) via Lowe's Path; a round trip to the summit requires about 30 min.

Continuing southwest from Thunderstorm Junction and beginning to descend, Gulfside Trail passes a jct. on the left with Israel Ridge Path, which ascends a short distance to Lowe's Path and thence to the summit of Mt. Adams. For 0.5 mi., Gulfside Trail and Israel Ridge Path coincide, passing Peabody Spring (unreliable) just to the right in a small, grassy flat; more-reliable water is located a short distance beyond, at the base of a conspicuous boulder just to the left of the path. Soon the trail climbs easily across a small ridge, where Israel Ridge Path diverges right at 1.5 mi. from Madison Spring Hut. Just north of this jct. in wet weather is a small pool called Storm Lake. Gulfside Trail bears a bit left toward the edge of Jefferson Ravine and, always leading toward Mt. Jefferson, descends southwest along the narrow ridge that divides Jefferson Ravine from Castle Ravine, near the edge of the southeast cliffs, from which are fine views into the Great Gulf. This part of Gulfside Trail was never graded. At the end of this descent, the trail reaches Edmands Col at 2.2 mi. from the hut, with 3.8 mi. to go to Mt. Washington.

At Edmands Col (4,938 ft.) is a bronze tablet in memory of J. Rayner Edmands, who made most of the graded paths on the northern peaks. Gulfside Spring is 50 yd. south of the col on Edmands Col Cutoff, and Spaulding Spring (reliable) is 0.1 mi. north along Randolph Path, near its jct. with Castle Ravine Trail and the Cornice. The emergency shelter once located at this col has been dismantled, and none of the trails leaving this area are entirely satisfactory escape routes in bad weather. From the col, Edmands Col Cutoff leads south, entering scrub almost immediately, affording the quickest route to this rough form of shelter in dangerous weather; it then continues about 0.5 mi. to Six Husbands Trail leading down into the Great Gulf, but it is very rough, and Six Husbands Trail is very difficult to descend, making it a far less than ideal escape route unless the severity of the weather leaves no choice. Randolph Path leads north into the Randolph Valley, running above treeline with great exposure to northwest winds for more than 0.5 mi. Nevertheless, this is probably the fastest, safest route to civilization, unless high winds make it too dangerous to cross through Edmands Col. Branching from Randolph Path, 0.1 mi. north of the col, are the Cornice, a very rough trail leading west entirely above treeline to Castle Trail, and Castle Ravine Trail, which descends steeply over very loose talus and may be hard to follow.

Part II. Edmands Col–Sphinx Col

South of Edmands Col, Gulfside Trail ascends steeply over rough rocks, with Jefferson Ravine on the left. The trail passes flat-topped Dingmaul Rock, from which you have a good view down the ravine, with Mt. Adams on the left. This rock named for a legendary alpine beast to which the rock is reputed to bear a remarkable resemblance—the more remarkable because there has never been a verified sighting of the beast. In another 0.1 mi., Mt. Jefferson Loop branches right and leads 0.4 mi. to the summit of Mt. Jefferson (5,716 ft.). The views from the summit are excellent, and Mt. Jefferson Loop is only slightly longer than the parallel section of Gulfside Trail, although it requires about 300 ft. of extra climbing and about 10 min. more hiking time.

Gulfside Trail now rises less steeply. It crosses Six Husbands Trail and soon reaches its greatest height, about 5,400 ft., on Mt. Jefferson. Curving southwest and descending a little, the trail crosses Monticello Lawn, a comparatively smooth, grassy plateau. Here, Mt. Jefferson Loop rejoins Gulfside Trail about 0.3 mi. from the summit. A short distance beyond the edge of the lawn, the Cornice enters right from Caps Ridge Trail. Gulfside Trail descends to the south, and from one point, there is a view of the Sphinx down the slope to the left. A few yd. north of the low point in Sphinx Col, Sphinx Trail branches left (east) into the Great Gulf through a grassy passage between ledges. Sphinx Col is 3.7 mi. from Madison Spring Hut, with 2.3 mi. remaining to the summit of Mt. Washington. In bad weather, a fairly quick descent to sheltering scrub can be made via Sphinx Trail, although once treeline is reached, this trail becomes rather steep and difficult.

Part III. Sphinx Col–Mt. Washington

From Sphinx Col the path leads toward Mt. Washington, and soon Mt. Clay Loop diverges left to climb over the summits of Mt. Clay with impressive views into the Great Gulf. Mt. Clay Loop adds about 300 ft. of climbing and 10 min.; the distance is about the same. Gulfside Trail is slightly easier and passes close to a spring but misses the best views. It bears right from the jct. with Mt. Clay Loop, runs south, and climbs moderately, angling up the west side of Mt. Clay. About 0.3 mi. above Sphinx Col, a loop leads to water a few steps down to the right. The side path continues about 30 yd. farther to Greenough Spring (more reliable), then rejoins

Gulfside Trail about 100 yd. above its exit point. Gulfside Trail continues its moderate ascent, and Jewell Trail from Cog Railway Base Rd. enters from the right at 4.6 mi. Gulfside Trail swings southeast and soon descends slightly to a point near the Clay–Washington col (5,391 ft.), where Mt. Clay Loop rejoins the trail from the left.

SEC 2

The path continues southeast, rising gradually on Mt. Washington. About 0.1 mi. above the col, Westside Trail branches right, crosses under the Cog Railway, and leads to Crawford Path and Lakes of the Clouds Hut. Gulfside Trail continues southeast between the Cog Railway on the right and the edge of the gulf on the left, with magnificent views into the gulf and across to the northern peaks. If the path is lost, the railway can be followed to the summit. At the extreme south corner of the gulf, Great Gulf Trail joins Gulfside Trail from the left, 5.5 mi. from Madison Spring Hut. Here, Gulfside Trail turns sharply right, crosses the railroad, and continues south to the plateau just west of the summit where the trail passes a jct. with Trinity Heights Connector, a link in the AT, which branches left and climbs for 0.2 mi. to the true summit of Mt. Washington. In another 0.1 mi., Gulfside Trail meets Crawford Path. Now coinciding with Crawford Path, Gulfside Trail turns left (southeast) and passes through the old corral (outlined by rock walls) in which saddle horses from the Glen House were kept. The combined trails then swing left (northeast) and lead between the Yankee Building and the Tip Top House on the left and the Stage Office and Cog Railway track on the right. Follow the sign: "Crawford Path to Summit." The summit, also marked by a sign, is an outcrop between the Tip Top House and the Sherman Adams summit building.

Descending from the summit of Mt. Washington and coinciding with Crawford Path, Gulfside Trail is on the right (west) side of the Cog Railway track. The trail leads southwest between the buildings then swings to the right (northwest) at a sign for Crawford Path and a large cairn; avoid random side paths toward the south. After passing through the old corral, the path reaches a jct. where Gulfside Trail turns sharply right as Crawford Path turns left.

MT. JEFFERSON LOOP (AMC; MAP 1: F9)

Cumulative from north jct. with Gulfside Trail (5,200 ft.) to:	↕	↗	○
Mt. Jefferson summit (5,716 ft.)	0.4 mi.	500 ft.	0:25
South jct. with Gulfside Trail (5,375 ft.)	0.7 mi.	500 ft. (rev. 350 ft.)	0:35

This trail provides access to the summit of Mt. Jefferson from Gulfside Trail. It diverges right (southwest) from Gulfside 0.2 mi. south of Edmands

Col and climbs steeply up the slope. Just below the summit, Six Husbands Trail enters on the left then Castle Trail enters on the right, and soon the jct. with Caps Ridge Trail is reached at the base of the summit crag. The true summit is 40 yd. right (west) on Caps Ridge Trail; the high point is reached by a short scramble up to the right. Mt. Jefferson Loop then descends moderately, with reasonably good footing, to rejoin Gulfside Trail on Monticello Lawn.

Descending from the trail jct. near the summit crag, the northbound Mt. Jefferson Loop leads northeast, and the southbound Mt. Jefferson Loop leads south.

MT. CLAY LOOP (AMC; MAP 1: F9)

Cumulative from north jct. with Gulfside Trail (5,025 ft.) to:	↥↧	↗	○
Mt. Clay summit (5,533 ft.)	0.5 mi.	500 ft.	0:30
South jct. with Gulfside Trail (5,400 ft.)	1.2 mi.	600 ft. (rev. 250 ft.)	0:55

This trail traverses the summit ridge of Mt. Clay roughly parallel to Gulfside Trail, providing access to superb views into the Great Gulf from Clay's east cliffs. The entire trail (except for its end points) is within the Great Gulf Wilderness.

The trail diverges left (east) from Gulfside Trail about 0.1 mi. south of Sphinx Col and ascends a steep, rough slope to the ragged ridge crest. After crossing the summit and passing over several slightly lower knobs, Mt. Clay Loop descends easily to the flat col between Mt. Clay and Mt. Washington, where the loop rejoins Gulfside Trail.

EDMANDS COL CUTOFF (RMC; MAP 1: F9)

From Edmands Col (4,938 ft.) to:	↥↧	↗	○
Six Husbands Trail (4,925 ft.)	0.5 mi.	100 ft. (rev. 100 ft.)	0:20

This important link, connecting Gulfside Trail and Randolph Path at Edmands Col with Six Husbands Trail, makes possible a quick escape from Edmands Col into plentiful sheltering scrub on the lee side of Mt. Jefferson. Footing on this trail is very rough and rocky. It is almost entirely within the Great Gulf Wilderness.

Leaving Edmands Col, the trail passes Gulfside Spring in 50 yd. then begins a rough scramble over rockslides and through scrub, marked by cairns. The trail is generally almost level but has many small rises and falls over minor ridges and gullies, with good views to the Great Gulf and out to the east. Edmands Col Cutoff ends at Six Husbands Trail 0.3 mi. below that trail's jct. with Gulfside Trail.

THE CORNICE (RMC; MAP 1: F9)

Cumulative from Randolph Path (4,900 ft.) to:	↥↧	↗	⟳
Castle Trail (5,100 ft.)	0.6 mi.	250 ft. (rev. 50 ft.)	0:25
Caps Ridge Trail (5,025 ft.)	1.3 mi.	300 ft. (rev. 150 ft.)	0:50
Gulfside Trail (5,275 ft.)	1.8 mi.	550 ft.	1:10

This trail circles the west slope of Mt. Jefferson, running completely above treeline, with many interesting views. The Cornice starts near Edmands Col, crosses Castle Trail and Caps Ridge Trail, and returns to Gulfside at Monticello Lawn, linking the trails on the west and northwest slopes of Jefferson. The Cornice's southern segment, which has relatively good footing, provides an excellent shortcut from Caps Ridge Trail to Gulfside Trail on Monticello Lawn, south of Mt. Jefferson. The section leading from Edmands Col to Caps Ridge Trail is extremely rough, however, with a large amount of tedious and strenuous rock-hopping, which is very hard on knees and ankles. This section of the trail, therefore, may take considerably more time than the estimates above. As a route between Edmands Col and Caps Ridge Trail, the Cornice saves a little climbing compared with the route over the summit of Jefferson, but the Cornice is much longer, requires more exertion, and is just as exposed to the weather. This makes its value questionable as a route to avoid Jefferson's summit in bad weather.

The Cornice diverges west from Randolph Path near Spaulding Spring, 0.1 mi. north of Gulfside Trail in Edmands Col, where Castle Ravine Trail also diverges from Randolph Path. The Cornice crosses a small grassy depression where there may be no perceptible footway until it climbs the rocky bank on the other side. The trail then ascends moderately over large rocks, passing above a rock formation that resembles a petrified cousin of the Loch Ness monster, and circles around the north and west sides of Mt. Jefferson, crossing Castle Trail above Upper Castle. The Cornice continues across the rocky slope with minor ups and downs, intersects Caps Ridge Trail above the Upper Cap, and turns left (east) up Caps Ridge Trail for about 20 yd., diverges right (east), and climbs gradually with improved footing to Gulfside Trail just below Monticello Lawn.

LINKING TRAILS ON THE NORTH AND WEST SLOPES

RANDOLPH PATH (RMC; MAP 1: E9–F9)

Cumulative from Randolph East parking area (1,225 ft.) to:	⇅	↗	⟳
Valley Way (1,953 ft.)	1.5 mi.	750 ft.	1:05
Air Line (2,000 ft.)	1.6 mi.	800 ft.	1:10
Short Line, north jct. (2,275 ft.)	1.9 mi.	1,050 ft.	1:30
King Ravine Trail and Amphibrach (2,925 ft.)	3.1 mi.	1,700 ft.	2:25
Lowe's Path (3,600 ft.)	3.9 mi.	2,400 ft.	3:10
Perch Path (4,325 ft.)	4.9 mi.	3,100 ft.	4:00
Israel Ridge Path, north jct. (4,825 ft.)	5.4 mi.	3,600 ft.	4:30
Edmands Col and Gulfside Trail (4,938 ft.)	6.1 mi.	3,700 ft.	4:55
Mt. Washington summit (6,288 ft.) via Gulfside Trail and Crawford Path	9.9 mi.	5,500 ft. (rev. 450 ft.)	7:40

This graded path extends southwest from Pinkham B Rd. (Dolly Copp Rd.) near Randolph village, ascending diagonally up the slopes of Mt. Madison and Mt. Adams to Gulfside Trail in Edmands Col, between Mt. Adams and Mt. Jefferson. In addition to providing a route from Randolph to Edmands Col, Randolph Path crosses numerous other trails along the way and thus constitutes an important linking trail between them. Some sections are heavily used and well beaten, but others bear very little traffic and, though well cleared and marked, have a less obvious footway. J. Rayner Edmands made Randolph Path from 1893 to 1899. Parts of it were reconstructed in 1978 as a memorial to Christopher Goetze, an active RMC member and former editor of *Appalachia*, AMC's mountaineering and conservation journal.

The path begins at the parking area known as Randolph East, located on Pinkham B Rd. 0.2 mi. south of US 2. Coinciding with Howker Ridge Trail, Randolph Path quickly crosses the Presidential Rail Trail and 30 yd. beyond turns right (southwest), where Howker Ridge Trail diverges left (southeast). Randolph Path runs to the south of a power-line clearing for about 0.2 mi. then swings southwest and ascends to a brushy logged area, where the path bears right; follow markings carefully. Entering mature woods, the trail ascends moderately to cross Sylvan Way at 0.7 mi., and at 1.4 mi., Randolph Path reaches Snyder Brook, where Inlook Trail and Brookside join on the left. Brookside and Randolph Path cross the brook together on large stepping-stones (the former bridge at this crossing was washed out in 2005 and will not be replaced), before Brookside diverges right and leads down to Valley Way. After a short climb, Randolph Path crosses Valley Way and soon after joins Air Line, coincides with it for 20 yd., then leaves it on the right.

At 1.9 mi., Short Line enters right; by this shortcut route, it is 1.3 mi. to US 2 at Appalachia. Short Line coincides with Randolph Path for 0.4 mi. then branches left for King Ravine. Randolph Path descends slightly and crosses Cold Brook on Sanders Bridge; Cliffway diverges right just beyond. At 3.1 mi., King Ravine Trail is crossed at its jct. with the Amphibrach, an intersection called the Pentadoi. Randolph Path continues across Spur Brook on ledges just below some interesting pools and cascades, and just beyond the brook, Spur Trail diverges left. Randolph Path climbs around the nose of a minor ridge and becomes steeper and rougher. Soon, Log Cabin Cutoff diverges right and runs, nearly level but with rough footing, 0.2 mi. to the Log Cabin.

At 3.9 mi. from Randolph East, Lowe's Path is crossed, and the grade moderates as Randolph Path angles up the steep west side of Nowell Ridge, although the footing is rocky. At 4.7 mi., good outlooks begin to appear, providing particularly notable views of the Castles nearby and Mt. Lafayette in the distance to the southwest. At 4.9 mi., Perch Path crosses, leading left (north) to Gray Knob Trail and right (south) to the Perch and to Israel Ridge Path; a small brook runs across Perch Path about 60 yd. south of Randolph Path. Above this jct., Randolph Path rises due south through high scrub. At 5.4 mi., Gray Knob Trail from Crag Camp and Gray Knob enters left at about the point where Randolph Path rises out of the high scrub. In another 70 yd., Israel Ridge Path enters right (west), ascending from US 2, and the trails coincide for about 150 yd.; then Israel Ridge Path branches left for Mt. Adams in an area where views to Jefferson and the Castles are particularly fine. From this point, Randolph Path is nearly level to its end at Edmands Col, curving around the head of Castle Ravine and offering continuous excellent views; despite the easy grade, the footing is often rough. The trail is above treeline, much exposed to the weather, and its treadway is visible for a long distance ahead. Near Edmands Col is Spaulding Spring (reliable water), located in a small grassy valley on the right, where two trails enter Randolph Path from the right at nearly the same point: Castle Ravine Trail from US 2 comes up through the length of this little valley from the north, and the Cornice leading to the Caps and Castles runs west across the valley. In 0.1 mi. more, Randolph Path joins Gulfside Trail in Edmands Col.

SEC 2

THE LINK (RMC; MAP 1: E9–F8)

Cumulative from Appalachia parking area (1,306 ft.) to:	⇅	↗	○
Memorial Bridge (1,425 ft.)	0.7 mi.	100 ft.	0:25
Cliffway (2,170 ft.)	2.0 mi.	850 ft.	1:25
Lowe's Path (2,475 ft.)	2.7 mi.	1,150 ft.	1:55
Israel Ridge Path (2,800 ft.)	4.0 mi.	1,500 ft.	2:45
Castle Ravine Trail, lower jct. (3,125 ft.)	5.1 mi.	1,900 ft. (rev. 100 ft.)	3:30
Castle Trail (4,025 ft.)	6.0 mi.	2,800 ft.	4:25
Caps Ridge Trail (3,800 ft.)	7.6 mi.	2,950 ft. (rev. 350 ft.)	5:15

This path links the Appalachia parking area with the trails ascending Mt. Adams and Mt. Jefferson, connecting to Amphibrach, Cliffway, Lowe's Path, Israel Ridge Path, and Castle Ravine, Emerald, Castle, and Caps Ridge trails. The Link is graded as far as Cascade Brook. The section between Caps Ridge and Castle trails, although very rough, makes possible a circuit of the Caps and the Castles from Jefferson Notch Rd. Though some sections are heavily used, much of the trail is very lightly used and, although well cleared and marked, may have little evident footway.

The Link diverges right from Air Line 100 yd. south of Appalachia, just after entering the woods beyond the power-line clearing, and runs west, fairly close to the edge of this clearing. The trail crosses a small brook, passes under maple sap lines, and bears left twice where logging roads enter from the right. At 0.6 mi., Beechwood Way diverges left, and, just east of Cold Brook, Sylvan Way enters left. The Link crosses Cold Brook at 0.7 mi. on Memorial Bridge, where you have a fine view upstream to Cold Brook Fall, which can be reached in less than 100 yd. by Sylvan Way or by a spur from the Amphibrach. Memorial Bridge is a memorial to the pioneer path makers of the northern peaks.

Just west of the brook, the Amphibrach diverges left and the Link continues straight ahead. The Link then follows old logging roads southwest, crossing several small brooks, with gradually increasing grades and occasional wet footing. At 2.0 mi., Cliffway leads left (east) to White Cliff, a viewpoint on Nowell Ridge, and the Link swings to the south and climbs at easy grades, crossing Lowe's Path at 2.7 mi. The Link crosses the north branch of Mystic Stream at 3.1 mi. and the main Mystic Stream, in a region of small cascades, at 3.3 mi. The trail soon curves left, rounds the western buttress of Nowell Ridge, and becomes rougher, running southeast nearly level and entering Cascade Ravine on the mountainside high above the stream. At 4.0 mi., the trail joins Israel Ridge Path coming up on the right from US 2; the two trails coincide for 50 yd., before Israel Ridge Path diverges left for Mt. Adams, passing Cabin–Cascades Trail in about 60 yd. The Link continues straight from this jct., descending sharply for 60 yd. to Cascade Brook, which the trail crosses behind a large, flat ledge at the top of the First Cascade, where you have a view of Mt. Bowman. This crossing may be difficult at high water. The trail makes a steep climb up the bank of the brook then swings right and crosses an old landslide with very rough footing (follow markings carefully). The grade now eases and the footing gradually improves as the trail rounds the tip of Israel Ridge and runs generally south into Castle Ravine, with minor ups and downs.

At 5.1 mi., the Link joins Castle Ravine Trail, and the two trails pass the jct. with Emerald Trail on the left and cross Castle Brook. Just beyond the crossing, at 5.4 mi., the Link diverges sharply right from Castle Ravine Trail and ascends steeply west with difficult footing, angling up the very rough southwest wall of Castle Ravine. At 6.0 mi., the Link crosses Castle Trail below the first Castle at about 4,025 ft. then runs south, generally descending gradually with occasional minor ascents over a very rough pathway with countless treacherous roots, rocks, and hollows that are tricky and tedious to negotiate. At 6.5 mi., the trail crosses an old slide with views, then a steep brook widened into a slide by the 2011 storm (use caution), and at 7.0 mi., it crosses a fair-sized brook flowing over mossy ledges. At 7.6 mi., the trail turns sharply left uphill and in 50 yd. reaches Caps Ridge Trail 1.1 mi. above Jefferson Notch Rd., about 100 yd. above a ledge with several potholes that provides a fine view up to Mt. Jefferson.

PRESIDENTIAL RAIL TRAIL (FPRT; MAP 1: E9–E8)

Noncumulative segments from Randolph East (1,225 ft.) to:	⇅	↗	↺
Appalachia (1,310 ft.)	0.9 mi.	85 ft.	0:30
Appalachia (1,310 ft.) to Lowe's Path (1,450 ft.)	2.2 mi.	140 ft.	1:10
Lowe's Path (1,450 ft.) to Bowman (1,500 ft.)	0.9 mi.	50 ft.	0:30

This multiuse trail follows the roadbed of the former railroad right-of-way (tracks removed in 1997) that runs for 18.3 mi. from Gorham to Waumbek Junction near Cherry Pond. The trail is open to a variety of nonmotorized uses, including walking, snowshoeing, cross-country skiing, bicycling, and dogsled traveling; it is open to motorized uses in winter. In its own right, the trail has limited interest for hikers, but—running roughly parallel to US 2—it is useful as a connecting link between the trails on the northern edge of the Presidential Range. The trail provides an easy and also pleasant and safe (compared with the alternative of walking along high-speed US 2) pedestrian route between the Randolph East and Appalachia trailheads, Lowe's Path, and the Bowman trailhead—even at night. Although this trail will also be encountered near Cherry Pond in Section Twelve, only the small part that is useful to Northern Presidential hikers is covered here. As it is assumed that hikers will use only segments as required rather than the Northern Presidential section as a whole, segment distances and times—rather than cumulative ones—are given. For more information on the trail, visit friendsofthepresidentialrailtrail.org.

GREAT GULF WILDERNESS

GREAT GULF TRAIL (WMNF; MAP 1: F10–F9)

Cumulative from parking area on NH 16 (1,350 ft.) to:	⇅	↗	○
Osgood Trail (1,850 ft.)	1.8 mi.	500 ft.	1:10
Osgood Cutoff (2,300 ft.)	2.7 mi.	950 ft.	1:50
Madison Gulf Trail, south jct. (2,300 ft.)	2.8 mi.	1,000 ft. (rev. 50 ft.)	1:55
Six Husbands and Wamsutta trails (3,100 ft.)	4.5 mi.	1,800 ft.	3:10
Sphinx Trail (3,625 ft.)	5.6 mi.	2,350 ft.	4:00
Spaulding Lake (4,228 ft.)	6.5 mi.	2,950 ft.	4:45
Gulfside Trail jct. (5,925 ft.)	7.4 mi.	4,650 ft.	6:05
Mt. Washington summit (6,288 ft.) via Gulfside Trail and Trinity Heights Connector	7.8 mi.	5,000 ft.	6:25

This trail begins at the Great Gulf Wilderness parking area on the west side of NH 16, 1.9 mi. south of its jct. with Pinkham B Rd. (Dolly Copp Rd.) near Dolly Copp Campground. The trail follows the West Branch of the Peabody River through the Great Gulf, climbs up the headwall, and ends at a jct. with Gulfside Trail 0.5 mi. below the summit of Mt. Washington. Some of the brook crossings may be difficult or dangerous in moderate to high water conditions, and brooks can rise very quickly during heavy rains in this deep, steep-walled valley. Care is required to follow the trail at some of the crossings in the upper valley. Ascent on the headwall is very steep and rough. Except for the first 1.6 mi., this trail is in the Great Gulf Wilderness; camping is prohibited within 0.25 mi. of the trail above the jct. with Sphinx Trail, and below that point, camping is limited to designated trailside sites or sites at least 200 ft. away from the trail.

Leaving the parking lot, the trail leads north on an old road then turns left and descends slightly to cross the Peabody River on a suspension bridge. The trail then ascends to a jct. at 0.3 mi. with Great Gulf Link Trail from Dolly Copp Campground. Great Gulf Trail turns sharply left here and follows a logging road along the northwest bank of the West Branch of the Peabody River, at first close to the stream and later some distance away from it. At 0.6 mi., the trail bears left off the road (which continues ahead as a ski trail), crosses a small brook, passes a ledgy cascade and pool, and turns left at 1.0 mi. as the ski trail rejoins from the right. At 1.6 mi., Hayes Copp Ski Trail diverges right; Great Gulf Trail soon crosses into the Great Gulf Wilderness; and Osgood Trail diverges right at 1.8 mi. Osgood Campsite is 0.8 mi. from here via Osgood Trail.

Great Gulf Trail follows the West Branch, mostly staying back in the woods, and passes a scenic spot on the river at 2.4 mi. The trail then climbs rather steeply to the high gravelly bank called the Bluff, where there is a good view of the gulf and the mountains around it, especially from the top of a boulder on the right. The trail follows the edge of the Bluff; then at 2.7 mi., Osgood Cutoff (which is part of the AT) continues straight ahead and Great Gulf Trail descends sharply left. For a short distance, this trail is also part of the AT. In 50 yd., the trail crosses Parapet Brook (no bridge) then climbs to the crest of the little ridge that separates Parapet Brook from the West Branch, where Madison Gulf Trail enters right, coming down from the vicinity of Madison Spring Hut through Madison Gulf. The two trails coincide for a short distance, descending to cross the West Branch on a suspension bridge and ascending the steep bank on the south side. Here, Madison Gulf Trail branches left, continuing the AT in that direction, and Great Gulf Trail leaves the AT and turns right, becoming rougher and rockier and leading up the south bank of the river past Clam Rock, a huge boulder on the left, at 3.1 mi.

At 3.9 mi., Great Gulf Trail crosses Chandler Brook, and on the far bank, Chandler Brook Trail diverges left and ascends to Mt. Washington Auto Rd. Great Gulf Trail continues close to the river, passing in sight of the mouth of the stream that issues from Jefferson Ravine on the north, to meet Six Husbands Trail (right) and Wamsutta Trail (left) at 4.5 mi. Great Gulf Trail continues up the valley with glimpses of Jefferson's Knees, and at 5.2 mi., it climbs up wet, slippery ledges beside a cascade and continues past numerous other attractive cascades in the next 0.2 mi. After crossing over to the northwest bank of the West Branch (may be difficult in high water), the trail soon crosses the brook that descends from Sphinx Col and, at 5.6 mi., reaches the jct. where Sphinx Trail, leading to Gulfside Trail, diverges right. Camping is prohibited within 0.25 mi. of Great Gulf Trail above this jct. Great Gulf Trail soon crosses again to the southeast bank of the West Branch, passing waterfalls, including Weetamoo Falls, the finest in the gulf. From open points along the trail, you have remarkable views up to Mt. Adams and Mt. Madison. The trail crosses an eastern tributary and, after a rocky ascent, reaches the tiny tarn called Spaulding Lake (4,228 ft.), with the impressive headwall rising ahead. This point is 6.5 mi. from NH 16 and 1.3 mi. by trail from the summit of Mt. Washington.

Great Gulf Trail continues on the east side of the lake, a little beyond passes through a section that may be overgrown, and soon begins to ascend the very steep and rough headwall. In this section, up onto the lower part of the headwall, there is often water running down the trail. The trail runs south and then southeast, with magnificent views of the gulf and surrounding mountains, rising 1,600 ft. in about 0.8 mi. over fragments of stone, many of which are loose. Extra caution is needed in an area well up on the headwall where the trail crosses a rock slide caused by the 2011 storm; here the footing may be especially unstable. Below and above the slide, the route is partially marked by cairns and faded yellow blazes, but in places the trail may be difficult to follow. The trail generally curves a little to the left until within a few yd. of the top of the headwall; then, bearing slightly right, the trail emerges from the gulf and ends at Gulfside Trail near the Cog Railway. It is 0.4 mi. from here to the summit of Mt. Washington by Gulfside Trail and Trinity Heights Connector.

GREAT GULF LINK TRAIL (WMNF; MAP 1: F10)

From Dolly Copp Campground (1,250 ft.) to:	⇅	↗	↺
Great Gulf Trail (1,375 ft.)	0.9 mi.	150 ft.	0:30

This trail was formerly a segment of Great Gulf Trail. Great Gulf Link Trail leaves Dolly Copp Campground at a sign at the south end of the main camp road (which is a dead end) 0.2 mi. south of the trailhead for Daniel Webster–Scout Trail. Parking is available near the trail entrance. The trail enters the woods and turns left (arrow) in 0.1 mi. onto an old logging road that has cross-country ski markers in both directions. It follows the logging road south along the west bank of the Peabody River, passing some interesting pools. Great Gulf Link Trail ends at a jct. with Great Gulf Trail, which comes in on the left from the parking lot on NH 16 and continues straight ahead into the gulf.

MADISON GULF TRAIL (AMC; MAP 1: F9)

Cumulative from Mt. Washington Auto Rd. (2,675 ft.) to:	⬆⬇	↗	⟳
Great Gulf Trail, south jct. (2,300 ft.)	2.1 mi.	250 ft. (rev. 650 ft.)	1:10
Foot of Madison Gulf headwall at Sylvan Cascade (3,900 ft.)	4.1 mi.	1,850 ft.	3:00
Parapet Trail (4,850 ft.)	4.8 mi.	2,800 ft.	3:50
Madison Spring Hut (4,800 ft.) via Parapet and Star Lake trails	5.1 mi.	2,850 ft. (rev. 100 ft.)	4:00
From Pinkham Notch Visitor Center (2,032 ft.) to:			
Madison Spring Hut (4,800 ft.) via Old Jackson Road and Madison Gulf, Parapet, and Star Lake trails	7.0 mi.	3,550 ft. (rev. 800 ft.)	5:15

SEC 2

This trail begins on Mt. Washington Auto Rd. a little more than 2 mi. from the Glen House site, opposite Old Jackson Road. Madison Gulf Trail first crosses a low ridge then descends gently to the West Branch, where the trail meets Great Gulf Trail. Madison Gulf Trail then ascends along Parapet Brook through Madison Gulf to the Parapet, where the trail ends 0.3 mi. from Madison Spring Hut. Madison Gulf Trail is almost entirely within the Great Gulf Wilderness. From the Auto Rd. to its departure from Great Gulf Trail, Madison Gulf Trail is part of the AT, but because the trail is in a Wilderness Area, paint blazes (including the familiar white AT blazes) are not used. Care is required to follow the trail at several stream crossings where the trail follows Parapet Brook on the approach to the headwall.

Caution: The section of this trail on the headwall of Madison Gulf is one of the most difficult in the White Mountains, going over several ledge outcrops, boulder-strewn areas, and a rock chimney. The steep slabs may be slippery when wet, and several ledges require scrambling and the use of handholds. Stream crossings may be very difficult in wet weather. The trail is not recommended for the descent, for hikers with heavy packs, or in wet weather. Allow extra time and do not start up the headwall late in the day. The ascent of the headwall may require several hours more than the estimated time; parties frequently fail to reach the hut before dark due to slowness on the headwall.

This trail is well protected from storms and has plenty of water. Combined with Old Jackson Rd., this is the shortest route (7.0 mi.) from Pinkham Notch Visitor Center to Madison Spring Hut via the Great Gulf but not usually the easiest; there are several reasonable alternative routes, although none of them is without drawbacks. The route via Osgood Cutoff and Osgood Trail, 7.5 mi. long, is steep in parts but has no hard brook crossings or difficult scrambles; however, the route is very exposed to weather in the upper part, even if the rough but more sheltered Parapet Trail is used to bypass Mt. Madison's summit. The route via Buttress Trail is 8.4 mi. long; it has two significant and potentially dangerous brook crossings and somewhat more weather exposure than Madison Gulf Trail, though substantially less than the Osgood–Parapet route. In any event, parties traveling to the hut from the Great Gulf side cannot avoid the 0.3-mi. walk to Madison Spring Hut across the windswept col between Mt. Madison and Mt. Adams except by going over the summit of Mt. Madison, where conditions may well be much worse. Therefore, choice of route comes down to a trade-off among the factors of distance, weather exposure, brook crossings, and rock scrambles; hikers must consider which factors they feel better prepared to deal with, taking current and expected conditions into account. Hikers who are not prepared for this level of challenge would be well advised to change their plans rather than attempt any of the direct routes between Pinkham Notch Visitor Center and Madison Spring Hut in adverse conditions, and even in favorable conditions, Madison Gulf Trail must be approached with caution.

Madison Gulf Trail leaves the Auto Rd. above the 2-mi. mark, opposite the Old Jackson Road jct., and enters the Great Gulf Wilderness. After a climb of 0.2 mi., a side path branches right in a little pass west of Low's Bald Spot and climbs 0.1 mi., with a bit of ledge scrambling, to this little ledgy knob, an excellent viewpoint. Madison Gulf Trail bears left and ascends over a ledge with a limited view then descends, first rapidly for a short distance and later easily, crossing many small brooks. The trail ascends briefly, curves into the valley of the West Branch of the Peabody River, then descends gently until Madison Gulf Trail meets Great Gulf Trail on the south bank at 2.1 mi. The two trails run together, descending the steep bank to the West Branch, crossing a suspension bridge to the north bank, and climbing to the crest of the little ridge that divides Parapet Brook from the West Branch. Here, Great Gulf Trail continues straight ahead, leading to NH 16 or to Osgood Trail (via Osgood Cutoff) for Mt. Madison and Madison Spring Hut. Madison Gulf Trail (which here leaves the AT) turns left up the narrow ridge, passing a view of Mt. Adams, and continues between the two streams until the trail enters its former route near the bank of Parapet Brook at 2.5 mi. At 2.8 mi., the trail crosses one channel of the divided brook, runs between the two for 0.1 mi., then crosses the other to the northeast bank. The trail follows the brook bank for a little way before turning right, away from the brook, then left and, becoming rougher, ascends along the valley wall at a moderate grade. It comes back to the brook at the mouth of the branch stream from Osgood Ridge, which it crosses. From here, the trail follows Parapet Brook rather closely and, at 3.5 mi., crosses the brook for the first of three times in less than 0.5 mi., ascending to the lower floor of the gulf where the trail reaches Sylvan Cascade, a fine waterfall, at 4.1 mi.

Madison Gulf Trail then ascends to the upper floor of the gulf, where the trail crosses several small brooks; the trail must be followed with care at these crossings. From the floor, the trail rises gradually to Mossy Slide, a small cascade at the foot of the headwall, then ascends very rapidly alongside a stream, which becomes partly hidden among the rocks as the trail rises. The trail then reaches the headwall of the gulf and climbs very steeply, with some difficult scrambles on the ledges. This section has several fine views. As Madison Gulf Trail emerges on the rocks at treeline, it bears right, the grade moderates, and soon the trail ends at Parapet Trail. For the Parapet (0.1 mi.) and Madison Spring Hut (0.3 mi.), turn left; for Osgood Trail via Parapet Trail, turn right.

CHANDLER BROOK TRAIL (AMC; MAP 1: F9)

From Great Gulf Trail (2,800 ft.) to:	↕	↗	⟳
Mt. Washington Auto Rd. (4,125 ft.)	0.9 mi.	1,350 ft.	1:10

This steep and rough trail passes many cascades as it climbs from Great Gulf Trail to Mt. Washington Auto Rd., just above the 4-mi. post. Lying on a very steep slope, its brook crossings can quickly become difficult in rainy weather. Chandler Brook Trail is almost entirely within the Great Gulf Wilderness.

The trail diverges south from Great Gulf Trail 3.9 mi. beyond NH 16, just above its crossing of Chandler Brook. The trail rises moderately, crossing two small brooks, then becomes steep as it approaches the first of three crossings of Chandler Brook at 0.3 mi. The second crossing, at 0.4 mi., presents waterfalls and an impressive view of Mt. Adams. From the last crossing, the trail runs southeast, rising very steeply over a jumbled mass of stones with fine views across the Great Gulf, and keeps west of interesting rock formations. The trail enters the Auto Rd. near a ledge of white quartz at the Horn, 0.3 mi. above the 4-mi. post. About 125 yd. left down the road are a parking area and adjacent ledges with wide views. (Descending, look for this white ledge, which is close to the Auto Rd. The trail is marked by cairns here and is visible from the road.)

SEC 2

WAMSUTTA TRAIL (AMC; MAP 1: F9)

Cumulative from Great Gulf Trail (3,100 ft.) to:	⬇⬆	↗	⟳
Outlook on promontory (4,350 ft.)	0.9 mi.	1,250 ft.	1:05
Mt. Washington Auto Rd. (5,305 ft.)	1.7 mi.	2,200 ft.	1:55

This steep and rough trail begins on Great Gulf Trail and ascends to Mt. Washington Auto Rd. just above the 6-mi. marker and opposite Alpine Garden Trail, with which the trail provides routes to Tuckerman Junction, Lakes of the Clouds Hut, and other points to the south. Wamsutta Trail is almost entirely within the Great Gulf Wilderness. The trail was named for Wamsutta, the first of six successive husbands of Weetamoo, a queen of the Pocasset tribe, for whom a beautiful waterfall in the Great Gulf is named.

Leaving Great Gulf Trail opposite Six Husbands Trail, 4.5 mi. from NH 16, Wamsutta Trail crosses a small stream then ascends gradually. Soon the trail climbs the very steep and rough northerly spur of Chandler Ridge, with one difficult scramble up a chimney. Higher up, in an area with several more scrambles, are impressive views across the floor of the gulf to mts. Jefferson, Adams, and Madison. The trail continues up steeply then more gradually to a small, open promontory on the crest of the spur, which offers another good view, at 0.9 mi. The trail then ascends gradually through woods, passing a spring on the right side of the trail. Continuing along the ridge crest at a moderate grade, the trail emerges at treeline and climbs to a point near the top end of the winter shortcut route of the Auto Rd. After turning right along this road, the trail ends in another 100 yd. at the main route of the Auto Rd., just above the 6-mi. post.

SPHINX TRAIL (AMC; MAP 1: F9)

From Great Gulf Trail (3,625 ft.) to:	⬇⬆	↗	⟳
Gulfside Trail (4,975 ft.)	1.1 mi.	1,350 ft.	1:15

This steep and rough trail runs from Great Gulf Trail below Spaulding Lake to Gulfside Trail in Sphinx Col, between Mt. Jefferson and Mt. Clay. The trail's name is derived from the profile of a rock formation seen from just below the meadow where water is found. This trail is particularly important because it affords the quickest escape route for anyone overtaken by storm in the vicinity of Sphinx Col. For the descent, the trail diverges east from Gulfside Trail 40 yd. north of the lowest point in the col, running through a grassy, rock-walled corridor, and descends to Great Gulf Trail. Once below the col, a hiker is quickly protected from west and northwest winds. For a considerable part of its length, this trail climbs very steeply;

there is a long section of very slippery rocks in a brook bed, very tedious particularly on the descent, and some of the scrambles on the ledges in the upper part are challenging. The trail can be difficult to follow at the brook crossings. This trail is almost entirely within the Great Gulf Wilderness.

Sphinx Trail branches northwest from Great Gulf Trail 5.6 mi. from NH 16, just beyond the crossing of the brook that flows down from Sphinx Col, through the minor ravine between Mts. Clay and Jefferson. The trail soon turns due west and ascends close to the brook, first gradually then very steeply, crossing the brook four times (follow with care) and passing several attractive cascades and pools. Above the second brook crossing, the trail crosses the base of a landslide caused by the 2011 storm. Just before the third crossing, the trail runs along the steep edge of a flume-like formation. For about 100 yd. above the fourth crossing, the trail runs directly in the brook bed, where the rocks are extremely slippery. At 0.6 mi., at the foot of a broken ledge with several small streams cascading over it, the trail turns left, away from the brook, and angles up across two more small brooks, with a couple of short, tricky scrambles. It climbs a small, fairly difficult chimney, where views out from the scrubby slope start to appear, then scrambles up ledges with several rock pitches of some difficulty. About 100 yd. above the chimney, after a slight descent, the trail crosses a small meadow where you can usually see water under a rock just downhill to the north of the trail. The trail then climbs steeply up a rocky cleft, ascends easily over the crest of a small rocky ridge, and descends into a slight sag. The trail finally climbs to the ridge crest and traverses a grassy passage at the base of a rock wall to Gulfside Trail, just north of Sphinx Col.

SIX HUSBANDS TRAIL (AMC; MAP 1: F9)

Cumulative from Great Gulf Trail (3,100 ft.) to:	⇅	↗	○
Buttress Trail (3,350 ft.)	0.5 mi.	250 ft.	0:25
Edmands Col Cutoff (4,925 ft.)	1.7 mi.	1,850 ft.	1:45
Gulfside Trail (5,325 ft.)	2.0 mi.	2,250 ft.	2:10
Mt. Jefferson Loop (5,625 ft.)	2.3 mi.	2,550 ft.	2:25

This steep, rough, and challenging trail provides magnificent views of the inner part of the Great Gulf. The name honors the six successive husbands of Weetamoo, queen of the Pocasset tribe. The trail diverges from Great Gulf Trail 4.5 mi. from NH 16, opposite Wamsutta Trail, crosses the West Branch, climbs up the north knee of Jefferson, crosses Gulfside Trail, and ends at Mt. Jefferson Loop a short distance northeast of the summit. Six Husbands Trail is very steep and difficult and is not recommended for descent except to escape dangerous weather conditions above treeline. Up to the Gulfside Trail jct., Six Husbands Trail is entirely within the Great Gulf Wilderness.

Leaving Great Gulf Trail, Six Husbands Trail descends directly across the West Branch, avoiding side paths along the stream. In times of high water, this crossing may be very difficult, but there may be a better crossing upstream. The trail climbs easily northward across a low ridge to join Jefferson Brook, the stream that flows from Jefferson Ravine, and ascends along its southwest bank. At 0.5 mi., Buttress Trail branches right and crosses the stream. Six Husbands Trail swings left away from the brook (last sure water) and runs through an area containing many large boulders. Soon the trail begins to attack the very steep main buttress, the north knee of Jefferson, passing by one boulder cave and through another. At 1.0 mi., the trail ascends a steep ledge on a pair of ladders then climbs under an overhanging ledge on a second pair of ladders, with a traverse of a tricky sloping ledge at the top of the ladders that might be dangerous if wet or icy. The trail climbs another, recently placed ladder just above, and soon the trail reaches a promontory with a fine view before beginning a steep and difficult climb with several more scrambles up the crest of a rocky ridge.

At 1.3 mi., the trail reaches the top of the knee approximately at treeline, with magnificent views, and the grade moderates. The trail winds up through scrub and across bare stretches, where it is marked by cairns. At 1.7 mi., Edmands Col Cutoff branches right, leading in 0.5 mi. to Edmands Col, and Six Husbands Trail becomes steeper as it begins to climb the cone of Mt. Jefferson. Soon, the trail passes over a talus slope that is usually covered well into July by a great drift of snow, conspicuous for a considerable distance from viewpoints to the east. Marked by cairns, the trail crosses Gulfside Trail and climbs moderately west toward the summit of Mt. Jefferson, swinging right at the end and joining Mt. Jefferson Loop 0.1 mi. below the summit.

BUTTRESS TRAIL (AMC; MAP 1: F9)

Cumulative from Six Husbands Trail (3,350 ft.) to:	↕	↗	○
Star Lake Trail (4,900 ft.)	1.9 mi.	1,600 ft. (rev. 50 ft.)	1:45
Madison Spring Hut (4,800 ft.) via Star Lake Trail	2.2 mi.	1,600 ft. (rev. 100 ft.)	1:55

This trail leads from Six Husbands Trail to Star Lake Trail, near Madison Spring Hut, and is the most direct route from the upper part of the Great Gulf to Madison Spring Hut. Buttress Trail is mostly well sheltered until it nears the hut, and grades are moderate; although the footing is rough in the upper section, overall, this trail is easier than most other Great Gulf trails. In bad weather, for hikers with heavy packs, or for descending, this is probably the best route from the lower part of the Great Gulf to the hut, despite the somewhat greater distance. (See Madison Gulf Trail, the principal alternative, for a discussion of other options.) Buttress Trail is almost entirely within the Great Gulf Wilderness.

SEC 2

The trail diverges north from Six Husbands Trail 0.5 mi. from Great Gulf Trail and immediately crosses Jefferson Brook (last sure water), the brook that flows out of Jefferson Ravine. On the far side of the brook, Buttress Trail bears left through a wet area on bog bridges; avoid several beaten paths that diverge right into a camping area.

After 0.1 mi., the trail bears right (east) and, ascending moderately, climbs diagonally across a steep slope of large, loose, angular fragments of rock (care must be taken not to dislodge the loose rocks). At the top of this talus slope is a spectacular view up the Great Gulf and to the steep buttress of Jefferson's north knee, rising nearby across a small valley. The trail continues east, rising steadily along a steep, wooded slope. Then, at 0.5 mi., the trail reaches a ridge corner and swings left (north) and runs at easy grades across a gently sloping upland covered with trees, passing to the right of a spring (reliable water) at 1.0 mi. At 1.2 mi., the trail passes through a cave formed by a large boulder across the path then reaches the foot of a steep ledge, swings left, and climbs it. At 1.4 mi., the trail swings right after passing between two ledges; the ledge on the right provides a fine view. The trail now ascends less steeply (but with rough footing) on open rocks above the scrub line, with an excellent view across Madison Gulf to Mt. Madison. The trail crosses a minor ridge and descends moderately. After passing under an overhanging rock, the trail reenters high scrub that provides shelter almost all the way to the jct. with Star Lake Trail, which is reached in the gap between the Parapet and Mt. Quincy Adams, just southwest of Star Lake and 0.3 mi. from Madison Spring Hut.

OSGOOD TRAIL (AMC; MAP 1: F10–F9)

Cumulative from Great Gulf Trail (1,850 ft.) to:	⬆⬇	↗	⟳
Osgood Cutoff (2,486 ft.)	0.8 mi.	650 ft.	0:45
Osgood Junction (4,822 ft.)	2.8 mi.	2,950 ft.	2:55
Mt. Madison summit (5,366 ft.)	3.3 mi.	3,500 ft.	3:25
Madison Spring Hut (4,800 ft.)	3.8 mi.	3,500 ft. (rev. 550 ft.)	3:40

This trail runs from Great Gulf Trail, 1.8 mi. from the Great Gulf Wilderness parking area on NH 16, up the southeast ridge of Mt. Madison to the summit, then down to Madison Spring Hut. The upper 1.7 mi. is very exposed to the weather and has very rough footing. Made by Benjamin F. Osgood in 1878, this is the oldest trail now in use to the summit of Mt. Madison. Above Osgood Cutoff, Osgood Trail is part of the AT. Osgood Trail begins in the Great Gulf Wilderness, but for most of its length, the trail is just outside the boundary; in fact, it constitutes the northern section of Wilderness Area's eastern boundary.

Osgood Trail leaves Great Gulf Trail and ascends at an easy to moderate grade. At 0.3 mi., Osgood Trail crosses a small brook, follows it, recrosses it, and bears away from it to the left. At 0.8 mi., Osgood Cutoff comes in from the left, and a spur path leads right over a small brook (last sure water) and continues about 100 yd. to Osgood Tentsite.

At 1.4 mi., Osgood Trail begins to climb a very steep and rough section. At about 1.6 mi., it gradually but steadily becomes less steep; the grade is easy by the time the trail emerges on the crest of Osgood Ridge, at treeline, at 2.1 mi. Ahead, on the crest of the ridge, 10 or 12 small, rocky peaks curve to the left in a crescent toward the summit of Mt. Madison; the trail, marked by cairns, follows this ridge crest with rough footing. At 2.8 mi. from Great Gulf Trail, Osgood Trail reaches Osgood Junction in a small hollow. Here, Daniel Webster–Scout Trail enters on the right, ascending from Dolly Copp Campground, and Parapet Trail diverges left on a level path marked by cairns and passes around the south side of the cone of Madison with little change of elevation, making a very rough but comparatively sheltered route to Madison Spring Hut.

From Osgood Junction, Osgood Trail climbs over a prominent crag, turns left (west), crosses a shallow sag, and starts up the east ridge of Mt. Madison's summit cone, where the trail is soon joined on the right by Howker Ridge Trail at 3.1 mi. Hikers planning to descend on Howker Ridge Trail must take care to distinguish that trail from beaten side paths that lead back to Osgood Trail. Osgood Trail ascends to the summit of Mt. Madison at 3.3 mi., where Watson Path enters on the right. (In the reverse direction, Osgood Trail descends almost due east, and Watson Path descends northeast.) Osgood Trail then follows the crest of the ridge west past several large cairns, drops off to the left (south), and continues to descend westward just below the ridge crest and above the steep slopes falling off into Madison Gulf on the left. Soon Osgood Trail crosses to the north side of the ridge and descends steeply, and 30 yd. before the trail reaches the front of Madison Spring Hut, Pine Link joins on the right.

OSGOOD CUTOFF (AMC; MAP 1: F9)

From Great Gulf Trail (2,300 ft.) to:	⇅	↗	○
Osgood Trail (2,486 ft.)	0.6 mi.	200 ft.	0:25

This link trail, a part of the AT, provides a convenient shortcut from Great Gulf and Madison Gulf trails to Osgood Trail. Osgood Cutoff is entirely within the Great Gulf Wilderness. This trail leaves Great Gulf Trail on the Bluff, continuing straight ahead where Great Gulf Trail turns sharply left to descend to Parapet Brook. Osgood Cutoff climbs moderately for 0.2 mi., then turns sharply right; shortly before the turn, an unmarked side path leads 25 yd. left to an excellent view of the Great Gulf from an opening at the top of an old slide. From the turn, the trail runs nearly on contour east across several small brooks to its jct. with Osgood Trail; directly across Osgood Trail is the spur path leading to Osgood Tentsite, which has reliable water.

MT. MADISON

DANIEL WEBSTER–SCOUT TRAIL (WMNF; MAP 1: F10–F9)

Cumulative from Dolly Copp Campground (1,250 ft.) to:	⇅	↗	○
Foot of little buttress (2,800 ft.)	2.0 mi.	1,550 ft.	1:45
Osgood Junction (4,822 ft.)	3.5 mi.	3,550 ft.	3:30
Mt. Madison summit (5,366 ft.) via Osgood Trail	4.0 mi.	4,100 ft.	4:05

This trail, cut in 1933 by Boy Scouts from the Daniel Webster Council, leads from Dolly Copp Campground to Osgood Trail at Osgood Junction, 0.5 mi. below the summit of Mt. Madison. Daniel Webster–Scout Trail begins on the main campground road, 0.8 mi. south of the campground entrance on Pinkham B Rd. (Dolly Copp Rd.) and 0.4 mi. west of NH 16, with adequate parking available on the left in another 0.1 mi. For much of its length, the trail's grades are moderate, and its footing is somewhat rocky but not unusually rough; however, the upper part of this trail is very steep, with rough footing on talus, and is very exposed to the weather.

The trail starts out through a section of open woods with some very large trees, soon crosses Hayes Copp Ski Trail (which here is a grassy logging road), and swings northwest almost to the bank of Culhane Brook, passing numerous small logging cuts and crossing several old skid roads. Veering away from the brook just before reaching it, Daniel Webster–Scout Trail climbs moderately up the east slope of Mt. Madison, mostly angling upward and carefully avoiding a more direct assault on the steeper parts of the mountainside. At 2.0 mi., the trail reaches the base of a little buttress, where the forest changes rather abruptly from hardwoods to evergreens. The trail winds steeply up this buttress to its top, switchbacks upward a bit farther, then resumes its steady ascent, angling northwest across the steep slope, becoming steeper and rockier. At 2.9 mi., the trail begins a very steep and rough climb nearly straight up the slope, with ever-increasing amounts of talus and decreasing amounts of scrub, where views begin to appear and improve. At 3.2 mi., the trail reaches treeline and moderates somewhat, although it is still steep. (Descending, the trail enters the scrub at a lower left corner of a large, steep talus slope.) On the open talus, the trail is marked with cairns and both blue and yellow blazes, which must be followed with care. As it approaches the ridge crest, the trail turns left and directly ascends the slope for the last 100 yd. to Osgood Junction and Osgood Trail.

PARAPET TRAIL (AMC; MAP 1: F9)

Cumulative from Osgood Junction (4,822 ft.) to:	⇅	↗	⟳
Madison Gulf Trail (4,850 ft.)	0.8 mi.	150 ft. (rev . 100 ft.)	0:30
Star Lake Trail (4,900 ft.)	1.0 mi.	200 ft.	0:35
Madison Spring Hut (4,800 ft.) via Star Lake Trail	1.2 mi.	200 ft. (rev. 100 ft.)	0:40

This trail, marked with cairns and blue blazes, runs at a roughly constant elevation around the south side of the cone of Mt. Madison, from the Osgood and Daniel Webster–Scout trails at Osgood Junction to Star Lake Trail between the Parapet and Madison Spring Hut. Although above timberline and extremely rough, particularly in its eastern half, Parapet Trail is mostly sheltered from the northwest winds in bad weather. The rocks can be very slippery; the trail may be hard to follow if visibility is poor; and the extra effort of rock-hopping more than expends the energy saved by avoiding the climb of about 500 ft. over the summit of Mt. Madison. Therefore, this is probably a useful bad-weather route only if strong northwest or west winds are a major part of the problem.

From Osgood Junction, Parapet Trail leads west and rises very slightly, marked by cairns across the open rocks; at the start, care must be taken to distinguish its cairns from those ascending the ridge crest on the right, which belong to Osgood Trail. Parapet Trail traverses a large area of open talus then swings left and descends briefly into scrub. The trail continues along the steep slope with minor ups and downs, often in the open, with several minor scrambles. The trail passes to the right of a crag with excellent views and descends slightly to a jct. at 0.8 mi., where Madison Gulf Trail enters left at the bottom of a little gully. Parapet Trail ascends a ledge and then makes a sharp right turn at 0.9 mi., where a spur path leads left 30 yd. onto the Parapet, a ledge that commands excellent views over the Great Gulf and Madison Gulf to the mountains beyond. Parapet Trail then runs north, passing above Star Lake, and joins Star Lake Trail 0.2 mi. south of Madison Spring Hut.

**SEC
2**

PINE LINK (AMC; MAP 1: E10–F9)

Cumulative from Pinkham B Rd. (Dolly Copp Rd.; 1,650 ft.) to:	⇅	↗	○
Howker Ridge Trail, lower jct. (3,850 ft.)	2.4 mi.	2,300 ft. (rev. 100 ft.)	2:20
Watson Path (4,950 ft.)	3.5 mi.	3,400 ft.	3:25
Madison Spring Hut (4,800 ft.)	4.0 mi.	3,400 ft. (rev. 150 ft.)	3:40

Pine Link ascends Mt. Madison from the highest point of Pinkham B Rd. (Dolly Copp Rd.) almost directly opposite the private road to the Horton Center on Pine Mtn., 2.4 mi. from US 2 at the foot of the big hill west of Gorham and 1.9 mi. from NH 16 near Dolly Copp Campground. This interesting trail provides an unusual variety of views from its outlook ledges and from the section above the treeline on Mt. Madison's northwest slope. Combined with the upper part of Howker Ridge Trail, Pine Link provides a very scenic loop. In general, it is not unusually steep, but the footing is often rough and consumes an unusual amount of attention and energy in comparison with most trails of similar steepness. The part above treeline is continuously exposed to the full force of northwest winds for about 0.7 mi., might be difficult to follow if visibility is poor, and requires a considerable amount of fairly strenuous rock-hopping. The result is that the trail generally proves more challenging than its statistical details might indicate.

The trail first ascends the northwest slope of a spur of Howker Ridge, climbing by a series of short, steep pitches interspersed with level sections. At 1.0 mi., the trail crosses a flat, swampy area and ascends another steep pitch then climbs to the ridge crest of the spur and follows it. At 1.7 mi., the trail passes an overgrown outlook with restricted views from the south side of the trail, the result of a 1968 fire. At 1.9 mi., just before the trail descends into a sag, a spur path leads left 20 yd. to a bare crag with fine views up to Mt. Madison and out to the Carter Range. At 2.4 mi., after a fairly long section of trail that has a brook running in and out of it, Pine Link turns right and joins Howker Ridge Trail in a shady little glen. Turning left at this jct., Pine Link coincides with Howker Ridge Trail. The two trails pass over a ledgy minor knob (a "Howk") that offers a good view and then descend from the ledge down a steep cleft to a wet sag. After passing a small cave on the right side of the trail, Pine Link branches right at 2.7 mi., at the foot of the most prominent Howk. The fine viewpoint at the top of this crag is only about 0.1 mi. above the jct. and is well worth a visit. From the jct., Pine Link runs nearly level across a wet area before rising moderately then rather steeply on the slope above Bumpus Basin, crossing several small brooks and several sections of slippery rocks. Climbing out of the scrub at 3.3 mi., the trail runs above treeline at easier grades, with fine views and great exposure to the weather. After crossing Watson Path at 3.5 mi. (0.3 mi. below the summit of Mt. Madison), Pine Link descends gradually, frequently crossing jumbles of large rocks that require strenuous rock-hopping. The footing improves in the last 0.1 mi., where the trail crosses two small meadows with little evident footway and ends at Osgood Trail 30 yd. from the front of Madison Spring Hut.

HOWKER RIDGE TRAIL (RMC; MAP 1: E9–F9)

Cumulative from Pinkham B Rd. (Dolly Copp Rd.; 1,225 ft.) to:	⇅	↗	⟲
Hitchcock Fall (1,875 ft.)	1.0 mi.	650 ft.	0:50
First Howk (3,450 ft.)	2.3 mi.	2,200 ft.	2:15
Pine Link, lower jct. (3,850 ft.)	3.1 mi.	2,800 ft. (rev. 200 ft.)	2:55
Osgood Trail (5,100 ft.)	4.2 mi.	4,200 ft. (rev. 100 ft.)	4:10
Mt. Madison summit (5,366 ft.) via Osgood Trail	4.4 mi.	4,450 ft.	4:25

This wild, rough, very scenic trail was built by Eugene B. Cook and William H. Peek, although the lower part no longer follows the original route. The trail leads from Pinkham B Rd. (Dolly Copp Rd.) at the Randolph East parking area, 0.2 mi. south of US 2, to Osgood Trail, 0.2 mi. below the summit of Mt. Madison. This is an interesting trail with a great variety of attractive scenery and woods, passing cascades in the lower part of the trail and offering excellent outlooks at different elevations higher up. Howker Ridge is the long, curving northeast ridge of Mt. Madison that partly encloses the deep, bowl-shaped valley called Bumpus Basin. The trail follows the crest of the ridge, on which are four little peaks called the

Howks; there are several ups and downs along this crest. The ridge gets its name from a family named Howker who once had a farm at its base.

Coinciding with Randolph Path, Howker Ridge Trail quickly crosses Presidential Rail Trail and 30 yd. beyond diverges left (southeast) on a series of plank walkways where Randolph Path turns right (southwest). Howker Ridge Trail ascends gradually through partly logged areas, crossing several overgrown skid roads. At 0.4 mi., the trail reaches the bank of Bumpus Brook, where a side path leads to ledges and cascades. The trail follows the brook, passing Stairs Fall (on a side stream) at 0.5 mi. It quickly enters the WMNF (sign) and passes a rocky gorge called the Devil's Kitchen, as well as other interesting pools and cascades. At 0.7 mi., at Coosauk Fall (sign; mostly dry), Sylvan Way enters on the right, and in less than 0.1 mi., Kelton Trail diverges right. At 1.0 mi., Howker Ridge Trail descends to make a somewhat difficult crossing of Bumpus Brook at the foot of Hitchcock Fall then climbs steeply up the slope on the other side, following a relocation. The trail soon levels off, descends slightly, and reaches a jct. with a spur trail that leads right 40 yd. to the Bear Pit, a natural cleft in the ledge that forms a traplike box. The main trail climbs steeply through conifer woods then moderates, reaching a rocky shoulder and descending into a slight sag. The trail resumes climbing and passes over a ledgy ridge crest called Blueberry Ledge—now far too overgrown to produce many blueberries—then continues up the ridge. The trail continues to climb, steeply at first and then moderately, with occasional restricted views north, as it approaches the crest of the first Howk, a long, narrow, densely wooded ridge capped by a number of small peaks. Following the ridge at easy grades, the trail crosses the ledgy but viewless summit of the first Howk at 2.3 mi., passes a limited outlook ahead to Mt. Madison, then descends steeply for a short distance. After crossing through a long, fairly level sag, the trail climbs seriously again, and at 3.0 mi., it passes over the ledgy summit of the second Howk, where you have fine views up to Mt. Madison and out to the Crescent and Pliny ranges to the north and northwest. Descending into the woods again rather steeply, with one ledgy scramble, the trail passes through a shady glen where Pine Link enters on the left; water is down this trail in less than 100 yd.

From this jct., the two trails coincide for 0.3 mi., ascending over one of a group of several small, ledgy knobs that constitute the third Howk, affording another good view. Descending a steep cleft to a wet sag, the trail passes a small cave to the right of the path then ascends to a jct. where Pine Link branches right. Bearing slightly left, Howker Ridge Trail climbs steeply up ledges to the open summit of the highest, most prominent Howk

(4,315 ft.) at 3.5 mi., where you have fine views in all directions. The trail descends back into the scrub, climbs over another minor crag, and passes through one last patch of high scrub before breaking out above treeline for good. The ensuing section of trail is very exposed to northwest winds and may be difficult to follow in poor visibility; however, if the trail is lost in conditions that do not dictate a retreat below the treeline, it is easy enough to reach Osgood Trail simply by climbing up to the ridge crest, as Osgood Trail follows that crest closely. From treeline, Howker Ridge Trail climbs steeply up the rocks, generally angling to the southwest and aiming for the notch between the most prominent visible crag and the lower crag to its left. As it approaches the ridge crest, the trail bears more to the right, heading for the most prominent visible crag, then bends slightly left and enters Osgood Trail about 100 yd. above a small sag and 0.2 mi. below the summit of Mt. Madison.

On the descent, at the jct. of Howker Ridge and Osgood trails, care must be taken to avoid beaten paths that lead back into Osgood Trail. When leaving the jct., keep to the left, descending only slightly, until the RMC sign a short distance down the path is in sight.

KELTON TRAIL (RMC; MAP 1: E9)

Cumulative from Howker Ridge Trail (1,700 ft.) to:	⇅	↗	⟳
Kelton Crag (2,075 ft.)	0.3 mi.	400 ft.	0:25
Inlook Trail (2,732 ft.)	0.9 mi.	1,050 ft.	1:00
The Brookside (2,750 ft.)	1.7 mi.	1,100 ft. (rev. 50 ft.)	1:25

This path runs from Howker Ridge Trail just above Coosauk Fall to the Brookside just below Salmacis Fall, from which Watson Path and Valley Way can be quickly reached. Kelton Trail passes two fine viewpoints, the Overlook and the Upper Inlook.

The trail branches right from Howker Ridge Trail 0.8 mi. from Pinkham B Rd. (Dolly Copp Rd.). Kelton Trail climbs steeply with some slippery sections to Kelton Crag then ascends toward the fingerlike north spur of Gordon Ridge, reaching an upper crag at the edge of a very old burn. From both these crags, there are restricted views; usually you can find water on the right between them. The trail then ascends to the Overlook at the edge of the old burn, where good views can be seen north and east a few steps left of the trail. It then swings right (west) to the Upper Inlook (outlook to the west) at 0.9 mi., where Inlook Trail enters right from Dome Rock. Kelton Trail then runs south nearly level through dense woods. The trail crosses Gordon Rill (reliable water) and traverses a section where extensive trail work has made travel across a rough slope easier. At 1.7 mi., the trail descends to cross Snyder Brook, climbs a steep bank, and ends at the Brookside 0.1 mi. below the foot of Salmacis Fall.

INLOOK TRAIL (RMC; MAP 1: E9)

Cumulative from Randolph Path (1,900 ft.) to:	↻	↗	⟳
Dome Rock (2,662 ft.)	0.6 mi.	750 ft.	0:40
Kelton Trail (2,732 ft.)	0.7 mi.	850 ft.	0:45

This path ascends the ridge that leads northwest from the end of the fingerlike north spur of Gordon Ridge, offering excellent views from the brink of the line of cliffs that overlook Snyder Brook and culminate in Dome Rock. The trail begins at the jct. of Randolph Path and the Brookside on the east bank of Snyder Brook. Inlook Trail ascends, steeply at the start, and soon reaches the first of several "inlooks" up the valley of Snyder Brook to Mt. Madison, Mt. John Quincy Adams, and Mt. Adams. The trail then ascends alternately over open ledges and through the woods, steeply at times. After passing Dome Rock, which offers an excellent view north from the tip of the finger, the trail swings right, leaving from the back of the ledge (sign), and continues up to the Upper Inlook (good view west) near the crest of the finger, where Inlook Trail ends at its jct. with Kelton Trail.

THE BROOKSIDE (RMC; MAP 1: E9)

From Valley Way (1,900 ft.) to:	↻	↗	⟳
Watson Path (3,250 ft.)	1.7 mi	1,350 ft.	1:30

This trail follows Snyder Brook, offering views of many cascades and pools. The upper part is fairly steep and rough. The trail begins at the jct. with Valley Way, at the point where Valley Way leaves the edge of the brook 0.9 mi. from the Appalachia parking area, and climbs along the brook to Watson Path, a short distance north of Bruin Rock.

The Brookside leaves Valley Way about 30 yd. above Valley Way's jct. with Beechwood Way, continuing straight where Valley Way turns uphill to the right. After a short washed-out section, Randolph Path joins on the right, and the two trails cross Snyder Brook together on large stepping-stones (the former bridge at this crossing was washed out in 2005 and will not be replaced). Here, Randolph Path turns left; Inlook Trail leaves straight ahead; and the Brookside turns right, continuing up the bank of the brook. At 0.3 mi., the Brookside recrosses the brook and climbs along the west bank at a moderate grade with good footing, rising well above the brook through a fine birch forest, with occasional views through the trees to cliffs on the valley wall on the other side of the brook. Returning gradually to brook level, the trail comes to the jct. with Kelton Trail, which enters from the left at 1.2 mi. Above this point, the Brookside becomes steeper and rougher and again runs close to the brook, passing Salmacis Fall (limited view north from the top) at 1.3 mi. The trail continues along a wild and beautiful part of the brook, with cascades and mossy rocks in a fine forest. The trail then climbs away from the brook and finally ascends sharply to Watson Path a short distance north of Bruin Rock.

WATSON PATH (RMC; MAP 1: E9–F9)

Cumulative from Scar Trail (3,175 ft.) to:	⇅	↗	↺
Valley Way (3,175 ft.)	0.2 mi.	0 ft.	0:05
Pine Link (4,950 ft.)	1.4 mi.	1,800 ft.	1:35
Mt. Madison summit (5,366 ft.)	1.7 mi.	2,200 ft.	1:55
From Appalachia parking area (1,306 ft.) to:			
Mt. Madison summit (5,366 ft.) via Valley Way and Watson Path	3.9 mi.	4,050 ft.	4:00

The original Watson Path, completed by Laban M. Watson in 1882, led from the Ravine House to the summit of Mt. Madison. The present path begins at Scar Trail, leads across Valley Way to Bruin Rock, and then follows the original route to the summit. This is an interesting route to Mt. Madison, but it is very steep and rough, and, on the slopes above treeline, is exposed to the full fury of northwest winds in a storm. The cairns above treeline are not very prominent, and the trail may be hard to follow when visibility is poor. Therefore, in bad weather this is potentially one of the most dangerous routes on the Northern Presidentials.

Branching from Scar Trail 0.3 mi. from Valley Way, Watson Path runs level, crossing Valley Way at 0.2 mi., 2.4 mi. on that trail from the Appalachia parking area. This first section of Watson Path is seldom used and is rather difficult to follow. After crossing Valley Way, the trail continues at an easy grade (but with one rough scramble around a large boulder), passing the jct. with the Brookside on the left just before reaching Bruin Rock—a large, flat-topped boulder on the west bank of Snyder Brook. In another 80 yd., the Lower Bruin branches to the right toward Valley Way, and Watson Path crosses the brook at the foot of Duck Fall. The trail soon attacks the steep flank of Gordon Ridge on a very steep and rough footway. At 1.0 mi., the trail emerges from the scrub onto the grassy, stony back of the ridge, crosses Pine Link at 1.4 mi., and ascends southward to the summit of Mt. Madison over rough and shelving stones, swinging right (southwest) near the top.

Descending from the summit, Watson Path leads northeast, and Osgood Trail descends to the east and to the west.

SEC 2

VALLEY WAY (AMC; MAP 1: E9–F9)

Cumulative from Appalachia parking area (1,306 ft.) to:	⥮	↗	↻
Randolph Path crossing (1,953 ft.)	0.9 mi.	650 ft.	0:45
Watson Path crossing (3,175 ft.)	2.4 mi.	1,850 ft.	2:10
Upper Bruin jct. (4,150 ft.)	3.3 mi.	2,850 ft.	3:05
Madison Spring Hut (4,800 ft.)	3.8 mi.	3,500 ft.	3:40
Mt. Madison summit (5,366 ft.) via Osgood Trail	4.3 mi.	4,050 ft.	4:10

This is the most direct and easiest route from the Appalachia parking area to Madison Spring Hut, and the route is well sheltered almost to the door of the hut. The parking area is a stop of the AMC Hiker Shuttle. In bad weather, this is the safest route to or from the hut. J. Rayner Edmands constructed the trail in his unmistakable style from 1895 to 1897, using parts of earlier trails constructed by Laban Watson and Eugene Cook.

The trail, in common with Air Line, begins at Appalachia and crosses Presidential Rail Trail to a fork, where Valley Way leads to the left and Air Line to the right across the power-line clearing. Just into the woods, Maple Walk diverges left, and at 0.2 mi., Sylvan Way crosses. Valley Way soon enters the WMNF, and at 0.5 mi., Fallsway comes in on the left, soon departs on the left for Tama Fall and Brookbank, then reenters Valley Way at 0.6 mi.—a short but worthwhile loop.

Valley Way leads nearer Snyder Brook and is soon joined from the right by Beechwood Way. About 30 yd. above this jct. the Brookside continues straight. Valley Way turns right and climbs 100 yd. to the crossing of Randolph Path at 0.9 mi. then climbs at a comfortable grade high above Snyder Brook, crossing several small brooks at their confluence at 1.4 mi. before swinging east then south. At 2.1 mi., Scar Trail branches right, leading to Air Line via Durand Scar, an excellent outlook on Scar Loop only about 0.2 mi. above Valley Way that is well worth the small effort required to visit it. At 2.4 mi., Watson Path crosses, leading left to the summit of Mt. Madison. Valley Way angles up the rather steep slopes of Durand

Ridge at a moderate grade considerably above the stream. At 2.8 mi., Lower Bruin enters left, coming up from Bruin Rock and Duck Fall. At 3.2 mi., a side path on the right leads 150 yd. to Valley Way Tentsite. Soon the trail passes a spring to the right of the trail. At 3.3 mi., Upper Bruin branches steeply right, leading in 0.2 mi. to Air Line at the lower end of the knife-edge.

Now Valley Way becomes steep and rough and approaches nearer to Snyder Brook. High up in the scrub, the path swings to the right, away from the brook, then swings back toward the stream and emerges from the scrub close to the stream, reaching a jct. with Air Line Cutoff 45 yd. below the hut. Valley Way ends in another 10 yd. at a jct. with Gulfside Trail, which continues another 35 yd. to the hut. From the hut, the summit of Mt. Madison can be reached by ascending 0.5 mi. on Osgood Trail.

Descending, follow Gulfside Trail 35 yd. northwest from the hut to a jct. where Valley Way diverges right (north) as Gulfside Trail bears left (southwest). Bear right in another 10 yd. where Air Line Cutoff diverges left.

MT. ADAMS

LOWER BRUIN (RMC; MAP 1: E9)

From Watson Path (3,275 ft.) to:	⮁	↗	⏱
Valley Way (3,584 ft.)	0.2 mi.	300 ft.	0:15

This short trail branches right from Watson Path on the west bank of Snyder Brook, where Watson Path crosses the brook at Duck Fall. The trail climbs steeply with a fairly difficult scramble, passes through a small clearing, and turns right uphill, moving away from the brook. The trail soon turns left and continues to climb rather steeply then becomes gradual and ends at Valley Way. In the reverse direction, care should be taken to turn left into the small clearing rather than following a beaten path down to the brook.

UPPER BRUIN (RMC; MAP 1: F9)

From Valley Way (4,150 ft.) to:	⮁	↗	⏱
Air Line (4,400 ft.)	0.2 mi.	250 ft.	0:15

This short trail and its companion, Lower Bruin, are the remnants of the original trail to Mt. Adams from Randolph. Upper Bruin branches to the right from Valley Way 3.3 mi. from Appalachia and climbs moderately with rocky footing to Air Line near treeline, 3.1 mi. from Appalachia.

AIR LINE (AMC; MAP 1: E9–F9)

Cumulative from Appalachia parking area (1,306 ft.) to:	⥮	↗	↻
Randolph Path (2,000 ft.)	0.9 mi.	700 ft.	0:50
Scar Trail (3,700 ft.)	2.4 mi.	2,400 ft.	2:25
Chemin des Dames (4,475 ft.)	3.2 mi.	3,150 ft.	3:10
Air Line Cutoff (4,800 ft.)	3.5 mi.	3,500 ft.	3:30
Gulfside Trail (5,125 ft.)	3.7 mi.	3,800 ft.	3:45
Mt. Adams summit (5,799 ft.)	4.3 mi.	4,500 ft.	4:25
Madison Spring Hut (4,800 ft.) via Air Line Cutoff	3.7 mi.	3,500 ft.	3:35

This trail, completed in 1885, is the shortest route to Mt. Adams from a highway. The trail runs from the Appalachia parking area up Durand Ridge to the summit. The middle section is steep and rough, and the sections on the knife-edged crest of Durand Ridge and above treeline are very exposed to weather but afford magnificent views.

The trail, in common with Valley Way, begins at Appalachia and crosses Presidential Rail Trail to a fork near the edge of the power-line clearing, where Air Line leads right and Valley Way left. In 40 yd., just after Air Line enters the woods, the Link diverges right. Air Line crosses Sylvan Way at 0.2 mi. and Beechwood Way and Beechwood Brook at 0.6 mi. At 0.8 mi. from Appalachia, Short Line diverges right, and at 0.9 mi., Air Line enters Randolph Path, coincides with it for 20 yd., then diverges left uphill. At 1.6 mi., there may be water in a spring 30 yd. left (east) of the path. From here, Air Line becomes quite steep and rough for 0.5 mi. then eases up and reaches a site once known as Camp Placid Stream (water unreliable) at 2.4 mi., where Scar Trail enters on the left, coming up from Valley Way.

At 3.0 mi., after a moderate climb, Air Line emerges from the scrub, and at 3.1 mi., Upper Bruin comes up left from Valley Way. Air Line now ascends over the bare, ledgy crest of Durand Ridge known as the Knife Edge, passing over crags that drop off sharply into King Ravine on the right and descend steeply but not precipitously into Snyder Glen on the left. At 3.2 mi., just south of the little peak called Needle Rock, the Chemin des Dames comes up from King Ravine. Air Line now climbs steadily up the ridge toward Mt. Adams. From several outlooks along the upper part of this ridge, one can look back down the ridge for a fine demonstration of the difference between the U-shaped glacial cirque of King Ravine on the left (west) and the ordinary V-shaped brook valley of Snyder Glen on the right (east). At 3.5 mi., Air Line Cutoff diverges left (southeast) to Madison Spring Hut, which is visible from this jct. in clear weather.

Air Line Cutoff (AMC). This short branch path provides a direct route 0.2 mi. (10 min.) long, fully sheltered by scrub, from Air Line high on Durand Ridge to Valley Way just below Madison Spring Hut. Water may be obtained on this trail not far from Air Line.

Air Line now departs a little from the edge of the ravine, going left of the jutting crags at the ravine's southeast corner, and rises steeply. In this section, following the trail in poor visibility requires great care. At 3.7 mi., the trail passes the Gateway of King Ravine, where King Ravine Trail diverges right and plunges between two crags into that gulf. Here, you have a striking view of Mt. Madison. In 60 yd., the path enters Gulfside Trail, turns right, and coincides with it for 70 yd. on the high plateau at the head of the ravine. Then Air Line diverges to the left (southwest), passing northwest of Mt. Quincy Adams, and, marked by blue blazes and cairns, climbs steadily and at times steeply up a rough way over large, angular stones to the summit of Mt. Adams, where Air Line meets Lowe's Path and Star Lake Trail.

Descending from the summit, Air Line follows cairns slightly east of north down the rocky cone of the mountain.

SCAR TRAIL AND SCAR LOOP (RMC; MAP 1: E9)

Cumulative from Valley Way (2,811 ft.) to:	↕	◢	○
Durand Scar (3,150 ft.) via Scar Loop	0.2 mi.	350 ft.	0:15
Watson Path (3,175 ft.) via main trail	0.3 mi.	350 ft.	0:20
Air Line (3,700 ft.) via either main trail or loop	1.0 mi.	900 ft.	0:55
From Appalachia parking area (1,306 ft.) to:			
Mt. Adams summit (5,799 ft.) via Valley Way, Scar Trail or Scar Loop, and Air Line	5.0 mi.	4,500 ft.	4:45

This trail runs from Valley Way, 2.1 mi. from Appalachia, to Air Line, 2.4 mi. from Appalachia. Scar Trail provides a route to Mt. Adams that includes the spectacular views from Durand Ridge while avoiding the steepest section of Air Line, and Scar Trail also has an excellent outlook of its own from Durand Scar, reached by Scar Loop.

The trail ascends moderately and divides 0.2 mi. above Valley Way. Scar Loop, an alternative route to the right, climbs up a natural ramp between two sections of rock face, turns sharply left, and 40 yd. above the loop jct. reaches Durand Scar, which commands excellent views both up and down the valley of Snyder Brook; those up to Adams and Madison are especially fine. Scar Loop then scrambles up the ledge, climbs steeply, passes an outlook on the left up the Snyder Brook valley toward Mt. Madison, and descends over a ledge to rejoin the main path 0.4 mi. above Valley Way. Scar Loop is best done on the ascent: The steep, narrow footway below the main outlook can be tricky for a descending hiker.

The main Scar Trail, which is easier but misses the best views, bears left at the loop jct. In 0.1 mi., the trail turns sharply right (as Watson Path diverges left) then climbs across a small brook to the upper loop jct. where Scar Loop reenters. From here, the trail winds its way west and then south up the mountainside to Air Line with mostly moderate grades and good footing.

STAR LAKE TRAIL (AMC; MAP 1: F9)

Cumulative from Madison Spring Hut (4,800 ft.) to:	⇅	↗	⟳
Buttress Trail (4,900 ft.)	0.3 mi.	100 ft.	0:10
Mt. Adams summit (5,799 ft.)	1.0 mi.	1,000 ft.	1:00

This trail leads from Madison Spring Hut to the summit of Mt. Adams, much of the way angling up the steep southeast side of Mt. John Quincy Adams. This trail is often more sheltered from the wind than Air Line is, but Star Lake Trail is steep and rough, especially in the upper part, where it rock-hops a great deal of large talus and then tackles some fairly challenging rock scrambles on the steep section just below the summit ridge. Star Lake Trail may also be difficult to follow when descending.

The trail runs south from the hut, rising gently, and at 0.2 mi., Parapet Trail branches to the left, passing east of Star Lake and leading to the Parapet and to Madison Gulf and Osgood trails. Star Lake Trail passes along the west shore of the lake, and beyond it at 0.3 mi., Buttress Trail diverges left and descends into the Great Gulf. Star Lake Trail ascends southwest on the steep southeast slope of Mt. Quincy Adams, leaving the scrub and passing a good spring below the trail. It becomes progressively steeper and rougher as it angles up the rocky slope, and the rocks become larger and require more strenuous hopping. Approaching the crest of a minor easterly ridge, the trail turns right and climbs very steeply with some fairly difficult scrambles to the top of the shoulder then ascends moderately along the ridge crest to the summit of Adams, where the trail meets Lowe's Path and Air Line.

Descending from the summit, Star Lake Trail leads to the southeast down a shoulder of the mountain then bears left for the steep descent.

SHORT LINE (RMC; MAP 1: E9)

Cumulative from Air Line (1,825 ft.) to:	⇅	↗	○
Randolph Path, lower jct. (2,275 ft.)	0.5 mi.	450 ft.	0:30
Randolph Path, upper jct. (2,500 ft.)	0.9 mi.	700 ft.	0:50
King Ravine Trail (3,150 ft.)	1.9 mi.	1,350 ft.	1:40

This moderate, graded path, leading from Air Line to King Ravine Trail below Mossy Fall, was made from 1899 to 1901 by J. Rayner Edmands. Short Line offers direct access to Randolph Path and to King Ravine from the Appalachia parking area.

Short Line branches right from Air Line 0.8 mi. from Appalachia. At 0.5 mi., Short Line unites with Randolph Path, coincides with it for 0.4 mi., then branches left and leads south up the valley of Cold Brook toward King Ravine, keeping a short distance east of the stream. At 2.7 mi. from Appalachia, Short Line joins King Ravine Trail just below Mossy Fall.

KING RAVINE TRAIL (RMC; MAP 1: E9–F9)

Cumulative from Lowe's Path (2,575 ft.) to:	⇅	↗	○
Randolph Path and the Amphibrach (2,925 ft.)	1.0 mi.	450 ft. (rev. 100 ft.)	0:45
Short Line (3,150 ft.)	1.8 mi.	800 ft. (rev. 100 ft.)	1:20
Foot of King Ravine headwall (3,825 ft.)	2.5 mi.	1,450 ft.	2:00
Air Line (5,100 ft.)	3.1 mi.	2,700 ft.	2:55
From Appalachia parking area (1,306 ft.) to:			
Mt. Adams summit (5,799 ft.) via Air Line, Short Line, King Ravine Trail, and Air Line	4.6 mi.	4,500 ft.	4:35

This trail through King Ravine was constructed as a branch of Lowe's Path by Charles E. Lowe in 1876. King Ravine Trail is very steep and rough on the headwall of the ravine, but it is one of the most spectacular trails in the White Mountains, offering an overwhelming variety of wild and magnificent scenery. This is not a good trail to descend due to its steep, rough, slippery footing, and extra time should be allowed in either direction for the roughness—and the views. It is not recommended for hikers with dogs. The trip to the floor of the ravine is well worth the effort, even if you do not choose to ascend the headwall. Although King Ravine Trail begins on Lowe's Path, a more direct route to the most scenic part of the trail leads from Appalachia via Air Line and Short Line.

King Ravine Trail diverges left from Lowe's Path 1.8 mi. from US 2 and rises over a low swell of Nowell Ridge. King Ravine Trail then descends gradually, and at 0.8 mi., it crosses Spur Brook below some cascades known as Canyon Fall, swings right (south), and in another 0.2 mi., the trail crosses Randolph Path at its jct. with the Amphibrach; this five-way intersection is called the Pentadoi. Skirting the east spur of Nowell Ridge, King Ravine Trail enters King Ravine and descends slightly, crosses a western branch of Cold Brook, goes across the lower floor of the ravine, and crosses two branches of the main stream. At 1.8 mi., near the foot of Mossy Fall (last sure water), the trail is joined from the left by Short Line, the usual route of access from the Appalachia parking area. Just above this fall, Cold Brook, already a good-sized stream, gushes from beneath the boulders that have fallen into the ravine.

So far, the path has been fairly gradual, but in the next 0.3 mi., it becomes much rougher, rising about 500 ft., with several fairly difficult scrambles over large boulders, and gaining the upper floor of the ravine (about 3,700 ft.). The grandeur of the views of the ravine from the jumbled rocks that the trail passes around is ample reward for the trip to this area, even if one does not continue up the headwall. The Chemin des Dames, leading very steeply up to Air Line, branches sharply left at 2.2 mi. King Ravine Trail turns sharply right here, emerges into the open, and then divides in another 10 yd. An alternate route called the Subway—more interesting but very strenuous—leads to the right from this jct.; this is one of the celebrated features of White Mountain trails, winding through boulder caves over and under rocks ranging up to the size of a small house.

The main path, called the Elevated, leads to the left, avoiding many of the boulder caves, and is thus much easier; it also offers some good views of the ravine. The paths rejoin after 220 yd. on the Subway or 140 yd. on the Elevated; soon Great Gully Trail diverges right, and King Ravine Trail divides again. The left fork is the main trail, and the right is the rough Ice Caves Loop, about 30 yd. shorter than the main trail, leading through boulder caves near the foot of the headwall; these caves have ice that remains throughout the year. After the paths rejoin at about 0.7 mi. from Short Line jct., the ascent of the headwall begins. This trail is very steep and rough, rising about 1,100 ft. in 0.5 mi. over large blocks of rock marked with cairns and paint. The trail climbs to the Gateway, where the trail emerges from the ravine between two crags and immediately joins Air Line just below its jct. with Gulfside Trail. From the Gateway is a striking view of Mt. Madison. Madison Spring Hut is in sight and can be reached by taking Gulfside Trail left. The summit of Mt. Adams is 0.6 mi. away via Air Line.

CHEMIN DES DAMES (RMC; MAP 1: F9)

From King Ravine Trail (3,700 ft.) to:	⮃	↗	○
Air Line jct. (4,475 ft.)	0.4 mi.	800 ft.	0:35

This trail leads from the floor of King Ravine up its east wall and joins Air Line just above treeline. Chemin des Dames is the shortest route out of the ravine but is nevertheless very steep and rough, climbing about 800 ft. in 0.4 mi. over gravel and talus, some of which is loose; this is also a difficult trail to descend. Leaving King Ravine Trail just before the point where Subway and Elevated divide, Chemin des Dames winds through scrub and boulders to the east side of the ravine, where the trail climbs steeply over talus through varying amounts of scrub, permitting plentiful, though not constant, views. About halfway up the steep slope, the trail passes through a boulder cave called Tunnel Rock or the Orange Squeezer. Above this are many fine views out across King Ravine and up to the towering crags of Durand Ridge. High up, the trail angles to the right across the top of a small slide and along the base of a rock face, reaching Air Line in a little col.

GREAT GULLY TRAIL (RMC; MAP 1: F9)

From King Ravine Trail (3,775 ft.) to:	⮃	↗	○
Gulfside Trail (5,490 ft.)	1.0 mi.	1,700 ft.	1:20

This remarkably wild and beautiful trail provides an alternative route between the floor of King Ravine and Gulfside Trail, reaching the latter at Thunderstorm Junction. Great Gully Trail is extremely steep and rough, and, like the other trails in the ravine, especially difficult to descend. It is well marked but lightly used, and must be followed with some care. It has one particularly difficult scramble and should not be attempted in wet or icy conditions. On this shady north slope, large snowdrifts may cover the trail well into June.

Leaving King Ravine Trail just past the point where the Subway and Elevated rejoin, Great Gully Trail runs across the floor of the ravine at easy grades then ascends steadily through scrubby birches in a region damaged by an avalanche, and at 0.3 mi., reaches (but does not cross) the brook that flows down the gully. At the base of an attractive high cascade, the trail turns right, away from the brook, and climbs up rocks to the spine of a narrow ridge and to a promontory with a spectacular view. The trail then passes under an overhanging rock on a ledge with a high, sheer drop close by on the left, forcing the faint of heart to crawl on their bellies, possibly dragging their packs behind them. After negotiating this pitch, the climber is rewarded with a fine view of the cascade. Here, the trail turns sharply right and climbs past a sheer dropoff to another viewpoint then crosses the brook above the cascade at a spot where *Arnica mollis*, an herb of the Aster family sought by Henry David Thoreau on his trips to the mountains, grows in profusion. The trail continues to climb steeply to treeline, with several more scrambles, ascends over a talus slope, then exits left from the rocks (watch for cairns marking this turn). The trail then begins to moderate as it runs almost due south across a grassy area marked by cairns that might be hard to follow in poor visibility and finally meets Gulfside Trail and Lowe's Path at Thunderstorm Junction.

SEC 2

THE AMPHIBRACH (RMC; MAP 1: E9)

Cumulative from Memorial Bridge (1,425 ft.) to:	⇅	↗	○
Monaway (2,200 ft.)	1.1 mi.	800 ft.	0:55
Randolph Path and King Ravine Trail (2,925 ft.)	1.9 mi.	1,500 ft.	1:40

This moderately graded trail begins on the Link at the west end of Memorial Bridge, 0.7 mi. from the Appalachia parking area, then runs south near Cold Brook and its tributary Spur Brook to the five-way jct. with Randolph Path and King Ravine Trail known as the Pentadoi. The Amphibrach takes its unusual name from the marking that was used when the trail was first made, around 1883: three blazes—short, long, and short—arranged vertically. It is one of the kindest trails to the feet in this region.

From the Link at Memorial Bridge, the Amphibrach follows the course of Cold Brook, ascending west of the stream but generally not in sight of the water. At 20 yd. from the jct., a side trail branches left 50 yd. to the foot of Cold Brook Fall. Soon, the Amphibrach enters the WMNF. At 1.1 mi., Monaway crosses, leading right to Cliffway and left to Coldspur Ledges and to cascades at the confluence of Cold and Spur brooks, reached about 80 yd. from this jct.; the last short, steep drop to the view of the ledges requires caution. The Amphibrach soon crosses Spur Brook on the rocks and then bears away to the left (east), ascending the tongue of land between the two brooks and climbing moderately. At 1.5 mi., the Amphibrach crosses Cliffway, which leads right (west) less than 0.2 mi. to picturesque Spur Brook Fall. Becoming a bit rougher, the Amphibrach continues upward to join King Ravine Trail a few steps below the Pentadoi.

CLIFFWAY (RMC; MAP 1: E9)

Cumulative from the Link (2,170 ft.) to:	⇅	↗	○
White Cliff (2,484 ft.)	0.7 mi.	300 ft.	0:30
Spur Brook Fall (2,550 ft.)	1.7 mi.	500 ft. (rev 100 ft.)	1:05
Randolph Path (2,575 ft.)	2.1 mi.	500 ft.	1:20

This path begins on the Link, 2.0 mi. from the Appalachia parking area, and runs across the Amphibrach to Randolph Path, 2.0 mi. from Appalachia via Air Line and Short Line. Many of Cliffway's former viewpoints from the cliffs and ledges of the low swell of Nowell Ridge are now overgrown, but White Cliff still offers a view of the Randolph Valley and the Pliny and Crescent ranges to the north, and Bog Ledge has an interesting view of King Ravine. The trail has generally easy grades and is well marked, but it is very lightly used, and care may be required to follow it.

Leaving the Link, Cliffway climbs gradually with several turns to the viewpoint at White Cliff at 0.7 mi., where the trail turns sharply right. Here, two trails diverge. To the left, Along the Brink (RMC), a trail just 20 yd. long, descends a few steps to the most open view at White Cliff, at the edge of the dropoff, then continues along the edge through the woods. Caution is required on this trail, especially when it is wet. Continuing ahead where Cliffway turns sharply right is Ladderback Trail (RMC). This short link trail, named for Ladderback Rock, a large boulder in the woods, connects Cliffway to Monaway, permitting a short loop hike including White Cliff, Bog Ledge, and the overgrown King Cliff. The trail is rough and must be followed with care. It leaves White Cliff and, in a short distance as the trail turns sharply right, is joined from the left by Along the Brink. Ladderback Trail then descends gradually past Ladderback Rock to Monaway 0.2 mi. (5 min.) from White Cliff.

At 1.0 mi., after ascending a zigzag course, Cliffway crosses Bog Ledge, where you have a cleared view of King Ravine and mts. Adams and Madison, then descends sharply for a short distance, turns left, and crosses a boggy area on bog bridges. The trail then turns sharply left again, passes overgrown King Cliff, and in another 0.1 mi., at 1.3 mi., meets Monaway. Monaway continues straight, and Cliffway turns sharply right and drops onto a small broken ledge that resembles a ruined stairway then runs nearly level across a moist area to Spur Brook at the base of picturesque Spur Brook Fall. The trail then climbs beside the fall, crosses Spur Brook above the fall, and runs across the Amphibrach at 1.9 mi. to Randolph Path, at the west end of Sanders Bridge over Cold Brook.

MONAWAY (RMC; MAP 1: E9)

From the Amphibrach (2,200 ft.) to:	↥↧	↗	⟳
Cliffway (2,550 ft.)	0.4 mi.	350 ft.	0:25

This short link trail affords the shortest route from the Randolph area to Cliffway at White Cliff or King Cliff. Monaway begins on the Amphibrach just below that trail's crossing of Spur Brook. At this jct., a short segment of Monaway leads downhill (east) about 80 yd. to pleasant Cold-spur Ledges at the confluence of Cold and Spur brooks (use caution). The main part of Monaway runs uphill (west) from the Amphibrach at a moderate grade, passes a jct. on the right at 0.3 mi. with Ladderback Trail to White Cliff, then swings left (south) at an easier grade and meets Cliffway about 0.1 mi. east of overgrown King Cliff. Turn left here for Spur Brook Fall or turn right for Bog Ledge and White Cliff.

SPUR TRAIL (RMC; MAP 1: E9–F9)

Cumulative from Randolph Path (2,950 ft.) to:	↥↧	↗	⟳
Crag Camp (4,247 ft.)	0.9 mi.	1,300 ft.	1:05
Lowe's Path (5,425 ft.)	2.0 mi.	2,500 ft.	2:15
Mt. Adams summit (5,799 ft.) via Lowe's Path	2.4 mi.	2,850 ft.	2:40

This trail leads from Randolph Path, just above its jct. with King Ravine Trail and the Amphibrach, to Lowe's Path, just below Thunderstorm Junction. Spur Trail ascends the east spur of Nowell Ridge near the west edge of King Ravine, passing Crag Camp (cabin). At several points below treeline are fine outlooks into King Ravine, and above treeline, views into King Ravine and up to mts. Madison and Adams are continuous and excellent. The lower part of the trail is steep and rough, and the upper part runs completely in the open, very exposed to weather. The RMC rehabilitated sections of this trail in 2011 and 2015.

Spur Trail diverges south from Randolph Path about 100 yd. west of its jct. with King Ravine Trail and the Amphibrach, on the west bank of Spur Brook, and climbs rather steeply along Spur Brook past attractive cascades and pools. At 0.2 mi., a branch path leads left 90 yd. to Chandler Fall, where the brook runs down a steep, smooth slab of rock; from the base of the fall is a restricted view north. At 0.3 mi., Hincks Trail to Gray Knob cabin diverges right, and Spur Trail crosses to the east side of the brook, the last water until Crag Camp. The trail climbs steeply up the spur that forms the west wall of King Ravine, ascending several rock staircases and following a short relocation to the right at 0.8 mi., just before reaching a side path that leads left 10 yd. to the Lower Crag, a good outlook to the ravine and mts. Madison and Adams. At 0.9 mi., Spur Trail reaches the Upper Crag, where the trail passes in front of Crag Camp, swings right around the cabin, and soon reaches the jct. on the right with Gray Knob Trail, which leads west 0.4 mi. to Gray Knob cabin.

Spur Trail bears left at this jct. and continues to climb quite steeply up the ridge, but not so near the edge of the ravine. At 1.1 mi., a side path (sign, hard to see on the descent) leads left 100 yd. to Knight's Castle, a spectacular perch high up on the ravine wall. Here, Spur Trail passes into high scrub, and in another 0.2 mi., it breaks out above treeline, commanding excellent views: Those to King Ravine are better in the lower portion, and those to Mts. Madison and Adams are better higher up. The grade moderates as it joins Nowell Ridge, ascending well to the east of the crest. Spur Trail finally merges with Lowe's Path 100 yd. below Gulfside Trail at Thunderstorm Junction. Descending, Spur Trail diverges right at a fork where Lowe's Path continues ahead on the left fork.

HINCKS TRAIL (RMC; MAP 1: E9–F9)

From Spur Trail (3,450 ft.) to:	⇅	↗	○
Gray Knob cabin (4,375 ft.)	0.7 mi.	950 ft.	0:50

This short link trail connects Spur Trail and Randolph Path to Gray Knob cabin. Hincks Trail is fairly steep and rough. It diverges right from Spur Trail immediately before the crossing of Spur Brook, about 0.3 mi. above Randolph Path. Soon, Hincks Trail comes to the edge of Spur Brook near a pleasant little cascade over mossy rocks then winds rather steeply up the valley, passing through several patches of woods damaged by wind, to Gray Knob.

GRAY KNOB TRAIL (RMC; MAP 1: E9–F9)

Cumulative from Spur Trail (4,250 ft.) to:	⇅	↗	○
Lowe's Path (4,400 ft.)	0.5 mi.	150 ft.	0:20
Randolph Path (4,825 ft.)	1.7 mi.	600 ft.	1:10

This trail connects three of the four RMC camps (Crag Camp, Gray Knob, and the Perch) with one another. The trail also links the upper parts of Spur Trail and Lowe's, Randolph, and Israel Ridge paths, affording a route from Crag Camp and Gray Knob to Edmands Col without loss of elevation. Grades are mostly easy, but the footing is frequently rough, and south of Lowe's Path, Gray Knob Trail has substantial weather exposure, although some sheltering scrub is usually close by.

Leaving Spur Trail 25 yd. west of Crag Camp, Gray Knob Trail climbs over a knoll with limited views then passes a side path on the right, leading down 25 yd. to a good piped spring. The trail traverses a rough slope nearly on the level; then, soon after passing a spring (left), the trail ascends a short pitch to Gray Knob cabin (left) at 0.4 mi., where Hincks Trail enters on the right. Gray Knob Trail then runs almost level, passing Quay Path, a short-cut on the right that runs 50 yd. to Lowe's Path at a fine outlook ledge called the Quay. Gray Knob Trail crosses Lowe's Path at 0.5 mi. and almost immediately enters scrub of variable height, offering a mixture of shelter and weather exposure with nearly constant views, and begins to climb moderately. At 0.8 mi., Perch Path diverges right. Gray Knob Trail continues to climb moderately up the slope then levels off and runs nearly on contour to Randolph Path just before its jct. with Israel Ridge Path.

PERCH PATH (RMC; MAP 1: F9)

Cumulative from Gray Knob Trail (4,550 ft.) to:	⇅	↗	○
The Perch (4,313 ft.)	0.4 mi.	0 ft. (rev. 250 ft.)	0:10
Israel Ridge Path jct. (4,300 ft.)	0.5 mi.	0 ft.	0:15

This path runs from Gray Knob Trail across Randolph Path and past the Perch (lean-to) to Israel Ridge Path. Perch Path diverges right (south) from Gray Knob Trail 0.3 mi. south of Lowe's Path then descends moderately, with rough footing and some views, and crosses Randolph Path at 0.3 mi. Perch Path soon crosses a small brook then passes the Perch and its tent platforms running nearly level to Israel Ridge Path at a sharp curve.

LOWE'S PATH (RMC; MAP 1: E9–F9)

Cumulative from US 2 near Lowe's Store (1,385 ft.) to:	⇅	↗	○
The Link (2,475 ft.)	1.7 mi.	1,100 ft.	1:25
King Ravine Trail (2,575 ft.)	1.8 mi.	1,200 ft.	1:30
Log Cabin (3,263 ft.)	2.4 mi.	1,900 ft.	2:10
Randolph Path (3,600 ft.)	2.7 mi.	2,200 ft.	2:25
Gray Knob Trail (4,400 ft.)	3.2 mi.	3,000 ft.	3:05
Mt. Abigail Adams (5,355 ft.)	4.1 mi.	3,950 ft.	4:00
Gulfside Trail (5,490 ft.)	4.4 mi.	4,150 ft. (rev. 50 ft.)	4:15
Mt. Adams summit (5,799 ft.)	4.7 mi.	4,450 ft.	4:35

This trail, cut from 1875 to 1876 by Charles E. Lowe and Dr. William G. Nowell from Lowe's house in Randolph to the summit of Mt. Adams, is the oldest of the mountain trails that ascend the peaks from the Randolph Valley. The trail begins on the south side of US 2, 150 yd. west of Lowe's Store, at which cars may be parked (small fee); no parking is available at the trailhead. This is perhaps the easiest way to climb Mt. Adams, with mostly moderate grades (although the middle section is steep and rough) and excellent views, but it still has considerable exposure to weather in the part above treeline.

Leaving US 2, Lowe's Path follows a broad woods road for 100 yd. then diverges right at a sign giving the history of the trail. It crosses a snowmobile trail, Presidential Rail Trail, then the power lines and ascends through woods at a moderate grade, heading at first southwest and then southeast, and crossing several small brooks. At 1.7 mi., the Link crosses, and at 1.8 mi., King Ravine Trail branches left. Lowe's Path continues to ascend, making a switchback out to the left, then becoming steeper and rougher, and at 2.4 mi., it passes just to the right of the Log Cabin. Here, Log Cabin Cutoff, nearly level but rough, runs left 0.2 mi. to Randolph Path, and the very rough Cabin–Cascades Trail to Israel Ridge Path in Cascade Ravine leaves on the right. Water (reliable) is found at the Log Cabin. Lowe's Path now begins to ascend more seriously and crosses Randolph Path at 2.7 mi. At this jct., Randolph Path, angling up to the right, is more obvious than Lowe's Path, which climbs straight ahead up some rocks. Lowe's Path climbs steeply up to the crest of Nowell Ridge then moderates. This section is often icy during cold seasons. At a fine outlook ledge called the Quay at 3.2 mi., the very short Quay Path diverges left to Gray Knob Trail, and 30 yd. farther, Gray Knob Trail crosses. The cabin at Gray Knob is 0.1 mi. left (east) by either route.

Soon Lowe's Path breaks out of the scrub, and from here on, the trail is above treeline and completely exposed to wind. Views are very fine. At 4.1 mi., after a steady ascent up Nowell Ridge, the trail passes just to the left of the 5,355-ft. crag formerly known as Adams 4 and recently renamed Mt. Abigail Adams in honor of the wife of President John Adams. The trail descends into a little sag then rises moderately again, keeping to the left (east) of Mt. Sam Adams. Spur Trail joins on the left, 100 yd. below Thunderstorm Junction, the major intersection with Gulfside Trail at 4.4 mi., where Great Gully Trail also enters on the left. After crossing Gulfside Trail, Lowe's Path climbs moderately up the jumbled rocks of the cone of Mt. Adams, passing the jct. where Israel Ridge Path enters right at 4.5 mi. Climbing almost due east over the rocks (follow cairns carefully),

Lowe's Path reaches the summit of Mt. Adams at 4.7 mi., where the trail meets Air Line and Star Lake Trail.

Descending from the summit, Lowe's Path leads slightly north of west.

CABIN–CASCADES TRAIL (RMC; MAP 1: E9–F9)

From Lowe's Path (3,263 ft.) to:	⇅	↗	○
Israel Ridge Path (2,825 ft.)	1.0 mi.	0 ft. (rev. 450 ft.)	0:30

Constructed in 1881 by AMC, Cabin–Cascades Trail leads from the Log Cabin on Lowe's Path to Israel Ridge Path near the cascades on Cascade Brook, descending almost all the way. Cabin–Cascades Trail is generally rough, with one rather steep, very rough section.

The trail begins at Lowe's Path 2.4 mi. from US 2, opposite the Log Cabin. Cabin–Cascades Trail runs gradually downhill, with minor ups and downs, crossing the Mystic Stream at 0.3 mi. At 0.7 mi., the trail enters Cascade Ravine and descends a steep pitch, passing a limited outlook to the Castles and Mt. Bowman rising over Israel Ridge. The trail then begins the final steep, rough descent to Cascade Brook, ending at Israel Ridge Path just above its upper jct. with the Link. The First Cascade can be reached by descending on Israel Ridge Path 60 yd. to the Link then following it downward to the left another 60 yd. to the ledges at the top of the cascade. The Second Cascade can be seen by following Israel Ridge Path about 150 yd. upward (left).

ISRAEL RIDGE PATH (RMC; MAP 1: E8–F9)

Cumulative from Castle Trail (1,900 ft.) to:	⇅	↗	○
Castle Ravine Trail (2,100 ft.)	0.4 mi.	200 ft.	0:20
The Link (2,800 ft.)	1.2 mi.	900 ft.	1:05
Perch Path (4,300 ft.)	2.4 mi.	2,400 ft.	2:25
Randolph Path, lower jct. (4,825 ft.)	2.8 mi.	2,950 ft.	2:55
Edmands Col (4,938 ft.) via Randolph Path	3.5 mi.	3,050 ft.	3:15
Gulfside Trail (5,250 ft.)	3.3 mi.	3,350 ft.	3:20
Mt. Adams summit (5,799 ft.) via Lowe's Path	4.1 mi.	3,900 ft.	4:00

This trail runs to the summit of Mt. Adams from Castle Trail, 1.3 mi. from US 2 at Bowman (which is 1.0 mi. west of Lowe's Store). Beginning in 1892, J. Rayner Edmands constructed Israel Ridge Path as a graded path. Although hurricanes and slides have severely damaged the original trail, and there have been many relocations, the upper part is still one of the finest and most beautiful of the Randolph trails. Some brook crossings are difficult in high water, and parts of the trail are steep and rough.

From Bowman, follow Castle Trail for 1.3 mi. Here, Israel Ridge Path branches left, and at 0.1 mi., the path makes a double crossing to the east bank of the Israel River. The trail follows the river, passing several small cascades, then turns left up the bank at 0.4 mi., where Castle Ravine Trail diverges right and continues along the river. Israel Ridge Path bears southeast up the slope of Nowell Ridge into Cascade Ravine, climbing moderately at first then becoming steeper and rougher. At 1.2 mi., the Link enters left. The trails coincide for 50 yd., and then the Link diverges right to cross Cascade Brook. The top of the First Cascade can be reached by following the Link 60 yd. downhill to the right. In another 60 yd., Cabin–Cascades Trail enters left from the Log Cabin. Israel Ridge Path now enters virgin growth. From this point to treeline, the forest has never been disturbed by lumbering, although slides and windstorms have done much damage.

The path ascends steeply on the northeast side of Cascade Brook, climbing one ledge on ladders. The path passes open sloping ledges beside the Second Cascade, with a view to the northwest, crosses the brook at the head of this cascade at 1.4 mi. (difficult in high water), turns right downstream for a short distance, then turns left and climbs. The trail ascends steeply up Israel Ridge (sometimes called Emerald Tongue), which rises between Cascade and Castle ravines. At 2.2 mi., after a long, mostly moderate sidehill section along the east side of the ridge with two more ladders up steep ledges, the path turns sharply left (east) where Emerald Trail diverges right to descend steeply into Castle Ravine. Emerald Bluff, a remarkable outlook to the Castles and Castle Ravine that is well worth a visit, can be reached from this jct. in less than 0.2 mi. by following Emerald Trail and a spur path that turns right before the main trail begins its steep descent.

Israel Ridge Path angles up a steep slope then turns right at 2.4 mi., where Perch Path enters left (east), 0.1 mi. from the Perch. Israel Ridge Path ascends steadily south to treeline, where it joins Randolph Path at 2.8 mi. The jct. of Gray Knob Trail with Randolph Path is 70 yd. to the left (north) at this point. For 0.1 mi., Israel Ridge and Randolph paths coincide, then Israel Ridge Path branches to the left and, curving east, ascends the southwest ridge of Mt. Adams—where you have fine views of Castle Ravine, the Castellated Ridge, and Mt. Jefferson—and joins Gulfside Trail at 3.3 mi., just south of Storm Lake. Israel Ridge Path coincides with Gulfside Trail for 0.5 mi., running northeast past Peabody Spring to the Adams–Sam Adams col. At 3.8 mi., with the cairn at Thunderstorm

Junction in sight ahead, Israel Ridge Path branches right from Gulfside Trail and enters Lowe's Path at 3.9 mi., which leads to the summit of Mt. Adams at 4.1 mi. The cairns between Gulfside Trail and Lowe's Path are not very prominent, so in poor visibility it might be better to follow Lowe's Path from Thunderstorm Junction to the summit.

SEC 2

EMERALD TRAIL (RMC; MAP 1: F9)

Cumulative from Castle Ravine Trail and the Link (3,225 ft.) to:	↕	↗	○
Emerald Bluff (4,025 ft.)	0.5 mi.	800 ft.	0:40
Israel Ridge Path (4,050 ft.)	0.6 mi.	850 ft.	0:45

This steep, rough trail connects Israel Ridge Path with Castle Ravine Trail, passing Emerald Bluff, a fine viewpoint to the Castles and Castle Ravine. The short section of Emerald Trail between Israel Ridge Path and Emerald Bluff is uncharacteristically gradual and easy. The path is lightly used and must be followed with some care. Emerald Bluff can be visited from US 2 by a wild, scenic, 7.5-mi. loop hike using Castle Trail, Castle Ravine Trail, Emerald Trail, and Israel Ridge Path.

This trail leaves the combined Castle Ravine Trail and Link 0.2 mi. southeast of their lower jct. and descends slightly across a channel of Castle Brook then climbs a very steep and rough slope, although there are no difficult scrambles. As the trail levels off on the crest of Israel Ridge just south of Emerald Bluff, it turns sharply right. Here, a side path turns left and leads 50 yd. to the viewpoint on Emerald Bluff. The main trail runs at easy grades to Israel Ridge Path 0.2 mi. below its jct. with Perch Path.

MT. JEFFERSON

CASTLE RAVINE TRAIL (RMC; MAP 1: E8–F9)

Cumulative from Israel Ridge Path (2,100 ft.) to:	↕	↗	○
The Link, lower jct. (3,125 ft.)	1.5 mi.	1,050 ft.	1:15
Roof Rock (3,600 ft.)	2.1 mi.	1,500 ft.	1:50
Randolph Path (4,900 ft.)	2.8 mi.	2,800 ft.	2:50

This scenic, challenging trail diverges from Israel Ridge Path 1.7 mi. from US 2 at Bowman and leads through wild and beautiful Castle Ravine to Randolph Path near Edmands Col. Although Castle Ravine Trail is reasonably well sheltered except for the highest section, parts of the trail are very rough, especially where it crosses a great deal of unstable talus on the headwall, which makes footing extremely poor for descending or when the rocks are wet. The trail is well marked (yellow blazes below treeline, orange markings above) but lightly used, and must be followed with some care—particularly at the brook crossings, which are marked with "Path" signs and blazes, and on the headwall, where winter avalanches may remove the markings. Some of the brook crossings may be very difficult at moderate to high water, and the ravine walls are very steep, making rapid flooding likely during heavy rain. Except for very experienced hikers, it would be a very difficult escape route from Edmands Col in bad-weather conditions.

From Bowman, follow Castle Trail and then Israel Ridge Path to a point 1.7 mi. from Bowman. Here, Israel Ridge Path turns left up a slope, and Castle Ravine Trail leads straight ahead near the river. It crosses to the west bank (difficult at high water and not easy at other times) and soon reaches a point abreast of the Forks of Israel, where Cascade and Castle brooks unite to form the Israel River. The trail crosses to the east bank of Castle Brook, passes a fine cascade, and recrosses to the west bank below another cascade. In general, the trail follows the route of an old logging road, now almost imperceptible. After entering Castle Ravine, the trail crosses to the east bank and climbs at a moderate grade well above the brook. At 1.5 mi., the Link enters from the left, and the two trails coincide on a rougher footway. About 0.1 mi. beyond this jct., avoid a beaten path that descends right toward the brook. At 1.7 mi., shortly after a small channel of Castle Brook is crossed, Emerald Trail diverges left (north) for Israel Ridge. After crossing to the southwest side of the main brook in a tract of enchanted, cool, virgin forest beloved of *Musca nigra* (a.k.a. black flies), the Link diverges right for Castle Trail at 1.8 mi., and Castle Ravine Trail continues up the ravine close to the brook, at one point following its bed for about 30 yd. then turning right off it. Near the foot of the headwall, the trail crosses Castle Brook, where an avalanche swept down in 2010, leaving a swath of woody debris on the brook bed; use caution. In 50 yd., the trail recrosses the brook where the avalanche has opened a view up to the Castellated Ridge. On the south side of the brook, the trail winds briefly through a rocky area where water can often be heard running underground then turns left and mounts the steep slope. At 2.1 mi., the trail passes under Roof Rock, a large, flat-bottomed boulder that would provide some shelter in a rainstorm.

Rising very steeply southeast with very rough footing, the trail soon winds up a patch of bare rocks marked by small cairns and dashes of orange paint, where you have good views up to the Castles and down the valley northward to the Pliny Range. The trail reenters the scrub at a large cairn, and in 100 yd. reemerges from the scrub at the foot of a steep slope of very loose rock (use extreme care, particularly when descending). The trail climbs very steeply to the top of the headwall, marked by cairns and paint on rocks, then ascends gradually in a grassy valley with little evident footway and sparsely placed cairns, passing Spaulding Spring on the right and joining Randolph Path (sign) on the rocks to the left of the grassy valley, 0.1 mi. north of Edmands Col. Here, also, the Cornice joins from the right.

Descending, follow Randolph Path north from Edmands Col to the small grassy valley then descend north along it until the line of cairns is found leading down the headwall.

CASTLE TRAIL (AMC; MAP 1: E8–F9)

Cumulative from Bowman (1,500 ft.) to:	⇅	↗	○
Israel Ridge Path (1,900 ft.)	1.3 mi.	400 ft.	0:50
The Link (4,025 ft.)	3.5 mi.	2,550 ft.	3:00
First Castle (4,450 ft.)	3.8 mi.	2,950 ft.	3:20
Mt. Jefferson summit (5,716 ft.)	5.0 mi.	4,200 ft.	4:35

This trail follows the narrow, serrated ridge that runs northwest from Mt. Jefferson, providing magnificent views in a spectacular setting. The part that traverses the Castles is rough with some difficult rock scrambles. In bad weather, Castle Trail can be dangerous due to long and continuous exposure to the northwest winds at and above the Castles. The path was first cut from 1883 to 1884, but much of it has since been relocated.

Castle Trail begins at Bowman on US 2, 3.0 mi. west of the Appalachia parking area and 4.2 mi. east of the jct. of US 2 and NH 115. Park on the north side of Presidential Rail Trail (the former railroad grade). Castle Trail follows the railroad grade to the right (west) for 100 yd. and turns left into the woods just past a gate. The trail crosses a pipeline clearing and then traverses an area of small trees. At 0.3 mi., the trail enters the WMNF, crosses a power line, and soon reaches the bank of the Israel River. Here, the trail turns sharply left and runs along the bank for 60 yd. then crosses the river (may be difficult at high water) at 0.4 mi. (The easiest crossing may be where the trail first comes to the river; on the far side, a beaten path leads left back to where the trail crosses.) On the far side, the trail turns left and parallels the stream for 100 yd. then bears right up a bank and rises at an easy grade through a hardwood forest.

At 1.3 mi., Israel Ridge Path branches left (east) toward the brook. The last sure water is a short distance along this trail. Castle Trail continues to rise above the brook on the northeast flank of Mt. Bowman, and at 1.5 mi., the trail turns sharply right, going away from the brook. Now climbing up the slope at a steeper angle, the trail ascends a long series of rock steps, passes to the right of a very large boulder at 2.2 mi., and becomes much steeper for the next 0.3 mi. At 2.5 mi., the trail enters a blowdown area near the crest of the ridge connecting Mt. Bowman and the Castellated Ridge and becomes almost level. Soon, the trail ascends easily with excellent footing through open woods with abundant ferns and gradually becomes steeper again as it climbs the main ridge below the Castles to a densely wooded shoulder with a sharp, ragged crest. Here, the trail winds along the steep slopes near the ridge crest to a little gap at 3.5 mi., where the Link crosses, coming up from Castle Ravine on the left and leading off to Caps Ridge Trail on the right.

The ridge becomes very narrow, and the trail becomes steep and rough with some difficult scrambles. After passing over two ledges with good outlooks from both, the trail reaches treeline and climbs to the foot of the first and most impressive Castle, a pair of 20-ft. pillars, at 3.8 mi. The view is very fine, especially into Castle Ravine. The trail leads on past a slightly higher but less impressive Castle, runs through a small col filled with scrub that would provide reasonable shelter in a storm, and continues to ascend over and around several higher but lesser crags as the Castellated Ridge blends into the main mass of Mt. Jefferson. At 4.5 mi., the Cornice crosses, leading northeast to Randolph Path near Edmands Col, and south to Caps Ridge and Gulfside trails. Castle Trail ascends moderately over the rocks and joins Mt. Jefferson Loop in a small flat area just northeast of the summit crag.

Descending, Castle Trail leads slightly west of north from the jct. with Mt. Jefferson Loop.

ROLLO FALL PATH (RMC; MAP 1: E8)

From Bowman (1,500 ft.) to:	⇅	↗	↻
Rollo Fall (1,570 ft.)	0.4 mi.	50 ft.	0:15

Near Bowman is Rollo Fall, an attractive cascade on the Moose River, now within the Randolph Community Forest and easily accessible by an unmarked footpath. From parking for Castle Trail at Bowman on the south side of US 2, walk across Presidential Rail Trail and immediately turn left on a grassy woods road that descends gently east. At 0.2 mi. the road swings right (south) and crosses a pipeline clearing. In another 0.1 mi. it crosses a power-line swath, beyond which it becomes a somewhat brushy footpath, bearing left at a fork and ascending to a bank near Rollo Fall at 0.4 mi. Here the path drops to the left and reaches rocks at the base of the falls in 30 yd.

CAPS RIDGE TRAIL (AMC; MAP 1: F8–F9)

SEC
2

Cumulative from Jefferson Notch Rd. (3,008 ft.) to:	⇅	↗	○
The Link (3,800 ft.)	1.1 mi.	800 ft.	0:55
Lower Cap (4,422 ft.)	1.5 mi.	1,400 ft.	1:25
Upper Cap (4,830 ft.)	1.9 mi.	1,800 ft.	1:50
The Cornice (5,025 ft.)	2.1 mi.	2,000 ft.	2:05
Mt. Jefferson summit (5,716 ft.)	2.5 mi.	2,700 ft.	2:35
Jct. with Mt. Jefferson Loop (5,700 ft.)	2.6 mi.	2,700 ft.	2:40
Gulfside Trail (5,275 ft.) via Cornice	2.6 mi.	2,250 ft.	2:25
Mt. Washington summit (6,288 ft.) via Cornice, Gulfside Trail, and Trinity Heights Connector	5.3 mi.	3,650 ft. (rev. 350 ft.)	4:30
Cumulative distance for loop over Caps, Mt. Jefferson, and Castles (via Castle Trail, Link, and Caps Ridge Trail)	6.8 mi.	2,850 ft.	4:50

Caps Ridge Trail makes a direct ascent of Mt. Jefferson from the height-of-land (3,008 ft.) on the road through Jefferson Notch, the pass between Mt. Jefferson and the Dartmouth Range. (This road is closed in winter.) This is the highest trailhead on a public through-road in the White Mountains, making it possible to ascend Mt. Jefferson with much less elevation gain than on any other trail to a Presidential peak over 5,000 ft., except for a few trails that begin high on Mt. Washington Auto Rd. Caps Ridge Trail is steep and rough, however, with numerous ledges that require rock scrambling and are slippery when wet, and the upper part is very exposed to weather. Therefore, the route is more strenuous than might be anticipated from the relatively small distance and elevation gain. (It is not easier to ascend Mt. Washington via Caps Ridge Trail than via Jewell Trail because the descent from Monticello Lawn to Sphinx Col mostly cancels out the advantage of the higher start.)

The south end of Jefferson Notch Rd. is located directly opposite Mt. Clinton Rd. at a crossroads on Cog Railway Base Rd. (the road that runs from US 302 to the Cog Railway). The north end is on Valley Rd. in Jefferson (which runs between US 2 and NH 115). The high point in the notch is about 5.5 mi. from Valley Rd. on the north and 3.4 mi. from Cog Railway Base Rd. on the south. Jefferson Notch Rd. is a good gravel road, open in summer and early fall, but because of the high elevation it reaches, snow and mud disappear late in spring, and ice returns early. Drive with care, as it is winding and narrow in places, and watch out for logging trucks. The southern half is usually in better condition than the northern half, which is often very rough (but still sound).

The trail leaves the parking area and crosses a wet section on log bridges then ascends steadily up the lower part of the ridge. At 1.0 mi., an outcrop of granite on the right provides a fine view, particularly of the summit of Jefferson and the Caps Ridge ahead. Several potholes in this outcrop were formed by glacial meltwater.

About 100 yd. beyond this outcrop, the Link enters from the left, providing a nearly level but very rough path that runs 1.6 mi. to Castle Trail just below the Castles, making possible a very scenic though strenuous loop over the Caps and Castles. Caps Ridge Trail follows the narrow crest of the ridge, becoming steeper and rougher as the trail climbs up into scrub, and views become increasingly frequent. At 1.5 mi., the trail reaches the lowest Cap after a steep scramble up ledges, and it runs entirely in the open from here on. The trail ascends very steeply up the ridge to the highest Cap at 1.9 mi. then continues to climb steeply as the ridge blends into the summit mass. At 2.1 mi., the Cornice enters left, providing a very rough route to Castle Trail and Edmands Col, and then diverges right in 20 yd., providing a relatively easy shortcut to Gulfside Trail at Monticello Lawn and points to the south. Caps Ridge Trail continues climbing steadily northeast and then east over the rocks, keeping a little south of the crest of the ridge, to the summit of Mt. Jefferson (the high point is reached by a short scramble to the left) then descends east 40 yd. to the base of the little conical summit crag, where Caps Ridge Trail meets Mt. Jefferson Loop just above the latter trail's jct. with Castle Trail.

Descending from the summit crag, Caps Ridge Trail leads slightly south of west.

BOUNDARY LINE TRAIL (WMNF; MAP 1: F8)

From Jewell Trail (2,525 ft.) to:	�);↑	↗	↻
Jefferson Notch Rd. (2,525 ft.)	0.8 mi.	50 ft. (rev. 50 ft.)	0:25
From Cog Railway Base Rd. parking area (2,500 ft.) to:			
Caps Ridge Trail (3,008 ft.) via Jewell Trail, Boundary Line Trail, and Jefferson Notch Rd.	2.6 mi.	600 ft.	1:35

This trail connects Jewell Trail, 0.4 mi. from the hikers parking area on Cog Railway Base Rd., with Jefferson Notch Rd., 1.4 mi. south of Caps Ridge Trail. Boundary Line Trail thus provides a shortcut between the trailheads of Caps Ridge Trail and Jewell Trail or Ammonoosuc Ravine Trail (Section One), although Boundary Line Trail is lightly used and must be followed with care. It diverges left (north) from Jewell Trail 0.4 mi. from the Cog Railway Base Rd. parking lot and runs north, nearly level, closely following the straight boundary line between two unincorporated townships. At 0.5 mi., Boundary Line Trail crosses Clay Brook then continues to its end at Jefferson Notch Rd.

MT. CLAY

JEWELL TRAIL (WMNF; MAP 1: F8–F9)

Cumulative from Cog Railway Base Rd. parking area (2,500 ft.) to:	⇅	↗	↻
Clay Brook crossing (2,850 ft.)	1.1 mi.	400 ft. (rev. 50 ft.)	0:45
Gulfside Trail (5,400 ft.)	3.7 mi.	2,950 ft.	3:20
Mt. Washington summit (6,288 ft.) via Gulfside Trail and Trinity Heights Connector	5.0 mi.	3,900 ft. (rev. 50 ft.)	4:25

This trail begins at a parking area on Cog Railway Base Rd., 1.1 mi. from its jct. with Jefferson Notch Rd. and Mt. Clinton Rd. (Cog Railway Base Rd. is the road that leads from US 302 to the Cog Railway Base Station at Marshfield.) The trail ascends the unnamed ridge that leads west from Mt. Clay and ends at Gulfside Trail high on the west slope of Mt. Clay, 0.3 mi. north of the Clay–Washington col and 1.4 mi. north of the summit of Mt. Washington. The grade is constant but seldom steep, there are no rock scrambles, and the footing is generally good below treeline and only moderately rough and rocky in the last section below Gulfside. In combination with Gulfside Trail and Trinity Heights Connector, Jewell Trail provides the easiest route to Mt. Washington from the west, featuring a great length of ridge walking above treeline with fine views, but this part is also greatly exposed to the weather and offers no shelter between the summit and treeline. In bad weather, or if afternoon thunderstorms threaten, it may be safer to descend from Mt. Washington via the Lakes of the Clouds Hut and Ammonoosuc Ravine Trail, despite the steep and slippery footing on the latter; descent by Jewell Trail offers much easier footing and thus may be preferred when the weather cooperates. The trail is named for Sergeant Winfield S. Jewell, once an observer for the Army Signal Corps on Mt. Washington, who perished on the Greely expedition to the Arctic in 1884.

Jewell Trail enters the woods directly across the road from the parking area, descends slightly to cross the Ammonoosuc River on a bridge at 0.1 mi. then swings northeast and ascends at an easy grade. At 0.4 mi., Boundary Line Trail diverges left, and Jewell Trail ascends the crest of the low ridge between the Ammonoosuc River and Clay Brook, joining the old route of the trail at 1.0 mi. Here a link path from the Cog Railway joins on the right (sign: Cog R.R.).

Jewell Link. Jewell Trail can be accessed from the Cog Railway Base Station by this link path. Parking (fee charged) is available in a lower gravel lot on the right (south) side of the Base Rd. (sign: Hiker Parking), 0.4 mi. east of the WMNF trailhead parking area. Elevation is 2,640 ft. (The upper lots are reserved for Cog Railway customers.) Proceed on foot up the walkway on the left side of the access road, through a parking lot on the left, and walk up past the left side of the main Base Station building. The link path (sign: Jewell Trail) starts on the left just beyond Platform A, 0.2 mi. from hiker parking. Elevation is 2,700 ft. Cross the tracks with care and descend a wooden stairway. In 40 yd. the path swings right behind a WMNF welcome sign and crosses the Ammonoosuc River (no bridge; difficult in high water). The unmarked but well-beaten path climbs by switchbacks, passes a closed former route on the right, then ascends easily and swings left to meet Jewell Trail, 0.3 mi. from the Base Station, ascent 200 ft. (15 min.). From hiker parking, 0.5 mi., 250 ft., 20 min.

From the jct. with the link, **Jewell Trail** descends slightly to Clay Brook, crosses on a footbridge at 1.1 mi., then climbs northeast by long switchbacks. At 2.0 mi., the trail passes through a blowdown patch at the edge of the steep wall of Burt Ravine, where you have limited views. The trail then swings somewhat to the north side of the ridge and climbs east, staying well below the ridge crest until near treeline. Reaching treeline at about 3.0 mi., the trail zigzags at a moderate grade with rough, rocky footing up the ridge crest, which quickly becomes less prominent and blends into the slope of Mt. Clay. At 3.5 mi., the trail swings to the right, going away from what remains of the ridge, and angles up the slope at an easy grade to Gulfside Trail. To ascend Mt. Washington, follow Gulfside Trail to the right (south).

PINE MTN.

PINE MTN. TRAIL (WMNF; MAP 5: E10)

From gravel pit on Promenade St. (820 ft.) to:	⮏⮑	⬈	↻
Pine Mtn. summit (2,405 ft.)	2.7 mi.	1,650 ft. (rev. 50 ft.)	2:10

This trail was reopened in the 1990s to restore an abandoned section of Pine Link that once linked an old route of the AT in Gorham with the Northern Presidentials via Pine Mtn. Reach the trailhead by turning west onto Promenade St. from NH 16 at a point 0.25 mi. south of its jct. with US 2, at the eastern edge of the Gorham business district. Follow this road through a residential area and then past a large cemetery on the right at 0.5 mi. from NH 16. The road becomes gravel, rough, and narrow at 0.6 mi. and continues to the edge of a gravel pit at 0.7 mi. from NH 16, where cars may be parked on the left (sign for trail), just before a fork in the road. This parking area is not plowed in winter, at which time hikers should use public parking in the business district.

The trail ascends on a narrow path south through the woods, reaching a natural gas pipeline clearing used as a snowmobile trail in 0.1 mi. (In the reverse direction, look carefully for the left turn off the pipeline clearing; the trail sign is down at the lower edge.) Follow the brushy pipeline clearing right (west) for another 0.1 mi., then Pine Mtn. Trail turns left (south) into the woods (sign). Pine Mtn. Trail now follows an old road (also a snowmobile trail), bearing left at a fork in 50 yd. and bearing left at a second fork in another 200 yd. At 0.5 mi. the trail turns right off this road (sign) and passes through an old logging cut then swings left onto a small ridge (arrow) and ascends. At 1.3 mi., the trail descends briefly to a swampy saddle, enters the WMNF, and angles up the northwest slope of Pine Mtn., crossing several old logging roads. At 2.1 mi., a spur path leads 50 yd. left to a limited view to the north. At 2.3 mi., the grade eases and the trail swings left under utility lines; here, at a sign for Chapel Rock, a well-constructed path ascends to the left and in 0.1 mi. reaches the northeast summit and the Horton Center worship area, where there is an excellent view from a rocky pinnacle called Chapel Rock; ascent is 100 ft.

Enjoy the views and meditate, but please avoid disturbing religious activities that may be in progress there (at which times the side path may be roped off). The main trail follows bog bridges under the utility lines for 60 yd. then bears right into the woods at a sign and ascends to a four-way jct. at 2.4 mi.; straight ahead (sign) yellow-blazed Pine Mtn. Loop Trail leads 0.2 mi. to Pine Mtn. Rd. The portion of the old tractor road diverging sharply right here leads to the private Horton Center and is not open to the public. Hikers are requested to use Pine Mtn. Loop Trail and not follow the road past the buildings of the Horton Center. Turning left here, Pine Mtn. Trail ascends the old tractor road (also signed as Pinkham Ledge Trail) 0.3 mi. to the summit of Pine Mtn., passing three signed side paths left to eastern outlooks: Chapel View, which leads 60 yd. to a ledge with an impressive view of Chapel Rock; Gorham View; and Angel View. From the viewless summit, where footings from an old fire tower remain, Ledge Trail descends 0.1 mi. ahead to the south cliffs and excellent views.

PINE MTN. ROAD AND PINE MTN. LOOP TRAIL (HC; MAP 1: E10)

Cumulative from Pinkham B Rd. (Dolly Copp Rd.; 1,650 ft.) to:	⇅	↗	○
Ledge Trail (1,800 ft.)'	0.9 mi.	200 ft. (rev. 50 ft.)	0:35
Pine Mtn. summit (2,405 ft.) via Pine Mtn. Loop Trail and Pine Mtn. Trail	2.0 mi.	800 ft.	1:25
Loop to Pine Mtn. via Ledge Trail, with return via Pine Mtn. Trail, Pine Mtn. Loop, and Pine Mtn. Road	3.5 mi.	850 ft.	2:10

This trail uses the private automobile road to the Horton Center on Pine Mtn. most of the way to the summit of Pine Mtn. The road begins a little northwest of the highest point of Pinkham B Rd. (Dolly Copp Rd.), opposite the Pine Link trailhead, where parking is available. This trailhead is 2.4 mi. from US 2 (at the foot of the big hill west of Gorham) and 1.9 mi. from NH 16 near Dolly Copp Campground. Pine Mtn. Road is closed to public vehicular use and has a locked gate but is open to the public as a foot trail to the summit, using Pine Mtn. Loop Trail and Pine Mtn. Trail for the upper part of the climb; hikers should watch out for Horton Center–affiliated cars along the road. Ledge Trail diverges from the road and runs over the top of the south cliff and to the summit; it is frequently used to make a loop over the summit.

The views from the summit area are fine, both to the much higher surrounding peaks—particularly Mt. Madison—and to the valleys of the Androscoggin, Moose, and Peabody rivers. The Horton Center, a private center for renewal and education operated by the New Hampshire Conference of the United Church of Christ (Congregational), occupies a tract of 100 acres on the summit. The center consists of six buildings and an outdoor chapel on the northeast peak, which has excellent views and can be reached by a spur path from Pine Mtn. Trail. Please avoid disturbing religious activities that may be in progress. Hikers are requested to use Pine Mtn. Loop Trail and not follow Pine Mtn. Road past the buildings of the Horton Center.

The road runs northeast from Pinkham B Rd., descends across a shallow col, and winds its way up the south and west flanks of the mountain. At 0.9 mi., Ledge Trail branches right to climb to the summit by way of the south cliff. The road now climbs more steadily, and at 1.5 mi. from Pinkham B Rd., the route to Pine Mtn. turns right into the woods on yellow-blazed Pine Mtn. Loop Trail; there is a large yellow sign just before the junction. Pine Mtn. Loop Trail climbs along the slope to the east of the road, bypassing the Horton Center and reaching a four-way jct. at 1.7 mi. To the right, Pine Mtn. Trail (also signed as Pinkham Ledge Trail) leads 0.3 mi. to the summit and the upper end of Ledge Trail, passing three signed side paths left to eastern outlooks; reach the excellent views from the south cliff by descending Ledge Trail for 0.1 mi. Continuing straight from the four-way jct., Pine Mtn. Trail leads 0.1 mi. to the side path to Chapel Rock. The trail leading sharply left from the four-way jct. to the Horton Center is not open to the public.

SEC 2

LEDGE TRAIL (WMNF; MAP 1: E10)

From Pine Mtn. Road (1,800 ft.) to:	⇅	↗	○
Pine Mtn. summit (2,405 ft.)	0.6 mi.	600 ft.	0:35

This trail, sparsely blazed in yellow, runs to the summit of Pine Mtn. from Pine Mtn. Rd. (a private road, closed to public vehicles), making possible an attractive loop with a sporty ascent past excellent views and an easy return. Ledge Trail diverges right from Pine Mtn. Rd. 0.9 mi. from Pinkham B Rd. (Dolly Copp Rd.), ascends through woods to the base of the south cliff, then swings left up a ledge with a fine view south at 0.3 mi. It climbs steeply through woods to the east of the cliff with several easy scrambles then swings left up broad glacier-scraped ledges to the cliff top, where you have beautiful views to the south and west. The trail then ascends gradually through woods for 0.1 mi. and meets Pine Mtn. Trail at the wooded summit, where footings from an old fire tower remain.

PLEASURE PATHS ON THE LOWER NORTH SLOPES

TOWN LINE BROOK TRAIL (RMC; MAP 1: E10)

From Pinkham B Rd. (Dolly Copp Rd.; 1,475 ft.) to:	⇅	↗	○
End of path above Triple Falls (1,725 ft.)	0.2 mi.	250 ft.	0:15

This short but steep yellow-blazed path gives access to Triple Falls from Pinkham B Rd. (Dolly Copp Rd.) 1.9 mi. southeast of US 2. Triple Falls are beautiful cascades on Town Line Brook named Proteus, Erebus, and Evans. The watershed is steep, and the rainwater runs off very rapidly, so the falls should be visited during or immediately after a rainfall. Parking is at a pulloff on the north side of the road, just west of the bridge over the brook. The trail starts at a sign on the south side of the road just east of the brook. It climbs moderately then steeply along the brookbank, and at

0.1 mi. a side path leads 20 yd. right to a view of Proteus Fall (sign). Above here the trail remains steep and runs along the edge of a gorge with a steep dropoff; use caution, especially in wet weather. It climbs past Erebus Fall and soon reaches Evans Fall (sign). The trail continues another 50 yd. upstream and ends at an RMC trail sign.

SEC 2

SYLVAN WAY (RMC; MAP 1: E9)

From Memorial Bridge (1,425 ft.) to:	⇅	↗	↻
Howker Ridge Trail (1,625 ft.)	1.7 mi.	250 ft. (rev. 50 ft.)	1:00

Sylvan Way departs from the Link at the east end of Memorial Bridge, 0.7 mi. from the Appalachia parking area, and leads over Snyder Brook to Howker Ridge Trail just above Coosauk Fall. Leaving Memorial Bridge, after 80 yd., Sylvan Way turns left away from Cold Brook at the base of Cold Brook Fall, where a beaten path continues ahead up the brook. Sylvan Way descends across Beechwood Way at 0.1 mi. then runs nearly level and crosses Air Line at 0.6 mi. and Valley Way 100 yd. farther. At 0.7 mi., within a space of 30 yd., Maple Walk enters left, Fallsway crosses, Sylvan Way crosses Snyder Brook on ledges 60 yd. above Gordon Fall, and Brookbank crosses. From here, Sylvan Way ascends gradually, crossing Randolph Path at 1.1 mi. Sylvan Way then passes through a brushy logged area and continues to Howker Ridge Trail.

FALLSWAY (RMC; MAP 1: E9)

From Appalachia parking area (1,306 ft.) to:	⇅	↗	↻
Valley Way jct. above Tama Fall (1,700 ft.)	0.7 mi.	400 ft.	0:35

Fallsway is an attractive alternative route to the first 0.6 mi. of Valley Way, following close to Snyder Brook and passing several falls. From the east end of the Appalachia parking area, the trail goes east for 60 yd. then turns right onto a gravel road and crosses Presidential Rail Trail (where Brookbank diverges left) and the power lines, then enters the woods and continues straight ahead. At 0.2 mi. from Appalachia, Fallsway reaches Snyder Brook and soon passes Gordon Fall. In 60 yd., Sylvan Way crosses and Maple Walk enters right as the trail continues up the west bank of the brook in hemlock woods. Lower and Upper Salroc Falls are passed, and soon Fallsway enters Valley Way at 0.6 mi., below Tama Fall. In 30 yd., Fallsway leaves Valley Way and passes Tama Fall, where Brookbank enters left, and in another 60 yd., Fallsway ends at Valley Way.

BROOKBANK (RMC; MAP 1: E9)

From lower jct. with Fallsway (1,310 ft.) to:	↥↧	↗	↻
Upper jct. with Fallsway (1,675 ft.)	0.7 mi.	350 ft.	0:30

Brookbank follows the lower part of Snyder Brook on the opposite side from Fallsway. Brookbank leaves Fallsway on the left, 100 yd. from Appalachia, and follows Presidential Rail Trail east for 0.1 mi. to a bridge over Snyder Brook. Across the bridge, Brookbank turns right and in 70 yd. reaches a power line. Here, the trail turns right again and then, in 20 yd., swings left and enters the woods. It runs up the east side of the brook, passing Gordon Fall, Sylvan Way, Lower and Upper Salroc Falls, and Tama Fall. Above Tama Fall, the trail recrosses the brook on ledges and reenters Fallsway.

MAPLE WALK (RMC; MAP 1: E9)

From Valley Way (1,310 ft.) to:	↥↧	↗	↻
Sylvan Way and Fallsway (1,400 ft.)	0.2 mi.	100 ft.	0:10

Maple Walk diverges left from Valley Way, a few yd. beyond the power line crossing just south of the Appalachia parking area, and runs at easy grades to the jct. of Fallsway and Sylvan Way just above Gordon Fall.

BEECHWOOD WAY (RMC; MAP 1: E9)

From the Link (1,400 ft.) to:	↥↧	↗	↻
Valley Way (1,850 ft.)	0.8 mi.	450 ft.	0:40

This path runs from the Link, 0.6 mi. from Appalachia, to Valley Way, 0.9 mi. from Appalachia, just below its jct. with the Brookside and Randolph Path. Beechwood Way follows a good logging road with moderate grades. The trail leaves the Link, crosses Sylvan Way in 100 yd. and then Air Line at 0.6 mi., passes through a fine stand of tall sugar maples, and ends at Valley Way.

SECTION THREE
FRANCONIA, TWIN, AND WILLEY RANGES

INTRODUCTION

The central region of the White Mountains is a great wooded area studded with fine peaks, with no through-highways and only a few gravel roads near the edges. The vast expanses of unbroken forest compensate for mountains that are, except for the Franconia Range and the cliffs of Mt. Bond, generally less rugged than the Presidentials. The region is bordered on the west and northwest by US 3 and I-93, on the northeast by US 302, on the east by NH 16, and on the south by the Kancamagus Highway (NH 112). Section Three includes the west and northwest portion of this central region, including the Franconia Range, Twin Range, and Willey Range. Most of the 45,000-acre Pemigewasset Wilderness is also covered here. (The southeastern part of the Pemigewasset Wilderness, including Mt. Hancock and Mt. Carrigain, is covered in Section Four.) All of Section Three is covered by AMC's *White Mountains Trail Map 2: Franconia–Pemigewasset*. In this section, the AT follows Liberty Spring Trail and Franconia Ridge Trail over Little Haystack Mtn. and Mt. Lincoln to Mt. Lafayette. The AT then runs along Garfield Ridge Trail to AMC's Galehead Hut, passing close to the summit of Mt. Garfield along the way. After following Twinway over South Twin Mtn. and Mt. Guyot and passing near the summit of Zealand Mtn., the AT reaches AMC's Zealand Falls Hut, then takes Ethan Pond Trail to US 302 in Crawford Notch.

FRANCONIA NOTCH AND THE FLUME

Franconia Notch lies between the Franconia Range on the east and the Kinsman Range and Cannon Mtn. on the west. The notch is traversed by a section of I-93 known as the Franconia Notch Parkway; there are several trailheads off the Parkway. The region includes many interesting and accessible natural features, such as Indian Head; Profile, Echo, and Lonesome lakes; and the Flume, the Pool, and the Basin. The most famous of all Franconia Notch features—the Profile (Old Man of the Mountain)— was destroyed by the natural forces that created it, gravity and erosion, in May 2003. The Flume and the Pool are described later; the others, which are west of US 3, are discussed in Section Five. From the Flume area north to Echo Lake, the valley bottom and lower slopes on both sides of it lie within Franconia Notch State Park. Information regarding trails and other facilities is available during the summer and fall tourist season at the Flume Visitor Center at the south end of the park and throughout the year (except for the late-fall and early-spring off-seasons) at the Cannon Mtn. Tramway. Information is also available from the information center in Lincoln, located opposite the Exit 32 I-93 northbound exit ramp. Hiker parking is available at the Flume Visitor Center, Whitehouse Trail, Basin, Lafayette Place, Old Man, Cannon Mtn. Tramway, and Echo Lake parking lots. No parking is available at the AT crossing near the former Whitehouse Bridge site, which is reached by Whitehouse Trail from the hikers parking lot on US 3, just north of the Flume Visitor Center. A paved bike path (Franconia Notch Recreation Path, in places signed as the "F.N.S.P. Multi-Use Trail") runs the entire length of the notch, from the parking area at the Flume to Skookumchuck Trail, and is available for pedestrian use, although those on foot should be careful not to impede bicycle traffic unnecessarily. A brief description of this path is provided in the Section Three Trail Descriptions. Concord Coach Lines has daily bus service from Boston at Logan Airport and South Station to Lincoln and Franconia. In summer, connections to trailheads can be made by using the AMC Hiker Shuttle.

The Flume, one of the best-known features in the Franconia region, is a narrow gorge that can be reached from the Flume Visitor Center by graded trails or by an NHDP bus. A network of graded trails connects points of interest, and a boardwalk runs up through the Flume itself. The center is open to visitors from about May 15 to October 15; an admission fee for the Flume and the Pool is charged during this time. In the Flume, one can see broad ledges that have been worn smooth by the action of the water and that were scoured by an avalanche in June 1883 that swept away the once famous suspended boulder. Avalanche Falls at the upper end is also worth visiting. The Pool is an interesting pothole formation in the Pemigewasset River, more than 100 ft. in diameter and 40 ft. deep; the Pool can be reached in 0.6 mi. from the visitor center via Flume Path and Wildwood Path. Flume Path, Rim Path, Ridge Path, and Wildwood Path can be used to make a 2.1-mi. loop walk (500 ft. of elevation gain, 1 hr. 20 min.) from the visitor center that visits the Flume, Liberty Gorge and Cascade, and the Pool, with a view of Mt. Liberty and Mt. Flume. In winter, this is an easy, popular, and beautiful area to walk or snowshoe in and has no admission fee; however, several of the boardwalks are removed for the season, restricting access to some parts of the Flume. From the south end of the Flume parking lot, Roaring River Memorial Nature Trail (no fee) makes a 0.3-mi. loop through the woods, passing a gazebo with a view of Mt. Liberty and Mt. Flume.

ROAD ACCESS

Several seasonal gravel roads maintained by the WMNF provide access to trails on the northern side of Section Three. Gale River Loop Rd. (FR 25 and FR 92) makes a 4.4-mi. loop on the south side of US 3, passing trailheads for Gale River Trail and Garfield Trail. Its eastern terminus is across from the jct. of US 3 with Trudeau Rd. (a location sometimes called Five Corners), 4.4 mi. east of the jct. of US 3 and NH 141 and 5.3 mi. west of the stoplight in Twin Mountain. The western terminus is 0.3 mi. from the eastern terminus. Haystack Rd. (FR 304) runs 2.5 mi. from US 3, 2.5 mi. west of the stoplight in Twin Mountain, to the trailhead for North Twin Trail. Zealand Rd. (FR 16) runs 3.5 mi. from US 302, starting 2.2 mi. east of the stoplight in Twin Mountain, leading to trailheads for Sugarloaf Trail, Hale Brook Trail, and Zealand Trail. None of these roads is maintained for winter travel.

SEC 3

GEOGRAPHY

The 45,000-acre Pemigewasset Wilderness is a vast forested area surrounded by tall mountains and drained by the East Branch of the Pemigewasset River. In the late nineteenth century, this was an untracked wilderness, but lumber operations from about 1890 to 1940 left it logged and burned, in places a virtual wasteland. Although the birch forests that clothe its slopes in many areas still testify subtly to the devastation of the not-so-distant past, the beauty of the area is almost completely restored. The history of the logging, and of the railroads that made it possible, is recounted in C. Francis Belcher's *Logging Railroads of the White Mountains* (AMC Books, 1980, currently out of print) and *J. E. Henry's Logging Railroads,* by Bill Gove (Bondcliff Books). Many of the valley trails in this region follow the beds of the old logging railroads, providing some of the easiest walking in the White Mountains. The trailhead at Lincoln Woods, on the Kancamagus Highway, 5.6 mi. east of the information center at I-93's Exit 32 in Lincoln, is the major gateway to this network of valley trails. In accordance with USFS Wilderness policy, the trails in the Pemigewasset Wilderness are generally maintained to a lower standard than are trails outside Wilderness Areas. Considerable care may be required to follow them.

The main part of the Pemigewasset Wilderness, north of the East Branch, is divided into two lobes by the long ridge of Mt. Bond.

The Franconia Range and the Twin Range are the two high ridges that form a great horseshoe enclosing the western lobe of the Pemigewasset Wilderness. This lobe is drained by Franconia and Lincoln brooks, which almost encircle the long wooded ridge called Owl's Head Mtn. Starting at the southwest end of the horseshoe and running almost due north, the main ridge rises over several lower mountains to the high peaks of the Franconia Range: mts. Flume, Liberty, Little Haystack, Lincoln, and Lafayette—the high point on the ridge. Swinging around to the east, the ridge crosses Mt. Garfield, Galehead Mtn., and South Twin Mtn., passing its lowest point (other than the ends), about 3,400 ft., between Garfield and Galehead. Rising again to South Twin Mtn., where a major spur ridge leads north to North Twin Mtn., the main ridge runs southeast to Mt. Guyot.

Here, another major spur, Zealand Ridge, runs east. Before Zealand Ridge comes to an abrupt end at Zealand Notch, another ridge runs north from Zealand Ridge over the Little River Mtns., which consist of Mt. Hale and the Sugarloaves. From Mt. Guyot, the main ridge runs south over Mt. Bond and Bondcliff before dropping to the East Branch. To the east of the great horseshoe lies the Willey Range, forming the west wall of Crawford Notch and the east wall of the broad, flat eastern lobe of the Pemigewasset Wilderness. The Rosebrook Range is a lower northwest spur of the Willey Range. Running south from the Willey Range is the broad plateau that connects the Willey Range to the Nancy Range and Mt. Carrigain. Slopes rise steeply to this plateau from Crawford Notch, bearing the highest waterfalls in the White Mountains, then incline gradually westward into the Pemigewasset Wilderness.

The Franconia Range ranks second among the ranges of the White Mountains in elevation. Its sharp, narrow ridge contrasts strikingly with the broad, massive Presidential Range. Once called "Great Haystack" on Carrigain's map of 1816, Mt. Lafayette (5,260 ft.) was renamed in honor of the Marquis de Lafayette, in gratitude for his assistance in the War of Independence. Its rocky, serrated crest descends gently north to the mountain's North Peak (5,060 ft.). The main part of the ridge, extending south from Mt. Lafayette over Mt. Lincoln (5,089 ft.) to Little Haystack Mtn. (4,780 ft.), rises well above treeline. This part of the ridge is a gothic masterpiece. Especially when seen from the west (particularly from North Kinsman), the ridge suggests the ruins of a gigantic medieval cathedral. The peaks along the high, serrated ridge are like towers supported by soaring buttresses that rise from the floor of the notch. Part of the ridge between Lincoln and Little Haystack is a knife-edge with interesting rock formations. To the south rise the sharp, ledgy peaks of Mt. Liberty (4,459 ft.) and Mt. Flume (4,328 ft.), which are connected to each other and to Little Haystack Mtn. by long, graceful wooded ridges. Both of these peaks have very fine views in all directions, particularly to the east, to rugged Mt. Bond and over the vast expanse of the Pemigewasset Wilderness. Eagle Cliff (3,420 ft.), a northwesterly spur of Mt. Lafayette, is remarkable for its sheer cliffs and for the "Eaglet," a detached finger of rock that is seen best from the vicinity of the Cannon Mtn. Tramway parking area. At the south end of the range are Whaleback Mtn. (3,586 ft.), Big Coolidge Mtn. (3,294 ft.), and Little Coolidge Mtn. (2,421 ft.), whose south ledges overlook the town of Lincoln; there are no maintained trails to these peaks.

The Twin Range is connected to the Franconia Range by Garfield Ridge. This jumbled, mostly densely wooded ridge runs north from Lafayette then swings to the east and culminates in the fine rocky peak of Mt. Garfield (4,500 ft.). Rising like a watchful sphinx over the valleys of Franconia Brook and Lincoln Brook to the south, Garfield provides one of the finest views in the White Mountains, including a spectacular panorama of the higher Franconias to the southwest. After passing Galehead Mtn. (4,024 ft.), a wooded hump with an outlook over the Twin Brook valley from near the edge of its summit plateau, the ridge reaches South Twin Mtn. (4,902 ft.), where the views from the open summit are similar to Garfield's and equally fine, but from a different perspective. The summit of North Twin Mtn. (4,761 ft.) is densely wooded, but a ledge almost at the summit on the west and another a short distance northeast provide magnificent views. Haystack Mtn. (2,713 ft.), sometimes also called the Nubble, is a small but very prominent rocky peak that rises sharply from the lower end of North Twin's north ridge; it has no maintained trail.

The main ridge swings southeast from South Twin, then south, crossing the bare summits of Mt. Guyot (4,580 ft.) and Mt. Bond (4,698 ft.), and then Bondcliff (4,265 ft.), the fine series of crags and ledges southwest of Mt. Bond. These three peaks, in addition to the spur of Bond called West Bond (4,540 ft.), command views unequaled in the White Mountains for their expansive vistas of forests and mountains with virtually no sign of roads or buildings. Arnold Guyot was the geographer who made the first accurate map of the White Mountains, supplanting the previous best map, the work of Professor G. P. Bond of Harvard; thus, the most remote set of peaks in the White Mountains bear the names of these two pioneer mapmakers. Guyot himself named several important White Mountains peaks, including Mt. Tripyramid. Wherever there were mountains to be explored, Guyot could be found: Mountains are also named for him in the Great Smoky Mtns., the Colorado Rockies, and the Sierra Nevada of California. Even a crater on the moon bears his name.

The interior of the western lobe of the Pemigewasset Wilderness is a relatively narrow valley surrounded by steep slopes and occupied mainly by the long wooded ridge of Owl's Head Mtn. (4,025 ft.), one of the more

SEC 3

remote major peaks in the White Mountains, named for the shape of its south end. The flat summit is wooded, but a slide on its western slope provides fine views up to the Franconia Ridge and the isolated valley of Lincoln Brook.

The high point of Zealand Ridge, Zealand Mtn. (4,260 ft.), is wooded and viewless, but there is a magnificent outlook from Zeacliff (3,600 ft.), a crag that overlooks Zealand Notch and the eastern part of the Pemigewasset Wilderness from the east end of the ridge. Originally called the New Zealand Valley, presumably owing to its remoteness, the name was shortened to Zealand for the convenience of the railroad and post office. Much of Zealand Notch and the area to the north was reduced to a jumble of seared rock and sterile soil by intensely hot forest fires in 1886 and 1903. Except for the open rocks of Whitewall Mtn. on the east side of the notch, this area has made a reasonably complete recovery, a remarkable and outstanding testimony to the infinite healing powers of nature. Nowhere else in New England is there a better example of regeneration after disaster. At the height-of-land at the north end of Zealand Notch is Zealand Pond, which has beaver dams as well as outlets at both ends; its waters eventually flow to the sea in the Merrimack and Connecticut rivers.

The Little River Mtns., lying between the Zealand River and Little River, offer excellent and easily attained panoramas of the surrounding summits from Middle Sugarloaf (2,539 ft.) and North Sugarloaf (2,310 ft.). The steady growth of a fringe of trees around the open summit of Mt. Hale (4,054 ft.) has almost totally obscured what was once an extensive view from this peak—the highest summit of this minor range—which was named for the Rev. Edward Everett Hale, author of the well-known patriotic tale "The Man without a Country."

The Willey Range is a high ridge that rises sharply out of Crawford Notch. The ridge is rather narrow with steep sides, giving it a rugged appearance from many viewpoints, but its crest undulates gently for about 2.5 mi. with relatively broad summits and shallow cols. The main peaks (from south to north) are Mt. Willey (4,285 ft.), named for the family whose members were all killed by a landslide that swept down its very steep east face in 1826; Mt. Field (4,340 ft.), named for Darby Field, leader of the first recorded ascent of Mt. Washington; and Mt. Tom (4,051 ft.), named for Thomas Crawford, younger brother of Ethan Allen Crawford and fellow White Mountain innkeeper. All of these peaks are wooded to the top, but Mt. Willey has fine outlooks to the east over Crawford Notch and to the southwest, into the eastern lobe of the Pemigewasset Wilderness. Mt. Tom temporarily offers a good view south and east from a blowdown patch near the summit; a view from a similar blowdown patch on the west side, at the true summit, is now partly obscured. Near the summit of Mt. Field is an outlook to the northeast and a restricted view west. A westerly spur of the Willey Range ends abruptly at Zealand Notch with the cliffs and talus slopes of trailless Whitewall Mtn. (3,405 ft.). The easterly spurs of Mt. Avalon (3,442 ft.) and Mt. Willard (2,865 ft.) offer fine views for relatively little exertion; perhaps no other spot in the White Mountains affords so grand a view with so little effort as Mt. Willard. The Rosebrook Range continues northwest from Mt. Tom over Mt. Echo (3,084 ft.), Mt. Stickney (3,043 ft.), Mt. Rosebrook (3,004 ft.), and Mt. Oscar (2,746 ft.). These peaks have no hiking trails, but the summit ledges of Mt. Oscar, with magnificent views over the Zealand Valley, can be reached by following ski slopes of the West Mtn. section of Bretton Woods Ski Area to a point near the summit of Mt. Oscar; the ledges are a short distance behind the top of the ski slopes.

SEC 3

Arethusa Falls and Ripley Falls are situated on brooks that flow down the steep west side of Crawford Notch; in times of high water, these waterfalls can be spectacular. Between them stands Frankenstein Cliff, named for Godfrey N. Frankenstein, an artist whose work in the White Mountains was once well known. A network of trails connects these features and affords the opportunity for a variety of shorter day hikes.

The interior of the eastern lobe is broad and relatively flat, with several low, wooded ridges that are both trailless and nameless, but Thoreau Falls, Ethan Pond, and Shoal Pond are interesting features. This region was the site of the most extensive logging in the White Mountains; in the wake of the devastation that resulted, part of the eastern lobe was commonly referred to as the Desolation region.

HUTS

For more than 125 years, AMC's White Mountain hut system has offered hikers a bunk for the night in spectacular locations, with home-cooked dinners and breakfasts, cold running water, and composting or waterless toilets. Reservations are highly recommended; limited drinks, snacks, and gear are available for purchase by day visitors. For information concerning AMC's huts or the Highland Center Lodge at Crawford Notch, including opening and closing schedules and pricing, contact AMC's Reservations Office (603-466-2727) or visit outdoors.org/lodging.

Greenleaf Hut (AMC)

Greenleaf Hut was built in 1929 and is located at an elevation of 4,220 ft. at the jct. of Old Bridle Path and Greenleaf Trail on Mt. Lafayette, overlooking Eagle Lake. Reach Greenleaf Hut from US 3 via Greenleaf Trail (2.7 mi.) or Old Bridle Path (2.9 mi.); the hut is 1.1 mi. from the summit of Mt. Lafayette and 7.7 mi. from Galehead Hut. Greenleaf Hut accommodates 48 guests in three bunkrooms and is open to the public from mid-May to mid-October (caretaker basis in May). Pets are not permitted in the hut.

Galehead Hut (AMC)

Galehead Hut, built in 1932 and completely rebuilt in between 1999 and 2000, is located at an elevation of 3,780 ft. on a little hump on Garfield Ridge, near Twinway and Garfield Ridge, Frost, and Twin Brook trails. Reach the hut in 4.7 mi. from Gale River Loop Rd. (FR 25 and FR 92) via Gale River and Garfield Ridge trails. Galehead Hut accommodates 38 guests in four bunkrooms and is open to the public from mid-May to mid-October (caretaker basis in May). Pets are not permitted in the hut.

Zealand Falls Hut (AMC)

This hut, built in 1932, is located at an elevation of 2,640 ft. beside Zealand Falls on Whitewall Brook, at the north end of Zealand Notch, near Twinway, Zealand, and Ethan Pond trails. Reach the hut from Zealand Rd. via Zealand Trail and Twinway in 2.7 mi.; in winter, Zealand Rd. is closed, which increases the approach walk to 6.5 mi. The hut accommodates 36 guests in four bunkrooms and is open to the public from early June to mid-October on a full-service basis with meals available, and on a caretaker basis the rest of the year. Pets are not permitted in the hut.

Highland Center at Crawford Notch
and Shapleigh Bunkhouse (AMC)

Located on 26 acres of private land at the head of Crawford Notch, the Highland Center is a lodging and education center open to the public year-round. It is located at the site of the former Crawford House grand hotel on US 302, about 20 mi. west of North Conway and 8.7 mi. east of the stoplight in Twin Mountain. The Highland Center is a stop on the AMC Hiker Shuttle routes during summer and on fall weekends. Read more about Highland Center programs and accommodations, including the Shapleigh Bunkhouse, on p. 14.

CAMPING

Pemigewasset Wilderness

In accordance with USFS Wilderness policy, hiking group size may not exceed ten people, and no more than ten people may occupy any designated or non-designated campsite. Camping and wood or charcoal fires are not allowed within 200 ft. of any trail in the Pemigewasset Wilderness except at designated campsites. See p. xiii for more information on Wilderness Area regulations.

SEC
3

Forest Protection Areas

The WMNF has established a number of FPAs, where camping and wood or charcoal fires are prohibited throughout the year. See p. xxiv for general FPA regulations.

No camping is permitted above treeline (where trees are less than 8 ft. tall), except in winter, and then only in places where there is at least 2 ft. of snow cover on the ground—but not on any frozen body of water.

No camping is permitted within 0.25 mi. of any trailhead, picnic area, or any facility for overnight accommodation, such as a hut, cabin, shelter, tentsite, or campground, except as designated at the facility itself. In the area covered by Section Three, camping is also forbidden within 0.25 mi. of Thoreau Falls, or within 0.25 mi. of the East Branch of the Pemigewasset River (including islands) from the Kancamagus Highway to Franconia Brook.

No camping is permitted within 200 ft. of certain trails, except at designated sites. In 2016, designated trails included those portions of Old Bridle Path, Falling Waters Trail, and Liberty Spring Trail that are not in Franconia Notch State Park (where trailside camping is absolutely prohibited), Franconia Falls Trail, and all trails in the Pemigewasset Wilderness. Camping is also prohibited within 200 ft. of Black Pond and within 200 ft. of the East Branch of the Pemigewasset River, from the Wilderness boundary to its crossing with Thoreau Falls Trail, including islands.

No camping is permitted on WMNF land within 0.25 mi. of certain roads except at designated sites (camping on private roadside land is illegal except by permission of the landowner). In 2016, these roads included US 302, Haystack Rd. (FR 304), Gale River Loop Rd. (FR 25 and FR 92), Zealand Rd. (FR 16), and the Kancamagus Highway (NH 112).

Franconia Notch State Park

Camping and fires are prohibited in Franconia Notch State Park, except at Lafayette Place Campground (NHDP; fee charged; nhstateparks.org) on the west side of the parkway.

Established Trailside Campsites

To reduce overcrowding, during peak summer and fall periods, groups of six or more planning to use AMC-managed backcountry campsites are required to use AMC's group notification system. For more information, visit outdoors.org/group_notification. In summer and fall, some of these campsites fill up quickly; when capacity is reached, the caretaker will direct backpackers to a designated overflow area.

13 Falls Tentsite (AMC), located at the jct. of Franconia Brook, Lincoln Brook, and Twin Brook trails, has nine tent pads. A caretaker is present during the summer months, and a fee is charged.

Franconia Brook Tentsite (WMNF) is located on Pemi East Side Trail, 2.7 mi. from the Kancamagus Highway. There are 24 tentsites and platforms; reservations can be made in advance or at the site itself. It is dangerous to cross to the trails on the west side of the East Branch in times of high water.

Guyot Campsite (AMC), located on a spur path that diverges from Bondcliff Trail between its jct. with Twinway and the summit of Mt. Bond, has an open log shelter accommodating 12, and six tent platforms. A fine spring is reliable in summer but may not always flow in the cold seasons. A caretaker is present during the summer months, and a fee is charged. In 2016 significant improvements were underway for this campsite, including construction of an additional platform.

Liberty Spring Tentsite (AMC), located near a fine spring on Liberty Spring Trail, 0.3 mi. below its jct. with Franconia Ridge Trail, has 10 tent platforms. A caretaker is present during the summer months, and a fee is charged.

Garfield Ridge Campsite (AMC), located near a fine spring on a spur path from Garfield Ridge Trail, 0.4 mi. east of Mt. Garfield, has seven tent platforms and one 12-person shelter, newly constructed in 2011 to replace an older shelter. A caretaker is present during the summer months, and a fee is charged.

Ethan Pond Campsite (AMC) is located near the shore of Ethan Pond, 2.7 mi. from the Willey House Station via Ethan Pond Trail and a spur path. The campsite has one shelter that sleeps eight and five tent platforms that sleep 20 total. Water (which is not fit to drink without treatment) may be obtained where the side path crosses the inlet brook. A caretaker is present during the summer months, and a fee is charged. Fires are not permitted.

SUGGESTED HIKES

■ Easy Hikes

MT. WILLARD

⬤ 👣 🐕 📷 ⛄

	⬆⬇	↗	○
RT via Mt. Willard Trail	3.2 mi.	900 ft.	2:05

This low peak has long been celebrated for the view of Crawford Notch from the brink of Willard's impressive cliffs. See Mt. Willard Trail, p. 180.

ARETHUSA FALLS AREA

▨ 👣 🐕 📷 ⛄

	⬆⬇	↗	○
RT to Arethusa Falls via Bemis Brook Trail	3.0 mi.	950 ft.	2:00
RT to Ripley Falls via Ethan Pond and Arethusa–Ripley Falls trails	1.0 mi.	400 ft.	0:40
LP to to Arethusa and Ripley falls via Arethusa Falls, Arethusa–Ripley Falls, and Ethan Pond trails	4.5 mi.	1,600 ft.	3:05
LP to Frankenstein Cliff and Arethusa Falls via Frankenstein Cliff, Arethusa–Ripley Falls, and Arethusa Falls trails	4.9 mi.	1,650 ft.	3:15

Arethusa Falls and Ripley Falls are two of the highest waterfalls in New Hampshire, with the hike to Arethusa somewhat more demanding than that to Ripley. On a visit to Arethusa Falls, Bemis Brook Trail can be used either ascending or descending to obtain additional views of other falls in Bemis Brook (see Bemis Brook Trail, p. 186). With a car spot, both of the big falls can be visited in one trip using Arethusa Falls, Arethusa–Ripley Falls, and Ethan Pond trails (to begin, see Arethusa Falls Trail, p. 185). You can also use Frankenstein Cliff Trail to make a loop that includes Frankenstein Cliff and Arethusa Falls (see Frankenstein Cliff Trail, p. 187).

LINCOLN WOODS AREA TRAILS

	↕	↗	○
RT to river overlook via Lincoln Woods Trail	3.6 mi.	150 ft.	1:50
RT to Black Pond via Lincoln Woods and Black Pond trails	6.8 mi.	450 ft.	3:35
RT to Franconia Falls via Lincoln Woods and Franconia Falls trails	6.6 mi.	350 ft.	3:30
LP via Pemi East Side Trail and Pine Island Trail	3.1 mi.	100 ft.	1:35
RT to Pemigewasset Wilderness via Pemi East Side Trail	6.4 mi.	350 ft.	3:15

From the Lincoln Woods parking area on the Kancamagus Highway, trails on either side of the East Branch of the Pemigewasset River provide easy, scenic walks. On the west side, Lincoln Woods Trail can be followed to a riverside viewpoint (see Lincoln Woods Trail, p. 189) or can be used to reach side trails to Black Pond (also see Black Pond Trail, p. 192) or Franconia Falls (also see Franconia Falls Trail, p. 192). On the east side, Pemi East Side Trail and Pine Island Trail can be used for a pleasant loop (to begin, see Pemi East Side Trail, p. 199). Pemi East Side Trail can also be followed to an attractive pool in the river just inside the Pemigewasset Wilderness.

CLOUDLAND FALLS

	↕	↗	○
RT via Falling Waters Trail	2.6 mi.	900 ft.	1:45

The lower part of Falling Waters Trail leads past three waterfalls; the highest, Cloudland Falls, is a good turnaround point. See Falling Waters Trail, p. 162.

EAGLE PASS

	↕	↗	○
RT via Greenleaf Trail	3.0 mi.	1,100 ft.	2:05

This narrow, rocky cleft between Mt. Lafayette and Eagle Cliff merits exploration. See Greenleaf Trail, p. 165.

■ Moderate Hikes
THE SUGARLOAVES

	↕	↗	○
RT via Sugarloaf Trail	3.4 mi.	1,100 ft.	2:15

These two open summits near the village of Twin Mountain offer excellent views for modest effort. See Sugarloaf Trail, p. 178.

ZEALAND FALLS

	⇅	↗	○
RT to Zealand Falls Hut via Zealand Trail and Twinway	5.4 mi.	650 ft.	3:00
RT to Zealand Notch via Zealand and Ethan Pond trails	7.6 mi.	550 ft.	4:05
RT to Thoreau Falls via Zealand, Ethan Pond, and Thoreau Falls trails	9.4 mi.	600 ft.	5:00

The gentle hike to AMC's Zealand Falls Hut leads past beaver ponds and meadows, ending with a short, steep climb on Twinway to a waterfall just outside the hut (see Zealand Trail, p. 176). As longer alternatives to visiting the hut, one can follow Ethan Pond Trail out into spectacular Zealand Notch (see Ethan Pond Trail, p. 182) or continue through the notch and down a short distance on Thoreau Falls Trail to the view ledge atop Thoreau Falls (see Thoreau Falls Trail, p. 203).

**SEC
3**

ETHAN POND

	⇅	↗	○
RT via Ethan Pond Trail	5.4 mi.	1,550 ft.	3:30

A moderate climb leads to this attractive backcountry pond with a view of the Twin Range. See Ethan Pond Trail, p. 182.

MT. AVALON

	⇅	↗	○
RT via Avalon Trail and spur path	3.7 mi.	1,550 ft.	2:40

The best view available from the Willey Range is found on this little crag, reached by the steep Avalon Trail and the spur path to the summit; visitors should make the short side loop en route to Beecher and Pearl cascades. See Avalon Trail, p. 180.

OLD BRIDLE PATH OUTLOOKS

	⇅	↗	○
RT via Old Bridle Path	4.0 mi.	1,600 ft.	2:50

A series of ledges partway up this route offers spectacular views of Franconia Ridge. See Old Bridle Path, p. 164.

MT. TOM

🏔️🚶🎿🐕✂️🥾	↕️	↗️	🕐
RT via Avalon Trail, A–Z Trail, and Mt. Tom Spur	5.8 mi.	2,250 ft.	4:00
LP to Tom and Field via Avalon and A–Z trails, Mt. Tom Spur, and Willey Range and Avalon trails	7.2 mi.	2,850 ft.	5:00
LP to Tom, Field, and Willey via Avalon and A–Z trails, Mt. Tom Spur, and Willey Range and Avalon trails	10.0 mi.	3,600 ft.	6:50

An open blowdown area offers good views atop this Willey Range peak (to begin, see Avalon Trail, p. 180). This route can be extended for a more strenuous trip including Mt. Field or mts. Field and Willey.

■ Strenuous Hikes

ZEACLIFF

🏔️💧🛶🐕✂️🥾	↕️	↗️	🕐
RT via Zealand Trail and Twinway	7.8 mi.	1,600 ft.	4:40

This perch at the northern end of the Pemigewasset Wilderness commands one of the finest outlooks in the White Mountains. See Zealand Trail, p. 176.

SOUTH TWIN MTN.

🚶🛶✂️🥾	↕️	↗️	🕐
RT via Gale River Trail, Garfield Ridge Trail, and Twinway	11.0 mi.	3,450 ft.	7:15

This high, open peak affords panoramic views. Ascend directly via the route above, passing Galehead Hut on the way. To begin, see Gale River Trail, p. 171.

MT. GARFIELD

🚶🎿🐕✂️🥾	↕️	↗️	🕐
RT via Garfield Trail and Garfield Ridge Trail	10.0 mi.	3,100 ft.	6:35

This peak's summit ledges are perched high above the Pemigewasset Wilderness and offer one of the best views in the White Mountains. Garfield Trail, though long, has generally good footing and moderate grades. The last 0.2 mi. to the summit is fairly steep and rough, with some scrambling. See Garfield Trail, p. 170.

FRANCONIA RIDGE

🏔️❄️🥾🎿⛸️🚶🧗

	↥↧	↗	⏱
LP to Lincoln and Lafayette via Falling Waters, Franconia Ridge, and Greenleaf trails and Old Bridle Path	8.9 mi.	3,950 ft.	6:25
RT to Lafayette via Skookumchuck and Garfield Ridge trails	10.2 mi.	3,750 ft.	7:00

The usual loop over Mt. Lincoln and Mt. Lafayette (to begin, see Falling Waters Trail, p. 162) is a good trip in either direction, though many hikers prefer a direct ascent via the steep and sometimes slippery Falling Waters Trail. A less crowded alternative is to climb Mt. Lafayette via Skookumchuck and Garfield Ridge trails, including a traverse of the mountain's open north ridge (see Skookumchuck Trail, p. 166).

SEC 3

MT. LIBERTY

🥾⛺🐕🎿🚶

	↥↧	↗	⏱
RT via Whitehouse, Liberty Spring, and Franconia Ridge trails	8.0 mi.	3,250 ft.	5:40
RT to Liberty and Flume via Whitehouse, Liberty Spring, and Franconia Ridge trails	10.2 mi.	4,250 ft.	7:15
RT to Mt. Flume via Lincoln Woods, Osseo, and Franconia Ridge trails	11.2 mi.	3,150 ft.	7:10

This rocky, open summit offers excellent views (to begin, see Whitehouse Trail, p. 162). Mt. Flume can be added to this trip, with a return over Mt. Liberty; the steep and difficult Flume Slide Trail is not recommended for descent. The separate ascent of Mt. Flume via Osseo Trail is another good option (see Osseo Trail, p. 191).

SEC 3

TRAIL DESCRIPTIONS

FRANCONIA RIDGE AND THE WEST SLOPES

FRANCONIA RIDGE TRAIL (AMC; MAP 2: H5)

Cumulative from Mt. Lafayette summit (5,260 ft.) to:	↕	↗	○
Mt. Lincoln summit (5,089 ft.)	1.0 mi.	300 ft.	0:40
Falling Waters Trail (4,765 ft.)	1.7 mi.	350 ft.	1:00
Liberty Spring Trail (4,260 ft.)	3.5 mi.	550 ft.	2:00
Mt. Liberty summit (4,459 ft.)	3.8 mi.	750 ft.	2:15
Mt. Flume summit (4,328 ft.)	4.9 mi.	1,200 ft.	3:05
Flume Slide Trail–Osseo Trail jct. (4,240 ft.)	5.0 mi.	1,200 ft.	3:05

FRANCONIA RIDGE TRAIL, IN REVERSE (AMC; MAP 2: H5)

Cumulative from Flume Slide Trail–Osseo Trail jct. (4,240 ft.) to:	↕	↗	○
Mt. Flume summit (4,328 ft.)	0.1 mi.	100 ft.	0:05
Mt. Liberty summit (4,459 ft.)	1.2 mi.	650 ft.	0:55
Liberty Spring Trail (4,260 ft.)	1.5 mi.	650 ft.	1:05
Falling Waters Trail (4,765 ft.)	3.3 mi.	1,350 ft.	2:20
Mt. Lincoln summit (5,089 ft.)	4.0 mi.	1,750 ft.	2:55
Mt. Lafayette summit (5,260 ft.)	5.0 mi.	2,200 ft.	3:35

This heavily used trail follows the backbone of the ridge that runs south from Mt. Lafayette, beginning on the summit of Lafayette at the jct. of Garfield Ridge and Greenleaf trails; passing over Mt. Lincoln, Little Haystack Mtn., Mt. Liberty, and Mt. Flume; and ending at a jct. with Flume Slide Trail and Osseo Trail just south of Mt. Flume. Much work has been done to define and stabilize the trail and to reduce erosion; the late Guy Waterman and Laura Waterman, authors of several books on hiking and backcountry ethics in the Northeast, spent many hours observing each step taken by passing hikers to determine the best placement of individual rocks. Hikers are urged to stay on the trail to save the thin alpine soils and fragile vegetation. From Mt. Lafayette to Liberty Spring Trail, this trail is part of the AT.

Caution: The portion of Franconia Ridge above treeline from Lafayette to Little Haystack does not involve any unusually difficult or hazardous climbing, but it is almost constantly exposed to the full force of any storms and is dangerous in bad weather or high winds. In particular, due to the sharpness, narrowness, and complete exposure to weather of the ridge crest on Mt. Lafayette, Mt. Lincoln, and Little Haystack Mtn., the danger from lightning is unusually great, and this portion of the ridge should be avoided when thunderstorms appear to be brewing.

The following description of the path is in the southbound direction (away from Mt. Lafayette). Distances, elevation gains, and times are also given for the reverse direction.

Leaving the signs at the three-way jct. with Greenleaf and Garfield Ridge trails just north of the summit of Mt. Lafayette, Franconia Ridge Trail leads south, passing to the left of the foundation of an 1850s summit house. The trail descends at a moderate grade to the first sag, where the trail passes through a small scrub patch that might provide some shelter in bad weather. The trail then climbs across a prominent hump (unofficially known as "Mt. Truman"), descends to another sag, and climbs again, with one ledge scramble, to the summit of Mt. Lincoln at 1.0 mi., with the high point just to the right of the trail. From there, the trail descends sharply with rough footing, keeping mostly just to the east of the crest of the knife-edged ridge between Mt. Lincoln and Little Haystack Mtn., which has steep slopes on both sides. At the base of this knife-edged section, the ridge becomes nearly level and much broader, and the trail continues on the ridge crest in the open, with minor ups and downs, to the jct. with Falling Waters Trail on the right at 1.7 mi., just under the summit rock of Little Haystack Mtn.

Franconia Ridge Trail continues to the south end of the Little Haystack summit ridge, enters the scrub and descends steeply over ledges for a short distance, with one fine view to the south, then moderates and follows the long, fairly gradual wooded ridge down to the Little Haystack–Liberty col at 2.8 mi. The trail then ascends easily to a jct. with Liberty Spring Trail on the right at 3.5 mi.; water can be found at Liberty Spring Tentsite, 0.3 mi. down this trail. Franconia Ridge Trail ascends to a small, ledgy crest then swings right up ledges to the rocky summit of Mt. Liberty at 3.8 mi. The trail then makes a hairpin turn to the left and descends into the woods to the east and then northeast. The descent is steep at first over ledges and large rocks then moderates as the trail descends southeast toward the col. The trail passes through two small sags and ascends moderately over a knob then continues up to the open summit of Mt. Flume. The trail traverses the level crest then descends along the edge of the west-facing cliff (use extra caution in windy or slippery conditions, especially where the trail crosses the top of a steep gully) and enters the woods. The trail ends 0.1 mi. south of the summit of Flume in a little col, at the jct. with Osseo Trail straight ahead and Flume Slide Trail on the right.

FLUME SLIDE TRAIL (AMC; MAP 2: H4–H5)

Cumulative from Liberty Spring Trail (1,800 ft.) to:	↧↥	↗	⟳
Foot of slide (2,850 ft.)	2.6 mi.	1,100 ft. (rev. 50 ft.)	1:50
Franconia Ridge Trail (4,240 ft.)	3.3 mi.	2,500 ft.	2:55

This trail runs from Liberty Spring Trail, 0.6 mi. from its jct. with Cascade Brook and Whitehouse trails, to Franconia Ridge Trail, 0.1 mi. south of the summit of Mt. Flume. Flume Slide Trail's upper section is extremely steep and rough, with polished rock slabs that are very slippery when wet (and they are nearly always wet due to the many seep springs on these steep slopes). This is one of the most difficult sections of trail in the White Mtns.; there have been several serious injuries here. This trail is not recommended for descent, and its use is discouraged in wet weather, when the ledges are more than ordinarily dangerous. Views from the trail itself are limited, as it ascends an old slide that is almost completely overgrown, well to the south of the prominent open slides on the west face of Mt. Flume. The route over the slide is poorly marked and must be followed with care.

The trail leaves Liberty Spring Trail on an old logging road that contours to the right (south). Soon the trail swings left off the logging road in a more easterly direction and begins a gradual ascent on the southwest shoulder of Mt. Liberty, with occasional slight descents. At 0.3 mi., the trail crosses a small brook, and about 0.1 mi. farther on, it crosses a larger brook. After rising from the brook bed, the trail climbs gradually, crossing several more small brooks. At 1.5 mi., the trail crosses a small brook, bears right after 40 yd., then turns left in another 20 yd. At 1.9 mi., the trail crosses to the south side of Flume Brook and follows it closely then crosses back to the north side in about 0.1 mi.; avoid a beaten path continuing ahead on the south side. In this region, the trail should be followed carefully.

At 2.4 mi., the trail crosses the north branch of Flume Brook, follows the south branch briefly, then ascends and leaves the remnants of the brook behind as slide gravel becomes more prominent underfoot. At 2.6 mi., the climbing begins in earnest, and the first ledges are soon reached. (Beaten side paths run through the woods alongside the ledges and bypass some of the worst spots.) While on the slide, be careful not to dislodge stones that might endanger climbers below and beware of rockfall from above. After struggling up the smooth, wet ledges with occasional restricted outlooks, the trail turns left at 3.1 mi. and continues on a steep, rocky, rooty path through the woods to the main ridge crest, where Franconia Ridge Trail leads left (north) and Osseo Trail leads right (south). A few steps before this jct. is reached, a rough and overgrown beaten path leads 30 yd. right (south) to a small crag with an excellent view.

SEC 3

LIBERTY SPRING TRAIL (AMC; MAP 2: H4–H5)

Cumulative from Whitehouse Trail (1,420 ft.) to:	⇅	↗	⟳
Sharp left turn (2,375 ft.)	1.4 mi.	950 ft.	1:10
Liberty Spring Tentsite (3,870 ft.)	2.6 mi.	2,450 ft.	2:30
Franconia Ridge Trail (4,260 ft.)	2.9 mi.	2,850 ft.	2:55
Mt. Liberty summit (4,459 ft.) via Franconia Ridge Trail	3.2 mi.	3,050 ft.	3:10

This trail climbs past Liberty Spring Tentsite to Franconia Ridge Trail, 0.3 mi. north of Mt. Liberty. Liberty Spring Trail begins on the Franconia Notch bike path, just north of the bridge over the Pemigewasset River, near the site of the former Whitehouse Bridge (parking no longer available); Cascade Brook Trail (Section Five) begins just south of this bridge. This trailhead is reached from the hikers parking lot on US 3, just north of the Flume Visitor Center by Whitehouse Trail (this parking area is a stop for the AMC Hiker Shuttle) or from the Flume or Basin parking areas by the paved bike path. Liberty Spring Trail ascends steadily and rather steeply at times, with some moderately rough footing. This trail is part of the AT.

From the bike path, the trail climbs moderately northeast through hardwood forest. At 0.4 mi., the trail turns sharply right, joining the old main logging road from the former Whitehouse mill, and soon levels off. At 0.6 mi., Flume Slide Trail leaves right (south). Liberty Spring Trail bears left, ascending gradually, and crosses a fairly large brook at 1.1 mi. The trail then climbs moderately, turns sharply left off the logging road at 1.4 mi., and soon swings right for a long, steady climb; the footing is rough in places. At 2.2 mi., the trail bears right and continues up rather steeply by switchbacks. At 2.6 mi., the trail reaches Liberty Spring Tentsite on the left and the spring (last sure water) on the right. The path then ascends fairly steeply through conifers and ends in 0.3 mi. at Franconia Ridge Trail; turn left (north) for Mt. Lafayette or right (south) for Mt. Liberty.

WHITEHOUSE TRAIL (AMC; MAP 2: H4)

From hikers parking area off US 3 (1,420 ft.) to:	⇅	↗	⟳
Liberty Spring Trail (1,420 ft.)	0.8 mi.	100 ft. (rev. 100 ft.)	0:25

This blue-blazed trail connects the hikers parking lot off US 3, just north of the Flume Visitor Center, with Liberty Spring Trail and Cascade Brook Trail (Section Five), near the site known as Whitehouse Bridge (where parking is not available). This is the usual route to these trails for hikers who arrive in the area by automobile. Up to the jct. with Cascade Brook Trail, Whitehouse Trail coincides with Pemi Trail (Section Five).

Whitehouse Trail leaves the parking lot and runs north, parallel to the main highway, passing over a minor ridge. The trail descends to the bike path at 0.6 mi. (signs for both Whitehouse Trail and Pemi Trail) and follows it left, across a bridge over a brook, to the jct. with Cascade Brook Trail, which, along with Pemi Trail, diverges left just before (south of) a bridge over the Pemigewasset River. Whitehouse Trail continues across the bridge and officially ends in another 50 yd., where Liberty Spring Trail diverges right off the bike path.

FALLING WATERS TRAIL (AMC; MAP 2: H4–H5)

Cumulative from Lafayette Place parking area (1,790 ft.) to:	⇅	↗	⟳
Dry Brook (2,000 ft.)	0.7 mi.	250 ft. (rev. 50 ft.)	0:30
Base of Cloudland Falls (2,600 ft.)	1.3 mi.	850 ft.	1:05
Shining Rock side path (4,170 ft.)	2.8 mi.	2,450 ft.	2:40
Franconia Ridge Trail (4,765 ft.)	3.2 mi.	3,050 ft.	3:10

This trail begins at the Lafayette Place parking lots (located on each side of the Franconia Notch Parkway) and climbs to Franconia Ridge Trail at the summit of Little Haystack Mtn., passing several waterfalls in its lower part. Falling Waters Trail is steep and rough in parts and better for ascent than descent but isn't usually dangerous unless there is ice on the ledgy sections near the brook. The Lafayette Place parking lots fill up early on fine summer and fall days, and later-arriving hikers will need to carefully park on the grassy shoulder of the parkway, sometimes a significant distance from the trailhead.

The trail leaves the parking lot on the east side of the parkway (reached from the west side by a paved path 0.1 mi. long) near the hiker information kiosk, in common with Old Bridle Path. Falling Waters Trail passes through a clearing into the woods and leads around a short section that was severely eroded by 2011's Tropical Storm Irene. At 0.2 mi., the trail turns sharply right from Old Bridle Path and immediately crosses Walker Brook on a bridge, climbs upstream past a cascade, and leads away from the brook heading east then south. At 0.7 mi., after a slight descent, Falling Waters Trail crosses Dry Brook (use care if the water is high), turns left (avoid a blocked-off path diverging to the right), and follows the south bank up to a beautiful cascade known as Stairs Falls.

Above the falls, the trail passes beneath Sawteeth Ledges and crosses the brook to the north bank just below Swiftwater Falls, which descends 60 ft. in a shady glen, then ascends a slippery ledge and a steep rock staircase to the north bank. It follows an old logging road that rises gradually in the narrow gorge of Dry Brook, passing more cascades, then leaves the old road at a steep embankment and ascends more roughly to the foot of Cloudland Falls (80 ft. high) at 1.3 mi. The trail climbs steeply up the bank of the brook beside the falls, with a dropoff to the right; this area is subject to occasional rockfall. Cut rock steps aid in a ledgy scramble to the top of the falls. Here, a viewpoint looks out over the valley toward Mt. Moosilauke on the skyline.

At the head of Cloudland Falls are two small (25 ft.) falls practically facing each other. The one to the south, which emerges from the woods, is on the branch of Dry Brook that runs down from Little Haystack Mtn., and the other is on the Mt. Lincoln branch. The trail continues steeply on the north bank of the Mt. Lincoln branch, soon crosses to the south bank and traverses slippery ledges, then crosses back to the north side. It climbs to and follows an old logging road, and recrosses to the south bank at 1.6 mi. Here, the trail swings to the right, away from the brook, and angles uphill on an old logging road. Soon the trail takes the left fork of the old road then diverges to the left off the road just before reaching the south branch of Dry Brook and ascends the ridge via a series of switchbacks.

**SEC
3**

At the south end of the last switchback, at 2.8 mi., a side trail leads right (south) downhill about 100 yd. to the northeast corner of Shining Rock, where you have fine views south and west over Franconia Notch. This steep granite ledge, more than 200 ft. tall and nearly 800 ft. long, is usually covered with water from springs in the woods above and, seen from the mountains across the notch, shines like a mirror in the sunlight. (*Caution:* Climbing Shining Rock without rock-climbing equipment and training is extremely dangerous. This steep ledge is wet and very slippery; several serious injuries have occurred here when hikers tried to scramble up the rock.) From the Shining Rock spur jct., the main trail continues north for a short distance then turns right and climbs steeply with rough footing east to Franconia Ridge Trail at the summit of Little Haystack Mtn.; the last 70 yd. of the trail is above treeline.

Descending, the trail runs slightly south of west down the open slope, bends right into the scrub, and soon swings left.

OLD BRIDLE PATH (AMC; MAP 2: H4–H5)

Cumulative from Lafayette Place parking area (1,790 ft.) to:	⇅	↗	↻
First outlook (3,280 ft.)	1.9 mi.	1,500 ft.	1:40
Greenleaf Hut (4,220 ft.)	2.9 mi.	2,450 ft.	2:40
Mt. Lafayette summit (5,260 ft.) via Greenleaf Trail	4.0 mi.	3,550 ft. (rev. 50 ft.)	3:45

This yellow-blazed trail runs from the Lafayette Place parking lots (located on each side of the Franconia Notch Parkway) to Greenleaf Hut, where the path joins Greenleaf Trail. Old Bridle Path affords fine views, particularly down into and across Walker Ravine and up to Franconia Ridge, from many outlooks in the upper half of the trail. For some of its length, the path follows the route of a former bridle path. The Lafayette Place parking lots fill up early on fine summer and fall days, and later-arriving hikers will need to park carefully on the grassy shoulder of the parkway, sometimes a significant distance from the trailhead.

The trail leaves the parking lot (which is a stop for the AMC Hiker Shuttle) on the east side of the parkway (reached from the west side by a paved path 0.1 mi. long) near the hiker information kiosk, in common with Falling Waters Trail. Old Bridle Path passes through a clearing into the woods and leads around a short section that was severely eroded by the 2011 storm. At 0.2 mi., Falling Waters Trail turns sharply right and immediately crosses Walker Brook on a bridge, but Old Bridle Path continues along the brook for 50 yd. then swings left away from the brook and starts to climb at a moderate grade. Old Bridle Path swings back to the right, and at 1.1 mi., it enters the WMNF (sign) and soon comes to the edge of the bank high above Walker Brook before swinging away again. At 1.6 mi., the path makes a sharp left turn via rock steps at the edge of the ravine, where you can catch a glimpse of Mt. Lincoln through the trees, then turns right, scrambles up some ledges, and soon gains the ridge.

At 1.9 mi., the first of the spectacular outlooks from the brink of the ravine is reached, and several more are passed in the next 0.1 mi. The trail then begins to ascend the steep part of the ridge, sometimes called Agony Ridge (a name that originated with hut staff who had to pack heavy loads up this steep section). At one point, the trail struggles up a steep dike of slippery red-brown rock known as Red Rocks; at the top of this pitch is a fine outlook south and west on the right. Still climbing—with steep and rough pitches alternating with short, easier sections—the trail passes several more views, crosses a small sag through a patch of dead trees, and soon descends slightly to Greenleaf Hut.

GREENLEAF TRAIL (AMC; MAP 2: G4–H5)

Cumulative from Cannon Mtn. Tramway parking area (1,970 ft.) to:	⇅	↗	↻
Eagle Pass (2,980 ft.)	1.5 mi.	1,050 ft. (rev. 50 ft.)	1:15
Greenleaf Hut (4,220 ft.)	2.7 mi.	2,300 ft.	2:30
Mt. Lafayette summit (5,260 ft.)	3.8 mi.	3,400 ft. (rev. 50 ft.)	3:35

This trail runs from the Cannon Mtn. Tramway parking lot on the west side of the Franconia Notch Parkway to Greenleaf Hut, where Old Bridle Path joins, and thence to the summit of Mt. Lafayette, where Greenleaf Trail ends at the jct. of Franconia Ridge and Garfield Ridge trails. Until Greenleaf Trail reaches the hut, the trail is almost completely in the woods with few views. The one exception is where it traverses Eagle Pass, a wild, narrow cleft between Eagle Cliff and the west buttress of Mt. Lafayette that has many interesting cliff and rock formations.

From the parking lot, the blue-blazed trail follows a sidewalk through the parkway underpass, turns left and follows the northbound ramp for 25 yd., then turns right across a ditch into the woods (sign). The trail runs southeast, parallel to the parkway, with rocky footing and minor ups and downs, crosses the gravel outwash of a slide at 0.7 mi., then turns sharply left and climbs moderately by numerous switchbacks to Eagle Pass at 1.5 mi. The path leads northeast nearly on the level through the pass under a high cliff, where a boulder on the right offers a unique view of Cannon

SEC 3

Cliff. A slide that fell in 2009 can be seen on the south side of the pass. The trail soon swings more to the east then south and rises steadily by long switchbacks, angling up a northwest shoulder over loose rocks that are slippery in wet weather. The trail finally reaches the top of the shoulder, passes a side path that descends on the right 90 yd. to a ledge with a restricted view northwest, and continues a short distance to reach Greenleaf Hut at 2.7 mi.

At the hut, Old Bridle Path enters on the right from Lafayette Place. Greenleaf Trail heads toward Mt. Lafayette, enters the scrub, and dips slightly, passing south of the Eagle Lakes, two picturesque shallow tarns (although the upper lake is rapidly becoming a bog). The trail rises, passing over several minor knobs, and at 3.2 mi., swings left after passing an open, sandy area on the right. The trail soon climbs above the scrub into the open and ascends at a moderate grade, sometimes on rock steps between stone walls. At 3.6 mi., the trail bears left around a prominent large ledge on the right side of the trail from which a remarkable spring issues, very small but fairly reliable. Now the trail turns right and soon reaches the trail signs just north of the summit of Mt. Lafayette; the summit ledge and the foundation of an 1850s summit house are just to the right (south). At this jct., Garfield Ridge Trail leads north (left), and Franconia Ridge Trail leads south (right).

Descending from the signs at this three-way jct., Greenleaf Trail follows cairns slightly north of west for 250 yd. then swings right (north) and then left (southwest) around the large ledge mentioned above.

SKOOKUMCHUCK TRAIL (WMNF; MAP 2: G4–G5)

Cumulative from US 3 (1,710 ft.) to:	⇅	⬈	⟳
Garfield Ridge Trail (4,730 ft.)	4.3 mi.	3,050 ft. (rev. 50 ft.)	3:40
Mt. Lafayette summit (5,260 ft.) via Garfield Ridge Trail	5.1 mi.	3,650 ft. (rev. 50 ft.)	4:25

This is an attractive and less frequently used route with generally good footing from the Franconia Notch area to the north ridge of Mt. Lafayette, 0.8 mi. below the summit. The trail begins on US 3 at a parking lot that also serves the north end of the Franconia Notch bike path, located 0.3 mi. south of the jct. of US 3 and NH 141 and just north of the point where US 3 divides at its northern jct. with I-93 and the Franconia Notch Parkway at Exit 35.

Leaving the parking lot, the trail climbs away from the highway, crosses a snowmobile trail, and runs generally south, descending to cross Jordan Brook at 0.6 mi. At 1.1 mi., the trail reaches the old route at the edge of Skookumchuck Brook and swings left to follow the brook upstream. At 1.8 mi., the trail crosses a small tributary on a rock bridge, climbs steeply away from the brook on rock steps, then continues up the valley well above the brook at a moderate grade through a fine stand of birch. At 2.5 mi., the trail passes a small brook (unreliable), soon reaches the crest of the ridge, and continues to a shoulder at 3.6 mi., where you can catch a glimpse ahead to Lafayette's North Peak. After a short, gradual descent, the trail angles to the northeast at mostly easy grades then swings right, scrambles up a tricky ledge, and emerges above treeline just before reaching its jct. with Garfield Ridge Trail.

Descending, Skookumchuck Trail runs generally northwest for about 60 yd. then swings more to the west (left), quickly reaching the shelter of the scrub.

SEC 3

FRANCONIA NOTCH RECREATION PATH (NHDP; MAP 2: H4–G4)

Cumulative from Flume Visitor Center parking area (1,340 ft.) to:	↥↧	↗	↺
Whitehouse Bridge–Liberty Spring Trail (1,420 ft.)	1.0 mi.	150 ft. (rev. 50 ft.)	0:35
The Basin viewing area (1,520 ft.)	1.8 mi.	300 ft. (rev. 50 ft.)	1:05
Lafayette Place–Lonesome Lake Trail (1,760 ft.)	3.4 mi.	550 ft.	2:00
Profile Lake, south end parking area (1,950 ft.)	4.8 mi.	800 ft. (rev. 50 ft.)	2:50
Cannon Mtn. Tramway–Greenleaf Trail (1,970 ft.)	5.9 mi.	850 ft. (rev. 50 ft.)	3:20
NH 18, north end of Echo Lake (1,930 ft.)	6.7 mi.	850 ft. (rev. 50 ft.)	3:45
Lafayette Brook bridge (1,890 ft.)	7.3 mi.	950 ft. (rev. 150 ft.)	4:05
Skookumchuck Trail parking area (1,710 ft.)	8.8 mi.	950 ft. (rev. 200 ft.)	4:50

This paved path (commonly known as the "bike path," and in places signed as the "F.N.S.P. Multi-Use Trail") extends for 8.8 mi. from the north end of the parking area at the Flume Visitor Center off US 3 (Exit 34A off I-93) north to the Skookumchuck Trail parking area on US 3, just north of Franconia Notch. Franconia Notch Recreation Path is shown as a double red line on AMC's *White Mountains Trail Map 2: Franconia–Pemigewasset*.

The trail is open to both bicycle and pedestrian use, but hikers should keep to the right and be alert for bicycle traffic approaching from either direction, particularly on the hilly, winding sections of the path. In winter, the trail is heavily used by snowmobilers. The path passes several of the major trailheads and scenic attractions in the notch, including the Basin, Whitehouse Bridge (AT crossing), Lafayette Place, Profile Lake, Cannon Mtn. Tramway, Echo Lake, and the Lafayette Brook bridge vista. For hikers, its primary use is as a connecting route for loop hikes on the Franconia Range or the Cannon–Kinsman Range. Distances, elevation gains, and times are given here from south to north.

GARFIELD RIDGE AND THE NORTH SLOPES

GARFIELD RIDGE TRAIL (AMC; MAP 2: H5–G6)

Cumulative from Mt. Lafayette summit (5,260 ft.) to:	⬍	↗	○
Skookumchuck Trail (4,730 ft.)	0.8 mi.	50 ft.	0:25
High point on Mt. Garfield (4,470 ft.)	3.5 mi.	1,050 ft.	2:15
Garfield Ridge Campsite spur path (3,930 ft.)	3.9 mi.	1,050 ft.	2:30
Franconia Brook Trail (3,420 ft.)	4.4 mi.	1,050 ft.	2:45
Gale River Trail (3,410 ft.)	6.0 mi.	1,500 ft.	3:45
Galehead Hut (3,780 ft.)	6.6 mi.	1,850 ft.	4:15

GARFIELD RIDGE TRAIL, IN REVERSE (AMC; MAP 2: H5–G6)

Cumulative from Galehead Hut (3,780 ft.) to:	⬍	↗	○
Gale River Trail (3,410 ft.)	0.6 mi.	0 ft.	0:20
Franconia Brook Trail (3,420 ft.)	2.2 mi.	450 ft.	1:20
Garfield Ridge Campsite spur path (3,930 ft.)	2.7 mi.	950 ft.	1:50
High point on Mt. Garfield (4,470 ft.)	3.1 mi.	1,500 ft.	2:20
Skookumchuck Trail (4,730 ft.)	5.8 mi.	2,750 ft.	4:15
Mt. Lafayette summit (5,260 ft.)	6.6 mi.	3,350 ft.	5:00

This trail runs from the signs at the jct. with Franconia Ridge and Greenleaf trails, just north of the summit of Mt. Lafayette, to Twinway near Galehead Hut, traversing the high ridge that joins the Franconia Range to South Twin Mtn. and passing near the summit of Mt. Garfield on the way.

The Garfield Ridge Trail footway is rough, and the trail has numerous minor gains and losses of elevation, so this route is more difficult than one might gather from a glance at the map. Extra time should be allowed, particularly by those carrying heavy packs.

The following description of the path is in the northbound direction (away from Mt. Lafayette). Distances, elevation gains, and times are also given for the reverse direction.

The trail leaves the signs at the three-way jct. just north of the summit of Mt. Lafayette and runs north along the open ridge over several minor knobs; climbs over the bare, rounded North Peak; then descends steeply to a jct. on the left with Skookumchuck Trail on an open shoulder at 0.8 mi. Swinging northeast, Garfield Ridge Trail then drops steeply for 250 yd. to timberline and continues to descend at a moderate grade near the crest of the ridge to a sag at 1.7 mi. From here, the trail climbs over a minor knob and then a large wooded hump, with a scramble up a ledge that offers a view back to Mt. Lafayette. The trail descends the rough end of the hump to a tangled col at 2.5 mi. then climbs gradually toward Mt. Garfield.

At 3.0 mi., near the foot of Garfield's cone, the trail passes to the right (south) of Garfield Pond, where a side path descends 35 yd. left to the shore. It then climbs steeply, with many rock steps, to its high point on Mt. Garfield at 3.5 mi.; the bare summit and its old fire lookout foundation, with magnificent views, are 60 yd. to the right (south) over open ledges. The trail then descends steeply, bearing right at 3.7 mi., at the jct. where Garfield Trail enters on the left. At 3.9 mi., where a small brook is beside the trail, a side path runs left 200 yd. (with 100 ft. of ascent) to AMC's Garfield Ridge Campsite, passing an outlook east (reached by a short ladder) on the way.

Garfield Ridge Trail continues to descend steeply with rough footing, including one tricky section of wet ledge where water runs down the trail. The trail crosses a small brook and reaches a major col at 4.4 mi., where Franconia Brook Trail leaves right and descends to 13 Falls. From this jct., Garfield Ridge Trail runs along the bumpy ridge with significant ups and downs. In this section, the trail climbs over three humps on an eastern spur of Mt. Garfield, descends to a col, climbs around the north side of another knob, passes a southeast outlook, descends steeply, and passes over one final hump before descending to the jct. with Gale River Trail on the left at 6.0 mi. Garfield Ridge Trail contours around the steep slope of Galehead Mtn., passing a restricted outlook north at 6.3 mi., then turns right and climbs to a jct. with Twinway and Frost Trail 40 yd. from Galehead Hut; turn right for the hut.

GARFIELD TRAIL (WMNF; MAP 2: G5)

Cumulative from Gale River Loop Rd.
(FR 92; 1,520 ft.) to:

	⇅	↗	⟳
Garfield Ridge Trail (4,260 ft.)	4.8 mi.	2,800 ft. (rev. 50 ft.)	3:50
Mt. Garfield summit (4,500 ft.) via Garfield Ridge Trail	5.0 mi.	3,050 ft.	4:00
Garfield Ridge Campsite (3,930 ft.) via Garfield Ridge Trail	5.0 mi.	2,800 ft. (rev. 350 ft.)	3:50

This trail runs from Gale River Loop Rd. (FR 92) to Garfield Ridge Trail 0.2 mi. east of the summit of Mt. Garfield, which is bare rock with magnificent views. Most of the way the trail follows an old road used for access to the former fire lookout, and its grades are easy to moderate all the way to Mt. Garfield, except for the short steep pitch on Garfield Ridge Trail just below the summit. The trailhead is reached by leaving US 3 at a small picnic area 0.3 mi. west of its intersection with Trudeau Rd. (a location sometimes called Five Corners) and 4.1 mi. east of its jct. with NH 141. Avoiding a right fork, follow FR 92 south for 1.2 mi. then swing left and cross a bridge to a parking lot on the right. (Straight ahead on this road, it is 1.6 mi. to the trailhead for Gale River Trail.) Garfield Trail lies within the watershed of a municipal water supply, and hikers and campers should take care not to pollute any of the streams in this watershed.

The trail begins to the right of the parking lot, climbing an embankment and following the top of the north bank of the South Branch of Gale River through fine woods with many large hemlocks. At 0.7 mi., the trail descends and swings right toward the river then turns left onto the old fire lookout access road. The trail now climbs slowly away from the river, heading generally south. The trail crosses Thompson Brook and two branches of Spruce Brook and then a snowmobile trail. Garfield Trail then recrosses Spruce Brook at 1.2 mi. and continues its long, gradual climb. (Although these three crossings usually are not difficult, in high water, you can use the snowmobile trail to avoid all three by bushwhacking up the east side of Thompson Brook, turning right on the snowmobile trail, and crossing bridges over both brooks—and also crossing Garfield Trail between the bridges—then bushwhacking up the west side of Spruce Brook back to Garfield Trail.)

At 2.6 mi. the trail crosses a small brook by a large flat rock, and at 3.0 mi. it crosses a ridge (once burned over and known as Burnt Knoll) in a birch forest and descends slightly. At 3.3 mi. the trail swings left and ascends moderately by several sweeping switchbacks in mostly coniferous woods and reaches a blowdown patch at 4.1 mi. Here, the trail turns sharply left and climbs easily to the east then swings south around the east side of the cone of Mt. Garfield to a jct. with Garfield Ridge Trail, which enters from the left, ascending from Garfield Ridge Campsite. The summit of Mt. Garfield is reached in 0.2 mi. by turning right and following a steep, rocky section of Garfield Ridge Trail to its high point then scrambling over the ledges on the left for another 60 yd. to the foundation of the old fire lookout.

GALE RIVER TRAIL (WMNF; MAP 2: G5–G6)

Cumulative from Gale River Loop Rd. (FR 92; 1,600 ft.) to:	⇅	↗	⟳
Garfield Ridge Trail (3,410 ft.)	4.1 mi.	1,850 ft. (rev. 50 ft.)	3:00
Galehead Hut (3,780 ft.) via Garfield Ridge Trail	4.7 mi.	2,250 ft.	3:30

This trail runs from the gravel-surface Gale River Loop Rd. (FR 92) to Garfield Ridge Trail 0.6 mi. west of Galehead Hut. The Gale River Trail trailhead is reached by leaving US 3 at its intersection with Trudeau Rd.; this intersection, sometimes called Five Corners, is 5.3 mi. west of the stoplight in Twin Mountain and 4.4 mi. east of the jct. of US 3 and NH 141, and has signs for Trudeau Rd. and Gale River Trail. Follow FR 25 southeast, bearing left at 0.6 mi., then turn sharply right at 1.3 mi. on FR 92 and continue to the parking area on the left at 1.6 mi. (Straight ahead on the road, it is 1.6 mi. from here to the Garfield Trail parking lot.) The parking area is a stop for the AMC Hiker Shuttle. Gale River Trail lies within the watershed of a municipal water supply, and hikers and campers should take care not to pollute any of the streams in this watershed.

From the parking area, the trail enters the woods, and in 40 yd., a path from the AMC Hiker Shuttle stop joins from the left. At 0.2 mi., the trail descends a bank and crosses a tributary brook then turns right on an old logging road that climbs easily along the west side of the North Branch of Gale River, some distance away from the stream. At 1.4 mi., the trail comes near the edge of the stream, and at 1.7 mi., the trail turns sharply right onto a relocated section more than 1 mi. long that was constructed in 2011 to bypass two difficult crossings of the North Branch. The trail swings right then left up a bank and left again as it heads south up the valley, high above the North Branch, at easy to moderate grades. At 2.2 mi., the trail descends slightly to cross Garfield Stream, a tributary of the North Branch (may be difficult in high water), then continues to climb through fine woods. The trail then swings left and descends gradually to rejoin the original route of the trail at 2.8 mi. (In the reverse direction, bear left and uphill on the relocated section.) After crossing several small brooks and passing the gravel outwash of an overgrown slide, the trail emerges at 3.2 mi. on a gravel bank above the stream at the base of a slide, where you have views down to the North Branch and up to the high ridges of the Twins. The trail now becomes significantly steeper and rougher and ends with a fairly steep climb, with many rock steps, to Garfield Ridge Trail.

FROST TRAIL (AMC; MAP 2: G6)

From Galehead Hut (3,780 ft.) to:	⇅	↗	↺
Galehead Mtn. summit (4,024 ft.)	0.5 mi.	250 ft.	0:25

This short trail leads from Galehead Hut to the summit of Galehead Mtn. Leaving the hut clearing, the trail descends into a sag then turns sharply right at a jct. where Twin Brook Trail enters left. After a short distance, Frost Trail ascends a steep pitch, at the top of which a side path leads left 30 yd. to an excellent outlook over the Twin Brook valley. The main trail continues at a moderate grade to the rather flat and viewless summit.

TWIN–ZEALAND RANGE

TWINWAY (AMC; MAP 2: G6–G7)

Cumulative from Galehead Hut (3,780 ft.) to:	⇅	↗	↺
South Twin Mtn. summit (4,902 ft.)	0.8 mi.	1,150 ft.	1:00
Bondcliff Trail (4,508 ft.)	2.8 mi.	1,400 ft.	2:05
Zealand Mtn. summit spur (4,250 ft.)	4.1 mi.	1,700 ft.	2:55
Zeacliff Trail (3,750 ft.)	5.7 mi.	1,800 ft.	3:45
Zealand Falls Hut (2,640 ft.)	7.0 mi.	1,800 ft.	4:25
Ethan Pond Trail–Zealand Trail jct. (2,460 ft.)	7.2 mi.	1,800 ft.	4:30

TWINWAY, IN REVERSE (AMC; MAP 2: G6–G7)

Cumulative from Ethan Pond Trail–Zealand Trail jct. (2,460 ft.) to:	⇅	↗	↺
Zealand Falls Hut (2,640 ft.)	0.2 mi.	200 ft.	0:10
Zeacliff Trail (3,750 ft.)	1.5 mi.	1,300 ft.	1:25
Zealand Mtn. summit spur (4,250 ft.)	3.1 mi.	1,900 ft.	2:30
Bondcliff Trail (4,508 ft.)	4.4 mi.	2,450 ft.	3:25
South Twin Mtn. summit (4,902 ft.)	6.4 mi.	3,100 ft.	4:45
Galehead Hut (3,780 ft.)	7.2 mi.	3,150 ft.	5:10

This trail extends from Galehead Hut to a jct. with Zealand Trail and Ethan Pond Trail 0.2 mi. beyond Zealand Falls Hut, forming an important ridge crest link along the north edge of the Pemigewasset Wilderness that connects the mountains of the western part of the region—the Franconia Range, Mt. Garfield, and the Twins—to the Bonds, the Zealand–Hale region, the Willey Range, and the northern parts of the Pemigewasset Wilderness. Twinway offers magnificent views from the summits of South Twin Mtn. and Mt. Guyot and from the outlook at Zeacliff, and connecting trails lead to a number of other superb outlooks. For its entire length, Twinway is part of the AT.

The following description of the path is in the eastbound direction (from Galehead Hut to Zealand Falls Hut). Distances, elevation gains, and times are also given for the reverse direction. From the jct. of Frost and Garfield Ridge trails 40 yd. from Galehead Hut, Twinway passes over a ledgy hump, descends to a sag, then climbs steadily and steeply on a rocky footway up the cone of South Twin to the south knob of the open summit at 0.8 mi. North Twin Spur begins here, running straight ahead 40 yd. to the north knob and then on to North Twin. Twinway turns right (south), enters the woods, and descends along the broad ridge toward Mt. Guyot, with easy to moderate grades after an initial steep pitch below the summit. At 1.8 mi., the trail crosses a ledgy hump with restricted views. The trail descends easily to the main col between South Twin and Guyot then climbs out of the scrub to open rocks on the side of Guyot and reaches the jct. with Bondcliff Trail on the right at 2.8 mi. Guyot Campsite is 0.8 mi. from this jct. via Bondcliff Trail and a spur path.

Twinway turns left and ascends in the open to the flat northeast summit of Guyot at 2.9 mi.; hikers should take care to stay on the marked trail and avoid trampling fragile alpine vegetation. The trail reenters the woods and descends at a moderate grade with some rough footing on the long ridge leading northeast toward Zealand Mtn., reaching the col at 3.9 mi. The trail then climbs rather steeply, and at 4.1 mi., a few yards before reaching the height-of-land, the trail passes a small cairn marking a side path on the left that runs nearly level 0.1 mi. to the true summit of Zealand Mtn. (sign), wooded and viewless. The main trail continues at mostly easy grades down the ridge, passes a ledge with a view southeast at 5.1 mi., then descends a steep pitch with a ladder, and in a sag at 5.3 mi. passes a side path that diverges right and descends to the shore of tiny, boggy Zeacliff Pond in 0.1 mi. (100 ft. descent). The main trail ascends over a scrubby hump and passes the jct. right with Zeacliff Trail at 5.7 mi.

In another 0.1 mi., Twinway reaches a loop side path that leads 75 yd. right to the magnificent Zeacliff outlook then turns sharply left and runs

70 yd. to rejoin the main trail 50 yd. east of its point of departure. Between the loop jcts., Twinway climbs over a ledge with views that are good but greatly inferior to those from the Zeacliff outlook. At the farther loop jct., Twinway turns left, ascends slightly, then descends steadily with rocky footing. At 6.9 mi., the trail crosses two branches of Whitewall Brook on ledges (use caution in high water), and Lend-a-Hand Trail immediately enters on the left. Twinway passes in front of Zealand Falls Hut at 7.0 mi., where a short side path leads right to scenic ledges on Whitewall Brook; from the hut is a good view of Zealand Notch and Mt. Carrigain. The main trail then descends steeply on rock steps, passing a side path right to a viewpoint for Zealand Falls, then crosses the outlet of Zealand Pond and reaches the grade of the old logging railroad. Here, Zealand Trail turns left and Ethan Pond Trail turns right, both on the railroad grade.

NORTH TWIN SPUR (AMC; MAP 2: G6)

From South Twin Mtn. summit (4,902 ft.) to:	⇅	↗	⟳
North Twin Mtn. summit (4,761 ft.)	1.3 mi.	300 ft. (rev. 450 ft.)	0:50

This trail connects Twinway on the bare summit of South Twin with North Twin Trail near the summit of North Twin. North Twin Spur leaves Twinway at the south knob of South Twin, crosses the north knob in 40 yd., traverses an open shoulder, then descends moderately to the fern-filled col at 0.8 mi. From here, North Twin Spur ascends moderately, with occasional views, to the summit of North Twin, where North Twin Trail continues straight ahead, and a spur path leads left 60 yd. over the wooded true summit, to a fine outlook from the western edge of the summit area.

NORTH TWIN TRAIL (WMNF; MAP 2: G6)

Cumulative from Haystack Rd. (1,850 ft.) to:	⇅	↗	⟳
Third crossing of Little River (2,390 ft.)	1.9 mi.	550 ft.	1:15
North Twin summit (4,761 ft.)	4.3 mi.	2,900 ft.	3:35

This trail ascends to the summit of North Twin from Haystack Rd. (FR 304, marked by a hiker symbol), which begins on US 3, 2.5 mi. west of the stoplight in Twin Mountain, and runs south 2.5 mi. to a parking area just past its crossing of Little River. (*Caution:* The three crossings of Little River on this trail are very difficult or impassable at high water; the third is the least difficult, and the first two can be avoided by staying on the east bank, bearing left at the first crossing and following a well-beaten path along the river, crossing a tributary stream partway along. Avoid an unmaintained trail that diverges left uphill after the tributary crossing.) North Twin Trail is in the watershed of a municipal water supply, and hikers and campers should take care not to pollute the streams.

The trail leaves the parking area and crosses the river three times, at 0.8 mi. (where the alternate path diverges left), 1.3 mi. (after which the alternate path rejoins from the left), and 1.9 mi., ascending easily on an old railroad grade with occasional bypasses. After the third crossing, the trail begins to climb away from the river and railroad grade, crossing and recrossing a tributary brook. The long, steady climb continues, and at 3.5 mi., the trail becomes quite steep and eroded, reaching the ledgy end of the ridge at 4.0 mi. The trail now climbs easily, passes a superb outlook ledge on the left at 4.2 mi., and reaches the summit of North Twin at 4.3 mi. North Twin Spur continues straight ahead to South Twin, and a side path leads right 60 yd. over the wooded true summit to a fine outlook from the western edge of the summit area.

SEC 3

ZEACLIFF TRAIL (AMC; MAP 2: G7)

From Ethan Pond Trail (2,448 ft.) to:	↕	↗	↻
Twinway (3,750 ft.)	1.4 mi.	1,500 ft. (rev. 200 ft.)	1:25

This trail runs from Ethan Pond Trail, 1.3 mi. south of its jct. with Zealand Trail, to Twinway, 0.1 mi. west of the Zeacliff outlook. Zeacliff is an attractive trail, much less frequently used than most trails in this area, but very steep and rough in parts and not recommended for hikers with heavy packs. Practically all of the trail is in the Pemigewasset Wilderness.

The trail leaves Ethan Pond Trail and descends west over open talus, soon bearing right (northwest); here, Zeacliff Trail must be followed with care. The trail then bears left and drops very steeply through the woods to cross Whitewall Brook at 0.2 mi. (In the reverse direction, ascending from the brook, bear right partway up the slope.) It then climbs to the west very steeply, up an old slide at first. The grade eases at 0.6 mi., and soon the trail reaches the top of the ridge, where it ascends northwest gradually through a beautiful birch forest. The trail then angles along the left edge of the ridge crest, descends slightly, and scrambles up to the left of a ledge. The trail winds upward to the northwest through rough, ledgy terrain, then at 1.1 mi., it turns right and scrambles up a steep, fairly difficult ledge, with a view of Mt. Bond at the top. Above this point, the trail ascends steadily to the ridge crest and Twinway. To reach the Zeacliff outlook, turn right at this jct.

ZEALAND TRAIL (WMNF; MAP 2: G7)

Cumulative from end of Zealand Rd. (2,020 ft.) to:	⇅	↗	↺
A–Z Trail (2,460 ft.)	2.3 mi.	450 ft.	1:25
Ethan Pond Trail–Twinway jct. (2,460 ft.)	2.5 mi.	450 ft.	1:30
Zealand Falls Hut (2,640 ft.) via Twinway	2.7 mi.	650 ft.	1:40

Zealand Trail runs from the end of Zealand Rd. to a jct. with Ethan Pond Trail and Twinway just below Zealand Falls Hut. Zealand Trail is reached by following Zealand Rd. (FR 16), which leaves US 302 at Zealand Campground 2.2 mi. east of the stoplight in Twin Mountain, to a parking area on the left 3.5 mi. from US 302. The parking area is a stop for the AMC Hiker Shuttle. Zealand Rd. is gated and closed to public vehicular use from mid-November to mid-May, and at those times hikers and skiers must not park at the gate or along the highway but instead use the parking area across US 302, 0.2 mi. east of Zealand Rd. Zealand Trail is attractive and relatively easy, following an old railroad grade much of the way, and passing through an area of beaver swamps, meadows, and ponds, with views of the surrounding mountains. The major brook crossings have bridges, but several smaller brooks must be crossed, and the upper part of the trail is subject to occasional beaver flooding.

Leaving the parking area, the trail bears left at a fork in 50 yd. (sign for Zealand Falls Hut) and follows an extension of the road for 0.2 mi. then bears right on a bypass 0.4 mi. long, much of which is rough and rocky. The trail then joins the railroad grade and approaches the Zealand River at 0.8 mi., near some ledges in the stream reached by a side path on the left. Here, the trail diverges right from the grade, climbs through the woods for 0.2 mi., then rejoins the grade and continues up the valley, crossing Zealand River on a bridge at 1.5 mi. The trail then crosses a brook, Zealand River on another bridge, and then another brook, and at 1.7 mi., it enters an open area of beaver ponds and meadows with fine views. The trail crosses a boardwalk across a swamp then turns left and follows the railroad grade along the west edge of the swamps, crossing two brooks and making one bypass to the right. At 2.3 mi., just beyond a beaver meadow with a view of Mt. Tom, A–Z Trail enters from the left. Zealand Trail crosses the outlet brook on a bridge and skirts Zealand Pond, with two side paths leading to views from the shore, and ends at 2.5 mi., where Ethan Pond Trail continues straight ahead on the old railroad grade and Twinway turns right to Zealand Falls Hut, 0.2 mi. away.

MT. HALE AND THE SUGARLOAVES

LEND-A-HAND TRAIL (AMC; MAP 2: G7–G6)

From Twinway (2,690 ft.) to:	⮁	⬈	⟳
Mt. Hale summit (4,054 ft.)	2.7 mi.	1,400 ft. (rev. 50 ft.)	2:05

This attractive trail connects Zealand Falls Hut with the summit of Mt. Hale, which offers only very restricted views over trees that are steadily growing taller. The grade is fairly easy, but the footing is rather rough for a good part of its distance. The trail takes its name from a journal for charitable organizations that was edited by Edward Everett Hale, the Boston pastor and author for whom Mt. Hale was named.

This trail diverges right (north) from Twinway 0.1 mi. above Zealand Falls Hut and climbs steadily, crossing a small brook three times. After about 0.5 mi., the grade becomes easy in a long section with numerous plank walkways, where small brooks flow in and through the trail. At 1.5 mi., the trail enters a scrubby, ledgy area with limited views and ascends moderately. In a rocky area at 1.9 mi., an opening 30 yd. right of the trail offers a good outlook toward Carrigain Notch. The trail then traverses a long, level shoulder, descending slightly. At 2.4 mi., the trail climbs another rocky pitch and continues in open conifers to the summit clearing, marked by a large cairn, where Hale Brook Trail leaves east (right). Many of the rocks around the former fire tower site are reputed to be strongly magnetic.

HALE BROOK TRAIL (WMNF; MAP 2: G7–G6)

From Zealand Rd. (1,770 ft.) to:	⮁	⬈	⟳
Mt. Hale summit (4,054 ft.)	2.2 mi.	2,300 ft.	2:15

This trail climbs from Zealand Rd. (FR 16), at a parking area 2.5 mi. from US 302, to the clearing at the summit of Mt. Hale, which provides only very restricted views over trees that have been steadily reclaiming the formerly bare summit. The trail has steady, moderate grades and passes through a fine birch forest in its middle section.

The yellow-blazed trail leaves the parking area, crosses a cross-country ski trail, then ascends steadily to cross Hale Brook at 0.8 mi. The trail continues the steady climb then swings left at 1.1 mi. and ascends gradually across the steep slope above Hale Brook (a difficult sidehill in winter), recrossing the brook in its rocky bed at 1.3 mi. The trail ascends by several switchbacks, crossing a small brook at 1.7 mi. Still ascending and curving

SEC
3

gradually to the right, the trail enters the conifers, passes a restricted view southeast to Mt. Willey, and attains the summit (where a clearing has a large cairn) from the east.

SUGARLOAF TRAIL (WMNF; MAP 2: F6)

From Zealand Rd. (1,644 ft.) to:	⮃	↗	⏱
Middle Sugarloaf summit (2,539 ft.)	1.4 mi.	900 ft.	1:10
North Sugarloaf summit (2,310 ft.)	1.2 mi.	700 ft. (rev 50 ft.)	0:55
Round trip to both summits	3.4 mi.	1,100 ft.	2:15

This trail ascends both North Sugarloaf and Middle Sugarloaf from Zealand Rd. (FR 16), just south of the bridge over the Zealand River, 1.0 mi. from US 302. Parking is just north of the bridge. These two little peaks offer excellent views from their open, ledgy summits for a relatively small effort.

Leaving the road, Sugarloaf Trail (which here coincides with Trestle Trail) follows the river for 0.2 mi., skirting a washout from the 2011 storm near the start. As Trestle Trail continues straight ahead along the river, Sugarloaf Trail swings left, immediately crosses a snowmobile trail and a logging road, and climbs gradually, passing a few large boulders, where Sugarloaf Trail turns sharply right (arrow). At 0.7 mi., it makes an abrupt ascent with many rock steps toward the notch between North and Middle Sugarloaf. In this notch, at 0.9 mi., the trail divides. The left branch traverses the flat ridge between the peaks for 0.2 mi. then turns sharply right and climbs by switchbacks to the summit of Middle Sugarloaf at 0.5 mi. from the notch, becoming very steep in the last ledgy section, which includes a ladder. The right branch descends slightly, circles the west side of North Sugarloaf, and then climbs to the ridge crest. Here, with an outlook to the left, the trail turns right and leads through scrub to open ledges at the south edge of the summit of North Sugarloaf at 0.3 mi. from the notch.

TRESTLE TRAIL (WMNF; MAP 2: F6)

From Zealand Rd. (1,644 ft.) for:	⮃	↗	⏱
Complete loop	1.0 mi.	100 ft.	0:35

This short loop trail, which runs at mostly easy grades with minor ups and downs but which has a difficult unbridged river crossing in the middle, begins and ends at the bridge over Zealand River on Zealand Rd. (FR 16), 1.0 mi. from US 302. (Parking is at the north end of the bridge.) The trail leaves the road at the south end of the bridge and follows the river, coinciding with Sugarloaf Trail for 0.2 mi., skirting a washout from the 2011 storm near the start. After Sugarloaf Trail diverges left, Trestle Trail continues briefly along the river, bears left away from the river, crosses a snowmobile trail, then turns sharply right at a large boulder to join and follow the snowmobile trail for a short distance. Then the trail turns sharply right on an old railroad grade, crosses the Zealand River at 0.6 mi. (may be very difficult or dangerous; the bridge at this crossing was washed out in 2005), and ascends to Sugarloaf II Campground. After following the campground road for 0.1 mi., the trail reenters the woods and returns to Zealand Rd. at the north end of the bridge.

Another short trail, signed "Wildlife Pond," leaves the east side of Zealand Rd. just north of the trailhead and follows a nearly level old logging road 0.2 mi. southeast to the open shore of a small pond with an impressive view of the cliffs on Middle Sugarloaf.

WILLEY RANGE

AROUND-THE-LAKE TRAIL AND RED BENCH TRAIL (AMC; MAP 2: G8–G7)

From Highland Center at Crawford Notch (1,900 ft.) for:	⇅	↗	⟳
Complete loop around Ammonoosuc Lake	1.2 mi.	100 ft.	0:40
Complete loop including Red Bench viewpoint	1.8 mi.	250 ft.	1:00

This yellow-blazed trail provides an easy, scenic loop hike around Ammonoosuc Lake, a small, secluded pond located near AMC's Highland Center. A spur trail leads to Red Bench, a restricted viewpoint. The trail starts behind the left (west) end of the Highland Center. Parking is available at AMC's Macomber Family Information Center hikers lot, or across US 302 at the north end of Saco Lake; follow paths across the field and walk to the left of the Highland Center. The trail (sign) begins a short distance down a spur road that diverges left off the main service road looping around the lodge. (The trail has two signed entrances; the paths soon unite.) Around-the-Lake Trail descends into the woods along an old road and in 60 yd. bears left off the road onto a footpath. (A few steps ahead on the old road, Stewardship Trail diverges right at a sign; this interpretive path leads 0.2 mi. back to the rear of the Highland Center.) Around-the-Lake Trail enters the WMNF and reaches the loop jct. at 0.3 mi. Taking the left (west) branch, the path crosses Crawford Brook on a plank bridge, descends past Merrill Spring, and runs along the west shore of the lake.

At 0.6 mi., Red Bench Trail, a spur path 0.3 mi. long, departs on the left (north) and runs parallel to the railroad, ascending and then descending gradually, then crosses the tracks diagonally (caution: active tourist railroad) and leads to a bench with a restricted view of Mt. Washington (ascent 50 ft., rev. 100 ft.). From the jct. with this spur, Around-the-Lake Trail bears right, soon passing the Down to the Lake Spur on the right. This short side path descends to the north shore of the lake, where you have a view of mts. Webster and Willard. The main trail swings around the northeast shore, crosses a small dam and field at the outlet, follows an old road across a bridge and uphill away from the lake, and finally bears right off the road (sign) into the woods on a footpath, ascending gently back to the loop jct.

SEC 3

MT. WILLARD TRAIL (AMC/NHDP; MAP 2: G8)

From Macomber Family Information Center (Crawford Depot; 1,900 ft.) to:	⇅	↗	⟳
Ledges near Mt. Willard summit (2,800 ft.)	1.6 mi.	900 ft.	1:15

This path runs from AMC's Macomber Family Information Center (Crawford Depot), on the west side of US 302 across from Saco Lake, to the ledges above the cliffs of Mt. Willard overlooking Crawford Notch. Parking is available at AMC's Macomber Family Information Center hikers lot, or across US 302 at the north end of Saco Lake. The upper part of this trail was formerly a carriage road, and the trail has easy to moderate grades, fairly good footing, and magnificent views from the ledges, offering one of the finest views in the White Mountains for the effort required.

The trail begins across the railroad tracks (caution: active tourist railroad) just south of the information center. The trail coincides with Avalon Trail for 0.1 mi., where Mt. Willard Trail diverges to the left and runs on the level, crosses a small brook, and soon turns right to begin the ascent. In another 100 yd., the trail bears right, bypassing to the west a severely washed-out portion of the old carriage road. At 0.5 mi., the trail passes to the left of Centennial Pool (sign), a pleasant spot on the small brook that the trail follows. The trail then bears left away from the brook and ascends fairly steeply, and at 0.7 mi., it turns right, rejoining the old carriage road. The trail ascends moderately, swinging left at 1.2 mi. and then right, and continues at easy grades to the ledges just east of the true summit.

AVALON TRAIL (AMC; MAP 2: G8–G7)

Cumulative from Macomber Family Information Center (Crawford Depot; 1,900 ft.) to:	⇅	↗	⟳
A–Z Trail (2,740 ft.)	1.3 mi.	850 ft.	1:05
Mt. Avalon spur path (3,350 ft.)	1.8 mi.	1,450 ft.	1:40
Willey Range Trail (4,280 ft.)	2.8 mi.	2,400 ft.	2:35

This trail runs from AMC's Macomber Family Information Center (Crawford Depot) on the west side of US 302 to Willey Range Trail, 90 yd. north of the summit of Mt. Field, passing a spur path to the fine outlook on Mt. Avalon along the way. Some parts of Avalon Trail are steep and rough. For parking, see Mt. Willard Trail.

Avalon Trail begins across the railroad tracks (caution: active tourist railroad) just south of the information center. Avalon Trail coincides with Mt. Willard Trail for 0.1 mi., continuing ahead where Mt. Willard Trail leaves left. Avalon Trail ascends gradually and crosses Crawford Brook (may be difficult in high water) at 0.3 mi. Just beyond this crossing, a loop path 0.1 mi. long (sign: Cascade Loop) diverges left, passes by Beecher and Pearl Cascades, and shortly rejoins the main trail. Avalon Trail climbs at a moderate grade, bears right away from the brook at 0.6 mi., recrosses the brook at 0.8 mi., and continues its moderate ascent. At 1.3 mi., after a steeper pitch, A–Z Trail to Zealand Trail and Zealand Falls Hut diverges right. Avalon Trail bears left and soon begins a sustained steep, rocky climb, and at 1.8 mi., in the small col just below Mt. Avalon's summit, a side path, 100 yd. long, diverges left and climbs steeply with several ledge scrambles to this fine ledgy viewpoint. The main trail passes through a flat, ledgy area with restricted views, climbs easily through a switchback, then swings right for a steep, rough climb, with some slippery ledges and restricted views to the northeast. The trail then continues with easier grades to Willey Range Trail. For the summit of Mt. Field, go left (south) 90 yd.

A–Z TRAIL (AMC; MAP 2: G7)

Cumulative from Avalon Trail (2,740 ft.) to:	↥↧	↗	⟳
Willey Range Trail (3,700 ft.)	1.0 mi.	1,000 ft. (rev. 50 ft.)	1:00
Zealand Trail (2,460 ft.)	3.7 mi.	1,100 ft. (rev. 1,350 ft.)	2:25
Zealand Falls Hut (2,640 ft.) via Zealand Trail and Twinway	4.2 mi.	1,300 ft.	2:45

This trail runs to Zealand Trail from Avalon Trail, 1.3 mi. from AMC's Macomber Family Information Center (Crawford Depot), crossing the Willey Range at the Field–Tom col, and thus provides a route between Zealand Falls Hut and US 302 at the high point of Crawford Notch, and access to the north end of the Willey Range from either starting point. The footing is often wet on some sections of the trail west of the Willey Range.

A–Z Trail diverges right from Avalon Trail and soon descends to cross a deep, steep-walled gully then climbs steadily, angling up along the side of the brook valley that has its head at the Field–Tom col. At 0.6 mi., A–Z

SEC 3

Trail crosses the brook, swings right, and soon begins to climb more steeply. The trail bears left to reach the height-of-land at 1.0 mi., where Mt. Tom Spur diverges right. A–Z Trail starts to descend gradually, and in 80 yd., Willey Range Trail enters on the left. A–Z Trail now descends more steeply with rougher footing for 0.5 mi. before the grade eases. The trail crosses a snowmobile trail and two branches of Mt. Field Brook, traverses a long easy section with a slight ascent, and recrosses the snowmobile trail at 2.4 mi. A–Z Trail descends moderately through a beautiful birch forest, crossing several small brooks, then descends more steeply to cross a larger brook at 3.0 mi. The trail climbs over a low ridge and continues down at easy grades, skirting a beaver pond, and reaches Zealand Trail 2.3 mi. from the end of Zealand Rd.; Zealand Falls Hut is 0.5 mi. left via Zealand Trail and Twinway.

ETHAN POND TRAIL (AMC; MAP 2: H8–G7)

Cumulative from Willey House Station site
(1,440 ft.) to:

	⇅	↗	○
Willey Range Trail (2,650 ft.)	1.6 mi.	1,200 ft.	1:25
Side trail to Ethan Pond Campsite (2,860 ft.)	2.6 mi.	1,450 ft. (rev. 50 ft.)	2:00
Shoal Pond Trail (2,510 ft.)	4.6 mi.	1,450 ft. (rev. 350 ft.)	3:00
Thoreau Falls Trail (2,460 ft.)	5.1 mi.	1,450 ft. (rev. 50 ft.)	3:15
Zeacliff Trail (2,448 ft.)	5.9 mi.	1,450 ft.	3:40
Zealand Trail–Twinway jct. (2,460 ft.)	7.2 mi.	1,500 ft. (rev. 50 ft.)	4:20
Zealand Falls Hut (2,640 ft.) via Twinway	7.4 mi.	1,700 ft.	4:35

This scenic trail begins at the Willey House Station site in a parking area just below the railroad tracks, reached by the paved Willey House Station Rd. (0.3 mi. long; not plowed in winter), which leaves the west side of US 302 directly opposite Webster Cliff Trail, 1.0 mi. south of the Willey House site. Ethan Pond Trail ends at the jct. of Zealand Trail and Twinway, 0.2 mi. below Zealand Falls Hut, and is part of the AT.

Ethan Pond Trail crosses the tracks and ascends on an old logging road, from which Arethusa–Ripley Falls Trail diverges left in 0.2 mi. Ethan Pond Trail bears right and climbs steadily then becomes more gradual, and at 1.3 mi., Kedron Flume Trail enters on the right. At 1.6 mi., Willey Range Trail leaves straight ahead, and Ethan Pond Trail turns left and climbs steadily to the broad height-of-land at 2.1 mi., passing from Crawford Notch State Park into the WMNF. The trail then follows an old logging road gently downhill to a point close to the southeast corner of Ethan Pond, which, however, is not visible from the trail. This pond is named for its discoverer, Ethan Allen Crawford. Here, at 2.6 mi. from Willey House Station, a side trail on the right descends 140 yd. to the inlet of Ethan Pond (where you have a view of the Twin Range over the pond), crosses the inlet, then ascends another 80 yd. to Ethan Pond Campsite.

Ethan Pond Trail descends gradually with many plank walkways, passing through semi-open bogs and beautiful spruce forest. At 3.3 mi., the trail bears right onto a relocated section that meanders to the north then rejoins the old route at 3.9 mi. At 4.4 mi., the trail bears right then left onto a spur of the old Zealand Valley railroad and follows it to the main line at 4.6 mi., where Shoal Pond Trail enters from the left. At 4.9 mi., Ethan Pond Trail crosses the North Fork on a wooden bridge, and at 5.1 mi., Thoreau Falls Trail diverges left to continue down the North Fork. (The top of Thoreau Falls, with fine views, is reached by descending 0.1 mi. on this trail.) Ethan Pond Trail soon crosses a small brook and follows the old railroad grade on a gradual curve into Zealand Notch, with its steep, fire-scarred walls. The trail crosses the talus slopes of Whitewall Mtn., coming into the open with fine views, and at 5.9 mi., in the middle of this section, Zeacliff Trail diverges left. Ethan Pond Trail soon reenters the woods and continues on the remains of the railroad grade (which is badly washed out in places) to the jct. with Zealand Trail and Twinway. For Zealand Falls Hut, turn left onto Twinway and follow it for 0.2 mi.

SEC
3

KEDRON FLUME TRAIL (AMC; MAP 2: G8)

Cumulative from Willey House site (1,320 ft.) to:	⇅	↗	○
Kedron Flume (2,000 ft.)	1.0 mi.	700 ft.	0:50
Ethan Pond Trail (2,450 ft.)	1.3 mi.	1,150 ft.	1:15

This blue-blazed trail runs from the Willey House site on US 302 in Crawford Notch, 2.9 mi. south of AMC's Highland Center, to Ethan Pond Trail 0.3 mi. south of its jct. with Willey Range Trail, passing Kedron Flume, an interesting cascade. Parking is available to the left of the main building at the Willey House site. As far as Kedron Flume, the trail has mostly easy to moderate grades with fairly good footing, but past the flume, it is very steep and rough.

Follow a driveway on the left (south) side of the main building for 40 yd. to the trail sign. The trail passes through a picnic area and enters the woods, soon passing a side path on the right (sign: Willey Boulders) that descends 80 yd. to a viewing platform with a vista to the Webster Cliffs; behind the platform are the Willey Boulders, around which the famed

Willey Slide of 1826 is said to have split, sparing the house below but not its occupants, who fled into the path of the slide. The main trail climbs the steep slope by long, gravelly switchbacks. At 0.2 mi., just after a right turn, the new West Side Trail diverges left. At 0.4 mi., the trail crosses the railroad tracks, where you can catch a glimpse of Mt. Willard; on the far side of the tracks is a steep, rough pitch. The trail turns left and climbs moderately, and at 1.0 mi., after a short descent, it crosses Kedron Brook. Above the crossing are an interesting flume and cascade; below, looking beyond the top of a waterfall, is a view across the notch. Use care on the slippery ledges. From here, the trail makes a very steep and rough climb, following a small brook part of the way, then becomes easier as the trail approaches Ethan Pond Trail.

WILLEY RANGE TRAIL (AMC; MAP 2: G8–G7)

Cumulative from Ethan Pond Trail (2,650 ft.) to:	↥↧	↗	⟳
Mt. Willey summit (4,285 ft.)	1.1 mi.	1,650 ft.	1:25
Mt. Field summit (4,340 ft.)	2.5 mi.	2,050 ft. (rev. 350 ft.)	2:15
A–Z Trail (3,700 ft.)	3.4 mi.	2,050 ft. (rev. 650 ft.)	2:45

This trail begins on Ethan Pond Trail, 1.6 mi. from the Willey House Station site, then runs over the summits of Mt. Willey and Mt. Field to A–Z Trail in the Field–Tom col. In combination with Ethan Pond, A–Z, and Avalon trails, Willey Range Trail makes possible various trips over the Willey Range to or from the Willey House Station site, AMC's Macomber Family Information Center (Crawford Depot), and Zealand Falls Hut. The section on the south slope of Mt. Willey is very steep and rough.

This trail continues straight ahead where Ethan Pond Trail turns left, crosses Kedron Brook in 100 yd., climbs moderately, and at 0.2 mi., turns left and crosses a smaller brook. At 0.4 mi., the trail crosses another small brook then makes a long, steep, and rough climb with occasional restricted outlooks; a series of wooden ladders is located partway up this slope. The best view is from the east outlook, just before the summit of Mt. Willey, reached by a side path that leaves on the right 40 yd. below the summit cairn. The main trail swings left over the summit at 1.1 mi. and circles around to the southwest outlook, which affords a sweeping view over the northeastern part of the Pemigewasset Wilderness. The trail then turns right (north) and descends gradually, swinging over to the east side of the ridge then back to the west side. The trail climbs over a knob and descends to the Field–Willey col at 2.0 mi. It then climbs, steeply at times, along the west side of the ridge, passing a partial view into the Pemigewasset Wilderness. At 2.5 mi., the trail reaches a clearing with a large cairn at the summit of Mt. Field, where a short side path on the right leads to a northeast outlook. Just north of the summit is a partial view west, and after a short, steep descent, Avalon Trail diverges right. Willey Range Trail then climbs over a small knob and descends gradually northwest to A–Z Trail, just below the Field–Tom col at 3.4 mi. Turn left for Zealand Falls Hut or right for Mt. Tom Spur, Macomber Family Information Center (Crawford Depot), and US 302.

MT. TOM SPUR (AMC; MAP 2: G7)

From A–Z Trail (3,700 ft.) to:	↕	↗	◯
Mt. Tom summit (4,051 ft.)	0.6 mi.	350 ft.	0:30

This short trail runs from A–Z Trail to the summit of Mt. Tom. Mt. Tom Spur leaves A–Z Trail at the height-of-land, 80 yd. east of the Willey Range Trail jct., and climbs at easy grades with one steep, rocky pitch to a false summit, where a side path on the right leads 70 yd. to an open blowdown area with good views east and south. Here, the main path swings left and reaches the true summit in another 60 yd. The former open view west from a blowdown patch has become limited due to tree growth.

ARETHUSA FALLS REGION

ARETHUSA FALLS TRAIL (NHDP; MAP 2: H8)

Cumulative from Arethusa Falls parking area (1,260 ft.) to:	↕	↗	◯
Arethusa–Ripley Falls Trail (2,100 ft.)	1.3 mi.	850 ft.	1:05
Arethusa Falls (2,000 ft.) via spur trail	1.5 mi.	850 ft. (rev. 100 ft.)	1:10

This trail is the direct route to Arethusa Falls, which at nearly 200 ft. is the highest falls in New Hampshire. The trail begins at the Arethusa Falls parking lot, located at the top of a 0.2-mi. spur road (Arethusa Falls Rd.; sign for Arethusa Falls) off the west side of US 302, 3.4 mi. south of the Willey House site in Crawford Notch State Park. (Plenty of parking space is available in the lot just off US 302 if the upper lot spaces are full.)

The trail crosses the railroad and leads left (south) for 50 yd. then turns right into the woods. The trail soon passes a spur path left to some cascades then follows old roads above the north bank of Bemis Brook. Bemis Brook Trail, which diverges left at 0.1 mi. and rejoins at 0.5 mi., provides an attractive but rougher alternative route closer to the brook. At the upper jct., Arethusa Falls Trail turns right and, in 50 yd., swings left and climbs moderately on a well-constructed footway, following an old logging road. At 1.0 mi., the trail crosses the first of two bridges over tributary brooks. After the second bridge, it climbs steadily and swings right to a three-way jct., where Arethusa–Ripley Falls Trail continues ahead and a spur trail to Arethusa Falls diverges left. Turn left and descend 0.2 mi. southwest (with 100 ft. of elevation loss) on the spur trail to reach the falls; you have a good view of the falls where the trail emerges at the edge of the brook. For the closest views, one must cross Bemis Brook, which is potentially difficult in the high-water conditions when the falls are most impressive.

BEMIS BROOK TRAIL (NHDP; MAP 2: H8)

From lower jct. with Arethusa Falls Trail (1,320 ft.) to:	⇅	↗	⏱
Upper jct. with Arethusa Falls Trail (1,670 ft.)	0.5 mi.	350 ft.	0:25

This is a slightly longer and rougher alternative route to the lower part of Arethusa Falls Trail, running closer to Bemis Brook. Bemis Brook Trail departs to the left from Arethusa Falls Trail 0.1 mi. from its start at the railroad, angles toward the brook, and then follows close to the brook, passing spur paths leading left to Fawn Pool, Coliseum Falls, and Bemis Brook Falls. Bemis Brook Trail then swings right and climbs very steeply up the bank to rejoin Arethusa Falls Trail.

ARETHUSA–RIPLEY FALLS TRAIL (AMC/NHDP; MAP 2: H8)

Cumulative from Arethusa Falls Trail (2,100 ft.) to:	⇅	↗	⏱
Frankenstein Cliff Trail (2,420 ft.)	1.1 mi.	500 ft. (rev. 200 ft.)	0:50
Ripley Falls (1,750 ft.)	2.3 mi.	600 ft. (rev. 750 ft.)	1:25
Ethan Pond Trail (1,570 ft.)	2.6 mi.	650 ft. (rev. 250 ft.)	1:40
Willey House Station site (1,440 ft.) via Ethan Pond Trail	2.8 mi.	650 ft. (rev.150 ft.)	1:45

These two spectacular waterfalls in Crawford Notch are connected by a blue-blazed trail that starts at the upper end of Arethusa Falls Trail. (From this jct., a spur path descends 0.2 mi. southwest, with 100 ft. of elevation loss, to the base of Arethusa Falls, as described earlier.)

From the upper end of Arethusa Falls Trail, Arethusa–Ripley Falls Trail descends slightly then climbs to the west on the south side of a brook, which the trail soon crosses. Becoming rougher, the trail leads northeast across several small watercourses, with several ups and downs, then climbs steeply to the plateau behind Frankenstein Cliff. Turning east, the trail descends easily then rises slightly to the jct. on the right with Frankenstein Cliff Trail at 1.1 mi. Arethusa–Ripley Falls Trail soon turns sharply left and ascends gradually northwest across the plateau. The trail descends gradually and then more steeply, crossing a small brook, then continues by switchbacks down to the bank of a brook. Here it turns left and follows a narrow, rooty path across a steep slope to the top of Ripley Falls, which are about 100 ft. high. The ledges just off the path near the top of the falls are dangerously slippery and should be avoided. The trail swings right here and descends a steep slope by rough switchbacks to cross Avalanche Brook (difficult at high water) at the foot of the falls at 2.3 mi. The trail climbs a short, steep pitch then descends gradually to the northeast with fairly rough footing to join Ethan Pond Trail 0.2 mi. above the Willey House Station site, which is reached by continuing straight ahead.

FRANKENSTEIN CLIFF TRAIL (NHDP; MAP 2: H8)

Cumulative from Arethusa Falls parking area (1,260 ft.) to:	⬆⬇	↗	↻
Frankenstein Cliff outlook (2,150 ft.)	1.3 mi.	1,000 ft. (rev. 100 ft.)	1:10
Arethusa–Ripley Falls Trail (2,420 ft.)	2.1 mi.	1,350 ft. (rev. 100 ft.)	1:45

This yellow-blazed trail provides access to Frankenstein Cliff, a prominent bluff that juts out from the tableland south of Mt. Willey and affords excellent views of the lower part of Crawford Notch. The trail begins at the top of a 0.2 mi. spur road (Arethusa Falls Rd.; sign for Arethusa Falls) off the west side of US 302, 3.4 mi. south of the Willey House site in Crawford Notch State Park. Plenty of parking space is available in the lot just off US 302 if the upper lot spaces are full.

Leaving the upper parking area, Frankenstein Cliff Trail descends to a jct. at 0.1 mi., where a green-blazed connecting path 0.1 mi. long from the lower parking lot enters on the right. The main trail swings left to cross a small brook then runs north below and roughly parallel to the railroad grade with many minor ups and downs. At 0.3 mi., blue-blazed Frankenstein Cutoff (sign) joins from the right. (This connecting path, 0.1 mi. long, leaves the west side of US 302 0.3 mi. south of the entrance to Dry River Campground, follows an old paved roadbed south for 100 yd., then turns right and climbs steeply to meet Frankenstein Cliff Trail.) At 0.6 mi., Frankenstein Cliff Trail turns sharply left and passes under the Frankenstein railroad trestle near the south abutment. (Trespassing on the railroad right of way, including the use of its bed as a footway, is extremely dangerous and is prohibited; the tracks are actively used by excursion trains from May through October.)

The trail ascends by switchbacks, steeply in places, with gravelly footing that is especially slippery on the descent. At 0.8 mi., the trail traverses below two cliff faces (use caution); when descending, avoid a beaten path leading left down a rocky gully beneath the lower cliff. In another 0.1 mi. the trail swings left and continues ascending generally southwest through hardwood forest. At 1.2 mi., after a scramble up a ledgy slot, the trail turns sharply left and continues through a fine forest of spruce and balsam to a cliff-top outlook similar to that on Mt. Willard, with a view south along the notch, at 1.3 mi. To the right, Arethusa Falls can be seen at the head of the Bemis Brook valley.

Leaving the outlook, the trail ascends gradually through a fine stand of spruce in a west-northwest direction, skirting the top of the cliffs and offering occasional restricted views of Mt. Bemis and the Bemis Brook valley. At 1.5 mi., a spur path called Falcon Cliff Trail (sign) diverges right and ascends north, first easily and then more steeply. It then turns sharply right, runs along the edge of a wooded bluff, and makes a short descent at 0.2 mi. to a partially open south-facing viewpoint atop a crag called Falcon Cliff, with a 150-ft. ascent from the main trail. The main trail continues to ascend and passes just south of the summit of a small knob. Near the height-of-land, the trail levels off, passes a restricted outlook to Mt. Washington and Montalban Ridge over the Dry River Valley on the right at 1.8 mi., then descends the ridge for a short distance and winds gradually downward to meet Arethusa–Ripley Falls Trail.

WEST SIDE TRAIL (NHDP; MAP 2: G8)

From Kedron Flume Trail (1,460 ft.) to:	⥮	↗	↻
US 302/Willey House Station Rd. (1,260 ft.)	1.2 mi.	250 ft. (rev. 450 ft.)	0:45

This new yellow-blazed trail along the lower western slopes of Crawford Notch, under development in 2016–2017, will link Kedron Flume Trail, 0.2 mi. above its trailhead at the Willey House site, with the trailhead for the Appalachian Trail at the jct. of Willey House Station Rd./US 302 and the north end of Maggie's Run at the Pleasant Valley picnic area on US 302. The section between Kedron Flume Trail and the AT trailhead was cut and blazed in 2016. Leaving Kedron Flume Trail on the left just above a sharp right turn, it runs south across the slope with several turns and numerous ups and downs, including several short, steep pitches; follow blazes carefully. It crosses two channels of Kedron Brook at 0.4 mi., descends to a low spot at 0.7 mi., ascends steeply, then descends again, crosses two small gullies, and runs at easy grades to the jct. of US 302 and Willey House Station Rd. From here the trail will be extended about 1 mi. southeast to US 302 at the point where it crosses the Saco River, about 100 yd. northwest of the north trailhead for Maggie's Run.

MAGGIE'S RUN (NHDP; MAP 2: H8)

From Pleasant Valley picnic area (1,206 ft.) to:	⇅	⬈	◔
South terminus on US 302 (1,180 ft.)	0.8 mi.	0 ft.	0:25
Saco River Trail (1,220 ft.) via link trail	0.6 mi.	0 ft.	0:20

This new trail provides an attractive walk along the Saco River on the floor of Crawford Notch, with a spur path connecting with Saco River Trail. The north end of the trail starts at the Pleasant Valley picnic area on the west side of US 302, 2.1 mi. south of the Willey House site and 0.8 mi. north of the entrance to Dry River Campground. The south terminus is about 0.1 mi. north of the campground entrance, diagonally across from a picnic area and historic sign for Frankenstein Trestle. From Pleasant Valley, the blue-blazed trail runs 0.2 mi. south between US 302 and the Saco River to a jct. where a link trail diverges left, crosses US 302, turns right and then left, and winds along the floor of the notch for 0.4 mi., ending at a jct. with Saco River Trail 0.4 mi. north of Dry River Trail. The main trail continues south along the attractive river. At 0.6 mi. it emerges on a dry brookbed, turns right and follows the bed for 15 yd., then turns left back into the woods. At 0.8 mi. Maggie's Run turns sharply left across a sandy area and soon reaches US 302. At the left turn a spur called Maggie's Extension, 0.2 mi. long, continues ahead (south) along the river, soon passing a sign, then swings left and climbs a grassy embankment to US 302, 0.1 mi. south of the entrance to Dry River Campground.

PEMIGEWASSET WILDERNESS

LINCOLN WOODS TRAIL (WMNF; MAP 2: I5–H6)

Cumulative from Lincoln Woods parking area (1,160 ft.) to:	⇅	⬈	◔
Osseo Trail (1,300 ft.)	1.4 mi.	150 ft.	0:45
Black Pond Trail (1,410 ft.)	2.6 mi.	250 ft.	1:25
Franconia Brook Trail and Pemigewasset Wilderness boundary (1,440 ft.)	2.9 mi.	300 ft.	1:35

Lincoln Woods Trail runs for 2.9 mi. along the west side of the East Branch of the Pemigewasset River, from the Kancamagus Highway (NH 112) to a footbridge over Franconia Brook, forming a central artery from which several trails diverge and lead to various destinations near and in the western part of the Pemigewasset Wilderness. Lincoln Woods Trail follows the wide bed of a logging railroad that last operated in 1948. The trail begins at a large parking area with a USFS information center on the north side of the road (sign: Lincoln Woods), just east of the highway bridge over the East Branch, 5.6 mi. from the information center at I-93, Exit 32 in Lincoln and 0.3 mi. beyond the Hancock Campground. This trail receives extremely heavy use, and camping is strictly regulated. (See p. 151 for camping regulations.) The area along the East Branch was heavily damaged by the 2011 storm, and in many places, the high, steep riverbanks have been severely undercut, creating a serious hazard for hikers who approach too close to the edge.

Note: The suspension footbridge that crossed the East Branch 5.4 mi. from the Lincoln Woods trailhead was removed in 2009. Advance route planning is essential. If you are starting your hike at Lincoln Woods, be sure to start on the correct side of the East Branch, depending on your destination. Hikers planning to reach Osseo Trail, Black Pond Trail, Franconia Falls Trail, Franconia Brook Trail, or Bondcliff Trail should start on Lincoln Woods Trail (west side of the river), and hikers planning to use Cedar Brook Trail, Wilderness Trail, Thoreau Falls Trail, Shoal Pond Trail, Carrigain Notch Trail, or points beyond should start on Pemi East Side Trail (east side of the river). Do not rely on crossing the river at either the Franconia Brook Tentsite or the site of the former suspension bridge. A former 0.7-mi. section of Wilderness Trail on the north side of the river and west of the bridge site has been closed. (This bridge removal does not affect the suspension bridge located at the Lincoln Woods trailhead.)

Leaving the parking lot, Lincoln Woods Trail runs across the deck of the information center and descends a wooden stairway to the left, swings left past a kiosk and crosses the East Branch on a suspension bridge, then turns right and follows the railroad bed along the river, climbing almost imperceptibly. At 0.7 mi., the trail skirts to the left of a major washout from the 2011 storm, with a view over the river to Mt. Hitchcock. Soon the trail crosses Osseo Brook over a culvert and follows it upstream, and at 1.4 mi., Osseo Trail diverges left to follow Osseo Brook up its valley. Lincoln Woods Trail soon passes the old logging camp 8 clearing on the left, and at 1.8 mi., by a piece of old rail, the trail comes close to the river's edge, where a fine view upstream to Bondcliff can be obtained from the rocks just off the trail.

Soon the trail crosses Birch Island Brook on a bridge, and a long straightaway leads to the jct. with Black Pond Trail on the left at 2.6 mi. At 2.9 mi., just before the bridge across Franconia Brook, Franconia Falls Trail diverges left. From this jct., Lincoln Woods Trail descends ahead to cross Franconia Brook on a footbridge. About 50 yd. beyond the Franconia Brook footbridge, Lincoln Woods Trail ends at the Pemigewasset Wilderness boundary. Here, Franconia Brook Trail climbs the bank on the left (north) and Bondcliff Trail (formerly a section of Wilderness Trail) diverges right (east). (*Note:* Use of a former route leading from the north end of the footbridge to a crossing of the East Branch is discouraged because the step stones have mostly been swept away, and the river crossing is often dangerous.)

SEC 3

OSSEO TRAIL (AMC; MAP 2: I6–H5)

Cumulative from Lincoln Woods Trail (1,300 ft.) to:	↕	↗	⟳
Downlook viewpoint (3,500 ft.)	3.2 mi.	2,200 ft.	2:40
Flume Slide Trail–Franconia Ridge Trail jct. (4,240 ft.)	4.1 mi.	2,950 ft.	3:30
From Lincoln Woods parking area (1,160 ft.) to:			
Mt. Flume summit (4,328 ft.) via Lincoln Woods Trail, Osseo Trail, and Franconia Ridge Trail	5.6 mi.	3,150 ft.	4:25

This trail connects Lincoln Woods Trail with the south end of Franconia Ridge, near the summit of Mt. Flume. Osseo Trail has mostly moderate grades with good footing. The trail begins on the west side of Lincoln Woods Trail, 1.4 mi. north of the parking area on the Kancamagus Highway. Osseo Trail heads west, following Osseo Brook in a flat area, then climbs the bank to the right and follows old logging roads up the valley at easy to moderate grades with good footing, including one section where it briefly follows an old inclined logging railroad grade at one of its switchbacks. At 2.1 mi., the trail turns right and climbs by switchbacks to the top of the ridge above the valley to the north then ascends the ridge—winding about at first and climbing by zigzags as the ridge becomes steeper. At the top of this section are several wooden staircases, and at 3.2 mi., a short side path (sign) leads right to a "downlook" with a fine view into the Pemigewasset Wilderness.

The trail ascends more staircases, passing a side path leading 10 yd. left to a south viewpoint, and soon reaches the top of the ridge. Its grade becomes easy until it reaches the crest of Franconia Ridge in an unusually flat area at 3.7 mi. The trail turns sharply right here and ascends steadily near the crest of a narrow ridge to a jct. with Flume Slide Trail on the left and Franconia Ridge Trail straight ahead.

BLACK POND TRAIL (WMNF; MAP 2: H6)

From Lincoln Woods Trail (1,410 ft.) to:	⇅	↗	↻
Black Pond (1,590 ft.)	0.8 mi.	200 ft.	0:30

This easy yellow-blazed spur trail leaves Lincoln Woods Trail 2.6 mi. from the Kancamagus Highway and ends at Black Pond, where you have a view of Bondcliff from the shore. Diverging left (west) from Lincoln Woods Trail by an old logging camp site, Black Pond Trail first follows a former logging railroad spur then leaves it on the left after 150 yd. and skirts the north shore of an old ice pond, which is in sight but not actually reached. The trail then meanders to the right of a beaver-flooded area, making several turns. At 0.2 mi. it turns right onto an old logging road, crosses an overgrown logging camp clearing, approaches Birch Island Brook, then bears slightly right away from it up a moderate incline. At 0.5 mi., the trail makes a short, sharp descent to cross the outlet brook from Black Pond then recrosses it at a boggy spot. Soon the trail crosses the outlet brook for the third time and follows it to the outlet of Black Pond, where there is a view of Owl's Head Mtn. In another 100 yd. the maintained trail ends at the viewpoint on the southwest shore.

FRANCONIA FALLS TRAIL (WMNF; MAP 2: H6)

Cumulative from Lincoln Woods Trail (1,420 ft.) to:	⇅	↗	↻
Franconia Falls (1,500 ft.)	0.4 mi.	100 ft.	0:15
End of trail (1,520 ft.)	0.5 mi.	100 ft.	0:20

This easy spur trail leads to Franconia Falls, where Franconia Brook falls over broad ledges with fine cascades and pools. Visitors to Franconia Falls should use great caution in times of high water because the ledges are slippery when wet and the current is very powerful. The trail leaves Lincoln Woods Trail on the left, 2.9 mi. from the Kancamagus Highway parking area, just before the footbridge over Franconia Brook. Franconia Falls Trail climbs gradually along Franconia Brook, at first close by it then some distance away. At 0.4 mi., side paths on the right lead out to the ledges beside Franconia Falls; from the upper ledges is a view of North Hancock. The trail continues another 0.1 mi. to a high bank overlooking a gorge and pool where there is an "End of Trail" sign.

FRANCONIA BROOK TRAIL (WMNF; MAP 2: H6–G5)

Cumulative from Bondcliff Trail (1,440 ft.) to:	⇅	↗	↻
Lincoln Brook Trail, south jct. (1,730 ft.)	1.7 mi.	300 ft.	1:00
13 Falls Campsite (2,196 ft.)	5.2 mi.	750 ft.	3:00
Garfield Ridge Trail (3,420 ft.)	7.4 mi.	2,000 ft.	4:40

SEC 3

This trail runs from a jct. with Lincoln Woods Trail and Bondcliff Trail, 2.9 mi. from the Kancamagus Highway, to Garfield Ridge Trail, 0.9 mi. east of the summit of Mt. Garfield, thus connecting the Pemigewasset East Branch valley with the Franconia–Garfield ridge crest. Practically the entire Franconia Brook Trail is in the Pemigewasset Wilderness. The many significant brook crossings may be difficult at high water.

The trail diverges north from the jct. about 50 yd. beyond the footbridge across Franconia Brook, at the boundary of the Pemigewasset Wilderness, and climbs up a steep bank to an old railroad grade, which the trail follows north. The trail crosses Camp 9 Brook at 0.5 mi. and 0.7 mi., and swings right at 1.0 mi. off the railroad grade onto a muddy bypass around a section flooded by an enthusiastic beaver colony, with glimpses of Owl's Head Mtn. across the swamp. The trail crosses Camp 9 Brook again, turns sharply left back along the brook (avoid the beaten path leading ahead into another swamp), climbs its bank, and soon rejoins the railroad grade, turning sharply right onto the grade at 1.3 mi. In the reverse direction, take care to make the left turn off the railroad grade and the right turn at the brook crossing. The trail continues to the jct. with Lincoln Brook Trail, which diverges left (west) at 1.7 mi.

Franconia Brook Trail next passes to the left of several beaver ponds and open swamps, with views of the lower ridges of the Bond range to the east; beaver flooding may affect the trail in this area. The trail continues to ascend gradually on the old railroad grade, crossing Hellgate Brook at 2.6 mi. (the best crossing is on a short path that diverges right), Redrock Brook at 3.5 mi., a nameless brook at 4.4 mi., and Twin Brook at 4.7 mi., and passing the sites of logging camps 10, 12, and 13. At 5.2 mi., the trail reaches 13 Falls, a series of beautiful waterfalls and cascades, and turns right, leaving the railroad grade on an old logging road. In 100 yd., Lincoln Brook Trail reenters from the left (west); 25 yd. to the left on this trail is a scenic ledgy area on Franconia Brook. Franconia Brook Trail continues ahead and, in quick succession, a spur path leads right to 13 Falls Campsite, and Twin Brook Trail branches off to the right. Franconia Brook Trail continues on an old logging road at easy grades, following a branch of Franconia Brook, then turns left to cross the brook at 6.2 mi. The trail then climbs more steeply along old logging roads, where the trail is often rough, muddy and obscure, to the top of the ridge, ending at Garfield Ridge Trail in the deep col east of Mt. Garfield. Garfield Ridge Campsite is 0.6 mi. to the left (west) by Garfield Ridge Trail and a spur path; Galehead Hut is 2.2 mi. to the right.

SEC 3

LINCOLN BROOK TRAIL (WMNF; MAP 2: H6–H5)

Cumulative from Franconia Brook Trail, south jct. (1,730 ft.) to:	⇅	↗	↺
Owl's Head Path (2,560 ft.)	3.4 mi.	900 ft. (rev. 50 ft.)	2:10
Height-of-land (3,210 ft.)	5.0 mi.	1,550 ft.	3:15
Franconia Brook Trail near 13 Falls Campsite (2,196 ft.)	6.9 mi.	1,550 ft. (rev. 1,000 ft.)	4:15

This trail begins and ends on Franconia Brook Trail, and together these two trails make a complete circuit around the base of Owl's Head Mtn. The south jct. is 1.7 mi. north of the bridge over Franconia Brook, and the north jct. is near 13 Falls Campsite, 5.2 mi. from the bridge. (*Caution:* Several of the brook crossings on this trail—in particular the southernmost crossing of Franconia Brook and the first crossing of Lincoln Brook—may be very difficult and potentially dangerous at high water. North of the jct. with Owl's Head Path, sections of this trail may be difficult to follow.) The entire trail is in the Pemigewasset Wilderness.

Turning left (west) off Franconia Brook Trail at the south jct., Lincoln Brook Trail leads southwest through the woods above an area flooded by beavers then descends gradually and bears right onto an old railroad bed just before the crossing of Franconia Brook at 0.5 mi. In another 0.4 mi., after crossing a minor brook, the trail crosses Lincoln Brook from the north to the south side. These two major crossings are not easy even at moderate water levels and are very difficult and potentially dangerous in high water, at which time other hiking options should be considered. If water levels are high, it may be safer for hikers who are traveling south on Lincoln Brook Trail from the Owl's Head area to bushwhack south along the west side of Lincoln Brook and Franconia Brook, at times following obscure paths, eventually reaching either Franconia Falls Trail or Black Pond Trail.

Beyond the Lincoln Brook crossing, Lincoln Brook Trail follows the brook upstream on a long northward curve, at 1.8 mi. passing the first of several small but attractive cascades. The trail traverses a rough section along the bank then crosses a brook at 2.2 mi. After a short climb it bears left onto an old railroad grade that is muddy in places and then crosses the larger Liberty Brook at 2.8 mi. Soon the trail swings left and right through the small Camp 12 clearing, climbs left to bypass a muddy stretch, rejoins the road, and crosses Lincoln Brook (sometimes difficult) to the east side at 3.0 mi. After a rougher stretch, at 3.4 mi. the trail passes the jct. on the right with Owl's Head Path, marked only by a cairn, beyond which Lincoln Brook Trail receives much less use. It climbs the slope well above the brook, becoming rough at times, then descends to cross Lincoln Brook again at 4.3 mi.

The trail continues north, climbing moderately, then runs across a plateau at easy grades. At 5.0 mi., the trail swings right and descends slightly to cross a small branch of Lincoln Brook at the height-of-land. For the next 0.2 mi., the trail is very muddy and obscure and requires great care to follow through a boggy area along the divide between the Lincoln Brook and Franconia Brook drainages, with glimpses of the Franconia Range (west) and Mt. Garfield (north). After crossing three more small brooks, the trail returns to drier ground along a section with old yellow blazes. The trail climbs a short pitch and descends northeast then east on a rough footway where again the trail must be followed with care, particularly where it runs in and out of a small brook bed several times. The trail then becomes better defined and the footing improves, and at 6.4 mi., the trail swings left and descends moderately to cross a west branch of Franconia Brook at 6.6 mi. The trail then turns sharply right and continues down the north bank of this tributary past cascades and pools. The trail crosses the main branch of Franconia Brook at an open ledgy area just above the confluence with the western tributary, with a view up to Owl's Head Mtn., and in 25 yd. rejoins Franconia Brook Trail near 13 Falls Campsite.

OWL'S HEAD PATH (MAP 2: H5)

From Lincoln Brook Trail (2,560 ft.) to:	⇅	↗	⟳
Owl's Head summit (4,025 ft.)	1.0 mi.	1,450 ft.	1:15
From Lincoln Woods parking area (1,160 ft.) to:			
Owl's Head summit (4,025 ft.) via Lincoln Woods Trail, Franconia Brook Trail, Lincoln Brook Trail, and Owl's Head Path	9.0 mi.	2,900 ft. (rev. 50 ft.)	5:55

This unofficial, unmaintained path ascends the slide on the west side of this remote mountain, starting from Lincoln Brook Trail 3.4 mi. from its south jct. with Franconia Brook Trail and 0.4 mi. beyond the second crossing of Lincoln Brook. At the slide, Lincoln Brook is nearby on the west, and the steep mountainside rises immediately to the east. In 2016 this jct. was marked by a cairn, but USFS regulations prohibit the marking of unofficial paths in Wilderness Areas, so hikers should be prepared to find the beginning of the path—and the path itself—without signs or other markings. The path begins just beyond a mossy flat area to the right of the trail. *Caution:* The slide is very steep and rough, and though considerably overgrown, it is still potentially dangerous due to loose rock and smooth ledges, especially when wet. Great care should be taken both ascending and descending.

Leaving Lincoln Brook Trail, Owl's Head Path climbs through dense evergreens, briefly to the right of the narrow slide track, then joins it and soon emerges on a steep swath of gravel and loose rock. Owl's Head Path quickly reaches the open part of the slide, which provides good views of the Lincoln Brook valley and Franconia Range. The slide has no well defined path; the most-used route, marked by occasional cairns, follows a winding course with a few ledge scrambles. Open ledges at about 2,950 ft. offer the best views and a convenient spot for a rest stop. Above here, one route enters the woods on the right and follows a steep and eroded beaten path, while another climbs the upper open part of the slide to the left. Above the top of the slide, 0.3 mi. and 700 ft. above Lincoln Brook Trail, is a small spring spurting from the rock like a fountain, which unfortunately is not completely reliable. The two routes rejoin, and the path continues up a very steep and rough pitch on an old section of the slide track that trees have reclaimed.

Higher up, the path exits to the left from the track (on the descent, avoid a beaten path continuing ahead at a point where the main path bears right and down) and climbs steeply northeast on a well-trodden but very rough footway usually littered with numerous blowdowns. The path continues climbing steadily up to the ridge, which is reached at 0.7 mi., then swings left and runs near the crest with minor ups and downs. At 0.8 mi., after climbing a short pitch, the path crosses a small clearing at the top of a 4,005-ft. knob, which had been regarded as the true summit for many years. The well-beaten path continues meandering north along the ridge, descending slightly and rising easily to the true summit (4,025 ft.), marked by a cairn in 2016, at 1.0 mi. (This or other markings may not always be present in the future.)

The path continuing north from the "old" true summit to the "new" true summit is now easy to follow for experienced hikers, although there are occasional faint paths that diverge and merge; in particular, in the reverse direction there is a fork where a false path diverges left and the correct path leads to the right. Interesting though restricted views are sometimes obtained around the summit area from blowdown patches; if this summit was not densely wooded, it would afford one of the finest views in the mountains due to its strategic location in the center of the great horseshoe formed by the ridge running from the Franconias to the Bonds.

TWIN BROOK TRAIL (AMC; MAP 2: H5–G6)

Cumulative from 13 Falls Campsite (2,196 ft.) to:	⥮	↗	⟳
Frost Trail (3,750 ft.)	2.6 mi.	1,550 ft.	2:05
Galehead Hut (3,780 ft.) via Frost Trail	2.7 mi.	1,600 ft.	2:10

This trail connects 13 Falls Campsite to Galehead Hut, running almost entirely within the Pemigewasset Wilderness. The trail diverges from Franconia Brook Trail near the campsite and rises gradually east-northeast, soon entering beautiful birch woods. At the start, take care to identify Twin Brook Trail at sharp bends, avoiding several old logging roads. After 0.4 mi., the trail swings to the northeast and heads up the valley of Twin Brook, keeping to the left (west) of the brook, which is occasionally audible but not visible. After traversing four distinct minor ridges of Galehead Mtn. in the next mile, the trail eventually climbs more steeply, swinging left and then right, and in another 0.1 mi. reaches its terminus on Frost Trail, 0.1 mi. from Galehead Hut. For the hut, make a right turn onto Frost Trail.

BONDCLIFF TRAIL (AMC; MAP 2: H6–G6)

Cumulative from Lincoln Woods Trail–Franconia Brook Trail jct. (1,440 ft.) to:	⥮	↗	⟳
Camp 16 site (1,600 ft.)	1.8 mi.	150 ft.	1:00
Bondcliff summit (4,265 ft.)	6.2 mi.	2,900 ft. (rev. 50 ft.)	4:35
Mt. Bond summit (4,698 ft.)	7.4 mi.	3,550 ft. (rev. 200 ft.)	5:30
Guyot Campsite spur (4,360 ft.)	8.1 mi.	3,600 ft. (rev. 400 ft.)	5:50
Twinway (4,508 ft.)	8.7 mi.	3,800 ft. (rev. 50 ft.)	6:15

This trail begins at a jct. with Lincoln Woods Trail and Franconia Brook Trail just north of the bridge over Franconia Brook, 2.9 mi. from the parking area on the Kancamagus Highway. Bondcliff Trail leads along the East Branch to the site of old logging camp 16 on a section that was formerly part of Wilderness Trail, ascends over Bondcliff and Mt. Bond, and ends at Twinway just west of the summit of Mt. Guyot. Bondcliff Trail connects the

Pemigewasset East Branch valley with the high summits of the Twin Range, and the entire trail is in the Pemigewasset Wilderness except for a short segment at the north end. The long section on Bondcliff and one shorter section on Guyot are above treeline, with great exposure to the weather. The views from this trail are unsurpassed in the White Mountains.

From the jct. on the north side of the Franconia Brook bridge, Bondcliff Trail bears right, bypassing a wet section of railroad grade, then joins the grade and continues to swing to the east. The trail crosses a brook at 1.0 mi. and reaches the camp 16 clearing (where camping is no longer permitted) at 1.8 mi. (Until this point, the trail was formerly part of Wilderness Trail; the section of Wilderness Trail that continued ahead for 0.7 mi. on the railroad grade to the site of the suspension bridge over the East Branch—which was removed in 2009—has been closed.) Here Bondcliff Trail turns left, runs level for 100 yd., turns sharply left just before reaching Black Brook, and climbs a bank to an old logging road. The trail then leaves the logging road and climbs well up on the slope to the west of the brook. At 2.9 mi., after a slight descent, the trail bears left to rejoin the logging road along the brook and ascends easily, although parts of the road are severely eroded.

The trail then makes the first of four crossings of the brook at 3.2 mi.; the second crossing, at 3.7 mi., provides the last sure water. At the third crossing, at 4.3 mi., the trail turns right and crosses the brook bed (often dry). In 40 yd.—a tricky spot—the trail reaches another brook bed (usually dry), descends along it to the right for 20 yd., then swings sharply left out of the brook bed and climbs a steep slope on rock steps. (Descending, the trail swings right at the bottom of the steps into the brook bed, ascends along it for 20 yd., then turns sharply left out of it.) The trail then swings left to another old logging road and crosses a gravel bank where one can look almost straight up to the summit of Bondcliff. In a short distance, the trail makes the last brook crossing in a steep, south-facing ravine; if the brook is dry here, water can sometimes be found a short distance farther up in the streambed. The trail winds up a small, prow-shaped, "hanging" ridge that protrudes into the main ravine then swings left at 5.0 mi. and begins a long sidehill ascent of the steep slope on a logging road, heading back to the southwest. At 5.9 mi., the trail reaches the crest of Bondcliff's south ridge, swings north, and ascends the ridge to a short, difficult scramble up a ledge. Soon the trail breaks out of the scrub and climbs along the edge of the cliffs, with spectacular views, reaching the summit of Bondcliff at 6.2 mi. (*Caution:* The trail runs above treeline for about a mile and is potentially dangerous in bad weather, particularly high winds. When visibility is poor, stay well to the right [east] of the edge of the precipices.)

The trail now descends the open ridge into a long, flat col then ascends the steep, rough slope of Mt. Bond, reentering scrubby woods about half-way up. At 7.4 mi., the trail passes just west of the summit of Mt. Bond, which commands a magnificent unrestricted view of the surrounding wilderness and mountains. Here, the trail bears left (northwest); in the reverse direction, it bears right (southwest) off the summit area. The trail descends north, crossing a minor knob, then drops down rather steeply past West Bond Spur on the left at 7.9 mi. and leaves the Pemigewasset Wilderness. The trail reaches the Bond–Guyot col at 8.1 mi., where a spur path descends right (east) 0.2 mi. and 200 ft. to Guyot Campsite and its spring. Bondcliff Trail then ascends to the bare south summit of Mt. Guyot and continues mostly in the open 0.2 mi. to its jct. with Twinway, 0.1 mi. west of the less-open north summit of Guyot. Go straight ahead here for the Twins and Galehead Hut, or turn right for Zealand Mtn. and Zealand Falls Hut.

SEC 3

WEST BOND SPUR (AMC; MAP 2: H6)

From Bondcliff Trail (4,490 ft.) to:	⇅	↗	⏱
West Bond summit (4,540 ft.)	0.5 mi.	200 ft. (rev. 150 ft.)	0:20

This short path provides access to the sharp, rocky summit of the West Peak of Mt. Bond, which is perched high above the deep valleys of an extensive Wilderness Area, commanding magnificent views. The entire trail is in the Pemigewasset Wilderness. The trail leaves Bondcliff Trail 0.5 mi. north of the summit of Mt. Bond and 0.2 mi. south of the spur to Guyot Campsite, descends moderately for 0.3 mi. to the col at the foot of West Bond, and ascends moderately for a short distance. West Bond Spur then climbs the steep cone to the summit, which is the most easterly of several small peaks on a ridge running east and west.

PEMI EAST SIDE TRAIL (WMNF; MAP 2: I5–H6)

Cumulative from Lincoln Woods parking area (1,160 ft.) to:	⇅	↗	⏱
Gate at wilderness boundary (1,420 ft.)	2.9 mi.	300 ft. (rev. 50 ft.)	1:35
Cedar Brook Trail–Wilderness Trail (1,716 ft.)	5.2 mi.	600 ft.	2:55

This trail, a former truck road used to haul timber out of the Pemigewasset Wilderness in the 1940s, provides easy, scenic walking along the east and south sides of the East Branch of the Pemigewasset River. The trail begins at the Lincoln Woods parking area off NH 112 (the Kancamagus

Highway), just east of the highway bridge over the East Branch and 5.6 mi. from the information center at the I-93 exit in Lincoln. From here, it leads into the Pemigewasset Wilderness, ending at a jct. with Cedar Brook Trail and Wilderness Trail. The area along the East Branch was heavily affected by the 2011 storm, and in many places the high, steep riverbanks have been severely undercut, creating a serious hazard for hikers who approach too close to the edge.

Note: The suspension footbridge that crossed the East Branch 5.8 mi. from the Lincoln Woods trailhead was removed in 2009. Advance route planning is essential. If you are starting your hike at Lincoln Woods, be sure to start on the correct side of the East Branch, depending on your destination. Hikers planning to access Osseo Trail, Black Pond Trail, Franconia Falls Trail, Franconia Brook Trail, or Bondcliff Trail should start on Lincoln Woods Trail (west side of the river), and hikers planning to use Cedar Brook Trail, Wilderness Trail, Thoreau Falls Trail, Shoal Pond Trail, Carrigain Notch Trail, or points beyond should start on Pemi East Side Trail (east side of the river). Do not rely on crossing the river at the Franconia Brook Tentsite or the site of the former suspension bridge. A former 0.7-mi. section of Wilderness Trail on the north side of the river and west of the bridge site has been closed.

The first 2.9 mi. of Pemi East Side Trail (also known as East Branch Truck Rd., FR 87), up to a gate marking the Wilderness boundary, is a gravel road occasionally used by USFS vehicles for administrative purposes but not open to public vehicular use. This section provides hikers access to Franconia Brook Tentsite (24 sites) at 2.7 mi. The entire trail receives far less use than the parallel Lincoln Woods Trail and Bondcliff Trail on the opposite side of the East Branch. Leaving the parking area, the trail runs across the deck of the Lincoln Woods information center and descends a short path to the gravel road, where the trail turns right and crosses a bridge. The road ascends gently, and at 0.2 mi. it turns right onto a relocated section that ascends easily past a large clearing on the right, descends slightly and crosses two wide bridges, then rejoins the original route at 0.7 mi. (To the left, the old route is now the start of Pine Island Trail, descending 50 yd. and then turning sharply right.) The trail ascends then descends briefly at 1.1 mi., crosses a brook on a bridge, and meanders past small beaver meadows, passing the north jct. with Pine Island Trail on the left at 1.5 mi.

Pemi East Side Trail climbs over a knoll, and at 2.6 mi., an opening on a bank above the river provides a limited view of the mountains to the west. After passing through the Franconia Brook Tentsite area, the trail reaches the gate and the Pemigewasset Wilderness boundary at 2.9 mi. Just before the gate, a spur road descends left to a former rock-hop crossing of the East

Branch, whose use is discouraged, as the step stones have mostly been swept away and crossing the river is often dangerous.

Beyond the gate, Pemi East Side Trail enters the Wilderness Area, swings east, and narrows to a footway. At 3.2 mi., a side path descends 25 yd. left to an attractive pool and cascade. The trail follows the East Branch closely, passing flat ledges fringing a pool at 3.5 mi., then pulls away from the river and follows a relocation, 0.1 mi. long, up to the right. The trail crosses Cedar Brook (difficult in high water) at 4.0 mi. and makes a sharp right turn at 4.1 mi. At 4.3 mi. it bears right at a fork where a beaten path leads left across a brook. The trail continues at easy grades through the woods, with occasional glimpses of the river, then bears right at 5.0 mi. and climbs moderately to a jct. with Cedar Brook Trail (right) and Wilderness Trail (left).

SEC 3

PINE ISLAND TRAIL (WMNF; MAP 2: I6)

From south jct. with Pemi East Side Trail (1,220 ft.) to:	⇅	↗	↺
North jct. with Pemi East Side Trail (1,260 ft.)	0.9 mi.	50 ft.	0:30
From Lincoln Woods parking area (1,160 ft.) for:			
Loop via Pemi East Side Trail and Pine Island Trail	3.1 mi.	100 ft.	1:35

This short yellow-blazed trail provides pleasant walking along the East Branch of the Pemigewasset River, making possible an easy loop hike in combination with Pemi East Side Trail. Two sections of the trail that were washed away by the 2011 storm have been relocated away from the river. Although the storm opened some interesting views near the trail, the riverbank is severely undercut in places, and caution is advised. Pine Island Trail diverges sharply left (sign) from Pemi East Side Trail, 0.7 mi. north of the Lincoln Woods parking area. It descends for 50 yd. on a section of road that was formerly part of Pemi East Side Trail then turns sharply right. It briefly follows an old logging road then bears left to cross Pine Island Brook (may be difficult in high water) and a second, smaller brook.

The trail soon swings right (north) and follows the wide, rocky river. At 0.3 mi., at a point near the riverbank with views of the mountains upstream, it bears right onto a relocated section. In 0.1 mi. it rejoins the original route, passes a side path descending 15 yd. left to a stony area with a view of Scar Ridge, and passes through a red pine grove. At 0.6 mi. it continues ahead on another relocated section, recrosses Pine Island Brook, runs through coniferous woods, and again rejoins the original route, passing a partial view of Owl's Head Mtn. It passes a short side path (left), dropping down a bank to an open sandy area where there are good views of the river and surrounding mountains, then turns right (east) and in 50 yd. ends at its northern jct. with Pemi East Side Trail.

WILDERNESS TRAIL (WMNF; MAP 2: H6–H7)

Cumulative from jct. with Pemi East Side Trail–Cedar Brook Trail (1,716 ft.) to:	⇅	↗	○
Thoreau Falls Trail (1,743 ft.)	1.5 mi.	100 ft. (rev. 100 ft.)	0:50
Stillwater Junction (2,050 ft.)	4.1 mi.	400 ft.	2:15

This trail now begins on the south side of the East Branch, at a jct. with Pemi East Side Trail (5.2 mi. from the Lincoln Woods parking area) and Cedar Brook Trail. (*Note:* There was formerly a 2.5-mi. section of Wilderness Trail on the north side of the East Branch. The western 1.8 mi. of that section is now part of Bondcliff Trail; the eastern 0.7 mi. of that section, which led to the suspension footbridge that was removed in 2009, has been closed.) The entire trail is in the Pemigewasset Wilderness.

Leaving the jct. with Pemi East Side Trail and Cedar Brook Trail, Wilderness Trail descends gradually east and northeast on an old railroad grade that was formerly part of Cedar Brook Trail, crossing two brooks. Before the first crossing is a large, deep washout from the 2011 storm that is bypassed on the right; use caution. At 0.6 mi., just before reaching the site of the former footbridge over the East Branch, Wilderness Trail bears right onto a short new segment of trail, and in 70 yd. the trail bears right onto the main railroad grade, which once crossed the East Branch at the site of the footbridge. Wilderness Trail now follows the grade upstream along the East Branch, skirting the end of the long north ridge of Mt. Hancock. Just after crossing a small slide, the trail reaches North Fork Junction at 1.5 mi., where Thoreau Falls Trail diverges left (north) and Wilderness Trail continues straight ahead. At 2.4 mi., the trail diverges from the railroad grade (which crossed the river here), crosses Crystal Brook, and soon rejoins the grade, which has crossed back to this bank.

After passing through the clearing of old logging camp 18, the trail leaves the railroad for the last time at 3.2 mi., following a path along the bank that provides scenic views of the East Branch, and crosses over a low ridge of spruce and pine. The trail descends to cross Carrigain Branch (may be difficult at high water) at 3.9 mi., cuts through a dense conifer thicket, and soon reaches Stillwater Junction beside the East Branch, coming into the jct. at a right angle to the stream. Here, Carrigain Notch Trail (Section Four) leads right (southeast), and Shoal Pond Trail crosses the East Branch directly ahead at an old dam (no bridge). (Avoid the path angling left, down to the stream, which is an abandoned section of Wilderness Trail.)

THOREAU FALLS TRAIL (WMNF; MAP 2: H6–G7)

From Wilderness Trail (1,743 ft.) to:	⇅	↗	↻
Ethan Pond Trail (2,460 ft.)	5.1 mi.	900 ft. (rev. 200 ft.)	3:00

This trail runs from Wilderness Trail at North Fork Junction (6.7 mi. from the Lincoln Woods parking area via Pemi East Side Trail) past Thoreau Falls to Ethan Pond Trail, roughly halfway between Ethan Pond Campsite and Zealand Falls Hut. The lower part of Thoreau Falls Trail follows an old railroad grade, but the upper part of the trail has a few steep and rough sections. Practically the entire trail is in the Pemigewasset Wilderness. Tropical Storm Irene caused some erosion and a major washout in the middle section of this trail.

The trail diverges left (north) from Wilderness Trail on a railroad bed, which the trail leaves after 0.4 mi. to cross the East Branch of the Pemigewasset on a 60-ft. bridge, where you have views of Bondcliff and Mt. Carrigain. (The bridge was badly damaged by the 2011 storm, and the USFS is assessing crossing options. As of late 2016, a final decision had not yet been made to either replace the bridge or permanently remove it and construct a rock crossing, which would be difficult in high water. In the interim, a load limit of one person at a time has been posted as an added safety precaution; for current status, check with the WMNF Pemigewasset Ranger District.)

On the north side of the river, the trail crosses a rocky brook bed, climbs to the left, and soon turns right to rejoin the railroad grade. The trail follows the grade along the North Fork, passing the old logging camp 22 clearing on the right at 1.1 mi. At 2.1 mi., the trail leaves the railroad grade for good and runs along the river with minor ups and downs; in this section there is a washout from the 2011 storm that must be traversed with care. The trail soon turns right and climbs fairly steeply northeast on a narrow footway and then descends, following a bypass that avoids two former crossings of the North Fork.

The trail rejoins the old route at 2.9 mi. and follows old logging roads and sections of footpath with some minor ups and downs, making several turns that must be followed carefully. At 4.0 mi., the trail turns right next to a ledge on the edge of the North Fork then continues up the valley at easy to moderate grades, crossing several small brooks. At 4.6 mi., the trail bears away from the North Fork and soon begins a steeper climb on a rough footpath to the right of, but out of sight of, Thoreau Falls. The trail descends to cross the North Fork at the top of the falls (use caution) at 5.0 mi., where a broad ledge offers a fine view up to mts. Bond and Guyot

SEC
3

and down to the beautiful curving waterfall. (In high water, this crossing is dangerous; there may be a better and safer brook crossing just upstream from the trail.) Leaving the stream, the trail ascends 0.1 mi. to Ethan Pond Trail, 0.2 mi. west of the latter's bridge over the North Fork. Turn left for Zealand Falls Hut or right for Ethan Pond Shelter.

SHOAL POND TRAIL (AMC; MAP 2: H7–G7)

Cumulative from Stillwater Junction (2,050 ft.) to:	↥↧	↗	⟳
Shoal Pond (2,550 ft.)	3.5 mi.	550 ft. (rev. 50 ft.)	2:00
Ethan Pond Trail (2,510 ft.)	4.0 mi.	550 ft. (rev. 50 ft.)	2:15

This trail runs through remote, wild country from its jct. with Wilderness Trail and Carrigain Notch Trail (see Section Four) at Stillwater Junction to Ethan Pond Trail, between Zealand Falls Hut and Ethan Pond Campsite. Practically the entire Shoal Pond Trail is in the Pemigewasset Wilderness. Parts of the trail are very wet, and some sections may be overgrown, littered with blowdowns, and difficult to follow.

At Stillwater Junction, the trail leads north across the East Branch at the site of an old dam (no bridge; may be difficult in moderate water and dangerous in high water), immediately turns left on a narrow footway on an old railroad bed, and turns right off the bed in 40 yd., onto a narrow section that may be overgrown. The trail soon joins another railroad bed, where the footway becomes easier to follow. Leaving the railroad grade temporarily, the trail descends to cross Shoal Pond Brook at 0.6 mi.; this crossing may be difficult if the water is high. The trail rejoins the railroad bed, passes the old logging camp 21 clearing on the left, and passes a spur path on the right at 1.0 mi. that leads to The Pool, an attractive ledgy cascade and pool. At 1.2 mi., the trail bears left off the railroad bed and follows old logging roads and occasional bypasses, crossing Shoal Pond Brook from west to east at 1.4 mi. The trail crosses a tributary at 1.7 mi., recrosses Shoal Pond Brook at 2.4 mi., and traverses many bog bridges (slippery when wet) in a shrubby, boggy area. At 3.2 mi., the trail crosses the brook for the last time, from west to east, and soon reaches Shoal Pond. Due to bogginess caused by beaver activity, the trail runs a short distance to the east of the pond, but a short side path at 3.5 mi. leads to the south shore of the pond and a view of Zealand Notch. The trail passes another short side path to the shore and continues on an old railroad grade, with wet footing in places, to Ethan Pond Trail.

SECTION FOUR

CARRIGAIN AND MOAT REGIONS

Map 3: Crawford Notch–Sandwich Range

INTRODUCTION

This section covers the eastern portion of the central region of the White Mountains (that part not included in Section Three), consisting of the areas bounded on the north by US 302, on the east by NH 16, and on the south by the Kancamagus Highway (NH 112); at its western edge, this section includes all areas and trails south and east of Wilderness Trail. (For a more precise description of the western boundary of Section Four, see the first paragraph of Section Three.) Section Four includes Mt. Carrigain and Mt. Hancock, the lesser mountains that surround them, and the lower but interesting mountains that rise to the east between the Saco and Swift rivers, principally Mt. Tremont and the Moat Range. The area is covered by AMC's *White Mountains Trail Map 3: Crawford Notch–Sandwich Range.* The AT does not pass through this section.

SEC 4

ROAD ACCESS

Important access roads in this area include the Kancamagus Highway (NH 112), which connects I-93 and US 3 in Lincoln to NH 16 in Conway and is a regular state highway that is paved and well maintained, open in winter except during the worst storms. Bear Notch Rd. runs 9 mi., from US 302 at the crossroads in Bartlett village to the Kancamagus Highway in Albany Intervale about 13 mi. west of Conway. Bear Notch Rd. is paved but not plowed in winter, except for the 1-mi. section immediately north of the Kancamagus Highway. North of Bear Notch, the road closely follows the line of an old railroad, and there are several excellent outlooks. Paved Passaconaway Rd. (formerly Dugway Rd.) runs west from West Side Rd. in Conway for 6.6 mi. to the Kancamagus Highway, 6.0 mi. west of its jct. with NH 16. The west half of this road is not plowed in winter, except for a short section leading from the Kancamagus Highway to a plowed parking area by the Albany Covered Bridge. The gravel Sawyer River Rd. (FR 34) begins on US 302 0.1 mi. north of the major bridge over the Sawyer River, 1.6 mi. north of the Sawyer Rock picnic area and 7.9 mi. south of the Willey House site in Crawford Notch State Park. There is a road sign and a brown post with FR 34 on it. This road is closed by a locked gate during snow season.

GEOGRAPHY

Mt. Carrigain (4,700 ft.) is the central and highest point of a mass of jumbled ridges that divides the watershed of the East Branch of the Pemigewasset River from that of the Saco River and its tributary, the Swift River.

The mountain was named for Philip Carrigain, New Hampshire secretary of state from 1805 to 1810. Carrigain made a map of the whole state in 1816, which included an early attempt to portray the White Mountains region that can best be described as imaginative. He was one of the party that named mts. Adams, Jefferson, Madison, and Monroe from the summit of Mt. Washington in 1820. The view from the observation tower on Mt. Carrigain takes in a wide area and includes most of the important peaks of the White Mountains, making this peak one of the competitors for the title of the finest viewpoint in the White Mountains. The view from Signal Ridge (4,420 ft.), Mt. Carrigain's open southeasterly spur, is also magnificent. The trailless northeasterly spur, Vose Spur (3,862 ft.), forms the west wall of the deep cleft of Carrigain Notch, facing Mt. Lowell on the east.

Mt. Hancock rises to the west of Mt. Carrigain. This is a long ridge with several summits, of which the most important are the North Peak (4,420 ft.) and the South Peak (4,319 ft.). Both peaks are wooded, but there is an outlook ledge near the summit of the North Peak and a restricted outlook from the South Peak. At one time, this was one of the most inaccessible mountains in the White Mountains, remote and trailless with slopes devastated by logging, but Mt. Hancock is now routinely ascended via Hancock Loop Trail.

The ridge between Mt. Carrigain and Mt. Hancock has no trail, and travel along the ridge is extremely difficult; the line along this ridge shown on many maps is part of the Lincoln–Livermore town boundary. Carrigain Pond, a beautiful and remote mountain pond that is one of the higher sources of the Pemigewasset River, lies just north of the ridge between Carrigain and Hancock at an elevation of about 3,200 ft. The Captain (3,540 ft.), located only 0.3 mi. from Carrigain Pond, is a striking little trailless peak, a miniature Half Dome with sheer cliffs overlooking the Sawyer River valley; however, the Captain is well hidden at the end of this isolated valley and can be seen from only a few viewpoints.

The group of peaks northeast of Carrigain Notch that rise along the ridge forming the watershed divide between the Saco and the East Branch of the Pemigewasset include Mt. Lowell (3,740 ft.), Mt. Anderson (3,740 ft.), Mt. Nancy (3,926 ft.), and Mt. Bemis (3,725 ft.). None of these peaks is reached by an officially maintained trail. The region is remarkable for its four picturesque ponds—Nancy Pond, Norcross Pond, Little Norcross Pond, and Duck Pond—which lie at the unusually high elevation of about 3,100 ft. A stand of virgin spruce just south of Nancy Pond on the north slopes of Duck Pond Mtn. is one of the largest remaining areas of virgin forest in the state, although the hurricane of 1938 did great damage,

SEC 4

felling many of the older trees. In 1991, the USFS established the 1,385-acre Nancy Brook Research Natural Area, to be maintained as nearly as possible in an undisturbed condition.

The tallest of several lesser peaks that rise in the region around Sawyer Pond, west of Bear Notch Rd., is Mt. Tremont (3,371 ft.). Mt. Tremont lies south of the big bend in the Saco River above Bartlett; this mountain has a narrow ridgecrest that runs north and south, with three conspicuous summits, of which the southernmost is the highest. Still farther south is a prominent spur peak, Owl's Cliff (2,940 ft.), with cliffs on its south and west faces. The main summit of Tremont has fine views to the south, west, and north; Owl's Cliff has a good outlook to the southwest. Southwest of both Mt. Tremont and Sawyer Pond is Green's Cliff (2,926 ft.), with cliffs on its south and east faces; Green's Cliff is very prominent from the overlooks on the eastern half of the Kancamagus Highway. Ledges near its summit provide views, but there is no trail. Sawyer Pond, which lies in a steep-walled basin on the southwest side of Mt. Tremont, and Church Pond, which lies in a flat area north of the Kancamagus Highway and southeast of Green's Cliff, are attractive objectives reached by relatively short, easy trails.

Bear Notch, crossed by the scenic Bear Notch Rd. from Bartlett village to the Kancamagus Highway in Albany Intervale, lies between Bartlett Haystack and Bear Mtn. The WMNF Bartlett Experimental Forest occupies a large area on the north slopes of these mountains. Bartlett Haystack (2,980 ft.), an aptly named mountain that was sometimes called Mt. Silver Spring in the days when hazy elegance was preferred to plain and effective description, is another interesting trailless peak that rises east of Mt. Tremont. A ledge just a few feet west of the summit, shaped like the prow of a ship, affords a magnificent view to the south, west, and north.

Moat Mtn. is a long ridge that rises impressively to the west of the Saco River nearly opposite North Conway. The whole ridge was burned over in the 1850s, and all the major summits are still bare, with magnificent views; numerous outlooks are scattered along the wooded parts of the ridge. There has been some uncertainty about the names of the summits in the range, but in this guide, the peaks are called North Moat Mtn. (3,196 ft.), Middle Moat Mtn. (2,805 ft.), and South Moat Mtn. (2,770 ft.). The peak at the apex of the Red Ridge (2,785 ft.) has sometimes also been called Middle Moat. From North Moat, a ridge runs west to densely wooded Big Attitash Mtn. (2,910 ft.), sometimes called West Moat; from there, the ridge passes over the lesser summits of Big Attitash and swings southwest to Table Mtn. (2,675 ft.), which has fine views to the south from several open ledges just below the summit. Next, the ridge swings west again to the trailless, wooded Bear Mtn. (3,220 ft.), which forms the east side of Bear Notch. South of Bear Mtn. and very close to the Kancamagus Highway are picturesque Rocky Gorge on the Saco River and nearby Falls Pond, a small scenic body of water reached by a short, easy trail from the highway. An unnamed rocky southern spur of the Moat group, which affords excellent views, is ascended by the moderately strenuous Boulder Loop Trail. On the east side of the Moat Range are White Horse Ledge (1,450 ft.) and Cathedral Ledge (1,159 ft.), two detached bluffs that present impressive cliffs to the Saco Valley. They are popular destinations for rock climbers but offer views for hikers as well. An auto road ascends to the summit of Cathedral Ledge. Echo Lake is an attractive small pond at the base of White Horse Ledge. Farther to the north, Little Attitash Mtn. (2,504 ft.) is a trailless peak on a long, curving ridge that extends northeast from Big Attitash to end in Humphrey's Ledge (1,510 ft.). Pitman's Arch, a shallow cave in the face of Humphrey's Ledge, was once reached by a toll path that is now completely overgrown. Diana's Baths is a set of very scenic cascades, located on Moat Mtn. Trail near West Side Rd., where Lucy Brook runs over ledges and through large potholes. A 4 mi. network of easy trails in the Albany Town Forest includes Swift River Trail, which offers fine views of the Swift River and South Moat Mtn. Trailhead parking is on the north side of the Kancamagus Highway, 0.7 mi. west of the WMNF Saco Ranger Station.

SEC 4

Several trails in the Mt. Carrigain region are partly within the eastern section of the Pemigewasset Wilderness. In accordance with USFS Wilderness policy, the trails in the Pemigewasset Wilderness are generally maintained to a lower standard than are non-Wilderness trails. Considerable care may be required to follow them.

CAMPING
Pemigewasset Wilderness
In accordance with USFS Wilderness policy, hiking group size may not exceed ten people, and no more than ten people may occupy any designated or non-designated campsite. Camping and wood or charcoal fires are not allowed within 200 ft. of any trail in the Pemigewasset Wilderness except at designated campsites. See p. xiii for more information about Wilderness Area regulations.

Forest Protection Areas
The WMNF has established a number of FPAs, where camping and wood or charcoal fires are prohibited throughout the year. See p.xxiv for general FPA regulations.

In the area covered by Section Four, camping and fires are also prohibited within 0.25 mi. of the Big and Little Sawyer Ponds (except at shelter and tent platforms) and Diana's Baths (located on Moat Mtn. Trail). Likewise, camping is not permitted in the Bartlett Experimental Forest and the Rocky Gorge Scenic Area. No wood or charcoal fires are permitted in the Nancy Brook Research Natural Area and the Church Pond Bog Candidate Research Natural Area.

No camping is permitted within 200 ft. of certain trails. In 2016, designated trails included Cedar Brook Trail between its jcts. with Hancock Notch and Hancock Loop trails, and all trails in the Pemigewasset Wilderness.

No camping is permitted on WMNF land within 0.25 mi. of certain roads (camping on private roadside land is illegal except by permission of the landowner). In 2016, these roads included US 302, Sawyer River Rd., the Kancamagus Highway, Bear Notch Rd., and Passaconaway (Dugway) Rd. from the Kancamagus Highway to the picnic area.

Established Trailside Campsites

Sawyer Pond Campsite (WMNF) is located on Sawyer Pond, reached by Sawyer Pond Trail. Six tent platforms are located on the northwest side of the pond, as is a shelter that accommodates eight.

SUGGESTED HIKES

■ **Easy Hikes**
FALLS POND

▒ ● ♦ ☎ ♿ (accessible to Falls Pond) 🐾	↺	↗	○
LP via Lovequist Loop	1.0 mi.	150 ft.	0:35

A short hike from the Rocky Gorge picnic area circles this pond. See Lovequist Loop, p. 228.

SAWYER POND

● ◁ ▲ ♦ ☎ ※	↺	↗	○
RT via Sawyer Pond Trail	3.0 mi.	350 ft.	1:40

This attractive and popular mountain pond situated at the base of Mt. Tremont is easily reached from Sawyer River Rd. See Sawyer Pond Trail, p. 224.

■ Moderate Hikes
BOULDER LOOP CLIFFS

🚶🐕🎿❄️

	⇅	↗	⏲
LP via Boulder Loop Trail	3.1 mi.	950 ft.	2:00

A moderately graded trail ascends a low spur of the Moat group and offers fine views from open ledges. See Boulder Loop Trail, p. 228.

TABLE MTN.

🎿🎿🚶🐕❄️

	⇅	↗	⏲
RT via Attitash Trail	3.8 mi.	1,350 ft.	2:35

This less visited peak offers good views from its south ledges. Start at Bear Notch Rd.; see Attitash Trail, p. 232.

SOUTH MOAT MTN.

🎿🎿🐕🎿❄️

	⇅	↗	⏲
RT via Moat Mtn. Trail	5.2 mi.	2,300 ft.	3:45

This bare summit has excellent views in all directions. See Moat Mtn. Trail, p. 229.

MT. TREMONT

🎿🎿🐕❄️

	⇅	↗	⏲
RT via Mt. Tremont Trail	5.6 mi.	2,550 ft.	4:05

The trail is steep in places and must be followed with care, but this infrequently climbed peak offers fine views. See Mt. Tremont Trail, p. 227.

■ Strenuous Hikes
NANCY CASCADES AND NORCROSS POND

🎿⬤🎿🎿🎿❄️

	⇅	↗	⏲
RT to Nancy Cascades via Nancy Pond Trail	4.8 mi.	1,550 ft.	3:10
RT to Nancy Cascades and Norcross Pond via Nancy Pond Trail	8.6 mi.	2,350 ft.	5:30

The trip to Nancy Cascades is attractive in itself, but it is worth the effort to continue to the unusual ledge that dams Norcross Pond and affords a fine view into the Pemigewasset Wilderness. See Nancy Pond Trail, p. 215.

SEC
4

MT. CARRIGAIN

	$\smile\!\!\!\downarrow$	$\nearrow$	$\circlearrowleft$
RT via Signal Ridge Trail	10.6 mi.	3,500 ft.	7:05

The tower on this peak offers what many people believe is the best view of all in the White Mountains. See Signal Ridge Trail, p. 212.

MT. HANCOCK

	$\smile\!\!\!\downarrow$	$\nearrow$	$\circlearrowleft$
LP via Hancock Notch, Cedar Brook, and Hancock Loop trails	9.8 mi.	2,700 ft.	6:15

An interesting route over a remote mountain, this loop offers partial outlooks from the north and south summits. To begin, see Hancock Notch Trail, p. 219.

NORTH MOAT

	$\smile\!\!\!\downarrow$	$\nearrow$	$\circlearrowleft$
LP via Red Ridge and Moat Mtn. trails	10.2 mi.	2,900 ft.	6:35

The rugged circuit over this mountain is one of the most beautiful trips in the region, traversing large amounts of open ledge. See Red Ridge Trail, p. 231.

TRAIL DESCRIPTIONS

MT. CARRIGAIN REGION

SIGNAL RIDGE TRAIL (WMNF/CAMP PASQUANEY; MAP 3: I8–H7)

Cumulative from Sawyer River Rd. (1,380 ft.) to:	$\smile\!\!\!\downarrow$	$\nearrow$	$\circlearrowleft$
Carrigain Notch Trail (1,920 ft.)	2.0 mi.	550 ft.	1:15
Signal Ridge (4,420 ft.)	4.8 mi.	3,100 ft. (rev. 50 ft.)	3:55
Mt. Carrigain summit (4,700 ft.)	5.3 mi.	3,400 ft. (rev. 50 ft.)	4:20
From US 302 (897 ft.) to:			
Mt. Carrigain summit (4,700 ft.)	7.3 mi.	3,900 ft. (rev. 100 ft.)	5:35

This trail ascends to the summit of Mt. Carrigain by way of Signal Ridge, starting from Sawyer River Rd. (FR 34) 2.0 mi. from its jct. with US 302, which is 1.6 mi. north of the Sawyer Rock picnic area. The trail begins on the right, just past the bridge over Whiteface Brook; a parking lot is on the left, also just beyond the bridge. The trail climbs moderately for most of its distance, using old roads that once provided access to the fire warden's cabin. The views from the observation tower on the summit and from Signal Ridge are magnificent. The loop back to Sawyer River Rd. via Desolation and Carrigain Notch trails is interesting but much longer, rougher, and more strenuous. Several relocations were made on the lower half of Signal Ridge Trail in 2012.

Leaving the road on a relocated section, Signal Ridge Trail ascends along the south side of Whiteface Brook. It joins the older route of the trail at 0.3 mi. and follows the south bank of the attractive brook, passing small cascades and pools, then turns left onto another relocated section at 0.6 mi. It rejoins the older route at 0.8 mi. and begins to climb steadily away from the brook then levels and crosses a flat divide. At 1.4 mi., Carrigain Brook Rd., an overgrown logging road, crosses the trail at a right angle. (This road is not passable by vehicles, but it can be followed south 1.6 mi. to Sawyer River Rd. about 0.3 mi. before the gate at the end of that road; however, there is a difficult brook crossing just before Sawyer River Rd. is reached.) At 1.7 mi., Signal Ridge Trail turns right, and in 60 yd. it crosses Carrigain Brook; care is required to find the trail on the opposite bank at this crossing, going either way. (At this right turn, the trail formerly continued ahead, but it has been relocated to follow what was formerly the lower part of Carrigain Notch Trail.) Continuing on logging roads at easy grades, Signal Ridge Trail passes to the right of an area of beaver activity. Then at 2.0 mi. it turns left onto a new section of trail at a jct. where Carrigain Notch Trail continues ahead. It swings left and climbs over a small ridge, crosses a small brook on a log bridge, and rejoins the older route at 2.3 mi. It now begins to ascend, gradually at first. At 2.7 mi., it turns sharply left where an old road continues straight up the valley. The trail angles up the end of a ridge, turns right to climb, then makes another sharp left turn (arrow) at the site of an old camp and angles up again.

At 3.1 mi., Signal Ridge Trail turns sharply right into a birch-lined straight section 1.0 mi. long with rocky footing that rises steadily at an angle up the steep side of the valley, with occasional restricted views. At the end of this section, the trail turns sharply left and zigzags up the nose of Signal Ridge, reaching the high point of the bare crest of the ridge at 4.8 mi. Views are excellent, particularly to the cliffs of Mt. Lowell across Carrigain Notch. The trail descends slightly, enters the woods, and angles left around to the south slope of the summit cone, climbing gradually to the site of the old fire warden's cabin, where there is a well on the right (water unsafe to drink without treatment). Bearing left from the small clearing, the trail soon swings right and climbs steeply to the small sag between Carrigain's two summit knobs then turns right and soon reaches

SEC 4

the summit, where an observation tower provides magnificent views. Here, Desolation Trail enters from the Pemigewasset Wilderness.

CARRIGAIN NOTCH TRAIL (AMC/CAMP PASQUANEY; MAP 3: I8–H7)

Cumulative from Signal Ridge Trail (1,920 ft.) to:	↟↡	↗	↺
Carrigain Notch (2,637 ft.)	2.0 mi.	700 ft.	1:20
Nancy Pond Trail (2,140 ft.)	3.8 mi.	700 ft. (rev. 500 ft.)	2:15
Desolation Trail (2,210 ft.)	4.6 mi.	750 ft.	2:40
Stillwater Junction (2,050 ft.)	5.4 mi.	750 ft. (rev. 150 ft.)	3:05

This trail begins on Signal Ridge Trail 2.0 mi. from Sawyer River Rd., runs through Carrigain Notch, and ends at Stillwater Junction, where Carrigain Notch Trail meets Wilderness and Shoal Pond trails (see Section Three). The section of Carrigain Notch Trail northwest of Carrigain Notch lies within the Pemigewasset Wilderness. (*Note:* Carrigain Notch Trail formerly extended 0.3 mi. farther south, but due to a 2012 relocation, that section is now part of Signal Ridge Trail.)

Carrigain Notch Trail diverges right from Signal Ridge Trail and leads north up the valley at easy grades on old logging roads. It crosses several washed-out stony areas, where care is required to follow the trail, and at 1.3 mi. it turns left off the road to bypass a muddy section. Here, just to the right of the trail, beside Carrigain Brook, you have a view of the ledges of Vose Spur, which form the west side of Carrigain Notch. Soon returning to the road, the trail climbs more steeply and, at 2.0 mi., reaches its height-of-land well up on the west wall of the notch, where it enters the Pemigewasset Wilderness. Very soon, the trail joins and follows an old logging road on the north side of the notch, descending moderately. At 2.8 mi., the trail turns left off the logging road and follows a path through the woods that avoids the wet sections of the old road while continuing to use some of the dry parts; in places, care is required to follow the trail.

At 3.8 mi., shortly after crossing a brushy area, the trail enters an old railroad grade and turns sharply left on it; Nancy Pond Trail follows the grade to the right from this point. At 4.6 mi., Carrigain Notch Trail bears left off the railroad grade then soon turns sharply right where Desolation Trail continues straight across a brook. In another 0.1 mi., Carrigain Notch Trail bears left where a blocked-off path diverges right. At 4.8 mi., the trail bears to the right, away from the Carrigain Branch, and descends gradually to Stillwater Junction on the East Branch; here Wilderness Trail turns sharply left, and Shoal Pond Trail turns right and immediately crosses the East Branch of the Pemigewasset.

DESOLATION TRAIL (AMC/CAMP PASQUANEY; MAP 3: H7)

Cumulative from Carrigain Notch Trail (2,210 ft.) to:	↿⇂	↗	⟳
Upper end of old logging road (3,530 ft.)	1.3 mi.	1,300 ft.	1:20
Mt. Carrigain summit (4,700 ft.)	1.9 mi.	2,500 ft.	2:10
From Sawyer River Rd. (1,380 ft.) for:			
Loop over Mt. Carrigain (4,700 ft.) via Signal Ridge, Carrigain Notch, Desolation, and Signal Ridge trails	13.8 mi.	3,900 ft.	8:50

This trail ascends to the summit of Mt. Carrigain from Carrigain Notch Trail, 0.8 mi. southeast of Stillwater Junction. The upper part of the trail is very steep and rough and requires great care, particularly on the descent or with heavy packs; substantial extra time may be required in either direction. Almost the entire trail is in the Pemigewasset Wilderness.

Desolation Trail leaves Carrigain Notch Trail to the southwest at a sharp turn near the edge of a tributary of the Carrigain Branch and crosses the brook. Desolation Trail follows a railroad grade for 60 yd. then diverges left and climbs moderately, at times on old logging roads. The trail climbs into a stand of birches and merges into an unusually straight old logging road on the west side of the ridge crest. The old road crosses to the east side of the ridge, deteriorates, and ends at 1.3 mi. The trail crosses a short section of slippery rock blocks and continues through an area where many rock steps have been built then swings directly up the slope into virgin woods and climbs a very steep and rough section. The grade gradually eases, and the footing slowly improves as the trail reaches the crest of the steep ridge. At 1.8 mi., the trail abruptly reaches the top of the steep section, swings left, and angles around the cone at an easy grade until reaching and climbing the last short, steep pitch to the summit observation tower, where the trail meets Signal Ridge Trail.

SEC 4

NANCY POND TRAIL (CAMP PASQUANEY/WMNF; MAP 3: H8–H7)

Cumulative from US 302 (940 ft.) to:	↿⇂	↗	⟳
Foot of Nancy Cascades (2,400 ft.)	2.4 mi.	1,500 ft. (rev. 50 ft.)	1:55
Nancy Pond (3,100 ft.)	3.4 mi.	2,200 ft.	2:50
Norcross Pond outlet (3,120 ft.)	4.3 mi.	2,250 ft. (rev. 50 ft.) ft.	3:15
Carrigain Notch Trail (2,140 ft.)	7.1 mi.	2,250 ft. (rev. 1,000 ft.)	4:40
Stillwater Junction (2,050 ft.) via Carrigain Notch Trail	8.7 mi.	2,300 ft. (rev. 150 ft.)	5:30

This trail begins at a parking pulloff on the west side of US 302, 2.8 mi. north of the Sawyer Rock picnic area and 6.7 mi. south of the Willey House site in Crawford Notch State Park. The trail passes Nancy Cascades and Nancy and Norcross ponds, and ends on Carrigain Notch Trail 0.8 mi. east of the jct. with Desolation Trail. The climb along the cascades is steep and rough. The section of the trail from Norcross Pond west lies within the Pemigewasset Wilderness. Deep snow or ice may remain in the shady ravine above Nancy Cascades late in spring.

Leaving US 302, Nancy Pond Trail follows an assortment of paths and old roads but is well marked with yellow blazes and signs. It first follows a logging road for 250 yd., passing a kiosk, diverges left and crosses a small brook, then joins a logging road along Halfway Brook, and soon turns right off the road and crosses the brook at 0.3 mi. The trail crosses an unmarked path, and then a private woods road joins from the right (descending, bear right here). The trail continues to the WMNF boundary, marked by a large pile of red-painted stones, at 0.8 mi. Just before the boundary marker, an unsigned path joins from the right; descending, bear right here. Another path (sign: To Inn) diverges to the right at the boundary marker. Here, Nancy Pond Trail joins and follows an old logging road along the south side of Nancy Brook, crossing the brook on the rocks at 1.6 mi. (may be difficult at high water; this crossing was washed out by the 2011 storm). The trail turns left and continues upstream on the road, entering the Nancy Brook Research Natural Area and passing the remains of the Lucy Mill at 1.8 mi. At 1.9 mi. it turns sharply right onto a relocation that climbs high up on the slope by switchbacks, bypassing major washouts from the 2011 storm, then makes a short, steep descent to rejoin the old route at 2.2 mi. The trail recrosses Nancy Brook and soon reaches the foot of Nancy Cascades at 2.4 mi., where the stream falls over a high, steep ledge into a beautiful pool.

The trail turns sharply left at the pool and ascends the steep, rough slope by switchbacks, providing another outlook at the middle of the cascades and then a view of the Giant Stairs and Mt. Resolution, and passes near the top of the cascades, which are several hundred feet high, at 2.8 mi. From the top of the cascades, the trail winds through the moss-carpeted virgin spruce forest on a footway crisscrossed by numerous roots. It crosses and recrosses the dwindling brook and continues past a small overgrown tarn to the northeast shore of Nancy Pond (4 acres in area) at 3.4 mi. Continuing along the north shore over numerous wooden walkways, the trail crosses the swamp at the upper end then passes over the almost imperceptible height-of-land that divides the Saco from the Pemigewasset drainage and reaches Little Norcross Pond (left).

Skirting the north shore, the trail then climbs over another small rise, entering the Pemigewasset Wilderness and descending to Norcross Pond (7 acres in area). By the northeast corner of the pond, where you have a fine view of the Twin Range, the trail bears right into the woods on the first of three relocations away from the old route on the shore, which has been flooded in places by beaver activity. In a clearing at the northwest corner of the pond, the trail turns sharply left and in 25 yd. reaches the ledgy natural dam at the west end of Norcross Pond at 4.3 mi. (In the reverse direction, turn right 25 yd. from the ledgy dam, where an old logging road continues ahead into a campsite area, and follow the trail along the shore of the pond.) At the ledges, you have a commanding outlook to Mt. Bond and the Twin Range, with the Franconias in the distance.

After crossing the stream at the outlet of Norcross Pond, Nancy Pond Trail descends gradually west on a logging road, passing a spring (iron pipe) on the south side of the trail at 5.5 mi. At 6.0 mi., the trail veers right, crosses Norcross Brook (may be difficult in high water), then shortly reaches an old railroad bed and swings left onto it. At 6.4 mi., the trail crosses Anderson Brook (may be difficult in high water) then passes along the south side of the old logging camp 19 clearing. At 6.8 mi., the trail turns left off the railroad grade and crosses the East Branch of the Pemigewasset River (may be difficult in high water), just a short distance below the point where the East Branch begins at the confluence of Norcross and Anderson brooks. On the other side, the trail follows another railroad grade, bearing right at a fork. The trail then crosses Notch Brook (may be difficult in high water) and ends in 25 yd., where Carrigain Notch Trail enters sharply left from Sawyer River Rd. and continues straight ahead on the railroad grade to Desolation Trail and Stillwater Junction.

SEC 4

MT. HANCOCK REGION

CEDAR BROOK TRAIL (WMNF; MAP 3: I6–H6)

Cumulative from Hancock Notch Trail (2,520 ft.) to:	↥↧	↗	◴
Hancock Loop Trail (2,720 ft.)	0.7 mi.	200 ft.	0:25
Height-of-land (3,100 ft.)	1.4 mi.	600 ft.	1:00
Camp 24A (2,500 ft.)	2.9 mi.	600 ft. (rev. 600 ft.)	1:45
Camp 24 (1,940 ft.)	4.3 mi.	600 ft. (rev. 550 ft.)	2:25
Pemi East Side Trail and Wilderness Trail (1,716 ft.)	5.5 mi.	600 ft. (rev. 200 ft.)	3:05

This trail runs from Hancock Notch Trail, 1.8 mi. from the Kancamagus Highway, to a jct. with the east end of Pemi East Side Trail and the west end of Wilderness Trail. (*Note:* Cedar Brook Trail formerly extended another 0.6 mi. at its north end, meeting Wilderness Trail by a suspension footbridge over the East Branch of the Pemigewasset; the bridge was removed in 2009, and a river crossing is no longer available at that location. This section of trail is now part of Wilderness Trail.) In combination with Hancock Notch and Hancock Loop trails, the southern portion of this trail affords the most direct route to Mt. Hancock. The trail formerly made five potentially difficult crossings of the North Fork of the Hancock Branch between Hancock Notch Trail and Hancock Loop Trail, but four of these are now bypassed, and the fifth could be avoided by bushwhacking along the east bank to Hancock Loop Trail (beyond the point where that trail makes an additional crossing, soon after its divergence from Cedar Brook Trail).

Leaving Hancock Notch Trail, Cedar Brook Trail immediately crosses a small brook and climbs moderately on an old logging road for 0.2 mi. to the former first crossing of the North Fork. Here the trail turns right and follows the start of a long-established bypass, and in 35 yd. it continues ahead (right) on a new relocation, which winds upward through spruce woods, descends to cross a small brook, and turns right onto the original route at 0.5 mi. In another 0.1 mi. the trail makes its only crossing of the North Fork, and the beginning of Hancock Loop Trail is reached on the right at 0.7 mi. Beyond here, Cedar Brook Trail receives much less use.

Cedar Brook Trail climbs moderately on a somewhat rough footway that in places must be carefully distinguished from miscellaneous brooks and muddy abandoned routes of the trail. The trail reaches the height-of-land between Mt. Hancock and Mt. Hitchcock at 1.4 mi., where it enters the Pemigewasset Wilderness, and descends on logging roads, swinging out to the west then back to the east and crossing a branch of Cedar Brook at 2.1 mi. Here, the trail turns left and heads north down the valley, crossing several brooks. The trail reaches the site of old logging camp 24A at 2.9 mi. then continues to descend on old roads, swinging south briefly and then northwest, and at 4.1 mi., the trail drops down a bank to the old logging railroad at the edge of Cedar Brook and turns sharply right onto the railroad grade. (In the reverse direction, bear left off the grade where the trail comes to the edge of the brook.)

Soon the trail passes through the extensive clearings of old logging camp 24 and continues down the railroad grade toward the East Branch of the Pemigewasset. At 5.5 mi., Cedar Brook Trail reaches its northern terminus at a jct. with Pemi East Side Trail (left, leading 5.2 mi. to the Lincoln Woods parking area on the Kancamagus Highway) and Wilderness Trail (right, leading into the eastern portion of the Pemigewasset Wilderness).

HANCOCK NOTCH TRAIL (WMNF; MAP 3: I6–I7)

Cumulative from Kancamagus Highway (2,129 ft.) to:	⇅	↗	↻
Cedar Brook Trail (2,520 ft.)	1.8 mi.	400 ft.	1:05
Hancock Notch (2,830 ft.)	2.7 mi.	750 ft. (rev. 50 ft.)	1:45
Sawyer River Trail (1,780 ft.)	6.9 mi.	750 ft. (rev. 1,050 ft.)	3:50

This trail begins at the Kancamagus Highway at the hairpin turn, 4.7 mi. east of the Lincoln Woods parking area, passes through Hancock Notch between Mt. Hancock and Mt. Huntington, then descends along the Sawyer River to Sawyer River Trail. At the Kancamagus Highway terminus, parking is available at the Hancock Overlook, just above the trailhead; parking is prohibited at the hairpin turn. Combined with Cedar Brook and Hancock Loop trails, this trail provides the easiest and most popular route to Mt. Hancock. From the Kancamagus Highway to Cedar Brook Trail, Hancock Notch Trail is heavily used, wide, and easily followed; from Cedar Brook Trail to Sawyer River Trail, Hancock Notch Trail is lightly used and in places requires care to follow, especially in areas damaged by the 2011 storm. The rough, wet section through and east of the notch had been badly overgrown in recent years but was well brushed out in 2016.

To reach the trail, descend a path from a sign and gate at the west end of the Hancock Overlook parking area and carefully cross the Kancamagus Highway at the hairpin turn. From the hairpin, the trail drops down a bank and follows an old logging railroad bed with good footing. It leaves the grade and descends to cross a brook at 0.6 mi. then climbs back to the grade and gradually approaches the North Fork of the Hancock Branch, passing a view of Mt. Hitchcock across the stream at 1.3 mi. The trail stays on the same side of the North Fork, swinging right and slightly uphill at 1.5 mi. to enter an old logging road at the point where the railroad grade (overgrown beyond this point) crossed the river. The trail follows the logging road at an easy grade then descends slightly, crosses three brooks in less than 0.1 mi., and soon reaches the jct. with Cedar Brook Trail at 1.8 mi. (For Mt. Hancock, turn left onto this trail across a small brook.)

Hancock Notch Trail now rises somewhat more steeply and bears left (northeast) on a relocation at 2.0 mi. The trail climbs over a rise and descends gradually southeast, crossing four small brooks and rejoining the original route at 2.4 mi. The trail climbs gradually again, reaching the broad, flat floor of Hancock Notch at 2.7 mi. For 0.2 mi., the trail runs nearly level through spruce woods, becoming quite wet and in places obscure at the east end of this section, passing an open spot with a glimpse of the talus slopes on Mt. Huntington at 2.8 mi.

SEC
4

East of the notch, the trail descends gradually and then steadily through a dense stand of spruce on a rough footway, requiring care to follow at times. At 3.4 mi. it turns right onto a running brook and follows it for 35 yd. then bears right off it. (Avoid beaten paths to a campsite on the left.) In another 0.1 mi. it crosses this brook and then crosses to the north side of the Sawyer River. The trail remains rough until a tributary brook is crossed at 4.1 mi. Here, the grade eases and the footing improves. The trail recrosses the tributary and then crosses back to the south side of the Sawyer River at 4.2 mi. Soon the trail diverges from the river, passes to the left of a beaver pond at 4.9 mi., rises slightly, and then descends to cross a major south branch of the river, where much damage from the 2011 storm is seen, at 5.2 mi. It descends along the right (east) side of this stream, passing through several rocky washouts. It exits right from the last rocky washout and in 40 yd., at 5.5 mi., emerges at the top of a high, washed-out bank at the third crossing of the Sawyer River. Descend carefully down the steep, gravelly bank and cross the river to a cairn on the far side. (In the reverse direction, the trail climbs the bank at a cairn, to the left of an uprooted tree.) Continuing to descend easily, the trail swings right to the fourth river crossing at 6.0 mi. It crosses a loop of the river, runs straight across an area of sand and rubble from the 2011 storm, and in 80 yd. crosses the main branch of the river. (Both the third and fourth crossings of the river may be difficult at high water.) The trail now follows old logging roads, with one small brook crossing, to its end at Sawyer River Trail at Hayshed Field, a small clearing 1.2 mi. from Sawyer River Rd.

HANCOCK LOOP TRAIL (AMC; MAP 3: I6–17)

Cumulative from Cedar Brook Trail (2,720 ft.) to:	↥	↗	↺
Loop jct. (3,400 ft.)	1.1 mi.	700 ft.	0:55
North Hancock summit (4,420 ft.) via North Link	1.8 mi.	1,800 ft. (rev. 100 ft.)	1:50
South Hancock summit (4,319 ft.) via South Link	1.6 mi.	1,600 ft.	1:35
Loop over both summits from:			
Cedar Brook Trail (2,720 ft.) in either direction	4.8 mi.	2,100 ft.	3:25
Kancamagus Highway (2,129 ft.)	9.8 mi.	2,700 ft.	6:15

This trail makes a loop over both the major summits of Mt. Hancock. The trail is steep and rough ascending to the peaks but well trodden and easy to follow, although the part on the ridge between the peaks is subject to blowdowns. The trail is most easily reached from the hairpin turn on the Kancamagus Highway by following Hancock Notch and Cedar Brook trails for 2.5 mi. Cedar Brook Trail has one brook crossing that may be difficult in high water.

Leaving Cedar Brook Trail on the right (east), 150 yd. north of that trail's only crossing of the North Fork of the Hancock Branch, Hancock Loop Trail follows an old logging road and soon recrosses the North Fork then passes over a steep, rocky brook bed and a wet area. It ascends at a gradual to moderate grade to the south of the main brook, coming beside it at 0.4 mi. and then keeping some distance away from it and considerably higher, and reaches the loop jct. at 1.1 mi. From this point, the circuit over the two main summits of Mt. Hancock can be made in either direction, so for convenience of description, the trail is divided into three segments: North Link, Ridge Link, and South Link.

SEC 4

North Link diverges left from the logging road at the loop jct. and descends moderately at an angle, offering a glimpse of the Arrow Slide. Soon the trail crosses a flat gravel area, usually dry but often with water flowing into it from the brook bed above and disappearing into the sand, where the overgrown track of the Arrow Slide is visible about 50 yd. to the left. The trail then climbs roughly parallel to the slide, first at a moderate grade angling across the hillside, then straight up, very steep and rough, although reconstruction by AMC's trail crew has improved the footway. Near the top, the trail veers left and becomes less steep. At the wooded summit of North Hancock, a side path leads left 40 yd. to a ledge with a view south to the Sandwich Range and Mt. Osceola, and Ridge Link turns right.

South Link continues along the logging road from the loop jct. for another 0.1 mi. then swings right up the mountainside. The climb to South Hancock is unrelievedly steep, crossing several old logging roads. (These are some of the roads that are prominent as light-green lines across the dark slope when seen from other peaks.) The upper part of the climb is badly eroded with loose rock and poor footing. At the summit, Ridge Link enters on the left (north), and a short path descends straight ahead (east) to a restricted viewpoint overlooking the Sawyer River valley.

Ridge Link connects the summits of North and South Hancock. From the summit of North Hancock, Ridge Link starts almost due north and curves to the right (east then south), descending to a col and traversing the generally broad, bumpy ridge with several minor ups and downs. From a minor summit, the trail swings right (southwest), descends to a final col, then climbs the last narrow section of ridge to the south peak at 1.4 mi., where South Link enters on the right (northwest).

FOREST DISCOVERY TRAIL (WMNF; MAP 3: I6)

From parking area on Kancamagus Highway (1,520 ft.) for:	⬆⬇	↗	↺
Complete loop, including spur loop path	1.4 mi.	200 ft.	0:50

This graded gravel, universally accessible path provides an easy loop hike on the north side of the Kancamagus Highway, starting at a parking area 2.2 mi. east of the Lincoln Woods trailhead and 0.1 mi. east of Big Rock Campground. Interpretive panels along Forest Discovery Trail explain the various forest management techniques used in the WMNF. From the parking area, the trail angles to the right for 80 yd. then turns left at an arrow and left again at a T intersection. The trail ascends easily, swinging right to a clear-cut area at 0.6 mi., where you have a view of Mt. Osceola. The trail descends by switchbacks to a jct. at 0.8 mi., where the main trail turns right, and a spur path (sign: Riparian Area & Softwood Groups) diverges left. The spur path crosses a bridge over a small brook and quickly reaches a jct. where a loop path makes a circuit through a conifer forest; distance for the spur path, including the loop and return, is 0.3 mi. From the jct. with the spur, the main trail descends gradually for 0.2 mi., passing a connecting path on the right, then turns right and returns to the parking area.

SAWYER RIVER TRAIL (WMNF; MAP 3: I8–I7)

Cumulative from Sawyer River Rd. parking area (1,610 ft.) to:	⬆⬇	↗	↺
Hancock Notch Trail (1,780 ft.)	1.2 mi.	150 ft.	0:40
Kancamagus Highway (1,806 ft.)	3.8 mi.	300 ft. (rev. 100 ft.)	2:05

This trail leads from Sawyer River Rd. (FR 34), at the end of the section open to public vehicular use 3.7 mi. from US 302, to a small parking area on the Kancamagus Highway, 3.1 mi. west of the Sabbaday Falls parking area and 0.6 mi. east of Lily Pond. Almost all the way, the trail follows the bed of an old logging railroad at easy grades.

The trail follows the gravel road past the gate, and in 100 yd., Sawyer Pond Trail turns left to cross the Sawyer River on a footbridge. Sawyer River Trail continues ahead, taking the left of two logging roads at a fork in 70 yd., crosses the Sawyer River on the logging-road bridge at 0.2 mi., and diverges right onto the old railroad grade 100 yd. beyond the bridge. (The grassy logging road can be followed 1.1 mi. to the jct. of Sawyer River Trail and Hancock Notch Trail, where the road meets Sawyer River Trail at a right angle; you have limited views from this road.) The railroad grade continues along the Sawyer River, with a rough 70-yd. bypass to the left around a section washed out by the 2011 storm at 0.4 mi. At 0.9 mi. it begins to swing to the south, away from the river. The trail runs through a washed-out area for 125 yd. then bears left and in 10 yd. makes an obscure crossing of a brook just below a beaver dam. The trail winds through the woods to the left of the washed-out railroad grade for 80 yd. then bears left onto the grade and in 10 yd. crosses a brook. (In the reverse direction, bear right into the woods 10 yd. after crossing the brook.) The trail continues on the grade to a four-way jct. in a small clearing called Hayshed Field at 1.2 mi., where Hancock Notch Trail diverges sharply right and the logging road described earlier enters on the left.

Sawyer River Trail follows the old railroad bed south across an imperceptible divide in the flat region west of Green's Cliff and enters an extensive wetland area at 1.8 mi., with occasional views of surrounding ridges. It crosses Meadow Brook on a bridge (views) at 2.5 mi. and follows the west bank of this stream for some distance, passing a jct. where a snowmobile trail diverges left at 3.2 mi. In another 60 yd., Nanamocomuck Ski Trail (X-C) enters on the left. The hiking and ski trails coincide, swinging southwest, and the ski trail diverges right just before Sawyer River Trail crosses the Swift River (which can be very difficult in high water) at 3.5 mi. The trail now ascends easily upstream along the river, passing a fine cascade and pool then climbs up the bank, bearing left twice, passes to the right of a skid road and logging yard, and reaches the Kancamagus Highway. In the reverse direction, from the trailhead follow a logging road (FR 158) to the left of the logging yard and skid road for 130 yd. and bear right at an arrow where a beaten path diverges left.

SEC 4

MT. TREMONT REGION

CHURCH POND TRAIL (WMNF; MAP 3: J8–I8)

From Passaconaway Campground (1,251 ft.) to:	⇅	↗	↻
Knoll above Church Pond (1,257 ft.)	1.1 mi.	0 ft.	0:35

Note: The east branch of Church Pond Trail has been closed due to the extremely wet and boggy terrain the trail traversed; the west branch of the trail remains open, ending at a knoll above the shore of the pond.

This trail provides an interesting short, level walk to Church Pond, passing through a flat and poorly drained region of pine and spruce swamps and bogs. The traverse is very wet at times, with several sections likely to be muddy. (*Caution:* The crossing of the Swift River near the trailhead almost always requires wading and can be dangerous at high water.) The trail begins in Passaconaway Campground just off the Kancamagus Highway, at the far end of the west loop road near site 19. Parking at the trailhead is limited to two vehicles, and the campground is closed much of the year, so you may have to use the Downes Brook Trail parking lot on the south side of the highway.

Church Pond Trail descends slightly and fords the Swift River to the north side, where the trail follows an often-dry streambed left for 20 yd. then turns to the right into the woods and soon crosses another channel of the Swift River that is usually not as difficult as the main channel. On the far bank, the trail angles left through dense, fast-growing streamside vegetation and may require considerable care to follow. At 0.3 mi., the former loop jct. is reached; the right fork is the eastbound Nanamocomuck Ski Trail (X-C). Church Pond Trail bears left here, following an old logging road through a pine forest for 0.4 mi. to a jct. where the westbound Nanamocomuck Ski Trail (X-C) diverges left. Church Pond Trail continues ahead and soon reaches an extensive series of bog bridges leading through a wetland area. The trail swings right past a view of Green's Cliff then swings left as it climbs to a low knoll covered with red pines overlooking Church Pond. Here the maintained trail ends; several side paths descend to the shore, where there are views of the surrounding mountains. (In the reverse direction, at the foot of the short descent from the knoll, bear right at an arrow where a beaten path runs straight ahead into a swamp.)

SAWYER POND TRAIL (WMNF; MAP 3: J8–I8)

Cumulative from parking area off Kancamagus Highway (1,225 ft.) to:	⇅	↗	↻
Brunel Trail (1,330 ft.)	1.1 mi.	100 ft.	0:35
Sawyer Pond (1,940 ft.)	4.5 mi.	900 ft. (rev. 200 ft.)	2:40
Sawyer River Rd. parking area (1,610 ft.)	6.0 mi.	900 ft. (rev. 350 ft.)	3:25

This trail (which has easy grades through most of its length) begins at a parking area 0.2 mi. in on a side road (FR 302) that leaves the north side of the Kancamagus Highway 0.6 mi. east of Passaconaway Campground and 1.4 mi. west of Bear Notch Rd. After passing Sawyer Pond and its campsite, the trail ends at Sawyer River Rd. (FR 34), near the gate that marks the end of public vehicular access at 3.7 mi. (*Caution:* The crossing of the Swift River near the Kancamagus Highway almost always requires wading and can be dangerous at high water.)

From the parking area, the trail passes through a clearing, angles right to the bank of the Swift River, and fords the stream to a sandbar. The trail passes through a brushy area and enters the woods, quickly bearing left at a fork, and soon Nanamocomuck Ski Trail (X-C) joins on the right. Sawyer

Pond Trail runs through a beautiful pine grove; at 0.7 mi., the ski trail diverges left (leading 1.1 mi. to Church Pond Trail; in 0.3 mi. it passes a fine view of the Swift River and Mt. Passaconaway). At 1.1 mi., Brunel Trail diverges right. At 1.7 mi., Sawyer Pond Trail crosses a logging road then rises along the west slope of Birch Hill, descends gently, and crosses a grass-grown logging road (marked as a snowmobile trail) diagonally at 2.6 mi.

The trail then comes close to a small brook, bears left away from it, passes over a flat divide, and descends to Sawyer Pond. As the pond is approached, there are a number of conflicting side paths; use care to stay on the correct path. At a point 15 yd. from the pond, the trail turns left and crosses the outlet brook at 4.5 mi. Here, a path leads to the right along the shore, passing the tentsites of Sawyer Pond Campsite on the left and providing several good views up to Mt. Tremont and Owl's Cliff, and reaches the shelter in 0.15 mi. The main trail passes to the left of the campsite area, and in 0.1 mi., it passes another side path that leads right 0.1 mi. to the shelter. Sawyer Pond Trail then descends gradually on an old logging road, turns sharply left off the road at 5.7 mi., and recrosses the Sawyer Pond outlet brook on a bridge. From there, the trail runs to the bank of the Sawyer River, descends the bank and turns right to cross the river on a footbridge, turns right again on the gravel extension of Sawyer River Rd. (which Sawyer River Trail follows to the left), and continues 100 yd. to the gate (where there is a sign for Sawyer Pond Trail) and the parking area beyond.

RAIL AND RIVER TRAIL (WMNF; MAP 3: J8)

From Passaconaway Historic Site parking lot (1,240 ft.) for:	⇅	↗	↻
Complete loop	0.6 mi.	0 ft.	0:20

This graded gravel, accessible path provides a short, easy loop through attractive pine and spruce woods near the Swift River, with interpretive panels describing the farming and logging history of the area. The trail starts at the parking lot for the Passaconaway Historic Site, which includes the nearby Russell–Colbath House (open in summer and fall) on the north side of the Kancamagus Highway, 0.5 mi. west of its jct. with Bear Notch Rd. From the parking area, the trail runs briefly west past a barn then swings right to the loop jct. The east end of the loop continues ahead, briefly follows the bed of an old logging railroad, bears left at 0.1 mi., and turns left again onto the bank of the Swift River at 0.2 mi. The trail runs alongside the river for 60 yd., with a view back to Bear Mtn., then bears left and continues through several more turns back to the loop jct. To return to the parking lot, bear right.

ROB BROOK TRAIL (WMNF)

Due to extensive beaver flooding, this trail is no longer maintained for hiking. The eastern 1-mi. section of the trail is maintained as part of Nanamocomuck Ski Trail (X-C).

BRUNEL TRAIL (WMNF; MAP 3: I8)

Cumulative from Sawyer Pond Trail (1,330 ft.) to:	↥↧	↗	↻
Departure from Rob Brook Rd. (1,350 ft.)	1.2 mi.	0 ft.	0:35
Owl's Cliff spur (2,820 ft.)	3.1 mi.	1,500 ft.	2:20
Mt. Tremont summit (3,371 ft.)	3.9 mi.	2,250 ft. (rev. 200 ft.)	3:05
Cumulative from Bear Notch Rd. (1,338 ft.) to:			
Departure of Brunel Trail from Rob Brook Rd. (1,350 ft.) via Rob Brook Rd.	2.6 mi.,	100 ft. (rev. 100 ft.)	1:20
Mt. Tremont summit	5.3 mi.	2,350 ft. (rev. 200 ft.)	3:50

This little-used trail runs from Sawyer Pond Trail 1.1 mi. north of the Kancamagus Highway to the summit of Mt. Tremont. The most frequently used approach to this trail, however, is the WMNF's Rob Brook Rd. (FR 35), which leaves Bear Notch Rd. 0.8 mi. north of the Kancamagus Highway. Rob Brook Rd. is closed to public vehicular travel, but it provides the easiest route to the point where Brunel Trail departs, 2.6 mi. from Bear Notch Rd. The remainder of Brunel Trail south of this point to the Kancamagus Highway is seldom used, largely because the ford of the Swift River near the start of Sawyer Pond Trail is frequently difficult. Parts of Brunel Trail are very steep and rough; the footway may be obscure in some areas, so the yellow blazes must be followed with care. The views to the west from Mt. Tremont, and to the southwest from Owl's Cliff, are excellent.

The trail diverges right (northeast) from Sawyer Pond Trail, and at 0.3 mi., Brunel Trail turns right onto the extension of Rob Brook Rd. and follows this road past the former jct. with the abandoned, beaver-flooded section of Rob Brook Trail on the right at 0.9 mi. At 1.1 mi., Brunel Trail bears right at a jct. with another logging road, crosses Rob Brook on a bridge, and soon a snowmobile trail diverges sharply left. At 1.2 mi., Brunel Trail (sign) turns left off the road; this point is 2.6 mi. from Bear Notch Rd. via Rob Brook Rd. (If approaching from Bear Notch Rd., turn right off Rob Brook Rd. onto Brunel Trail.)

Leaving Rob Brook Rd., Brunel Trail passes through a stand of large conifers then rises moderately through hardwoods, crossing the snowmobile trail at 2.3 mi. At 2.5 mi., Brunel Trail crosses a small brook and soon passes several large boulders that announce the approach to the east end of Owl's Cliff. At 2.8 mi., the trail swings left and climbs a very steep section. The grade moderates and finally becomes easy as the height-of-land is reached. At 3.1 mi. (1.9 mi. from Rob Brook Rd.), a spur path (sign) diverges left and climbs to a point just below the summit of Owl's Cliff then descends over a steep ledge to a fine southwest outlook (use caution if wet or icy) 0.2 mi. from the main trail (spur trail ascent 100 ft., rev. 50 ft.). From the jct., Brunel Trail soon swings right and descends at a moderate grade into the sag, passes through a section where the footway may be overgrown and obscure (watch carefully for blazes), and then ascends very steeply; sections running straight up the slope alternate with old logging roads angling to the left. At 3.9 mi. (2.7 mi. from Rob Brook Rd.), the trail scrambles up a ledge and reaches the summit ledges of Mt. Tremont, where Mt. Tremont Trail enters from the north.

SEC 4

MT. TREMONT TRAIL (WMNF; MAP 3: I8)

From US 302 (820 ft.) to:	⇅	↗	○
Mt. Tremont summit (3,371 ft.)	2.8 mi.	2,550 ft.	2:40

This trail begins on the south side of US 302 (roadside parking, limited in winter), 0.5 mi. west of the Sawyer Rock picnic area and 0.1 mi. west of the bridge over Stony Brook, and climbs, steeply at times, to the summit of Mt. Tremont, where you have fine views, especially to the west over the Sawyer Pond area.

Leaving US 302, the trail soon reaches and follows the west side of Stony Brook, passing several cascades. At 0.7 mi., the trail runs briefly on a narrow, eroded section on the edge of the brook bank, crosses a tributary, then swings right and climbs for 0.3 mi. to the top of a ridge (watch for a sharp right turn up a steep bank, shortly after crossing a seasonal brook). The trail then levels off, swings left and crosses an old logging road, and passes through a rough, muddy section where blazes should be followed with care. The trail then turns sharply right, crosses a small brook, and, in about 0.1 mi., turns sharply right again and climbs. At 1.5 mi., the trail bears left and makes a slight descent to cross a major branch of Stony Brook. The trail now climbs the steep northeast side of the mountain, first at a moderate grade, passing from birch woods into conifers at 2.4 mi. The trail then ascends a steep, rough section with many switchbacks to the ridge top, passes two side paths to an outlook on the right, and continues another 15 yd. to the ledgy summit.

MOAT MTN. REGION

LOVEQUIST LOOP (WMNF; MAP 3: I9)

From Rocky Gorge Picnic Area (1,120 ft.) to:	⇅	↗	↻
Complete loop	1.0 mi.	150 ft.	0:35

This short, fairly easy loop path, with several minor ups and downs and some rooty footing, provides access to scenic Falls Pond from the Rocky Gorge Picnic Area, which is located on the Kancamagus Highway 8.4 mi. west of NH 16 and 3.4 mi. east of its jct. with Bear Notch Rd. From the parking area at Rocky Gorge, follow the paved walkway 0.1 mi. to the bridge across the gorge. From the far end of the bridge, a graded gravel, accessible path ascends 125 yd. to the loop jct.; here a 35-yd. accessible side path descends ahead to the shore of Falls Pond, where you have a view of the lower ridges of Bear Mtn. The section of the loop on the east shore of the pond is also part of Lower Nanamocomuck Ski Trail (X-C). Turn left to follow the loop in a clockwise direction. The trails coincide for about 100 yd. then the pond loop turns right at the south end of the pond and swings around its west shore. After traveling 0.4 mi. from the ski trail jct., the pond loop rejoins the ski trail at the north end of the pond, turns sharply right, and returns to the loop jct. near the bridge across the Swift River.

BOULDER LOOP TRAIL (WMNF; MAP 3: I10)

Cumulative from Passaconaway Rd. (860 ft.) to:	⇅	↗	↻
Loop jct. (910 ft.)	0.2 mi.	50 ft.	0:10
Spur path to ledges (1,750 ft.)	1.3 mi.	900 ft.	1:05
Complete loop, including spur to ledges	3.1 mi.	950 ft.	2:00

This is a loop trail to ledges on a southwest spur of the Moat Range, starting from the north side of Passaconaway Rd. (formerly Dugway Rd.) just east of the Albany Covered Bridge and just west of the entrance to the WMNF Covered Bridge Campground. A parking area is on the south side of the road. Passaconaway Rd. leaves the Kancamagus Highway just east of the entrance to Blackberry Crossing Campground, passes through the Albany Covered Bridge, turns right, and reaches the trailhead parking on the right at 0.2 mi. (This part of Passaconaway Rd. is closed to vehicles from November to May; at these times, parking is available on the right off Passaconaway Rd., a short distance in from the Kancamagus Highway.) The trail offers excellent views for a relatively modest effort. In late fall of 2016, a brush fire burned over much of the trail.

The trail leaves Passaconaway Rd. and ascends to the loop jct. at 0.2 mi. From here, the loop is described in the clockwise direction. Taking the left-hand branch, the trail shortly passes a large rock face (left), where the trail turns right and climbs moderately. At 0.8 mi., the trail turns sharply left where a side path leads right to an outlook south. The main trail runs at easy grades then bears right and climbs again. It swings left and right, and at 1.3 mi., at the main trail's high point, a spur path (sign: View) diverges right, climbs a ledgy pitch, and leads southeast 0.15 mi. to clifftop ledges that afford a fine view of the Swift River valley and the Sandwich Range. The main trail continues behind the ledges and descends fairly steeply toward Big Brook then turns right (southwest) below the ledges and, running at an easier grade, crosses a stream and passes an overhanging boulder (left) at 2.3 mi. The trail weaves through more boulders, swings left over a low ridge, and returns to the loop jct. at 2.6 mi., 0.2 mi. from Passaconaway Rd.

SEC 4

MOAT MTN. TRAIL (WMNF; MAP 3: I11–J10)

Cumulative from West Side Rd. (550 ft.) to:	⇅	↗	↺
Red Ridge Trail, lower jct. (750 ft.)	1.2 mi.	200 ft.	0:40
Attitash Trail (1,080 ft.)	2.4 mi.	550 ft.	1:30
North Moat summit (3,196 ft.)	4.3 mi.	2,650 ft.	3:30
Red Ridge Trail, upper jct. (2,760 ft.)	5.4 mi.	2,800 ft.	4:05
Middle Moat summit area (2,800 ft.)	6.4 mi.	3,150 ft.	4:45
South Moat summit (2,770 ft.)	7.0 mi.	3,250 ft.	5:10
Passaconaway Rd. (650 ft.)	9.6 mi.	3,350 ft.	6:30
Cumulative from Passaconaway Rd. (650 ft.) to:			
South Moat summit (2,770 ft.)	2.6 mi.	2,200 ft.	2:25
Middle Moat summit area (2,800 ft.)	3.2 mi.	2,350 ft.	2:45
Red Ridge Trail, upper jct. (2,760 ft.)	4.2 mi.	2,650 ft.	3:25
North Moat summit (3,196 ft.)	5.3 mi.	3,250 ft.	4:15
Attitash Trail (1,080 ft.)	7.2 mi.	3,250 ft.	5:15
Red Ridge Trail, lower jct. (750 ft.)	8.4 mi.	3,250 ft.	5:50
West Side Rd. (550 ft.)	9.6 mi.	3,250 ft.	6:25

This trail traverses the main ridge of Moat Mtn., providing magnificent views from numerous outlooks. Parts of the ridge are very exposed to weather, particularly the section that crosses Middle Moat and South Moat. The trail can be hard to follow along the open ridge sections in poor visibility; look carefully for cairns and blazes, many of which are faded.

The south terminus of the trail is located on Passaconaway Rd. (formerly Dugway Rd.). At the lights on NH 16 in Conway village, turn north (directly opposite NH 153) onto Washington St., which becomes West Side Rd. Go left at a fork, then at 0.9 mi., turn left onto Passaconaway Rd. Moat Mtn. Trail (sign) leaves Passaconaway Rd. at a trailhead parking area on the right, 3.2 mi. from West Side Rd. Passaconaway Rd. continues west another 3.4 mi. and joins the Kancamagus Highway near Blackberry Crossing Campground (but the west part of Passaconaway Rd. is closed to vehicles from November to May).

The northeast terminus of the trail is reached from Conway village via Washington St. and West Side Rd., or from North Conway (just north of the Eastern Slope Inn) by following River Rd. west for 1.0 mi. across the Saco River to West Side Rd. Bear right on West Side Rd. and drive north for another 1.4 mi. to a large parking lot on the left (west) side of the road.

Starting from the northeast terminus, a wide, graded, universally accessible path descends slightly then turns left and winds through coniferous woods for 0.6 mi., intersecting the former route (a gravel road) at the clearing just below the mill site at Diana's Baths, a series of scenic cascades where Lucy Brook runs over ledges and through large potholes. Moat Mtn. Trail bears right and leaves the upper end of the clearing, close to the baths, then bears left at a fork onto a logging road that follows the north bank of Lucy Brook, crossing a tributary just before reaching another fork (sign) at 1.2 mi. Here, Red Ridge Trail turns left across the brook, eventually rejoining Moat Mtn. Trail at the apex of Red Ridge, making possible a fine loop hike.

Moat Mtn. Trail crosses Lucy Brook (difficult at high water) at 1.5 mi. and follows the south bank, passing an attractive cascade. At 2.4 mi., it turns abruptly left uphill, away from the stream (last sure water), at the point where Attitash Trail continues straight ahead along the stream toward Big Attitash Mtn. Moat Mtn. Trail ascends steadily through the woods and, at 2.8 mi., begins to pass over scrubby, ledgy areas, where the trail must be followed with care, reaching the first good outlook at 3.6 mi. After a steeper section, the trail reaches a shoulder at 4.0 mi. and runs nearly level through a patch of larger trees then climbs fairly steeply through decreasing scrub and increasing bare ledge to the summit of North Moat at 4.3 mi., where you have an unobstructed view in all directions.

From the summit of North Moat, the trail descends sharply to the base of the cone then easily along a shoulder with occasional views. At the end of the shoulder, the trail drops steeply, passing over several ledges that require some scrambling, traverses another shoulder where you have a fine outlook to the right in a ledgy area, then descends steeply over more ledges to a col in a fine spruce forest. Ascending again, the trail passes the jct. with

Red Ridge Trail left (northeast) at 5.4 mi., just below several large rocks that provide good views. Moat Mtn. Trail descends to the major col on the ridge then climbs up the northwest side of Middle Moat to low scrub, followed by open ledges with continuous views, and passes east of the summit of Middle Moat (which can be reached in 80 yd. over open ledges) at 6.4 mi. The trail descends to a col with a patch of woods that would provide some shelter in a storm, turns sharply right, climbs over an open ledgy knob, and ascends to the summit of South Moat at 7.0 mi.

The trail descends into scrub with intermittent views for 0.3 mi. then enters woods with many beautiful red pines. At 7.6 mi., the trail crosses a large open ledge with southwest views (on the ascent from the south terminus, this is the first good outlook reached), and the trail becomes steep with rough footing. Below this section, the grade eases somewhat (although there are a number of rough ledges), and at 8.3 mi., the trail turns right onto a wide, well-constructed relocation. The trail runs generally west, descending at easy grades with occasional minor ascents, crosses Dry Brook on a bridge at 8.6 mi., swings left and then right over a small ridge, and crosses a small brook at 9.3 mi. The trail climbs over another low ridge then turns left and runs 0.1 mi. to the parking area on Passaconaway Rd. In 2016 the last 0.1 mi. followed a temporary reroute to the right of an active log landing. (Starting from the trailhead, the reroute went left into the woods.) When the timber harvest is completed, the trail will resume its former route for the southernmost 0.1 mi. on a logging road beyond the gate at the trailhead.

RED RIDGE TRAIL (WMNF; MAP 3: I10)

Cumulative from Moat Mtn. Trail, lower jct. (750 ft.) to:	⇅	↗	○
Red Ridge Link (970 ft.)	0.8 mi.	200 ft.	0:30
Crossing of Moat Brook (1,160 ft.)	2.0 mi.	500 ft. (rev. 100 ft.)	1:15
Moat Mtn. Trail, upper jct. (2,760 ft.)	3.6 mi.	2,100 ft.	2:50

This trail ascends Red Ridge, with magnificent views, leaving Moat Mtn. Trail 1.2 mi. from West Side Rd. and rejoining Moat Mtn. Trail at the unnamed peak at the apex of Red Ridge, 1.1 mi. south of the summit of North Moat. With Moat Mtn. Trail, Red Ridge Trail provides a very attractive loop over the open summit of North Moat.

This trail, marked with yellow blazes (and some orange blazes north of the jct. with Red Ridge Link) branches left (south) from Moat Mtn. Trail and immediately crosses Lucy Brook, a difficult crossing in high water. Red Ridge Trail ascends generally south at a gentle grade, crossing a yellow-blazed snowmobile trail at 0.5 mi. Red Ridge Link leaves on the left for White Horse Ledge at 0.8 mi., and Red Ridge Trail descends gradually until it crosses the gravel FR 379 (the continuation of the snowmobile trail mentioned above) at 1.5 mi. The trail soon turns sharply right, approaches Moat Brook and follows it, then turns left and crosses the brook at 2.0 mi., zigzagging steeply upward and climbing to a gravel bank (use caution here, particularly on the descent) where you have good views. Continuing upward rather steeply, the trail ascends a steep ledge by means of an eroded trap dike and soon attains the crest of Red Ridge, where the grade moderates. Passing alternately through scrub and over ledges with good views, the trail reaches the bottom of an extensive open ledge section with magnificent views at 3.0 mi. At 3.4 mi., the trail reenters scrub and soon rejoins Moat Mtn. Trail at the foot of several little rock knobs atop a small peak on the main ridge crest between North Moat and Middle Moat.

RED RIDGE LINK (NHDP; MAP 3: I10)

From Red Ridge Trail (970 ft.) to:	⇅	↗	⟳
White Horse Ledge Trail (1,370 ft.)	0.4 mi.	400 ft.	0:25

This short orange-blazed path links Red Ridge Trail with White Horse Ledge Trail, connecting the trails on Moat Mtn. with those on White Horse and Cathedral ledges. Red Ridge Link leaves Red Ridge Trail on the left (east) 0.8 mi. from the latter trail's lower jct. with Moat Mtn. Trail, just past the top of a small rise; the sign is a few yards up the trail. The trail ascends through open hemlock forest at a moderate grade, turning sharply left then sharply right 60 yd. farther, at the tops of two wooded ledges. These turns may be difficult to see, particularly descending, if the trail blazes are faded. Red Ridge Link ends at White Horse Ledge Trail 0.2 mi. below the summit ledges.

ATTITASH TRAIL (WMNF; MAP 3: I9–I10)

Cumulative from Bear Notch Rd. (1,260 ft.) to:	⇅	↗	⟳
High point on Table Mtn. (2,610 ft.)	1.9 mi.	1,350 ft.	1:40
Big Attitash Mtn. summit (2,910 ft.)	4.7 mi.	2,350 ft. (rev. 700 ft.)	3:30
Moat Mtn. Trail (1,080 ft.)	7.2 mi.	2,450 ft. (rev. 1,950 ft.)	4:50

This trail runs from Bear Notch Rd., 2.7 mi. south of its jct. with US 302 in Bartlett village, to Moat Mtn. Trail, 2.4 mi. west of West Side Rd. The trail is well trodden from Bear Notch Rd. to the ledges of Table Mtn., where you have good views from an area burned by a small forest fire in October 1984. Except for these ledges, the trail is in the woods all the way, and the section east of Table Mtn. is wild, rough, and very lightly used. This part of the trail has prolific vegetation, and hikers may encounter blowdowns and overgrown sections. Though it was well-cleared in 2016, this section is not recommended for inexperienced hikers. The trail is marked with yellow blazes of various ages, although not all sections are marked well.

Leaving the small parking area on the east side of Bear Notch Rd., the trail follows a logging road that crosses a major branch of Louisville Brook in about 120 yd. At 0.3 mi., the trail bears right on an older road. At 0.6 mi., the trail comes to the edge of Louisville Brook at a small, ledgy cascade and follows near the brook. In less than 0.1 mi., the trail crosses a branch of the brook then turns left (arrow) at a logging road fork and ascends moderately to the col between Bear Mtn. and Table Mtn. at 1.3 mi. The trail turns sharply left here and climbs more steeply; loose gravel on ledges makes for frequently slippery footing, particularly on the descent. Soon reaching the edge of the burned area, the trail crosses several ledges with excellent views to the south and southwest, with one fairly steep scramble. At 1.9 mi., the trail reaches its high point on Table Mtn. and passes somewhat south of the summit, with views available a short distance to the right from a large ledge at the edge of the south cliff.

From this point, the trail is very lightly used, and although experienced hikers should have little trouble following it, care is required at times. The trail descends easily then steadily into a col at 2.5 mi., where there is a brook (unreliable), passes a ledgy spot with a glimpse back to Table Mtn., and soon climbs a very steep pitch to the main ridge of Big Attitash. From here, the trail runs along the north side of the ridge, crossing the west and middle knobs of Big Attitash with short intervening descents. On the final approach to the summit of Big Attitash, the trail crosses a boggy, muddy area where considerable care is required to follow it. At 4.7 mi., the trail passes very close to the summit of Big Attitash; the high point is to the right of the trail. Then it descends, moderately at first then steeply and roughly on a sidehill slope, into the valley of Lucy Brook, which is crossed at 5.9 mi., where the brook may be dry. The trail soon turns right onto a relocated section, climbs and descends on the slope above the brook, crosses a side stream and two branches of the main brook, then follows a logging road and crosses back over Lucy Brook just before reaching the jct. with Moat Mtn. Trail at 7.2 mi. (These crossings may be difficult in high water.) Moat Mtn. Trail can be followed to the right, to North Moat, or straight ahead to Diana's Baths and West Side Rd.

MOAT MINERAL SITE TRAIL (WMNF; MAP3: I10)

Cumulative from parking area at end of FR 380 (890 ft.) to:	⬆⬇	↗	⏱
Moat Mtn. mineral collecting area (1,030 ft.)	0.9 mi.	150 ft.	0:30
FR 379 (640 ft.)	1.9 mi.	150 ft. (rev. 400 ft.)	1:00

This yellow-blazed trail leads from the end of High St. (FR 380) to a designated mineral collecting site at the eastern base of Moat Mtn. then descends to FR 379, which can be used to connect with Thompson Falls Trail and Red Ridge Trail. This multiuse trail also connects with several mountain-biking trails, so hikers should be prepared to yield to oncoming riders, especially on the northern section. To reach the trailhead, take Passaconaway Rd. west from West Side Rd. for 1.2 mi. and turn right onto High St. (gravel). At 0.9 mi. from Passaconaway Rd., continue straight where Crossover Rd. joins from the left. Pass through a gate (closed in winter) at 1.5 mi., bear left at a fork at 1.8 mi., and continue to trailhead parking at 2.6 mi.

Leaving the parking area, the trail follows an old road through a brushy area and bears right (arrow) at a fork at 0.1 mi. (Left at this fork is a mountain-biking trail.) The trail ascends gently, with occasional brief descents, crossing a gullied brook bed at 0.5 mi. and passing the jct. with another mountain biking trail on the left at 0.7 mi. At 0.9 mi., Moat Mineral Site Trail enters the mineral collecting area (sign) then soon turns right and descends by numerous switchbacks to FR 379. To the right, this road descends 0.3 mi. to the lower (east) end of Thompson Falls Trail. To the left, the road ascends 0.2 mi. to the upper (west) end of Thompson Falls Trail and continues another 0.8 mi. to a point where the road is crossed by Red Ridge Trail, 0.7 mi. south of that trail's jct. with Red Ridge Link.

THOMPSON FALLS TRAIL (WMNF; MAP 3: I10)

Cumulative from lower jct. with FR 379 (530 ft.) to:	⬆⬇	↗	⏱
Thompson Falls (660 ft.)	0.3 mi.	150 ft.	0:15
Upper jct. with FR 379 (760 ft.)	0.5 mi.	250 ft.	0:25
From parking area at end of FR 380 (890 ft.) for:			
Round trip with loop past Thompson Falls via Moat Mineral Site Trail, FR 379, and Thompson Falls Trail	4.8 mi.	800 ft.	2:50

This short trail provides access to Thompson Falls, a fine cascade on Moat Brook set amid a beautiful hemlock forest. The trail connects on both ends with FR 379, making a loop possible from Moat Mineral Site Trail. To reach the lower (east) end of Thompson Falls Trail, follow Moat Mineral Site Trail for 1.9 mi. from its trailhead to its northern terminus on FR 379. Turn right on FR 379 and descend for 0.3 mi. to a point where the road swings right, 0.1 mi. beyond a gate. Thompson Falls Trail diverges sharply left here, at first coinciding with Lower Stony Ridge Trail (mountain biking). The coinciding trails swing left in 30 yd., and Lower Stony Ridge Trail soon diverges right. Thompson Falls Trail continues ahead, crossing a brook at 0.1 mi. The trail ascends gently toward Moat Brook then swings left and climbs moderately on the bank above the brook, passing an outlook on the right to Thompson Falls at 0.3 mi. The trail briefly ascends alongside the brook past smaller cascades then bears left and ascends easily to its upper jct. with FR 379. Turn left to descend to the northern terminus of Moat Mineral Site Trail in 0.2 mi.

SEC 4

PATHS ON WHITE HORSE LEDGE AND CATHEDRAL LEDGE

ECHO LAKE TRAIL (NHDP; MAP 3: I11)

From Echo Lake State Park parking area (490 ft.) for:	↕	↗	↻
Complete loop around Echo Lake	0.9 mi.	0 ft.	0:25

This short, easy trail provides a scenic loop around Echo Lake, a sandy kettle pond at the base of White Horse Ledge, and provides access to White Horse and Cathedral ledges via Bryce Path. Leave Main St. in North Conway just north of the Eastern Slope Inn and take River Rd., which runs west across the Saco River. Turn left at 1.0 mi. onto West Side Rd. then right at 1.4 mi. onto Echo Lake Rd., following signs for Echo Lake State Park, and reach the park gate at 1.5 mi. (Admission charged in season.) If the park is closed, parking is available on an old segment of road to the left, and the park road can be followed on foot from the gate to the trailhead (signs).

From here, Echo Lake Trail descends 60 yd. nearly to the south edge of Echo Lake then (going in the clockwise direction) bears left and runs along the west shore of the lake, some distance away but mostly in sight of it. At 0.4 mi., Bryce Path (sign) diverges left, and Echo Lake Trail continues around the north end of the lake and returns to the trailhead at the parking area in another 0.5 mi.; the trail is poorly marked and its footway is not always defined well, particularly in the vicinity of the main beach, but its route along the shore is fairly obvious, and good views of the White Horse and Cathedral cliffs can be seen from the east shore.

BRYCE PATH (NHDP; MAP 3: I11–I10)

Cumulative from Echo Lake Trail (490 ft.) to:	↥↧	↗	↻
White Horse Ledge Trail, lower jct., and Bryce Link (570 ft.)	0.3 mi.	100 ft.	0:10
White Horse Ledge Trail, upper jct. (900 ft.)	0.6 mi.	400 ft.	0:30
Top of Cathedral Ledge Rd. (1,120 ft.)	1.0 mi.	650 ft.	0:50
From Echo Lake parking area (490 ft.) to:			
Top of Cathedral Ledge Rd. (1,120 ft.) via Echo Lake Trail and Bryce Path	1.4 mi.	650 ft.	1:00

This trail leads from Echo Lake Trail on the northwest side of Echo Lake to the col between White Horse Ledge and Cathedral Ledge and then on to the upper end of Cathedral Ledge Rd., near the summit of Cathedral Ledge. Bryce Path connects with Bryce Link and both ends of White Horse Ledge Trail, making possible a variety of hikes in this interesting area. Leaving Echo Lake Trail 0.4 mi. from the parking area (via the west shore), Bryce Path ascends gradually northwest for 0.3 mi. to a four-way jct. To the left is the lower end of White Horse Ledge Trail, and to the right is Bryce Link. Bryce Path continues ahead, passing near the foundation of an old sugarhouse, then swings left and climbs steeply, reaching a rock slab in the woods and then ascending for about 0.1 mi. up rock steps and two wooden stairways.

The trail then bears right and runs at easy grades to a jct. in the col between White Horse Ledge and Cathedral Ledge. Here, the upper end of White Horse Ledge Trail leads left (south) to the summit of White Horse Ledge. Bryce Path turns right at the jct. and leads north across a flat, wooded upland for 0.2 mi. then turns sharply right and climbs rather steeply for another 0.2 mi. to a T intersection, where the path turns left and reaches the turnaround at the top of Cathedral Ledge Rd. in another 40 yd. (trail sign). A right at the T leads to the south outlook in 80 yd. (The summit area is interlaced with countless beaten paths.) The true summit is a wooded ledge, but there are several fine viewpoints from the rim of the summit area, including the fenced east outlook at the top of the main cliff.

BRYCE LINK (NHDP; MAP 3: I11)

From either entrance on Cathedral Ledge Rd. (535 ft.) to:	⇅	↗	◷
Bryce Path and lower end of White Horse Ledge Trail (570 ft.)	0.3 mi.	50 ft.	0:10

This short path has two entrances on Cathedral Ledge Rd. and provides a shorter but less scenic approach (compared with the approach via Echo Lake Trail) to the trails that ascend White Horse and Cathedral ledges; Bryce Link also avoids park admission fees in season. The signs at both entrances are for Bryce Path, but this trail is referred to here and on Map 3 as Bryce Link to distinguish it from the Bryce Path proper. Leave Main St. in North Conway just north of the Eastern Slope Inn and take River Rd., which runs west across the Saco River. At 1.0 mi., bear right onto West Side Rd. then turn left onto Cathedral Ledge Rd. at 1.5 mi. from Main St. Follow Cathedral Ledge Rd. (which ends in another 1.8 mi. just below the summit of Cathedral Ledge) for 0.3 mi. The first entrance (sign: Bryce Path; yellow blazes, wooden posts) is a dirt road on the left, directly across from a private dirt road. The second entrance (signs: Bryce Path, Perimeter Trail, and Echo Lake; yellow blazes) is about 100 yd. farther west on Cathedral Ledge Rd. Ample roadside parking is available at either entrance. The two routes converge in less than 0.1 mi. from either entrance. Bryce Link then continues as a single yellow-blazed route, avoiding branching roads and footpaths, to a four-way jct. with Bryce Path and the lower end of White Horse Ledge Trail; turn right onto Bryce Path to ascend to the col between the ledges.

SEC 4

WHITE HORSE LEDGE TRAIL (NHDP; MAP 3: I10–I11)

Cumulative from upper jct. with Bryce Path (900 ft.) to:	⇅	↗	◷
White Horse Ledge (1,450 ft.)	0.6 mi.	550 ft.	0:35
Lower jct. with Bryce Path (570 ft.)	2.4 mi.	650 ft. (rev. 1,000 ft.)	1:30
From Echo Lake parking area (490 ft.) for:			
Loop over White Horse Ledge via Echo Lake Trail, Bryce Path, and White Horse Ledge Trail	4.1 mi.	1,050 ft.	2:35
Loop over White Horse Ledge with side trip to Cathedral Ledge	4.9 mi.	1,300 ft.	3:05

This trail, in combination with Bryce Path, provides a loop hike over White Horse Ledge, passing several viewpoints. White Horse Ledge Trail is described starting at its upper jct. with Bryce Path in the col between Cathedral and White Horse ledges. (This jct. can be reached in 1.0 mi. from the Echo Lake parking area via Echo Lake Trail and Bryce Path, or in 0.6 mi. from Cathedral Ledge Rd. via Bryce Link and Bryce Path.) From the jct., White Horse Ledge Trail heads uphill to the south. It then turns right at a group of large boulders and climbs steeply for a short distance then swings left and climbs moderately. At 0.2 mi. from the jct. in the col, the trail reaches an open ledge that provides a fine vista east across the valley to Kearsarge North and the Green Hills and down to Echo Lake. The trail soon reenters the woods and climbs moderately.

At 0.6 mi., on the crest of the ridge, the trail turns left (sign) where a short connecting path continues ahead, descends slightly, and in 100 yd. swings sharply right and emerges on a large ledge, where you have a view east to the Green Hills. The trail follows the crest of the ledge for 60 yd. west to the summit, where Upper Stony Ridge Trail (mountain biking) comes up from the left. A few steps beyond the high point, White Horse Ledge Trail turns right into the woods (follow yellow blazes on the rocks); a ledge 25 yd. to the left at this turn provides a fine view of Moat Mtn. The trail soon passes the other end of the short connecting path on the right and descends easily northwest and then west before turning sharply left where Red Ridge Link enters on the right at 0.8 mi.

White Horse Ledge Trail descends moderately to the south, and at 1.0 mi. Upper Stony Ridge Trail joins from the left and in 20 yd. diverges right as the yellow-blazed hiking trail continues ahead. The trail then swings left and bears left again at 1.2 mi., angling down along the south slope of the ridge. The trail turns left, climbs briefly on a sidehill, then descends and turns sharply right where a climbers path diverges left to the cliffs. The trail descends by switchbacks then swings north and weaves through large boulders at the base of the cliffs, with minor ups and downs. The trail dips right to a low point, then climbs and turns sharply left near the edge of a green on a private golf course. The trail runs through a narrow strip of woods behind the White Mountain Hotel, and at 2.2 mi., a rock climbers path to the base of White Horse Ledge enters on the left; the steep slab, whose base is 80 yd. from this jct., is worth a visit, but its ascent is a technical climb that must be left to properly trained and equipped rock climbers. From here, White Horse Ledge Trail continues north at easy grades to the four-way jct. at its lower end, where the trail meets Bryce Path and Bryce Link.

SECTION FIVE
CANNON AND KINSMAN

Map 4: Moosilauke–Kinsman Ridge

INTRODUCTION

This section covers the trails on Kinsman Mtn., Cannon Mtn., and the lower peaks in the same range on the west side of Franconia Notch, principally Mt. Wolf, the Cannon Balls, and Mt. Pemigewasset. The section also covers trails on several smaller mountains to the west and north, including Bald Mtn. and Artists Bluff, Cooley Hill, Kilburn Crags, and a spur of Gardner Mtn. The area is bounded on the east by I-93, US 3, and Franconia Notch Parkway, and on the south by NH 112 (Lost River Rd.). Nearly the entire section is covered by AMC's *White Mountains Trail Map 4: Moosilauke–Kinsman Ridge*. Most of the trails in this section are also shown on AMC's *White Mountains Trail Map 2: Franconia–Pemigewasset*.

The paved Franconia Notch Recreation Path (commonly known as the "bike path," and in places signed as "F.N.S.P. Multi-Use Trail") runs 8.8 mi. through the notch, from the parking area at the Flume to Skookumchuck Trail, and is available for pedestrian use, although those on foot should be careful not to impede bicycle traffic unnecessarily. For hikers, its primary use is as a connecting path for loop hikes on the Franconia Range or the Cannon–Kinsman Range. (See Section Three for description and mileages.) Information regarding trails and other facilities is available during the summer and fall tourist season at the Flume Visitor Center at the south end of the park and throughout the year (except for the late-fall and early-spring off-seasons) at the Cannon Mtn. Tramway. Information is also available from the information center in Lincoln, located opposite the I-93 northbound exit ramp. Concord Coach Lines has daily bus service from Boston at Logan Airport and South Station to Lincoln and Franconia. In summer, connections to several trailheads can be made by using the AMC Hiker Shuttle (outdoors.org/shuttle).

In this section, the AT follows Kinsman Ridge Trail from Kinsman Notch to Kinsman Junction (near Kinsman Pond), Fishin' Jimmy Trail from Kinsman Junction to Lonesome Lake Hut, and Cascade Brook Trail from Lonesome Lake Hut to a trail jct. near the former Whitehouse Bridge site, which is reached by Whitehouse Trail (Section Three) from the hikers parking area just north of the Flume Visitor Center or by the bike path from the Basin parking lots.

ROAD ACCESS

Most of the trails in this section start from the major roads that run through the valleys: I-93 (Franconia Notch Parkway), US 3, NH 112, NH 116, and NH 18. Road access for other trails is given in individual trail descriptions.

GEOGRAPHY

The heart of this region is the Cannon–Kinsman Range. The northern half of the range is a high, well-defined ridge, of which Cannon Mtn. and the two peaks of Kinsman Mtn. are the most important summits. The southern half of the range is broad, with only one significant summit, Mt. Wolf.

At the north end of the range is Cannon Mtn. (4,100 ft.). This dome-shaped mountain was long famous for its magnificent profile, Old Man of the Mountain (which fell in May 2003 due to the natural forces of weathering and erosion), and for its imposing east cliff. The mountain, also sometimes known as Profile Mtn., takes its officially recognized name from a natural stone table resting on a boulder that resembles a cannon when seen from Profile Clearing. The Great Stone Face (the name by which the Old Man was immortalized in a story by Nathaniel Hawthorne) was formed by three ledges at the north end of the east cliff that were not in a vertical line but appeared to be a profile when viewed from the vicinity of Profile Lake. For many years, state park personnel protected the Old Man from the otherwise inexorable forces of ice and gravity by filling cracks with cement and maintaining a system of cables and turnbuckles, but on the night of May 3, 2003, the forces of nature finally prevailed. Cannon Mtn. has a major ski area operated by the state of New Hampshire, with an aerial tramway (the successor to the first such passenger tramway in North America) that extends from a valley station (1,970 ft.) just off the parkway to a mountain station (4,000 ft.) just below the main summit. The tramway is operated in summer and fall for tourists and for skiers in the winter. Hiking is not permitted on ski trails, with the exception of yellow-blazed Mittersill-Cannon Hiking Trail, opened in 2013. This route, 2.5 mi. long with 2,350-ft. elevation gain (rev. 150 ft.) to the summit of Cannon Mtn., follows ski trails and service roads starting at parking lot 1, at the base of Mittersill Ski Area, located off NH 18 0.7 mi. west of I-93 Exit 34C. It ascends over Mittersill Peak (3,630 ft.), the northwestern spur of Cannon Mtn., which offers interesting views. Mittersill-Cannon Hiking Trail was closed in 2016 due to ski area construction; for current status, visit cannonmt.com or call 603-823-8800.

On the ridge southwest of Cannon Mtn. are three humps called the Cannon Balls (east to west: 3,769 ft., 3,660 ft., and 3,693 ft.). All are wooded, but the highest, the northeast Cannon Ball, has several restricted outlooks. Attractive Bridal Veil Falls is located on Coppermine Brook in the ravine between Cannon Mtn. and the Cannon Balls on the northwest side of the ridge. Lonesome Lake (2,740 ft.) is located on the high plateau south of the ridge between Cannon Mtn. and the Cannon Balls. Trails completely encircle the lake, which has excellent views from its shores. The whole area around the lake is in Franconia Notch State Park, and camping is not permitted.

Kinsman Mtn. rises to the south of the Cannon Balls, and its two peaks are the highest points on the ridge. North Kinsman (4,293 ft.) is wooded, and its true summit is actually a pointed boulder in the woods beside the trail, but ledges just to the east of the summit command magnificent views. The view of Mt. Lafayette and Mt. Lincoln across Franconia Notch is particularly impressive. South Kinsman (4,358 ft.) has a broad, flat summit with two knobs of nearly equal height. The USGS Lincoln quad puts the summit elevation on the north knob, which is just off the main trail, but the south knob bears the cairn and is preferred by most hikers. Views are fine from the open south knob (take care not to trample fragile alpine vegetation). The best views south are from ledges along the Kinsman Ridge Trail, 0.1 mi. south of the summit. Kinsman Mtn. shelters two very beautiful small ponds: Kinsman Pond (3,740 ft.) under the east cliffs of North Kinsman, and Harrington Pond (3,380 ft.) under the bluff at the end of South Kinsman's south ridge.

Two spurs of the Kinsman group are especially notable. On the west, Bald Peak (2,470 ft.) is a flat, ledgy knob with good views, reached by a short spur path from Mt. Kinsman Trail. On the east, lying below the massive southeast ridge of South Kinsman, is Mt. Pemigewasset (2,557 ft.), with its famous natural rock profile, Indian Head; the ledgy summit affords excellent views, and its ascent requires only a modest effort.

South of Kinsman Mtn., only Mt. Wolf (3,500 ft.) has much claim to prominence. Its summit bears a ledge with a restricted view to the east and northeast. Although lacking in impressive peaks, the southern part of the range does have several interesting aquatic attractions, including Lost River, Gordon Pond, Gordon Falls, and Georgiana Falls. The Lost River Reservation, property of the Society for the Protection of New Hampshire Forests (SPNHF), lies in Kinsman Notch about 6 mi. west of North Woodstock on NH 112 (Lost River Rd.). Here, Lost River, one of the tributaries of Moosilauke Brook, flows for nearly 0.5 mi. through a series of caves and large potholes, for the most part underground. At one place, the river falls 20 ft. within one of the caves, and at another, known as Paradise Falls, the river falls 30 ft. in the open. Trails, boardwalks, and ladders make the caves accessible; the trip through the gorge is about 1 mi. long with 300 ft. of elevation gain on the return. To protect the forest and gorge, SPNHF began to acquire the surrounding land in 1912, and it now owns 157 acres bordering the highway on both sides. SPNHF maintains a nature garden and Kinsman Notch Ecology Trail, a 0.4-mi. interpretive loop. The very strenuous Dilly Trail, described in this section, is also accessed from the Lost River parking area. The reservation is open from May through October; an admission fee is charged for access to the gorge and caves.

This section also includes several scattered peaks and trails. Just northeast of Cannon Mtn. are Bald Mtn. (2,340 ft.) and Artists Bluff (2,340 ft.), two small but very interesting peaks at the north end of Franconia Notch that offer excellent views for little exertion. Bald Mtn. is a striking miniature mountain with a bold, bare, rocky cone, whereas Artists Bluff is a wooded dome that bears the fine cliff for which the peak is named on its southeast face. A proposed expansion of Franconia Notch State Park may result in additional trails on the northern slopes of Bald Mtn. Between the villages of Franconia and Bethlehem, Mt. Agassiz (2,369 ft.) is reached by a paved road 0.8 mi. long (formerly an auto toll road) that leaves NH 142 1.0 mi. south of its jct. with US 302 in Bethlehem village. An extensive view can be seen from the summit. The former restaurant and observation tower are now a private residence, so hikers, who are currently welcome to enjoy the views from the summit (on foot only), should exercise great care to respect the rights of the property owner by staying away from all buildings. Cooley Hill (2,485 ft.) is a wooded peak west of Kinsman Mtn. with limited views; a new trail connects its summit with a trail network in the 840-acre Cooley–Jericho Community Forest in Easton. The Kilburn Crags (1,350 ft.) above the town of Littleton provide an easily visited viewpoint with an excellent view of the White Mountain high peaks. A viewpoint on a spur of Gardner Mtn. above the village of Woodsville is accessible by the new Lone Oak Trail.

HUTS
Lonesome Lake Hut (AMC)
For more than 125 years, AMC's White Mountain hut system has offered hikers a bunk for the night in spectacular locations, with home-cooked dinners and breakfasts, cold running water, and composting or waterless toilets. Lonesome Lake Hut, at an elevation of 2,760 ft., is located on the southwest shore of Lonesome Lake, with superb views of the Franconia Range. The hut was built in 1964, replacing cabins on the northeast shore. The hut accommodates 48 guests in two bunkhouses, with rooms for four to seven people, and is open to the public year-round (full-service with meals available early June through mid-October, and on a caretaker basis in late fall, winter, and spring). Reservations are highly recommended; limited drinks, snacks, and gear are available for purchase by day visitors. Pets are not permitted in the hut. The hut can be reached by Lonesome Lake Trail or by Cascade Brook Trail (via Whitehouse Trail or Basin–Cascades Trail) from the Franconia Notch Parkway; by Fishin' Jimmy

SEC 5

Trail from Kinsman Junction; or by Dodge Cutoff from Hi-Cannon Trail. Camping is not permitted around the hut or the lake, or anywhere else in Franconia Notch State Park except at Lafayette Campground. For schedules and information, contact AMC's Reservations Office at 603-466-2727 or visit outdoors.org/lodging.

CAMPING
Forest Protection Areas
The WMNF has established a number of FPAs, where camping and wood or charcoal fires are prohibited throughout the year. See p. xxiv for general FPA regulations.

In the area covered by Section Five, camping is also forbidden within 200 ft. of the Woodsville water supply dam on the Wild Ammonoosuc River and within 0.25 mi. of NH 112 (Lost River Rd.) between Lincoln and Woodsville.

Franconia Notch State Park
No camping is permitted in Franconia Notch State Park except at Lafayette Place Campground (see p. 152). In this section, the areas included in the park consist mostly of the northeast slopes of Cannon Mtn. and the regions surrounding Lonesome Lake and extending east from the lake to the Franconia Notch Parkway.

Established Trailside Campsites
To reduce overcrowding, during peak summer and fall periods, groups of six or more planning to use AMC-managed backcountry campsites are required to use AMC's group notification system. For more information, visit outdoors.org/group_notification.

Eliza Brook Campsite (AMC), with a shelter and four tent pads, is located on Kinsman Ridge Trail at its crossing of Eliza Brook, between Mt. Wolf and Kinsman Mtn.

Kinsman Pond Campsite (AMC), with a shelter and four tent platforms, is located on Kinsman Pond near Kinsman Junction, where Kinsman Ridge, Kinsman Pond, and Fishin' Jimmy trails meet. There is a caretaker in summer, and a fee is charged. Water is available from the pond but is not potable without treatment. In summer and fall this campsite fills up quickly; when capacity is reached, the caretaker will direct backpackers to a designated overflow area.

Coppermine Shelter (WMNF) is located on Coppermine Trail just west of Bridal Veil Falls.

SUGGESTED HIKES

■ Easy Hikes

BALD MTN. AND ARTISTS BLUFF

	↕	↗	○
RT to Bald Mtn. via Bald Mtn.–Artists Bluff Path	0.8 mi.	350 ft.	0:35
LP to Bald Mtn. and Artists Bluff via Bald Mtn.–Artists Bluff Path and Loop Trail	1.6 mi.	600 ft.	1:05

Bald Mtn. is a scale-model mountain: Impressive in appearance, with excellent views, it easily can be climbed with a bit of ledge scrambling at the top. Enjoy additional views from low, ledgy Artists Bluff. See Bald Mtn.–Artists Bluff Path, p. 252.

CASCADE BROOK AND ROCKY GLEN FALLS

	↕	↗	○
RT via Basin–Cascades Trail	2.4 mi.	600 ft.	1:30

A sometimes rough trail follows Cascade Brook from the Basin area all the way to Rocky Glen Falls. There are many broad ledges and small cascades, and one can turn back at any point. See Basin–Cascades Trail, p. 257.

KILBURN CRAGS

	↕	↗	○
RT via Kilburn Crags Trail	1.8 mi.	400 ft.	1:05

This easy trip to a viewpoint overlooks the town of Littleton and many high peaks. See Kilburn Crags Trail, p. 270.

LONESOME LAKE

	↕	↗	○
RT via Lonesome Lake, Cascade Brook, Fishin' Jimmy, and Around-Lonesome-Lake trails	3.2 mi.	1,000 ft.	2:05

This very popular objective offers fine views of the Kinsmans and the Franconia Range. This trip makes a circuit around the lake, including Lonesome Lake Hut. To begin, see Lonesome Lake Trail, p. 253.

■ Moderate Hikes
MT. PEMIGEWASSET

RT via Mt. Pemigewasset Trail	3.6 mi.	1,300 ft.	2:25

Leaving from the Flume Visitor Center, access an excellent outlook from a prowlike cliff atop Indian Head. See Mt. Pemigewasset Trail, p. 260.

BRIDAL VEIL FALLS

RT via Coppermine Trail	5.0 mi.	1,100 ft.	3:05

This attractive waterfall is reached by a pleasant walk uphill along Coppermine Brook. See Coppermine Trail, p. 264.

BALD PEAK

RT via Mt. Kinsman Trail and side path	4.6 mi.	1,450 ft.	3:00

This rocky spur of Kinsman Mtn. has fine views. See Mt. Kinsman Trail, p. 265.

CANNON MTN.

RT to east peak via Kinsman Ridge Trail	3.0 mi.	1,850 ft.	2:25
RT to summit via Kinsman Ridge Trail and Rim Trail	4.4 mi.	2,250 ft.	3:20
RT to summit via Lonesome Lake, Hi-Cannon, Kinsman Ridge, and Rim trails	5.6 mi.	2,350 ft.	4:00

The rough and rocky Kinsman Ridge Trail provides access to a fine broad ledge on the east peak of Cannon Mtn. that commands a spectacular view across Franconia Notch; one can easily extend the trip to the tramway-accessible summit (see Kinsman Ridge Trail, p. 247). Another good route to the summit is Hi-Cannon Trail, with a bird's-eye view of Lonesome Lake en route (to begin, see Lonesome Lake Trail, p. 253).

■ Strenuous Hikes
KINSMAN MTN.

	⇅	↗	○
RT to North Kinsman via Mt. Kinsman and Kinsman Ridge trails	8.2 mi.	3,250 ft.	5:45
RT to North and South Kinsman via Mt. Kinsman and Kinsman Ridge trails	10.0 mi.	3,900 ft.	6:55

North Kinsman has a spectacular view out to the Franconia Range and almost straight down to Kinsman Pond at the foot of its cliffs; an interesting trip can be made using Mt. Kinsman Trail from NH 116, with the option to add the spur paths to Kinsman Flume and Bald Peak, as well as a side trip to Kinsman Pond (not included in totals). South Kinsman, with its fine views, particularly to the south, can be added to this trip. To begin, see Mt. Kinsman Trail, p. 265.

SEC 5

TRAIL DESCRIPTIONS

MAIN RIDGE

KINSMAN RIDGE TRAIL (AMC; MAP 4: I3–G4)

Cumulative from NH 112 in Kinsman Notch (1,870 ft.) to:	⇅	↗	○
Dilly Trail (2,650 ft.)	0.6 mi.	800 ft.	0:40
Gordon Pond Trail (2,670 ft.)	3.3 mi.	1,450 ft.	2:25
Reel Brook Trail (2,600 ft.)	6.5 mi.	2,500 ft.	4:30
Eliza Brook Shelter spur (2,400 ft.)	7.5 mi.	2,600 ft.	5:05
Harrington Pond (3,400 ft.)	8.9 mi.	3,600 ft.	6:15
South Kinsman summit (4,358 ft.)	10.0 mi.	4,550 ft.	7:15
North Kinsman summit (4,293 ft.)	10.9 mi.	4,850 ft.	7:50
Mt. Kinsman Trail (3,850 ft.)	11.3 mi.	4,850 ft.	8:05
Kinsman Junction (3,750 ft.)	11.5 mi.	4,850 ft.	8:10
Lonesome Lake Trail (3,400 ft.)	13.9 mi.	5,700 ft.	9:50
Hi-Cannon Trail (3,900 ft.)	14.3 mi.	6,200 ft.	10:15
Rim Trail jct. near Cannon Mtn. summit (4,050 ft.)	14.7 mi.	6,350 ft.	10:30
Side path to ledges (3,800 ft.)	15.4 mi.	6,400 ft.	10:55
Cannon Mtn. Tramway parking area (1,970 ft.)	16.9 mi.	6,400 ft.	11:40

KINSMAN RIDGE TRAIL, IN REVERSE (AMC; MAP 4: I3–G4)

Cumulative from Cannon Mtn. Tramway parking area (1,970 ft.) to:	⇅	↗	○
Side path to ledges (3,800 ft.)	1.5 mi.	1,850 ft.	1:40
Rim Trail jct. near Cannon Mtn. summit (4,050 ft.)	2.2 mi.	2,150 ft.	2:10
Hi-Cannon Trail (3,900 ft.)	2.6 mi.	2,150 ft.	2:20
Lonesome Lake Trail (3,400 ft.)	3.0 mi.	2,150 ft.	2:35
Kinsman Junction (3,750 ft.)	5.4 mi.	3,350 ft.	4:20
Mt. Kinsman Trail (3,850 ft.)	5.6 mi.	3,450 ft.	4:30
North Kinsman summit (4,293 ft.)	6.0 mi.	3,900 ft.	4:55
South Kinsman summit (4,358 ft.)	6.9 mi.	4,250 ft.	5:35
Harrington Pond (3,400 ft.)	8.0 mi.	4,250 ft.	6:05
Eliza Brook Shelter spur (2,400 ft.)	9.4 mi.	4,250 ft.	6:50
Reel Brook Trail (2,600 ft.)	10.4 mi.	4,550 ft.	7:30
Gordon Pond Trail (2,670 ft.)	13.6 mi.	5,650 ft.	9:40
Dilly Trail (2,650 ft.)	16.3 mi.	6,300 ft.	11:20
NH 112 in Kinsman Notch (1,870 ft.)	16.9 mi.	6,300 ft.	11:35

This trail follows the crest of the main ridge from the height-of-land on NH 112 in Kinsman Notch north to the Cannon Mtn. Tramway parking lot, just off Franconia Notch Parkway at Exit 34B. At its south end, the trail leaves NH 112 just to the north of the height-of-land, 0.5 mi. north of the Lost River entrance and almost directly opposite the parking area at the north terminus of Beaver Brook Trail. At its north end, the trail begins near a designated hikers parking area at the southeast end of the Cannon Mtn. Tramway parking lot. From NH 112 to Kinsman Junction, Kinsman Ridge Trail is part of the white-blazed AT. For much of its length, Kinsman Ridge Trail is a more difficult route than one might infer from the map; footing is often rough, with many minor ups and downs. Hikers with heavy packs should allow considerable extra time for many parts of the trail. Little water exists on or near several long sections of the trail and none that a cautious hiker will drink without treatment.

The trail is described in the northbound direction (from Kinsman Notch to the Cannon Mtn. Tramway parking lot); distances, elevation gains, and times are given for both the northbound and southbound directions. The trail leaves NH 112 and climbs a steep sidehill, bearing gradually away from the road for 0.1 mi., then swings right and climbs very steeply northeast with many rock steps. At 0.4 mi., the grade relaxes, and the trail soon crosses a swampy sag on log bridges and reaches a jct. on the right at 0.6 mi. with Dilly Trail from the SPNHF Lost River Reservation. At 0.9 mi., Kinsman Ridge Trail crosses the summit of a wooded knob, passes a restricted southeast outlook, descends steeply by zigzags, soon passes a small stream (unreliable), and follows the ridge over several minor humps. At 2.4 mi., the trail passes an outlook to the east then crosses a larger wooded hump and descends steadily. At 3.3 mi., the trail reaches its low point south of Mt. Wolf, crossing a stagnant brook in a ravine, then ascends 30 yd. to the jct. where Gordon Pond Trail enters on the right, 0.3 mi. from Gordon Pond.

Kinsman Ridge Trail now climbs by short, steep sections alternating with easy sections and occasional minor descents, crosses a small brook (reliable water) at 3.9 mi., and ascends to a point just below the summit of the west knob of Mt. Wolf. Then the trail descends slightly into a shallow sag and climbs to a point near the summit of the east knob of Mt. Wolf at 4.6 mi., where the trail makes a sharp left turn. Here, a side path leads to the right 60 yd. to the summit of the east knob, where you have a restricted view of the Franconias and the peaks to the east and southeast. The main trail then descends the east side of Mt. Wolf's north ridge at a moderate grade but with a rough footway and two significant ascents along the way. At 5.4 mi., where the trail turns left for the second of these ascents, a side path descends 20 yd., right to the edge of a bog known as Failing Water Pond, where you have a view of South Kinsman. At 6.0 mi., the trail turns left, runs almost level, then descends and meets Reel Brook Trail, which enters left at 6.5 mi., just south of the col between Mt. Wolf and Kinsman Mtn. (this was the original Kinsman Notch). Kinsman Ridge Trail continues along the ridge top with several ups and downs, crosses under power lines (bearing right and then left) where there is a view southeast at 7.0 mi., and descends moderately to the bank of Eliza Brook at 7.5 mi., passing two side paths that lead 60 yd. left to Eliza Brook Campsite.

Kinsman Ridge Trail crosses Eliza Brook, turns left and then quickly right, and in 50 yd. bears left onto an old logging road. (In the reverse direction, the trail turns right off the road to descend to Eliza Brook.) The trail follows the road for 0.3 mi. then turns left off it and descends to the bank of Eliza Brook. It climbs, roughly at times, along a scenic section of the brook, with several attractive cascades and pools. At 8.6 mi., the trail recrosses Eliza Brook and soon climbs steeply, passing through a rocky portal at the top, where it levels to cross the bog at the east end of Harrington Pond on log bridges; the footing in this area may be very wet. Here, at 8.9 mi., is an interesting view of the rugged shoulder of South Kinsman rising above the beautiful pond. (*Note:* The section of the trail between

SEC 5

Harrington Pond and South Kinsman may require much extra time, particularly for those with heavy packs, and is also somewhat exposed to weather.) The trail continues at a moderate grade for 0.3 mi. then climbs a steep and rocky pitch with a partial outlook at the top at 9.5 mi. It runs nearly level across a shoulder then struggles up a very steep and rough pitch with several scrambles to an excellent outlook where the climbing becomes somewhat easier. It runs briefly in the open, reenters the scrub, and ascends easily to another open ledge where it turns left at a cairn; here a fine outlook ledge is 10 yd. to the right. Kinsman Ridge Trail continues another 140 yd. to the bare south knob of South Kinsman's summit, which is very exposed to weather, at 9.9 mi.; here there is a large cairn.

From here, Kinsman Ridge Trail crosses a scrub-filled sag, passes 15 yd. to the west of the north knob of South Kinsman at 10.0 mi., and descends moderately to the col between South and North Kinsman at 10.5 mi. The trail climbs easily at first then steadily with some minor ledge scrambling past two viewpoints to a side path (sign) that leads to the right at 10.9 mi.; this side path runs 25 yd. to a fine outlook to the Franconias. From the north side of this broad ledge, the path descends via a steep, rough scramble another 70 yd. to a ledge that looks directly down on Kinsman Pond. The true summit of North Kinsman is a pointed boulder on the right (east) side of the main trail, 30 yd. north of the outlook spur. Kinsman Ridge Trail now descends steeply, with several ledge scrambles, to the jct. with Mt. Kinsman Trail on the left at 11.3 mi., then continues down to Kinsman Junction at 11.5 mi. Here, Fishin' Jimmy Trail continues the AT ahead to Lonesome Lake, and Kinsman Pond Trail bears right, leading in 0.1 mi. to Kinsman Pond and Kinsman Pond Shelter.

Kinsman Ridge Trail, from here on blazed in blue, turns sharply left at Kinsman Junction, and after a brief descent, rises abruptly 100 ft. to a hump (3,812 ft.) on the ridge. The trail then continues over the Cannon Balls, the three humps that make up the ridge leading to Cannon Mtn. After passing near the top of the first (west) Cannon Ball at 12.5 mi., the trail descends sharply to a deep ravine where a small, sluggish brook usually contains some water. The trail circles to the north of the second (middle) Cannon Ball and enters the next col with very little descent. After passing several scattered viewpoints while climbing over the third (northeast) Cannon Ball at 13.7 mi., the trail descends steeply and roughly to the jct. at 13.9 mi. with Lonesome Lake Trail, which leads right (southeast) 1.0 mi. to Lonesome Lake Hut (water can be found 0.2 mi. down this trail).

In a few yards, the trail reaches the low point in Coppermine Col, at the base of Cannon Mtn., then climbs a very steep and rough pitch among huge boulders, with several fairly difficult scrambles and a bypass around a large rock that fell onto the trail in 2016. At 14.3 mi., Hi-Cannon Trail enters right, and Kinsman Ridge Trail swings left and climbs gradually up the ridge to the gravel Rim Trail at 14.7 mi., where Kinsman Ridge Trail encounters the maze of trails in the summit area. The true summit, with its observation platform and lookout tower, is reached in 100 yd. by following the gravel path straight ahead from this jct. (From the tower, a path signed Short Trail continues 250 yd. down to the rear of the Cannon Mtn. Tramway summit station.)

Kinsman Ridge Trail bears right at the jct. and coincides with Rim Trail for about 0.2 mi., descending easily around the edge of the summit plateau, affording excellent views from several ledges, then turns sharply right downhill (sign), as Rim Trail continues on toward the tramway terminal (reaching it in 100 yd.). Descending the semi-open east flank of the main peak over rocks and ledges then through scrub, Kinsman Ridge Trail crosses a moist sag and ascends slightly to the east summit. At the point where the main trail makes a 90-degree turn left (north), a side trail turns sharply right and descends easily southeast for 60 yd., emerging on ledges where you have a magnificent view across the notch to the Franconia Range. The main trail descends easily at first then steadily, and at 15.7 mi., it turns right onto a ski trail (on the ascent, turn left off the ski trail here) and descends along its right edge.

Soon the trail descends steeply through a semi-open area of ski glades, with rough and rocky footing including some slippery ledges. The hiking trail crosses the ski route four times, with occasional views north; follow the blue blazes carefully. At 16.1 mi., Kinsman Ridge Trail continues steeply ahead, down into the woods, as the ski trail descends to the left. The descent remains steep with several switchbacks down through deeply eroded gravelly sections with slippery footing. Finally, the trail emerges in a clearing at the base of a steep slope, turns right and follows the right edge of the clearing for 70 yd., then turns left onto a service road and follows it for 120 yd. to the trail's end at the Cannon Mtn. Tramway parking lot. In the reverse direction, from the southeast corner of the Tramway parking area (sign: Kinsman Ridge Trail), follow a service road southeast for 120 yd. to a clearing on the right, then turn right follow the left edge of the clearing for 70 yd., and turn left (sign) into the woods.

SEC 5

WEST SIDE OF FRANCONIA NOTCH

BALD MTN.–ARTISTS BLUFF PATH (NHDP/TRAILWRIGHTS; MAP 4: G4)

Cumulative from Peabody Slopes parking area (2,000 ft.) to:	⇅	↗	↺
Fork in trail (2,180 ft.)	0.3 mi.	200 ft.	0:15
Bald Mtn. (2,340 ft.) via spur path	0.4 mi.	350 ft.	0:25
Echo Lake beach parking area (1,960 ft.) direct via Artists Bluff	0.9 mi.	350 ft.	0:40
Echo Lake beach parking area (1,960 ft.) via side trip to Bald Mtn. and Artists Bluff	1.2 mi.	500 ft.	0:50
Complete loop, including side trip to Bald Mtn., via Loop Trail	1.6 mi.	600 ft.	1:05

The cliff called Artists Bluff and the summit of Bald Mtn. provide fine views for very little effort. The trail begins and ends on NH 18 just west of its jct. with Franconia Notch Parkway (I-93) at Exit 34C, north of Echo Lake. The west trailhead is located at the edge of the large gravel parking lot for the Roland Peabody Memorial Slope section of Cannon Mtn. Ski Area, on the north side of NH 18, 0.5 mi. from the parkway. This parking lot is sometimes closed when the ski area is not open, at which times cars must be parked in a designated area just off the highway (sign). The east trailhead is on NH 18, 0.4 mi. east of the west trailhead. There is no parking here; the nearest parking is at the Echo Lake beach parking lot, 140 yd. to the west.

From parking for the west trailhead, walk 100 yd. across the Peabody Slopes parking lot to the trail sign. The red-blazed trail follows an old carriage road, passing a jct. with the west end of Loop Trail on the right in 25 yd., and climbs steadily to the top of the ridge at 0.3 mi. At this point, Bald Mtn. spur path diverges left (sign) and climbs through the woods, with one scramble up a ledge, then ascends steeply up the open rocky cone of Bald Mtn., reaching the top in another 0.1 mi. About 25 yd. beyond the jct. with the spur to Bald Mtn., the main trail turns right from the old road (avoid a false path that leads ahead) and runs over two wooded humps, passing an outlook ledge on each. The trail then descends steeply to the top of a gravelly gully at 0.7 mi., where a path leads left 50 yd. to open ledges at the top of Artists Bluff. The main trail continues steeply down the gully over rock steps, passes the jct. with the eastern end of Loop Trail on the right, and in another 40 yd., at 0.9 mi., reaches NH 18.

Loop Trail is 0.4 mi. long and makes a loop hike possible over Bald Mtn. and Artists Bluff, avoiding a road walk along NH 18. From its eastern jct. with Bald Mtn.–Artists Bluff Path, 40 yd. in from NH 18, Loop Trail winds past several boulders, climbs over a bank with a view of Cannon

Mtn., and bears right at a fork at 0.2 mi. (sign; here the unmaintained Short Circuit path to NH 18 diverges left). Loop Trail climbs on a rocky sidehill, levels off, and descends slightly to its western jct. with Bald Mtn.–Artists Bluff Path, just above the Peabody Slopes parking lot.

LONESOME LAKE TRAIL (AMC; MAP 4: H4)

Cumulative from Lafayette Campground west side parking area (1,760 ft.) to:	⇅	↗	⟳
Hi-Cannon Trail (1,925 ft.)	0.4 mi.	150 ft.	0:15
Cascade Brook Trail–Dodge Cutoff (2,740 ft.)	1.2 mi.	1,000 ft.	1:05
Kinsman Ridge Trail (3,400 ft.)	2.3 mi.	1,650 ft.	2:00
Lonesome Lake Hut (2,760 ft.) via Cascade Brook Trail and Fishin' Jimmy Trail	1.5 mi.	1,000 ft.	1:15

This yellow-blazed trail begins on the west (southbound) side of Franconia Notch Parkway, at the end of the south parking lot at Lafayette Campground (the parking area is a stop for the AMC Hiker Shuttle), and runs past Lonesome Lake to Kinsman Ridge Trail at Coppermine Col. Lonesome Lake Trail follows the route of an old bridle path much of the way to Lonesome Lake, with fairly good footing and moderate grades; beyond the lake, the trail becomes fairly steep and rough with poor footing. The parking area is reached from the southbound lane of the parkway (off the left side of the campground exit ramp). Additional parking is available at the north end of the campground exit ramp, or one may park in the Old Bridle Path lot on the east (northbound) side of the parkway and walk to the west side through a pedestrian tunnel, which leads to the northern parking area. The Lafayette Place parking lots fill up early on fine summer and fall days, and later-arriving hikers will need to carefully park on the grassy shoulder of the Parkway, sometimes a significant distance from the trailhead.

The trail leaves the parking lot at a large trail sign, crosses the Pemigewasset River on a footbridge, and then crosses Pemi Trail (which here follows a paved road). Lonesome Lake Trail follows a yellow-blazed path through the campground, crossing two more roads, and climbs at a moderate grade, soon swinging left. At 0.3 mi., a bridge crosses a small brook at a sharp left turn in the trail, and at 0.4 mi., Hi-Cannon Trail leaves right. From this point, Lonesome Lake Trail ascends steadily by long switchbacks, swinging right at 0.6 mi. and left at the edge of a ravine at 0.9 mi. Above this turn it climbs rather steeply with rocky footing then descends slightly to a jct. at 1.2 mi. near the shore of Lonesome Lake; here, Cascade Brook Trail diverges left and Dodge Cutoff diverges sharply right. A few steps ahead is a fine view of North and South Kinsman across the lake.

SEC 5

For the shortest route to Lonesome Lake Hut, follow Cascade Brook and Fishin' Jimmy trails. Lonesome Lake Trail turns right and continues along the north shore on plank walkways, coinciding with Around-Lonesome-Lake Trail, which diverges left after 0.2 mi. and leads to Lonesome Lake Hut in another 0.3 mi. Lonesome Lake Trail continues northwest at easy grades, soon climbs a steep and rough section, then eases again before ending at Kinsman Ridge Trail in Coppermine Col, 0.8 mi. southwest of the summit of Cannon Mtn.

AROUND-LONESOME-LAKE TRAIL (AMC; MAP 4: H4)

From any starting point (2,740 ft.) for:	⥮	↗	⏱
Complete loop	0.8 mi.	0 ft.	0:25

This trail, composed mostly of portions of other trails, encircles Lonesome Lake and affords fine views, especially of the Franconia Range. The part on the west shore of the lake is subject to flooding in wet seasons, although an extensive set of plank walkways installed in 2009 has made passage easier.

Starting at the jct. of Dodge Cutoff and Lonesome Lake and Cascade Brook trails, Around-Lonesome-Lake Trail follows Cascade Brook Trail south along the east shore. Around-Lonesome-Lake Trail then turns west and, following Fishin' Jimmy Trail, crosses the outlet of the lake on a bridge and continues across the open beach area with views of Franconia Ridge at 0.3 mi. as Fishin' Jimmy Trail bears left to ascend to the hut. Around-Lonesome-Lake Trail continues north past more viewpoints then leads through the open bogs along the west side of the lake (the only section not shared with another trail), crosses several inlet brooks, and meets Lonesome Lake Trail at 0.6 mi., shortly after entering the woods. Here, Around-Lonesome-Lake Trail turns right on Lonesome Lake Trail and continues to the jct. with Dodge Cutoff and Cascade Brook Trail, completing the circuit.

HI-CANNON TRAIL (NHDP; MAP 4: H4)

Cumulative from Lonesome Lake Trail (1,925 ft.) to:	⥮	↗	⏱
Dodge Cutoff (2,840 ft.)	0.8 mi.	900 ft.	0:50
Kinsman Ridge Trail (3,900 ft.)	2.0 mi.	1,950 ft.	2:00
From Lafayette Campground west side parking area (1,760 ft.) to:			
Cannon Mtn. summit (4,100 ft.) via Lonesome Lake, Hi-Cannon, Kinsman Ridge, and Rim trails	2.8 mi.	2,350 ft.	2:35

This blue-blazed trail begins at Lonesome Lake Trail, 0.4 mi. from the parking area at Lafayette Campground, and ends on Kinsman Ridge Trail, 0.4 mi. south of the summit of Cannon Mtn. Hi-Cannon Trail is steep near Cliff House, rough at times, and potentially dangerous if there is ice on the ledges above Cliff House. The trail passes several fine viewpoints, particularly the ledges overlooking Lonesome Lake.

The trail diverges right (west) from Lonesome Lake Trail and begins to ascend steadily by numerous short switchbacks, in places with gravelly, eroded footing that is slippery on the descent; please do not shortcut the switchbacks, as this causes further erosion. Watch carefully for a sharp right switchback at 0.1 mi., where an old logging road continues straight ahead. Use caution where the trail crosses a steep brookbed at 0.2 mi. At 0.8 mi., Dodge Cutoff from Lonesome Lake enters on the left at the top of a ridge. Soon Hi-Cannon Trail becomes significantly steeper and rougher. At 1.2 mi., shortly after the trail crosses a gravelly washout, is a fine outlook across Franconia Notch. The trail turns left here, and 100 yd. farther, passes Cliff House (up above the trail on the right)—a natural rock shelter—and ascends a ladder with a tricky, narrow ledge traverse to the left at the top (dangerous if icy). The trail then passes through woods along a cliff edge with three fine outlooks over Lonesome Lake in the next 0.2 mi. (use caution on the ledges, as cliffs drop off sharply). Then the trail ascends moderately with rough footing and occasional easier sections to the top of the ridge, turns right, and ends at its jct. with Kinsman Ridge Trail at 2.0 mi. For the summit of Cannon Mtn., follow Kinsman Ridge Trail and then Rim Trail straight uphill for 0.4 mi.

SEC 5

DODGE CUTOFF (NHDP; MAP 4: H4)

From Lonesome Lake Trail (2,740 ft.) to:	⇅	↗	○
Hi-Cannon Trail (2,840 ft.)	0.3 mi.	100 ft.	0:15

This short link between Lonesome Lake and Hi-Cannon trails provides a shortcut between Lonesome Lake and Cannon Mtn. It was named in honor of Joe Dodge, a legendary White Mountain character who is known as the longtime manager of AMC's hut system.

The trail leads northeast (sign) from the jct. of Lonesome Lake and Cascade Brook trails on the east shore of the lake, 0.3 mi. from Lonesome Lake Hut. After climbing over a low ridge and crossing a moist sag, Dodge Cutoff ascends by switchbacks, rather steeply for a while, to Hi-Cannon Trail, 0.8 mi. above the jct. of Lonesome Lake and Hi-Cannon trails and 1.6 mi. below the summit of Cannon Mtn.

PEMI TRAIL (NHDP; MAP 4: H4)

Cumulative from Old Man parking area on west side of parkway (1,990 ft.) to:	⇅	↗	⟲
Lafayette Campground (1,760 ft.)	2.0 mi.	100 ft. (rev. 350 ft.)	1:05
Basin-Cascades Trail (1,540 ft.)	3.9 mi.	100 ft. (rev. 200 ft.)	2:00
Cascade Brook Trail (1,470 ft.)	4.7 mi.	100 ft. (rev. 50 ft.)	2:25
Whitehouse Trail (1,400 ft.) via Cascade Brook Trail	4.9 mi.	100 ft. (rev. 100 ft.)	2:30
Flume hikers parking lot (1,420 ft.) via Whitehouse Trail	5.6 mi.	200 ft. (rev. 100 ft.)	2:55

This trail extends from a parking lot near Profile Lake to the hikers parking area just north of the Flume Visitor Center, providing a fairly easy footpath that is an alternative route to the bike path along the central part of Franconia Notch. The trail makes various loop hikes possible on the east side of the Cannon–Kinsman range. The markings are not always obvious, and signs are not always present at intersections with roads and the bike path, so following Pemi Trail requires some care, particularly at points where it diverges from these other routes and at stream crossings. In 2016, several stretches of the trail were overgrown, particularly in the northern section. The crossings of Cascade Brook and Whitehouse Brook near the south end of the trail may be difficult in high water.

Pemi Trail leaves the southeast corner of the Old Man site parking area on the west side of Franconia Notch Parkway (0.3 mi. off Exit 34B), ascends granite steps into the woods, rises slightly, then turns sharply left across a brook bed and descends to the west shore of Profile Lake at 0.3 mi. The trail skirts up and down along the west shore of the lake, with views of Eagle Cliff rising above the parkway. The trail crosses a wet area south of the lake on log bridges then, in 40 yd., where a climbers access path joins from the left after crossing the lake's outlet brook, Pemi Trail turns right to cross a minor branch of the outlet brook on bog bridges. On the west bank, Pemi Trail turns left to follow the main outlet brook as the climbers path continues ahead up the slope. In another 100 yd., at 0.7 mi., Pemi Trail enters the paved bike path, follows it right for 40 yd., then turns left off it and reenters the woods (signs at both intersections).

Pemi Trail runs close to the parkway, passing a short alternate route for cross-country skiers on the right, then descends to cross the Pemigewasset River on a bridge at 1.2 mi. The trail continues down the valley, with occasional short ascents, then runs above an extensive beaver wetland. At 1.8 mi., a side path (sign: 5) diverges sharply right and leads in 40 yd. to a fine view of Cannon Cliff from the open wetland. In another 60 yd., the trail crosses through an area of beaver activity with more views. It crosses a wet area on bog bridges, then recrosses the Pemigewasset on another bridge. In another 100 yd., the trail crosses the bike path. (This crossing is signed only in the northbound direction; going south, the trail reenters the woods directly across the bike path.) The trail then soon turns right onto a paved road that leads into Lafayette Campground, just below the headquarters buildings, at 2.0 mi.

In 15 yd., the trail turns left (south) on the paved campground road (signs for Pemi Trail and Sites 45–70) that follows most closely along the west bank of the river, crosses Lonesome Lake Trail, and enters the woods (sign) between campsites 67 and 68. Pemi Trail continues for 1.7 mi. close to the river at easy grades with good footing then becomes rougher as the trail descends to intersect a tourist path by a bridge, 50 yd. west of the Basin.

In 20 yd., at 3.9 mi., Pemi Trail turns left onto Basin–Cascades Trail, then in 50 yd. turns right onto a paved path, with the Basin a short distance to the left. In 70 yd., where the paved path bears left, Pemi Trail diverges right into the woods (sign). The trail descends easily along the river, passing the "Baby Flume" and some cascades, and crosses Cascade Brook (may be very difficult at high water) at 4.3 mi.; follow blazes carefully at this crossing. The trail soon begins to swing away from the river, crosses Whitehouse Brook (may be difficult at high water), then ascends briefly to join Cascade Brook Trail at 4.7 mi. and follows it to the left, passing under both lanes of I-93 to the bike path. From there, Pemi Trail turns right and follows Whitehouse Trail (Section Three) for 0.2 mi. along the bike path and then 0.6 mi. on a footpath on the right (signs for Pemi and Whitehouse trails) to the hikers parking lot just north of the Flume.

SEC 5

BASIN–CASCADES TRAIL (NHDP; MAP 4: H4)

From trailhead near the Basin (1,540 ft.) to:	⇅	↗	↺
Cascade Brook Trail (2,084 ft.)	1.0 mi.	550 ft.	0:45

This trail starts at the Basin parking areas on either side of Franconia Notch Parkway and ascends along the beautiful lower half of Cascade Brook to Cascade Brook Trail. The brook is scenic, and trail grades are mostly moderate, but the footing is often fairly rough; use caution where Basin–Cascades Trail passes along steep banks above the brook. From the parking areas on either side of the parkway, follow the tourist paths past the Basin and onto the west bank of the Pemigewasset River, about 0.2 mi.

from either starting point, where the trailhead is situated at the western edge of the maze of paths that surrounds the Basin.

From the trailhead (sign) at the jct. with Pemi Trail, Basin–Cascades Trail leads northwest, angles left toward Cascade Brook, then soon climbs along the brook past cascades, small falls, and ledges with views of the Franconia Range across the notch, reached by numerous unmarked side paths. At 0.3 mi. it enters the WMNF. At 0.4 mi., the trail passes a rough side path (sign) that leads down to a good view of Kinsman Falls, and 50 yd. farther up, as the main trail comes out on the bank of the brook, a ledge on the left provides a viewpoint at the top of these falls. In another 100 yd., the trail crosses Cascade Brook (may be difficult in high water) and continues with rough footing along the brook past more cascades and pools. The trail passes Rocky Glen Falls in a gorge to the right at 0.9 mi. then swings sharply left up through a small box canyon, passes abutments from a former footbridge, and soon ends at Cascade Brook Trail on the south bank of the brook.

CASCADE BROOK TRAIL (AMC; MAP 4: H4)

Cumulative from Whitehouse Trail jct. (1,400 ft.) to:	⇅	↗	↻
Basin–Cascades Trail (2,084 ft.)	1.5 mi.	700 ft.	1:05
Kinsman Pond Trail (2,294 ft.)	2.0 mi.	900 ft.	1:25
Fishin' Jimmy Trail (2,740 ft.)	2.8 mi.	1,350 ft.	2:05
Lonesome Lake Trail and Dodge Cutoff (2,740 ft.)	3.1 mi.	1,350 ft.	2:15

This relatively easy trail, a link in the AT, leads to Lonesome Lake from the bike path at the former Whitehouse Bridge site, just south of the bike path's bridge over the Pemigewasset River (Liberty Spring Trail begins just north of the bridge). No parking is available at the Whitehouse Bridge site, which is reached in 0.8 mi. from the hikers parking area, just north of the Flume Visitor Center via Whitehouse Trail (see p. 162) or in 0.7 mi. via the bike path from the Basin parking lot on the northbound side of the parkway.

From the jct. with the bike path, Cascade Brook Trail crosses under both lanes of the parkway (coinciding with Pemi Trail) then turns right at the edge of the parkway clearing and enters the woods; just after crossing a small brook at 0.2 mi., Pemi Trail leaves on the right. Cascade Brook Trail climbs at a moderate grade and crosses Whitehouse Brook at 0.4 mi., just above a fine cascade. The trail continues generally northwest at moderate and then easy grades, crossing numerous small brooks, and swings right to a jct. at 1.5 mi. at the edge of Cascade Brook, where Basin–Cascades Trail enters right.

Cascade Brook Trail immediately crosses Cascade Brook on rocks a short distance upstream from the site of a former footbridge that was washed away in 2011. This crossing is difficult and potentially dangerous in high water; as of 2016 the bridge had not been replaced. On the far side of the brook, the trail climbs easily along the northeast bank. At 2.0 mi., Kinsman Pond Trail diverges left and crosses the brook, and from this point, Cascade Brook Trail bears right and becomes rougher and rockier. It makes a short loop to the right on a relocation and continues at a moderate grade to the jct. with Fishin' Jimmy Trail on the left, at the outlet of Lonesome Lake at 2.8 mi. From here, Lonesome Lake Hut is 120 yd. to the left. Cascade Brook Trail bears right and continues along the east side of the lake and ends at a jct. with Lonesome Lake Trail and Dodge Cutoff at 3.1 mi., where there is a fine view of North and South Kinsman a few steps to the left.

SEC
5

FISHIN' JIMMY TRAIL (AMC; MAP 4: H4)

Cumulative from Cascade Brook Trail (2,740 ft.) to:	⇅	↗	○
Lonesome Lake Hut (2,760 ft.)	0.1 mi.	0 ft.	0:05
Kinsman Junction (3,750 ft.)	2.0 mi.	1,200 ft. (rev. 200 ft.)	1:35

This trail, a link in the AT, leads from Lonesome Lake to Kinsman Ridge Trail at Kinsman Junction, near Kinsman Pond. Parts of Fishin' Jimmy Trail are steep and rough, with wooden steps on ledges. The trail received its peculiar name from a well-known local character called Fishin' Jimmy—his real name was James Whitcher—who lived in the Franconia area and was featured in a story by Annie Trumbull Slosson, once a popular New England author.

Diverging from Cascade Brook Trail at the south end of Lonesome Lake, Fishin' Jimmy Trail crosses the outlet brook on a bridge, passes the jct. on the right with Around-Lonesome-Lake Trail near the beach at the southwest corner of the lake, and climbs a wooden stairway, reaching Lonesome Lake Hut in 120 yd. Fishin' Jimmy Trail runs around the lower end of a ridge coming down from Middle Cannon Ball, making several ascents and descents and passing over a ledgy ridge crest at 0.6 mi. The trail then crosses several small brooks, with the last reliable water source in a small mossy, ledgy brook at 1.1 mi., and soon begins to climb, at times steeply, with wooden steps and cut steps aiding passage on the steepest ledges but with occasional minor descents as well. At 1.7 mi., the trail curls around a large boulder on the left and passes through a fairly flat area. At 1.9 mi., the trail reaches the top of the serious climbing and ascends gradually to Kinsman Junction and Kinsman Ridge Trail at 2.0 mi., 0.1 mi. north of Kinsman Pond Shelter on Kinsman Pond Trail.

KINSMAN POND TRAIL (AMC; MAP 4: H4)

From Cascade Brook Trail (2,294 ft.) to:	⇅	↗	↻
Kinsman Junction (3,750 ft.)	2.5 mi.	1,500 ft. (rev . 50 ft.)	2:00

This blue-blazed trail leads to Kinsman Pond and Kinsman Junction from Cascade Brook Trail, 2.0 mi. from its beginning on the bike path at the Whitehouse Bridge site, and 0.5 mi. above its jct. with Basin–Cascades Trail. The lower half of Kinsman Pond Trail has reasonably good footing, but the upper part is wet, steep, rocky, and very rough, and at times the trail shares the footway with small brooks, making rocks slippery; it may also be difficult to follow for short stretches.

Leaving Cascade Brook Trail, Kinsman Pond Trail immediately crosses to the southwest side of Cascade Brook (may be difficult in high water) and proceeds west on old logging roads. Soon the trail crosses a small brook and begins to rise moderately, following a brook past several small but attractive cascades and passing into dense boreal forest. At 1.3 mi., the trail crosses the brook and soon runs in its bed for 0.1 mi. From here on, the trail is very rough and eroded. At 1.6 mi., the grade becomes easy, and the trail crosses the outlet brook from the pond at 1.9 mi., passes a water source left (sign), and reaches the foot of the pond at 2.1 mi. The trail climbs roughly up and down on the ledgy east shore of the pond, with the impressive bulk of North Kinsman rising from the opposite shore, and passes Kinsman Pond Shelter at 2.4 mi. and then several tent platforms. Water in this area is unsafe to drink unless treated. Kinsman Junction, where Kinsman Pond Trail meets Kinsman Ridge and Fishin' Jimmy trails, is 0.1 mi. beyond the shelter.

MT. PEMIGEWASSET TRAIL (NHDP; MAP 4: H4)

From Flume Visitor Center parking area (1,340 ft.) to:	⇅	↗	↻
Mt. Pemigewasset summit (2,557 ft.)	1.8 mi.	1,250 ft. (rev. 50 ft.)	1:30

This blue-blazed trail runs from the north end of the Flume Visitor Center parking area (on US 3 at Exit 34A off Franconia Notch Parkway) to the summit of Mt. Pemigewasset (Indian Head), where excellent views can be obtained from a large open ledge with modest effort. Grades are easy to moderate and the footing is generally good. The Trailwrights have made many improvements on the trail in recent years. The trail reaches the vertical summit cliffs very abruptly, so care should be exercised, particularly with small children or in slippery conditions.

The trail follows the bike path (Franconia Notch Recreation Path) north from the parking lot for 150 yd., turns left (sign) on a gravel path, and passes under US 3 in a tunnel then turns left again and crosses a brook on a bridge. The trail descends a short distance then turns sharply right and ascends under both lanes of Franconia Notch Parkway. The trail enters the woods at 0.4 mi., crosses a small brook and swings right, and ascends gradually northwest through hardwood forest, crossing several small brooks. At 0.7 mi. it crosses another brook on a log bridge, swings left, and begins climbing more steadily. It ascends along a small brook then turns sharply right away from it at 1.0 mi. At 1.3 mi., the trail passes to the left of a large boulder and swings left uphill, climbing a bit more steeply to the ridge crest, where it turns left (south) at 1.6 mi. and enters conifer forest. It passes the jct. with Indian Head Trail on the right at 1.7 mi. and reaches the summit ledges at 1.8 mi. At the true summit, which is 90 yd. beyond the first ledges and around to the left (follow blue blazes and avoid old yellow blazes from an abandoned trail that lead southeast), there is a restricted northeast view toward the Franconia Range. Use caution if the sloping ledges are wet or icy.

SEC
5

INDIAN HEAD TRAIL (AMC; MAP 4: I4–H4)

From US 3 (1,000 ft.) to:	⇅	↗	↺
Mt. Pemigewasset summit (2,557 ft.)	1.9 mi.	1,550 ft.	1:45

This yellow-blazed trail runs to the summit of Mt. Pemigewasset (Indian Head), where open ledges afford excellent views. (See Mt. Pemigewasset Trail description for cautionary notes about the summit ledges.) The trail begins on the west side of US 3, 0.2 mi. south of the Indian Head Resort at a small parking area reached by a short gravel road (sign: Trailhead Parking). This trail is much less heavily used than Mt. Pemigewasset Trail; the footway may be wet and obscure in places, and markings should be followed with care.

The trail leaves the parking area and soon crosses a small field then turns left and accompanies Hanson Brook under both lanes of I-93, reentering the woods at 0.3 mi. It ascends by easy to moderate grades through hardwoods on an old logging road along the brook, crossing a tributary and then passing a small cascade at 0.8 mi. The trail then ascends more steeply with rougher footing. At 1.1 mi., it turns right onto another old woods road then soon leaves that road and climbs moderately, with wet footing in places and occasional bypasses, circling well around the south side of the cliffs that form Indian

Head. The trail then enters conifer forest and ascends steeply for a short distance, swings right, and at 1.8 mi., just below the summit ledges, joins Mt. Pemigewasset Trail and follows it to the right, toward the summit.

SOUTHEAST SIDE OF KINSMAN RIDGE

GEORGIANA FALLS PATH (MAP 4: I4)

Cumulative from Hanson Farm Rd. (900 ft.) to:	⇅	↗	○
Lower Georgiana Falls (1,250 ft.)	0.8 mi.	350 ft.	0:35
Upper Georgiana Falls (1,640 ft.)	1.2 mi.	750 ft.	1:00

SEC 5

Georgiana Falls is a series of cascades on Harvard Brook. The two major waterfalls, sometimes called the lower Georgiana Falls and the upper Georgiana or Harvard Falls, are about 0.4 mi. apart. The USGS applies the name "Georgiana Falls" to the more imposing upper waterfall. The path is located in Second Presidential State Forest but is not officially maintained. From US 3, 0.2 mi. north of the I-93 Exit 33 northbound exit ramp and opposite the Longhorn Restaurant, turn west onto Hanson Farm Rd. Where Hanson Farm Rd. turns right, continue across Hanson Brook on Georgiana Falls Rd., to a parking area on the right at the end of pavement, 0.1 mi. from US 3.

From the parking area (sign for hiking trail), follow a dirt road ahead (west) through a tunnel under the northbound lanes of I-93 and bear right at a fork (snowmobile and hiking trail signs) then swing left through the tunnel under the southbound lanes. At 0.5 mi., where the road bears right and becomes overgrown, the trail (marked only with an occasional faded yellow or red blaze but well beaten) turns left into the woods and follows the north side of Harvard Brook. At 0.7 mi., the trail crosses a rocky brook bed (follow with care), climbs steeply on sloping ledges beside cascades (a rough alternate path runs parallel through the woods), briefly reenters the woods on the right, and emerges on ledges beside a pool at the base of the lower Georgiana Falls.

Above these falls, the trail is minimally maintained, although it is marked with dark red blazes, which must be followed carefully. It reenters the woods to the right of the pool and follows a steep, sometimes slippery route up the east side of the brook on a network of interlacing beaten paths through a hemlock forest, to the upper Georgiana Falls. In general, the marked route stays higher up on the slope to the right. After passing a side view of the falls, Georgiana Falls Path turns left and makes a steep scramble up to ledges at the top of this waterfall (use caution), where you have a view of the Pemigewasset River valley and the Loon Mtn. range.

GORDON POND TRAIL (WMNF; MAP 4: I4–I3)

Cumulative from NH 112 (900 ft.) to:	⇅	↗	↻
Gordon Falls (2,200 ft.)	3.9 mi.	1,400 ft. (rev. 100 ft.)	2:40
Gordon Pond (2,567 ft.)	4.7 mi.	1,750 ft.	3:15
Kinsman Ridge Trail (2,670 ft.)	5.0 mi.	1,850 ft.	3:25

This blue-blazed trail runs from from the north side of NH 112, 1.7 mi. west of its jct. with US 3 in North Woodstock, to Kinsman Ridge Trail south of Mt. Wolf, passing Gordon Falls and Gordon Pond. Much of the trail provides pleasant woods walking. Gordon Pond Trail is lightly used, however, and must be followed with care, and the section between Gordon Falls and Gordon Pond is muddy, rough, and at times obscure. The trailhead on NH 112 (where the WMNF trail sign was missing in 2016) is located at a private driveway (sign: Mountain Side Rd.) opposite the site of a former restaurant. Park in a gravel area on the south side of the road, west of the trailhead. (*Note:* The WMNF may relocate this trailhead in the future.)

This trail follows the paved driveway for 60 yd. between the buildings on the north side of NH 112 (No Trespassing signs do not apply to hikers who stay on the trail) then continues ahead up a gravel road past a garage on the right, and at 0.1 mi., the trail turns right at a crossroads and follows the gravel road along an old railroad grade. At 0.4 mi., follow an older road ahead past a gate as the gravel road bears left and uphill. At 0.6 mi., the trail reaches the power lines, turns left (arrow), and follows the power-line clearing uphill on a rough track for 0.2 mi. then turns right (arrow) and crosses under the lines into the woods, descending to the old railroad grade at 1.0 mi. and turning left (arrow) onto it. At 1.3 mi., turn left where another road enters on the right. (In the opposite direction, bear right here, following blue blazes.) At 1.8 mi., the trail approaches Gordon Pond Brook; a logging road crosses the brook, but the trail remains on the southwest bank and swings to the northwest to recross the power lines at 2.0 mi.

The trail finally crosses Gordon Pond Brook (may be difficult at high water) at 2.2 mi. and continues along the north side through a fine hardwood forest, crossing a tributary at 2.8 mi., then swings left to recross the main brook at 3.5 mi., at the top of a small cascade (use caution). The trail continues on an old road, becoming somewhat steeper, and crosses a minor ridge to the southerly branch of Gordon Pond Brook, where the trail passes several small cascades and then Gordon Falls. Crossing the brook on a ledge at the top of the falls at 3.9 mi. (use caution), the trail soon recrosses, leads through a flat area where the trail was cleared in 2016 with bypasses made around muddy areas, then crosses Gordon Pond Brook at 4.6 mi. Just before the trail recrosses the main brook at 4.7 mi., an unsigned path leads right through a campsite to the shore of the pond, where there is an interesting view of the steep face of Mt. Wolf. The main trail does not come within sight of the pond but continues at a level grade, bears left where an unsigned path enters right, and climbs easily to Kinsman Ridge Trail.

DILLY TRAIL (SPNHF; MAP 4: I3)

Cumulative from Lost River Reservation parking lot (1,790 ft.) to:	⇅	➚	⟳
Lookout over Lost River (2,520 ft.)	0.4 mi.	750 ft.	0:35
Kinsman Ridge Trail (2,650 ft.)	0.5 mi.	850 ft.	0:40

This short but challenging trail (Dilly Cliff Trail on some signs) runs from Lost River Reservation, which is on NH 112 just east of the height-of-land in Kinsman Notch, to Kinsman Ridge Trail, 0.6 mi. from NH 112. Dilly Trail is open only during the hours and season when Lost River is open (summer and fall, daytime) and closed to the public at all other times. The trail is extremely steep and rough but offers an interesting outlook across the valley. The trailhead, shared with Kinsman Notch Ecology Trail, is on a parking area access road, directly across from a gazebo. In 25 yd. from the road, Ecology Trail leaves on the left, making a somewhat rough 0.4-mi. loop through the woods back to the other side of the parking area. Here, Dilly Trail continues ahead and soon begins to ascend by short switchbacks a very steep, badly eroded gully with large boulders and some very loose footing, requiring caution, particularly when descending. At 0.4 mi., where the trail reaches the top rim of the steep slope, a side path leads sharply right 40 yd. to an outlook from the rim. The main trail turns sharply left, soon crosses an unmarked path, and continues at moderate grades through a section that may be obscure and overgrown to Kinsman Ridge Trail.

WEST SIDE OF KINSMAN RIDGE

COPPERMINE TRAIL (WMNF; MAP 4: G3–H4)

From parking area off NH 116 (994 ft.) to:	⇅	➚	⟳
Bridal Veil Falls (2,100 ft.)	2.5 mi.	1,100 ft.	1:50

This attractive and relatively easy trail to Bridal Veil Falls begins on Coppermine Rd. (sign), which leaves the east side of NH 116 3.4 mi. south of NH 18 in Franconia (and 1.0 mi. south of the Franconia Airport) or 7.7 mi. north of NH 112 at Bungay Corner. Park on the left near NH 116 (public vehicle access is not allowed beyond this point) and follow Coppermine Rd. ahead on foot, past Beechwood Lane on the left. At 0.3 mi., the trail bears left off Coppermine Rd. onto an older road (hiker logo sign and yellow blazes). At 1.0 mi., the trail joins Coppermine Brook, where a side path descends right for 40 yd. through open hemlock woods to a cascade. Coppermine Trail continues ahead, where a cross-country ski trail diverges left and uphill, and follows along the north side of the brook, climbing at easy to moderate grades and passing an attractive ledgy area on the brook at 1.3 mi. It crosses to the south side on a bridge at 2.3 mi., swings left, passes to the right of the WMNF Coppermine Shelter, crosses a branch of the brook, and ends at the base of Bridal Veil Falls. The sloping ledges above this point are slippery and potentially dangerous.

MT. KINSMAN TRAIL (WMNF; MAP 4: H3–H4)

Cumulative from parking area off NH 116 (1,030 ft.) to:	⥮	↗	◐
Bald Peak spur trail (2,400 ft.)	2.1 mi.	1,350 ft.	1:45
Kinsman Ridge Trail (3,850 ft.)	3.7 mi.	2,800 ft.	3:15
North Kinsman summit (4,293 ft.) via Kinsman Ridge Trail	4.1 mi.	3,250 ft.	3:40

This trail climbs from the east side of NH 116 to Kinsman Ridge Trail, 0.4 mi. north of North Kinsman. The trailhead, with a short road leading into a large dirt parking area (usually not plowed in winter), is 4.7 mi. south of NH 18 in Franconia village, just beyond the Tamarack Tennis Camp, and 1.7 mi. north of the Easton town hall. Mt. Kinsman Trail climbs at mostly moderate grades and is blazed in blue.

The trail leaves the southeast corner of the parking area and, in 20 yd., turns sharply left and ascends moderately through a brushy area. At 0.2 mi., the trail enters an attractive hemlock forest, dips to cross a small brook, and ascends generally eastward. At 0.5 mi., the trail swings left and levels off, crossing an unmarked mountain bike trail, and in another 30 yd. turns right onto a logging road, joining an older route. (In the reverse direction, turn left off the road onto a footpath at a sign.) The trail soon swings left, passes an old sugarhouse on the left at 0.6 mi., and swings right again.

The trail enters the WMNF at 1.1 mi. and turns right off the road (cairn and arrow) then in 30 yd. turns left onto another road. This road, older and steeper, crosses a brook at 1.5 mi. near the site of the former Kinsman Cabin (up on the left). At 1.8 mi., Mt. Kinsman Trail crosses Mossy Falls Brook, which falls over a mossy ledge to the left of the trail, then crosses Kendall (Flume) Brook at 2.1 mi. Just over the brook, a side path on the right descends close to the brook bank for 150 yd. to the top edge of small, steep-walled Kinsman Flume, a classic eroded dike. (Use caution here.) The main trail continues on the road for another 70 yd. then turns sharply left at the point where a yellow-blazed spur path (sign) 0.2 mi. long diverges sharply right, descends briefly, then makes an easy ascent to Bald Peak, a bare ledgy dome with fine views that crowns a western spur of Kinsman Mtn.

The trail now winds up the mountainside at easy to moderate grades, with relatively good footing except for short, scattered steep pitches with rough footing. The trail crosses several small brooks, follows a short relocation to the right at 3.2 mi., and at 3.5 mi. swings right and angles upward, then swings left and climbs straight up to the ridge top, where Mt. Kinsman Trail meets Kinsman Ridge Trail. For North and South Kinsman, turn right; for Kinsman Pond and Kinsman Junction, turn left.

REEL BROOK TRAIL (WMNF; MAP 4: H3)

From road fork near field (1,400 ft.) to:	⇅	↗	↻
Kinsman Ridge Trail (2,600 ft.)	2.9 mi.	1,250 ft. (rev. 50 ft.)	2:05

This lightly used trail ascends to Kinsman Ridge Trail in the col between Mt. Wolf and South Kinsman (the original Kinsman Notch), 1.0 mi. south of Eliza Brook Shelter. Reel Brook Trail begins on gravel Reel Brook Rd. (sign: Trailhead Parking and hiker logo), which leaves NH 116 3.7 mi. north of the jct. with NH 112 at Bungay Corner and 1.1 mi. south of the Easton town hall. The road, which is not plowed in winter, is rough but passable for cars to a fork (hiker logo on post) at 0.6 mi. from NH 116, where the rocky left branch (not recommended for low-clearance vehicles) leads to a small open field (parking); a more accessible parking spot is located on the right at 0.4 mi. The grades on this trail are easy to moderate, with one section of poor footing.

From the field, Reel Brook Trail enters the woods (sign) and follows an old logging road with good footing southeast, parallel to but some distance northeast of Reel Brook, crossing several small brooks. At 1.2 mi., it bears right and descends, and very shortly, the trail diverges left from the old road, crosses a small brook, and turns left onto a wide logging road at 1.3 mi. (In the opposite direction, this turn could easily be missed; be sure to turn sharply right off the wide logging road 100 yd. after leaving the power-line clearing.) In 100 yd., the trail enters the brushy, grassy power-line clearing, crosses it on a diagonal (avoid a path diverging left up along the lines), and reenters the woods. The trail crosses a tributary, then Reel Brook itself twice, and meets a grassy logging road that descends from the left just before the third and last crossing of Reel Brook at 1.9 mi. Here, the trail turns right and follows the logging road across the brook and then away from the brook, climbing steadily with wet, rocky footing. The trail climbs to a fork at 2.4 mi., where an overgrown road diverges left to the power lines. Here the trail, with improved footing, forks right on another old logging road. In another 100 yd., it diverges right off this road, which swings left. From here, the trail runs nearly level through a wet area then climbs gradually to the jct. with Kinsman Ridge Trail on the ridge crest.

WEST OF NH 116

JERICHO ROAD TRAIL (WMNF; MAP 4: H3)
From NH 116
(1,385 ft.) to:

	⇅	↗	↻
Cooley Hill (2,480 ft.)	3.2 mi.	1,250 ft. (rev. 150 ft.)	2:15

SEC 5

Note: A major WMNF timber harvest is planned along this trail, beginning in 2017 and continuing for several years. During road construction (on the lower 1.3 mi.) and timber harvest activities, the trail may be temporarily closed. A new trailhead parking area will be constructed off NH 116.

This yellow-blazed trail ascends to the site of the Cooley Hill fire tower from a point just north of the height-of-land on the west side of NH 116, 1.9 mi. north of its jct. with NH 112 at Bungay Corner, starting (sign) on a gated gravel logging road (FR 480) with limited roadside parking. The trail was originally constructed as a horse trail and mostly follows logging roads of varying ages. Views are limited, but some sections, particularly in the upper half, are quite pleasant for walking.

The trail follows the gravel road uphill, swings to the right (north), and then continues straight (marked by a hiker logo and blaze) on an older road (FR 480A) at 0.3 mi., where the newer road bears right. At 1.3 mi., the trail crosses a ditch and narrows, soon passing an old cellar hole on the right. The trail then swings north around the west side of a hump and descends into a sag at 2.3 mi. Here, the trail turns right (arrow) off the road and continues to descend gradually then climbs moderately. At 2.6 mi., the trail turns sharply left (arrow) onto another old road that ascends from the right and follows the road up the crest of the ridge. At 3.1 mi., an unmarked spur path leads 25 yd. right to a restricted view of the Kinsman and Franconia ranges, and the main trail soon reaches a small wooded ledge near the concrete piers of the old fire tower. It continues 25 yd. ahead to a fork where a snowmobile trail diverges left and Yellow Trail (marked with yellow diamonds) diverges right into the Cooley-Jericho Community Forest, leading 3.0 mi. to a trailhead on Trumpet Round Rd.

COOLEY-JERICHO COMMUNITY FOREST TRAIL SYSTEM (ACT; MAP: COOLEY-JERICHO.ORG)

This conserved 840-acre tract includes the summits of Cooley Hill and Cole Hill and surrounding slopes. It is jointly owned by the towns of Easton, Franconia, Landaff, and Sugar Hill and is managed by the Ammonoosuc Conservation Trust (ACT). A trail system for hiking and mountain biking is under development, with Blue Trail and Yellow Trail (may be renamed) open in 2016 and more trails planned for the future. Maps are available at cooley-jericho.org. To reach the trailhead, turn northwest from NH 116 onto Sugar Hill Rd. (which becomes Easton Rd.), 0.7 mi. north of the Easton Town Hall. At 2.2 mi. from NH 116 turn left onto Dyke Rd. Turn left onto Jericho Rd. at 2.9 mi. and left again onto Trumpet Round Rd. at 3.2 mi. Continue 0.1 mi. to trailhead parking at the end of the maintained road.

The trailhead (1,650 ft.), where there is a view east, is reached on foot by following a rough road ahead for 75 yd. Blue Trail, marked with blue diamonds, makes a 2.5-mi. loop on the north slopes of Cole Hill with 900 ft. elevation gain (1 hr. 40 min.), passing several viewpoints from ledges and clearings along logging roads. Yellow Trail, marked with yellow diamonds, ascends by many switchbacks through young forest, crossing Blue Trail at 0.2 mi. then meeting Blue Trail again at 1.1 mi. and coinciding with it for 0.3 mi., passing a ledge with a restricted view east. At the upper jct. Yellow Trail bears left into mature woods and slabs around the east slope of Cole Hill, descending and then ascending to the ridge between Cole Hill and Cooley Hill. At 2.1 mi., it enters the WMNF, passes through a fern-filled glade, and meanders along the ridgecrest. At 2.6 mi., it reenters the community forest, winds up through brushy cutover areas, skirting to the east of the summit of Cooley Hill, and ends at a jct. where a snowmobile trail diverges sharply right and the WMNF Jericho Road Trail continues ahead, leading 25 yd. to the remains of the fire tower. Distance from the community forest trailhead to Cooley Hill is 3.0 mi. with 950 ft. elevation gain (rev. 100 ft.), 2 hr.

COBBLE HILL TRAIL (WMNF; MAP 4: H2)

From NH 112 (1,017 ft.) to:	⇅	↗	⟳
South Landaff Rd. (1,260 ft.)	0.7 mi.	250 ft.	0:30
WMNF boundary (1,800 ft.)	2.1 mi.	800 ft.	1:25

Note: A major WMNF timber harvest is planned along this trail, beginning in 2017 and continuing for several years. During timber harvest activities, the trail may be temporarily closed.

This trail begins at a small parking area on the north side of NH 112, 1.4 mi. west of its western jct. with NH 116, and follows a gated logging road (FR 310) and older woods roads up the valley of Dearth Brook to the WMNF boundary at the height-of-land between Cobble Hill and Moody Ledge. Grades are easy to moderate. From the gate, the trail climbs moderately, passing an attractive cascade on the right about 100 yd. from NH 112. The trail bears left at a utility pole, and at 0.6 mi., continues straight on FR 310A as a grassy road diverges right across the brook. At 0.7 mi., the abandoned South Landaff Rd. leaves left. (This woods road, parts of which are muddy during wet seasons, leads about 2 mi. through an extensive area of old farmsteads. Here are many stone walls, cellar holes, and other remnants of a hill farm community that flourished in the nineteenth century, as well as several apple orchards maintained by the WMNF.) Cobble Hill Trail passes a wildlife opening on the left and continues climbing up the valley, crossing a branch brook on a bridge and passing numerous stone walls. After a muddy stretch, the trail ends at a small clearing near the WMNF boundary; from here the old road continues north through logged areas for another 1.4 mi. down across private land to Mill Brook Rd., south of Landaff Center.

SEC
5

LONE OAK TRAIL (UVLT; USGS WOODSVILLE QUAD)

From Abbott Ave. (470 ft.) to:	↕	↗	○
Viewpoint on spur of Gardner Mtn. (1,190 ft.)	0.8 mi.	700 ft.	0:45

This short but steep trail leads to an open ledgy area on a southern spur of Gardner Mtn. in Bath with good views south. It is located on private land conserved by the Upper Valley Land Trust. In 2015–2016 rock steps and switchbacks were constructed by Woodsville High School JAG (Jobs for America's Graduates) students in cooperation with AMC Trails. Additional improvements are planned in the future. To reach the trailhead, follow NH 135 north from its jct. with US 302 in the village of Woodsville. In 0.3 mi. turn right on Abbott Ave., and drive another 0.2 mi. to parking (two cars) at a trail sign on the left. Additional parking is available at a large pulloff on the right (south) side of Abbott Ave., 0.2 mi. east of the trailhead. From the trailhead, the blue-blazed trail ascends moderately then gradually on an old logging road. At 0.3 mi. it turns sharply right onto another road then in 80 yd. turns left off the road, climbs a steep switchback, and ascends steadily northeast along a well-defined ridge. At 0.7 mi. it turns right and climbs a steep slope by six switchbacks then descends slightly past the "lone oak" to the viewpoint overlooking the village of

Woodsville, the Connecticut River valley, and the Middle Connecticut River Mountains.

KILBURN CRAGS TRAIL (LCC; MAP 2: F3)

From NH 18/135 (1,050 ft.) to:	↕	↗	○
Kilburn Crags viewpoint (1,350 ft.)	0.9 mi.	350 ft. (rev. 50 ft.)	0:40

This trail, maintained by the Littleton Conservation Commission, offers easy access to a ledge with a fine view over the town of Littleton, to the Presidential and Franconia ranges. Take I-93 to Exit 43 and proceed to the jct. of NH 18 and NH 135, just south of the exit. Turn right (west) onto the combined NH 18/135, also called St. Johnsbury Rd., and follow it 0.5 mi. to the trailhead (sign) on the left (south) side of the road, with parking available for two cars. Please stay on the designated trail, which is partly on private land.

From the parking area, the trail climbs along the left edge of a field; the footway may be obscure in tall grass. The trail enters the woods on a well-defined road at the upper left corner of the field, and at 0.2 mi., another old road joins from the left. (Bear left here on the descent.) The trail climbs moderately, passing a bench, then levels at 0.4 mi. The trail bears left at a fork at 0.5 mi. (arrow), traverses a wet section, and bears left again at 0.6 mi. (arrow). The trail passes another bench then swings left (east) at 0.7 mi. and climbs to a high point on a north spur of Walker Mtn. It then descends slightly to the ledge.

SECTION SIX
MOOSILAUKE REGION

INTRODUCTION

This section covers Mt. Moosilauke and several lower ranges and peaks, including the Benton Range, the Stinson–Carr–Kineo area, and the chain of medium-sized mountains that rises east of and roughly parallel to the Connecticut River between Hanover and Glencliff. The area is bordered on the west by the Connecticut River, on the north by NH 112, on the east by US 3 (and I-93), and on the south by NH 25, NH 118, and US 4. Most of this section is covered by AMC's *White Mountains Trail Map 4: Moosilauke–Kinsman Ridge*.

In this section, the AT, maintained by the DOC, begins at the New Hampshire boundary, at the bridge over the Connecticut River, close to the western edge of both the town of Hanover and the campus of Dartmouth College. The AT follows Velvet Rocks Trail, Hanover Center Trail, and Moose Mtn. Trail over Moose Mtn.; Holts Ledge Trail over Holts Ledge; and, after a short section parallel to Dorchester Rd., Lambert Ridge Trail to the summit of Smarts Mtn. From there, the AT follows J Trail and Kodak Trail to Mt. Cube and Mt. Cube Trail, Atwell Hill Trail, Ore Hill Trail, and Wachipauka Pond Trail to NH 25. The AT leaves NH 25 on Town Line Trail, runs along Long Pond Rd. (formerly North and South Rd.) and High St. (formerly Sanatorium Rd.) for short distances then follows Glencliff Trail and Moosilauke Carriage Road to the summit of Mt. Moosilauke and descends on Beaver Brook Trail to Kinsman Notch.

ROAD ACCESS

Many of the trails on the east side of Mt. Moosilauke begin at a trailhead on Ravine Lodge Rd., the access road to the DOC Ravine Lodge (which is open to the public). The road (sign: Ravine Rd.; not plowed in winter) leaves NH 118 on the north, 5.8 mi. east of its northern jct. with NH 25 and 7.2 mi. west of its jct. with NH 112; elevation here is 2,082 ft. From NH 118, it is 1.6 mi. to the turnaround at the end of the road, where the trails begin. Parking is prohibited in the turnaround and along the last 0.2 mi. section of the road, which is reserved for Ravine Lodge guests. Hikers must parallel park on the west side of the road, south of a service road that diverges left 1.4 mi. from NH 118. For the start of Gorge Brook Trail and Asquam–Ridge Trail, continue 0.2 mi. ahead up the main road on foot. (*Note:* The original Ravine Lodge building was dismantled in late 2016. While the new Ravine Lodge is under construction in summer 2017, hiker parking temporarily will be farther south on Ravine Lodge Rd., 0.7 mi. from NH 118.) Directions for other access roads are provided in individual trail descriptions.

SEC 6

GEOGRAPHY

The farthest west of White Mountain peaks more than 4,000 ft. tall, Mt. Moosilauke (4,802 ft.) is the dominant peak of the region between Franconia Notch and the Connecticut River. People disagree about whether *Moosilauke* should be pronounced to rhyme with "rock" or with "rocky." At one time, Mt. Moosilauke was commonly referred to as "Moosehillock," but the name actually means "a bald place" and has no reference to large, antlered beasts. The broad, bare summit, once the site of a stone lodge called the Tip-Top House, commands an extremely fine view over ridge after ridge of the White Mountains to the east, and across the Connecticut Valley to the west. The summit of Mt. Moosilauke is very exposed to weather, with no shelter available. The mountain has a fairly extensive alpine zone, and hikers should take care to stay on the marked and defined trails to avoid trampling fragile vegetation.

Moosilauke is a massive mountain with several subsidiary summits, the most important being the South Peak (4,523 ft.), an excellent viewpoint with unique views into Tunnel Brook Notch, the deep valley that lies between Mt. Moosilauke and its trailless western neighbor, Mt. Clough (3,561 ft.). Hurricane Mtn. (3,015 ft.) is a minor knob on Mt. Moosilauke's long south ridge. To the northeast of Mt. Moosilauke's summit are two prominent wooded humps, the trailless Mt. Blue (4,529 ft.) and Mt. Jim (4,172 ft.), which form the upper part of the ridge that encloses Jobildunk Ravine, a glacial cirque on the east side of the mountain, through which the headwaters of the Baker River flow from their source in a bog that was once Deer Lake. This ridge continues to the southeast and then south over Mt. Waternomee (3,940 ft.) and several lesser peaks. Other ravines on Mt. Moosilauke include Gorge Brook Ravine on the southeast, Slide Ravine on the southwest, Benton or Tunnel Ravine on the northwest, and Little Tunnel Ravine on the north.

SEC 6

The Benton Range, which rises to the west of Mt. Clough, is composed of Black Mtn. (2,830 ft.), Sugarloaf Mtn. (2,609 ft.), the Hogsback (2,810 ft.), Jeffers Mtn. (2,994 ft.), Blueberry Mtn. (2,662 ft.), and Owls Head (1,967 ft.). Of these peaks, all but Jeffers Mtn. provide excellent views, although only Black and Blueberry mtns. have maintained trails.

Stinson Mtn. (2,900 ft.), Carr Mtn. (3,453 ft.), Rattlesnake Mtn. (1,594 ft.), and trailless Mt. Kineo (3,313 ft.) rise in the angle formed by the Pemigewasset and Baker rivers. Stinson Mtn. and Carr Mtn. offer partly restricted views from summits that once bore fire towers. Although Rattlesnake Mtn. is best known for its outstanding rock-climbing opportunities, it also offers hikers excellent views from its summit ledges for a modest effort. Short walks are available at two properties owned by the Pemi-Baker Land

Trust at the southern base of Stinson Mtn.; trail maps are available at quincybog.org. Quincy Bog Natural Area is a small preserve with a variety of wetlands. Kent Ecological Trail makes a 1.3-mi. loop around the perimeter of Quincy Bog. Trailhead parking is on Quincy Bog Rd., a short spur road off Quincy Rd., 2.1 mi. east of Rumney village. Just to the north is Quincy Pasture Forest, with a small network of trails accessed from a parking area on the north side of East Rumney Rd., 0.6 mi. north of Quincy Rd. A 2-mi. loop hike with 600-ft. ascent and a view over Loon Lake is possible.

The chain of medium-sized mountains that rises east of and roughly parallel to the Connecticut River between Hanover and Glencliff—sometimes called the Middle Connecticut River Mtns.—begins at the Hanover (south) end with a region of low hills then finally reaches Moose Mtn., the southernmost mountain of consequence in the chain. From here northward, the AT is never far from the divide between the Connecticut and Pemigewasset drainages, but the mountains that the AT passes over do not really form a range because they are mostly separate peaks rising from a hilly upland with no significant connecting ridges between them. This chain of mountains is traversed by the AT and the network of side trails maintained by the DOC. Velvet Rocks (1,243 ft.) is a low ridge in Hanover named for its moss-covered ledges; its western knob has a limited outlook southeast. Moose Mtn. (North Peak, 2,313 ft.; South Peak, 2,293 ft.) is located in Hanover; Moose Mtn. Trail crosses the South Peak and passes near the summit of the North Peak. There are partial views from both peaks. Passing through the notch between the two peaks is old Province Rd. (known in the Hanover area as Wolfeboro Rd.), laid out in 1772 to connect Governor Wentworth's residence in Wolfeboro with the Connecticut Valley towns, where the residents were becoming disaffected with the royal government in New Hampshire.

Holts Ledge (2,110 ft.) has good views to the east and southeast, although access to some of the outlooks is restricted during the peregrine falcon nesting season (April 1 to August 1). Smarts Mtn. (3,238 ft.), a massive wooded peak located in Lyme, affords interesting views of a lesser-known country from its fire tower, which was renovated in 2016. Its southwest spur, Lambert Ridge (2,390 ft.), is ledgy with good views. Located in Orford, Mt. Cube (2,909 ft.) has excellent views from ledges on both its south and north peaks and is one of the more rewarding small mountains in this part of New Hampshire. Sunday Mtn. (1,823 ft.) is a small, isolated mountain west of Mt. Cube with restricted but interesting views. Webster Slide Mtn. (2,184 ft.) rises steeply above Wachipauka Pond, with excellent views from the top of the cliff overlooking the pond, and nearby Mt. Mist (2,230 ft.) is wooded with a restricted outlook. West of Webster Slide Mtn. is Lake Constance, a fine mountain pond that can be reached from NH 25C, 6.2 mi.

east of NH 10, by following a rocky logging road that leaves from the west side of the bridge over Eastman Brook for 0.3 mi. At a clearing, the logging road turns left (north) onto an older road that climbs steeply, easing and narrowing to an unmaintained footpath that leads through red pines and over quartzite ledges above the west side of the pond. The path descends to the shore at 1.2 mi. from NH 25C.

Cross Rivendell Trail extends 36 mi. from the summit of Mt. Cube across the Connecticut River valley to Flagpole Hill in Vershire, Vermont. The trail is managed by the Rivendell Trails Association (RTA) and the Rivendell Interstate School District. Most of this trail is on private land, and camping and fires are not allowed. The only sections covered in this guide are those ascending Mt. Cube and traversing over Sunday Mtn. A waterproof map of the trail can be purchased at some area stores. Numerous conservation areas are located in the Connecticut River Valley towns on the west side of the AT; many have walking trails. Maps and descriptions can be found on the town of Hanover's website (hanovernh.org/conservation-commission/pages/trail-maps) and on the website of the Upper Valley Land Trust (uvlt.org/public -access-trails/). The 1.8-mi. loop hike to Trout Pond in Lyme is particularly rewarding. On the lower south slope of Mt. Moosilauke, the town of Warren maintains the McVetty Recreational Trails, a network of walking and biking paths, one of which provides access to the Baker River. Trailhead parking is on the east side of NH 118, 0.6 mi. south of the jct. with Ravine Lodge Rd.

The northeastern part of Section Six, including all the trails described in this section that are located north of NH 25A, is shown on AMC's *White Mountains Trail Map 4: Moosilauke–Kinsman Ridge.* The region south of NH 25A is covered by USGS quads, but the most useful additional maps for this section are the National Geographic Trails Illustrated White Mountain National Forest, West Half Map (#740), and the ATC maps of the AT from Hanover to Glencliff.

CAMPING

Most of this section south of NH 25A is private land, where camping and fires are permitted only at official campsites. On the publicly owned lands of the AT corridor—all the way from Hanover to Mt. Moosilauke—camping is permitted but not within 200 ft. of the AT itself, except at the official campsites. The part of Section Six north of NH 25A is mostly in the WMNF, where camping is permitted in accordance with the usual restrictions (which include no camping in the alpine zone on Mt. Moosilauke). Much of the land on Mt. Moosilauke itself is owned by Dartmouth College. No camping or fires are permitted on Dartmouth College land, which lies east and south of the summit of Mt. Moosilauke, roughly bounded by a line starting just south of Hurricane Mtn. and following the ridge crest over South Peak, Mt. Moosilauke, Mt. Blue, Mt. Jim, and Mt. Waternomee and then south from Mt. Waternomee to NH 118.

Forest Protection Areas

The WMNF has established a number of FPAs, where camping and wood or charcoal fires are prohibited throughout the year. See p. xxiv for general FPA regulations.

Camping and fires are prohibited above treeline (where trees are less than 8 ft. tall), except in winter, when camping is permitted above treeline in places where snow cover is at least 2 ft. deep and not on any frozen body of water.

In the area covered by Section Six, camping is also prohibited within 0.25 mi. of Long Pond (including islands).

No camping is permitted within 200 ft. of certain trails. In 2016, designated trails included the entire AT, from the summit of Mt. Moosilauke to the Connecticut River (except at shelters and designated sites).

No camping is permitted on WMNF land within 0.25 mi. of certain roads (camping on private roadside land is illegal except by permission of the landowner). In 2016, these roads included Breezy Point Rd. (FR 186), NH 112 between Lincoln and Bath, Stinson Lake Rd. (FR 113) where it crosses Brown Brook, and Tunnel Brook Rd. (FR 700).

Established Trailside Campsites

Velvet Rocks Shelter (DOC) is located north of the center of Hanover on a loop path 0.2 mi. from Velvet Rocks Trail (AT). The shelter was rebuilt in 2006.

Moose Mtn. Shelter (DOC), with two nearby tentsites, is located on a loop path off Moose Mtn. Trail (AT), 0.1 mi. north of the crossing of Old Wolfeboro Rd.

Trapper John Shelter (DOC) is near Holts Ledge, 1.1 mi. from Dorchester Rd. via Holts Ledge Trail (AT) and a spur path.

Smarts Campsite (DOC) is near the summit of Smarts Mtn. The former fire warden's cabin is also maintained as a shelter by the DOC and was renovated in 2016.

Hexacuba Shelter (DOC) is an innovative hexagonal shelter for 8 people on a spur path 0.2 mi. off Kodak Trail (AT), 1.5 mi. south of the south peak of Mt. Cube.

Ore Hill Tentsite (DOC), with two tentsites, is on a short spur path off Ore Hill Trail (AT), 0.6 mi. north of Cape Moonshine Rd. *Note:* The former shelter at this site was destroyed by fire in the fall of 2011; there are no plans to rebuild it.

Jeffers Brook Shelter (DOC) is located just off Town Line Trail (AT), 0.1 mi. south of Long Pond Rd.

Beaver Brook Shelter (DOC), with two nearby tent platforms, is located on Beaver Brook Trail (AT), 1.5 mi. from NH 112 in Kinsman Notch.

Three Ponds Shelter (WMNF) is located on a knoll above the middle pond, on a side trail from Three Ponds Trail, 2.3 mi. from Stinson Lake Rd.

SUGGESTED HIKES

■ Easy Hikes

RATTLESNAKE MTN.

LP via Rattlesnake Mtn. Trail	2.5 mi.	1,050 ft.	1:45

The fairly steep loop trail over this small, ledgy mountain offers good views of the Baker River valley. See Rattlesnake Mtn. Trail, p. 294.

SEC
6

THREE PONDS LOOP

LP via Three Ponds Trail, Donkey Hill Cutoff, and Mt. Kineo Trail	5.2 mi.	550 ft.	2:55

This interesting loop cuts through a region of ponds and swamps; add 0.4 mi. total for a side trip via Three Ponds Trail to the upper pond. See Three Ponds Trail, p. 296.

HOLTS LEDGE

RT via Holts Ledge Trail	2.8 mi.	1,050 ft.	1:55

Ascend from the north to a short side path leading to excellent eastern views; stay behind the fence to avoid disturbing nesting peregrine falcons (April 1 to August 1). Additional views are found a short distance to the north and south. See Holts Ledge Trail, p. 306.

■ Moderate Hikes

BEAVER BROOK CASCADES

RT to first cascade via Beaver Brook Trail	0.8 mi.	200 ft.	0:30
RT to top of cascades via Beaver Brook Trail	2.2 mi.	1,250 ft.	1:45

A short, moderate climb reaches the first cascade; a longer and very steep climb leads to the top of the series of picturesque cascades. See Beaver Brook Trail, p. 280.

STINSON MTN.

	$\circlearrowleft$	$\nearrow$	$\circlearrowright$
RT via Stinson Mtn. Trail	3.6 mi.	1,400 ft.	2:30

A fairly easy climb leads to views south and northwest from this former fire tower peak. See Stinson Mtn. Trail, p. 293.

BLACK MTN.

	$\circlearrowleft$	$\nearrow$	$\circlearrowright$
RT via Chippewa Trail	3.6 mi.	1,600 ft.	2:35

This fine viewpoint in the Benton Range is reached by a steep but attractive ascent. See Chippewa Trail, p. 292.

BLUEBERRY MTN.

	$\circlearrowleft$	$\nearrow$	$\circlearrowright$
RT via Blueberry Mtn. Trail	4.0 mi.	1,200 ft.	2:35

Starting at Long Pond Rd., this hike delivers views from both sides of this mountain's broad, ledgy ridgecrest; turn around at the western view ledges. See Blueberry Mtn. Trail, p. 290.

TUNNEL BROOK NOTCH

	$\circlearrowleft$	$\nearrow$	$\circlearrowright$
RT via Tunnel Brook Trail	5.8 mi.	900 ft.	3:20

Also leaving from Long Pond Rd., this hike provides the best access to a scenic area of slides and beaver ponds. Turn around at the northern ponds, where there are views of Mt. Clough. See Tunnel Brook Trail, p. 281.

EAST RIDGE OF MOOSILAUKE

	$\circlearrowleft$	$\nearrow$	$\circlearrowright$
LP via Al Merrill Loop and Asquam–Ridge Trail	5.5 mi.	1,050 ft.	3:15

A pleasant wooded loop passes a restricted but interesting outlook toward Mt. Moosilauke. See Al Merrill Loop, p. 290.

MOOSE MTN.

	〵〴	∿	○
RT to North Peak via Moose Mtn. Trail	3.4 mi.	1,350 ft.	2:25
RT to North and South peaks via Moose Mtn. Trail	7.4 mi.	2,150 ft.	4:45

Enjoy two viewpoints along the north section of trail, from Goose Pond Rd. to the north knob of the North Peak. The trip can easily be extended to the South Peak and another view. See Moose Mtn. Trail, p. 304.

LAMBERT RIDGE

	〵〴	∿	○
RT via Lambert Ridge Trail	4.0 mi.	1,400 ft.	2:40

Head to the north end of the ledgy ridge for several good views. See Lambert Ridge Trail, p. 307.

MT. CUBE

	〵〴	∿	○
RT via Mt. Cube Section, Mt. Cube Trail, and North Cube Side Trail	5.0 mi.	1,600 ft.	3:20

Enjoy expansive views from both the south and north summits. See Mt. Cube Section, p. 312.

SEC 6

WACHIPAUKA POND AND WEBSTER SLIDE MTN.

	〵〴	∿	○
RT via Wachipauka Pond Trail, spur path, and Webster Slide Trail	6.4 mi.	1,900 ft.	4:10

Starting from NH 25, visit the attractive pond before continuing on for a bird's-eye view from the summit of Webster Slide. See Wachipauka Pond Trail, p. 314.

■ Strenuous Hikes
SMARTS MTN.

	〵〴	∿	○
LP via Ranger Trail and Lambert Ridge Trail	7.5 mi.	2,400 ft.	4:55

Ascend the sometimes wet and slippery Ranger Trail to the summit fire tower and wide views then descend over the open ledges of Lambert Ridge Trail, enjoying several more vistas. To begin, see Ranger Trail, p. 308.

MT. MOOSILAUKE
❄ 🐾 🔍 🧗

	↕	↗	○
LP via Gorge Brook Trail, Moosilauke Carriage Road, South Peak spur, and Snapper Trail	8.3 mi.	2,650 ft.	5:30
RT via Glencliff Trail, South Peak spur, and Moosilauke Carriage Road	8.2 mi.	3,400 ft.	5:50
LP via Glencliff Trail, Moosilauke Carriage Road, Benton and Tunnel Brook trails, Long Pond Rd., and High St.	13.3 mi.	4,000 ft.	8:40

This bald dome, the dominant peak of the region, offers extensive views. An interesting loop with moderate grades from the east side, including a short side trip to unusual views from the South Peak, can be made using the first route above (to begin, see Gorge Brook Trail, p. 287). The second, a popular hike with a steady ascent from the southwest, also includes a side trip to the South Peak (see Glencliff Trail, p. 284). The third, a good, long loop with a wide variety of scenery, involves some road walking (to begin, see Glencliff Trail).

SEC 6

TRAIL DESCRIPTIONS
MT. MOOSILAUKE
BEAVER BROOK TRAIL (DOC; MAP 4: I3)

Cumulative from NH 112 (1,870 ft.) to:	↕	↗	○
Beaver Brook Shelter (3,750 ft.)	1.5 mi.	1,900 ft.	1:40
Asquam–Ridge Trail (4,050 ft.)	1.9 mi.	2,200 ft.	2:05
Benton Trail (4,570 ft.)	3.4 mi.	2,800 ft. (rev. 100 ft.)	3:05
Mt. Moosilauke summit (4,802 ft.)	3.8 mi.	3,050 ft.	3:25

This trail, which climbs to the summit of Mt. Moosilauke from NH 112 at a large parking area near the height-of-land in Kinsman Notch, 6.2 mi. from US 3 in North Woodstock, is a link in the AT. The trail passes the beautiful Beaver Brook Cascades, but the section along the cascades is very steep and rough, making this trail the most arduous route to Mt. Moosilauke despite its relatively short distance. (*Caution:* In wet or icy conditions, this part of the trail may be dangerous.) The upper part of the trail coincides with Benton Trail for the last 0.4 mi. to Mt. Moosilauke's summit, ascending the mountain's open north ridge; this part may be dangerous in bad weather.

From the parking area, follow a path for 20 yd. past a kiosk and turn left onto the trail proper (which begins 90 yd. to the right at NH 112). Beaver

Brook Trail crosses Beaver Brook on rocks and a small stream on a bridge, swings left, and recrosses the small stream on rocks and Beaver Brook on a bridge. The trail swings right past a sign and soon begins the climb along Beaver Brook, reaching the first of the Beaver Brook Cascades on the right at 0.4 mi. The trail then rises very steeply past the long series of cascades, with many rock steps, wooden steps, and hand rungs; in several places, the trail passes near the edge of steep dropoffs. At 1.1 mi., the cascades end, and the trail bears left along a tributary, climbs a steep and rocky section, then moderates. At 1.5 mi., the trail passes a side path that leads right in 80 yd. to Beaver Brook Shelter (DOC). Here is a view to the northeast, and a small stream 60 yd. farther along provides water (may not be reliable).

The main trail continues to climb steadily for a short distance then the grade eases, and at a jct. in a flat area at 1.9 mi., Asquam–Ridge Trail turns sharply left. Here, Beaver Brook Trail bears right and ascends easily then skirts the edge of Jobildunk Ravine with rough and rocky footing, passing a restricted viewpoint over the valley. Just beyond, at 2.5 mi., the trail turns right uphill then immediately turns left and climbs fairly steeply, with some views to a point high up on the side of Mt. Blue. Beaver Brook Trail then descends to a col, climbs over another knob with several outlooks, descends to a second col, and climbs to the jct. where Benton Trail joins from the right at 3.4 mi. (Descending, turn right here.) From this point, the two trails coincide, reaching treeline at 3.6 mi. and ascending the open, very exposed ridge crest to the summit. Descending from the summit, the trail leads briefly northeast then generally north, following cairns along the broad, open ridge. In this section, hikers are urged to stay on the well-defined footway to avoid trampling fragile alpine vegetation.

SEC 6

TUNNEL BROOK TRAIL (WMNF; MAP 4: I2)

Cumulative from Long Pond Rd. (1,393 ft.) to:	↑↓	↗	↻
Viewpoint at Mud Pond (2,280 ft.)	2.3 mi.	900 ft.	1:35
South end of Tunnel Brook Rd. (1,880 ft.)	4.4 mi.	900 ft. (rev. 400 ft.)	2:40
Benton Trail (1,675 ft.)	5.2 mi.	900 ft. (rev. 200 ft.)	3:05
Parking on Tunnel Brook Rd. (1,400 ft.)	6.7 mi.	900 ft. (rev. 300 ft.)	3:50

This trail runs between Long Pond Rd. (FR 19) and a gate on Tunnel Brook Rd. (FR 700), through the deep valley (the "tunnel") between Mt. Moosilauke and Mt. Clough. The south trailhead is located on Long Pond Rd., 0.4 mi. north of the point where it leaves High St., 1.0 mi. from NH 25 in Glencliff; there is limited roadside parking. To reach the north trailhead, follow Tunnel Brook Rd., which leaves the south side of NH 112 at a historical marker, 0.3 mi. east of its eastern jct. with NH 116 and 1.9 mi. west of the WMNF Wildwood Campground. Follow the road to a jct. at 1.4 mi., where the road ahead (south) is blocked by boulders. Beyond the boulders, Tunnel Brook Rd. was severely washed out by Tropical Storm Irene in 2011 and was subsequently rehabilitated, but it is no longer open for public vehicle travel. Hikers must park here and proceed on foot up the revegetating road (and occasional sections of bypass trail, through woods on the right) another 2.3 mi., to the start of the trail proper at the former north trailhead. Logging is scheduled for the near future along this section. Tunnel Brook Rd. and Long Pond Rd. are closed in winter. The central portion of this trail is subject to disruption by beaver activity, and short sections could become very wet or obscure. This section—now most easily reached from the south trailhead—is very scenic with numerous views of beaver ponds and the slides on Mt. Clough, and grades are mostly easy. Some of the brook crossings may be difficult in high water.

From Long Pond Rd., the trail follows an old road at easy grades, crossing Jeffers Brook by a cascade at 0.2 mi. It crosses a tributary and Slide Brook at 0.6 mi. then recrosses Slide Brook and passes to the left of a small reservoir at 1.1 mi., where it bears left at a fork. Care should be taken not to pollute Slide Brook, the water supply for the state of New Hampshire's Glencliff Home. Soon the trail begins a moderate ascent, following a very old road to a broad height-of-land. It then descends gently to an open spot on the west shore of Mud Pond at 2.3 mi., where there is a view up to the South Peak of Mt. Moosilauke. It continues nearly level past more beaver ponds, follows a bypass to the left of a flooded area, and crosses an open grassy spot with views, where it must be followed with care. At 2.8 mi. it crosses Tunnel Brook (may be obscure), swings left past a campsite, and runs along the east side of several more ponds with views of the Clough slides.

Leaving the ponds, the trail crosses Tunnel Brook at 3.1 mi., becomes rougher in an area of old landslides, and recrosses the brook at 3.6 mi. It passes a beaver meadow and crosses a rocky outwash then descends gradually down logging roads to the former north trailhead at the end of Tunnel Brook Rd., at 4.4 mi. The trail follows the decommissioned road north, passing the jct. with Benton Trail on the right at 5.2 mi. It ascends slightly then continues down the road, in the last 0.7 mi. following occasional marked sections of trail through the woods to the left around erosion control areas, and ends at the boulders at the end of the drivable section of Tunnel Brook Rd.

BENTON TRAIL (WMNF; MAP 4: I2–I3)

Cumulative from Tunnel Brook Trail (1,675 ft.) to:	↥↧	↗	↻
Little Tunnel Ravine outlook (2,720 ft.)	1.3 mi.	1,050 ft.	1:10
Beaver Brook Trail jct. (4,570 ft.)	3.2 mi.	2,900 ft.	3:05
Mt. Moosilauke summit (4,802 ft.)	3.6 mi.	3,150 ft.	3:25
From parking on Tunnel Brook Rd. (1,400 ft.) to:			
Mt. Moosilauke summit (4,802 ft.)	5.1 mi.	3,400 ft.	4:15

This trail climbs to the summit of Mt. Moosilauke from the northern portion of Tunnel Brook Trail that follows the decommissioned section of Tunnel Brook Rd. (FR 700). The trail follows the route of an old bridle path with moderate grades and good footing, making this a pleasant and fairly easy route to the magnificent views from Mt. Moosilauke's summit, although the brook crossing 0.2 mi. from the start is difficult when the water level is high. For the last 0.2 mi., Benton Trail (coinciding with Beaver Brook Trail) ascends the open north ridge of Mt. Moosilauke, where the trail is greatly exposed to the elements, so this section may be dangerous in bad weather.

To access the start of Benton Trail, park by the gate on Tunnel Brook Rd. 1.4 mi. from NH 112, and continue on foot up Tunnel Brook Trail (which here follows the decommissioned section of road and occasional bypass footpaths) for 1.5 mi. with 300-ft. ascent. Benton Trail diverges left at a sign and descends slightly from the former parking lot to an old logging road. It follows the road south along Tunnel Brook for 0.2 mi. then crosses the brook (may be difficult at high water) and bears right on an old logging road, crossing a newer logging road, and then ascending the wooded spur that forms the south wall of Little Tunnel Ravine. At 1.3 mi. from Tunnel Brook Trail is a splendid view to the left into the ravine. The trail passes an unreliable spring on the right at 2.2 mi. then soon turns sharply right and climbs at moderate grades through a beautiful evergreen forest, passing an outlook west on a short side path to the right at 3.0 mi. Beaver Brook Trail (a part of the AT) enters from the left at 3.2 mi. and in another 0.2 mi. the combined trails break out from the scrubby trees. The two trails ascend the bare north ridge, marked by cairns, to the summit. Descending from the summit, Benton Trail leads briefly northeast then north along the broad, open ridge. In this section, hikers are urged to stay on the well-defined footway to avoid trampling fragile alpine vegetation.

SEC 6

GLENCLIFF TRAIL (DOC; MAP 4: J2–I2)

Cumulative from trailhead parking area on High St. (1,520 ft.) to:	⬆⬇	↗	⟳
Moosilauke Carriage Road (4,450 ft.)	3.0 mi.	2,950 ft.	3:00
Mt. Moosilauke summit (4,802 ft.) via Moosilauke Carriage Road	3.9 mi.	3,300 ft.	3:35

This trail runs from High St. (formerly Sanatorium Rd.), 1.2 mi. from its jct. with NH 25 in Glencliff village, to Moosilauke Carriage Road in a sag just north of Mt. Moosilauke's South Peak. The trail is part of the AT. There is only one steep section, and the footing is generally good on the lower half, though quite rocky on the upper half. The trailhead parking area, where most hikers begin, is on the right, 100 yd. past (north of) the trail sign; from here, one may follow an old farm road past a gate, crossing a brook on a bridge and joining the trail in 0.1 mi.

The trail proper leaves High St., passes a gate, enters an overgrown pasture, and soon crosses a small brook on a bridge. At 0.1 mi., the trail joins the farm road on the left that ascends from the parking area, follows a cart track along the right edge of a field, crosses a brook on a bridge, runs along the left edge of another field, and enters the woods at 0.4 mi., where Hurricane Trail immediately diverges right (east). Here Glencliff Trail crosses a small brook and quickly passes an unmarked path leading left to the DOC Great Bear Cabin (open to the public by reservation only). The main trail ascends steadily on an old logging road that gradually fades away then slabs up across the slope, crossing several small brooks. Then the trail swings right, going straight up the slope, and at 2.5 mi. becomes quite steep and rocky, passing a talus slope on the right at 2.9 mi. that offers good views to the west. At the top of the ridge, the trail levels and reaches the jct. with a spur path (sign) that leads right 0.2 mi. (80-ft. ascent, rather steep and rough near the top) to the open summit of South Peak. In a few more steps, the trail enters Moosilauke Carriage Road; for the main summit, turn left.

TOWN LINE TRAIL (DOC; MAP 4: J2)

From NH 25 (1,000 ft.) to:	⬆⬇	↗	⟳
Long Pond Rd. (1,340 ft.)	1.1 mi.	400 ft. (rev. 50 ft.)	0:45

This trail, a short link in the AT constructed mainly to eliminate a road walk for AT hikers, runs from the northeast side of NH 25, just southeast of the Warren–Benton town line (parking 100 yd. farther southeast on the southwest side of NH 25), to Long Pond Rd. (formerly North and South Rd.), 0.1 mi. north of the point where that road leaves High St.

SEC
6

(formerly Sanatorium Rd.), 1.0 mi. from NH 25 in Glencliff. In times of high water, the crossing of Oliverian Brook next to NH 25 is dangerous, and in such conditions, hikers traveling between Mt. Moosilauke and points to the south on the AT should follow High St. and NH 25 rather than attempting to use this trail. Erosion caused by the 2011 storm has made this crossing even more difficult.

The trail drops down a steep bank and crosses Oliverian Brook (fairly difficult even at moderate water levels) and follows the bank of the brook downstream then swings left away from the brook, climbs moderately over a narrow ridge crest, and continues across low ridges and shallow sags. At 0.9 mi., the trail crosses a good-sized brook on a bridge, and in another 90 yd. a side path leaves left and runs north 0.1 mi. to Jeffers Brook Shelter. The main trail passes an unmarked path that leads 40 yd. right to cascades on Jeffers Brook then passes another side path that leads 70 yd. left to the shelter and continues to Long Pond Rd. To reach the start of Glencliff Trail, turn right onto Long Pond Rd. and follow it for 0.1 mi. then turn left onto High St. and ascend for 0.2 mi. to the trail sign on the right.

HURRICANE TRAIL (DOC; MAP 4: J3–J2)

Cumulative from Gorge Brook Trail (2,380 ft.) to:	⇅	↗	⟲
Moosilauke Carriage Road, upper jct. (2,340 ft.)	1.0 mi.	50 ft. (rev. 100 ft.)	0:30
Spur to viewpoint (3,000 ft.)	2.7 mi.	950 ft. (rev. 250 ft.)	1:50
Glencliff Trail (1,660 ft.)	4.3 mi.	950 ft. (rev. 1,350 ft.)	2:35

This lightly used trail runs around the lower south end of Mt. Moosilauke, making possible a number of loop trips by linking the lower end of Glencliff Trail, the lower part of Moosilauke Carriage Road, and the complex of trails that leave Ravine Lodge Rd. East of Moosilauke Carriage Road, Hurricane Trail is level and clear; some parts to the west, up and over the ridge, are moderately steep and rough. In 2016 DOC made major improvements on the section ascending the ridge from the east.

Hurricane Trail continues straight where Gorge Brook Trail turns right, 0.5 mi. from hiker parking on Ravine Lodge Rd. Hurricane Trail crosses Gorge Brook on a high log bridge and descends to the bank of Baker River, where the trail picks up a logging road with good footing and follows it on a long curve away from the river, crossing two brooks. At 1.0 mi., the trail reaches Moosilauke Carriage Road and turns left (downhill). The two trails coincide for 0.3 mi., crossing Big Brook on a bridge, then Hurricane Trail turns right (west) off Carriage Rd. and follows a logging road into a small, moist clearing (an old logging camp site) at 1.5 mi. Here, the trail turns sharply left and climbs moderately with a few steeper pitches, with a relocation to the right around a wet, eroded section, to the height-of-land at 2.6 mi. The trail then runs nearly level across the broad ridgecrest, with minor ups and downs. At 2.7 mi. a new spur path (sign: View) diverges left and leads 100 yd. to a ledge with a view south. The main trail passes north of the little hump called Hurricane Mtn. then follows a relocation to the right that descends by switchbacks past a restricted view west, rejoining the original route in 0.1 mi. The trail now descends rather steeply with rough footing for about 0.3 mi. before the footing improves. At 3.3 mi., the grade eases on a plateau, and the descent is easy to moderate to Glencliff Trail, 0.4 mi. from High St.

MOOSILAUKE CARRIAGE ROAD (WMNF/DOC; MAP 4: J3–I3)

Cumulative from Breezy Point trailhead (1,720 ft.) to:	⇅	↗	⟳
Snapper Trail (3,360 ft.)	3.0 mi.	1,650 ft.	2:20
Glencliff Trail (4,450 ft.)	4.2 mi.	2,750 ft.	3:30
Mt. Moosilauke summit (4,802 ft.)	5.1 mi.	3,100 ft.	4:05

This former carriage road climbs to the summit of Mt. Moosilauke from Breezy Point, a large clearing with good views, the former site of the Moosilauke Inn. Breezy Point Rd. (sign for Moosilauke Carriage Road) leaves NH 118 2.5 mi. north of its northern jct. with NH 25 (which is 1.0 mi. north of Warren village). Follow the road (paved for 0.5 mi. then gravel) for 1.5 mi. to the left-branching overgrown driveway of the former inn, where parking is available across from a Forest Protection Area sign. In 2016, the road was drivable to this point, though rough near the end; at times in the past it has not been maintained this far, making it necessary to park on the shoulder, lower on the road. Beyond the sign, the road becomes rougher, but you may be able to drive another 0.1 mi. and park to the left just before the trail sign, where mileages begin. Grades are easy to moderate, and the footing is generally good, although there are several wet stretches in the lower section. The trail is intermittently marked with DOC orange-and-black blazes. The upper part is above treeline and greatly exposed to the elements, so it can be dangerous in bad weather. The lower part, up to a barricade at 4.1 mi., receives heavy snowmobile use in winter.

From the trail sign, Moosilauke Carriage Road continues on the grassy road, crossing Merrill Brook and another brook on bridges. The trail passes through a brushy clearing at 0.3 mi., traverses several wet sections, and crosses Little Brook on a bridge. Hurricane Trail enters left at 1.3 mi., and the two trails cross Big Brook together on the Camp Misery Memorial Bridge. Hurricane Trail diverges right to Ravine Lodge Rd. at 1.6 mi., and the old carriage road begins to climb, by a series of switchbacks, through a beautiful mature hardwood forest with easy to moderate grades and excellent footing. At 3.0 mi., Snapper Trail enters right.

The next section of the road has been widened and improved, eliminating what was formerly a washed-out section with poor footing. Starting at 3.5 mi., you have occasional views back to the south and east. At 4.1 mi., the old road is blocked by a row of boulders to prevent further vehicular use. At 4.2 mi., Glencliff Trail enters from the left; a few steps along Glencliff Trail, a spur trail leads left 0.2 mi. (80-ft. ascent) to South Peak, a fine viewpoint. The old road, now part of the AT, continues along the ridge, with a narrow fringe of trees on each side, passing a short side path right to a viewpoint over the Gorge Brook ravine. At 4.9 mi., the old road reaches treeline and, marked by cairns and low rock walls, ascends northeast along the windswept ridge to the summit. Descending from the summit, the trail leads briefly west then southwest down the broad, open ridge. In this section, hikers are urged to stay on the well-defined footway to avoid trampling fragile alpine vegetation.

SEC
6

GORGE BROOK TRAIL (DOC; MAP 4: J3–I3)

Cumulative from hiker parking on Ravine Lodge Rd. (2,440 ft.) to:	⇅	↗	○
Lower jct. with Snapper Trail (2,660 ft.)	0.8 mi.	300 ft. (rev. 100 ft.)	0:35
McKenney Forest plaque (3,250 ft.)	1.8 mi.	900 ft.	1:20
Mt. Moosilauke summit (4,802 ft.)	3.9 mi.	2,450 ft.	3:10

This trail runs from the end of Ravine Lodge Rd. to the summit of Mt. Moosilauke. This relatively easy trail affords some interesting views as it climbs.

Leaving the turnaround at the end of Ravine Lodge Rd., 0.2 mi. from hiker parking, Gorge Brook Trail follows the gravel logging road (which is also the start of Asquam–Ridge Trail) northeast for 100 yd. then turns left (sign) and left again, descending rather steeply past a recently built bunkhouse (left) to Baker River, where a road descending from Ravine Lodge joins from the left. The trail crosses the river on a footbridge and immediately turns left at 0.4 mi. from hiker parking, where a former section of Asquam–Ridge Trail diverged right. (This section of Asquam–Ridge Trail has been closed due to washouts from the 2011 storm.) In a short distance, Gorge Brook Trail bears right where a path leads 70 yd. left to the Class of '97 Swimhole. In another 90 yd., at 0.5 mi., Hurricane Trail continues straight ahead, whereas Gorge Brook Trail turns sharply right uphill and follows a rocky footway along Gorge Brook then crosses it on a bridge at 0.8 mi. On the far side, Gorge Brook Trail meets Snapper Trail and coincides with it, continuing straight ahead; the former section of Gorge Brook Trail that led to the right along the west bank of the brook has been closed due to damage from the 2011 storm.

At 1.0 mi. Gorge Brook Trail diverges right from Snapper Trail and follows a relocated section, climbing well above the brook at easy grades. It rejoins the older route at 1.4 mi. and crosses back over the brook on a bridge at 1.5 mi. At 1.8 mi., the trail passes the memorial plaque for the Ross McKenney Forest; here, the trail swings right, away from the brook, and ascends east and northeast. At 2.3 mi., the trail turns left onto an old logging road, passes a cleared outlook to the south at 2.5 mi., then turns left off the road and winds uphill at moderate grades, passing more outlooks to the south and east. At 3.5 mi., the trail reaches a shoulder covered with low scrub that affords a view to the summit ahead and soon breaks into the open on the grassy ridge crest. The trail continues to the base of the summit rocks then clambers up the last rocky 50 yd. to the summit. On the descent, although the trails are fairly well signed, the maze of beaten paths (including several abandoned trails) in this area might prove confusing in poor visibility. From the summit, Gorge Brook Trail descends briefly eastward down the rocks and then runs southeast along a grassy shoulder until the trail reaches the scrub. In this area, hikers are urged to stay on the well-defined footway to avoid trampling fragile alpine vegetation.

SNAPPER TRAIL (DOC; MAP 4: J3–J2)

From lower jct. with Gorge Brook Trail (2,660 ft.) to:	⇅	↗	↻
Moosilauke Carriage Road (3,360 ft.)	1.1 mi.	700 ft.	0:55
From hiker parking on Ravine Lodge Rd. (2,440 ft.) to:			
Mt. Moosilauke summit (4,802 ft.) via Gorge Brook Trail, Snapper Trail, and Moosilauke Carriage Road	4.0 mi.	2,450 ft. (rev. 100 ft.)	3:15

This trail was originally cut as a downhill ski trail, but it was almost completely relocated in 1991 and features less steep grades and drier footing than before. The trail runs from a bridge on Gorge Brook Trail 0.8 mi. from hiker parking on Ravine Lodge Rd. to Moosilauke Carriage Road 2.1 mi. below the summit of Mt. Moosilauke. This makes possible a number of loop hikes from Ravine Lodge Rd.; particularly attractive is the circuit over the summit of Mt. Moosilauke that combines the Snapper Trail–Moosilauke Carriage Road route with Gorge Brook Trail; these two routes are approximately equal in distance and difficulty. Snapper Trail begins at the first bridge over Gorge Brook on Gorge Brook Trail and in its lower section coincides with that trail. The combined trails immediately pass a closed section of Gorge Brook Trail on the right and ascend northwest along a tributary. At 0.2 mi. Gorge Brook Trail diverges right onto a relocated section, and Snapper Trail continues ahead, crossing the tributary at 0.3 mi. Snapper Trail swings left then right, crosses another tributary, then angles up the slope in a southwest direction at a moderate grade. At 0.9 mi., Snapper Trail crosses the old trail route and continues to its jct. with Moosilauke Carriage Road.

ASQUAM–RIDGE TRAIL (DOC; MAP 4: J3–I3)

Cumulative from hiker parking on Ravine Lodge Rd. (2,440 ft.) to:	⇅	↗	○
Beaver Brook Trail (4,050 ft.)	4.1 mi.	1,750 ft. (rev. 150 ft.)	2:55
Mt. Moosilauke summit (4,802 ft.) via Beaver Brook Trail	6.0 mi.	2,600 ft. (rev. 100 ft.)	4:20

This trail (Ridge Trail on some signs) runs from the end of Ravine Lodge Rd., 0.2 mi. from hiker parking, to Beaver Brook Trail between Mt. Jim and Mt. Blue, providing a long but rather easy route to Mt. Moosilauke's summit. The former lower 0.5 mi. of this trail, which ran along the west side of the Baker River from a jct. with Gorge Brook Trail, has been closed due to a major washout from the 2011 storm. Asquam–Ridge Trail now starts from the turnaround at the end of Ravine Lodge Rd. The trail follows a gravel logging road northeast, coinciding with Gorge Brook Trail and Al Merrill Loop. In 100 yd., Gorge Brook Trail diverges left, and at 0.3 mi. from hiker parking, Al Merrill Loop diverges right at a fork in the road. Asquam–Ridge Trail follows the left fork and ascends gradually, crossing the Baker River on a footbridge at 0.7 mi.

On the far side of the bridge, the trail bears right onto the original route and rises gradually along the west bank of the river. At 1.1 mi. it bears left onto a relocation (sign: Traps Turnpike) around a badly eroded section of the old road. The trail returns to the road at 1.25 mi. (in the reverse direction, bear right off the road at a small fence and arrow), crosses to the east side of the river on a footbridge at 1.7 mi., and turns sharply right to ascend gradually away from the river. At 2.1 mi., Asquam–Ridge Trail turns sharply left, where Al Merrill Loop continues straight ahead, then follows another logging road very gradually upward. Eventually, Asquam–Ridge Trail encounters some steeper pitches, climbs by switchbacks, passes a few yd. left of the wooded summit of Mt. Jim at 3.8 mi., then descends easily to a col and rises slightly to Beaver Brook Trail.

SEC 6

AL MERRILL LOOP (DOC; MAP 4: J3–I3)

Cumulative from hiker parking on Ravine Lodge Rd. (2,440 ft.) to:	⇅	↗	⟳
10th Mtn. Division outlook (3,460 ft.)	2.6 mi.	1,000 ft.	1:50
Asquam–Ridge Trail, upper jct. (3,130 ft.)	3.4 mi.	1,100 ft. (rev. 400 ft.)	2:15
Complete loop via Asquam–Ridge Trail	5.5 mi.	1,100 ft.	3:20

This trail follows old logging roads from the end of Ravine Lodge Rd. to the trail's upper jct. with Asquam–Ridge Trail and, although it was originally intended mostly as a ski trail, Al Merrill Loop is excellent for hiking. Up to the height-of-land (just past the 10th Mtn. Division memorial outlook), the loop provides easy grades and footing, affording a hike of about 5-mi. round trip, while rising only about 1,000 ft. to a partly restricted but interesting viewpoint. A loop hike that is a bit longer with slightly rougher footing can be made by continuing to the upper jct. with Asquam–Ridge Trail and following that trail back to the starting point.

Leaving the turnaround at the end of Ravine Lodge Rd., 0.2 mi. from hiker parking, this trail coincides at first with Asquam–Ridge Trail, continuing on the gravel logging road past the jct. where Gorge Brook Trail diverges from the road on the left, 100 yd. from the turnaround. Al Merrill Loop takes the right fork of the road at 0.3 mi., where Asquam–Ridge Trail follows the left fork. Al Merrill Loop continues on a wide road past a spur path that leads left to the DOC John Rand Cabin (open to the public by reservation only) at 0.7 mi. and climbs to a fork in a clearing at 1.4 mi., where the trail bears left and becomes narrower as a dead-end ski trail goes to the right. Still ascending easily by long switchbacks, at 2.6 mi. the loop reaches the 10th Mtn. Division memorial outlook, with a restricted but unusual view up to the summit ridge of Mt. Moosilauke. Soon the trail crosses the height-of-land and descends with somewhat less easy footing to its upper jct. with Asquam–Ridge Trail, which the loop enters at a switchback; left (downhill) leads toward Ravine Lodge Rd., whereas right (uphill) leads toward Mt. Jim and the summit of Mt. Moosilauke

BENTON RANGE

BLUEBERRY MTN. TRAIL (WMNF; MAP 4: I2–I1)

Cumulative from Long Pond Rd. (1,558 ft.) to:	⇅	↗	⟳
Ridge crest near Blueberry Mtn. summit (2,635 ft.)	1.7 mi.	1,100 ft.	1:25
Gate on FR 107 (1,176 ft.)	4.5 mi.	1,100 ft. (rev. 1,450 ft.)	2:50

This trail crosses the ridge of Blueberry Mtn., affording interesting views from scattered ledges on both sides of the broad crest. The east terminus is reached by following High St. for 1.0 mi. from NH 25 in Glencliff then turning left (north) on Long Pond Rd. (closed in winter) and following it for 0.7 mi. to a parking area on the left. The west terminus is reached by taking Lime Kiln Rd. north from NH 25 in East Haverhill, 5.2 mi. north of Glencliff and 0.4 mi. north of a power-line crossing. Keep straight ahead on Page Rd. at a jct. 1.4 mi. from NH 25, where Lime Kiln Rd. turns left, and continue to FR 107, which leaves left at 2.2 mi. (sign: Trail). Parking is available on the left 0.1 mi. up this road, just before a gate on private land that one should not drive past, even if the gate is open. Do not block this gate or the one on the right side of the road. The lower sections of both the east and west sides of the trail pass through areas that have been logged in recent years; follow markings carefully. The western section is lightly used, but the footway is fairly easy to follow for experienced hikers.

Starting at Long Pond Rd., Blueberry Mtn. Trail follows a relatively new logging road through logging cuts, bearing left at 0.1 mi. At 0.2 mi., it turns sharply right up a short, steep bank and follows an older logging road, crossing the newer road at 0.4 mi. The trail ascends through hardwoods then enters coniferous woods at 0.8 mi. and begins to climb ledges with restricted views before turning sharply right at 1.2 mi. and continuing to climb. Soon it reaches ledges that are more open with views south along the trail, as well as an unusual view into the slide-scarred ravine of Slide Brook on Mt. Moosilauke from a broad ledge 15 yd. to the right at 1.6 mi. At 1.7 mi., the trail reaches the crest of the main ridge, where a side path leads right (north) 90 yd. up to the ledges of the true summit, which offers restricted views over trees. The start of the side path is marked only by a small cairn, just past a boulder.

The main trail (this part receives less use; follow cairns and blazes carefully) then descends gradually across the broad ridge crest through scrubby trees and ledges with limited views, crossing a small moist glen then rising slightly and turning sharply right at a cairn. At 2.0 mi, it reaches ledges with views west across the Connecticut Valley to Vermont and north to Black Mtn., Sugarloaf, and the Hogsback. In the next 100 yd. other views are passed as the trail descends on ledges then continues down through a scrubby, ledgy area. The trail drops into moss-carpeted coniferous woods at 2.2 mi. then enters mixed woods with a large logging cut to the left. At 2.8 mi. the grade eases and the trail crosses two small brooks in a wet area. It soon runs through a strip of birch woods between two logging cuts then follows an old road through a region of abandoned farms, where many stone walls and cellar holes remain. At 3.4 mi. a branch road diverges sharply right

SEC 6

(in the reverse direction, continue straight ahead, avoiding the left fork), and at 3.5 mi. the trail turns right onto a wide and much newer logging road (FR 107A). At 4.0 mi., the trail turns left onto another wide logging road (FR 107) and follows it gradually downward, passing the WMNF boundary in 125 yd. and reaching the gate at the western trailhead at 4.5 mi. In the reverse direction, from the gate follow FR 107 for 0.5 mi. then turn right onto FR 107A (sign: Trail). At 1.0 mi., the trail bears left off this road into the woods at a yellow blaze; it is the middle of three forks at this jct.

BLACK MTN. TRAIL (WMNF; MAP 4: H2–I1)

From end of maintained section of Howe Hill Rd. (1,550 ft.) to:	⇅	↗	⟳
Black Mtn. summit (2,830 ft.)	2.4 mi.	1,300 ft.	1:50

This trail ascends Black Mtn. from the north, using old logging roads and the old tractor road to the former fire tower. This is a fairly easy way to ascend this attractive small mountain, although there are no views before reaching the summit. From the four-way intersection on NH 116 in Benton village, 2.9 mi. west of the western jct. of NH 112 and NH 116, follow Howe Hill Rd., which runs uphill approximately south. The road changes to gravel at 0.6 mi., and the maintained section ends at 0.8 mi., where a much rougher, often muddy, section continues ahead. Vehicles with low clearance should park here, in front of a fence to the left of the trail sign and the continuation of the road, taking care not to block driveways. High clearance vehicles may be able to drive another 0.2 mi. to a parking area.

From the end of the maintained section of Howe Hill Rd., the trail follows the rougher road, bearing left at a jct. at 0.5 mi. (arrow). The trail passes through an old log yard, crosses the WMNF boundary, and begins to climb easily. The trail then bears left in an overgrown clearing (sign and arrow), soon bears slightly right, and winds steadily uphill. At 1.4 mi., the trail swings right (southwest) and angles up the slope at easier grades. At 2.4 mi., Chippewa Trail joins from the right, and the open, ledgy ridge crest at the old fire tower site is another 40 yd. ahead. You have good views from the ridge crest both east and west of the tower site; Tipping Rock, which has more good views, is 150 yd. to the east via a faint path over ledges and through scrubby areas.

CHIPPEWA TRAIL (WMNF; MAP 4: I1)

From parking area off Lime Kiln Rd. (1,320 ft.) to:	⇅	↗	⟳
Black Mtn. summit (2,830 ft.)	1.8 mi.	1,550 ft. (rev. 50 ft.)	1:40

This steep but very scenic trail ascends Black Mtn. from Lime Kiln Rd., which leaves NH 25 in East Haverhill 5.2 mi. north of Glencliff and 0.4 mi. north of a power-line crossing. Bear left at a major fork at 1.4 mi. and continue to the trailhead, 3.1 mi. from NH 25, just past a sharp left turn in the road. In the other direction, the trailhead is 1.8 mi. from the jct. of Lime Kiln Rd. and NH 116. The trail, blazed in yellow, begins on the east side of the road at a small parking area; in 2016, there was a trail sign at the edge of the woods.

The trail descends a fairly steep pitch over log steps through a brushy area, crosses two small brooks, and skirts a beaver wetland. The trail soon dips to cross another small brook on a bog bridge next to an abandoned beaver dam then climbs to a T intersection with a logging road at 0.2 mi. (The Lime Kilns are located on a signed side trail that can be reached by following this road 90 yd. to the left; from the sign, the side trail follows a diverging logging road to the right for 50 yd. to the first kiln then a path for another 50 yd. to a larger kiln and interpretive sign.) Chippewa Trail turns right onto the logging road at the T intersection, follows it for 60 yd., then diverges left from this road on an older road and begins the ascent of the mountain. At 0.6 mi., the trail passes to the left of a cellar hole in an overgrown pasture and, after passing through a shallow sag, begins to climb more steeply.

The trail passes a State Forest Boundary sign and then turns sharply left, just before a rock outcrop on the ridge crest, continuing to climb among ledges in woods dominated by red pines and passing two side paths leading 50 yd. right to ledges with good views. At 1.1 mi., the main trail turns sharply left where a side path leads right 25 yd. to a ledge that affords fine views south and west. In this area, the blue blazes of the state forest property line must not be confused with trail blazes, which are yellow. After 1.3 mi., the trail climbs mostly on ledges past excellent outlooks scattered along the way until it reaches a knob with an interesting view of the summit rocks ahead then crosses a shallow, moist sag in the woods and reaches the jct. with Black Mtn. Trail from Benton village. The open ridge crest at the old fire tower site is 40 yd. up to the right, with good outlook points on the ridge crest both east and west of the tower site. Tipping Rock, on a ledge with good views, is 150 yd. east of the tower site via a faint path over ledges and through scrubby areas.

STINSON–CARR–KINEO REGION

STINSON MTN. TRAIL (WMNF; MAP 4: K3)

From parking lot (1,495 ft.) to:	↧↥	↗	↻
Stinson Mtn. summit (2,900 ft.)	1.8 mi.	1,400 ft.	1:35

SEC 6

The fire tower on this small, relatively easy mountain was dismantled many years ago, but good views south are still available, and metamorphosed strata make the summit ledge geologically interesting. The trail is reached by following Main St., which becomes Stinson Lake Rd., north from NH 25 in Rumney. Main St. leaves NH 25 7.3 mi. west of Exit 26 on I-93. At the foot of the lake, 5.0 mi. from NH 25 and 0.1 mi. south of the Stinson Lake General Store and Post Office, turn right uphill on Cross Rd. for 0.8 mi. then turn right again on Lower Doe Town Rd. (sign for trail) and follow it for 0.3 mi. to a parking area on the left. Lower Doe Town Rd. is not plowed in winter.

The trail leaves the parking area and soon enters and follows an old farm road at easy grades between stone walls. After crossing a snowmobile trail at 0.4 mi. and passing a cellar hole on the left side of the trail, it becomes steeper, and at 0.9 mi., it bears left, joining a snowmobile trail that comes up from the right (descending, turn right here). At 1.1 mi., the trail takes the right fork at a jct.; left is the old tractor road (now a snowmobile trail) to the summit; the snowmobile trail is 0.1 mi. longer, muddy in places, and has one very wet stretch on the ridge crest. The hiking trail ascends steadily with rocky footing then swings left, climbs by switchbacks, and rejoins the old tractor road just below the summit (note the left turn here for the descent). From here, either of two routes, which together make a very short loop, climbs to the summit ledges. From the right branch of the summit loop, 15 yd. before its upper jct. with the left branch, an unmarked spur path leads southwest about 80 yd. to a cleared view of Stinson Lake and Mt. Moosilauke.

RATTLESNAKE MTN. TRAIL (WMNF; MAP 4: L2)

Cumulative from Buffalo Rd. (630 ft.) to:	⇅	↗	○
Rattlesnake Mtn. summit (1,594 ft.)	1.3 mi.	1,000 ft.	1:10
Complete loop	2.5 mi.	1,050 ft.	1:45

This trail climbs moderately to a loop over the ledges of Rattlesnake Mtn., providing excellent views over the Baker River Valley for a modest effort. From NH 25, 3.3 mi. west of the traffic circle and jct. with NH 3A in West Plymouth, turn right (north) at the flashing light onto Main St. in Rumney (the road leading to Stinson Lake). In 0.7 mi., turn left onto Buffalo Rd. and follow it along the north bank of the Baker River, passing parking areas for rock climbers at 1.5 mi. and 1.8 mi. from NH 25. The trailhead (sign) is on the right (north) at 3.3 mi., just before the Rumney Transfer Station; the parking area is small and rough. Additional parking is available 75 yd. east on the north side of Buffalo Rd. Parking is not allowed along the edge of the road. Buffalo Rd. may also be reached from NH 25 via Sand Hill Rd. in West Rumney; turn right (east) to reach the trailhead in 1.2 mi.

Entering a pine grove, the trail soon swings right on an old road, and in 125 yd., a path from the alternate parking area enters from the right. The trail then swings left near a brook, crosses a minor tributary, and climbs rather steeply on a wide footway with good footing. The grade eases on the ridge crest, and at 0.8 mi., the west end of the summit loop diverges right. In another 80 yd., the east end of the summit loop turns right off the old road, meanders through the woods, and crosses a ledge with a view of Stinson Mtn. Rattlesnake Mtn. Trail soon bears right and dips, entering an area burned by a forest fire in 2008, and ascends ledges to the open, rocky summit at 1.3 mi. The trail descends and then turns sharply right at the base of the summit ledge, where a faint spur path leads 40 yd. left to a view west, and returns over a rocky knob to the old road at 1.7 mi. Turn left here to return to the parking area.

CARR MTN. TRAIL (WMNF; MAP 4: K3–K2)

Cumulative from Three Ponds Trail (1,505 ft.) to:	⇅	↗	⟳
Carr Mtn. summit side path (3,440 ft.)	2.9 mi.	2,100 ft. (rev. 150 ft.)	2:30
Parking area on Clifford Brook Rd. (880 ft.)	5.8 mi.	2,100 ft. (rev. 2,550 ft.)	3:55

SEC 6

This trail provides access to the summit of Carr Mtn., where several rounded rock knobs provide good, though somewhat restricted, views. The trail begins on Three Ponds Trail, 0.5 mi. from the parking area on Stinson Lake Rd., ascends to the ridge crest where a short spur trail leads to the summit of Carr Mtn., and descends to a small parking area on Clifford Brook Rd. in Warren. Carr Mtn. Trail is sparsely marked, but the footway is generally clear and easy to follow. For the west trailhead, turn off NH 25 into the Warren Fish Hatchery and Wildlife Center, follow a paved road south for 0.1 mi., then turn left onto Clifford Brook Rd. at a trail sign. This gravel road may be driven for 0.7 mi. to a marked grassy parking area on the right; do not park near the house at the end of the road.

The trail diverges sharply left (south) from Three Ponds Trail and descends to cross Sucker Brook at 0.2 mi. (This crossing is difficult at high water; it can be avoided by following Three Ponds Trail to its bridge over Sucker Brook then returning back southeast along the brook on an old logging road, with wet footing in places, to Carr Mtn. Trail. This route is about 0.8 mi. longer than the direct trail route.)

Once across Sucker Brook, Carr Mtn. Trail crosses the aforementioned old logging road in 25 yd. and ascends moderately to the west with good footing through a fine hardwood forest, crossing several small brooks. The trail swings left at 1.2 mi., turns sharply right at an unmarked jct. at 1.4 mi. (avoid a snowmobile trail that continues ahead), swings back to the left at 1.7 mi., then winds upward near the crest of a shoulder close to a small brook. (The USFS plans to clear a helicopter landing zone beside the trail at about 1.9 mi.) Higher up, the trail approaches and crosses a very small mossy brook then zigzags upward with some wet, rough footing. At 2.5 mi., the trail swings left and ascends close to the crest of the main ridge. The ascent becomes gradual through dense, moist coniferous woods, and at 2.9 mi., a side path leads 70 yd. left to the flat, open summit area, where standing views to the north and northeast are available from several rock knobs and the concrete steps of the former fire tower. (The USFS plans to install a small radio repeater between the fire tower footings.)

The main trail descends, reaching a small brook that the trail crosses twice on slippery rocks. It continues to descend moderately on old logging roads that gradually become more and more discernible. It leaves the WMNF at 4.6 mi. and soon swings right (northeast) and descends through a wet section. At 4.8 mi., the trail turns sharply left onto a newer woods road; leading right from this jct. (straight ahead, ascending) is a signed but obscure footpath that runs to the base of a small waterfall at 0.1 mi. After crossing this waterfall's brook and passing over a low ridge, the spur path reaches the top of Waternomee Falls at 0.2 mi. At 5.5 mi., the road crosses a long meadow (follow yellow blazes on posts), passes to the left of a house, and becomes an obvious gravel road that reaches the parking area on the left at 5.8 mi.

In the reverse direction, from the end of the gravel road by the house, ascend straight through the meadow, with Carr Mtn. in sight ahead, to a yellow-blazed post where the trail joins the old logging road in the woods.

SEC
6

THREE PONDS TRAIL (WMNF; MAP 4: K3–J3)

Cumulative from Stinson Lake Rd. (1,330 ft.) to:	↥↧	↗	⟳
Side path to Three Ponds Shelter (1,725 ft.)	2.3 mi.	450 ft. (rev. 50 ft.)	1:20
Height-of-land (2,360 ft.)	5.1 mi.	1,200 ft. (rev. 100 ft.)	3:10
Hubbard Brook Trail (1,450 ft.)	7.2 mi.	1,200 ft. (rev. 900 ft.)	4:10

This yellow-blazed trail starts on the west side of Stinson Lake Rd. at a parking lot 6.9 mi. north of NH 25 and 1.8 mi. north of the Stinson Lake General Store and Post Office. The trail passes attractive ponds with several interesting outlooks to Carr Mtn. and Mt. Kineo, crosses a low ridge, and descends to the gravel road used by Hubbard Brook Trail, 0.2 mi. from NH 118. This gravel road (FR 211, marked by a hiker symbol and a sign: 922) leaves NH 118 4.4 mi. northeast of the northern jct. of NH 118 and NH 25, which is about 1 mi. north of Warren village. Drive in 0.1 mi. and park on the right before a gate. South of the ponds, Three Ponds Trail mostly coincides with a snowmobile trail. The northern part of this trail, between the ponds and NH 118, is seldom used. In 2016 it was thoroughly cleared but still requires some care to follow.

Leaving the parking lot, the trail rises moderately and passes jcts. with Mt. Kineo Trail on the right at 0.1 mi. and Carr Mtn. Trail on the left at 0.5 mi. then descends gently. At 1.0 mi., Three Ponds Trail crosses Sucker Brook on a snowmobile bridge and turns right (upstream) along the brook, following an old logging road. At 1.3 mi. it turns right onto a relocation along the brook, passing several small cascades. At 1.5 mi. it passes a view over a beaver meadow and returns to the road, soon crossing a tributary and the main brook on snowmobile bridges. The trail continues along the east bank of the brook, and at 2.0 mi. it turns right onto a wide new snowmobile trail, ascends along it for 150 yd., then turns left onto a footpath (yellow blazes). In another 50 yd. it turns right at a Forest Protection Area sign, as an abandoned route continues ahead. Three Ponds Trail climbs up and across a slope then descends to join the older route of the trail by the southeast corner of the Middle Pond at 2.3 mi. (In the reverse direction, bear left at the fork.) In 100 yd., a side path 80 yd. long diverges right, passes Three Ponds Shelter on a knoll above the pond, and descends steeply to rejoin the main trail 50 yd. from its point of departure, at an open spot with a view of the pond. The main trail continues along the shore of the pond, passing two more viewpoints and bearing right at a fork.

At 2.5 mi., Donkey Hill Cutoff diverges right, whereas Three Ponds Trail turns left across Sucker Brook on a beaver dam (this area may be flooded and difficult to cross with dry feet). On the far side it turns right then in 20 yd. turns left and climbs over a knoll to the northeast corner of the Middle Pond, with a view of Carr Mtn. It then picks up an old logging road and follows it to a point 80 yd. from the Upper Pond. Here, at 2.7 mi., the road continues ahead as a spur to the edge of the pond (view of Mt. Kineo), but the main trail turns sharply left and starts to ascend. At 2.9 mi. the trail turns right onto another old logging road (where an abandoned snowmobile trail joins from the left) and crosses a brook at 3.1 mi.

At 3.4 mi. the trail corridor leads along the edge of the bog at Foxglove Pond for 75 yd.; this wet stretch can be avoided by an obscure bypass through the woods to the right. The WMNF plans future trail work at this

SEC 6

location, where there is a fine view of Carr Mtn. across the bog. The trail crosses Brown Brook for the first of three times at 3.8 mi., and at 4.0 mi. it crosses a wide snowmobile trail. Beyond here, Three Ponds Trail narrows and requires some care to follow. It ascends to a high plateau on the side of Whitcher Hill, with minor ups and downs, crosses the height-of-land at 5.1 mi., then descends steadily. At the bottom of the slope, the trail turns right and runs through a partly logged area, crossing a skid road. At 6.4 mi., the trail merges with the Warren–Woodstock snowmobile trail (in the reverse direction, bear left at this fork, which is signed). The trail crosses two branches of Blodgett Brook on bridges, runs straight across an overgrown field at 6.9 mi., soon bears right where a private trail diverges left, and continues to Hubbard Brook Trail, 0.1 mi. east of the gate on FR 211.

DONKEY HILL CUTOFF (WMNF; MAP 4: K3)

From Three Ponds Trail (1,740 ft.) to:	⇅	↗	○
Mt. Kineo Trail (1,700 ft.)	1.0 mi.	50 ft. (rev. 100 ft.)	0:30

This rough, wild trail links Three Ponds Trail, 2.5 mi. from Stinson Lake Rd. parking area, to Mt. Kineo Trail, 1.7 mi. from the parking area, making possible a loop hike. Leaving Three Ponds Trail, Donkey Hill Cutoff skirts an area flooded by beaver activity and leads northeast, crossing a low ridge dividing the drainages of Sucker Brook and Brown Brook. At 0.7 mi., the trail swings southeast, crossing several small ridges as it follows the edge of an extensive beaver swamp with views of Mt. Kineo; the best view is at 0.8 mi., where a side path descends a short distance left to the edge of the swamp. Donkey Hill Cutoff ends where Mt. Kineo Trail crosses Brown Brook on a large snowmobile bridge; turn right onto the Mt. Kineo hiking trail along the brook for the Stinson Lake Rd. parking area. In the reverse direction, the start of Donkey Hill Cutoff is marked by a yellow blaze at the south end of the bridge.

MT. KINEO TRAIL (WMNF; MAP 4: K3–J3)

Cumulative from Three Ponds Trail (1,370 ft.) to:	⇅	↗	○
Donkey Hill Cutoff (1,700 ft.)	1.6 mi.	450 ft. (rev. 100 ft.)	1:00
Height-of-land (2,880 ft.)	4.0 mi.	1,700 ft. (rev. 100 ft.)	2:50
Hubbard Brook Rd. spur (1,920 ft.)	5.2 mi.	1,700 ft. (rev. 950 ft.)	3:25

This trail begins on Three Ponds Trail, 0.1 mi. from the parking lot on Stinson Lake Rd., crosses the ridge of Mt. Kineo almost 1.0 mi. east of the true summit, and descends to the end of a spur road off Hubbard Brook Rd. (FR 22; closed in winter); this spur, 0.5 mi. long and passable by cars, leaves Hubbard Brook Rd. at a sign for Mt. Kineo Trail, 6.3 mi. from US 3 in West Thornton. An easy loop can be made using the south part of this trail, Donkey Hill Cutoff, and Three Ponds Trail. The middle section of Mt. Kineo Trail coincides with a wide snowmobile trail. The section south of the Mt. Kineo ridge crest is a lightly used footpath and requires care to follow.

Leaving Three Ponds Trail, Mt. Kineo Trail proceeds north over several minor ups and downs and bears left onto an older route of the trail (a logging road along Brown Brook) at 1.0 mi.; in the reverse direction, turn right here (signs). For the next 0.5 mi., the trail coincides with a wide snowmobile trail that is sometimes muddy, climbing along the attractive brook. Where the snowmobile trail diverges left uphill, Mt. Kineo Trail continues ahead past a line of boulders, passing a fine cascade (a short side path leads to a pool at the base) and crossing a loop of the brook twice. At 1.6 mi., where the snowmobile trail rejoins from the left and Donkey Hill Cutoff then diverges left, Mt. Kineo Trail crosses the brook on a large new snowmobile bridge. (In the reverse direction from this jct., the hiking trail stays to the left along the brook through an open area [sign], whereas the much wider snowmobile trail bears right and uphill.)

Across the bridge, Mt. Kineo Trail, which formerly followed a footpath left (north) along the brook, now follows a wide new snowmobile trail that ascends steadily to the right then swings left, crosses a small saddle, and descends to rejoin the original route, which comes in from the left at 2.0 mi. The combined hiking/snowmobile trail crosses a brook on a bridge at 2.3 mi., at the edge of an extensive beaver wetland. In 0.1 mi., the trail swings right, away from the swamp, crosses a small brook on a bridge, and at 2.6 mi. there is a major intersection where a new snowmobile trail diverges left (northwest). Here Mt. Kineo Trail bears right (southeast), recrosses the brook on a bridge, and swings left (north), ascending to a jct. at 2.8 mi., where the snowmobile trail bears right and the less obvious hiking trail diverges left (sign). Now once again a footpath, Mt. Kineo Trail continues north for another 0.2 mi. The trail then swings right and makes a long eastward traverse across the slope, alternately angling up on old logging roads and climbing straight up on steeper sections. At 4.0 mi., it crosses the ridge in a small col then descends to an old logging road, which it follows steadily downward through several muddy stretches to the end of the gravel spur road off Hubbard Brook Rd.

SEC 6

HUBBARD BROOK TRAIL (WMNF; MAP 4: J3)

Distance from gate on FR 211 (1,430 ft.) to:	⤒⤓	↗	⟳
Hubbard Brook Rd. (1,850 ft.)	2.4 mi.	550 ft. (rev. 150 ft.)	1:30

This trail provides an attractive woods walk through the notch between Mt. Cushman and Mt. Kineo, passing several interesting beaver wetlands. The west trailhead is at a gate on a gravel logging road (FR 211), 0.1 mi. from NH 118. The entrance to FR 211 (hiker symbol and sign: 922) is 4.4 mi. northeast of the northern jct. of NH 118 with NH 25 (this jct. is 1.0 mi. north of Warren village). Park on the right before the gate. The east trailhead, with roadside parking, is on Hubbard Brook Rd. (FR 22; closed in winter) at a hairpin turn across Hubbard Brook, 7.6 mi. from US 3 in West Thornton. The trail is lightly used and requires care to follow in some places, but it was cleared and freshly blazed in 2016.

The trail crosses a bridge beyond the gate on FR 211 and in 150 yd. passes a jct. with Three Ponds Trail on the right. Hubbard Brook Trail continues ahead, climbing easily up the overgrown road, and turns right into the woods (sign) at 0.4 mi. In 75 yd. it turns left and crosses a brook, and at 0.6 mi. it skirts the right edge of a beaver swamp. Running nearly level, it crosses two more brooks, and at 0.8 mi., just after the second crossing, it turns left near the edge of a beaver meadow. In another 0.1 mi. it makes an obscure crossing of a small brook between two meadows then swings left and climbs moderately through fine hardwood forest, reaching the height-of-land at 1.5 mi. It soon runs along the left edge of a beaver swamp for 0.1 mi., bears left into the woods, then reaches the west end of an attractive beaver pond and meadow at 1.8 mi. The trail skirts the north shore, with one short bypass to the left, crosses two small brooks, and at 2.1 mi. turns left on a new (2016) relocation around an area of recent beaver activity. This blazed route, with little footway, must be followed with great care as it crosses a small brook, swings right through an area of beaver cuttings, and rejoins the original trail in 0.1 mi. From here the trail descends gradually, crossing a brook just before reaching Hubbard Brook Rd.

PEAKED HILL POND TRAIL (WMNF; MAP 4: K4)

From gate (820 ft.) to:	⤒⤓	↗	⟳
Peaked Hill Pond (1,200 ft.)	1.6 mi.	450 ft. (rev. 50 ft.)	1:00

This trail follows a logging road to Peaked Hill Pond from US 3, 2.1 mi. north of Exit 29 of I-93, at the Shamrock Motel. Though poorly marked, the trail is easy, and the route is fairly obvious and has a pleasant view of

Peaked Hill from the shore of the pond. Portions of the access road and trail may occasionally be disrupted by logging. The trail begins and ends on private land; the middle section is within the WMNF. From US 3, follow Peaked Hill Pond Rd. (sign for trail) west. Parking is available on the right at 0.25 mi.; careful drivers may continue, passing under I-93, turning right at 0.4 mi. where Lumber Dr. diverges left (parking also available at jct.), and parking on the left just before a steel gate at 0.6 mi. from US 3 (do not block gate). The road bears left 35 yd. beyond the gate, ascends a short washed-out section, and continues up gradually to a fork at 0.5 mi. from the gate. The left branch leads along the north side of an old pasture, and the right branch (sign for trail) continues ahead through the woods; the two routes rejoin in 0.1 mi. The road bears left at 0.9 mi. and climbs moderately, and at 1.5 mi., it passes through a small clearing and then a larger clearing. In another 50 yd., the trail diverges right from the main road on a branch road (sign for pond) and descends to the shore of the pond, where the trail ends.

MIDDLE CONNECTICUT RIVER MTNS.

VELVET ROCKS TRAIL (DOC; ATC/NGTI MAPS)

Cumulative from Connecticut River Bridge (390 ft.) to:	↕	↗	○
Velvet Rocks Trail, official west end (530 ft.)	1.4 mi.	150 ft.	0:45
Velvet Rocks Shelter Loop Trail, southern jct. (910 ft.)	2.1 mi.	500 ft.	1:20
High point on Velvet Rocks ridge (1,243 ft.)	3.3 mi.	1,000 ft. (rev. 150 ft.)	2:10
Trescott Rd. (925 ft.)	5.2 mi.	1,200 ft. (rev. 500 ft.)	3:10

This section of the AT, described south to north, passes through the town of Hanover, climbs over the interesting low ridge called Velvet Rocks, passes a loop path to Velvet Rocks Shelter, and ends on Trescott Rd. opposite the western terminus of Hanover Center Trail, 0.9 mi north of the jct. of Trescott Rd. and Hanover Center Rd. Along its route, the trail passes jcts. with a number of local connecting paths, most of which are shown on the Town of Hanover online trail map.

The main purpose of Velvet Rocks Trail and Hanover Center Trail is to take the AT across the Connecticut Valley and connect the mountains of Vermont and New Hampshire. This part of the AT passes through a moderately populated area, but over the years, relocations have eliminated road walks except for the 1.4 mi. section from the Connecticut River bridge to the official west end of Velvet Rocks Trail. No parking is available at or

SEC 6

near the official west terminus of the trail; hikers must find legal parking in downtown Hanover (inquire at the DOC office in Robinson Hall at the town common). For directions to the east terminus, see Hanover Center Trail (west terminus); one can also follow East Wheelock St. and its continuation, Trescott Rd., 3.0 mi. from its jct. with NH 120 at the north edge of the Dartmouth athletic complex.

Beginning at the state line on the Connecticut River bridge between Hanover, New Hampshire, and Norwich, Vermont, the white-blazed AT follows the north side of West Wheelock St. to the square at the town common in Hanover. The trail turns right onto the west side of South Main St. then soon turns left onto the north side of Lebanon St., which merges into NH 120 (South Park St.) at 1.2 mi. Just before the merge, the trail turns left and crosses through a parking lot and crosswalk to the east side of NH 120. The trail turns right to follow NH 120 south, and in 100 yd., just beyond a service station, turns left (signs and double blaze) and runs along a hedge, traversing the south end of Chase Field, then enters the woods at 1.4 mi.

At this point, the segment officially known as Velvet Rocks Trail (sign) begins. The trail swings left then right and ascends moderately. At 2.1 mi., blue-blazed Velvet Rocks Shelter Loop Trail diverges left.

Velvet Rocks Shelter Loop Trail. This easy trail climbs 0.2 mi. to Velvet Rocks Shelter, where a connecting path diverges left and descends steeply to Low Rd. The loop trail passes to the left of the shelter and continues up a ridge, passing a limited outlook southeast at 0.3 mi., just beyond its high point. The trail then descends to a jct. at 0.4 mi., where a spur trail on the left descends 0.3 mi. to East Wheelock St., just west of Balch Hill Lane. Here, the loop trail turns right and descends a short, steep pitch to rejoin Velvet Rocks Trail in a sag at 0.5 mi.; 15 yd. before the jct., a blue-blazed spur diverges left, leading 0.2 mi. to Ledyard Spring. (From the spring, Ledyard Link, blue-blazed and lightly used, descends 0.4 mi. north to Trescott Rd.—the continuation of East Wheelock St.—just east of its jct. with Grasse Rd., and a short connecting path leads left to the spur that descends to East Wheelock St.) Velvet Rocks Shelter Loop Trail ascent is 150 ft. (rev. 150 ft.).

From its southern jct. with the shelter loop trail, **Velvet Rocks Trail** descends, swings left, and ascends easily to its northern jct. with the shelter loop trail, which rejoins from the left in a sag at 2.6 mi. Turning right (east), the main trail climbs over a knoll then ascends steeply, with a rope for assistance in one spot, through a hemlock forest to the highest knob (no views) on the Velvet Rocks ridge at 3.3 mi.; a short distance before the high point, Trescott Spur (no sign; blue blazed) diverges left and descends 0.4 mi. to Trescott Rd., 0.3 mi. east of Grasse Rd. The main trail swings right and descends moderately with several switchbacks, passing by a series of beautiful mossy ledges that provide the name "velvet rocks"; at the first turn to the left, Oli's Trail diverges right and descends 0.6 mi. through the Greensboro Ridge Natural Area to a parking area at the end of Velvet Rocks Rd. At 4.5 mi., Velvet Rocks Trail crosses a cattail marsh on a footbridge, and at 4.8 mi., the trail crosses a well-worn connecting trail. Velvet Rocks Trail then climbs over a knoll and rises gently to Trescott Rd.; a hikers parking lot is located 50 yd. to the left on the east side of the road.

HANOVER CENTER TRAIL (DOC; ATC/NGTI MAPS)

Cumulative from Trescott Rd. (925 ft.) to:	↕	↗	↻
Hanover Center Rd. (845 ft.)	1.3 mi.	150 ft. (rev. 250 ft.)	0:45
Three Mile Rd. (1,400 ft.)	3.8 mi.	800 ft. (rev. 100 ft.)	2:20

This is the section of the AT between Trescott Rd. and Three Mile Rd. The trail is described south to north. Parking is available at both ends of the trail. For the west terminus, follow Greensboro Rd. east from NH 120 at the traffic lights at the bottom of the hill, south of downtown Hanover (this is 3.5 mi. north of I-89 Exit 18). At 1.9 mi. from NH 120, at a T intersection, turn left on Etna Rd. then turn left on Trescott Rd. at 2.6 mi., just before reaching the center of Etna village. The trailhead is on the right (east) at 3.5 mi. For the crossing of Hanover Center Rd. in the middle of this section, continue on Etna Rd. through Etna village and then on Hanover Center Rd. to the trail crossing just before a cemetery at 3.6 mi. For the east terminus, continue on Etna Rd. through Etna village; at 3.3 mi., turn right onto Ruddsboro Rd., and at 4.8 mi., turn left onto unpaved Three Mile Rd. and continue to the trailhead on the left (west) at 6.1 mi.

From Trescott Rd., the trail passes a spur on the left from the parking area, ascends gradually through a pine plantation, runs along the edge of a field, and swings left into the woods. The trail descends, passes through a stone wall, and climbs briefly. At 0.7 mi., the trail turns left on an old logging road, follows it for 90 yd., then turns right and descends. The trail crosses a brook, a field, and another brook (both crossings are bridged), passes to the right of a cemetery, and reaches Hanover Center Rd. (limited parking) at 1.3 mi. The trail crosses the road and ascends moderately then gradually through old pasture pines, crossing a stone wall. At 1.9 mi., the trail enters a large open field with a view southwest, follows blazed posts across it, then reenters the woods in 0.2 mi. The trail continues an easy to moderate ascent, with occasional short descents, and at 3.4 mi. turns right onto an old trail segment (going south, bear left here). Hanover Center

SEC 6

Trail crosses a woods road (Corey Rd.), passes through a wet section, bears right at 3.7 mi., and soon reaches Three Mile Rd.

MOOSE MTN. TRAIL (DOC; ATC/NGTI MAPS)

Cumulative from Three Mile Rd. (1,400 ft.) to:	⇅	↗	↻
South Peak, Moose Mtn. (2,290 ft.)	1.9 mi.	1,000 ft. (rev. 100 ft.)	1:25
Old Wolfeboro Rd. (2,000 ft.)	2.4 mi.	1,000 ft. (rev. 300 ft.)	1:40
North Peak, Moose Mtn. (2,300 ft.)	3.9 mi.	1,400 ft. (rev. 100 ft.)	2:40
Goose Pond Rd. (950 ft.)	5.6 mi.	1,400 ft. (rev. 1,350 ft.)	3:30

This is the AT section that crosses over Moose Mtn.; the trail is described south to north. The southern terminus is on Three Mile Rd.; follow Greensboro Rd. east from NH 120 at the traffic lights at the bottom of the hill, south of downtown Hanover (this is 3.5 mi. north of I-89 Exit 18). At 1.9 mi. from NH 120, at a T intersection, turn left onto Etna Rd. and continue through Etna village; at 3.3 mi., turn right onto Ruddsboro Rd., and at 4.8 mi., turn left onto unpaved Three Mile Rd. and continue to the trailhead at 6.1 mi., with parking available on the left (west) side of the road. The northern terminus is on Goose Pond Rd., 3.7 mi. east of NH 10, with parking available on the north side of the road at the south end of Holts Ledge Trail.

Leaving Three Mile Rd., the trail climbs briefly then descends to cross Mink Brook on a footbridge and ascends to a jct. at 0.4 mi., where Fred Harris Trail (an old woods road that is frequently muddy) leaves left. Moose Mtn. Trail climbs moderately, with one steeper section, and swings left across a wet area at 1.3 mi. as an unmarked trail diverges right, leading south down the ridge. Moose Mtn. Trail climbs northeast to a clearing and sign at 1.9 mi., where you have a view east and southeast. In 40 yd., Nat Thompson Trail (sign) diverges left, and in another 100 yd., Moose Mtn. Trail passes just to the right of the wooded summit of the South Peak of Moose Mtn. The trail then descends to the notch between the two peaks of Moose Mtn., where it crosses historic Old Wolfeboro Rd. (Province Rd.) at 2.4 mi.

The trail now ascends moderately. In 0.2 mi., a loop path 0.1 mi. long diverges right, passing the Moose Mtn. Shelter in 75 yd. and continuing past side paths to the privy and two tentsites, then rejoins the main trail. The main trail climbs over a knob, swings right below wooded cliffs, and reaches the north end of the shelter loop path at 2.7 mi. In 50 yd., the trail crosses a small brook then ascends easily along the ridge. The trail passes over the southern knob of the North Peak, descends slightly, and reaches its high point on the North Peak of Moose Mtn. at 3.9 mi., where you have a restricted view to the southwest from quartzite ledges on the left. The trail then descends past a fine northeast outlook toward Smarts Mtn. at 4.3 mi. (the best viewpoint on the mountain), continues down the ridge, then descends steadily by long switchbacks. The trail crosses a branch of Hewes Brook at 5.2 mi. and continues to Goose Pond Rd.

NAT THOMPSON TRAIL (DOC; ATC/NGTI MAPS)

Cumulative from Three Mile Rd. (1,400 ft.) to:	⇅	↗	◷
Start of Nat Thompson Trail (1,460 ft.) via Moose Mtn. Trail, Fred Harris Trail, and Class of '66 Lodge access trail	0.8 mi.	150 ft. (rev. 100 ft.)	0:30
Moose Mtn. Trail (2,290 ft.)	2.0 mi.	1,000 ft.	1:30
Complete loop over South Peak of Moose Mtn. with descent via Moose Mtn. Trail	3.9 mi.	1,100 ft.	2:30

This trail, opened by DOC in 2010, leads to the South Peak of Moose Mtn. from the DOC Class of '66 Lodge at the western base of the mountain. Used in combination with Moose Mtn. Trail, Fred Harris Trail, and the access trail to the lodge, Nat Thompson Trail makes possible a loop hike over the South Peak. To reach the beginning of the trail, follow Moose Mtn. Trail 0.4 mi. from its trailhead on Three Mile Rd. and turn left onto Fred Harris Trail, an old woods road. In another 0.1 mi., bear left at a fork (the right fork is an abandoned ski route) and cross a brook. At 0.6 mi. from Three Mile Rd., the lodge access trail joins from the left. (To the left, this path runs 0.5 mi. to a parking area on Three Mile Rd., 0.2 mi. north of Moose Mtn. Trail trailhead.)

Continue ahead on the combined Fred Harris and lodge access trails for 100 yd. then turn right at a sign and follow the access trail to the lodge, which is reached at 0.8 mi., just beyond a brook crossing on a bridge. Nat Thompson Trail (sign) begins behind the left side of the lodge. The trail climbs steadily then turns left onto an old woods road (the upper end of the abandoned ski route) at 1.0 mi. and ascends at easy grades to the right of a brook; this section may be muddy during wet seasons. At 1.3 mi., the trail leaves the road on a short bypass to the right then soon swings left (northeast). At 1.7 mi., the trail bears right (east) and climbs moderately to Moose Mtn. Trail; from this jct., Moose Mtn. Trail can be followed 40 yd. right (south) to the South Peak viewpoint clearing and summit sign, or 100 yd. left (north) to the wooded summit of South Peak and on to Moose Mtn. Shelter and North Moose Mtn.

SEC 6

HOLTS LEDGE TRAIL (DOC; ATC/NGTI MAPS)

Cumulative from Dorchester Rd. (870 ft.) to:	⇅	↗	↻
Side trail to outlook (1,930 ft.)	1.4 mi.	1,050 ft.	1:15
Crest of Holts Ledge (2,100 ft.)	1.7 mi.	1,250 ft.	1:30
Goose Pond Rd. (950 ft.)	3.7 mi.	1,350 ft. (rev. 1,250 ft.)	2:30

This segment of the AT crosses between Goose Pond Rd. and Dorchester Rd., passing over Holts Ledge. The endangered peregrine falcon has nested there in recent years, and some of the outlooks may be closed during the nesting season (April 1 to August 1) to prevent disturbing the birds. The northern terminus is on Dorchester Rd. at its jct. with Grafton Turnpike (which diverges right and leads a short distance to the Dartmouth Skiway), 3.2 mi. east of NH 10 in Lyme. Park in the Skiway parking lot; parking is not allowed at the road fork. The south terminus is on Goose Pond Rd., 3.7 mi. east of NH 10, where a small parking area is located on the north side of the road. Because Holts Ledge is more frequently ascended from the north, this trail is described in the north-to-south direction.

Leaving Dorchester Rd., Holts Ledge Trail ascends moderately through hardwoods. At 0.7 mi., it crosses a ski area access road, and at 0.8 mi., a side path to the right descends 0.3 mi. to Trapper John Shelter. The main trail climbs, turning right to cross a small brook and then left to cross a tributary. At 1.4 mi., the trail reaches the brink of the cliff and turns sharply right; to the left, a side path leads 70 yd. to a clearing behind a fence that protects the falcon nesting area, with excellent views to the east. Additional views to the west and north are available from the top of the ski trails of Dartmouth Skiway, which can be reached by following a grassy path 90 yd. northwest from the north end of the fenced clearing. The main trail ascends through woods along the edge of the cliffs, passing two more outlooks, the second of which affords a particularly fine unobstructed view to the east, and reaches the wooded crest of Holts Ledge at 1.7 mi. The trail descends, turns sharply right at 1.9 mi., and continues down the east side of a ridge. At 2.3 mi., the trail swings right where a side path leads 25 yd. left to an outlook south and east. Holts Ledge Trail crosses a snowmobile trail and descends rather steeply. At the bottom, Holts Ledge Trail follows a woods road, swinging east and then south along the edge of a beaver flowage with wet footing before ascending gradually for 0.3 mi. to Goose Pond Rd.

Note: For AT thru-hikers or others interested in a walking route between the north trailhead of Holts Ledge Trail and the south trailhead of Lambert Ridge Trail, a 1.9-mi.-long section of the AT runs roughly parallel to Dorchester Rd. At the jct. of Dorchester Rd. and Grafton Turnpike,

3.2 mi. east of NH 10, near the base of Dartmouth Skiway, the trail follows Dorchester Rd. (the left fork) for a short distance then swings right off the road and runs across a field to the left of a pond. The trail soon enters the woods and ascends at mostly easy grades for 1.2 mi. then descends and crosses a brook at an overhanging ledge. The trail descends gradually until it swings right onto an old road at a granite AT mileage post. The trail follows this old road to Dorchester Rd., where the trail turns left and crosses a bridge to the trailhead for Lambert Ridge Trail (AT) and Ranger Trail. Elevation gain is 400 ft. (rev. 150 ft.).

LAMBERT RIDGE TRAIL (DOC; ATC/NGTI MAPS)

Cumulative from Dorchester Rd. (1,110 ft.) to:	⇅	↗	○
Ranger Trail (2,700 ft.)	3.3 mi.	1,900 ft. (rev. 300 ft.)	2:35
J Trail–Daniel Doan Trail jct. (3,230 ft.)	3.9 mi.	2,400 ft.	3:10

This scenic trail, with several viewpoints, is the segment of the AT between Dorchester Rd. and the summit of Smarts Mtn. The trail is described south to north. To reach the trailhead, follow Dorchester Rd. east from NH 10 in Lyme. At 3.2 mi., bear left where Grafton Turnpike diverges right to the Dartmouth Skiway and continue on a gravel section of Dorchester Rd. to a small parking area on the left at 5.1 from NH 10.

From the parking area, Lambert Ridge Trail (sign) leaves on the left and ascends moderately by switchbacks through a fine hardwood forest, passing through a stone wall at 0.4 mi. After a steeper pitch, the trail crosses a ledge with a southwest view and soon reaches an extensive ledgy area with a view east at 0.8 mi. Here, the trail turns sharply left at the edge of a cliff and continues climbing along the ridge, alternately through the woods and over ledges, with occasional views. At 1.8 mi., you have a fine view of the summit of Smarts ahead, and in the next 0.2 mi., the trail passes several more outlooks, with minor ups and downs between the ledges.

From the highest ledge, the trail descends steeply then gradually, swinging right into a wet sag with a small stream at 2.3 mi. The trail then bears right (northeast) and ascends gradually along a shoulder, with occasional brief descents; parts of this section are often muddy. The trail then climbs a fairly steep and rough section with several slippery ledges to join Ranger Trail, which comes in from the right at 3.3 mi. The combined trails climb rather steeply by switchbacks up the west side of the mountain; at the first right turn, the trails ascend a steep, wet slab via log and rock stairs and iron rungs. At 3.8 mi., the grade eases, and a spur leads right 50 yd. to a tentsite with a view south, and at 3.9 mi., a short side path leads left to the recently

SEC 6

restored fire tower. The combined Lambert Ridge and Ranger trails continue another 15 yd. to a jct. where J Trail diverges right, carrying the AT northward, and blue-blazed Daniel Doan Trail diverges left, reaching the warden's cabin in 30 yd. and Mike Murphy Spring in 0.2 mi.

RANGER TRAIL (DOC; ATC/NGTI MAPS)

Cumulative from Dorchester Rd. (1,110 ft.) to:	⇅	↗	○
Lambert Ridge Trail (2,700 ft.)	3.0 mi.	1,600 ft.	2:20
J Trail–Daniel Doan Trail jct. (3,230 ft.)	3.6 mi.	2,100 ft.	2:50

This trail, the old warden's trail to the fire tower on Smarts Mtn., ascends to the summit from Dorchester Rd., 5.1 mi. east of NH 10 (the same place where Lambert Ridge Trail begins). The upper 0.6 mi. coincides with Lambert Ridge Trail and is part of the AT. After receiving no official maintenance for a number of years, the lower part of Ranger Trail is once again being maintained; the lower part is blazed in blue. Portions of this trail, especially in the middle section, are very wet, and the section that ascends to the jct. with Lambert Ridge Trail has poor footing. Ranger Trail does provide the opportunity for an interesting partial loop hike in combination with Lambert Ridge Trail.

From the parking area, Ranger Trail (sign) starts ahead up a woods road and ascends at mostly easy grades, coming beside Grant Brook on the right (east) at 0.9 mi. At 1.1 mi., the trail bears left away from the brook, and good footing alternates with rough, muddy sections. The road ends at the former fire warden's garage at 1.9 mi., and the trail turns right across the brook. After a gradual section, the trail crosses a tributary at 2.3 mi. (last reliable water) and swings right; here, care must be taken to distinguish the trail from adjacent brook beds. The grade steepens as the trail becomes rough, eroded, and slippery in places. After climbing over numerous wet slabs, Ranger Trail reaches the jct. with Lambert Ridge Trail (AT) on the left at 3.0 mi., and the two trails coincide from here to the summit, as described previously.

DANIEL DOAN TRAIL (DOC; ATC/NGTI MAPS)

Cumulative from parking area on Mousley Brook Rd. (1,310 ft.) to:	⇅	↗	○
Mousley Brook crossing (1,980 ft.)	1.9 mi.	650 ft.	1:15
J Trail–Lambert Ridge Trail jct. (3,230 ft.)	3.2 mi.	1,900 ft.	2:35

This blue-blazed trail follows the route of the former Mousley Brook Trail (once the AT route north of Smarts Mtn.), ascending Smarts Mtn. from the northwest along the valley of Mousley Brook. Daniel Doan Trail is named in honor of Daniel Doan, the author of the first of the popular *50 Hikes* series, a Dartmouth alumnus who spent his adolescent years in nearby Orford. Doan also wrote a novel, *Amos Jackman* (Beacon Press), in which most of the action takes place within a short distance of this trail's Quinttown trailhead.

The trail is frequently wet in its lower and upper sections, although recent work and relocations have alleviated the problem. In recent years there has been active logging along the lower part of the trail. From NH 25A, 3.9 mi. east of its jct. with NH 10 (with signs for Quinttown Rd. and Thomson Tree Farm), follow Quinttown Rd. 1.8 mi. east to a jct. at a nearly deserted farming village, also called Quinttown. Quinttown Rd. continues east (straight ahead) toward a locked gate and the trailhead for J Trail (AT south) and Kodak Trail (AT north). For Daniel Doan Trail, follow Mousley Brook Rd. right (south) from this jct. for 0.7 mi., passing Marsh Rd. (which diverges left) and a farm, to a gate at the end of the public section of road, where a small parking area is located on the left (DOC sign for trailhead parking). The road may not be passable in winter, so you may have to walk at least part of the way from Quinttown. Most of this trail is on private land, and near its beginning, the trail passes a house whose residents keep horses; hikers' dogs should be leashed here.

Continue on foot up the main road past the gate, taking the right fork where two parallel bridges cross Mousley Brook, to a jct. at 0.2 mi. that has a sign for Daniel Doan Trail and Smith Mtn. Trail. A house is on the left, and Smith Mtn. Trail (a snowmobile route) diverges right. Daniel Doan Trail continues straight ahead up an old woods road, passing a driveway diverging sharply left to the house, then bears right (sign) at 0.4 mi., just before the road reaches a gate and bridge. The trail ascends easily up an old farm road, wet and eroded in places, crossing a skid road leading from a log yard on the right at 0.8 mi. At 1.5 mi., the trail bears left to bypass a wet, eroded section of the old trail then rejoins the old route and crosses Mousley Brook at 1.9 mi. The trail ascends along the south bank of the brook past several cascades then veers away to the right and becomes steeper, narrowing to a footpath and crossing the boundary of the AT corridor.

The next section is steep and rough, as Daniel Doan Trail ascends over several slippery ledges. At 2.9 mi., the grade eases, and the trail soon passes Mike Murphy Spring (sign) in a wet area. At 3.2 mi., the trail passes in front of the recently restored warden's cabin and swings right, and in 30 yd. reaches the summit ridge and a jct. where J Trail turns left and Lambert Ridge Trail (along with the coinciding Ranger Trail) continues straight, reaching the side path to the fire tower on the right in 15 yd.

SEC 6

J TRAIL (DOC; ATC/NGTI MAPS)

From Quinttown Rd. at locked gate (1,300 ft.) to:	↯	↗	↺
Lambert Ridge Trail (3,230 ft.)	4.3 mi.	2,000 ft. (rev. 50 ft.)	3:10

This trail, with easy to moderate grades throughout, is the segment of the AT from the summit of Smarts Mtn. to Quinttown Rd., 2.9 mi. from NH 25A. Quinttown Rd. leaves NH 25A 3.9 mi. east of its jct. with NH 10 (with signs for Quinttown Rd. and Thomson Tree Farm); at 1.8 mi., at the crossroads called Quinttown where Mousley Brook Rd. diverges right (south), Quinttown Rd. continues straight through the crossroads and becomes rougher shortly before reaching a locked gate at 2.4 mi. Park on the left before the gate, taking care not to block the road. The trailhead is 0.5 mi. up the road past the gate, across from the start of Kodak Trail; in winter or mud season, you may have to walk the entire 1.1 mi. from Quinttown. Watch for barbed wire when passing through a second gate. This trail is described from north to south, ascending Smarts Mtn.; mileages are given from the parking area before the first gate.

The trail descends gradually a short distance, crosses the South Branch of Jacobs Brook on a footbridge, and ascends through hardwood forest that has reclaimed old pasture land. At 2.3 mi., the trail reaches evergreen woods as the grade remains easy to moderate on the J-shaped ridge. In places, the footing may be wet and muddy. At 4.0 mi., the trail swings right (west) across the east summit knob and descends slightly, passes a spring located on the left, ascends briefly, and bears right at a jct. on the left with the abandoned DOC Clark Pond Loop (which descended southeast to Dorchester Rd.; in the reverse direction, bear left here). J Trail then continues to a jct. on the summit ridge at 4.3 mi. Ahead, the combined Lambert Ridge and Ranger trails continue the AT south, passing a short spur to the fire tower on the right in 15 yd. Here, also, the blue-blazed Daniel Doan Trail diverges right, reaching the warden's cabin in 30 yd. and Mike Murphy Spring in 0.2 mi. Daniel Doan Trail descends to Mousley Brook Rd. and offers an alternative return route to the J Trail parking spot via a 1.3-mi. road walk.

KODAK TRAIL (DOC; ATC/NGTI MAPS)

From Quinttown Rd. at locked gate (1,300 ft.) to:	↯	↗	↺
Mt. Cube summit (2,909 ft.)	3.5 mi.	1,800 ft. (rev. 200 ft.)	2:40

This scenic trail, with moderate grades and occasionally rough footing, is the segment of the AT from Quinttown Rd., 2.9 mi. from NH 25A, to the main (south) peak of Mt. Cube. The trail is described south to north, ascending Mt. Cube. The many smooth quartzite ledges are slippery when wet. Parking is the same as for J Trail (above); see that description for driving directions. The trailhead is 0.5 mi. up Quinttown Rd. from the parking spot before the first gate, across from the start of J Trail; mileages are given from the parking spot.

The trail ascends moderately from the road, swinging right as it climbs to the top of Eastman Ledges at 1.1 mi., which have a fine view of Smarts Mtn. The trail then swings to the north, passing over a low ridge and descending to cross the North Branch of Jacobs Brook at 1.6 mi.; an attractive cascade can be seen 30 yd. left along an old road. At 2.0 mi., a spur path leads right uphill 0.2 mi. to hexagonal Hexacuba Shelter; the water source for the shelter is the brook at the spur path jct. The main trail crosses the brook on a log bridge and soon ascends the southwest ridge of Mt. Cube. At 2.6 mi., after several rough, rocky switchbacks, the trail reaches ledges with southwest views, and at 2.8 mi. are more views. The trail crosses a ledge with a view of the summit ahead, descends into a sag at 3.1 mi., and then climbs moderately to the bare summit of Mt. Cube, where Mt. Cube Section enters from the left and Mt. Cube Trail from the right.

SEC 6

MT. CUBE TRAIL (DOC; ATC/NGTI MAPS)

From NH 25A (900 ft.) to:	⇅	↗	⟳
Mt. Cube summit (2,909 ft.)	3.4 mi.	2,100 ft. (rev. 100 ft.)	2:45

This is the segment of the AT from the main (south) summit of Mt. Cube to NH 25A, 4.6 mi. west of its jct. with NH 25 and 1.9 mi. east of its high point near Mt. Cube Farm. Parking is on the roadside. The trail is described north to south, ascending Mt. Cube.

Leaving NH 25A, the trail crosses a brook in 150 yd. and ascends gradually on an old woods road past stone walls and a cellar hole then crosses a gravel road at 0.5 mi, swings right, and narrows. The trail ascends easily, crossing two branches of Brackett Brook, then descends at 1.5 mi., soon turns left onto an old logging road and follows it for 50 yd. then turns right and descends by a switchback to cross the main branch of Brackett Brook. The trail crosses another brook in 50 yd., then ascends through open hardwoods, crossing two small brooks. At 2.3 mi., the trail turns sharply left and ascends by a series of longer then shorter switchbacks, with rough footing in places. At 3.3 mi., the trail reaches the ridge crest between the two peaks of Mt. Cube. Here, yellow-blazed North Cube Side Trail (DOC), rough and overgrown in places, leads 0.3 mi. right to the open quartzite ledges of the north peak, where wide views north and east prominently feature Mt. Moosilauke. Mt. Cube Trail turns left at this jct. and ascends to the summit of the bare south peak, where the trail meets Kodak Trail and Mt. Cube Section.

MT. CUBE SECTION (RTA; NGTI MAP/CROSS-RIVENDELL TRAIL MAP)

From Baker Rd. (1,400 ft.) to:	↥↧	↗	↺
Mt. Cube summit (2,909 ft.)	2.1 mi.	1,550 ft. (rev. 50 ft.)	1:50

This route to the main (south) summit of Mt. Cube is a section of Cross Rivendell Trail. It provides a pleasant route to Mt. Cube with moderate grades and two viewpoints along the way. It is mostly on private land.

The trailhead is on Baker Rd., a gravel road that runs south from NH 25A, 8.3 mi. west of NH 25 in Wentworth and 7.1 mi. east of NH 10 in Orford. The trailhead (sign and kiosk) is on the left (east) side of the road 0.9 mi. from NH 25A; park north of the trailhead on the west side of the road. The blue-blazed trail leaves Baker Rd. on an old logging road. At 0.1 mi., it swings left and ascends by many switchbacks. After entering a beautiful spruce forest, it ascends past a cleared westward outlook at 1.3 mi. and climbs short switchbacks with many rock steps to a ledge with a view west at 1.5 mi. It turns left here and descends slightly for 0.2 mi., crossing a small brook, then resumes the ascent, reaching steep quartzite ledges 100 yd. below the bare summit. From the summit, Kodak Trail runs south, and Mt. Cube Trail north; the fine northeast outlook from the north peak can be reached by following Mt. Cube Trail and North Cube Side Trail north for 0.4 mi.

SUNDAY MTN. SECTION (RTA; NGTI MAP/CROSS RIVENDELL TRAIL MAP)

Cumulative from eastern trailhead on Dame Hill Rd. (1,039 ft.) to:	↥↧	↗	↺
Spur trail to Sunday Mtn. summit (1,675 ft.)	1.8 mi.	750 ft. (rev. 100 ft.)	1:15
Norris Rd. (900 ft.)	3.4 mi.	750 ft. (rev. 800 ft.)	2:05

This section of Cross Rivendell Trail traverses Sunday Mtn. (1,823 ft.), a small peak with limited but interesting views. The entire section is on private land, so landowners' rights must be respected. Parking (sign and kiosk) for the eastern trailhead is on the right (east) side of Dame Hill Rd., a short distance from its eastern jct. with NH 25A; this is 5.7 mi. east of NH 10 in Orford and 9.7 mi. west of NH 25 in Wentworth. The western trailhead (limited roadside parking) is on Norris Rd.; from NH 10 in Orford, follow Archertown Rd. for 1.9 mi. then turn right onto Norris Rd. and follow it to the trailhead on the left at 2.2 mi. from NH 10.

From the eastern trailhead, walk back to Dame Hill Rd., follow it to the right for 60 yd., then turn right onto Indian Pond Rd. At 0.2 mi., turn left off the road (sign) onto the blue-blazed trail (no parking here). The trail follows a farm road for 20 yd. then bears right and runs through a narrow swath of woods along the edge of a field. At 0.3 mi. from the parking area, the trail turns left and follows the edge of another field for 100 yd. then turns right through a stone wall. The trail descends slightly and turns left onto an old woods road for 50 yd. then turns right off it through another stone wall. The trail descends to a sag; crosses a small brook, a knoll, and another brook; and at 0.7 mi. bears slightly right onto a woods road that comes from a field to the left. (Avoid the road that turns sharply right.)

The trail descends gradually to the north along this road then swings left at 0.9 mi. and ascends. At 1.1 mi. the trail bears left onto a footpath and climbs by long switchbacks. At 1.6 mi., it swings right at a ledgy spot with a view of Mt. Cube (Smarts Mtn. can also be seen a few steps down from the trail) and climbs through a fine oak forest to a signed jct. at 1.8 mi. Here, a spur trail diverges left and climbs 0.2 mi. and 150 ft. to the wooded summit (sign), passing a framed view of Mt. Moosilauke near the top. The main trail bears right and descends to a level shoulder then turns left off the shoulder at 2.4 mi.; here, a side path descends 40 yd. ahead to a view of Mt. Moosilauke. The main trail descends moderately, crossing numerous old logging roads, runs through a stone wall at 3.3 mi., and continues to Norris Rd.

ATWELL HILL TRAIL (DOC; MAP 4: K1)

From NH 25A (905 ft.) to:	↕	↗	○
Cape Moonshine Rd. (1,425 ft.)	1.7 mi.	500 ft.	1:05

This segment of the AT runs from NH 25A, 4.5 mi. west of NH 25 and 0.1 mi. east of Mt. Cube Trail, to Cape Moonshine Rd. opposite the south end of Ore Hill Trail; this point on Cape Moonshine Rd. is 3.3 mi. south of NH 25C and 2.1 mi. north of NH 25A. Atwell Hill Trail is described south to north. From NH 25A, the trail crosses a muddy spot and ascends gradually, bearing left onto an old woods road at 0.2 mi. Good footing alternates with muddy, rough sections. At 1.2 mi., the trail bears right (east) off the woods road, crosses an extensive swampy area with many stepping-stones, and ascends to Cape Moonshine Rd.

SEC 6

ORE HILL TRAIL (DOC; MAP 4: K1–J1)

From Cape Moonshine Rd. (1,425 ft.) to:	⇅	↗	⟳
NH 25C (1,550 ft.)	3.4 mi.	800 ft. (rev. 650 ft.)	2:05

This segment of the AT runs from Cape Moonshine Rd. opposite Atwell Hill Trail, 3.3 mi. south of NH 25C and 2.1 mi. north of NH 25A, to NH 25C, 3.5 mi. west of NH 25 and 0.1 mi. west of Wachipauka Pond Trail. Ore Hill Trail is described south to north. The trail passes under a small power line and ascends through mixed forest and a beautiful spruce grove. At 0.6 mi., a spur path leads right 100 yd. to Ore Hill Tentsite (the former shelter here was destroyed by fire in 2011 and will not be rebuilt); water is available by following a path 150 yd. south from the tentsite. The main trail crosses the height-of-land on Sentinel Mtn. at 0.8 mi. then descends, crossing an old woods road at 1.4 mi. At 2.0 mi., after an extensive muddy section, the trail crosses a small stream, swings right (east) for 0.1 mi., turns left (north), and passes a small pond on the right. The trail ascends to its high point on Ore Hill in a fine stand of sugar maples at 2.8 mi., where the trail bears right and descends to NH 25C.

WACHIPAUKA POND TRAIL (DOC; MAP 4: J1–J2)

Cumulative from NH 25 (1,030 ft.) to:	⇅	↗	⟳
Webster Slide Trail (1,660 ft.)	2.3 mi.	900 ft. (rev. 250 ft.)	1:35
NH 25C (1,520 ft.)	4.9 mi.	1,550 ft. (rev. 800 ft.)	3:15

This segment of the AT, which runs from NH 25C to NH 25, leaves NH 25C 3.4 mi. west of NH 25 and 0.1 mi. east of Ore Hill Trail. The Wachipauka Pond Trail trailhead on NH 25 is 4.4 mi. north of the northern jct. of NH 25 and NH 118, 0.5 mi. north of the jct. of NH 25 and High St., and 120 yd. south of the western terminus of Town Line Trail. Wachipauka Pond Trail also provides access to Wachipauka Pond and Webster Slide Trail, and because the north trailhead is used most often to reach these features, Wachipauka Pond Trail is described here from north to south.

Leaving NH 25, the trail crosses an old railroad grade and climbs easily then turns sharply right at 0.5 mi. and ascends steadily to its high point on Wyatt Hill at 1.2 mi. The trail descends west gradually to a swampy area then contours and climbs with rough footing along the base of Webster Slide Mtn. above the west shore of Wachipauka Pond. (An obscure side path, a former route of the AT, diverges left and runs along the shore of the pond, ending at a clearing reached by another side path described below.)

At a four-way jct. at 2.3 mi., Webster Slide Trail leaves right (west) for the summit of Webster Slide Mtn., and an unmarked but obvious side path descends 0.2 mi. (with 150-ft. elevation loss) left (east) to a clearing at the northwest corner of the pond. Wachipauka Pond Trail continues ahead (south) from the jct., passing Hairy Root Spring on the right, then climbs moderately, passing a short spur path left to a restricted east outlook at 2.6 mi. The trail crosses the wooded summit of Mt. Mist (sign) at 3.1 mi. and descends gradually, crossing an old woods road at 3.6 mi., then rises slightly as the trail passes around a low hill. The trail descends to cross Ore Hill Brook then rises a short distance to NH 25C.

WEBSTER SLIDE TRAIL (DOC; MAP 4: J1)

From Wachipauka Pond Trail (1,660 ft.) to:	↕	↗	○
Webster Slide Mtn. main outlook (2,130 ft.)	0.7 mi.	500 ft. (rev. 50 ft.)	0:35

The unusual outlook from this mountain, looking straight down on Wachipauka Pond, is reached by a blue-blazed spur trail that leaves Wachipauka Pond Trail right (west) at a four-way jct. 2.3 mi. from NH 25. Webster Slide Trail is lightly used and requires some care to follow through brushy areas near the top. The trail follows a woods road up through two muddy spots, swings right across a flat area, ascends moderately, and at 0.3 mi. turns sharply right, climbing a steep, eroded pitch with poor footing. The trail then climbs easily to a point just south of the wooded summit (sign) at 0.6 mi. and descends slightly to a clearing (the site of a former shelter). The best viewpoint over the pond is reached by a beaten path descending 30 yd. to the left from the clearing; use caution. For the descent, Webster Slide Trail leaves the upper left (southwest) corner of the old shelter clearing and, in 10 yd., bears right where a beaten path diverges left; the left-branching path leads 0.1 mi. down to a southwestern outlook (sign) that can be reached only by a very steep and potentially dangerous descent.

SEC 6

SECTION SEVEN

WATERVILLE VALLEY AND SQUAM LAKE REGIONS

Map 3: Crawford Notch–Sandwich Range
Map 4: Moosilauke–Kinsman Ridge

INTRODUCTION

This section covers the mountains that surround the valley of the Mad River, commonly called the Waterville valley, including Mt. Tecumseh, Mt. Osceola, Mt. Tripyramid, Sandwich Mtn., and their subordinate peaks. Waterville Valley, the town, should be distinguished from the Waterville valley (the valley of the Mad River); a significant part of the Waterville valley is in the town of Thornton, and the town of Waterville Valley includes the summits of Mts. Whiteface and Passaconaway, which are not considered part of the Waterville valley by even the broadest definition.

This section also covers the lower ranges to the south and southwest, including the mountains in the vicinity of Squam Lake: the Squam Range, the Rattlesnakes, and Red Hill. This region is bounded on the west by the Pemigewasset River (and I-93, which follows the river fairly closely), on the north by the Kancamagus Highway (NH 112), and on the south by NH 25. This is the western part of a larger mountainous region bounded on the east by NH 16; it extends nearly 30 mi. from Lincoln to Conway without being crossed from north to south by any road. Mt. Tripyramid and Sandwich Mtn. are the westernmost high peaks of the Sandwich Range; the rest of the Sandwich Range, extending east to Mt. Chocorua, is covered in Section Eight. The other mountains covered in Section Seven have not customarily been considered as belonging to the Sandwich Range.

Many of the trails on Mt. Tripyramid and Sandwich Mtn. are partly or entirely within the 35,800-acre Sandwich Range Wilderness. In accordance with USFS Wilderness policy, the trails in the Sandwich Range Wilderness are generally maintained to a lower standard than trails outside the Wilderness Area. Considerable care may be required to follow them.

Almost the entire section is covered by AMC's *White Mountains Trail Map 3: Crawford Notch–Sandwich Range* coverage of the Squam Range extends a bit farther south on AMC's *White Mountains Trail Map 4: Moosilauke–Kinsman Ridge*. The trails on Cotton Mtn. at the south end of the Squam Range, and most of the trails on Red Hill, are not shown on the AMC maps. The Squam Lakes Association (SLA), which maintains most of the trails on the Squam Range, publishes a trail guide and map that covers the entire Squam Range, the Rattlesnakes, Red Hill, Sandwich Mtn., and Mt. Israel. The guide (new edition due in 2017) can be ordered from the SLA.

SEC 7

ROAD ACCESS

From I-93 at Exit 28 near Campton, NH 49 runs northeast beside the Mad River to Waterville Valley. At 10.6 mi. from I-93, where Tripoli Rd. (see below) diverges left at a ski area sign, NH 49 ends, and Valley Rd.

continues ahead into the town center. At 11.6 mi., where Snows Brook Rd. continues ahead, Boulder Path Rd. diverges right and leads 0.3 mi. to a jct. with West Branch Rd., on the left, by the Osceola Library; a short distance further on Boulder Path Rd. is a trailhead parking area on the right, at the base of Snows Mtn. Ski Area. From this jct., West Branch Rd. leads 0.7 mi. to the large Livermore Rd. (FR 53) trailhead parking area (plowed in winter, also referred to as Depot Camp) on the right then immediately crosses a bridge and ends at Tripoli Rd.

From its jct. with NH 49, Tripoli Rd. (FR 30) leads toward the Mt. Tecumseh slopes of the Waterville Valley Ski Area. At 1.3 mi. from NH 49, Tripoli Rd. diverges right as the more prominent ski area access road continues ahead. (The ski area access road continues 0.7 mi. to a one-way loop road around the ski area parking lots; the trailhead for Mt. Tecumseh Trail is 0.2 mi. along the right side of the loop.) At 1.9 mi., West Branch Rd. diverges right, immediately crosses a bridge, and passes the Livermore Rd. parking area on the left. From its jct. with West Branch Rd., Tripoli Rd. (narrow and winding, drive with caution) climbs northwest to Thornton Gap (2,280 ft.), the pass between Mts. Osceola and Tecumseh. Here the road crosses a gate and changes to gravel, passes the Mt. Osceola Trail parking area at 4.7 mi., and descends past the Mt. Tecumseh Trail trailhead at 5.9 mi. and the East Pond Trail trailhead at 6.2 mi. The road becomes paved again at 9.5 mi. (where Russell Pond Rd. diverges right), continuing down to I-93 (Exit 31) at 11.4 mi. and its western terminus, just beyond, at NH 175. Tripoli Rd. is unplowed and gated from late fall through spring between its jct. with West Branch Rd. and a point 0.3 mi. east of I-93.

Sandwich Notch is crossed by Sandwich Notch Rd., a very rough, interesting gravel road that passes through a farming region that flourished in the mid-1800s but has almost completely reverted to forest and is now a part of the WMNF. The road, which runs northwest from Center Sandwich to NH 49 between Campton and Waterville Valley, is sound but narrow, steep, rough, and very slow going; the road is maintained this way to protect it from becoming an attractive route for through traffic. It is not recommended for low-clearance vehicles. Numerous historic sites are located along the road, and several attractive ponds are reached by unmarked side roads and footpaths.

Unlike other White Mountain notches, Sandwich Notch is a complex notch made up of two distinct mountain passes: The one on the south (1,460 ft.), between Mt. Israel and the eastern end of the Squam Range, separates the watershed of the Bearcamp River (a Saco tributary) from the valley of the Beebe River (a Pemigewasset tributary); the one on the north (1,780 ft.), between Sandwich Mtn. and Mt. Weetamoo, separates the valley of the Beebe River from the valley of the Mad River (another Pemigewasset tributary). At its eastern end, the road through Sandwich Notch starts from NH 113 in Center Sandwich. Take Grove St. northwest from the village, bear left at 0.4 mi. onto Diamond Ledge Rd. and keep left on Sandwich Notch Rd. at 2.5 mi., where Diamond Ledge Rd. bears right (north), leading 0.4 mi. to Mead Base Conservation Center, the trailhead for Wentworth Trail to Mt. Israel. From this jct., Sandwich Notch Rd. runs northwest—past trailheads for Bearcamp River Trail at 3.2 mi., Crawford–Ridgepole Trail at 3.7 mi., Guinea Pond Trail at 5.4 mi., and Algonquin Trail at 6.9 mi.—and ends at NH 49 at 10.5 mi.; this jct. is 3.2 mi. north of the jct. of NH 49 and NH 175 in Campton. In winter, the road through Sandwich Notch is open for about only 1 mi. from its west end and 2.5 mi. from its east end.

GEOGRAPHY

As discussed in this section's first paragraph, on p. 317, some features are in the Waterville valley but not in Waterville Valley, and vice versa. The original name of the town was plain Waterville; it was changed to Waterville Valley in 1967 to share in the publicity that the major ski area of that name had generated. *The Waterville Valley* (1952, North Country Press), by Nathaniel Goodrich (who participated in the scouting and building of many White Mountain trails and also was the first person to suggest the creation of a 4,000-footer club), recounts the history of the Waterville valley from its first settlers up to a time just before the modern major tourist development started. It provides a fascinating picture of this place when it was a rustic backwater known only to a few people—who, however, loved it passionately—and of a period of history and a way of life that, among other things, produced many of the hiking trails we enjoy today.

The Waterville Valley Athletic & Improvement Association (WVAIA) maintains a system of local trails to points of interest. Trail information and a Tyvek WVAIA trail map (2017 edition) may be obtained at the Town Square retail complex. Some of these trails intersect or coincide with ski-touring trails that may have the same name as a hiking trail but follow a somewhat different route. A separate map of the extensive ski-touring network is available locally.

Named for the Shawnee leader, Mt. Tecumseh (4,003 ft.) is the highest and northernmost summit of the ridges that form the west wall of the Waterville valley, beneath which the Mad River flows. Good outlooks are at its summit and on Sosman Trail along its south ridge. A major ski area is on the eastern slopes. Thornton Gap, at the head of the northwestern branch of the Mad River, separates Mt. Tecumseh from Mt. Osceola to the northeast; to the west, southwest, and south, several long ridges—some of

SEC 7

them ledgy—run out from Mt. Tecumseh toward Woodstock and Thornton. On the end of the south ridge, the fine rocky peak of Welch Mtn. (2,605 ft.) forms the impressive northwest wall of the narrow south gateway to the upper Waterville valley. The views from Welch Mtn.'s open summit are excellent. Dickey Mtn. (2,734 ft.) is close to Welch Mtn. on the northwest, with many fine outlooks.

The tallest peak in the region, Mt. Osceola (4,340 ft.), lies north of the valley. The peak was named for the great chief of the Seminole people. This narrow, steep-sided ridge has a number of slides in its valleys and is particularly impressive when seen from the outlooks along the western half of the Kancamagus Highway. Its open summit ledge, once the site of a fire tower, commands magnificent views. Mt. Osceola has two subordinate peaks, the East Peak (4,156 ft.; wooded but with several nearby outlooks) and the trailless West Peak (4,114 ft.). Continuing the ridge of Mt. Osceola to the west is trailless Scar Ridge (3,774 ft.), which runs northwest parallel to the Hancock Branch and the Kancamagus Highway and ends with a group of lower peaks above Lincoln village; the most important is Loon Mtn. (3,065 ft.), which can be ascended via the major ski area on its north slope. At the far west end of the Loon group is trailless Russell Crag (1,926 ft.), rising directly above I-93 just north of the Tripoli Rd. exit; north of the crag is Russell Pond, with a WMNF campground reached by a paved side road (closed in winter) off Tripoli Rd. To the east of Mt. Osceola is Mad River Notch, in which the beautiful Greeley Ponds are located, and across that notch is Mt. Kancamagus (3,763 ft.), a trailless mass of rounded, wooded ridges named for a Pennacook chieftain.

Mt. Tripyramid, the rugged and very picturesque mountain that forms the east wall of the Waterville valley, also overlooks Albany Intervale, which lies to the north and east. Most of Mt. Tripyramid is within the Sandwich Range Wilderness. Mt. Tripyramid was named by the illustrious cartographer Arnold Guyot for the three pyramidal peaks that cap the narrow, steep-sided ridge. North Peak (4,180 ft.) is wooded, with a partial view northeast near the summit. Middle Peak (4,140 ft.), the most nearly symmetrical pyramid of the three, provides a view toward Mts. Passaconaway and Chocorua from the summit; a fine outlook over the Waterville valley toward Mts. Tecumseh and Osceola is located to the west of the trail near the summit. South Peak (4,100 ft.) is viewless.

From South Peak, the tall, rolling Sleeper Ridge (covered in Section Eight) connects Mt. Tripyramid with Mt. Whiteface and the eastern part of the Sandwich Range. Scaur Peak (3,605 ft.) caps the prominent northwestern spur of Mt. Tripyramid. Livermore Pass (2,900 ft.) lies between Mt. Tripyramid and Mt. Kancamagus. A major east spur of Mt. Tripyramid is called the Fool Killer (3,548 ft.) because it blends into the main mass when viewed from a distance. Incautious parties attempting to climb Mt. Tripyramid from the east before the construction of the trails found themselves on top of the Fool Killer instead, separated from their goal by a long, scrubby ridge with deep valleys on either side.

Mt. Tripyramid is best known for its slides—great scars visible from long distances—that provide excellent views. The North Slide, which occurred during heavy rains in August 1885, is located on the northwest slope of North Peak. This slide exposed a great deal of bedrock that is geologically interesting and is ascended mainly on steep ledges. The South Slide, located on the southwest face of the South Peak, fell in 1869 and again in 1885 and is mostly gravel and loose rock. Two smaller, revegetated slides descend into the valley of Sabbaday Brook from the east face of Middle Peak. Mt. Tripyramid is steep and rugged, and all routes to its summits have at least one rough section; consequently, the mountain is more difficult to climb than a casual assessment of the altitude, distance, and elevation gain might suggest.

Sabbaday Falls, a picturesque waterfall and pool formed by an eroded traprock dike, is reached from Sabbaday Falls Picnic Area on the Kancamagus Highway by a gravel pathway section of Sabbaday Brook Trail. Snows Mtn. (3,040 ft.) is a low wooded ridge southwest of Mt. Tripyramid with a small ski area on its western end. The summit is trailless; a loop trail along the west half of the ridge passes one limited viewpoint and one open outlook.

SEC 7

Sandwich Mtn. (3,980 ft.), sometimes called Sandwich Dome, is the westernmost major summit of the Sandwich Range; its western ridge forms the south wall of the Waterville valley. Sandwich Mtn. is mostly within the Sandwich Range Wilderness. The mountain looks over the lower Mad River to the west, and Sandwich Notch separates the mountain from the Campton and Holderness mountains on the south and southwest. Sandwich Mtn. was once called Black Mtn., a name that has also been applied to its southwest spur (3,500 ft.), which is ledgy with many fine outlooks, and to a nubble (2,732 ft.) at the end of this spur. According to the USGS, the nubble is officially entitled to the name Black Mtn., but the southwest spur is also commonly referred to as Black Mtn. To the northeast, a high pass separates Sandwich Mtn. from the long ridge of Flat Mtn. (3,331 ft.) in Waterville; Pond Brook has cut a deep ravine between its east shoulder and the rounded Flat Mtn. (2,940 ft.) in Sandwich.

Flat Mtn. Pond (2,320 ft.) lies east of Sandwich Mtn. and west of Mt. Whiteface, between the two Flat Mountains; originally two separate ponds, they have been united by the dam at their south end, making one larger pond. To the north of the pond is the remote gap known as Lost

Pass. The area has largely recovered from lumbering begun in 1920 and an extensive fire in 1923. In the flat region south of Sandwich Mtn. lie a number of attractive ponds, including Guinea Pond and Black Mtn. Pond. South of these ponds is Mt. Israel (2,630 ft.), which provides a fine panorama of the Sandwich Range from its north ledge and offers great rewards for the modest effort required to reach it. Southwest across Sandwich Notch from Sandwich Mtn. is the trailless Campton Range; its principal summits are Mt. Weetamoo (2,548 ft.) and Campton Mtn. (2,387 ft.). The northern slopes of this range are within the WMNF, and its southern slopes, as well as the northern slopes of the eastern Squam Range, including 2 mi. of Crawford–Ridgepole Trail, are now under conservation easement as part of the 5,435-acre Beebe River Tract.

Jennings Peak (3,460 ft.) and Noon Peak (2,976 ft.) form a ridge running north from Sandwich Mtn. toward Waterville Valley. Sandwich Mtn. has fine views north over the valley, but the views from the cliffs that drop from the summit of Jennings Peak into the valley of Smarts Brook are even better. Acteon Ridge runs from Jennings Peak to the west over sharp, bare Sachem Peak (2,860 ft.) and ends in the open rocky humps of Bald Knob (2,300 ft.), which faces Welch Mtn. across the Mad River Valley and forms the other half of the gateway; this ridge is occasionally traversed, although there is no path.

The Squam Range begins at Sandwich Notch across from Mt. Israel and runs roughly southwest toward Holderness. This area is almost entirely private property (much of which is now under conservation easements held by Lakes Region Conservation Trust and Squam Lakes Conservation Society), open to day-hikers by the gracious permission of the landowners, but camping is not permitted. The Squam Range peaks, from northeast to southwest, are an unnamed knob (2,218 ft.), Doublehead Mtn. (2,158 ft.), Mt. Squam (2,223 ft.), Mt. Percival (2,212 ft.), a knob sometimes called the Sawtooth (2,260 ft.) that is the actual high point of the range, Mt. Morgan (2,220 ft.), Mt. Webster (2,076 ft.), Mt. Livermore (1,500 ft.), and Cotton Mtn. (1,270 ft.).

Crawford–Ridgepole Trail crosses over or near all of these summits except for Cotton Mtn., and several trails ascend the ridge from NH 113; curiously, the Sawtooth, the high point of the range, is bypassed by the trail. By far the most popular hike on the range, often fairly crowded, is the loop over mts. Morgan and Percival, which offer superb views south over the lake and hill country and north to the higher mountains; the rest of the range is lightly visited, and the trails, including Crawford–Ridgepole Trail, often require some care to follow, although the rewards of pleasant walks to several excellent viewpoints are great.

The Rattlesnakes—West Rattlesnake (1,260 ft.) and East Rattlesnake (1,289 ft.)—are a pair of hills that rise just across the highway from mts. Morgan and Percival and offer excellent lake views for little effort. West Rattlesnake has fine views to the south and west from its southwest cliff. East Rattlesnake has a more limited but still excellent view over Squam Lake. Five Finger Point, which lies southeast of the Rattlesnakes and has a perimeter trail connected to the Rattlesnakes' trail network, offers attractive lakeside walking on undeveloped rocky shores. Note that some of the parking areas and trails on the Squam Range and Rattlesnakes are temporarily closed each year during the spring mud season.

Red Hill (2,030 ft.) and its ledgy northern spur, Eagle Cliff (1,410 ft.), rise between Squam Lake and Lake Winnipesaukee. The fire tower on the summit of Red Hill offers excellent views in all directions for very modest effort; Eagle Cliff offers interesting but much less extensive views and has a somewhat more challenging trail to ascend. The summit and most of the trails are within the 2,650-acre Red Hill Conservation Area, owned and managed by the Lakes Region Conservation Trust (LRCT), which publishes a Red Hill trail map. The LRCT also maintains a small, lightly used trail network, with some limited views, at its Sheridan Woods property on the northeastern slope of Red Hill. The trailhead (kiosk) is on Sheridan Rd. in Moultonborough, 1.4 mi. northwest of NH 25.

A number of public and quasi-public reservations in this region offer the opportunity for pleasant walking. Although the trail is no longer continuous, parts of Bearcamp River Trail (a 17-mi. route from Sandwich Notch to South Tamworth opened in the early 1990s) offer a variety of walks through woods, farmlands, and wetlands along or near the Bearcamp River, linking several reservations and parcels of land protected by conservation easements. About one-third of this route is on country roads. Some trail sections may be very obscure and difficult to follow, and others may be posted as closed by landowners. Maps may be available at the Sandwich town offices and at tamworthconservationcommission.org.

Of particular interest is the western end of the trail, located on public land, which passes by Beede Falls and Cow Cave. SLA manages several campsites and more than 4 mi. of trails in the Chamberlain–Reynolds Memorial Forest at the south end of Squam Lake. The trails, several of which reach the shore of the lake, can be reached from two parking areas on College Rd. between US 3 and NH 25B in Center Harbor. SLA also maintains a small trail network in its Belknap Woods reservation, including a 1.5-mi. loop around a beaver pond; the trailhead is on NH 25B in Center Harbor, 0.9 mi. east of US 3. For descriptions of many trails in the nearby Ossipee Range, see AMC's *Southern New Hampshire Trail Guide* (4th ed., 2015).

SEC 7

CAMPING
Sandwich Range Wilderness
All shelters have been removed from the Sandwich Range Wilderness. In accordance with USFS Wilderness policy, hiking groups may not exceed ten people, and no more than ten people may occupy any designated or non-designated campsite. See p. xiii for more information about Wilderness Area regulations.

Squam Lakes Region
The trails described in this guide on the Squam Range, the Rattlesnakes, and Red Hill are almost entirely on private land, and although the owners welcome hikers for day use, camping is not allowed.

Forest Protection Areas
The WMNF has established a number of Forest Protection Areas, or FPAs, where camping and wood or charcoal fires are prohibited throughout the year. See p. xxiv for general FPA regulations.

In the area covered by Section Seven, camping is forbidden within 0.25 mi. of Sabbaday Falls, East Pond, and Kiah Pond and at any point within the Greeley Ponds Scenic Area. No camping is permitted within 200 ft. of Black Mtn. Pond or Smarts Brook (along which Smarts Brook Trail runs) from NH 49 1.6 mi. to the large clearing.

No camping is permitted on WMNF land within 0.25 mi. of certain roads (camping on private roadside land is illegal except by permission of the landowner). In 2016, these roads included the Kancamagus Highway, NH 49 (Mad River Rd.), Beebe River Rd. (FR 400), Kiah Pond Rd. (FR 418), Sandwich Notch Rd. (FR 98), Upper Hall Pond Rd. (FR 422), and Lower Hall Pond Rd. (FR 417). Camping is permitted along Tripoli Rd. (fee charged), but not within 200 ft. of any trail or along the 0.5-mi. section east of the crossing of the West Branch of the Mad River and other areas as signed. In the near future, however, the USFS plans to close and rehabilitate these unofficial roadside campsites and replace them with designated sites along two spur roads off Tripoli Rd.: Mack Brook Rd. (FR 609) and Hix Mtn. Spur Rd. (FR 31A).

Established Trailside Campsites
Flat Mtn. Pond Shelter (WMNF) is located at the south end of Flat Mtn. Pond on Flat Mtn. Pond Trail, just outside the Sandwich Range Wilderness. A designated tentsite is located near the shelter.

Black Mtn. Pond Tentsite (WMNF/SLA), located above the east shore of Black Mtn. Pond on Black Mtn. Pond Trail, has two tent pads; the shelter formerly located on the south shore has been removed. This area is in the Sandwich Range Wilderness. Except at the designated site, camping and fires are not permitted within 200 ft. of the pond or in adjacent revegetation areas.

SUGGESTED HIKES

■ Easy Hikes
WEST RATTLESNAKE

	🔄	↗	⏱
RT via Old Bridle Path	1.8 mi.	400 ft.	1:05
RT via Pasture Trail	1.2 mi.	600 ft.	0:55

The first and very popular route provides an easy climb to ledges with beautiful views over Squam Lake (see Old Bridle Path, p. 367). For a good alternative to this busy route, try Pasture Trail (see p. 368).

SABBADAY FALLS

	🔄	↗	⏱
RT via Sabbaday Brook Trail and side trail	0.6 mi.	100 ft.	0:20

A gentle stroll up a partially graded route leads to an unusual waterfall. See Sabbaday Brook Trail, p. 348.

SMARTS BROOK LOOP

	🔄	↗	⏱
LP via Pine Flats, Yellow Jacket, and Smarts Brook trails	3.6 mi.	400 ft.	2:00

This easy walk leads past a scenic gorge, a beaver pond (via a short side trip), and a fine cascade and pool. To begin, see Pine Flats Trail, p. 352.

GREELEY PONDS

	🔄	↗	⏱
RT via Greeley Ponds Trail	4.4 mi.	450 ft.	2:25

This route from the Kancamagus Highway offers relatively easy access (with some rough footing) to these two remote ponds in beautiful Mad River Notch. See Greeley Ponds Trail, p. 340.

SEC 7

■ Moderate Hikes

RED HILL

		↻	↗	⊙
RT via Red Hill Trail		3.4 mi.	1,350 ft.	2:20
LP via Red Hill and Cabin trails		3.6 mi.	1,350 ft.	2:30

Follow an old Jeep road to a tower with wide views of the Lakes Region (see Red Hill Trail, p. 369). Make it a loop rather than an out-and-back via Cabin Trail (see p. 370).

EAST PONDS

	↻	↗	⊙
LP via East Pond Trail, Little East Pond Trail, and East Pond Loop	4.8 mi.	1,000 ft.	2:55

This pleasant hike visits two high mountain ponds. To begin, see East Pond Trail, p. 341.

MTS. PERCIVAL AND MORGAN

	↻	↗	⊙
LP via Mt. Morgan, Morse, Mt. Percival, Crawford–Ridgepole, and Mt. Morgan trails	5.4 mi.	1,600 ft.	3:30

This loop hike offers exceptional views for the effort. To begin, see Mt. Morgan Trail, p. 364.

MT. ISRAEL

	↻	↗	⊙
RT via Wentworth Trail	4.2 mi.	1,700 ft.	2:55
RT via Guinea Pond and Mead trails	6.8 mi.	1,300 ft.	4:05
LP via Wentworth Trail, Mead Trail, Guinea Pond Trail, Sandwich Notch Rd., and Bearcamp River Trail	8.2 mi.	1,850 ft.	5:00

Located south of the main peaks of the Sandwich Range, this summit offers an impressive view of its higher neighbors. The most direct ascent is via Wentworth Trail (see p. 359). For a longer, more varied route, ascend by Guinea Pond and Mead trails (see p. 359). The third option above makes a particularly fine loop with a great variety of scenery: a ledgy summit, open swamps, interesting rock formations along a brook, and a walk on a historic road through long-abandoned farmland (to begin, see Wentworth Trail, p. 359).

SEC
7

WELCH AND DICKEY MTNS.

	⇅	↗	⟳
LP via Welch-Dickey Loop Trail	4.4 mi.	1,800 ft.	3:05
RT to Welch ledge	2.6 mi.	800 ft.	1:40
RT to Dickey ledge	2.4 mi.	1,100 ft.	1:45

This loop offers a great deal of open-ledge walking and is one of the finest half-day hikes in the White Mountains, covering fairly rugged terrain with excellent views for an unusually large portion of the way. The ledges are slippery when wet. Shorter trips can be made to the first view ledge on either the Welch side or the Dickey side. See Welch–Dickey Loop Trail, p. 331.

MT. OSCEOLA

	⇅	↗	⟳
RT via Mt. Osceola Trail	5.8 mi.	2,050 ft.	3:55

This high peak with fine views can be ascended fairly easily from the high point on Tripoli Rd., although the footing is rough in places. See Mt. Osceola Trail, p. 339.

WATERVILLE VALLEY POINTS OF INTEREST

	⇅	↗	⟳
RT to Cascades via Cascade Path (see p. 333)	3.4 mi.	800 ft.	2:05
RT to Scaur (a ledgy outlook) via Livermore Trail and Kettles Path (to begin, see Livermore Trail, p. 343)	4.0 mi.	650 ft.	2:20
RT to Scaur and Waterville Flume via Livermore Trail, Kettles Path, and Irene's Path (see p. 343)	6.2 mi.	1,250 ft.	3:45
RT to Davis Boulders (large glacial erratics) and Goodrich Rock via Livermore, Greeley Ponds, and Goodrich Rock trails (see p. 343)	4.0 mi.	750 ft.	2:25
RT to Greeley Brook upper valley viewpoints via Livermore, Greeley Ponds, and Timber Camp trails (see p. 343)	5.8 mi.	950 ft.	3:25

A variety of interesting objectives can be reached via the fine network of trails in Waterville Valley.

SEC 7

FLAT MTN. POND

	🔁	🡕	⏱
RT via Flat Mtn. Pond and Bennett St. trails	9.0 mi.	1,250 ft.	5:10
RT via Flat Mtn. Pond Trail from Whiteface Intervale Rd.	8.4 mi.	1,550 ft.	5:00

This beautiful, remote pond in the Sandwich Range Wilderness can be reached from the Bennett St. trailhead or from the Whiteface Intervale Rd. trailhead. To begin either, see Flat Mtn. Pond Trail, p. 354. Add 2.2 mi. and 100 ft. round trip for a traverse along the western shore.

■ Strenuous Hikes

JENNINGS PEAK

	🔁	🡕	⏱
LP to Jennings Peak via Sandwich Mtn. Trail, Jennings Peak spur, and Drakes Brook Trail	6.5 mi.	2,150 ft.	4:20
LP to Jennings Peak and Sandwich Mtn. via Sandwich Mtn. Trail, Jennings Peak spur, and Drakes Brook Trail	8.7 mi.	2,850 ft.	5:45

This rocky spur of Sandwich Mtn. delivers fine views. The partly open summit of Sandwich Mtn. proper can also be included in this trip. To begin, see Sandwich Mtn. Trail, p. 349.

SEC 7

SANDWICH MTN.

	🔁	🡕	⏱
RT via Algonquin Trail	9.0 mi	2,850 ft.	5:55

A rugged and very scenic route leads directly to the summit from the south, via the trailhead on rough Sandwich Notch Rd. See Algonquin Trail, p. 356.

TRIPYRAMID SLIDES

	🔁	🡕	⏱
LP via Livermore and Mt. Tripyramid trails	11.0 mi.	3,000 ft.	7:00
LP via Livermore, Scaur Ridge, Pine Bend Brook, and Mt. Tripyramid trails	12.0 mi.	3,000 ft.	7:30

The first route makes for one of the most challenging and scenic trips in the White Mountains. The second avoids the steep slabs of the North Slide, as when wet or icy. To begin both, see Livermore Trail, p. 343.

TRAIL DESCRIPTIONS

MT. TECUMSEH AND VICINITY

MT. TECUMSEH TRAIL (WMNF; MAP 3: J6)

Cumulative from Mt. Tecumseh Ski Area parking lot (1,840 ft.) to:	⇅	↗	↻
Mt. Tecumseh summit (4,003 ft.)	2.5 mi.	2,200 ft. (rev. 50 ft.)	2:20
Tripoli Rd. (1,880 ft.)	5.6 mi.	2,400 ft. (rev. 2,300 ft.)	4:00

This trail ascends Mt. Tecumseh, starting at Waterville Valley Ski Area at the top right (northwest) edge of the ski area parking loop road, across from lot 1. The trail climbs the east slope of Mt. Tecumseh then descends the northwest ridge to a parking area just off Tripoli Rd. (FR 30), 5.5 mi. east of I-93 (Exit 31, northbound ramp) and 1.2 mi. west of the Mt. Osceola Trail parking area.

Starting at a trail sign at the edge of the ski area parking lot, the trail crosses a small brook and follows a relocation to the left on the south side of Tecumseh Brook, where the trail was washed out by Tropical Storm Irene in 2011. At 0.3 mi. the trail crosses the brook and follows a section of trail along a small ridge above the north side. At 1.1 mi., the trail drops and recrosses the brook then climbs by switchbacks to intersect the former route, an old logging road, about 20 yd. from the edge of the ski slope; good views can be obtained by following the old trail left to the edge of the open slope. The main trail turns right and follows the rocky old road, with many volunteer-built rock steps and drainages, angling upward along the south side of the Tecumseh Brook valley and passing two more paths leading to the ski slopes. It then climbs steadily to the main ridge crest south of Mt. Tecumseh, where the trail turns right in a flat area. Here, at 2.2 mi., Sosman Trail enters from the left, from the top of the ski area.

In another 120 yd., Sosman Trail forks left to ascend the summit from the west. Mt. Tecumseh Trail swings right, descends slightly to circle the base of the steep cone (passing a restricted view of Sandwich Mtn.), and finally climbs steeply to reach the summit from the north at 2.5 mi. The summit offers open views to the east. Care must be taken to follow the correct trail for the descent; new signage has improved the situation. Mt. Tecumseh Trail leaves north for the ski area and west-northwest for Tripoli Rd., whereas Sosman Trail runs almost due south along the ridge crest then turns sharply right (west) off the ridge and descends.

SEC 7

From the summit of Mt. Tecumseh, Mt. Tecumseh Trail descends briefly west then swings northwest past a restricted but interesting north outlook and descends steeply then moderately to a broad saddle. The trail ascends to the summit of the west ridge at 3.2 mi. and passes over three knobs; on the third, westernmost knob a side path leads left 30 yd. to a restricted view of Mt. Moosilauke from a blowdown patch. The trail then descends steadily to another saddle at 4.2 mi. Here, the trail turns right at a cairn and angles down the north slope of the ridge on an old logging road. Near the bottom of the slope, the trail swings left then right, crosses a tributary brook and then Eastman Brook (difficult at high water), and ends at the parking area off Tripoli Rd.

SOSMAN TRAIL (WVAIA; MAP 3: J6)

Cumulative from summit of Mt. Tecumseh (4,003 ft.) to:	⇅	↗	↻
Top of ski area (3,850 ft.)	0.8 mi.	100 ft. (rev. 250 ft.)	0:25
Ski area base lodge (1,840 ft.) via ski trails	2.6 mi.	100 ft. (rev. 2,000 ft.)	1:20

This trail connects the summit of Mt. Tecumseh with the top of the ski slopes. Sosman Trail is easy to follow from the summit of Mt. Tecumseh to the top of the slopes, but in the reverse direction, it can be difficult to find the beginning of the trail at the top of the slopes. The trail leaves the summit of Mt. Tecumseh along the ridge to the south (sign), soon passes a side path leading 70 yd. left to a south outlook, then turns to the west and switchbacks with rough footing down the slope and around the rocky nose of the ridge, with restricted views to the west. The trail turns to the right onto Mt. Tecumseh Trail at 0.2 mi.; then, after 120 yd., Sosman Trail diverges right and follows the ridge south. At 0.4 mi., the trail climbs a rocky hump with an interesting view of Mt. Tecumseh's summit cone. Just beyond is an outlook west, on the right; in another 10 yd. on the left are a bench and a restricted view northeast.

The trail runs south nearly level along the ridge, bearing left at 0.8 mi. and emerging beneath a transmission tower. Here, with an obscure footway, the trail bears left then right, coming out at the top of a chairlift. From the clearing next to the tower, you can follow a grassy road 100 yd. south then east to the top of the ski slopes. From either point, depending on the route chosen, ski trails lead about 1.5 to 2.0 mi. to the base lodge. To find the trail at the top of the ski area, where there is no sign, it is easiest to follow the grassy road to the transmission tower; the trail enters the woods to the right of the tower.

WELCH–DICKEY LOOP TRAIL (WVAIA; MAP 3: K5)

From Orris Rd. parking area (1,060 ft.) to:	⇅	↗	↻
Welch Mtn. summit (2,605 ft.) via Welch branch	1.9 mi.	1,550 ft.	1:45
Dickey Mtn. summit (2,734 ft.) via Dickey branch	2.1 mi.	1,650 ft.	1:55
Complete loop	4.4 mi.	1,800 ft.	3:05

This loop trail affords excellent views for a modest effort, with nearly 2 mi. of open ledge walking at relatively low elevations. On the south ledges of Welch Mtn., the trail runs through one of the few stands of jack pine *(Pinus banksiana)* that occur in New Hampshire; this tree commonly is found much farther north and benefits from fires because it releases its seeds most readily after its cones have been scorched. The section of trail that ascends Welch Mtn. is often one of the first to be clear of snow in spring. Some of the ledges, however, provide mildly challenging rock scrambles and may be very slippery when wet and dangerous in icy conditions, so they must be ascended with caution. Follow the yellow blazes carefully on the open ledge sections. From NH 49, 4.5 mi. from its jct. with NH 175, turn left onto Upper Mad River Rd., which runs northwest across the Mad River. In 0.7 mi., turn right onto Orris Rd. (sign) and follow this road for 0.6 mi. then take either of two short forks to the right into a large parking area, where the trail begins.

SEC
7

In 15 yd. from the parking area, the trail forks. This description follows the counterclockwise direction, first taking the right-hand fork leading toward Welch Mtn.; the ledges are steeper on this side and easier to ascend than descend for most hikers. This branch soon crosses a brook and follows its east side up the valley, between the south ridges of Welch Mtn. and Dickey Mtn. At 0.9 mi. it turns sharply right and angles up southeastward to reach the large, flat, open ledges on the south ridge of Welch Mtn. at 1.3 mi. On these ledges, hikers should avoid walking in delineated revegetation areas. You have fine views east across the valley to Mt. Tripyramid and Sandwich Mtn. and its rocky Acteon Ridge. The trail turns sharply left (north) on the ledges, and after a brief level traverse, it climbs, steeply at times, over open ledges interspersed with jack pines, spruces, and dwarf birches, traversing a side-sloping ledge followed by a climb up a large exposed slab. After several short scrambles and a passage through a rocky cleft in the woods, it continues up more ledges to the open summit of Welch Mtn. at 1.9 mi., with views in all directions.

From here, the loop drops steeply to a wooded notch (use caution, staying left of the top of the cliff) then rises steeply, skirting to the left around a high rock slab. Approaching the summit of Dickey Mtn., an obscure branch route intermittently marked with cairns, leads right 0.2 mi. over ledges to a fine north outlook from a large open ledge. The main loop continues over the partly open summit of Dickey at 2.4 mi. and descends a ledgy ridge to the southwest, soon angling down a large open slab that is often wet. The trail continues down alternately over ledges and through patches of scrub (follow markings carefully, especially where the trail turns left at a large cairn and climbs to a higher ledge), entering the woods to stay after descending along the upper edge of a particularly interesting ledge with an impressive dropoff at 3.2 mi. The trail drops over a ledge step and turns left along the base of a ledgy wall then descends steadily through oak woods. At 4.3 mi., the trail turns left onto a logging road (to the right, Brown Ash Swamp mountain bike trail leads 1.7 mi. through Dickey Notch to FR 23C, passing several small beaver ponds about halfway along) and soon reaches the loop jct. and the parking lot.

NEAR WATERVILLE VALLEY

TIMBER CAMP TRAIL (WVAIA; MAP 3: J6)

Cumulative from Greeley Ponds Trail (2,030 ft.) to:	↑↓	↗	○
Gravel bank (2,380 ft.)	0.6 mi.	350 ft.	0:30
End of maintained trail (2,540 ft.)	0.9 mi.	500 ft.	0:40

This trail leaves the west side of the relocated Greeley Ponds Trail, 1.7 mi. north of Livermore Trail, and follows old logging roads into the high basin of Greeley Brook on the east side of Mt. Osceola. Two open areas at the upper end of the trail offer interesting views.

Timber Camp Trail diverges left from Greeley Ponds Trail at a fork where Greeley Ponds Trail continues ahead. The trail climbs to a hairpin turn left (south) then loops back to the northwest. At 0.6 mi., it turns left along the base of a gravel bank, which provides views of Mt. Tripyramid, Mt. Kancamagus, and the Painted Cliff of Mt. Osceola. The trail continues up the logging road, with the footway becoming wet in places. After crossing two small brooks, it emerges in a stony clearing with a large cairn and more views, where the maintained trail ends; an unofficial path continues ahead up the valley, eventually swinging left to a limited viewpoint.

GOODRICH ROCK TRAIL (WVAIA; MAP 3: J6)

From Greeley Ponds Trail (1,700 ft.) to:	⬍	↗	◷
Goodrich Rock (2,325 ft.)	0.8 mi.	600 ft.	0:40

This trail leads from the west side of Greeley Ponds Trail, 0.9 mi. north of Livermore Trail, to the Davis Boulders and Goodrich Rock (one of the largest glacial erratics in New Hampshire) on a shoulder of East Osceola. Leaving Greeley Ponds Trail, Goodrich Rock Trail climbs steadily for 0.3 mi. on an old logging road then swings left and meanders to the first boulders. The trail turns left across a small streambed and passes through a split boulder and a boulder cave. Beyond the boulders, the trail bears left across a flat area then slabs easily before a short, rough pitch leads to the base of Goodrich Rock. Yellow blazes lead around the left side of the immense boulder and up to its back side, where a 20-ft. ladder provides access to the boulder's flat top and a view across the valley to Sandwich Mtn. Use great caution ascending and descending the ladder.

NORWAY RAPIDS TRAIL (WVAIA; MAP 3: J7)

Cumulative from Cascade Path (1,710 ft.) to:	⬍	↗	◷
Norway Rapids (1,760 ft.)	0.4 mi.	100 ft. (rev. 50 ft.)	0:15
Livermore Trail (1,780 ft.)	0.5 mi.	100 ft.	0:20

This short trail links Cascade Path with Livermore Trail, providing access to Norway Rapids, a scenic ledgy area on Slide Brook. Coinciding at first with the wide Snows Mtn. Ski Trail, Norway Rapids Trail leaves Cascade Path on the left, 1.2 mi. from the Snows Mtn. Ski Area parking lot, and crosses Cascade Brook on a bridge. In 60 yd., Norway Rapids Trail turns left off the ski trail, meanders up and across a plateau, and descends slightly to Norway Rapids at 0.4 mi. (difficult crossing at high water). On the far side of the brook, the trail turns sharply left along the bank then swings right and climbs gently to Livermore Trail, 1.8 mi. from the Livermore Rd. parking area.

CASCADE PATH (WVAIA; MAP 3: J6–J7)

Cumulative from Snows Mtn. Ski Area parking lot (1,540 ft.) to:	⬍	↗	◷
First cascade (1,780 ft.)	1.4 mi.	450 ft. (rev. 200 ft.)	0:55
Service road (1,940 ft.)	1.7 mi.	600 ft.	1:10

SEC 7

This trail provides easy access to a series of scenic waterfalls on Cascade Brook. The trail leaves the northeast corner of the large parking lot at the base of the Snows Mtn. Ski Area, located off Boulder Path Rd. just north of its jct. with West Branch Rd. by the Osceola Library.

From the parking area, the trail crosses Cascade Ridge Rd. (trail sign) and swings right, passing residences along the road, then continues up an old ski trail, passing the jct. with Boulder Path on the left at 0.2 mi. Here, Cascade Path bears right at a fence, soon crosses Cascade Ridge Rd., and then climbs up the continuation of the ski trail. At 0.3 mi., Cascade Path bears left off the ski trail at a sign, enters the woods, and ascends gently, crossing a cross-country ski trail in 75 yd. and passing the jct. with Elephant Rock Trail on the right at 0.5 mi. Cascade Path continues nearly level then descends along the lower slopes of Snows Mtn.

At 1.2 mi., the trail approaches Cascade Brook and turns right on a wide ski trail. (In the reverse direction, turn left off the ski trail at a signpost just beyond a bridge over a small brook.) In 70 yd., the ski trail and Norway Rapids Trail turn left across a bridge over Cascade Brook. Cascade Path continues up the west bank of the brook, climbing easily to the base of the first cascade at 1.4 mi. The main trail turns left here, crosses the brook (difficult in high water), and climbs along the east bank, passing several more cascades and pools before ending at the gravel Snows Mtn. service road (Upper Snows Mtn. Ski Trail [X-C]) at 1.7 mi. From the base of the first cascade, an alternate path (sign: Westside) continues 0.3 mi. up the west bank of the brook to the service road; both paths provide fine views of the cascades. From the top of Cascade Path, the service road can be followed left 0.6 mi. to Livermore Trail (2.2 mi. from the Livermore Rd. parking area), or right 0.5 mi. to a short connector to Snows Mtn. Trail on the left and another 0.3 mi. to the top of the Snows Mtn. ski lift, making possible loop hikes with other WVAIA trails.

BOULDER PATH (WVAIA; MAP 3: J6)

From Livermore Trail (1,580 ft.) to:	⇅	↗	○
Cascade Path (1,670 ft.)	0.7 mi.	150 ft. (rev. 50 ft.)	0:25

This trail leaves Livermore Trail on the right, 0.6 mi. from the Livermore Rd. parking area, and runs 70 yd. to a crossing of Slide Brook (difficult at high water) just downstream from a huge boulder. After crossing the brook, Boulder Path turns left and follows an old road along the brook for 0.1 mi. then turns right off the road (sign) and ascends moderately. At 0.3 mi. the trail turns right onto the wide Lower Snows Mtn. Ski Trail

(X-C), rises slightly, and descends gradually. At 0.6 mi., the trail leaves the WMNF (sign), crosses a private driveway, swings left, and continues to Cascade Path, 0.2 mi. above the Snows Mtn. Ski Area parking lot.

BIG PINES PATH (WVAIA; MAP 3: J6)

From Livermore Trail (1,620 ft.) to:	⬆⬇	↗	⏱
Big Pines (1,580 ft.)	0.2 mi.	0 ft. (rev. 50 ft.)	0:05

This short path leads to a stand of impressive white pines near the bank of the Mad River. The path leaves Livermore Trail 0.7 mi. from the parking area, runs nearly level for 100 yd., descends a steep pitch, and continues at easy grades, with a short final descent to the pines.

ELEPHANT ROCK TRAIL (WVAIA; MAP 3: J6–J7)

From Cascade Path (1,840 ft.) to:	⬆⬇	↗	⏱
Top of ski area (2,100 ft.)	0.4 mi.	250 ft.	0:20

This short trail links Cascade Path with the top of Snows Mtn. Ski Area and Greeley Ledge Trail. Elephant Rock Trail leaves Cascade Path on the right, 0.5 mi. from the Snows Mtn. Ski Area parking lot. In 100 yd., the trail passes Elephant Rock, a large boulder; the tree that formed the elephant's trunk is no longer present. The trail rises moderately, emerging near the top of the Beanbender ski slope. Walk left 100 yd. up the slope to reach the top of the lift (views of Mt. Osceola and Mt. Tecumseh) and Greeley Ledge Trail.

GREELEY LEDGE TRAIL (WVAIA; MAP 3: J7)

From Snows Mtn. hiking trail (1,950 ft.) to:	⬆⬇	↗	⏱
Top of ski area (2,100 ft.)	0.2 mi.	150 ft.	0:15

This short trail connects the Snows Mtn. hiking trail with the top of Snows Mtn. Ski Area. Greeley Ledge Trail leaves the north loop of the Snows Mtn. hiking trail on the left, 0.7 mi. from the parking area at the base of the ski slopes. The trail ascends through hardwoods then climbs into a rocky area of spruces. After passing viewless Greeley Ledge on the left, the trail rises a short distance to the top of the ski area behind the chairlift; from the top of the slopes there are views of Mt. Osceola and Mt. Tecumseh.

SEC 7

KETTLES PATH (WVAIA; MAP 3: J6-J7)

From Livermore Trail (1,640 ft.) to:	⇅	↗	⟳
The Scaur (2,230 ft.)	1.1 mi.	600 ft.	0:50

This trail leads from Livermore Trail, 0.9 mi. from the Livermore Rd. parking area, to the ledgy viewpoint known as the Scaur and provides access to the Waterville Flume on Flume Brook via Irene's Path. Kettles Path leaves the north side of Livermore Trail and runs nearly level for more than 0.1 mi. then follows a relocation to the right, ascending to the Kettles, seen on both sides of the trail at 0.4 mi. A third Kettle is seen on the right at 0.5 mi. The Kettles are dry, bowl-shaped hollows in the woods created at the end of the last ice age. Meltwater debris accumulated around ice blocks left by the retreating glacier; after the ice chunks melted, their kettle-shaped depressions remained. This type of formation is unusual in the White Mountains.

Beyond the Kettles, the trail climbs easily to a right turn at 0.9 mi. (the former jct. with Scaur Trail; the section of Scaur Trail that descended to the left to Greeley Ponds Trail has been closed). Now following the former upper section of Scaur Trail, Kettles Path climbs moderately to the east then swings south on a steep ascent up the back side of the knob known as the Scaur. At 1.1 mi. Irene's Path diverges left along the base of a rock face. Here Kettles Path bears right (sign: The Scaur) and climbs steeply through a ledgy slot to the open, south-facing outlook at the Scaur.

IRENE'S PATH (WVAIA; MAP 3: J7)

From Kettles Path (2,180 ft.) to:	⇅	↗	⟳
Waterville Flume (2,500 ft.)	1.1 mi.	450 ft. (rev. 150 ft.)	0:45

This new path was constructed in 2014 to replace Flume Brook Trail, which was severely washed out by Tropical Storm Irene in 2011 and permanently closed. It is part of the shortest route to the Waterville Flume. It diverges left from Kettles Path 1.1 mi. from Livermore Trail, runs alongside a rock face, and soon passes a ledge on the right with a view of Mt. Tecumseh and then passes a large prowlike rock on the left. It angles up to the crest of the ridge leading east from the Scaur and ascends at easy to moderate grades, keeping mostly to the south side of the ridge. At 0.6 mi. it angles left to the north side and descends into the valley of Flume Brook, gently at first then rather steeply by switchbacks on a well-constructed footway, passing an outlook with an interesting view of Mt. Osceola and Mad River Notch at 0.7 mi. It descends for another 0.1 mi. then ascends gradually to a junction with Old Skidder Path on the right at 1.0 mi. Irene's Path bears left here and, following a remaining short section of Flume Brook Trail, ascends 0.1 mi. to the base of the Flume. With a short climb up rocks, you can obtain a view of the Flume's rock walls and cascade. The former footway that continued up through the Flume along the right side was destroyed by the storm.

FLUME BROOK TRAIL

This trail was severely damaged by the 2011 storm and has been closed by the WMNF. The Waterville Flume is now most easily accessed via Livermore Trail, Kettles Path, and Irene's Path.

OLD SKIDDER TRAIL (WVAIA; MAP 3: J7)

From Irene's Path (2,400 ft.) to:	Distance	Elevation gain	Time
Livermore Trail (2,820 ft.)	0.8 mi.	400 ft.	0:35

This lightly used trail links Irene's Path, 0.1 mi. below the Flume, with Livermore Trail, 4.6 mi. from that trail's southern terminus at the Livermore Rd. parking area. Old Skidder Trail is narrow and may be overgrown in places, although the footway is well worn. This trail makes possible a pleasant 8.6-mi. loop hike in combination with Livermore Trail, Kettles Path, and Irene's Path, including the Scaur and the Waterville Flume. Leaving Irene's Path, Old Skidder Trail runs across a ferny clearing and climbs moderately northeast, following an old road across the steep slope above Flume Brook. The trail passes under a rock face and levels off at 0.2 mi., after providing a glimpse of Mt. Osceola. At 0.5 mi., at the end of a long straightaway, the trail turns right off the road (blazes) and makes a winding climb southeast through an area where the trail must be followed with care. The trail passes over a knoll carpeted with birch and ferns then swings east to Livermore Trail. Turn right for the Livermore Rd. parking area.

FLETCHER CASCADES TRAIL (WVAIA; MAP 3: J6–J7)

From Drakes Brook Trail (1,540 ft.) to:	Distance	Elevation gain	Time
Upper cascades (2,250 ft.)	1.2 mi.	700 ft.	0:55

This trail leads from Drakes Brook Trail, 0.4 mi. from the parking area off NH 49, to Fletcher Cascades, a series of waterfalls on the lower slope of Flat Mtn. Fletcher Cascade Trail bears left on a logging road (a ski trail in winter) where Drakes Brook Trail bears right off the road to cross Drakes Brook. Fletcher Cascade Trail follows the road for 100 yd. then turns right into the woods at a sign. The trail climbs easily along the north side of Drakes Brook, entering the Sandwich Range Wilderness. At 0.8 mi., the trail crosses the north fork of Drakes Brook and climbs steadily past some large hemlocks to the lower cascades at 1.1 mi. Above here, the trail becomes steep and rough, climbing another 0.1 mi. to the upper cascades. At the top of the climb, it turns left across the base of a lesser cascade (arrow) and continues a short distance to the base of the main upper cascade.

SNOWS MTN. TRAIL (WVAIA; MAP 3: J6–J7)

Cumulative from Snows Mtn. Ski Area parking lot (1,540 ft.) to:	⬆⬇	↗	⏱
Snows Mtn. viewpoint spur (2,780 ft.)	2.0 mi.	1,250 ft.	1:40
Complete loop, including spur	4.1 mi.	1,250 ft.	2:40

This loop trail follows the route of the former Woodbury Trail to the shoulder of Snows Mtn., ascends the ridge to a viewpoint spur path, and descends the west slope of the mountain. Snows Mtn. Trail is lightly used and in places requires care to follow, although it is well blazed in yellow.

The north end of the loop trail begins at the south end of a large parking lot at the base of the Snows Mtn. Ski Area, located off Boulder Path Rd. just north of its jct. with West Branch Rd., by the Osceola Library. Climb up along the left (north) side of the ski trail then angle up to the right beneath the chairlift. At 0.3 mi., the trail turns right into the woods at a sign and climbs for another 0.3 mi. then levels off. At 0.7 mi., Greeley Ledge Trail leaves left. At 1.0 mi., a short connecting path diverges left to Upper Snows Mtn. Ski Trail (X-C), and an unmaintained path diverges right. The hiking trail (sign) continues ahead on an easy traverse. At 1.2 mi., Snows Mtn. Trail reaches the end of the old Woodbury Trail section and turns right at a cairn, climbing steadily up the side of the ridge. Snows Mtn. Trail then ascends southeast along the ridge, winding back and forth across the crest. After a slight dip through a col with some large yellow birches, the trail climbs steadily to a jct. at a high point on the ridge, reached at 2.0 mi. Here, a side trail leads left 0.1 mi. to a ledge with a restricted view south to Sandwich Mtn.

From the jct., the south loop of Snows Mtn. Trail turns sharply right and descends, soon turning right again and passing a short side path left to a cleared southwest viewpoint at 2.1 mi. The trail drops steeply for a short distance then follows an old logging road along the mountain's west slope. Bearing left off the road, the trail descends through hardwood forest with many twists and turns, crossing an unmaintained path at 2.8 mi. The trail crosses a small brook, and at 3.5 mi., emerges at the driveway at 76 Snows

Mtn. Rd. Follow the road downhill for 0.3 mi. then turn right onto a paved path that leads 0.1 mi. north between tennis courts to the base of the chair-lift and the parking area beyond. (If ascending the south loop, the trail enters the woods at a blaze at the upper end of the driveway at 76 Snows Mtn. Rd., located at a sharp left curve. Hikers should park in the designated area at the base of the ski slopes and walk up the road.)

MT. OSCEOLA AND SCAR RIDGE

MT. OSCEOLA TRAIL (WMNF; MAP 3: J6–I6)

Cumulative from Tripoli Rd. (2,280 ft.) to:	⇅	↗	↻
Mt. Osceola summit (4,340 ft.)	2.9 mi.	2,050 ft.	2:30
Mt. Osceola, East Peak (4,156 ft.)	3.9 mi.	2,400 ft. (rev. 550 ft.)	3:10
Greeley Ponds Trail (2,300 ft.)	5.4 mi.	2,400 ft. (rev. 1,850 ft.)	3:55

This trail begins at a parking area on Tripoli Rd. (FR 30) near the height-of-land in Thornton Gap, 6.7 mi. from I-93 (Exit 31, northbound ramp) and 2.9 mi. from the Livermore Rd. parking area on West Branch Rd. The trail climbs over Mt. Osceola and East Osceola and descends to Greeley Ponds Trail at the height-of-land in Mad River Notch, 1.3 mi. south of the Kancamagus Highway. The trail from Thornton Gap to the summit of Mt. Osceola has easy to moderate grades, although the footing is rough in some places. The section between East Osceola and Greeley Ponds Trail is very steep and rough. This section may require considerable extra time, both ascending and descending.

The trail leaves Tripoli Rd. and climbs moderately with rocky footing, going east across the south slope of Breadtray Ridge and crossing several small brooks. At 1.2 mi., the trail begins to climb by switchbacks toward the ridge top, and the footing improves, although there are still occasional rough sections. At 2.1 mi., the trail swings right across a small brook (unreliable). The trail resumes its switchbacks, crossing numerous angled slabs that may be icy in cold seasons and passing a view southwest. It gains the summit ridge and turns right, and soon crosses a ledge at 2.9 mi. at the site of an older fire tower site (probably the true summit); here, a side path leads 20 yd. left to a ledge with a good view north. In another 50 yd., the trail reaches the large, open, east-facing ledge at the more recent fire tower site, with excellent views. The trail then turns left and descends from the summit, alternating easy stretches with steep, rocky descents.

Just before reaching the main col between Mt. Osceola and East Osceola, the trail descends a steep chimney (easier to climb than descend), which can

SEC
7

be avoided by a somewhat less difficult but still tricky detour to the left (north). (Just above the chimney is a view of East Osceola.) The trail crosses the col at 3.5 mi. and climbs moderately with steep pitches past a fine outlook on the left at 3.7 mi., reaching the wooded summit of East Osceola (marked by a small cairn) at 3.9 mi. Just beyond the summit there is a view east from a side path 15 yd. to the right. The trail then crosses a lower knob and descends steeply then moderately to a shoulder. At the top of a gully is an outlook west 25 yd. to the left on a side path. The main trail turns right and descends the steep, loose, washed-out gully then goes diagonally down and across a small, ledgy slide with good views (use caution). The trail continues to descend very steeply with rough footing past a sloping rock face, where it turns left. At 4.6 mi., the trail turns sharply left, with an abandoned route of the trail straight ahead, and descends moderately under the impressive cliffs of Mt. Osceola's north spur to Greeley Ponds Trail.

GREELEY PONDS TRAIL (WMNF; MAP 3: J6–I6)

Cumulative from Livermore Trail (1,580 ft.) to:	⇅	↗	⟳
Timber Camp Trail (2,030 ft.)	1.7 mi.	450 ft.	1:05
Lower Greeley Pond (2,180 ft.)	3.1 mi.	800 ft. (rev. 200 ft.)	1:55
Mt. Osceola Trail (2,300 ft.)	4.0 mi.	900 ft.	2:25
Kancamagus Highway (1,940 ft.)	5.3 mi.	900 ft. (rev. 350 ft.)	3:05

Note: The southern half of this trail was severely damaged by the 2011 storm, and several sections were relocated and reopened in 2014. The relocations have lengthened the trail by 0.2 mi.

This trail diverges from Livermore Trail 0.3 mi. from the parking area on Livermore Rd. (FR 53), leads past the Greeley Ponds and through Mad River Notch, and ends at a small parking area on the Kancamagus Highway (NH 112), 4.5 mi. east of the Lincoln Woods parking lot and 0.9 mi. west of the Hancock Overlook. (Note that there is a pull-off for the Greeley Ponds Ski Trail [X-C]—not suitable for summer hiking—0.3 mi. west of the hiking trailhead.) Near the ponds, the trail is crossed several times by a ski-touring trail marked with blue diamonds; the hiking trail is marked with yellow blazes. Grades are mostly easy, and the ponds are beautiful. Camping is not allowed within the Greeley Ponds Scenic Area.

The trail leaves Livermore Trail sharply left, just after the first bridge beyond the Depot Camp clearing, and follows a new gravel road and then two relocated sections. It rejoins the original route and passes Goodrich Rock Trail on the left at 0.9 mi. At 1.0 mi. it turns left on an old logging road, formerly the lower part of Timber Camp Trail. It ascends north along the road at easy grades, high above the river. At 1.7 mi. Timber Camp Trail diverges left and Greeley Ponds Trail continues ahead on a wide relocated section. As it approaches Greeley Brook, the trail turns sharply right and descends steadily to the Mad River, which it crosses on a new bridge at 2.2 mi. It turns left at a junction where Kancamagus Brook Ski Trail (not maintained for hiking) diverges right (south) downstream. Greeley Ponds Trail follows another wide relocation up and down the slope on the east side of the river then rejoins the original route at 2.6 mi., soon narrows to a footpath, and enters the Greeley Ponds Scenic Area at 2.8 mi. It soon turns left to cross the Mad River (no bridge); here, a well-beaten path (ski-touring trail) continues straight for 0.2 mi. to a fine viewpoint on the southeast shore of the lower pond.

The main trail reaches the southwest corner of the lower Greeley Pond at 3.1 mi., passes another viewpoint at the northwest corner on the right (reached by a side path 30 yd. long) at 3.3 mi., and climbs easily past two ski trail jcts. on the right to the upper pond at 3.6 mi. Here an unmarked path on the right crosses the upper pond outlet brook and continues 100 yd. to a fine view of East Osceola from a clearing on the shore. The main trail runs along a bank above the upper pond, passing a side path descending steeply right to the northwest shore. The trail soon crosses a bog bridge over the headwater of Mad River and passes a ski trail jct. on the right. It then ascends easily to Mad River Notch, bearing right where the ski trail diverges left, and meeting Mt. Osceola Trail on the left at the height-of-land at 4.0 mi. Leaving the Scenic Area, Greeley Ponds Trail descends easily on an old logging road, bears right off the road at 4.4 mi., and continues down at easy grades but with fairly rough footing and many bog bridges. At 5.0 mi., the trail crosses two branches of the South Fork of Hancock Branch (no bridges) and ends at the parking area off the Kancamagus Highway.

EAST POND TRAIL (WMNF; MAP 3: J5–I6)

Cumulative from parking area off Tripoli Rd. (1,800 ft.) to:	⬆️⬇️	📈	🕐
East Pond (2,600 ft.)	1.3 mi.	800 ft.	1:05
Height-of-land (3,100 ft.)	2.1 mi.	1,300 ft.	1:40
Kancamagus Highway (1,760 ft.)	5.0 mi.	1,300 ft. (rev. 1,350 ft.)	3:10

This trail passes scenic East Pond and climbs over the notch between Mt. Osceola and Scar Ridge. The southern trailhead is at a parking lot about 100 yd. up a gravel side road that leaves Tripoli Rd. (FR 30) 5.2 mi. east of I-93 (Exit 31, northbound ramp). The northern trailhead is at a

SEC
7

parking area off the Kancamagus Highway by the bridge over the Hancock Branch, 3.7 mi. east of the Lincoln Woods parking lot.

From the southern trailhead, the trail follows the gravel road past boulders and continues straight into the woods where the gravel road swings right into a brushy clearing. Just beyond, at 0.3 mi., near the site of the old Tripoli Mill (in the woods to the right), Little East Pond Trail turns left on an old railroad grade, whereas East Pond Trail continues ahead on a logging road. At 0.7 mi., East Pond Trail bears right and then left to cross East Pond Brook on a snowmobile bridge and climbs steadily. At 1.3 mi., near the point where East Pond Loop leaves left for Little East Pond, a side path leads right 40 yd. to the south shore of East Pond.

The main trail runs behind the west shore then swings to the left, away from the pond, and climbs moderately on old logging roads to the height-of-land at 2.1 mi. From here, it steadily on old logging roads, crossing Cheney Brook at 3.1 mi. and Pine Brook at 4.2 mi. Just after the latter crossing (which may be difficult at high water), the trail reaches an old logging railroad spur and follows it almost all the way to the parking area off the Kancamagus Highway.

LITTLE EAST POND TRAIL (WMNF; MAP 3: J6–I5)

From East Pond Trail (1,980 ft.) to:	⇅	↗	⟳
Little East Pond (2,596 ft.)	1.7 mi.	600 ft.	1:10

This trail, with mostly good footing, leaves East Pond Trail left (northwest) 0.3 mi. from Tripoli Rd. and follows an old railroad grade slightly uphill, soon crossing East Pond Brook. It passes through fine hardwood forest, crossing three small brooks and then Clear Brook in a small ravine at 0.7 mi. Soon the trail bears right from the end of the railroad grade and climbs moderately, swinging to the north. At 1.7 mi. it meets East Pond Loop, which diverges right where a spur path leads 25 yd. ahead to the south shore of Little East Pond; here you have a view up to Scar Ridge.

EAST POND LOOP (WMNF; MAP 3: I6–I5)

From East Pond Trail (2,600 ft.) to:	⇅	↗	⟳
Little East Pond Trail (2,596 ft.)	1.5 mi.	200 ft. (rev. 200 ft.)	0:50
From parking area off Tripoli Rd. (1,800 ft.) for:			
Complete loop to both ponds	4.8 mi.	1,000 ft.	2:55

This trail runs between East Pond and Little East Pond, going up and down over two minor ridges at easy grades and making possible a loop trip that visits both ponds. From East Pond Trail it climbs gradually across a ridge and descends to cross a dry brook bed at 0.6 mi. It climbs again, contours with minor ups and downs, swings right (northwest) around another ridge, and descends to meet Little East Pond Trail behind the south shore of Little East Pond, which is reached by a spur path leading 25 yd. to the right.

MT. TRIPYRAMID

LIVERMORE TRAIL (WMNF; MAP 3: J6–I7)

Cumulative from Livermore Rd. parking area (1,580 ft.) to:	⇅	↗	○
South end, Mt. Tripyramid Trail (2,000 ft.)	2.6 mi.	400 ft.	1:30
North end, Mt. Tripyramid Trail (2,400 ft.)	3.6 mi.	800 ft.	2:10
Livermore Pass (2,900 ft.)	5.6 mi.	1,300 ft.	3:25
Kancamagus Highway (2,060 ft.)	7.7 mi.	1,300 ft. (rev. 850 ft.)	4:30

Note: Some sections of this trail were severely eroded by the 2011 storm; several of these were repaired by the USFS in 2014.

This trail, which provides access to numerous other trails in the Waterville valley backcountry, begins at a large parking area at the beginning of Livermore Rd. near Waterville Valley and climbs through Livermore Pass (2,900 ft.) to the Kancamagus Highway across from Lily Pond, 2.7 mi. east of Kancamagus Pass; there is roadside parking on both sides of the road. Livermore Trail once connected Waterville Valley to the Sawyer River logging railroad, which led to the now deserted village of Livermore on the Sawyer River. (The present Sawyer River Trail was a part of this Waterville–Livermore route.) Livermore Trail consists of logging roads of various ages and conditions; the part through Livermore Pass is muddy and can be difficult to follow. The gravel-surface southern section, from Tripoli Rd. to Flume Brook Camp, is also called Livermore Rd. (FR 53); it is closed to public vehicular use. To reach the southern trailhead, take NH 49 for 10.6 mi. from I-93 and turn left onto Tripoli Rd. (sign: Ski Area). At 1.3 mi. from NH 49, bear right on Tripoli Rd. as the ski area access road continues ahead, and at 1.9 mi. turn right onto West Branch Rd. Cross a bridge over the West Branch of the Mad River, and immediately bear left into the parking area.

From the Livermore Rd. parking area, the trail passes a kiosk and in a short distance turns left and follows the gravel road through an open field (site of Depot Camp) and across a bridge over a branch of the Mad River. Greeley Ponds Trail diverges sharply left at 0.3 mi., 40 yd. past the bridge. Soon Livermore Trail crosses the main branch of the Mad River on another bridge. In the next 2.0 mi., several WVAIA local paths intersect the trail: Boulder Path diverges right at 0.6 mi. from the parking area; Big Pines Path diverges left at 0.7 mi.; Kettles Path diverges left at 0.9 mi.; Norway Rapids Trail diverges right at 1.8 mi.; and a service road (Upper Snows Mtn. Ski Trail [X-C]) diverges right at 2.2 mi. across a major logging road bridge, leading to the upper end of Cascade Path at 0.6 mi. and the top of the Snows Mtn. ski slopes at 1.4 mi.

Livermore Trail bears left at this jct. and soon passes attractive cascades on Slide Brook to the right. The trail then swings left (northeast), and at 2.6 mi. it passes the south end of Mt. Tripyramid Trail, which leads to the right across Avalanche Brook and provides access to the Tripyramid peaks via the South Slide. After passing the site of Avalanche Camp to the left of the trail at 3.1 mi., Livermore Trail reaches a hairpin turn to the left at 3.6 mi.; here, the northern part of Mt. Tripyramid Trail diverges right toward the peaks via the difficult North Slide. At 3.8 mi., Scaur Ridge Trail diverges right, offering a longer but safer and easier route to the summit of North Tripyramid. Livermore Trail climbs steadily through another hairpin turn and reaches a minor height-of-land at 4.6 mi., where Old Skidder Trail enters on the left, then descends gently and crosses a branch of Flume Brook at 4.8 mi.; just beyond is a trail sign on the left.

At 5.0 mi., the gravel road ends in the grassy Flume Brook Camp clearing; here Kancamagus Brook Ski Trail (too wet for summer hiking) diverges left (west) at the far end, whereas Livermore Trail (sign) bears slightly right (northeast) into the woods on an older road. (In the reverse direction, Livermore Trail continues south from the clearing.) The trail is obscure for a short distance where it crosses a grassy, muddy area. The next section is rough, often wet and muddy, sparsely marked, and must be followed with care. It climbs gradually into the very flat Livermore Pass (sign) at 5.6 mi., passes to the right of a small mountain meadow, and descends from the pass, slowly at first.

Livermore Trail runs in a dry rocky brook bed then descends steeply, angling down the east side of a deep, wooded gorge on a narrow, gravelly footway—a difficult section in winter; at 5.9 mi., the trail crosses the brook bed at the bottom of the gorge. The trail descends moderately, crosses several brooks, bears left off an old logging road at 6.7 mi., crosses another brook, and ascends slightly to a clearing at 7.1 mi. The trail turns right here and follows a grassy logging road. (In the reverse direction, the trail turns left off the road at an arrow.) The trail crosses a brushy wildlife opening and reaches the Kancamagus Highway across from Lily Pond.

MT. TRIPYRAMID TRAIL (WVAIA; MAP 3: J7)

Cumulative from Livermore Trail (2,400 ft.) to:	⬆⬇	↗	⟳
North Peak (4,180 ft.)	1.2 mi.	1,800 ft.	1:30
Sabbaday Brook Trail (3,850 ft.)	1.7 mi.	1,800 ft. (rev. 350 ft.)	1:45
Middle Peak (4,140 ft.)	2.0 mi.	2,100 ft.	2:05
South Peak (4,100 ft.)	2.4 mi.	2,200 ft. (rev. 150 ft.)	2:20
Kate Sleeper Trail (3,800 ft.)	2.6 mi.	2,200 ft. (rev. 300 ft.)	2:25
Livermore Trail (2,000 ft.)	4.9 mi.	2,200 ft. (rev. 1,800 ft.)	3:35
From Livermore Rd. parking area (1,580 ft.) for:			
Complete loop over Mt. Tripyramid via Livermore and Mt. Tripyramid trails	11.0 mi.	3,000 ft.	7:00

This trail makes a loop over the three summits of Mt. Tripyramid from Livermore Trail and is usually done from north to south to ascend the steep rock slabs of the North Slide and descend the loose gravel of the South Slide. Descent of the North Slide is more difficult than ascent and may be particularly daunting to hikers who have difficulty or lack experience on steep rock, whereas ascent of the South Slide can be very frustrating due to constant backsliding on the loose gravel. (*Caution:* The steep rock slabs of the North Slide are difficult, and they are dangerous in wet or icy conditions. At all times—but particularly in adverse conditions or for the descent—Scaur Ridge Trail is a much easier and safer route than the North Slide. The North Slide lies mostly in deep shade in seasons when the sun is low, so ice may form early in fall and remain late in spring. The loose footing on the South Slide may also be hazardous when wet or icy.) Allow plenty of time for the steep, rough trip over the Tripyramids via the slides. This trail is almost entirely within the Sandwich Range Wilderness.

The north end of the loop leaves Livermore Trail at a hairpin turn 3.6 mi. from the Livermore Rd. parking area. Mt. Tripyramid Trail descends sharply for 50 yd. to cross Avalanche Brook (last reliable water), enters the Sandwich Range Wilderness, ascends at a moderate grade, occasionally requiring some care to follow, and reaches the gravel outwash of the North Slide about 0.5 mi. from Livermore Trail. Swinging right (southeast), Mt. Tripyramid Trail now becomes extremely steep, climbing about 1,200 ft. in 0.5 mi. The lower part of the slide has the most difficult, slippery slabs; the upper part is more exposed, but the rough, normally dry rock offers comparatively good traction. Follow paint blazes (often faint and sparse) on the rocks. Soon the trail reaches the first open slabs, and views become steadily more extensive. Higher up, the trail ascends the right-hand track of the slide almost to its top then turns sharply left into the woods at a cairn and continues to climb steeply for 0.1 mi. to the jct. where Pine Bend Brook Trail enters from the left, 20 yd. below the summit of North Peak.

Mt. Tripyramid Trail and Pine Bend Brook Trail now coincide. They cross over the wooded summit of North Peak (where you have a partial view northeast from a short side path on the left) and descend at a moderate grade toward Middle Peak. Just north of the saddle between North and Middle Peaks, Sabbaday Brook Trail enters left from the Kancamagus Highway, and Pine Bend Brook Trail ends. Mt. Tripyramid Trail crosses the saddle and makes a steep and rough ascent of the cone of Middle Peak. At the top of the climb, the trail levels off and passes a west-facing outlook on the right. Just beyond, the true summit—a ledge that offers a view to the east—is a few yards to the left.

The trail descends steeply into the saddle between Middle and South Peaks then climbs moderately to the wooded summit of South Peak. From this summit, the trail starts to descend steeply and soon reaches the top of the South Slide, with excellent views south and southwest. In another 60 yd., Kate Sleeper Trail (Section Eight) to Mt. Whiteface diverges left at a three-way arrow painted on a ledge; a sign is located a short distance in on a scrubby tree. The descent to the foot of the slide at 3.0 mi. is very steep, alternately in the open and through scrub, with loose gravel footing becoming more prevalent as one descends. Mt. Tripyramid Trail enters the woods for good and continues down to a small open area at the bottom of the slide. Here, the trail turns right, ascends slightly, and descends on old logging roads at moderate grades. The trail swings left across a small brook, passes Black Cascade on the left at 4.1 mi., and soon crosses Cold Brook. Continuing on old roads at easy grades, the trail passes a small cascade on Slide Brook and crosses several small tributaries. The trail eventually crosses Avalanche Brook, leaving the Sandwich Range Wilderness, and ends in another 25 yd. on Livermore Trail, 2.6 mi. from the Livermore Rd. parking area.

SCAUR RIDGE TRAIL (WMNF; MAP 3: J7)

From Livermore Trail (2,500 ft.) to:	⇅	↗	↻
Pine Bend Brook Trail (3,440 ft.)	1.2 mi.	950 ft.	1:05
From Livermore Rd. parking area (1,580 ft.) for:			
Complete loop over Mt. Tripyramid via Livermore, Scaur Ridge, Pine Bend Brook, and Mt. Tripyramid trails	12.0 mi.	3,000 ft.	7:30

This trail runs from Livermore Trail to Pine Bend Brook Trail, affording an easier, safer alternative route to the North Slide. Scaur Ridge Trail is almost entirely within the Sandwich Range Wilderness. Scaur Ridge Trail diverges right (east) from Livermore Trail 3.8 mi. from the Livermore Rd. parking area. Following an old logging road at a moderate grade, the trail crosses a small brook at 0.9 mi. then soon bears left off the road. Now climbing somewhat more steeply, the trail turns right at 1.1 mi. then swings left and meets Pine Bend Brook Trail at the top of a narrow ridge at 1.2 mi. The summit of North Tripyramid is 0.8 mi. to the right via Pine Bend Brook Trail.

PINE BEND BROOK TRAIL (WMNF; MAP 3: J8–J7)

Cumulative from Kancamagus Highway (1,370 ft.) to:	⬆⬇	↗	⏱
Scaur Ridge Trail (3,440 ft.)	3.2 mi.	2,100 ft. (rev. 50 ft.)	2:40
North Peak (4,180 ft.)	4.0 mi.	2,850 ft.	3:25
Sabbaday Brook Trail (3,850 ft.)	4.5 mi.	2,850 ft. (rev. 350 ft.)	3:40

This trail ascends North Tripyramid from the Kancamagus Highway 1.0 mi. west of the Sabbaday Falls Picnic Area; parking is on the shoulder of the highway. Parts of the trail are steep and rough. In the lower part are numerous brook crossings; these are relatively easy at normal water levels. The upper part of the trail is in the Sandwich Range Wilderness.

The trail leaves the highway and in 80 yd. turns right onto the grade of the old Swift River logging railroad, follows it for 0.2 mi., then turns left off the railroad grade and follows a branch of Pine Bend Brook southwest, soon bearing right onto an old logging road. The trail crosses the brook at 0.8 mi., continues to follow it, passes a logging cut on the right, and bears right onto a relocated section 0.1 mi. long. The trail recrosses the brook at the end of the relocation (descending, bear left off the old route to cross the brook). Then, at 1.3 mi., the trail swings to the right (west) and makes a third crossing of the brook. The trail runs at easy grades, crossing several small tributaries, then passes over a minor divide and descends to a westerly branch of Pine Bend Brook, crossing it at 1.6 mi. and immediately turning left. After a short relocation, the trail recrosses this brook then ascends moderately and enters the Sandwich Range Wilderness at 2.1 mi.

The trail soon swings left and crosses a rocky brook bed (descending, bear right here, taking care not to follow either of two brook beds downhill), becoming rough and steep as it ascends along the north bank of the brook valley. Higher up, the trail swings left then right, climbing along the right edge of the brook bed for about 50 yd., then turns left and recrosses

SEC 7

the brook bed. The trail then angles up a steep slope, where recent rock step work has improved the footing; along the first set of steps, you see a glimpse of Mt. Carrigain and Mt. Lowell. At 2.7 mi., the trail reaches the crest of a minor easterly ridge and turns right to ascend it, with steady but less difficult climbing and restricted views north.

Eventually, the trail reaches the ridge running from Mt. Tripyramid north to Scaur Peak, crosses it, descends slightly to the west side, turns left, and continues almost level to the jct. on the right at 3.2 mi. with Scaur Ridge Trail. Rising gradually on the very narrow wooded ridge, Pine Bend Brook Trail provides a glimpse of the North Slide then descends slightly. Soon the trail attacks the final steep, rough, and rocky climb to North Peak with several scrambles over slippery ledges. Mt. Tripyramid Trail enters from the North Slide on the right, 20 yd. below this summit. (You have good views from the top of the slide, a steep 0.1 mi. and 250 ft. down from this jct. via Mt. Tripyramid Trail.) The two trails then coincide, passing the wooded summit of North Peak (where you have a partial view north-east along a short side path on the left) and descending at a moderate grade to the jct. with Sabbaday Brook Trail, just north of the saddle between North and Middle Peaks.

SEC 7

SABBADAY BROOK TRAIL (WMNF; MAP 3: J8–J7)

Cumulative from Sabbaday Falls Picnic Area (1,320 ft.) to:	⇅	↗	○
Fourth crossing of Sabbaday Brook (2,100 ft.)	2.8 mi.	800 ft.	1:50
Pine Bend Brook Trail–Mt. Tripyramid Trail (3,850 ft.)	4.9 mi.	2,550 ft.	3:45

This trail begins at the Sabbaday Falls Picnic Area on the Kancamagus Highway, 3.3 mi. west of Bear Notch Rd., and ascends to the saddle between North Tripyramid and Middle Tripyramid. The trail has numerous brook crossings, some of which may be difficult at high water. Except for the very steep, rough section just below the main ridge crest, grades are easy to moderate and the footing is mostly good. Most of the trail is in the Sandwich Range Wilderness.

From the parking area, follow a gravel tourist path along the west side of the brook. At 0.25 mi., a side path, 0.1 mi. long, descends left and then climbs staircases past several viewpoints over Sabbaday Falls, rejoining the main trail at 0.3 mi. Here, the gravel path ends, and the trail continues on an old logging road with easy grades. Just beyond the falls is a short, rough, eroded section along the bank. At 0.6 mi. the trail follows a rough course for 125 yd. along the bank beside a loop of the brook. At 0.7 mi., the trail makes the first of three crossings of Sabbaday Brook in 0.2 mi. (All three may be difficult in high water, but the first two can be avoided by a rough bushwhack along the west bank for 0.1 mi.) After the third crossing of the main brook, Sabbaday Brook Trail crosses a small brook, turns left up a bank, and crosses the small brook twice more.

At 1.2 mi., the trail bears right onto an old logging road on the east bank of Sabbaday Brook, soon enters the Sandwich Range Wilderness, and follows the road for more than 1.5 mi., crossing several small tributaries. At 2.8 mi., the trail crosses a tributary, turns sharply right, descends briefly, and makes a fourth crossing of Sabbaday Brook. Above this point, both the brook and trail swing to the west then northwest, up the narrow valley between Mt. Tripyramid and the Fool Killer. The trail climbs more steadily and crosses the brook twice more in an area that was washed out by the 2011 storm; follow with care.

The trail passes the base of a small slide on the Fool Killer at 3.7 mi., crosses the brook for the seventh and last time (last water) at a washed-out spot at the head of the ravine at 4.1 mi., swings back to the south, runs roughly across the slope, and soon rejoins the old route of the trail at an overgrown slide on the east slope of Tripyramid. The trail turns sharply right here and climbs steeply up slabs and broken rock, with a restricted view of Mt. Chocorua, then becomes a bit less steep but remains rough, with many rocks and roots. Finally, the trail levels off and meets Pine Bend Brook Trail and Mt. Tripyramid Trail just north of the saddle between North and Middle Tripyramid; turn right for North Peak (0.5 mi.) or left for Middle Peak (0.3 mi.).

SEC 7

SANDWICH MTN.

SANDWICH MTN. TRAIL (WMNF; MAP 3: J6–K7)

Cumulative from parking area off NH 49 (1,400 ft.) to:	⇅	↗	○
Outlook on Noon Peak (2,940 ft.)	1.6 mi.	1,550 ft.	1:35
Drakes Brook Trail (3,240 ft.)	2.7 mi.	1,950 ft. (rev. 100 ft.)	2:20
Sandwich Mtn. summit (3,980 ft.)	3.9 mi.	2,700 ft.	3:20

This trail runs to the partly open summit of Sandwich Mtn. from a parking lot just off NH 49, 0.4 mi. southwest of its jct. with Tripoli Rd. You have fine views from the trail at several different elevation levels. Most of the trail is in the Sandwich Range Wilderness.

The trail leaves the southwest corner of the parking lot, skirts left around a power station, and drops sharply to cross Drakes Brook. If the brook is very high and the crossing difficult, you can reach the trail on the other side of the brook by bushwhacking up the west bank from where Drakes Brook crosses under NH 49, just south of the parking lot. After crossing the brook, the trail climbs moderately, entering the Sandwich Range Wilderness at 0.6 mi. It passes a large boulder at 1.1 mi. then climbs, steeply at times, to an outlook with excellent views north and east at 1.6 mi.

The trail crosses the narrow ridge crest of Noon Peak, passes an outlook over the Drakes Brook valley, and descends gradually to a sag. The trail then follows a curving ridge covered with beautiful mosses, climbs a steep pitch to an outlook, and passes another outlook on the left at 2.3 mi. The best view is found by descending 70 yd. over the ledges. The trail passes an unreliable spring on the right, soon skirts the east slope of Jennings Peak, and Drakes Brook Trail enters on the left at 2.7 mi. At 2.8 mi., a spur path, steep at the top, leads right 0.2 mi. (with 150-ft. ascent) to the ledgy summit of Jennings Peak, which commands impressive views south and east. For the next 0.4 mi., the grades are easy across a shallow sag. Smarts Brook Trail enters on the right at 3.3 mi., and Sandwich Mtn. Trail ascends moderately to the summit of Sandwich Mtn. About 90 yd. below the summit, Algonquin Trail enters on the right, and 15 yd. below the summit, Bennett Street Trail enters on the right.

DRAKES BROOK TRAIL (WMNF; MAP 3: J6–K6)

Cumulative from parking area off NH 49 (1,400 ft.) to:	⇅	↗	↺
Sandwich Mtn. Trail (3,240 ft.)	3.2 mi.	1,850 ft.	2:30
Sandwich Mtn. summit (3,980 ft.) via Sandwich Mtn. Trail	4.4 mi.	2,600 ft.	3:30

This trail leaves the same parking lot off NH 49 as Sandwich Mtn. Trail and rejoins that trail near Jennings Peak, providing an alternate route for ascent or descent of Sandwich Mtn., as well as access to Fletcher Cascades. Grades are easy to moderate, and the footing is generally good. Most of Drakes Brook Trail is in the Sandwich Range Wilderness.

The trail leaves east from the north side of the parking lot and follows a gated logging road (FR 52) for 0.4 mi. At this point, the trail to Fletcher Cascades continues up the road, and Drakes Brook Trail diverges right and crosses Drakes Brook (difficult at high water). On the far bank the trail bears left, enters the Wilderness, and follows an old logging road at easy to moderate grades, climbing away from the brook and returning to its bank several times; use caution at a washout at 2.3 mi. At 2.6 mi., the trail turns right off the logging road and climbs by switchbacks, fairly steeply at times, up the west side of the ravine to join Sandwich Mtn. Trail just north of Jennings Peak, 1.2 mi. from the summit of Sandwich Mtn.

SMARTS BROOK TRAIL (WMNF; MAP 3: K6)

Cumulative from parking area on NH 49 (900 ft.) to:	⬍	↗	↻
Cascade on Smarts Brook (1,100 ft.)	1.2 mi.	200 ft.	0:40
Wilderness boundary (1,620 ft.)	2.6 mi.	700 ft.	1:35
Sandwich Mtn. Trail (3,380 ft.)	5.1 mi.	2,500 ft.	3:50
Sandwich Mtn. summit (3,980 ft.) via Sandwich Mtn. Trail	5.7 mi.	3,100 ft.	4:25

This trail provides a long but generally easy approach to the ridge of Sandwich Mtn., with moderate grades and mostly good footing. It follows the valley of Smarts Brook from NH 49, 4.0 mi. east of its jct. with NH 175, to Sandwich Mtn. Trail in the sag south of Jennings Peak. The upper half of the valley is in the Sandwich Range Wilderness. The trail leaves the east side of NH 49 from the south end of a parking area just northeast of the Smarts Brook bridge, crosses the brook on the highway bridge, and immediately turns left. (The trail that leaves the east side of the parking area heading north is Pine Flats Trail; see below.)

Smarts Brook Trail climbs a short, steep pitch to an old logging road and follows the road to the left. At 0.2 mi., where an alternate and slightly shorter cross-country ski route continues ahead, Smarts Brook Trail turns sharply right then in 100 yd. turns sharply left (north) onto a grassy, gravel logging road as Tri-Town Trail continues ahead. The alternate cross-country ski route soon joins from the left, and Smarts Brook Trail follows the road, swinging southeast and passing a fine cascade and pool on the left at 1.2 mi. The trail passes a side path leading 25 yd. left to another cascade, and at 1.3 mi., the other end of Tri-Town Trail enters from the right. At 1.4 mi., Yellow Jacket Trail diverges left across a bridge over Smarts Brook.

Smarts Brook Trail crosses a brook on a bridge and passes to the left of a beaver pond at 1.6 mi. In another 125 yd., the trail crosses along the right edge of a large brushy clearing. The trail then climbs easily with several muddy sections, and at 2.6 mi., shortly after passing a side path left to the bank of Smarts Brook, it enters the Sandwich Range Wilderness. The trail soon crosses a tributary and then climbs along the slope, well above the main brook. At 3.3 mi., you see a glimpse of the cliffs of Sachem Peak across the valley, and soon the trail crosses another tributary at a washout. At 3.7 mi., the trail passes several large boulders, crosses the main brook at 3.9 mi., and passes several more very large boulders. Then the trail turns left and climbs by a long switchback, swinging right at 4.6 mi. and left at 4.9 mi., to the ridge top, where Smarts Brook Trail meets Sandwich Mtn. Trail.

SMARTS BROOK AREA TRAILS (WMNF; MAP 3: K6, WVAIA MAP)

A network of easy trails originally developed for cross-country skiing provides opportunities for several loop hikes from the Smarts Brook Trail parking area in combination with Smarts Brook Trail. These trails are also popular for mountain biking; hikers should be alert for cyclists.

Tri-Town Trail provides a pleasant woods walk as an alternative to the logging road portion of Smarts Brook Trail. It diverges south from Smarts Brook Trail 0.3 mi. from the parking area, ascends gradually south then east over a low ridge, and descends to rejoin Smarts Brook Trail 1.3 mi. from that trail's start. From lower jct. with Smarts Brook Trail (980 ft.): 1.1 mi., 250 ft. (rev. 100 ft.), 0:40.

Pine Flats Trail leaves the southeast side of the parking area at a sign and leads north along Smarts Brook, passing two branches of Old Waterville Rd. and ascending alongside a beautiful gorge on the stream. It crosses a pine-wooded plateau, descends, and ascends briefly to a four-way jct. with Yellow Jacket Trail (right) and Old Waterville Rd. (left and ahead). From parking area on NH 49 (900 ft.): 0.7 mi., 100 ft., 0:25.

Yellow Jacket Trail diverges east from the four-way jct., ascends gradually, descends south across a bridge over a brook, and ascends easily southeast along Smarts Brook, crossing the brook on a bridge just before reaching Smarts Brook Trail 1.4 mi. from that trail's start. From Pine Flats Trail/Old Waterville Valley Rd. jct. (1,020 ft.): 1.2 mi., 250 ft. (rev. 100 ft.), 0:45.

Old Waterville Rd. follows part of the original highway route between Campton and Waterville Valley. It diverges left from Pine Flats Trail 0.1 mi. from the parking area, passes a short connecting path on the right, and descends to NH 49 at 0.3 mi. It follows the shoulder of the highway to the right (north) 250 yd., reenters the woods, ascends, and runs level past a short connector on the left to a four-way jct. with Yellow Jacket Trail (ahead) and Pine Flats Trail (right) at 0.7 mi. Here Old Waterville Rd. turns left (north) and ascends easily past a nineteenth-century homestead site and cemetery at 0.9 mi. The trail soon levels off, passes stone walls and cellar holes, swings northeast, and descends, meeting a power line at

2.0 mi. It crosses a small brook and the power-line clearing then ends at a gated logging road off NH 49, 0.1 mi. south of the High Brook picnic area. From Pine Flats Trail (900 ft.): 2.5 mi., 350 ft., (rev. 100 ft.), 1:25.

BENNETT STREET TRAIL (WODC; MAP 3: K7)

Cumulative from Flat Mtn. Pond Trail (1,200 ft.) to:	↥↧	↗	⏱
Crossing of Flat Mtn. Pond Trail (1,850 ft.)	1.6 mi.	650 ft.	1:10
Sandwich Mtn. summit (3,980 ft.)	4.0 mi.	2,800 ft.	3:25
From Bennett St. parking area (1,070 ft.) to:			
Sandwich Mtn. summit (3,980 ft.) via Flat Mtn. Pond and Bennett St. trails	4.5 mi.	2,900 ft.	3:40

This lightly used, pleasant trail runs to the summit of Sandwich Mtn. from Flat Mtn. Pond Trail, 0.3 mi. past Jose's (rhymes with "doses") bridge and 0.5 mi. from the parking area on Bennett St. (which is 2.2 mi. from NH 113A; for trailhead access directions, see Flat Mtn. Pond Trail, p. 354. The upper part of Bennett Street Trail is in the Sandwich Range Wilderness.

From the parking area, go west on Flat Mtn. Pond Trail past a gate and Jose's bridge to a signed jct. at 0.5 mi., where Bennett Street Trail begins on the right. It soon enters the WMNF and follows a logging road along the southwest bank of Pond Brook, crossing several small streams. At 0.6 mi. from Flat Mtn. Pond Trail, just after a sharp left turn, Gleason Trail diverges left. Bennett Street Trail crosses another stream, becomes rougher, and soon passes an unnamed cascade. At 0.9 mi. the trail follows a 2016 relocation to the left above a washout. In 0.1 mi. it descends briefly to rejoin the old route and soon passes Great Falls.

At 1.2 mi., Bennett Street Trail crosses a tributary and turns left to follow it. The trail recrosses the tributary, climbs a steep pitch, and at 1.6 mi. crosses Flat Mtn. Pond Trail, which at this point is an old railroad grade. The trail ascends the bank above the grade, soon entering the Sandwich Range Wilderness. The trail climbs steadily, and at 2.3 mi. turns sharply right onto an old logging road. At 2.9 mi., the trail turns left off the logging road, and at 3.5 mi., after turns to the right and left, it passes the jct. with the decommissioned upper section of Gleason Trail on the left. Bennett Street Trail soon turns left onto another old road and climbs to a jct. with Sandwich Mtn. Trail; the summit is 15 yd. to the right.

GLEASON TRAIL (WODC; MAP 3: K7)

From Bennett Street Trail (1,400 ft.) to:	↕	↗	↻
Flat Mtn. Pond Trail (1,740 ft.)	0.5 mi.	350 ft.	0:25

Note: The upper 1.7 mi. of this trail has been decommissioned due to wetness, steep grades, and severe erosion. The lower 0.5-mi. section remains open, offering the option for a lower-elevation loop hike.

The trail diverges left from Bennett Street Trail at 0.6 mi. (1.1 mi. from the Bennett St. parking area), ascends across a ledgy brook, and climbs moderately to Flat Mtn. Pond Trail (an old railroad grade) at 0.5 mi.

FLAT MTN. POND TRAIL (WMNF; MAP 3: K8–K7)

Cumulative from Whiteface Intervale Rd. (968 ft.) to:	↕	↗	↻
McCrillis Trail (1,250 ft.)	1.7 mi.	400 ft. (rev. 100 ft.)	1:05
Flat Mtn. Pond Shelter spur path (2,330 ft.)	5.3 mi.	1,500 ft. (rev. 50 ft.)	3:25
Guinea Pond Trail (1,560 ft.)	9.2 mi.	1,500 ft. (rev. 750 ft.)	5:20
Bennett St. parking area (1,070 ft.)	10.3 mi.	1,500 ft. (rev. 500 ft.)	5:55

SEC 7

This trail, with easy grades and generally good footing for most of its distance, begins on Whiteface Intervale Rd. at a parking area 0.3 mi. north of its intersection with Bennett St., ascends to Flat Mtn. Pond, then descends to Bennett St. at a parking area 2.2 mi. from NH 113A. To reach these trailheads, take Whiteface Intervale Rd., which leaves NH 113A 2.9 mi. north of the western jct. of NH 113 and NH 113A, where NH 113A bends from north–south to east–west. Bennett St. turns left from Whiteface Intervale Rd. 0.1 mi. from NH 113A and continues straight (left) past a jct. at 1.7 mi. (plowing ends here in winter), where the street becomes rougher. The road is gated at 2.2 mi., at a parking lot on the left, 0.2 mi. east of Jose's (rhymes with "doses") bridge. The upper section of Flat Mtn. Pond Trail, around and east of Flat Mtn. Pond, is in the Sandwich Range Wilderness. Some brook crossings may be difficult in high water.

The trail leaves the Whiteface Intervale Rd. parking area on a gated logging road and crosses a beaver pond outlet on a metal bridge at 0.4 mi.; in another 15 yd., a side path leads 20 yd. left to a bench with a good view of Sandwich Mtn. and the southern Flat Mtn. The trail soon bears left at a fork and turns sharply right off the road at 0.6 mi. Soon the trail reaches an older, grassy logging road and follows it left for 60 yd. then leaves this road to the right and passes an outlook to Mt. Whiteface at 0.9 mi. The trail ascends easily along a small ridge, dips to cross a small brook, climbs again, and then descends by switchbacks to the Whiteface River at the site of an old bridge abutment. The trail crosses the river (may be difficult at high water; the best crossing is 30 yd. upstream) at 1.6 mi., entering the Sandwich Range Wilderness, and immediately picks up the older route of the trail, a logging road the trail follows to the left (upstream), along the east bank.

At 1.7 mi., McCrillis Trail turns sharply right up the bank, and Flat Mtn. Pond Trail continues to ascend along the river at comfortable grades, crossing the river's East Branch at 1.9 mi., following a short relocation to the right at 2.1 mi., and traversing a rough section along the bank just beyond. After a nearly level section, it crosses a major branch at 3.1 mi. and then the main river 50 yd. beyond (difficult at high water). The trail climbs steadily for 0.5 mi. then eases, crossing a brook and a rocky area. It passes over a small hump and descends to the edge of Flat Mtn. Pond at 4.2 mi., where it enters the old Beebe River logging railroad grade. The trail follows the grade to a fork at the edge of the major inlet brook; the main trail follows the left fork across the stream, and the right fork runs about 125 yd. to the edge of a beaver pond with a view of the northern Flat Mtn. and Lost Pass.

Continuing along the shore of the long, narrow pond, the main trail soon diverges right on a rough footway to circle around an area in which the grade has been flooded. The trail passes a large boulder with a view of Mt. Whiteface at 4.8 mi. and traverses roughly on the slope above the pond, with several ups and downs; care is required to follow the trail in this section, particularly at a spot where a side path descends left and the main trail swings right. The trail returns to the grade at the south end of the pond at 5.3 mi., 70 yd. after leaving the Sandwich Range Wilderness. Straight ahead are two spur paths. The right fork leads 70 yd. to the Flat Mtn. Pond Shelter, worth visiting just for the view across the pond to South Tripyramid and Sleeper Ridge; the left fork leads 50 yd. to a designated tentsite and continues to a grassy area below the shelter. The main trail turns right on the railroad grade and descends gradually, with occasional washed-out sections, into the valley of Pond Brook.

At 6.3 mi., the grade makes a hairpin turn to the left at a beaver pond (with a potentially difficult crossing of a flooded area), soon crosses a tributary brook, and crosses Pond Brook twice within 100 yd. At 7.6 mi., the trail crosses a major tributary, and at 7.7 mi., it passes through a four-way jct. with Bennett Street Trail. After a wet section where the railroad ties remain, Gleason Trail diverges left at 8.2 mi. (To the right, the upper section of Gleason Trail has been decommissioned.) Either Bennett Street Trail or Gleason Trail can be used as an attractive shortcut to Jose's bridge

SEC 7

and the Bennett St. parking area. At 9.2 mi., Guinea Pond Trail continues ahead on the railroad grade, and Flat Mtn. Pond Trail turns left and descends moderately on a logging road, leaving the WMNF just before reaching a signed jct. at 9.8 mi., where Bennett Street Trail enters on the left. (In the reverse direction, bear right at a fork 40 yd. beyond the jct. with Bennett Street Trail). Flat Mtn. Pond Trail continues ahead on the road, passes Jose's bridge (private) on the left, and in another 0.2 mi. reaches a gate and the parking area beyond.

ALGONQUIN TRAIL (SLA; MAP 3: K6–K7)

Cumulative distances from Sandwich Notch Rd. (1,420 ft.) to:	⇅	↗	↻
Small pass (2,600 ft.)	2.1 mi.	1,200 ft.	1:40
Black Mtn. Pond Trail (3,280 ft.)	2.8 mi.	1,850 ft.	2:20
Sandwich Mtn. Trail (3,950 ft.)	4.5 mi.	2,700 ft. (rev. 150 ft.)	3:35

This trail ascends Sandwich Dome from the north side of the narrow, rough Sandwich Notch Rd., 1.4 mi. north of the power line along the Beebe River and 3.6 mi. south of NH 49. There is limited roadside parking at the trailhead. This trail provides many extensive views from open ledges on the southwest shoulder, sometimes called Black Mtn. The trail is steep and rough in parts, with one difficult rock scramble, and the ledges may be slippery when wet. It must be followed with care in the open ledgy areas. Almost the entire trail is in the Sandwich Range Wilderness.

The trail enters the Wilderness 100 yd. from the road and follows an old logging road at easy grades, crossing a brook at 0.4 mi. and passing a small meadow. At 0.9 mi., in a small clearing, it turns left off the road (watch carefully for yellow blazes). The trail begins to climb steeply then moderates and passes through a ledgy area with two small brooks before climbing steeply again to a small pass at 2.1 mi. Here, the trail turns right, descends slightly, then attacks the west end of the ridge, climbing steeply with one difficult rock scramble. Two other rock pitches farther up the trail can be bypassed by unblazed but well-beaten paths to the right; at the second, good views west are missed unless one walks back 20 yd. to the ledges on the blazed route of the trail.

The trail continues to climb steeply, with several short scrambles, before the grade moderates as the trail climbs largely in the open, and at 2.8 mi., Black Mtn. Pond Trail enters on the right. (Descending, Algonquin Trail turns right at this jct., and Black Mtn. Pond Trail continues ahead.) Algonquin Trail continues to ascend moderately past several viewpoints, including one looking down on Black Mtn. Pond and another to the west,

then descends steeply for a short distance into a sag at 3.5 mi. The trail
ascends easily along the ridge with a few minor dips then climbs moderately, passing an outlook south, and ends at Sandwich Mtn. Trail 90 yd.
below the summit.

BLACK MTN. POND TRAIL (SLA; MAP 3: K7–K6)

Cumulative from Guinea Pond Trail (1,430 ft.) to:	⤊	↗	◔
Black Mtn. Pond (2,220 ft.)	2.4 mi.	800 ft.	1:35
Algonquin Trail (3,280 ft.)	3.5 mi.	1,850 ft.	2:40

This trail runs from Guinea Pond Trail, 1.7 mi. from the parking area on
Beebe River Rd., past beautiful Black Mtn. Pond to Algonquin Trail,
1.7 mi. below the summit of Sandwich Mtn. Sections of the trail below
Black Mtn. Pond are wet, and the part from the pond to the ridge is very
steep and rough, with several difficult scrambles. The former Black Mtn.
Pond Shelter has been removed. Nearly the entire Black Mtn. Pond Trail
is in the Sandwich Range Wilderness.

This trail leaves the north side of Guinea Pond Trail almost directly
opposite Mead Trail, crosses the Beebe River (may be difficult at high
water), continues generally north to the west bank of the Beebe River
(which has turned to run north and south), and recrosses it below a beaver
pond at 0.5 mi. Black Mtn. Pond Trail passes several cascades and continues up the valley at mostly easy grades. At 1.9 mi., a side path leads left
0.1 mi. to the base of Mary Cary Falls. The main trail climbs more steeply
by a switchback then eases, recrosses the brook, and ascends to a signed
T jct. at 2.3 mi. Here the main trail turns left, and a spur path leads right
a short distance to two designated tent pads on a knoll above Black Mtn.
Pond. This area has been heavily affected by camping, which is now prohibited within 200 ft. of the pond and within marked revegetation areas.

The main trail can be difficult to follow here due to the ill-defined footway, diverging paths, and sparse blazing; at the T jct. it turns left, runs
across the knoll, soon turns right, and descends a short pitch to the west
edge of Black Mtn. Pond at 2.4 mi. The trail winds around in the spruce
woods near the pond then turns right to bypass a beaver pond. The trail
then begins the steep climb, with many twists and turns and several difficult scrambles; care is required to follow it here. About halfway up, the trail
reaches the first of several outlook ledges with good views south; views to
the west increase as the trail works around toward the west end of the
shoulder. At 3.3 mi., the trail passes a boulder cave, turns sharply right, and
continues up to meet Algonquin Trail on the ridge crest.

SEC
7

GUINEA POND TRAIL (WMNF; MAP 3: K6–K7)

Cumulative from parking area on Beebe River Rd. (1,320 ft.) to:	↕	↗	↻
Mead Trail–Black Mtn. Pond Trail (1,430 ft.)	1.7 mi.	100 ft.	0:55
Flat Mtn. Pond Trail (1,560 ft.)	4.1 mi.	250 ft.	2:10

This trail runs east from Sandwich Notch Rd. 5.4 mi. from Center Sandwich, just south of the bridge over the Beebe River, to Flat Mtn. Pond Trail 1.1 mi. from the Bennett St. parking area. The trailhead parking area is located on the north side of Beebe River Rd. (FR 400, the road that runs west from the crossroads just north of the bridge), about 100 yd. west of the crossroads and 0.1 mi. from the gate at the start of the trail. No parking is available at the trailhead. Distances are given from the designated parking area. Extensive sections of the trail west and east of Guinea Pond have been impacted by beaver flooding; bypasses skirt the worst sections.

From the parking area on Beebe River Rd., walk back 100 yd. to Sandwich Notch Rd., turn right and cross the bridge, and turn left onto Guinea Pond Trail at 0.1 mi. The trail follows a gated road to the old railroad grade in a power-line clearing at 0.2 mi. then enters the woods and follows the grade. At 1.1 mi. it enters an extensive wetland area along the Beebe River, and at 1.3 mi., the main trail continues ahead across a place where it may be flooded in wet seasons; here a high-water bypass has been flagged to the right. (This route crosses the power-line swath, swings left through the woods, and crosses back over the swath to meet the main route in 0.2 mi.) The main trail follows the grade ahead past an old gate and across a snowmobile bridge, with views of Sandwich Mtn. At 1.4 mi. it swings right and then left onto an older bypass of a flooded section of the grade; here the newer high-water bypass rejoins from the right.

The trail rejoins the railroad grade just before reaching the jcts. with Mead Trail on the right at 1.7 mi. and Black Mtn. Pond Trail on the left 10 yd. farther on. (In the reverse direction, turn left off the grade and onto the bypass after passing these jcts.) Continuing east, the trail crosses the Beebe River twice in 0.1 mi.; these crossings often require wading but may be bypassed by following a beaten path along the south bank. The trail then crosses a tributary brook, and at 1.9 mi. a side path (sometimes wet) runs left 0.2 mi., swinging right near the end, to the swampy shore of Guinea Pond, where there is a view of Sandwich Mtn. In 2016 the side path was marked by only a wooden post. The main trail continues on the railroad grade then swings left off it at 2.6 mi. to bypass a beaver swamp; this turn was poorly marked in 2016.

The bypass runs up and down through the woods to the left of the swamp then makes a tricky crossing of a wet area on logs and swings right across an open area to rejoin the grade at 2.8 mi.; here there is a view of Mt. Israel. (In the reverse direction, turn right off the grade and cross the open area, with little evident footway, to the log crossing.) At 2.9 mi., the trail crosses the Cold River (difficult in high water) and continues on the grade, crossing several small brooks, to the jct. with Flat Mtn. Pond Trail, which enters right from Jose's bridge and follows the railroad grade ahead to Flat Mtn. Pond.

MT. ISRAEL

MEAD TRAIL (SLA; MAP 3: K7)

From Guinea Pond Trail (1,430 ft.) to:	⇅	↗	↻
Wentworth Trail (2,610 ft.)	1.7 mi.	1,200 ft.	1:25

This trail, with easy to moderate grades and generally good footing, ascends to the summit of Mt. Israel (where you will find outstanding views, particularly to the higher peaks of the Sandwich Range close by to the north) from Guinea Pond Trail, 1.7 mi. from trailhead parking on Beebe River Rd.

Mead Trail leaves Guinea Pond Trail and crosses a small ridge, a sag, a power line, and then a brook at 0.3 mi. It ascends through hardwoods along the ravine of a branch of the brook, crossing it at 0.9 mi. The trail ascends moderately, swings left at 1.4 mi., and climbs through spruce forest past a small spring on the left (unreliable) to Wentworth Trail; the summit ledge, with fine views, is 70 yd. left.

WENTWORTH TRAIL (SLA; MAP 3: L7–K7)

From Mead Base (930 ft.) to:	⇅	↗	↻
Mt. Israel summit (2,630 ft.)	2.1 mi.	1,700 ft.	1:55

This trail ascends Mt. Israel from Mead Base Conservation Center—located at the end of Diamond Ledge Rd., 0.4 mi. north of its jct. with Sandwich Notch Rd. and 2.9 mi. from Center Sandwich—and affords splendid views of the Lakes Region and the Sandwich Range. Park in the field below the camp buildings. (The Friends of Mead Base Conservation Center maintains three campsites at this trailhead; for information, visit meadbase.org.)

SEC 7

Wentworth Trail, blazed in yellow, enters the woods at the left rear of the main camp building (sign) and leads directly uphill, following an old cart path through an opening in a stone wall 0.3 mi. above the camp. The trail turns right and angles up the hillside above the wall, crosses a brook and turns left to follow it, then turns right away from the brook at 0.8 mi. Soon the trail begins to switchback up the slope and, at 1.5 mi., passes a rock face right and a fine outlook (views over the Lakes Region) 10 yd. farther on the left. The trail reaches the ridge 100 yd. farther up, and climbing becomes easier. The trail soon becomes almost level in a dense coniferous forest then turns right at a ledge (good view north) near the summit of the west knob and continues along the ridge (follow markings with care), descending briefly before rising to the jct. on the left with Mead Trail; the summit is a ledge 70 yd. past the jct. Some cairns mark a lightly beaten path that leads about 100 yd. northeast from the summit to ledges with more views to the north and east.

BEARCAMP RIVER TRAIL (SCC; MAP 3: L7)

From Sandwich Notch Rd. (1,020 ft.) to:	⮑	↗	⟳
Mead Base (930 ft.)	0.6 mi.	0 ft. (rev. 100 ft.)	0:20

From Mead Base (930 ft.), Sandwich Town Park (1,020 ft.), or Guinea Pond Trail parking area (1,320 ft.) for:			
Complete loop over Mt. Israel via Wentworth Trail, Mead Trail, Guinea Pond Trail, Sandwich Notch Rd., and Bearcamp River Trail	8.2 mi.	1,850 ft.	5:00

One of the most interesting parts of this 17-mi. trail (sections of which have become obscure or have been closed by landowners) is the western-most portion, which runs 0.6 mi. from Mead Base to the Sandwich Town Park (parking) on Sandwich Notch Rd., 3.2 mi. from Center Sandwich. This easy section of trail can be hiked for its own sake or used as part of a very attractive and varied loop hike over Mt. Israel via Wentworth Trail, Mead Trail, Guinea Pond Trail, a 2.2-mi. section of Sandwich Notch Rd., and Bearcamp River Trail.

The following description is eastbound from Sandwich Notch Rd. to Mead Base. The yellow-blazed trail first descends gradually to the Bear-camp River at Beede Falls. The shallow pool at the foot of this beautiful cascade is a popular swimming hole in summer. It crosses the river on a new bridge. On the far side, a spur path on the right (sign) descends 125 yd. to ledges and cascades at Lower Falls. The main trail soon bears left, away from the river into a beautiful hemlock forest, and at 0.2 mi. it passes Cow Cave (left), where legend says a lost cow safely spent a winter. At 0.4 mi. it crosses a small stream and bears right onto a grassy road, passes tentsites (left) opposite an open field, and reaches Mead Base at 0.6 mi.

SQUAM LAKE AREA

CRAWFORD–RIDGEPOLE TRAIL (SLA; MAPS 3 & 4: L6, SLA MAP)

Cumulative from Sandwich Notch Rd. (1,240 ft.) to:	⇅	↗	⟳
East Doublehead summit (2,158 ft.)	1.9 mi.	1,100 ft. (rev. 200 ft.)	1:30
Mt. Squam, east summit (2,223 ft.)	3.0 mi.	1,450 ft. (rev. 300 ft.)	2:15
Mt. Percival summit (2,212 ft.)	4.4 mi.	1,750 ft. (rev. 300 ft.)	3:05
Upper jct. with Mt. Morgan Trail (2,170 ft.)	5.2 mi.	1,850 ft. (rev. 150 ft.)	3:30
Mt. Livermore summit (1,500 ft.)	10.0 mi.	2,500 ft. (rev. 1,300 ft.)	6:15
Spur of Cotton Mtn. (1,210 ft.)	11.3 mi.	2,850 ft. (rev. 650 ft.)	7:05

This trail follows the backbone of the Squam Range from Sandwich Notch Rd. to the south knob of Cotton Mtn. The trail starts on the southwest side of Sandwich Notch Rd., 3.7 mi. from NH 113 in Center Sandwich, 0.5 mi. beyond the Sandwich Town Park/Bearcamp River Trail parking area, and 1.8 mi. south of the power line along the Beebe River. There is space for one or two cars at the trailhead; other parking may be found a short distance east along the road. Except for the very popular segment between Mt. Percival and Mt. Morgan, the trail is used infrequently, despite fine views in the Squam–Doublehead section. The northern half of the trail is ledgy and rough in places and is more difficult than the statistics and map would suggest.

From the road (sign), the trail ascends steeply, with one difficult ledge scramble. Higher up, the grade eases, and the trail passes southeast of the summit of an unnamed wooded peak and continues along the ridge across a saddle to Doublehead Mtn., where you have a restricted view north, just before the summit of East Doublehead. At 1.9 mi., 80 yd. beyond the summit of East Doublehead, the trail bears right and descends where Doublehead Trail diverges left to NH 113. A very fine viewpoint, well worth the side trip, is located on Doublehead Trail, 0.1 mi. from this jct. After dropping steeply to a col and climbing over West Doublehead, where there is a limited outlook to the north, Crawford–Ridgepole Trail continues along the ridge, much of the way over ledges that are slippery when wet. The trail climbs steeply out of a muddy col, with one fairly difficult ledge scramble,

SEC 7

passes an excellent south outlook at 2.6 mi., then crosses an open ledgy area with fine views to the north.

The trail crosses the east summit of Mt. Squam, where you have a good view, at 3.0 mi. The trail continues along the ledgy ridge, in places requiring care to follow, crosses the west summit of Mt. Squam, passes an outlook south, descends through a notch, and climbs to Mt. Percival Trail and Mt. Percival's excellent views at 4.4 mi. Continuing along the ridge with minor ups and downs and occasional views, Crawford–Ridgepole Trail passes just west of the actual high point of the range (sometimes called the Sawtooth, it can be reached by a short but thick bushwhack and has a restricted view) and continues to a jct. with Mt. Morgan Trail at 5.2 mi. Here, Mt. Morgan Trail leads to the right 90 yd. to a fork; the left branch (almost straight ahead) leads another 50 yd. to a fine cliff-top viewpoint, whereas the right branch leads 50 yd. to the true summit of Mt. Morgan, where you have a restricted view north.

From this jct., Crawford–Ridgepole Trail and Mt. Morgan Trail coincide, bearing left and descending a set of steps. Shortly, a difficult spur path (use caution) branches right, ascends three ladders, and climbs about 100 yd. through a boulder cave and up steep ledges to the cliff-top viewpoint on Mt. Morgan. The main trail descends to a jct. at 5.6 mi., where Mt. Morgan Trail turns left to continue its descent to NH 113, and Crawford–Ridgepole Trail turns right to climb at mostly easy grades toward Mt. Webster, keeping to the west side of the ridge crest and passing below the wooded summit at 6.6 mi. At 7.1 mi., an unmarked spur path leads left 50 yd. to a fine outlook over Squam Lake; at 7.4 mi., an obscure side path leads right 20 yd. to a restricted view west; and at 7.5 mi., another unmarked spur leads left a few steps to a restricted eastern outlook.

The trail now descends at moderate and easy grades, passing an outlook east at 8.1 mi. The trail runs along a shoulder, bears right at 8.8 mi. where an unofficial red- and orange-blazed trail diverges left, and descends again before climbing slightly to the four-way jct. with Old Mtn. Rd. at 9.6 mi. Crawford–Ridgepole Trail continues ahead and ascends to the summit of Mt. Livermore (view east) at 10.0 mi. Coinciding with Prescott Trail, Crawford–Ridgepole Trail descends west from Mt. Livermore along a stone wall then turns left onto an old carriage road and descends by switchbacks. At 10.4 mi., Prescott Trail branches left; Crawford–Ridgepole Trail continues its steady descent, crosses two tiny streams near a low pass, then climbs through a rocky area in a beautiful hemlock grove to a south spur of Cotton Mtn., where the trail ends at its jct. with Cotton Mtn. Trail. Descent can be made by following Cotton Mtn. Trail down for 0.7 mi. to

NH 113 near the Old Highway trailhead; a spur path leads left to a view south a short distance ahead on this trail.

DOUBLEHEAD TRAIL (SLA; MAP 3: L6)

From trailhead on Thompson Rd. (840 ft.) to:	⇵	↗	↻
Crawford–Ridgepole Trail (2,120 ft.)	1.4 mi.	1,300 ft.	1:20

This trail, steep in its upper section, provides access to a ledge high on Doublehead Mtn. with one of the finest views in the Squam Range. The first section above Thompson Rd. was relocated in 2016. To reach the trailhead, turn west off NH 113 onto Thompson Rd., 3.5 mi. southwest of Center Sandwich and 8.4 mi. northeast of its jct. with US 3 in Holderness. Drive up gravel Thompson Rd. (narrow but sound in 2016), continuing straight ahead at a jct. with a gated logging road at 0.6 mi. A new trailhead parking area is on the left at 0.9 mi. from NH 113, just beyond a sign for Doublehead Preserve. The trail, marked with yellow diamonds, leaves Thompson Rd. (sign: Trail) across from the west end of the parking area. It follows a wide gravel road uphill for 0.1 mi. then bears right off the road (sign: Trail) at a three-way jct. Here a spur road (sign: View) diverges left and leads 50 yd. to a view south from the top of a field.

The main trail ascends along an older road, and at 0.3 mi. it bears left onto the original route of the trail. It ascends moderately up old woods roads, crosses a small brook bed three times, and passes through a stone wall at 0.7 mi. The trail climbs steadily, crosses an overgrown skid road, swings right at 1.1 mi., bears right at the base of wooded ledges, and ascends steeply. It bears right again and at 1.3 mi. reaches a ledge with excellent views to the south. The trail runs along the top edge of the ledge (descending, look carefully for a marker where the trail bears right off the ledge) then turns left off it and swings left again behind the ledge. The trail scrambles up the left side of another ledge, bears right across its top (cairn), and continues up to Crawford–Ridgepole Trail 80 yd. west of the summit of East Doublehead.

SEC 7

MT. PERCIVAL TRAIL (SLA; MAP 3: L6)

From NH 113 (800 ft.) to:	⇵	↗	↻
Mt. Percival summit (2,212 ft.)	2.0 mi.	1,450 ft. (rev. 50 ft.)	1:45

This trail provides access to fine views and interesting boulder caves on Mt. Percival and, in combination with Mt. Morgan Trail, Morse Trail, and

Crawford–Ridgepole Trail, offers one of the most popular and scenic loop hikes on the southern fringe of the White Mtns. The trail begins on the north side of NH 113, 0.3 mi. northeast of the Mt. Morgan–Rattlesnake parking areas. Parking for this trail (sign) is available at the end of a short gravel road.

The trail follows a logging road past a chain gate and ascends at an easy grade. At 0.2 mi., Morse Trail diverges left for Mt. Morgan Trail. Mt. Percival Trail passes through a clearing, and at 0.4 mi. the trail turns left onto a relocated section then loops back to rejoin the original route at 0.6 mi. At 0.9 mi., after a slight descent, the trail crosses a brook and climbs moderately. At 1.5 mi., the trail turns right (northeast) and traverses the south slope of Mt. Percival for 0.1 mi., descending slightly. The trail then swings left and climbs steeply to a fork at 1.9 mi. (From this fork, an alternate route diverges left and ascends a difficult and very strenuous route through a boulder cave [not recommended in wet weather] then continues up ledges to the summit.) Here the main trail turns right; struggles up a steep, rough, ledgy section; crosses a cliff top with a fine view of Squam Lake; and continues over ledges to join Crawford–Ridgepole Trail at the open summit.

MT. MORGAN TRAIL (SLA; MAP 3: L6)

From NH 113 (800 ft.) to:	↕	↗	↻
Mt. Morgan summit (2,220 ft.)	2.1 mi.	1,400 ft.	1:45

This trail, leading to a summit with fine views, leaves the west side of NH 113, 5.5 mi. northeast of its jct. with US 3 in Holderness and 6.3 mi. southwest of its jct. with NH 109 in Center Sandwich. From the parking area, the trail follows a logging road, turning left off it almost immediately. At 0.1 mi., Morse Trail diverges right, leading 0.5 mi. to Mt. Percival Trail. Mt. Morgan Trail climbs west at a moderate grade then swings right and traverses to the north. At 1.4 mi., the trail swings left to begin the steeper ascent of the southeast slope of the mountain. At 1.7 mi., Crawford–Ridgepole Trail enters left from Mt. Webster, and the two trails coincide, passing a difficult spur path (use caution) that branches left, ascends three ladders, and climbs about 100 yd. through a boulder cave and up steep ledges to the cliff-top viewpoint. After climbing a set of steps, the main trails soon reach a jct. where Crawford–Ridgepole Trail diverges right for Mt. Percival. Here, Mt. Morgan Trail leads 0.1 mi. left to the cliff-top viewpoint; partway along, a short spur leaves on the right and runs 50 yd. to the true summit, where you have a restricted view north.

MORSE TRAIL (SLA; MAP 3: L6)

From Mt. Morgan Trail (850 ft.) to:	⮑	↗	↻
Mt. Percival Trail (840 ft.)	0.5 mi.	0 ft.	0:15
From Mt. Morgan parking area (800 ft.) for:			
Complete loop over mts. Percival and Morgan via Mt. Morgan Trail, Morse Trail, Mt. Percival Trail, Crawford–Ridgepole Trail, and Mt. Morgan Trail	5.4 mi.	1,600 ft.	3:30

This trail links the lower ends of Mt. Morgan and Mt. Percival trails, making possible an excellent loop hike without a road walk on NH 113. Morse Trail diverges right from Mt. Morgan Trail 0.1 mi. from NH 113 and descends easily to cross a small brook. Morse Trail passes through a gap in a stone wall and ascends gradually, crosses a brook on a footbridge at 0.4 mi., passes through a gap in another stone wall, and bears right to meet Mt. Percival Trail, 0.2 mi. from NH 113.

OLD HIGHWAY (SLA; MAP 4: L6, SLA MAP)

Cumulative from NH 113 (585 ft.) to:	⮑	↗	↻
Prescott Trail (900 ft.)	0.9 mi.	300 ft.	0:35
Burleigh Farm Rd. (750 ft.)	1.4 mi.	300 ft. (rev. 150 ft.)	0:50

SEC 7

This trail, used for access to the lower ends of Prescott Trail and Old Mtn. Rd., continues straight where NH 113 bears right, 1.3 mi. northeast of Holderness and 0.2 mi. beyond a large pull-off (the trailhead for Cotton Mtn. Trail), where parking is available. A century ago, the old road, followed by Old Highway, was part of the main highway between Holderness and Center Sandwich. The trail leaves NH 113 at the same point as a paved driveway; there is no parking here. The trail climbs at moderate then easy grades through an area with many stone walls; parts of the old road are severely eroded. At 0.8 mi., the trail turns left onto a newer road. Prescott Trail diverges left (north) at the height-of-land at 0.9 mi., 100 yd. beyond the Prescott Cemetery, and after a short descent Old Mtn. Rd. diverges left at an acute angle at 1.1 mi. and runs near the edge of a large field. Old Highway continues ahead between two fields with a view east then descends past a sugarhouse to a locked gate (no parking here) at the edge of Burleigh Farm Rd., which runs 0.6 mi. to NH 113, 3.0 mi. from US 3. Parking is available on Burleigh Farm Rd. 0.2 mi. from NH 113, near the jct. with Laurence Rd.

PRESCOTT TRAIL (SLA; MAP 4: L6)

Cumulative from Old Highway (900 ft.) to:	↕	↗	↻
Crawford–Ridgepole Trail (1,220 ft.)	1.0 mi.	400 ft. (rev. 100 ft.)	0:40
Mt. Livermore summit (1,500 ft.)	1.4 mi.	700 ft.	1:05

This trail to Mt. Livermore turns left off Old Highway at the height-of-land 0.9 mi. from NH 113, 100 yd. beyond the Prescott Cemetery. Prescott Trail follows a logging road for 0.2 mi., turns sharply left off it, ascends gradually, and turns right uphill at 0.3 mi. The trail now climbs by switchbacks over a low ridge and descends gradually to Crawford–Ridgepole Trail, which enters left at 1.0 mi. From this point, the two trails ascend together via switchbacks. Just below the summit, they turn sharply right and ascend steeply to the summit, where you have a view over Squam Lake.

Descending headed south, Crawford–Ridgepole Trail and Prescott Trail leave the summit together, turn sharply right (west) and descend along an old stone wall, then turn left onto an old bridle trail. After 0.4 mi., Crawford–Ridgepole Trail leaves on the right.

OLD MTN. ROAD (SLA; MAP 4: L6)

From Old Highway (820 ft.) to:	↕	↗	↻
Crawford–Ridgepole Trail (1,285 ft.)	0.7 mi.	450 ft.	0:35

This trail leaves sharply left from Old Highway 1.1 mi. from its western end at NH 113. The trail ascends on an old road to the left of a field; from the top of the field is a view of Red Hill. The trail continues climbing at a moderate grade, with wet footing in places, to Crawford–Ridgepole Trail at the low point between Mt. Livermore and Mt. Webster. The old road continues from here, descending 0.5 mi. northwest to a parking area on Mountain Rd. (off Perch Pond Rd.), but this section is not an official trail.

COTTON MTN. TRAIL (SLA; SLA MAP)

From NH 113 (590 ft.) to:	↕	↗	↻
South spur of Cotton Mtn. (1,210 ft.)	0.7 mi.	600 ft.	0:40

This trail provides access to a ledge with a fine view located on a south spur of Cotton Mtn. and connects with the south end of Crawford–Ridgepole Trail. The trail (sign) starts at a pull-off on the west side of NH 113, 1.1 mi. north of its jct. with US 3 in Holderness. Cotton Mtn. Trail follows a dirt road through a brushy gravel pit, curving right at 0.2 mi. into an open area then left (cairns) to an SLA signpost, where the road bears left again and ends in 15 yd. at the top of the bank. Here the trail turns right into the woods (sign) and ascends, crossing an old road in 60 yd. The trail climbs rather steeply up the east slope of the mountain, with many rock steps, circling around to the south side to reach the summit of the south spur and the jct. with Crawford–Ridgepole Trail. A few yards before the jct., a spur path leads 20 yd. right to a ledge with a view over Squam Lake.

RATTLESNAKE PATHS (SLA; MAP 3: L6)

Old Bridle Path. This short and easy route to the excellent West Rattlesnake outlooks receives very heavy use. The path (yellow markers) leaves a parking area (sign: West Rattlesnake Parking) on the southeast side of NH 113, 5.5 mi. northeast of its jct. with US 3 in Holderness and 6.3 mi. southwest of its jct. with NH 109 in Center Sandwich, and across from the parking area for Mt. Morgan Trail. The trail follows an old cart road with wooden retaining steps at moderate then easy grades, swinging right at 0.3 mi. and reaching the cliffs near the summit at 0.9 mi. Near the top, an unsigned side path leads 70 yd. right to ledges with restricted views west. Ramsey Trail joins from the right just below the summit ledges. Descending, Old Bridle Path begins slightly northwest of the summit cliffs. From Rattlesnake parking area (820 ft.): 0.9 mi., 400 ft., 0:40.

Ramsey Trail. A much steeper route to West Rattlesnake. The trail (signs: Ramsey and Undercut trails; white markers to start) leaves Pinehurst Rd. (which begins on NH 113, 0.5 mi. west of the Mt. Morgan–Rattlesnake parking) 0.7 mi. from NH 113 and 90 yd. east of the entrance to Rockywold and Deephaven camps. Park off the road on the right, before the stone gate, 0.2 mi. farther east on Pinehurst Rd. and just past the Bacon Rd jct. In 0.1 mi. from Pinehurst Rd., Ramsey Trail (green markers) turns right; Undercut Trail continues on. Ramsey Trail climbs steeply for 0.4 mi., with ledge scrambles, to a point just north of the summit cliffs and joins Old Bridle Path. From parking on Pinehurst Rd. (620 ft.): 0.7 mi., 600 ft., 0:40.

Undercut Trail (white markers) continues straight where Ramsey Trail turns right. It then turns right 0.2 mi. from the Ramsey Trail jct. onto a driveway for 15 yd. then right again into the woods. (Left on this driveway leads 0.2 mi. to Pinehurst Rd., 80 yd. west of the Rockywold/Deephaven entrance.) Undercut Trail runs another 0.7 mi. (follow carefully, as it makes several turns on and off old woods roads) to NH 113, 0.1 mi. west of the Old Bridle Path parking. From Ramsey Trail jct. (680 ft.): 0.9 mi., 150 ft. (rev. 50 ft.), 0:30.

SEC 7

Pasture Trail. This trail (blue markers to Col Trail jct., then yellow) leads to West Rattlesnake from Pinehurst Rd., 0.95 mi. from NH 113. Park in the small area to the right before the stone gate, just past the jct. with Bacon Rd. The trailhead (sign) is on the left 100 yd. past the gate. Start on a road to the left then after 25 yd. turn right onto a footpath between Pinehurst Farm buildings. At 0.2 mi. East Rattlesnake and Five Finger Point trails diverge right across a brook, and in 15 yd. Pasture Trail bears left where Col Trail continues ahead. The cliffs are reached at 0.6 mi. after a moderate ascent. Descending, Pasture Trail leaves the east side of the lower (southern) of the two levels of ledge atop the cliffs. From parking on Pinehurst Rd. (620 ft.): 0.6 mi., 600 ft., 0:35.

Col Trail. This trail (blue markers) continues straight where Pasture Trail bears left, 0.2 mi. from the gate on Pinehurst Rd. Col Trail ascends moderately 0.3 mi. to Ridge Trail, which joins from the left. Col Trail turns right here, coincides with Ridge Trail for 30 yd., and diverges left. Col Trail passes over the height-of-land and descends (follow with care) to the edge of a beaver pond at 0.8 mi. from Pasture Trail. The trail skirts the east side of the pond, passing a view to the Squam Range, turns left onto an old road, dips across the pond outlet, rises slightly, and turns right onto a gravel road at 1.0 mi. It descends along this road then rises slightly across a bridge and passes a chain gate to the trailhead parking area on NH 113 at 1.2 mi. (This is 0.3 mi. east of the Holderness–Sandwich town line and 0.4 mi. west of Metcalf Rd.; elevation 740 ft.). To start from this trailhead (sign on left side of entrance: Col Trail), park on the right a short distance in from the highway and continue on foot 0.2 mi. on the gravel road, bearing left and slightly downhill at a fork where the road bears right. From Pasture Trail (720 ft.): 1.2 mi., 300 ft. (rev. 300 ft.), 0:45.

Ridge Trail. This trail (green markers) connects West and East Rattlesnake mtns. The trail begins just northeast of the cliffs of West Rattlesnake, ascends a short distance to the wooded summit, then swings right and descends moderately to a saddle at 0.4 mi., where Col Trail comes in from the right and, 30 yd. beyond, leaves again to the left. Ridge Trail ascends, and East Rattlesnake Trail enters right at 0.8 mi. Ridge Trail reaches the ledge overlooking Squam Lake at 0.9 mi. and continues to the summit of East Rattlesnake and Butterworth Trail. From West Rattlesnake cliffs (1,220 ft.): 1.0 mi., 350 ft. (rev. 300 ft.), 0:40.

East Rattlesnake Trail. This trail (red markers) branches right from Pasture Trail 0.2 mi. from the gate on Pinehurst Rd. In 25 yd., Five Finger Point Trail continues straight. East Rattlesnake Trail turns left and ascends steadily to Ridge Trail, 0.1 mi. west of the East Rattlesnake outlook. From Pasture Trail (720 ft.): 0.4 mi., 450 ft., 0:25.

Five Finger Point Trail. This trail (yellow blazes) leaves East Rattlesnake Trail and descends gradually then moderately along a slope with occasional rough footing, losing 150 ft. in elevation. At 0.7 mi., it reaches a 1.3-mi. loop path circling the edge of Five Finger Point, with several interesting viewpoints (two reached by side paths) and attractive small beaches where swimming is permitted (no lifeguards). Loop from East Rattlesnake Trail (720 ft.): 2.7 mi., 150 ft., 1:25.

Butterworth Trail. This trail (green markers) leads to East Rattlesnake from Metcalf Rd. (gravel), which leaves NH 113 0.7 mi. east of the Holderness–Sandwich town line. Butterworth Trail leaves Metcalf Rd. on the right, 0.5 mi. from NH 113 (no parking at trailhead; park on the right, 100 yd. beyond the trailhead, by a cove on Squam Lake) and climbs moderately to the summit. The East Rattlesnake viewpoint is 0.1 mi. farther via Ridge Trail. From Metcalf Rd. (580 ft.): 0.7 mi., 700 ft., 0:40.

RED HILL TRAIL (LRCT; SLA MAP, LRCT RED HILL MAP)

From parking area (680 ft.) to:	⮁	↗	⏱
Red Hill summit (2,030 ft.)	1.7 mi.	1,350 ft.	1:30

This trail mostly follows an old jeep road and provides a fairly easy route to the fire tower on Red Hill, where you have fine views from the tower and a good outlook south from the summit ledges. From NH 25, just north of its jct. with NH 25B in Center Harbor, go northwest on Bean Rd. 1.5 mi., turn right (east) and follow Sibley Rd. (sign: fire lookout) 1.1 mi., turn left onto Red Hill Rd., and continue 0.2 mi. to a parking area on the right with a LRCT kiosk (sign: fire lookout).

The trail leaves the northwest side of the parking lot on a footpath marked with red diamonds; the former section of trail starting up an eroded road has been closed. The trail swings right twice, and at 0.2 mi. it crosses the eroded road mentioned above.

Now marked with green diamonds, Red Hill Trail continues ahead and ascends steadily on another old road, crossing a brook on a bridge. At 0.4 mi., another old road joins from the right (bear right here on the descent). At 0.5 mi., Red Hill Trail passes through a fence, joins a newer road for 20 yd., and turns left off it at an LRCT kiosk. Here, Cabin Trail (sign), marked with blue diamonds, continues ahead on the road, providing an option for a loop hike to the summit. Red Hill Trail passes the Horne cellar hole on the left (sign), skirts a gate, and follows the old fire warden road for a moderate and winding ascent to the summit. At 1.0 mi., a piped spring is on the left. At 1.5 mi., an unmaintained path joins from the left, and Eagle Cliff Trail (sign) enters on the left just before the fire tower and fire warden cabin on the summit of Red Hill.

CABIN TRAIL (LRCT; LRCT RED HILL MAP)

From Red Hill Trail (1,040 ft.) to:	⇅	↗	↻
Red Hill summit (2,030 ft.)	1.4 mi.	1,000 ft.	1:10
Loop over Red Hill via Red Hill Trail and Cabin Trail	3.6 mi.	1,350 ft.	2:30

This recently opened trail, marked with blue diamonds, continues straight (northeast) where Red Hill Trail turns left at a kiosk, 0.5 mi. from the parking area. It follows a wide woods road at easy to moderate grades, passing through an area with large maples and old stone walls. At 0.6 mi. it swings left, passing two entrances to a snowmobile trail on the right, and runs through a brushy area. It then descends slightly to an old hunter's cabin in the col between Red Hill and its southeastern spur at 0.7 mi. Bearing left in front of the cabin, it narrows to a footpath and makes a steady winding ascent through a fine oak forest on the southeastern slope of Red Hill. At 1.2 mi. it swings left up onto a grassy shoulder then descends slightly, bears left, climbs a steep pitch, and soon reaches the northeast corner of the summit clearing. Descending, Cabin Trail leaves the summit clearing on the northeast side of the tower at a sign and several blue diamonds.

EAGLE CLIFF TRAIL (SLA; MAP 3: L7, SLA MAP, LRCT RED HILL MAP)

Cumulative from Bean Rd. (580 ft.) to:	⇅	↗	↻
Eagle Cliff viewpoint (1,220 ft.)	0.6 mi.	650 ft.	0:40
Red Hill fire tower (2,030 ft.)	2.7 mi.	1,750 ft. (rev. 300 ft.)	2:15

This trail ascends Red Hill via Eagle Cliff, providing fine views of Squam Lake and the Squam Range. The part of the path that ascends to the best viewpoints is steep and rocky, much more difficult than Red Hill Trail, and may be hazardous in wet or icy conditions. A bypass path—recommended in adverse conditions, particularly for the descent—avoids the most difficult and dangerous section. Teedie Trail is also available as an alternative descent route in hazardous conditions. From NH 25, just north of its jct. with NH 25B in Center Harbor, follow Bean Rd. north for 5.2 mi. to the trail sign on the right, 0.4 mi. north of the Moultonborough–Sandwich town line. There is room for several cars to park on the shoulder.

Eagle Cliff Trail begins by crossing a ditch in a thicket then ascends steadily by switchbacks. At 0.5 mi., after a steep pitch, a bypass trail leaves on the right; it is about 0.1 mi. longer than the main trail, which becomes steep and rough with several rocky scrambles as it gets well up on the ledge. The bypass trail rejoins the main trail just below the best viewpoint on Eagle Cliff, at 0.6 mi. Eagle Cliff Trail turns right above the viewpoint, scrambles up a higher ledge, then enters the woods and climbs to the summit of Eagle Cliff. The trail swings right, crosses a knob with a view ahead to the main ridge of Red Hill, then descends sharply to a small pass at 1.0 mi., where Teedie Trail enters right.

Eagle Cliff Trail crosses another knoll, descends, and ascends steadily through a mixture of young growth in cutover areas and mature woods, with one more intervening descent. The trail finally levels out and meets Red Hill Trail just below the summit of Red Hill. Descending, the trail diverges right from Red Hill Trail (Jeep road) just below the fire warden cabin (sign).

TEEDIE TRAIL (SLA; SLA MAP, LRCT RED HILL MAP)

From Eagle Cliff Trail (1,320 ft.) to:	↥↧	↗	⟳
Bean Rd. (580 ft.)	0.7 mi.	0 ft. (rev. 750 ft.)	0:20

SEC 7

This yellow-blazed path leaves Eagle Cliff Trail in the col south of Eagle Cliff and descends steadily west by switchbacks, crossing through gaps in several stone walls in its lower half, to a small field on Bean Rd. at the Moultonborough–Sandwich town line, 0.4 mi. south of the beginning of Eagle Cliff Trail. The trailhead (no parking here) is marked by a sign at the back edge of the field, where the trail enters the woods. Teedie Trail is much less scenic than Eagle Cliff Trail but avoids the descent over the Eagle Cliff ledges in adverse conditions.

SECTION EIGHT

MT. CHOCORUA AND THE EASTERN SANDWICH RANGE

INTRODUCTION

This section covers trails on Mts. Chocorua, Paugus, Passaconaway, and Whiteface and on their subsidiary peaks and ridges. The region is bounded on the north by the Kancamagus Highway (NH 112), on the east by NH 16, on the south by NH 25, and on the west by Section Seven (Waterville Valley and Squam Lakes Region). This division places Mt. Tripyramid in Section Seven and Mt. Whiteface and the Sleeper Ridge in Section Eight. The Sandwich Range Wilderness includes 35,800 acres on and around the principal peaks of the range. In accordance with USFS Wilderness policy, the trails in the Sandwich Range Wilderness are generally maintained to a lower standard than trails outside the Wilderness Area. Considerable care may be required to follow them.

The entire section is covered by AMC's *White Mountains Trail Map 3: Crawford Notch–Sandwich Range.* The CMC, WODC, and the WMNF maintain most of the trails in this area. The CMC marks its trails with yellow paint and signs, whereas the WODC trails have blue paint and signs; in the Sandwich Range Wilderness, most signs are unpainted wood; blazes, where still present, will be allowed to fade and will not be repainted unless deemed necessary for hiker safety or resource protection. The WODC publishes a contour map of the Sandwich Range Wilderness and the surrounding area, with short trail descriptions on the back, which covers all of Section Eight; the map can be obtained from the WODC or at area stores. The CMC publishes a contour map of the Chocorua–Paugus region that includes a peak-identifying panorama of the view from the summit of Mt. Chocorua; the map can be obtained from the CMC or at area stores.

SEC 8

ROAD ACCESS

Confusion in finding trailheads on the southern side of the Sandwich Range sometimes results from the rather erratic behavior of NH 113 and NH 113A, the alternate routes between North Sandwich and Tamworth. Both roads change direction frequently, and NH 113 unites with and then diverges from NH 25 between its two jcts. with NH 113A. Follow access directions very carefully for trailheads on the southeast slopes of the Sandwich Range.

Whiteface Intervale Rd. leaves NH 113A 2.9 mi. north of the western jct. of NH 113 and NH 113A, where NH 113A bends from north–south to east–west. Bennett St. turns left from Whiteface Intervale Rd. 0.1 mi. from NH 113A, and the trailhead for Flat Mtn. Pond Trail (leading to McCrillis Trail) is 0.3 mi. farther on Whiteface Intervale Rd. Ferncroft Rd. leaves NH 113A in Wonalancet village at a right-angle turn in the main highway; at 0.5 mi. from NH 113A, a gravel road (FR 337) turns right and reaches a parking area and kiosk in 0.1 mi. No parking is permitted on Ferncroft Rd. beyond this gravel road. This parking area is plowed in winter.

A gravel road runs between NH 16 (at the bridge that crosses the south end of Chocorua Lake, about 1.5 mi. north of Chocorua village) and NH 113A (3.3 mi. north of the eastern jct. of NH 113 and NH 113A in Tamworth, just north of the bridge over Paugus Brook). This road is known as Chocorua Lake Rd., from NH 16 to its jct. with Philbrick Neighborhood Rd., and as Fowler's Mill Rd., from that jct. to NH 113A. Paugus Rd. (FR 68) branches north (sign) from Fowler's Mill Rd., 1.2 mi. north of NH 113A and 3.4 mi. west of NH 16, and runs to a parking area for Brook, Liberty, and Bolles trails at 0.8 mi., beyond which the road is closed to vehicles. The last 0.6 mi. is not plowed in winter and parking is limited.

GEOGRAPHY

The Sandwich Range and the jumbled collection of ridges to its west compose a mass of mountains extending about 30 mi., from Conway on the Saco River to Campton on the Pemigewasset, with summits just over 4,000 ft. high rising abruptly from the lake country to the south. Although the Sandwich Range is not outstanding for its elevation—the North Peak of Mt. Tripyramid, at 4,180 ft., is its highest point—the mountains are nevertheless quite rugged, and their viewpoints offer interesting combinations of mountain, forest, and lake scenery.

The picturesque rocky cone at the east end of the range, Mt. Chocorua (3,500 ft.), is reputedly one of the most frequently photographed mountains in the world—and certainly one of the most frequently ascended peaks in the White Mountains. Mt. Chocorua has a substantial network of trails; several are very heavily used, but you can usually avoid crowds (up to the summit, at least) by taking less-popular trails. Piper Trail, Champney Falls Trail, and Liberty Trail are probably the most popular. Confusion sometimes occurs from the fact that several trails are thought to extend all the way to the summit. Multiple jcts. are below the summit, but only two trails (Piper Trail and Liberty Trail) reach the summit, and they coincide for the last 50 yd. up a small, steep gully.

In descending from the summit, go 50 yd. southwest on the only marked path, down the small gully to the first jct., where Liberty Trail turns left and Piper Trail turns right. Care should be taken to follow the correct trail on the descent, as one could easily end up on the wrong side of the mountain. The trails on the open rocks are marked with cairns and yellow paint, and jcts. are signed with WMNF signs or paint, or both. Many of the blazes are faded, so on the open ledges the trails must be followed with care. Camping on the upper slopes of Mt. Chocorua, a Forest Protection Area, is severely restricted to prevent damage to the mountain's natural qualities.

Caution: The extensive areas of open ledge that make Mt. Chocorua so attractive also pose a very real danger. Many of the trails have sections with ledges that are dangerous when wet or icy, and the summit and upper ledges are severely exposed to lightning during electrical storms. Despite its comparatively modest elevation, Mt. Chocorua is one of the most dangerous peaks in the White Mountains in a thunderstorm. Although Mt. Chocorua is relatively low compared with other major White Mountain peaks, its trailheads are also located at low elevations, resulting in a substantial amount of elevation gain that makes it as strenuous a trip as many much higher peaks. The safety of any untreated water source in this heavily used area is doubtful. In winter, the upper part of this mountain is potentially dangerous due to steep, icy slopes and exposure to weather; only those with proper winter mountaineering equipment and experience should attempt the ascent.

The Three Sisters, which form the northern ridge of Mt. Chocorua, are nearly as tall and have bare summits. First Sister (3,354 ft.) is the tallest of the three rocky knobs, and Middle Sister (3,340 ft.) bears the remains of an old stone fire lookout. Carter Ledge (2,420 ft.) is a prominent ledgy spur just east of the Three Sisters, with excellent views. White Ledge (2,010 ft.) is a bluff farther east of the Three Sisters, with a ledgy top from which you have a good view east. The rocky south shoulder of Mt. Chocorua is called Bald Mtn. (2,140 ft.). On the northwest side of the mountain is Champney Falls, named for Benjamin Champney (1817–1907), a pioneer White Mountain artist. These falls are beautiful when there is a good flow of water but meager in dry seasons.

SEC 8

A low but rugged and shaggy mountain once aptly called "Old Shag," Mt. Paugus (3,198 ft.), was named in 1875 by the poet Lucy Larcom for the Pequawket chief who led the Abenaki forces at the battle of Lovewell's Pond in 1725. Due to its lumpy shape and scarred sides, Mt. Paugus has been given many names; it may hold the record for having had the most names—both common and unusual—of any peak in the White Mountains, including Bald Mtn., Moose Mtn., Ragged Mtn., Deer Mtn., Hunchback, Middle Mtn., and Frog Mtn. All trails end at an overgrown ledge 0.3 mi. south of the wooded true summit, which is not reached by any trail; good views can be obtained by descending a short distance down the southwest side of this ledge. Paugus Pass (2,220 ft.) is the lowest pass on the ridge that connects Mt. Paugus with Mt. Passaconaway and the Wonalancet Range on the west.

A graceful peak, Mt. Passaconaway (4,043 ft.) was named for the great and legendary sachem of the Pennacooks (his name is thought to mean "child of the bear") who ruled at the time the first Europeans settled in New England. The mountain is densely wooded, with no view from the true summit, but a ledge on Walden Trail a short distance from the summit offers a fine outlook to the east and north, and a ledge near the top of Dicey's Mill Trail offers a view to the northwest. Another outlook on Walden Trail presents a fine view south. A side path diverges from Walden Trail between the summit and the east outlook and descends 0.3 mi. to the splendid, secluded north outlook.

A major ridge extends southeast to Paugus Pass over the two subpeaks that give the mountain its characteristic steplike profile when viewed from the lake country to the south. The first subpeak bears the unofficial name of Nanamocomuck Peak (3,340 ft.), after the eldest son of Passaconaway. Square Ledge (2,620 ft.) is a bold, rocky promontory that is a northeast spur of Nanamocomuck Peak. From the farther subpeak, which is sometimes called Mt. Hedgehog, or the Wonalancet Hedgehog (3,140 ft.) and which has two viewpoints, the Wonalancet Range runs south, consisting of Hibbard Mtn. (2,940 ft.) and Mt. Wonalancet (2,780 ft.); both of these peaks are wooded but have outlook ledges. Mt. Wonalancet is named for a Pennacook sachem who was a son of Passaconaway and succeeded his father as senior chieftain.

Another Hedgehog Mtn. (2,532 ft.) is located north of Mt. Passaconaway. This small but rugged mountain rises between Downes and Oliverian brooks and commands fine views over the Swift River Valley and up to Mt. Passaconaway; the best views are from ledges near the summit, on the east shoulder, and at Allen's Ledge. Potash Mtn. (2,700 ft.) lies to the west of Hedgehog Mtn., between Downes and Sabbaday brooks. The summit of Potash is open and ledgy and affords excellent views of the surrounding mountains and valleys in most directions.

The precipitous ledges on its south face doubtless gave Mt. Whiteface (4,020 ft.) its name. Its true summit is wooded, but the slightly lower south summit, 0.3 mi. from the true summit, affords magnificent views from the bare ledge at the top of the precipices. Two lesser ridges run south on either side of the cliffs, and the backbone of the mountain runs north then northeast, connecting Mt. Whiteface with Mt. Passaconaway. Sleeper Ridge on the northwest connects Mt. Whiteface to Mt. Tripyramid.

East of Mt. Whiteface lies the Bowl, a secluded valley of glacial origin encircled by the main ridge of Mt. Whiteface and the south ridge of Mt. Passaconaway. This area was never logged due to the efforts of many local people. Louis Tainter represented the Kennett lumber interests in negotiating the sale of this land to the WMNF in a virgin state. His ashes rest in a crypt cut into the ledge at the south summit of Mt. Whiteface. The Bowl was preserved for many decades as a special natural area, and the Bowl Research Natural Area is included within the Sandwich Range Wilderness.

West of Mt. Whiteface, the range sprawls: One major ridge continues northwest over the high, rolling Sleeper Ridge—composed of West Sleeper (3,881 ft.) and East Sleeper (3,860 ft.)—to Mt. Tripyramid then ends at Livermore Pass, the high notch (2,900 ft.) between Mt. Tripyramid and Mt. Kancamagus that is crossed by Livermore Trail. Although Sleeper Ridge could have been named quite aptly for the sleepy appearance of its two rounded, rather gently sloping domes, it is actually named for Katherine Sleeper Walden, a civic-minded local innkeeper whose efforts in trail building (she founded the WODC), conservation, and public improvements were so energetic and pervasive that she earned the sobriquet "matriarch of Wonalancet and the WODC." Walden was very active in preventing the Bowl from being logged. Two natural features (Sleeper Ridge and Mt. Katherine) and a trail (Kate Sleeper Trail) have been named for her, and Walden Trail memorializes her husband, Arthur Walden, founder of the famous Chinook husky kennels in Wonalancet.

Everything in the Sandwich Range west and southwest of the Sleeper Ridge is covered in Section Seven.

Several public and quasi-public reservations in this region offer the opportunity for pleasant walking. Of particular note is Hemenway State Forest, where fine views of the Sandwich Range can be obtained from the fire tower on Great Hill (1,300 ft.), which is reached in 0.5 mi. (300-ft. ascent) by old roads that leave gravel Great Hill Rd. (off NH 113A) at its jct. with Hemenway Rd. On foot, follow a road east for 0.2 mi., turn left then turn right at 0.3 mi. by a cabin, and continue to the tower. On the northeast side of Hemenway State Forest is the Big Pines Natural Area, an impressive stand of large white pine and hemlock. Several trails are maintained here by the Tamworth Conservation Commission, providing an attractive alternative route to Great Hill. (These are shown on Map 3: K9.)

The trailhead (sign: Big Pines Natural Area) is on the south side of NH 113A, 2.9 mi. northwest of its jct. with NH 113 in Tamworth village. An access trail descends 0.1 mi. to a bridge over the Swift River, passing two jcts. with an unmarked and obscure 0.2-mi. loop path to the left. On the south side of the bridge is the lower loop jct. of Betty Steele Loop Trail. The right (west) half of the loop, the direct route to Great Hill, ascends 0.3 mi. to the upper loop jct., passing the largest white pine in the stand. The rougher left (east) half of the loop reaches the upper loop jct. in 0.5 mi.

From the upper loop jct., Peg King Spur Trail, 0.6 mi. long, ascends easily then rather steeply to the tower on Great Hill. Ascent to Great Hill via the access trail, the west half of Betty Steele Loop Trail, and Peg King Spur Trail is 1.1 mi., 600 ft. (rev. 50 ft.), 0:50.

Another network of trails (shown on the WODC map and also on a map at chocorualakeconservancy.org/public-access/trail-map) is maintained in the 700-acre Chocorua Conservation Lands south of Mt. Chocorua. This area, managed by the Chocorua Lake Conservancy, includes TNC's Frank Bolles Reserve, the Clark Reserve, and the Mary P. Scott Reserve. An interesting 3.8-mi. loop, with 750-ft. elevation gain, visits several attractive natural features, including Heron Pond (Lonely Lake), a glacial kettle pond; Bickford Heights (1,080 ft.), a low ridge with a restricted view west; and a number of impressive glacial boulders. Use Old Mail Road and Highland, Hunter's, Bickford Heights, Middle, and Heron Pond trails. The ledges on the west side of Bickford Heights Trail are steep and slippery. The trails are marked with cairns and TNC markers. Best access is from the Hammond Trail parking area, starting on the south side of Scott Rd. at a sign for Bolles Reserve.

East of White Ledge is the Tin Mountain Conservation Center's Rockwell Sanctuary, located on the south side of Bald Hill Rd., 1.2 mi. west of NH 16. (Bald Hill Rd. leaves NH 16 0.4 mi. south of the jct. with NH 112.) A map of the trail system, which provides access to Chase Pond, an old quarry, and other features, is at tinmountain.org/wp-content/uploads/RockwellMap.pdf. At White Lake State Park, several miles farther south on the west side of NH 16 and just north of West Ossipee, there is a 2-mi. trail around the lake and a branch loop that passes through the Pitch Pine National Natural Landmark.

CAMPING
Sandwich Range Wilderness

In accordance with USFS Wilderness policy, hiking groups in the Sandwich Range Wilderness may not exceed ten people, and no more than ten people may occupy any designated or non-designated campsite. See p. xiii for more information on Wilderness Area regulations. All shelters within this Wilderness have been removed.

Forest Protection Areas

The WMNF has established a number of Forest Protection Areas, or FPAs, where camping and wood or charcoal fires are prohibited throughout the year. See p. xxiv for general FPA regulations.

In the area covered by Section Eight, camping is also forbidden within 0.25 mi. of Champney Falls and at any point within the Mt. Chocorua FPA, except at Jim Liberty Cabin (overnight use allowed inside the cabin only) and Camp Penacook. No wood or charcoal fires are allowed within the Bowl Research Natural Area.

No camping is permitted within 200 ft. of certain trails. In 2016, designated trails included Champney Falls Trail from the edge of the Kancamagus Highway FPA to the edge of the Champney Falls FPA. No camping is permitted on WMNF land within 0.25 mi. of certain roads, and camping on private roadside land is illegal, except by permission of the landowner. In 2016, these roads included the Kancamagus Highway.

Established Trailside Campsites

Camp Penacook (WMNF), located on a spur path off Piper Trail on Mt. Chocorua, is an open shelter that accommodates six to eight people, with a nearby tentsite. Water is nearby in a small stream.

Jim Liberty Cabin (WMNF) is located on a ledgy hump 0.5 mi. below the summit of Mt. Chocorua. Overnight use is allowed only inside the cabin, and fires are not allowed. The water source is scanty in dry weather.

Camp Rich (WODC), a shelter formerly located on the southwest side of Mt. Passaconaway on Dicey's Mill Trail at about 3,500 ft. elevation, has been removed. The latrine at the site has been retained, and camping is permitted. Water is available from a small brook on Dicey's Mill Trail just below the campsite.

Camp Shehadi (WODC), at the jct. of Rollins and Kate Sleeper trails, 0.1 mi. north of the south summit of Mt. Whiteface, has been removed. Camping at the site (which has no convenient water source) is discouraged.

Camp Heermance (WODC), near the south summit of Mt. Whiteface, has been removed. Camping at the site (which has no convenient water source) is discouraged.

SEC
8

SUGGESTED HIKES

■ Easy Hikes
MT. KATHERINE

🚶 🐕 📷 🥾   ↻   ↗   ○

RT via Blueberry Ledge Trail and Pasture Path	3.2 mi.	250 ft.	1:45

A gentle stroll leads to a ledge with a limited but picturesque view of Mt. Chocorua. See Blueberry Ledge Trail, p. 407.

CHAMPNEY AND PITCHER FALLS

	⤸	↗	⟳
RT via Champney Falls Trail and spur path	3.2 mi.	600 ft.	1:55

An easy-graded climb reaches a pair of waterfalls. See Champney Falls Trail, p. 382.

ALLEN'S LEDGE

	⤸	↗	⟳
RT via UNH Trail and spur path	2.2 mi.	600 ft.	1:25

A moderate climb delivers a good viewpoint. See UNH Trail, p. 404.

BIG ROCK CAVE

	⤸	↗	⟳
RT via Cabin and Big Rock Cave trails	3.8 mi.	1,250 ft.	2:30

This interesting boulder cave on a southern spur of Mt. Paugus is a good objective for children. See Cabin Trail, p. 396.

■ Moderate Hikes

WHITE LEDGE

	⤸	↗	⟳
LP via White Ledge Loop Trail	4.4 mi.	1,450 ft.	2:55

A loop over an eastern spur of Mt. Chocorua delivers several views. See White Ledge Loop Trail, p. 383.

POTASH MTN.

	⤸	↗	⟳
RT via Downes Brook and Mt. Potash trails	4.4 mi.	1,450 ft.	2:55 min

A moderate trek leads to a small, open peak on the north side of the Sandwich Range. See Downes Brook Trail, p. 411.

HEDGEHOG MTN.

	⤸	↗	⟳
LP via UNH Trail	4.7 mi.	1,400 ft.	3:05

Looping this low mountain north of Mt. Passaconaway offers three viewpoints. See UNH Trail, p. 404.

SEC
8

CARTER LEDGE

🌫️🏃‍♂️🐾   ↻   ↗   ○

RT via Piper, Nickerson Ledge, and Carter Ledge trails	5.6 mi.	1,650 ft.	3:40

A scenic route leads to this magnificent open ledge; the climb is steep near the top. To begin, see Piper Trail, p. 386.

WONALANCET RANGE

🏃‍♂️🌲🐾   ↻   ↗   ○

LP via Old Mast Road, Walden Trail, and Wonalancet Range Trail	6.2 mi.	2,200 ft.	4:10

A rugged loop hike traverses three spurs of Mt. Passaconaway with several views. To begin, see Old Mast Road, p. 399.

■ Strenuous Hikes

MT. CHOCORUA

❄️🌫️🏃‍♂️🛶△🐾   ↻   ↗   ○

RT via Champney Falls and Piper trails	7.6 mi.	2,250 ft.	4:55
LP via Brook and Liberty trails	7.5 mi.	2,750 ft.	5:05
LP via Piper, Nickerson Ledge, Carter Ledge, Middle Sister, Piper, Liberty, Hammond, Weetamoo, and Piper trails	9.6 mi.	3,200 ft.	6:25

There are several attractive routes up one of the most popular peaks in the White Mountains. The first, above, is moderate and leaves from the Kancamagus Highway (see Champney Falls Trail, p. 382). The second makes a fine loop, but with significantly steeper and rougher climbing from the southwest (see Brook Trail, p. 390). The third is even longer and even more challenging (to begin, see Piper Trail, p. 386).

SEC 8

MT. PAUGUS

🏃‍♂️🌲🐾   ↻   ↗   ○

LP via Bolles, Old Paugus, Lawrence, Cabin, and Whitin Brook trails	8.6 mi.	2,450 ft.	5:30

A fine loop over this interesting mountain starts at the Paugus Rd. trailhead. To begin, see Bolles Trail, p. 392.

MT. PASSACONAWAY

🏃 🎿 🏔 🦌 🔭

	⇅	↗	○
RT via Oliverian Brook Trail, Passaconaway Cutoff, Square Ledge Trail, and Walden Trail	10.0 mi.	2,900 ft.	6:25

The route ascending this wooded peak from the Kancamagus Highway offers several views; add 0.6 mi. and 200 ft. for a side trip to the spectacular north outlook. To begin, see Oliverian Brook Trail, p. 398.

MT. WHITEFACE

🥾 🏃 🏔 🔭

	⇅	↗	○
RT via Blueberry Ledge and Rollins trails	8.4 mi.	3,000 ft.	5:40
LP to Whiteface and Passaconaway via Blueberry Ledge Trail, Rollins Trail, Dicey's Mill Trail, Walden Trail, East Loop, and Dicey's Mill Trail	12.0 mi.	3,950 ft.	8:00
RT via Flat Mtn. Pond, McCrillis, and Rollins trails	10.4 mi.	3,350 ft.	6:55

The broad ledges of Whiteface's south summit offer an excellent view over the lake country to the south; the ledges and the wooded true summit can be reached by ascending the first route above, a scenic and challenging hike that can be extended into a scenic loop using the second route. (To begin either, see Blueberry Ledge Trail, p. 407). The third is a less-used route (see Flat Mtn. Pond Trail, p. 354).

SEC 8

TRAIL DESCRIPTIONS
MT. CHOCORUA AND VICINITY
CHAMPNEY FALLS TRAIL (WMNF; MAP 3: J9)

Cumulative from Kancamagus Highway (1,260 ft.) to:	⇅	↗	○
Champney Falls loop, lower end (1,750 ft.)	1.4 mi.	500 ft.	0:55
Piper Trail (3,180 ft.)	3.2 mi.	1,900 ft.	2:35
Mt. Chocorua summit (3,500 ft.) via Piper Trail	3.8 mi.	2,250 ft.	3:00

This heavily used trail runs from a large parking area off the Kancamagus Highway (sign: Champney Brook Trail), 10.5 mi west of NH 16 in Conway, to Piper Trail, in the flat saddle between Mt. Chocorua and the Three Sisters. Champney Falls is attractive, particularly when there is a good flow of water, and Champney Falls Trail has moderate grades all the way.

Leaving the parking area, the trail soon crosses Twin Brook on step stones and turns right; the former footbridge here was damaged by a flood and removed. (In high water, this crossing can be avoided by walking east along the highway across the bridge then turning right into the woods at a No Parking sign and following an old woods road to meet the trail in 90 yd.) The trail passes a jct. at 0.1 mi., where Bolles Trail diverges right, and proceeds south at easy grades, mostly on an old logging road, to Champney Brook. There, at 0.5 mi., Champney Falls Trail swings right and up onto a hemlock ridge to avoid an abandoned section of trail along the brook then descends left and returns to the old road along the brook at 0.7 mi.

Champney Falls Loop (WMNF). At 1.4 mi., this recently reconstructed loop diverges left, descends to cross a tributary, and ascends to the base of Champney Falls in 0.2 mi.; here, Pitcher Falls can be seen on a tributary brook in a gorge off to the left. The loop path then climbs steeply up rock steps beside Champney Falls and swings right back to the main trail; total distance: 0.4 mi., 250 ft., 20 min. (*Caution:* Many of the ledges in the area around the falls are very slippery; there have been serious accidents in this vicinity.)

Champney Falls Trail continues up the valley, and the loop path rejoins at 1.7 mi. The steady ascent continues, with rocky footing. At 2.4 mi., the trail turns right onto the first of several switchbacks, and at 3.0 mi. Champney Falls Cutoff diverges left toward Middle Sister.

Champney Falls Cutoff (WMNF). This short trail—which has also been called Middle Sister Cutoff—leads from Champney Falls Trail to the col between Middle Sister and First Sister, giving access to the fine views from the old fire lookout site on Middle Sister. Leaving Champney Falls Trail, the cutoff follows an old road past a fine outlook ledge at 0.1 mi. and climbs moderately on a side hill then swings right onto open ledges and soon reaches Middle Sister Trail; total distance: 0.3 mi., 200 ft., 15 min.

SEC 8

From this jct., **Champney Falls Trail** climbs past an outlook (sign) on a side path to the right and soon reaches a ledgy saddle. The trail then passes the jct. on the left with Middle Sister Trail, and in another 80 yd. ends at its jct. with Piper Trail, 0.6 mi. from the summit of Mt. Chocorua. Turn right on Piper Trail to continue to the summit.

WHITE LEDGE LOOP TRAIL (WMNF; MAP 3: J10)

Cumulative from White Ledge Campground (750 ft.) to:	⥮	↗	○
Loop jct. (840 ft.)	0.3 mi.	100 ft.	0:10
White Ledge summit (2,010 ft.) via east branch	2.7 mi.	1,450 ft. (rev. 200 ft.)	2:05
White Ledge summit (2,010 ft.) via west branch	1.7 mi.	1,250 ft.	1:30
Complete loop	4.4 mi.	1,450 ft.	2:55

This loop trail to White Ledge is reached from White Ledge Campground on NH 16, 5.0 mi. south of its jct. with NH 112; parking is available near the restrooms, 0.1 mi. from NH 16. (The entrance to the campground is gated from late fall through spring; only limited parking is available outside the gate, and in winter, there may be no plowed parking available.)

The trail diverges right from the north end of the main campground road, 0.1 mi. from parking, swings right, and reaches the loop jct. at 0.3 mi. The loop is described here in a counterclockwise direction. Taking the east branch to the right across a small brook, the trail turns left and then right and bears left onto an old road at 0.6 mi., where a former alternative access route (now closed) joined from the right. The trail now climbs steadily to the height-of-land east of the main bluff of White Ledge at 1.3 mi. then descends gradually through a brushy area. At 2.0 mi. it turns sharply left and then left again and climbs moderately up the east end of White Ledge, through woods and then across ledges with outlooks to the north; follow blazes and cairns carefully on the ledges, some of which are slippery.

The trail reaches the summit at 2.7 mi., where you have a restricted view east from a short spur path to the left; a better view east is reached by an obscure side path that leaves the main trail 60 yd. north of the high point and leads 50 yd. down to open ledges. The main trail descends over ledges past a restricted outlook to Mt. Chocorua, continues steadily down through woods, passes an unmarked side path that leads 30 yd. left to a fine southeast outlook at 3.2 mi., turns sharply left at 3.7 mi., descends across two brooks, and reaches the loop jct. at 4.1 mi.

CARTER LEDGE TRAIL (WMNF; MAP 3: J10–J9)

Cumulative from White Ledge Campground (750 ft.) to:	⇅	↗	⟳
Middle Sister Trail, lower jct. (1,350 ft.)	1.1 mi.	600 ft.	0:50
Nickerson Ledge Trail (1,740 ft.)	2.0 mi.	1,000 ft.	1:30
Carter Ledge (2,420 ft.)	2.8 mi.	1,700 ft.	2:15
Middle Sister Trail, upper jct. (3,150 ft.)	3.7 mi.	2,500 ft. (rev. 100 ft.)	3:05

This trail provides an attractive route to Middle Sister from White Ledge Campground (on NH 16, 5.0 mi. south of its jct. with NH 112) or from Piper Trail (via Nickerson Ledge Trail). It is steep and ledgy in places, with several fairly difficult scrambles in its upper section, and is better suited for ascent than descent. Carter Ledge, an interesting objective in its own right, is a fine open ledge with views of Mt. Chocorua and one of only a few colonies of jack pine *(Pinus banksiana)* that exist in the White Mountains. The trailhead is located on the left branch of the campground road; park in the parking lot at the campground picnic area. (See note under White Ledge Loop Trail about off-season parking.)

Carter Ledge Trail diverges west from the left branch road 0.1 mi. south of the main fork. The trail climbs moderately to the long southeast ridge of Carter Ledge, passing a jct. at 1.1 mi., where Middle Sister Trail diverges to the right. Carter Ledge Trail then continues to a flat, densely wooded shoulder and the jct. with Nickerson Ledge Trail, which enters on the left at 2.0 mi. After a short descent, Carter Ledge Trail crosses a small brook and soon ascends a steep, gravelly slope with poor footing then turns sharply right and up at a gravelly slide with a view of Mt. Chocorua; this turn is easily missed, especially on the descent.

Continuing to climb steeply through woods and then across ledges with many fine views, the trail passes through the jack pine stand and reaches the summit of the ledge at 2.8 mi., where you have a good view north a few steps to the right of the trail. The trail passes through a sag then climbs, steeply at times, up the slope of Third Sister, with several excellent outlooks, but with some ledges that can be dangerous in wet or icy conditions. Higher up is a particularly tricky scramble across a potentially slippery, downward sloping ledge (especially difficult on the descent), and, after several more scrambles, the trail reaches Middle Sister Trail 0.3 mi. northeast of Middle Sister.

MIDDLE SISTER TRAIL (WMNF; MAP 3: J10–J9)

Cumulative from lower jct. with Carter Ledge Trail (1,350 ft.) to:	⇅	↗	⏱
Middle Sister summit (3,340 ft.)	3.6 mi.	2,100 ft. (rev. 100 ft.)	2:50
Champney Falls Trail (3,180 ft.)	4.1 mi.	2,250 ft. (rev. 300 ft.)	3:10

SEC 8

This trail begins on Carter Ledge Trail 1.1 mi. from the WMNF White Ledge Campground, climbs over the Three Sisters, and ends at Champney Falls Trail in the saddle between the Sisters and Mt. Chocorua. In its upper part, Middle Sister Trail provides good views. Follow markings carefully across the open ledges of the Sisters.

Leaving Carter Ledge Trail, this trail ascends gradually with occasional minor descents through mixed hardwoods and softwoods and crosses Hobbs Brook at 1.3 mi. At 1.8 mi., Middle Sister Trail joins an older route of the trail, swinging left and climbing more steeply with rough footing to the col between the Three Sisters ridge and Blue Mtn. at 2.4 mi. Here, the trail turns sharply left and ascends steadily along the northeast spur of the Third Sister, passing a good outlook north at 2.9 mi. At 3.3 mi., Carter Ledge Trail enters on the left. Middle Sister Trail climbs steeply with good views and several ledge scrambles, crosses the ledgy summit of Third Sister and a small dip beyond, and reaches the summit of the Middle Sister at 3.6 mi.

The trail descends across ledges to a col, where it passes Champney Falls Cutoff (right), climbs over the open ledges of First Sister, and descends steeply in the open then moderately through woods to its terminus on Champney Falls Trail. From here, Champney Falls Trail leads 80 yd. left to Piper Trail, and then Piper Trail leads 0.6 mi. right to the summit of Mt. Chocorua.

PIPER TRAIL (WMNF; MAP 3: J10–J9)

Cumulative from WMNF parking area off NH 16 (780 ft.) to:	⇅	↗	↻
Nickerson Ledge Trail (1,380 ft.)	1.2 mi.	600 ft.	0:55
Chocorua River crossing (1,580 ft.)	1.8 mi.	800 ft.	1:20
Camp Penacook spur trail (2,500 ft.)	2.8 mi.	1,700 ft.	2:15
Champney Falls Trail (3,180 ft.)	3.6 mi.	2,400 ft.	3:00
Mt. Chocorua summit (3,500 ft.)	4.2 mi.	2,700 ft.	3:25

This heavily used trail to Mt. Chocorua from NH 16, first blazed by Joshua Piper in the 1870s, begins behind the sign for the former Davies General Store, which is located 6.2 mi. south of the east terminus of the Kancamagus Highway (NH 112). It is a scenic and well-constructed route with generally good footing. To reach the large trailhead parking area (not plowed in winter), drive on gravel Piper Trail Rd. to the right of the former store (sign: Piper Trail) for 0.2 mi.

The trail enters the woods at a kiosk, crosses a bridge over a small brook, swings right and follows it for 0.3 mi., then turns right to join a woods road that is the old route of the trail. (The section of the old route leading back from here to NH 16 is not open to the public.) Weetamoo Trail diverges left at 0.6 mi., and Piper Trail ascends moderately. Nickerson Ledge Trail diverges right at 1.2 mi., and grades are easy to a crossing of the Chocorua River (a small brook at this point) on a bridge at 1.8 mi. The trail now ascends moderately then climbs a series of switchbacks through spruce forest, with many stone steps. At 2.8 mi., a spur path (sign: Shelter) diverges left and climbs, steeply at times, 0.2 mi. and 200 ft. to Camp Penacook (an open shelter with a nearby tentsite, water, and a view southeast). About 50 yd. before reaching the shelter, the spur turns right, as an unmarked path leads 50 yd. left to a small brook.

The main trail turns sharply right at the shelter spur jct. and ascends, with more rock steps, reaching the first of several open ledges with spectacular views to the north, east, and south at 3.0 mi. After passing more outlooks, the trail reenters the woods and climbs to the ridge crest, where

Champney Falls Trail enters right at 3.6 mi. Here Piper Trail turns left (south) and skirts the east side of a hump, and in another 0.2 mi., West Side Trail enters on the right. Piper Trail soon emerges from the woods and, marked with cairns and faded yellow blazes (follow with care), continues south along the ridge over open ledges with occasional scrambles. After traversing along the east side of the crest, the trail swings right and climbs over a rocky knob, passes through a patch of scrub, and ascends along the west side of the summit cone to the jct. with Liberty Trail. Now coinciding with Liberty Trail, Piper Trail turns left (east) and climbs a small, steep rock gully to the summit; at the top, the high point is to the left.

Descending from the summit, go 40 yd. west on the only marked path, down the small, steep, ledgy gully to the first jct., where Liberty Trail turns left and Piper Trail turns right. Care should be taken to follow the correct trail on the descent, as one could easily end up on the wrong side of the mountain.

NICKERSON LEDGE TRAIL (WMNF; MAP 3: J10)

From Piper Trail (1,380 ft.) to:	⇅	↗	⟳
Carter Ledge Trail (1,740 ft.)	0.8 mi.	350 ft.	0:35

This trail connects Piper Trail with Carter Ledge Trail and Middle Sister, making possible loop hikes that include the attractive ledges on the northeast part of the mountain. Nickerson Ledge Trail leaves Piper Trail 1.2 mi. from the parking lot off NH 16 and climbs rather steeply for 0.2 mi. to Nickerson Ledge (on the right), which has a view south to the Ossipee Range and Bald Mtn., then continues along a broad, densely wooded ridge with a gradual ascent to Carter Ledge Trail, 2.0 mi. above White Ledge Campground.

WEETAMOO TRAIL (CMC; MAP 3: J10–J9)

From Piper Trail (960 ft.) to:	⇅	↗	⟳
Hammond Trail (2,200 ft.)	1.9 mi.	1,250 ft.	1:35

This attractive trail with moderate grades connects the lower part of Piper Trail, 0.6 mi. from the parking lot off NH 16, with Hammond Trail well up on Bald Mtn. and gives access to the open ledges of the south ridge of Mt. Chocorua from Piper Trail.

Weetamoo Trail diverges left from Piper Trail, ascends easily, descends slightly, and crosses the Chocorua River in a fine hemlock grove at 0.4 mi. Weetamoo Trail turns right and follows the river then a tributary upstream, swings left, and climbs a long switchback. The trail ascends through young hardwood growth, enters spruce woods, turns sharply left at 1.4 mi., and reaches Weetamoo Rock, an immense boulder on the left, at 1.7 mi. The trail ends at Hammond Trail, 2.0 mi. from the summit of Mt. Chocorua via Hammond Trail and Liberty Trail.

HAMMOND TRAIL (CMC; MAP 3: J10–J9)

Cumulative from parking area on Scott Rd. (610 ft.) to:	⇅	↗	⟳
Bald Mtn. (2,130 ft.)	1.9 mi.	1,500 ft.	1:40
Liberty Trail (2,550 ft.)	3.0 mi.	2,050 ft. (rev. 100 ft.)	2:30

This trail provides a route up Bald Mtn. and the ledgy south shoulder of Mt. Chocorua. The trailhead is on Scott Rd., a dirt road (sometimes plowed in winter) that leaves NH 16 at a road sign on the left (west), just north of a large boulder, 3.1 mi. north of the jct. with NH 113 in Chocorua village. Parking is on the right, 0.4 mi. from NH 16. If the small parking area (located on private land) is full, hikers should take care not to block access to the house at the end of the road.

The trail leaves the parking area, climbs over a small ridge, swings left and crosses Stony Brook, passes the WMNF boundary, then recrosses Stony Brook. At 0.8 mi., the trail crosses an old logging road then climbs steadily through a hardwood forest. After several switchbacks, the trail continues up over wooded ledges and passes a side path (left) to a ledge with a restricted view to the southwest shortly before reaching the crest of Bald Mtn. at 1.9 mi. The trail crosses a sag then ascends along the ridge. At 2.1 mi., Weetamoo Trail enters on the right, and Hammond Trail ascends through spruce woods, scrambling up through a rocky cleft at 2.3 mi. In another 35 yd. a side path ascends 25 yd. right to a large, ledgy area with views east and northeast. In the next 0.2 mi. there are two more outlooks to the right. The trail dips to a sag then ascends to a ledgy hump, where the summit of Mt. Chocorua is in sight ahead. The trail descends then rises slightly to its end at the jct. with Liberty Trail, 1.1 mi. from the summit.

LIBERTY TRAIL (WMNF; MAP 3: J9)

Cumulative from Paugus Rd. parking area (910 ft.) to:	⇅	↗	⟳
Hammond Trail (2,550 ft.)	2.7 mi.	1,700 ft. (rev. 50 ft.)	2:10
Jim Liberty Cabin (2,940 ft.)	3.3 mi.	2,150 ft. (rev. 50 ft.)	2:45
Brook Trail (3,100 ft.)	3.6 mi.	2,300 ft.	2:55
Mt. Chocorua summit (3,500 ft.)	3.8 mi.	2,700 ft.	3:15

SEC 8

This is the easiest route to Mt. Chocorua from the southwest, although some steep ledges in its upper part are potentially dangerous if wet or icy. The trail begins at the parking area just before the gate on Paugus Rd. (FR 68; see "Road Access" on p. 373 for trailhead directions). This is a very old path that was improved somewhat by James Liberty in 1887 and further developed as a toll bridle path by David Knowles and Newell Forrest in 1892. Knowles built the two-story Peak House on Mt. Chororua in 1892; the house was blown down in September 1915. The stone stable was rebuilt by the CMC in 1924 and named the Jim Liberty Shelter. This lasted until 1932, when spring winds blew off the roof, and in 1934, the WMNF replaced the shelter with an enclosed cabin with bunks. Overnight use is allowed only inside the cabin, and fires are not allowed.

Liberty Trail follows a woods road that branches right from the parking area just before the gate on the main road (which continues to the Bolles and Brook trails), and ascends at a steady, moderate grade, mostly along the route of the former bridle path. The trail descends slightly to cross Durrell Brook at 1.1 mi. Then the moderate climb resumes, with wet footing in one section, and at 2.7 mi., the trail reaches the ridge top, where Hammond Trail enters right. Liberty Trail climbs a hump, descends into the sag beyond, and climbs past an outlook ledge up on the right to Jim Liberty Cabin at 3.3 mi., where a side path on the right (sign) descends 0.1 mi. to a mediocre water source and a nearby ledge with a view east. Liberty Trail swings to the left (west) at the foot of a ledge and follows the old bridle path, which was blasted out of the rock in many places.

The trail circles around the southwest side of the cone, ascending moderately with some ledge scrambling (use caution if wet or icy; one high ledge step is particularly difficult), passing two outlooks to the south, and meets Brook Trail (left) on a ledge at 3.6 mi. Liberty Trail swings right, and in 35 yd. from this jct., West Side Trail, a bad-weather summit bypass leading to Piper Trail, diverges left (north). Liberty Trail climbs east over ledges then swings left (northeast) and ascends a steep, rough section through the woods over broken ledges to the jct. where Piper Trail enters left (sign). Now coinciding with Piper Trail, Liberty Trail turns right (east) and climbs to the summit through a small, steep rock gully; at the top, the high point is to the left.

Descending from the summit, go 40 yd. west on the only marked path, down the small, steep, ledgy gully to the first jct., where Liberty Trail turns left and Piper Trail turns right. Care should be taken to follow the correct trail on the descent, as one could easily end up on the wrong side of the mountain. At the jct. with Brook Trail at the southwestern base of the cone, Liberty Trail bears left (southeast), whereas Brook Trail continues ahead (south).

SEC 8

WEST SIDE TRAIL (WMNF; MAP 3: J9)

From Piper Trail (3,200 ft.) to:	⇅	↗	⟳
Liberty Trail (3,140 ft.)	0.5 mi.	100 ft. (rev. 150 ft.)	0:20

This trail runs from Piper Trail 0.4 mi. north of the summit of Mt. Chocorua to the ledge where Liberty and Brook trails meet. West Side Trail has easy grades, is well sheltered, and affords a route for avoiding the summit rocks in bad weather. The trail leaves Piper Trail in a flat wooded area north of the summit and descends, circling the west side of the cone, then ascends past a restricted outlook to Liberty Trail, 35 yd. above its jct. with Brook Trail.

BROOK TRAIL (CMC; MAP 3: J9)

Cumulative from Paugus Rd. parking area (910 ft.) to:	⇅	↗	⟳
Bickford Trail (1,180 ft.)	0.9 mi.	300 ft. (rev. 50 ft.)	0:35
Claybank Brook crossing (1,870 ft.)	2.5 mi.	1,000 ft.	1:45
Bee Line Trail (2,550 ft.)	3.0 mi.	1,700 ft.	2:20
Liberty Trail (3,100 ft.)	3.4 mi.	2,250 ft.	2:50
Mt. Chocorua summit (3,500 ft.) via Liberty Trail	3.6 mi.	2,650 ft.	3:10

This trail runs from the parking area at the end of Paugus Rd. (FR 68; see "Road Access" on p. 373 for trailhead directions) to Liberty Trail, 0.2 mi. below the summit of Mt. Chocorua. In 1892, local residents cut the trail to avoid paying a toll on Liberty Trail. High up, Brook Trail ascends steep ledges with excellent views; it is more scenic but also more difficult than Liberty Trail, and potentially dangerous in wet or icy conditions. An excellent loop trip can be made by ascending Brook Trail and descending Liberty Trail.

From the parking area on Paugus Rd., continue north on the gravel road (FR 68) past the gate. After 0.1 mi., Bolles Trail diverges left, and at 0.4 mi., just before the bridge over Claybank Brook, Brook Trail diverges to the right off the gravel road. The trail follows the east bank of the brook, soon turns right onto a relocated section, and ascends then swings left and descends back to the brook. The trail passes a jct. on the left with Bickford Trail at 0.9 mi. and climbs well above the brook. At 1.8 mi., the trail returns to the brook at a tiny waterfall then finally crosses the brook at 2.5 mi.

The trail becomes steeper, and the first ledge is reached at 3.0 mi.; just beyond here, Bee Line Trail enters from the left. From here, Brook Trail climbs steadily through the woods then ascends the steep, open ledges of Farlow Ridge, where the trail is marked with cairns and yellow paint; there is one fairly difficult scramble. At 3.4 mi., Liberty Trail joins from the right on a ledge. The summit of Mt. Chocorua is 0.2 mi. farther ahead (north) via Liberty Trail.

BETWEEN MT. CHOCORUA AND MT. PAUGUS

BEE LINE TRAIL (CMC; MAP 3: J9)

From Bolles Trail (1,300 ft.) to:	⇅	↗	↻
Brook Trail (2,550 ft.) via Chocorua Branch	1.7 mi.	1,250 ft.	1:30
Old Paugus Trail (2,450 ft.) via Paugus Branch	1.1 mi.	1,200 ft. (rev. 50 ft.)	1:10
From Paugus Rd. parking area (910 ft.) to:			
Mt. Chocorua summit (3,500 ft.) via Bolles, Bee Line, Brook, and Liberty trails	4.3 mi.	2,600 ft.	3:25
Ledge on south knob of Mt. Paugus (3,100 ft.) via Bolles, Bee Line, and Old Paugus trails	3.8 mi.	2,250 ft. (rev. 50 ft.)	3:00

This trail runs from Old Paugus Trail on the south ridge of Mt. Paugus to Brook Trail on the southwest side of Mt. Chocorua, linking the two summits almost by a beeline. Bee Line Trail crosses Bolles Trail well south of the height-of-land in the valley between the mountains, 2.0 mi. north of the Paugus Rd. parking area and 3.8 mi. south of Champney Falls Trail parking area on Kancamagus Highway (NH 112). Although Bee Line Trail was originally designed to provide a direct route between the two summits, nowadays the trail is most frequently used to ascend to or descend from one of the peaks rather than as a connector between them—that is, from the middle to either end rather than from one end to the other—so the trail will be described in that manner. Nearly the entire Paugus branch is in the Sandwich Range Wilderness, and the upper part of the Mt. Chocorua branch is in the Mt. Chocorua FPA.

Chocorua Branch. The trail leaves Bolles Trail and ascends gradually on an old logging road along the bank of a brook that originates high on the western slope of Mt. Chocorua. At 0.4 mi., Bee Line Trail turns right onto a relocated section higher up the slope then descends slightly to rejoin the original route. After crossing the brook at 0.7 mi. and again at 1.1 mi., the trail enters the Mt. Chocorua FPA (signs). Bee Line Trail ascends moderately away from the brook, becoming gradually steeper as the trail enters a mixed softwood forest. At 1.4 mi., the trail bears right off a former route

SEC
8

and traverses the wooded slope, climbing moderately, until it reaches the jct. with Brook Trail at 1.7 mi., just above that trail's lowest semi-open ledge. From here, it is 0.4 mi. to the jct. with Liberty Trail and 0.6 mi. to the summit of Mt. Chocorua.

Paugus Branch. Leaving Bolles Trail, Bee Line Trail soon crosses Paugus Brook, enters the Sandwich Range Wilderness, and runs over a small ridge. At 0.2 mi., Bee Line Cutoff departs left (southeast), providing a shortcut to Paugus Rd. Bee Line Trail crosses a small brook in a flat area, and in another 0.1 mi., the trail crosses a larger brook. The trail follows this brook up the valley then climbs by increasingly steep grades up the side of the mountain, making some use of old lumber roads, to Old Paugus Trail near the top of the ridge, 1.1 mi. from Bolles Trail and 0.7 mi. below the jct. with Lawrence Trail on the ledge on the south knob of Paugus.

BEE LINE CUTOFF (CMC; MAP 3: J9)

From Bolles Trail (1,100 ft.) to:	⇅	↗	○
Bee Line Trail (1,320 ft.)	0.6 mi.	200 ft.	0:25

This trail provides an easy shortcut from the Paugus Rd. parking area to the Paugus branch of Bee Line Trail. Bee Line Cutoff is almost entirely within the Sandwich Range Wilderness. The trail diverges left (northwest) from Bolles Trail 1.2 mi. from the parking area and follows an old lumber road. At 0.2 mi., Bee Line Cutoff bears right, crosses a brook, and continues at easy grades, crossing a small brook twice, to Bee Line Trail, 0.2 mi. west of the jct. of Bee Line and Bolles trails.

BOLLES TRAIL (WMNF; MAP 3: J9)

Cumulative from Brook Trail (940 ft.) to:	⇅	↗	○
Bickford Trail–Old Paugus Trail (1,000 ft.)	0.5 mi.	50 ft.	0:15
Bee Line Trail (1,300 ft.)	1.9 mi.	350 ft.	1:10
Kancamagus Highway (1,260 ft.)	5.7 mi.	1,300 ft. (rev. 1,000 ft.)	3:30

This trail connects the Paugus Rd. (FR 68) parking lot with the Champney Falls Trail parking lot on the Kancamagus Highway, passing between Mt. Chocorua and Mt. Paugus and using old logging roads most of the way. Bolles Trail is named for Frank Bolles, who reopened a very old road approximately along the route of this trail in 1892 and called it the "Lost Trail." South of the height-of-land, most of the trail borders the Sandwich Range Wilderness.

Bolles Trail diverges left from Brook Trail (which here is the gravel logging road extension of Paugus Rd.) 0.1 mi. north of the Paugus Rd. parking lot. At 0.2 mi. from Brook Trail, Bolles Trail crosses Paugus Brook on large stepping-stones (may be difficult at high water), and at 0.5 mi., shortly after a snowmobile trail diverges left across a bridge, Old Paugus Trail and Bickford Trail enter left. In 90 yd., Bickford Trail diverges right. Soon Bolles Trail passes the huge Paugus Mill sawdust pile (left), and at 1.1 mi., Bee Line Cutoff diverges left. Bolles Trail now crosses two branches of Paugus Brook on snowmobile bridges; the snowmobile trail diverges right 130 yd. after the second bridge. At 1.9 mi., Bolles Trail crosses Bee Line Trail and then a tributary brook.

The trail follows Paugus Brook closely at times, climbs briefly away from the brook, and dips to recross Paugus Brook on a bridge at 2.6 mi. It heads briefly southwest then turns right (northwest) in an old logging-camp site known as Mudgett's Camp, where berry bush growth often obscures the footway. It heads north through a flat area, running along and then crossing a small brook where a snowmobile trail (red diamonds) diverges right; follow yellow blazes carefully in this area.

The trail soon begins to climb more steeply, recrossing the brook, passing a jct. where the snowmobile trail rejoins from the right, and reaching the height-of-land at 3.7 mi. It runs nearly level through the pass then descends steeply to Twin Brook, crosses it on a bridge, and swings left along the bank where an overgrown snowmobile trail continues ahead.

Bolles Trail continues down the valley, crossing Twin Brook 10 more times and a tributary once; the last crossing is at 4.9 mi. The trail continues past the snowmobile trail diverging sharply right, bears right at 5.4 mi. where a former route of the trail crossed the brook to the left, and reaches Champney Falls Trail 0.1 mi. south of its trailhead parking lot on the Kancamagus Highway.

SEC 8

BICKFORD TRAIL (WODC; MAP 3: K9–J9)

Cumulative from NH 113A (1,170 ft.) to:	⥮	↗	↻
Bolles Trail (1,000 ft.)	2.0 mi.	400 ft. (rev. 550 ft.)	1:10
Brook Trail (1,180 ft.)	2.7 mi.	600 ft.	1:40

This trail runs from NH 113A (limited roadside parking) 1.1 mi. east of Wonalancet to the lower part of Brook Trail, offering a walking route from Wonalancet to Old Paugus, Bolles, and Brook trails to Mt. Paugus and Mt. Chocorua. Bickford Trail's blue blazes must be followed with care.

The trail leaves the north side of NH 113A (sign) and ascends easily on an old logging road, descends gently, and at 0.2 mi. turns left onto another logging road, follows it for 25 yd., then turns right twice, descending to cross a small brook. The trail ascends again, passes between several camps, crosses a driveway, and descends easily to a field with a private home at 0.7 mi. The trail bears left diagonally across the field, reenters the woods at the east edge of the field, enters the WMNF at 0.8 mi., and soon crosses a small brook. The trail then climbs moderately to a rocky ridge top, and descends on the other side, following and crossing a brook. Old Paugus Trail enters left 20 yd. west of Whitin Brook, and the two trails cross the brook and meet Bolles Trail at 2.0 mi.

Bickford Trail turns left (north) on Bolles Trail for 90 yd. then turns right (east), crosses Paugus Brook (may be difficult), climbs a steep pitch, and soon reaches a logging road (which can be followed to the right, to the Paugus Rd. parking area). Bickford Trail turns left and follows the road for 80 yd. then turns right (turns marked with arrows), ascends easily, and descends and crosses Claybank Brook to Brook Trail, where Bickford Trail ends.

MT. PAUGUS

OLD PAUGUS TRAIL (CMC; MAP 3: J9)

Cumulative from Bolles Trail (1,000 ft.) to:	⇅	↗	○
Bee Line Trail (2,450 ft.)	2.1 mi.	1,450 ft.	1:45
Ledge on south knob of Mt. Paugus (3,100 ft.)	2.8 mi.	2,150 ft. (rev. 50 ft.)	2:30

This trail runs to the south knob of Mt. Paugus from Bolles Trail 0.6 mi. from the Paugus Rd. parking area. Old Paugus Trail is almost entirely within the Sandwich Range Wilderness. Portions of the trail are very steep and rough, with poor footing, and may be dangerous in wet or icy conditions. It is sparsely marked and requires care to follow.

This trail leaves Bolles Trail along with Bickford Trail; the two trails cross Whitin Brook together, then Bickford Trail diverges left 20 yd. beyond the brook. Old Paugus Trail continues along Whitin Brook at easy grades, crosses it at 0.7 mi. (may be difficult at high water), and turns right at 1.0 mi., as Whitin Brook Trail continues straight ahead along the brook. Old Paugus Trail now climbs steeply, passes a jct. left with Big Rock Cave Trail at 1.3 mi., ascends at an easier grade for a while, and climbs into a very steep, rocky gully with poor footing. Partway up the gully, Old Paugus Trail swings right at a small cairn, climbs a gravelly pitch, and passes along the base of a rock face. It climbs steeply again, crosses a shoulder with many downed trees, and climbs along a sidehill to the jct. right with Bee Line Trail at 2.1 mi.

Old Paugus Trail ascends sharply with several short scrambles, passes an outlook south on the right, ascends a wet, steeply sloping ledge (use caution), eases up in spruce forest, descends slightly, and turns left where a side path leads right to the site of the former Old Shag Camp. Soon the trail crosses a small brook and climbs steeply; at the top of the pitch, a short side path leads right to a ledge with a view of Mt. Chocorua, and the main trail turns left then right and continues at easier grades to the ledgy south knob. Here, Old Paugus Trail ends, and Lawrence Trail continues ahead, leaving the clearing to the right (northwest). An excellent view to the west can be obtained by descending 50 yd. southwest from the knob over ledges, past a group of boulders and through a belt of scrub, to a large open ledge. Descending, Old Paugus Trail leaves the southeast side of the ledge on the south knob (sign).

WHITIN BROOK TRAIL (CMC; MAP 3: J9–J8)

From Old Paugus Trail (1,450 ft.) to:	⇅	↗	⏱
Cabin Trail (2,180 ft.)	1.6 mi.	750 ft.	1:10

This trail runs from Old Paugus Trail to Cabin Trail and gives access to points in the vicinity of Paugus Pass from the Paugus Rd. (FR 68) parking area. Whitin Brook Trail must be followed with care, particularly at the crossings of Whitin Brook, which may be difficult at high water. The trail is almost entirely within the Sandwich Range Wilderness.

The trail continues along Whitin Brook, where Old Paugus Trail turns right, upslope, 1.0 mi. above the jct. of Old Paugus and Bolles trails. In 0.2 mi., Big Rock Cave Trail crosses then Whitin Brook Trail crosses the brook three times. After the last crossing, at 0.7 mi., the trail continues up the valley at easy grades for 0.5 mi. then swings left away from the brook and climbs steadily through spruce woods with many blowdowns, swinging to the right near the top, and ends at Cabin Trail, 0.4 mi. south of its jct. with Lawrence Trail.

SEC 8

BIG ROCK CAVE TRAIL (WODC; MAP 3: K8–J9)

Cumulative from Cabin Trail (1,200 ft.) to:	⇅	↗	⏱
Big Rock Cave (1,700 ft.)	1.6 mi.	800 ft. (rev. 300 ft.)	1:10
Old Paugus Trail (1,720 ft.)	2.1 mi.	950 ft. (rev. 150 ft.)	1:30

This trail runs from Cabin Trail 0.3 mi. from NH 113A over the flat ridge of Mt. Mexico to Whitin Brook and Old Paugus trails. Big Rock Cave Trail provides access to Big Rock Cave, a boulder cave that invites exploration.

Diverging right from Cabin Trail, Big Rock Cave Trail ascends moderately on a logging road that fades away to a trail, reaching the very flat ridge crest of Mt. Mexico at 1.1 mi. and entering the Sandwich Range Wilderness. From here, the trail descends moderately then steeply and passes Big Rock Cave (right) at 1.6 mi. The trail swings left and continues down steeply, crosses Whitin Brook (may be difficult at high water) and Whitin Brook Trail at 1.7 mi., and climbs on a lightly used section to its end at Old Paugus Trail. Note that if descending Whitin Brook Trail, the sign for Big Rock Cave Trail is easily missed, as it faces the opposite direction.

CABIN TRAIL (WODC; MAP 3: K8–J8)

Cumulative from NH 113A (1,070 ft.) to:	↰↱	↗	○
Whitin Brook Trail (2,180 ft.)	2.2 mi.	1,100 ft.	1:40
Lawrence Trail (2,320 ft.)	2.6 mi.	1,250 ft.	1:55

This trail runs north from NH 113A 0.5 mi. east of the sharp turn at Wonalancet to Lawrence Trail 0.3 mi. east of Paugus Pass. Parking is available on the shoulder across from the trailhead; do not park on the driveway. The upper part of Cabin Trail is in the Sandwich Range Wilderness. The trail follows a private driveway for 60 yd., bears right onto another driveway and follows it for 150 yd., passing a house, and bears left into the woods on an older road. At 0.3 mi., Big Rock Cave Trail diverges right, and soon Cabin Trail bears right at a fork where an unmarked path diverges left.

Cabin Trail ascends easily along the west side of Whitin Ridge on a logging road, crossing several small brooks and entering the Sandwich Range Wilderness at 1.7 mi. At 2.2 mi., just after crossing to the east side of the ridge crest, the trail reaches a jct. where Whitin Brook Trail enters from the right. Cabin Trail continues on the east side of Whitin Ridge, soon passes an outlook to the cliffs and slides on Mt. Paugus, climbs along a narrow and rough side hill, and descends slightly to its end at Lawrence Trail.

LAWRENCE TRAIL (WODC; MAP 3: J8–J9)

Cumulative from Old Mast Road (2,360 ft.) to:	↰↱	↗	○
Cabin Trail (2,320 ft.)	0.6 mi.	100 ft. (rev. 150 ft.)	0:20
Ledge on south knob of Mt. Paugus (3,100 ft.)	2.2 mi.	1,100 ft. (rev. 200 ft.)	1:40

This trail runs from the four-way jct. with Old Mast Road, Walden Trail, and Square Ledge Trail, 2.0 mi. from the Ferncroft Rd. parking area (via Old Mast Road), to the jct. with Old Paugus Trail on the south knob of Mt. Paugus. Extensive relocations made in 2006 and 2008 bypassed two very steep and rough sections, making this a moderate route to Mt. Paugus. Lawrence Trail is entirely within the Sandwich Range Wilderness.

The trail leaves the four-way jct. at the north end of Old Mast Road and descends east into Paugus Pass at 0.3 mi., where Lawrence Trail is joined on the left (north) by Oliverian Brook Trail from the Kancamagus Highway and on the right (south) by Kelley Trail from Ferncroft. Lawrence Trail climbs to a knob at 0.6 mi., where Cabin Trail enters from the right. Lawrence Trail next descends to the southeast side of the ridge at the base of the Overhang, and at 0.9 mi., the trail continues ahead on a relocated gravelly footway where the old route turned left and uphill. The trail contours through dense hardwood growth well below the cliffs with good footing, passes a limited view of the cliffs on Mt. Paugus, then swings left and climbs by easy switchbacks to join the old route in a hollow at 1.4 mi.

Here Lawrence Trail bears right, crosses two small brooks, enters spruce forest, and soon turns right onto the first of several more relocated sections, ascending the steep slope by switchbacks and passing a view of Mt. Whiteface. At 1.8 mi., the trail swings right at an easier grade, crosses a small brook at 2.0 mi., and continues to the ledgy south knob of Mt. Paugus, where Old Paugus Trail continues ahead. An excellent view to the west can be obtained by descending 50 yd. southwest from the knob over ledges, past a group of boulders and through a belt of scrub, to a large open ledge. Descending, Lawrence Trail leaves the northwest side of the ledge at the top of the knob; the trail sign is set back a few steps into the woods.

SEC 8

PAUGUS PASS AND VICINITY

KELLEY TRAIL (WODC; MAP 3: K8–J8)

From Ferncroft Rd. parking area (1,140 ft.) to:	⇅	↗	⟳
Lawrence Trail and Oliverian Brook Trail (2,220 ft.)	2.3 mi.	1,100 ft.	1:40

This trail runs from the Ferncroft Rd. parking area through an interesting ravine to a jct. with Lawrence and Oliverian Brook trails at Paugus Pass. The upper part of Kelley Trail, which is in the Sandwich Range Wilderness, is rough with poor footing and numerous slippery rocks.

For a short time during the retreat of the last continental glacier, this ravine was the outlet of glacial Lake Albany, which occupied the Albany

Intervale, the broad valley to the north of the eastern Sandwich Range. This lake was contained by an ice dam at the east end, and until enough ice had melted from the ice dam to allow the meltwater to pass out by the present route of the Swift River, the water was forced through Paugus Pass and down this ravine in a torrential stream, which left evidence of significant carving by large and powerful waterfalls that the present small stream could not possibly have caused.

The trail leaves the Ferncroft Rd. parking area on a gated, gravel logging road (FR 337), coinciding with Old Mast Road, and soon bears left at a fork where Gordon Path follows the road that runs straight ahead. After passing the jct. with Wonalancet Range Trail on the left at 0.1 mi., the trails cross Spring Brook on a wooden bridge, and at 0.3 mi., Kelley Trail turns off Old Mast Road to the right and follows a woods road to a grassy logging road (FR 337) at 0.5 mi. Here the trail turns right and descends along this road for 0.1 mi. then turns left and ascends along a brook. Soon the trail begins to climb above the brook then enters the Sandwich Range Wilderness and returns to the brook at the top of a small cascade. The trail now crosses the brook (or its dry bed) three times, briefly runs in the brook bed, then climbs steeply out of a small box ravine—one of the remnants of the outflow of glacial Lake Albany—and ascends through a narrow cut to Paugus Pass.

OLIVERIAN BROOK TRAIL (WMNF; MAP 3: J8)

Cumulative from parking area off Kancamagus Highway (1,240 ft.) to:	↟↧	↗	↺
Passaconaway Cutoff (1,500 ft.)	1.9 mi.	250 ft.	1:05
Square Ledge Branch Trail (1,770 ft.)	3.3 mi.	550 ft.	1:55
Paugus Pass (2,220 ft.)	4.4 mi.	1,000 ft.	2:40

This trail runs from the Kancamagus Highway up the Oliverian Brook valley, to Lawrence and Kelley trails at Paugus Pass. Oliverian Brook Trail begins at a parking lot 0.1 mi. in from the Kancamagus Highway, on a gravel road that cuts off from the south side of the highway 1.0 mi. west of Bear Notch Rd. Grades are mostly easy and, except for a few wet sections, the footing is good. The part of the trail south of Passaconaway Cutoff is in the Sandwich Range Wilderness.

Oliverian Brook Trail follows the gravel road beyond the gate for 125 yd., turns sharply left (sign) for another 125 yd., then turns sharply right on the old route of the trail. Oliverian Brook Trail crosses an overgrown logging road, bears right onto an old railroad grade along the west side of Oliverian

Brook at 0.6 mi. (in the reverse direction, bear left here), and follows it for nearly 0.5 mi., soon passing a jct. with a cross-country ski trail on the right and then a beaver pond that sometimes floods the trail. At 1.1 mi., the trail turns left off the railroad grade, climbs gently along the brook, enters the Sandwich Range Wilderness at 1.7 mi., and crosses two small brooks. At 1.9 mi., Passaconaway Cutoff diverges right (southwest).

Oliverian Brook Trail continues south, soon following a relocation to the right around a muddy area. It swings left through a dip then right and crosses a major tributary at 2.2 mi. At 2.4 mi., the trail bears left off an old logging road (arrow), runs alongside the main brook, and crosses it at 2.7 mi. The trail now follows higher ground away from the brook to the east, crosses a tributary brook, and descends slightly to reach the jct. with Square Ledge Branch Trail, which leaves on the right and immediately crosses Oliverian Brook at 3.3 mi. Oliverian Brook Trail then crosses Oliverian Brook at 3.5 mi., ascends along the brook for a while, and continues to the multiple-trail jct. in Paugus Pass.

MT. PASSACONAWAY AND RIDGES

OLD MAST ROAD (WODC; MAP 3: K8–J8)

From Ferncroft parking area (1,140 ft.) to:	⇅	↗	⏲
Lawrence Trail–Walden Trail–Square Ledge Trail (2,360 ft.)	2.0 mi.	1,200 ft.	1:35

This trail, which has easy to moderate grades and good footing throughout, runs from the Ferncroft Rd. parking area to the jct. with the Walden, Square Ledge, and Lawrence trails 0.3 mi. west of Paugus Pass. The original road was reputedly built for hauling out the tallest timbers as masts for the British navy. The upper part of Old Mast Road is in the Sandwich Range Wilderness.

Leaving the parking area along with Kelley Trail on a gated, gravel logging road (FR 337), Old Mast Road follows the left-hand road at the first fork, where Gordon Path follows the road that continues straight ahead. At 0.1 mi., Wonalancet Range Trail diverges left, just before the bridge over Spring Brook, and at 0.3 mi., Kelley Trail diverges right. Soon Old Mast Road passes the WMNF boundary. At 0.9 mi., the trail crosses an overgrown logging road, soon enters another old road, and follows it for 0.1 mi. The trail continues to climb, entering the Sandwich Range Wilderness, then levels, passes to the right of a small brook, and ends at the multiple-trail jct.

SEC 8

DICEY'S MILL TRAIL (WODC; MAP 3: K8–J8)

Cumulative from Ferncroft Rd. parking area (1,140 ft.) to:	⮁	↗	⏲
Tom Wiggin Trail (1,950 ft.)	1.9 mi.	850 ft. (rev. 50 ft.)	1:25
Rollins Trail (3,250 ft.)	3.7 mi.	2,150 ft.	2:55
Mt. Passaconaway summit (4,043 ft.)	4.6 mi.	2,950 ft.	3:45

This trail ascends Mt. Passaconaway from the Ferncroft Rd. parking area, with moderate grades and mostly good footing. This was the first trail to be built on the mountain. Most of the trail is in the Sandwich Range Wilderness.

From the parking area, return to Ferncroft Rd. and turn right, following the gravel road past Squirrel Bridge, where Blueberry Ledge Trail turns left. Pass a gate (not intended to keep out hikers) and a house in a large clearing, and continue on the road, which becomes a logging road as it enters the woods. About 40 yd. before Dicey's Mill Trail enters the WMNF and Sandwich Range Wilderness at 0.8 mi., a marked path left crosses the Wonalancet River on a footbridge to Blueberry Ledge Cutoff on the opposite bank. Soon Dicey's Mill Trail swings right and becomes steeper. Then the grade becomes easy again and continues to the jct. on the left with Tom Wiggin Trail at 1.9 mi. At 2.3 mi., Dicey's Mill Trail crosses a branch of the river near the site of Dicey's Mill. Across the stream, the trail passes a large boulder and begins a long ascent, angling up the side of a ridge, following an old logging road at a moderate grade through hardwoods with occasional minor descents and glimpses of the steep-sided Wonalancet Range rising on the opposite side of the valley. At the ridge top, at 3.7 mi., Rollins Trail from Mt. Whiteface enters on the left. Dicey's Mill Trail then climbs through a rough and wet section, crosses a small brook, and reaches a jct. at 3.9 mi., where East Loop bears right.

SEC 8

East Loop. This short trail begins on Dicey's Mill Trail near the small brook, just below the former site of Camp Rich, and runs nearly level, with minor ups and downs, for 0.2 mi. (5 min.) to Walden Trail a short distance above the point where that trail makes a right turn at the base of its steep climb to the summit of Mt. Passaconaway. East Loop is entirely within the Sandwich Range Wilderness.

From the East Loop jct., **Dicey's Mill Trail** bears left, passes the site of the former Camp Rich (25 yd. left on a side trail), climbs moderately via wide switchbacks, then ascends steeply for 0.2 mi. to a northwest outlook. Here the trail turns right and meets Walden Trail in another 20 yd. The wooded summit is 40 yd. right on a spur path, and Walden Trail leads ahead, passing a spur trail left to the north outlook and reaching the east outlook in 90 yd.

WALDEN TRAIL (WODC; MAP 3: J8)

Cumulative from Old Mast Road (2,360 ft.) to:	↥↧	↗	⟳
Wonalancet Range Trail (3,100 ft.)	0.9 mi.	800 ft. (rev. 50 ft.)	0:50
Square Ledge Trail (3,380 ft.)	2.1 mi.	1,450 ft. (rev. 350 ft.)	1:45
Mt. Passaconaway summit (4,043 ft.)	2.8 mi.	2,100 ft.	2:25

This trail ascends Mt. Passaconaway from the jct. of Old Mast Road and Square Ledge and Lawrence trails via the southeast ridge. Walden Trail is a more interesting but longer, steeper, and rougher route to Mt. Passaconaway from Ferncroft Rd. (via Old Mast Road) than is the direct Dicey's Mill Trail; some of the pitches are among the steepest in the Sandwich Range. Much of Walden Trail was reconstructed from 1997 to 2001 by the WODC. The trail is entirely within the Sandwich Range Wilderness. The trail was named for Arthur Walden, founder of the Chinook Kennels in Wonalancet and a widely known handler and breeder of husky sled dogs.

The trail runs northwest from Old Mast Road, up a very steep slope where much trail work has been done. There are several rock scrambles, including one especially tricky, steep, broken ledge. At the top of the shoulder, the grade eases, and the trail crosses a minor knob and a sag. The trail climbs steeply again and at the top of a steep ledge passes a side path that leads right 20 yd. to a partly restricted outlook east to mts. Paugus and Chocorua. At 0.7 mi., the trail passes a side trail to the left (south) that leads about 100 yd. to a fine viewpoint to the south. The main trail passes just to the south of the large boulder that is the true summit of Wonalancet Hedgehog, and at 0.9 mi., Wonalancet Range Trail enters left. Walden Trail now descends steeply past a restricted outlook north to a col, descends to the left along a brook bed (possible water) for 50 yd., then swings right and climbs very steeply again, with several fairly difficult pitches, to the next subpeak, locally called Nanamocomuck Peak in honor of the eldest son of Passaconaway.

The trail descends easily to a col then climbs gradually to the jct. on the right with Square Ledge Trail at 2.1 mi. The trail now starts to angle upward around the south face of the mountain, makes a right turn up the slope at 2.2 mi., soon passes the jct. with East Loop on the left, and climbs steeply over a reconstructed footway, with one easier stretch partway up. At the top of a steep, rocky pitch, Walden Trail swings left to a fine south outlook then climbs a short, steep pitch to the excellent east outlook. The jct. with Dicey's Mill Trail is 90 yd. beyond the outlook, and the true summit is 40 yd. left from that jct. along a side path. Between the east outlook and Dicey's Mill Trail, a side path (sign: To View) descends right 0.3 mi. and 200 ft. to a spectacular north outlook.

WONALANCET RANGE TRAIL (WODC; MAP 3: K8–J8)

Cumulative from Old Mast Road (1,140 ft.) to:	⇅	↗	↺
Mt. Wonalancet summit (2,780 ft.)	1.8 mi.	1,650 ft.	1:45
Walden Trail (3,100 ft.)	3.2 mi.	2,150 ft. (rev. 200 ft.)	2:40

This trail ascends from Old Mast Road, 0.1 mi. from the Ferncroft Rd. parking area, over the Wonalancet Range to Walden Trail, 0.2 mi. west of the Wonalancet Hedgehog. You have good views from ledges on the way, and the trail offers an attractive but significantly longer and rougher alternative to Dicey's Mill Trail, the most direct route to Mt. Passaconaway from Ferncroft. Most of Wonalancet Range Trail is within the Sandwich Range Wilderness.

The trail diverges left from Old Mast Road just before the bridge over Spring Brook. The trail follows the brook for 30 yd., turns left on a relocation then left again to rejoin the older route. The trail climbs easily, entering the Sandwich Range Wilderness at 0.7 mi., then ascends more steeply with rocky footing. At 1.4 mi., after a very steep pitch, the trail passes a trail (sign: Shortcut) on the right that climbs 0.4 mi. and 250 ft. to rejoin the main trail 0.4 mi. north of the summit of Mt. Wonalancet, avoiding ledges that provide good views but that are slippery when wet or icy.

The main trail turns left and climbs steeply with rough footing, soon crossing a fine outlook ledge, then swings around to the south edge of Mt. Wonalancet and makes a hairpin turn north to pass over the flat, wooded summit at 1.8 mi. The trail passes the upper end of the short cut in a sag at 2.2 mi. then climbs steadily. The trail passes a short spur on the right, which leads to an outlook to the south, and soon reaches the inconsequential summit of Hibbard Mtn. at 2.7 mi., where the former view of Mt. Whiteface is overgrown. After a short descent, the trail continues to ascend moderately then descends slightly to the jct. with Walden Trail.

PASSACONAWAY CUTOFF (WMNF; MAP 3: J8)

From Oliverian Brook Trail (1,500 ft.) to:	⇅	↗	↺
Square Ledge Trail (2,550 ft.)	1.7 mi.	1,050 ft.	1:25
From parking area off Kancamagus Highway (1,240 ft.) to:			
Mt. Passaconaway summit (4,043 ft.) via Oliverian Brook Trail, Passaconaway Cutoff, Square Ledge Trail, and Walden Trail	5.0 mi.	2,850 ft. (rev. 50 ft.)	3:55

This trail provides the shortest route to Mt. Passaconaway from the north, running from Oliverian Brook Trail, 1.9 mi. from its parking lot off the

Kancamagus Highway, to Square Ledge Trail (and thence to the summit via Walden Trail). The entire Passaconaway Cutoff is in the Sandwich Range Wilderness. Leaving Oliverian Brook Trail, the cutoff follows an old logging road at easy grades, crosses the west branch of Oliverian Brook at 0.5 mi., and runs above the brook. At 0.9 mi., where an overgrown path leads ahead to the brook, the cutoff turns left and climbs steadily well above the brook, with glimpses of Mt. Passaconaway across the valley. At 1.5 mi., the trail climbs over a ledge and continues up to the jct. with Square Ledge Trail west of Square Ledge.

SQUARE LEDGE TRAIL (WODC; MAP 3: J8)

Cumulative from Old Mast Road–Lawrence Trail–Walden Trail (2,360 ft.) to:	↥↧	↗	↺
Square Ledge eastern outlook (2,550 ft.)	1.5 mi.	600 ft. (rev. 400 ft.)	1:05
Passaconaway Cutoff (2,550 ft.)	2.1 mi.	800 ft. (rev. 200 ft.)	1:25
Walden Trail (3,380 ft.)	2.8 mi.	1,700 ft. (rev. 50 ft.)	2:15

This trail begins at the jct. of Old Mast Road and Walden and Lawrence trails, climbs over Square Ledge, and ascends to Walden Trail just below the summit cone of Mt. Passaconaway. Square Ledge Trail is entirely within the Sandwich Range Wilderness. Peregrine falcons often nest on the cliff of Square Ledge, so access to the Square Ledge eastern viewpoint may be restricted during the nesting season (April 1 to August 1).

From the four-way jct. at its southern end, the trail descends from the height-of-land with several short ascents, crossing a small brook at 0.6 mi. At 1.1 mi., just before the trail crosses Square Ledge Brook, Square Ledge Branch Trail diverges right (east) to join Oliverian Brook Trail. A short distance farther, the main trail makes a sharp turn left (west) to ascend the ledge. Square Ledge Trail bears east for a short distance then climbs very steeply along the base of wooded cliffs, with one fairly difficult ledge scramble, to the shoulder. At 1.5 mi., at a sharp left turn, a spur leads right 20 yd. to Square Ledge outlook, where you have a partly restricted view east across the valley to Mt. Paugus.

Leaving the ledge, the trail ascends past a view left to Wonalancet Hedgehog to a point near the wooded summit of the knob above the ledge. Just past this summit, an unmarked side path diverges left and in 15 yd. swings left up a steep ledge then continues another 30 yd. through an overgrown section to a ledge with a view of Mt. Passaconaway. (Use caution: The edge of the cliff is partly obscured by scrubby growth.) The main trail descends alongside a rock face then climbs steeply up a shoulder, turns sharply right where you have a restricted view of Mt. Paugus, and descends to the jct. with Passaconaway Cutoff on the right at 2.1 mi. Here, Square Ledge Trail turns left (west), crosses a dip, passes through an old logging-camp site, and climbs across the base of a slide at 2.4 mi.; a view to Mt. Washington can be obtained by carefully scrambling a short distance up this slide. The trail then climbs steadily to Walden Trail.

SQUARE LEDGE BRANCH TRAIL (WMNF; MAP 3: J8)

From Oliverian Brook Trail (1,770 ft.) to:	↻	↗	○
Square Ledge Trail (2,100 ft.)	0.5 mi.	350 ft.	0:25
Loop over Square Ledge from parking area off Kancamagus Highway via Oliverian Brook Trail, Square Ledge Branch Trail, Square Ledge Trail, and Passaconaway Cutoff	8.4 mi.	1,550 ft.	5:00

This short trail, with good footing, begins on Oliverian Brook Trail 3.3 mi. from the Kancamagus Highway, immediately crosses Oliverian Brook, and ascends moderately to Square Ledge Trail below the steep section that ascends the ledge; its lower half follows Square Ledge Brook. Square Ledge Branch Trail is most frequently used to make a loop over Square Ledge from the Kancamagus Highway.

HEDGEHOG MTN. AND POTASH MTN.

UNH TRAIL (WMNF; MAP 3: J8)

Cumulative from parking lot off Kancamagus Highway (1,270 ft.) to:	↻	↗	○
East ledges (2,300 ft.)	2.1 mi.	1,100 ft. (rev. 50 ft.)	1:35
Hedgehog Mtn. summit (2,532 ft.) via east branch	2.9 mi.	1,400 ft. (rev. 100 ft.)	2:10
Complete loop	4.7 mi.	1,400 ft.	3:05

This loop trail to the ledges of Hedgehog Mtn. offers fine views from several viewpoints for a modest effort. The trail begins at the Downes Brook Trail parking lot, at the end of a 0.1-mi. gravel road (sign for UNH, Mt. Potash, and Downes Brook trails) that leaves the south side of the Kancamagus Highway opposite the WMNF Passaconaway Campground. The loop trail was named for the University of New Hampshire Forestry Camp, formerly located nearby.

The trail leaves Downes Brook Trail on the left 40 yd. from the edge of the parking lot and follows an old railroad grade 0.2 mi. to the former loop jct.; here, the trail turns right to ascend to the new loop jct., and the former east branch (no longer maintained for hiking) continues straight on the old railroad grade. The trail runs at easy grades, crosses a skid road, and climbs moderately past a clearcut area on the left. At 0.8 mi. it reaches the new loop jct.

From this point, the loop will be described in the clockwise direction (east branch to summit then west branch back), although the loop is equally good in the opposite direction. The east branch turns left here and descends gradually across the slope then turns right onto the older route at 1.1 mi. It follows an old logging road, climbing moderately, and swings right to cross White Brook at 1.4 mi. The trail climbs across the boulder-strewn northeast slope of the mountain, crosses a small brook, climbs by switchbacks through spruce forest, and swings left, descending slightly to a northeast outlook. Here the trail bears right and climbs, swinging right again up open rock to the east ledges at 2.1 mi., where you have fine views south and east, with an impressive view of nearby Mt. Passaconaway. The trail dips into a patch of woods then runs along the top of the open cliffs on the south face (follow blazes carefully) and enters the woods under the steep, ledgy south side of the main peak.

The trail descends and then ascends, bearing gradually toward the north onto the west slope of the main peak of Hedgehog Mtn., which the trail climbs in a series of short ledgy switchbacks, passing several outlooks. It reaches the summit at 2.9 mi., where nearby ledges provide views in most directions. The trail turns left here, drops off the summit ledge, bears right where a side path leads left to an outlook, and soon descends easily through an open area, with views to the north. It descends rather steeply with fairly rough footing then eases and passes a side path leading 15 yd. right to a ledge with a view of Mt. Chocorua at 3.6 mi. The main trail makes a sharp left turn at 3.7 mi. Here a side path (sign) climbs steeply right 60 yd. to Allen's Ledge, swinging left along the base of a rock face; by descending carefully 25 yd. to a lower ledge perch, one can obtain a wider view to the east and northeast. The main trail descends to cross a small brook then climbs a bank and turns right onto an old logging road (in the reverse direction, the trail descends left off the logging road) and follows the road down past the new loop jct. at 3.9 mi. to the railroad grade. Turn left to return to the parking area.

SEC 8

MT. POTASH TRAIL (WMNF; MAP 3: J8)

From Downes Brook Trail (1,285 ft.) to:	⇅	↗	↻
Potash Mtn. summit (2,700 ft.)	1.9 mi.	1,400 ft	1:40

This trail ascends to the open ledges of Potash Mtn., providing excellent views for a modest effort. The trail begins on Downes Brook Trail, 0.3 mi. from the parking area on the 0.1-mi. gravel road that leaves the

Kancamagus Highway, almost directly opposite the entrance to Passaconaway Campground.

Mt. Potash Trail turns right off Downes Brook Trail and heads southwest. After crossing Downes Brook (may be difficult) at 0.1 mi., Mt. Potash Trail turns sharply left and ascends, crossing a gravel logging road at 0.5 mi. (This road provides an alternate approach to the trail that avoids the often-difficult brook crossing; the road begins at a gate on the Kancamagus Highway 0.6 mi. west of the trailhead; take care not to block the gate when parking. The trail crossing is reached in 0.7 mi.) After traversing a slope among hardwoods, Mt. Potash Trail enters a beautiful hemlock forest, and at 0.9 mi., the trail turns sharply left and climbs on granite slabs and roots, making several turns. It crosses a southeast outlook at 1.3 mi., traverses a shoulder, ascends moderately, and at 1.6 mi. swings left and angles up the east side of the mountain, circling clockwise with rough, rocky footing around the cone to avoid the steepest ledges. The trail crosses a ledge with excellent views up the valley of Downes Brook then turns right and climbs steeply up open south-facing ledges to the summit.

MT. WHITEFACE AND VICINITY

ROLLINS TRAIL (WODC; MAP 3: J8)

From Blueberry Ledge Trail– McCrillis Trail jct. (3,990 ft.) to:	⇅	↗	↻
Dicey's Mill Trail (3,250 ft.)	2.5 mi.	300 ft. (rev. 1,050 ft.)	1:25

This trail runs along the high ridge that connects Mt. Whiteface to Mt. Passaconaway. The trail begins at a jct. with Blueberry Ledge and McCrillis trails on the open ledges of the south summit of Mt. Whiteface and ends on Dicey's Mill Trail 0.2 mi. below the site of the former Camp Rich. On the ridge of Mt. Whiteface, some sections are steep and rough. Rollins Trail is entirely within the Sandwich Range Wilderness.

Leaving the south ledges, Rollins Trail passes over a wooded ledge with a glimpse ahead to the true summit then descends sharply into the steep, narrow col between the true summit and the open south summit of Mt. Whiteface, passing the jct. with Kate Sleeper Trail at the site of the former Camp Shehadi on the left at 0.1 mi. From this col, Rollins Trail climbs north then runs along the ridge crest to the wooded true summit (no official marking) of Mt. Whiteface at 0.3 mi. The trail continues along the narrow ridge, descending gradually with occasional steep, rough pitches and several short ascents. There are outlooks to the east across the Bowl at 0.6 mi., beyond which a narrow traverse at the base of a ledge requires caution, and at 1.3 mi., after a fairly significant ascent. The trail then descends steadily, with several sharp turns near the bottom, to the broad, deep pass between Mts. White-face and Passaconaway. The trail then angles slightly upward around the south face of Passaconaway and descends slightly to meet Dicey's Mill Trail.

BLUEBERRY LEDGE TRAIL (WODC; MAP 3: K8–J8)

Cumulative from Ferncroft Rd. parking area (1,140 ft.) to:	⇅	↗	↻
Blueberry Ledge Cutoff, upper jct. (2,140 ft.)	2.0 mi.	1,000 ft.	1:30
South summit ledges of Mt. Whiteface (3,990 ft.)	3.9 mi.	2,850 ft.	3:25
True summit of Mt. Whiteface (4,020 ft.) via Rollins Trail	4.2 mi.	2,950 ft. (rev. 50 ft.)	3:35

This trail, which was opened in 1899, ascends Mt. Whiteface from the Ferncroft Rd. parking area, ending at a jct. with McCrillis and Rollins trails on the wide ledges of the lower south summit. Blueberry Ledge Trail is very scenic with excellent views, but the upper part is steep and requires some rock scrambling. Although rock steps have been drilled out in the ledges at some difficult spots, the wooden steps that were also installed on the steepest ledge on this trail have been removed. This trail is still one of the more challenging climbs in the White Mountains. It is particularly difficult on the descent, even more difficult when wet, and dangerous in icy conditions. Most of the trail is within the Sandwich Range Wilderness.

From the parking area, return to Ferncroft Rd. and follow it northwest to Squirrel Bridge Rd. at 0.3 mi., where Dicey's Mill Trail continues straight ahead. Blueberry Ledge Trail turns left across Squirrel Bridge, bears right in 30 yd. (sign: Trails), follows a private gravel road (avoid several branching driveways), and diverges left into the woods, where the road curves right to the last house. Here, at 0.5 mi., Pasture Path to Mt. Katherine leaves left. In 0.1 mi., the trail joins an old road, and soon Blueberry Ledge Cutoff diverges right to follow the bank of the Wonalancet River.

The trail crosses into the WMNF and the Sandwich Range Wilderness, and at 0.9 mi. continues straight where McCrillis Path to Whiteface Intervale Rd.—not to be confused with McCrillis Trail to Mt. Whiteface—follows the old road sharply left. Blueberry Ledge Trail now passes through a flat area, following relocations to the right then the left around wet areas, and ascends moderately. At 1.6 mi., the trail reaches the bottom of the Blueberry Ledges (with one limited view of Mt. Chocorua) and climbs to the top of the ledges at 2.0 mi., where you have a restricted view of the Ossipee Range. Blueberry Ledge Cutoff rejoins here on the right at a cairn and sign, and Blueberry Ledge Trail reenters the woods at the upper left corner of the ledge.

The trail climbs gently through open hardwoods then rises steeply, with many recently built rock steps, past restricted Wonalancet Outlook to the top of the ridge. The trail drops slightly into a hollow then ascends slightly to a jct. with Tom Wiggin Trail on the right at 3.2 mi. Now the trail climbs moderately then swings sharply right at an outlook at 3.6 mi., where it abruptly approaches the edge of a steep cliff and may be dangerous if slippery. Just beyond here, the trail climbs a steep ledge then continues to scramble up the steep, rough, rocky ridge, with several excellent viewpoints to the west and east (including a particularly fine ledge overlooking the Bowl on the right at 3.8 mi.), ending at the ledges of the lower south summit. McCrillis Trail enters from the left, just north of the ledges, and Rollins Trail continues north to the true summit of Mt. Whiteface and on toward Mt. Passaconaway.

BLUEBERRY LEDGE CUTOFF (WODC; MAP 3: K8)

From Blueberry Ledge Trail, lower jct. (1,220 ft.) to:	⇅	↗	○
Blueberry Ledge Trail, upper jct. (2,140 ft.)	1.7 mi.	900 ft.	1:20

This trail begins and ends on Blueberry Ledge Trail, providing an attractive alternative route. Blueberry Ledge Cutoff is slightly longer in distance and somewhat rougher than the parallel section of Blueberry Ledge Trail. The upper part of the trail is in the Sandwich Range Wilderness.

Blueberry Ledge Cutoff leaves Blueberry Ledge Trail on the right, 0.6 mi. from the Ferncroft Rd. parking area, and descends slightly to the riverbank. At 0.3 mi., a footbridge on the right leads across the river to Dicey's Mill Trail. Blueberry Ledge Cutoff continues ahead, soon climbs a small ridge, and returns to the bank high above the brook. The trail swings away from the brook again, meets and follows a small tributary, and enters the Sandwich Range Wilderness. Here the trail follows a relocation to the left (south) on a long, gentle switchback. It swings back to the right (north) then turns left onto the older route and climbs, steeply at times, through a bouldery area and across ledges. Marked by cairns and occasional blue blazes, Blueberry Ledge Cutoff climbs to meet Blueberry Ledge Trail at the western edge of the uppermost Blueberry Ledge at a cairn and sign.

TOM WIGGIN TRAIL (WODC; MAP 3: J8)

From Dicey's Mill Trail (1,950 ft.) to:	⇅	↗	○
Blueberry Ledge Trail (3,300 ft.)	1.1 mi.	1,400 ft. (rev. 50 ft.)	1:15

This steep, rough, lightly used trail, cut by Thomas Wiggin in 1895 and nicknamed the Fire Escape, connects Dicey's Mill Trail 1.9 mi. from the Ferncroft Rd. parking area with Blueberry Ledge Trail just below the upper ledges. Tom Wiggin Trail lies entirely within the Sandwich Range Wilderness.

Leaving Dicey's Mill Trail, Tom Wiggin Trail descends to cross the Wonalancet River (may be difficult at high water), bears left and ascends a little knoll, crosses a small brook, and bears right in old-growth hardwoods, climbing past a large boulder. The trail tends to angle to the right as it climbs steeply up the mountainside, with many sections of loose, gravelly footing that are particularly tedious on the descent. The trail enters conifers and reaches Blueberry Ledge Trail just north of a small hollow.

McCRILLIS TRAIL (WMNF; MAP 3: K8–J8)

Cumulative from Flat Mtn. Pond Trail (1,250 ft.) to:	⇅	↗	⏱
Base of steep climb (2,600 ft.)	2.0 mi.	1,350 ft.	1:40
Blueberry Ledge Trail–Rollins Trail (3,990 ft.)	3.2 mi.	2,750 ft.	3:00
From Whiteface Intervale Rd. (968 ft.) to:			
True summit of Mt. Whiteface (4,020 ft.) via Flat Mtn. Pond, McCrillis, and Rollins trails	5.2 mi.	3,200 ft. (rev. 150 ft.)	4:10

This trail ascends Mt. Whiteface—ending at the lower south summit—from Flat Mtn. Pond Trail (see Section Seven), 1.7 mi. from Whiteface Intervale Rd. McCrillis Trail is lightly used, and the lower part through hardwood forest requires care to follow due to luxuriant undergrowth. The upper part is fairly steep and rough but, unlike Blueberry Ledge Trail, does not require rock scrambling (except for one ledge at the top that can be tricky in wet or icy conditions) and is more sheltered in bad weather. McCrillis Trail is entirely within the Sandwich Range Wilderness. Be careful not to confuse this trail with McCrillis Path, which runs from Whiteface Intervale Rd. to Blueberry Ledge Trail.

Leaving Flat Mtn. Pond Trail on the east bank of the Whiteface River, McCrillis Trail ascends a bank then runs east nearly on the level (follow with care) to intersect the former route, an old logging road, at 0.4 mi. Turning left on this road, the trail climbs moderately through hardwoods, passes through a wet area, and at 2.0 mi., begins to climb steeply into a forest of conifers. At 2.6 mi., the trail passes the first of several outlooks, including one up on the left (reached by a short scramble) to the southwest, and others on the right, which provide good views southeast and a glimpse of the "white face."

SEC
8

The trail climbs steeply again and finally climbs along the edge of the southwest ledges (use caution) to a jct. with Rollins and Blueberry Ledge trails just north of the ledges of the lower south summit. The true summit is 0.3 mi. farther north via Rollins Trail. (To descend on McCrillis Trail, walk southwest from the highest rock of the south ledges along the southeast edge of the ledges. Once the first markings are found, the trail is easily followed.)

McCRILLIS PATH (WODC; MAP 3: K8)

Cumulative from Flat Mtn. Pond trailhead on Whiteface Intervale Rd. (968 ft.) to:	⇅	↗	○
WMNF boundary (1,450 ft.)	1.8 mi.	500 ft.	1:10
Tilton Spring Path (1,470 ft.)	3.1 mi.	650 ft. (rev. 150 ft.)	1:55
Blueberry Ledge Trail (1,370 ft.)	3.3 mi.	650 ft. (rev. 100 ft.)	2:00

This lightly used path connects the trailhead for Flat Mtn. Pond Trail on Whiteface Intervale Rd. with Blueberry Ledge Trail, 0.9 mi. from the Ferncroft parking area. By connecting these two trailheads, it makes possible a long loop hike over Mt. Whiteface using McCrillis Path, Blueberry Ledge Trail, McCrillis Trail, and Flat Mtn. Pond Trail. (Be careful not to confuse McCrillis Path with McCrillis Trail to Mt. Whiteface.) The western section of McCrillis Path is on private land and was closed for several years. It was relocated and reopened by the WODC and WMNF in 2012. The eastern part of McCrillis Path, which is in the Sandwich Range Wilderness, gives access to a network of minor trails via Tilton Spring Path and passes through the remains of old farms that can be explored. The trail is described from west to east. Hikers accessing the west end of McCrillis Path must park at the trailhead for Flat Mtn. Pond Trail; there is no public parking on Whiteface Intervale Rd. beyond this point, and hikers should take care to stay on the described route where it crosses private land.

From the trailhead for Flat Mtn. Pond Trail, the route follows Whiteface Intervale Rd. north (left) then east, with fine views of the surrounding mountains. At 0.6 mi. from trailhead parking, just past a cemetery, it turns left onto gravel Neal Brook Rd. It continues straight at a three-way junction, and at 0.8 mi. it turns left onto a woods road, soon passing a sign for the Ambrose Nature Preserve. Just beyond the sign, the trail bears left at a fork (the right fork is a ski trail); here there are blue blazes and a trail sign. It ascends steadily up a woods road then turns left onto a footpath at 1.3 mi. and in 50 yd. swings right along the edge of a small gorge on Captain Neal

Brook. In another 70 yd. it swings right again and climbs briefly to a plateau, where openings provide views of Mt. Israel and Sandwich Dome.

The trail now runs nearly level, staying just south of the WMNF boundary and passing the upper jct. with the ski trail on the right, swings left, and enters the WMNF at 1.8 mi. It descends, and at 2.3 mi. it bears left onto the original route of the trail, following a road between Birch Intervale (now known as Wonalancet) and Whiteface Intervale that is more than 200 years old. In 0.2 mi. it passes a small cellar hole on the left, and at 2.7 mi. it crosses Tewksbury Brook. The trail ascends to a height-of-land, passes the jct. with Tilton Spring Path on the right at 3.1 mi., and descends moderately to meet Blueberry Ledge Trail. Turn right for the Ferncroft parking area or left for the summit of Mt. Whiteface.

DOWNES BROOK TRAIL (WMNF; MAP 3: J8)

Cumulative from parking lot off Kancamagus Highway (1,270 ft.) to:	↥↧	↗	↺
Kate Sleeper Trail jct. (3,400 ft.)	5.2 mi.	2,150 ft.	3:40
True summit of Mt. Whiteface (4,020 ft.) via Kate Sleeper and Rollins trails	6.2 mi.	2,750 ft.	4:30
East Sleeper summit (3,860 ft.) via Kate Sleeper Trail and side path	6.1 mi.	2,600 ft.	4:20

This trail provides a long route to the main ridge crest of the Sandwich Range between Mt. Whiteface and Sleeper Ridge. Downes Brook Trail begins at a parking area 0.1 mi. from the Kancamagus Highway, on a gravel road that leaves on the south side of the highway almost directly opposite Passaconaway Campground. The trail crosses Downes Brook ten times, and several crossings may range from difficult to impassable at high water. Allow extra time for these wide crossings, even at lower water levels. Take extra care to find and follow the trail at several of the crossings where there are multiple streambeds. Grades are mostly easy to moderate with generally good footing; the upper section is steeper and rougher. Most of the trail is in the Sandwich Range Wilderness.

Leaving the parking area, the trail follows the edge of a gravel pit, and UNH Trail diverges left on an old railroad grade in 40 yd. After a short climb, Downes Brook Trail turns right, enters the woods, turns left, and follows an old logging road that runs along Downes Brook, at first some distance away and later mostly along the bank. At 0.3 mi., shortly after the left turn, Mt. Potash Trail diverges right, and at 0.7 mi., Downes Brook Trail makes the first of four crossings of Downes Brook in a span of 0.6 mi.; after the fourth crossing, it enters the Sandwich Range Wilderness. It then

SEC
8

follows a relocated section up to the left, crossing a small brook before rejoining the original route. At 2.3 mi., the trail crosses an extensive outwash from a tributary then crosses the main brook at 2.5, 2.8, and 3.1 mi. At 3.5 mi. it traverses the first of two short, washed-out sections along the west bank. It continues on that side to the eighth crossing at 3.9 mi., after which it climbs a narrow side-hill section high on the east bank, with one tricky scramble through another washout. The ninth crossing is at 4.2 mi., and at 4.5 mi. you have glimpses of the slides on the steep slope of Mt. Whiteface across the valley.

The trail now climbs more steeply, passing numerous small cascades, and crosses the brook for the last time in the flat pass between Sleeper Ridge and Mt. Whiteface. In another 100 yd., at 5.2 mi., with a swampy area visible straight ahead, Downes Brook Trail ends at the jct. with Kate Sleeper Trail. To reach Mt. Whiteface, turn left on Kate Sleeper Trail; for the Sleeper Ridge and Mt. Tripyramid beyond, turn right.

KATE SLEEPER TRAIL (WODC; MAP 3: J7–J8)

Cumulative from Rollins Trail jct. (3,940 ft.) to:	⇅	↗	⟳
Downes Brook Trail (3,400 ft.)	0.8 mi.	0 ft. (rev. 550 ft.)	0:25
Mt. Tripyramid Trail (3,800 ft.)	3.3 mi.	950 ft. (rev. 550 ft.)	2:10

This trail connects Mt. Tripyramid with Mt. Whiteface and the eastern peaks of the Sandwich Range. The trail begins at the little col between the summits of Mt. Whiteface and runs over the high, double-domed Sleeper Ridge to Mt. Tripyramid Trail, high on the South Slide. Kate Sleeper Trail is entirely within the Sandwich Range Wilderness. The only sure water on or near Kate Sleeper Trail is on Downes Brook Trail, just north of the jct. between the two trails in the sag between Mt. Whiteface and the Sleepers. In 2012 Hurricane Sandy caused massive blowdown along the southern slopes of East Sleeper; this was cleared from the trail in 2013 by WODC volunteers using only hand tools.

Kate Sleeper Trail leaves Rollins Trail in the col between the two summits of Mt. Whiteface and descends at a moderate grade 0.8 mi. to its jct. on the right with Downes Brook Trail. Kate Sleeper Trail then skirts to the north of a swampy area and soon begins to ascend East Sleeper. At 1.0 mi. it enters the blowdown area, passing through several corridors of sawn tree trunks; the areas adjacent to the trail in this section are scenes of impressive devastation. After a moderate ascent, the trail leaves the blowdown area and passes left (southwest) of the top of East Sleeper at 1.6 mi. Here a side path (no sign) leads right 0.1 mi. to this viewless summit, marked by a sign.

The main trail bears left, soon turns sharply right, descends into the col between the Sleepers, and climbs to a point 30 yd. south of the summit of West Sleeper at 2.6 mi.

After descending again and traversing a bit below the Tripyramid col, the trail bears west and contours roughly along South Tripyramid until the trail enters the South Slide on the smaller eastern slide. Small cairns and blue blazes mark the winding route on the slide, as the trail climbs very steeply on ledges and loose gravel about 100 yd., with fine views, then reenters the brush on the opposite side. After running about 50 yd. through this brushy area, the trail enters the larger western slide, where the trail meets Mt. Tripyramid Trail. To locate the beginning of the trail at the eastern edge of the western slide, 60 yd. below its top, look for a three-way arrow painted on a ledge and a sign located a short distance in, on a scrubby tree.

SHORTER PATHS IN THE FERNCROFT AREA (WODC; MAP 3: K8–K9)

	⇅	↗	↻
Brook Path	2.0 mi.	50 ft. (rev. 300 ft.)	1:00
Gordon Path	1.2 mi.	100 ft. (rev. 150 ft.)	0:40
Pasture Path	1.1 mi.	200 ft.	0:40
Red Path	0.7 mi.	200 ft.	0:25
Tilton Spring Path	0.9 mi.	200 ft.	0:35

SEC 8

These trails are often not as well beaten as the more important paths, and signs and other markings may be sparse or absent, so they must be followed with care. They frequently cross private property, and landowner rights and privacy must be respected. They provide opportunities for easy, low-elevation walking through attractive woods.

Brook Path. This scenic trail leaves the south side of NH 113A opposite Cabin Trail trailhead and follows the north side of the Wonalancet River for 0.9 mi., crossing two tributaries on bridges. It crosses the main brook on a bridge and ascends to a jct. with a logging road, where the path bears left and descends back near the brook. Becoming rougher, the path passes an old dam and then Wonalancet Falls (also called Locke Falls) at 1.1 mi. The path descends roughly a short distance past an old mill building then follows an old woods road along the brook. At 1.8 mi., the path climbs a steep bank, turns left onto a gravel road, and follows it for 0.2 mi. to a designated parking area on the left. This road leads another 0.1 mi. to NH 113A, just south of the bridge across the Wonalancet River and 1.7 mi. east of Cabin Trail trailhead.

Gordon Path. This trail begins at the Ferncroft Rd. parking area, taking the right fork (almost straight ahead) on the gravel road (FR 337) where Old Mast Road and Kelley Trail bear left, and soon crossing Spring Brook on a bridge. After 0.2 mi., Gordon Path turns to the right off this road, immediately passing a ski trail diverging right, then swings right along the edge of a clearing, crosses a small brook on a bridge, and climbs onto a low, wooded ridge. At 0.8 mi. it turns right onto an old logging road, descends, bears right again, crosses a branch of Spring Brook on a bridge, emerges in a yard (private property), and crosses along the yard's right edge. The trail bears right on a gravel driveway and follows it to NH 113A 0.2 mi. east of its jct. with Ferncroft Rd. and 0.3 mi. west of Cabin Trail trailhead. In the reverse direction, there is a sign for Gordon Path where the driveway leaves NH 113A. The trail can be difficult to follow where it bears left off the driveway and crosses the yard.

Pasture Path. This trail diverges left from Blueberry Ledge Trail 0.5 mi. from the Ferncroft Rd. parking area. Ascending gradually, Pasture Path leads past Tilton Spring on the right at 0.6 mi., passing through an intersection with Tilton Spring Path (right) and Red Path (left). Pasture Path continues ascending gently, crossing several overgrown logging roads, and bears left to the summit of Mt. Katherine (1,380 ft.), a broad ledge with a limited but attractive view of Mt. Chocorua beyond the fields of Wonalancet.

Red Path. This trail begins at the site of the former Wonalancet Post Office on Ferncroft Rd. 125 yd. north of its jct. with NH 113A; there is no parking here. The trail follows a gravel road past fields and houses then swings left and right. At 0.3 mi. it turns left off the road at a blue blaze on a telephone pole and leads west on a narrow path through the woods. In another 0.15 mi. it bears left onto a grassy track that soon becomes an old woods road with good footing. It climbs moderately and bears right near the top, soon reaching Tilton Spring, where Red Path meets Tilton Spring Path and Pasture Path.

Tilton Spring Path. This trail begins at Tilton Spring and ascends gradually to the west, entering the WMNF at 0.2 mi. It descends slightly, swings right (north) at 0.5 mi., and ascends easily to McCrillis Path 0.2 mi. from Blueberry Ledge Trail.

SECTION NINE

CARTER AND BALDFACE RANGES

Map 5: Carter Range–Evans Notch

INTRODUCTION

This section covers the Carter–Moriah Range and the Baldface Range, along with the broad valley of the Wild River that lies between these two high ranges, as well as the lower mountains on the long subsidiary ridges that extend south from them. In the Carter–Moriah Range, the major peaks are Wildcat Mtn., Carter Dome, Mt. Hight, South Carter Mtn., Middle Carter Mtn., North Carter Mtn., Mt. Moriah, and Shelburne Moriah Mtn.; in the Baldface Range, the major peaks are Eastman Mtn., North Baldface, South Baldface, Mt. Meader, West Royce Mtn., and East Royce Mtn.; and in the southern part of the section, the major peaks are Black Mtn., North and South Doublehead Mtns., Mt. Kearsarge North, Black Cap, Peaked Mtn., and Middle Mtn. The area is bounded on the west by NH 16, on the north by US 2, and on the east and south by NH/ME 113 (which crosses the state line several times). Many trails in this section coincide with or intersect cross-country ski or snowmobile trails, and care often must be taken to distinguish the hiking trails from the others. The entire area of Section Nine is covered by AMC's *White Mountains Trail Map 5: Carter Range–Evans Notch.*

Established in 2006, the Wild River Wilderness includes 23,700 acres in the great valley between the Carter and Baldface ranges. In accordance with USFS Wilderness policy, the trails in the Wild River Wilderness are generally maintained to a lower standard than are trails outside Wilderness Areas. Considerable care may be required to follow them.

In this section, the AT begins at NH 16 opposite AMC's Pinkham Notch Visitor Center and follows Lost Pond, Wildcat Ridge, Nineteen-Mile Brook, Carter–Moriah, Kenduskeag, and Rattle River trails to US 2 east of Gorham. The AT crosses the summits of Wildcat Mtn., Carter Dome, Mt. Hight, South Carter Mtn., Middle Carter Mtn., and North Carter Mtn., and passes near the summit of Mt. Moriah.

ROAD ACCESS

Trails on the western and northern sides of the Carter Range are reached from NH 16 and US 2. Trails on the eastern side of the Baldface–Royce Range are reached from NH/ME 113, the road that leads through Evans Notch. In winter, this road is not plowed between the road to Basin Pond and a gate 1.8 mi. south of US 2. The gravel Wild River Rd. (FR 12) leaves NH/ME 113 3.2 mi. south of US 2 and leads 5.7 mi. southwest up the Wild River valley; this road is not plowed in winter. Several roads lead to trailheads on the south side of the area covered in Section Nine. Carter Notch Rd. runs 5.2 mi. north from Jackson village, becoming gravel at

4.4 mi.; the last 0.5 mi. is not plowed in winter. Town Hall–Slippery Brook Rd. (FR 17) leads 7.3 mi. north from NH 16 in Intervale; at 5.9 mi., East Branch Rd. (FR 38) diverges left and runs northwest for 3.2 mi. Only the first 3.5 mi. of FR 17 is plowed in winter. Steep, winding Hurricane Mtn. Rd. provides a route between Intervale and South Chatham; in winter, the road is plowed for only 2 mi. from its west end. North of the east end of Hurricane Mtn. Rd., two trails are accessed by gravel roads off Green Hill Rd. Several trails in the Green Hills Preserve are accessed via Artist's Falls Rd. and Thompson Rd. off NH 16 in North Conway.

GEOGRAPHY

The Carter–Moriah Range would be a great deal more prominent among White Mountain ranges, were it not for those neighbors that rise 1,500 ft. higher across Pinkham Notch. On a high, mostly wooded ridge about 10 mi. long are eight significant peaks more than 4,000 ft. tall, as well as wild, dramatic Carter Notch. The finest views in the range are commanded by Mt. Hight, which remains bare after having been swept by fire in 1903. Views from Shelburne Moriah Mtn. and Mt. Moriah are also excellent, and you find several fine outlooks in various directions along the trails. To the east, the range overlooks the broad, forested valley of the Wild River and the rocky peaks of the Baldface group, and far beyond lies the Atlantic Ocean, which reflects the sun on the southeast horizon behind Sebago Lake on clear midmornings.

Rugged Wildcat Mtn. rises at the south end of the range. Of its numerous summits, the highest is the one nearest to Carter Notch; Wildcat Mtn.'s five most prominent summits are designated, from east to west: A Peak (4,422 ft.), B Peak (4,330 ft.), C Peak (4,298 ft.), D Peak (4,062 ft.), and E Peak (4,046 ft.). The mountain is heavily wooded but has magnificent outlook ledges on Wildcat Ridge Trail west of E Peak, a lookout platform with good (though increasingly restricted) views on D Peak near the top of Wildcat Ski Area (which is located on the northwest slopes of the mountain), and fine views straight down into Carter Notch from A Peak.

Carter Notch, the deep cleft between Carter Dome and Wildcat Mtn., includes some of the finest scenery in this region, particularly the two small, beautiful Carter Lakes that lie in the secluded hollow in the deepest part of the notch. The actual pass (3,388 ft.) in the main ridge connecting Carter Dome to Wildcat Mtn. is north of the lakes and 100 ft. higher than them, whereas the Rampart, a barrier of rocks that have fallen from the cliffs above on both Wildcat and Carter Dome, stretches across the floor of the notch, so that the lakes are totally enclosed by natural walls, and their outlet brook on the south side is forced to run underground. Above

SEC 9

the lakes, the impressive wooded cliffs of Wildcat Mtn. rise vertically nearly 1,000 ft. to the west, and to the east, Carter Dome also rises steeply, with the immense boulder called Pulpit Rock jutting out above the notch. A rough trail leaves Wildcat River Trail about 100 yd. south of AMC's Carter Notch Hut and runs east over the Rampart's huge rocks, where you have a good view toward Jackson. The many boulder caves among the fallen rocks, where ice sometimes remains through the summer, invite exploration (use caution).

Carter Dome (4,832 ft.) once bore a fire tower on its flat, scrub-fringed top. You have good views west and north from an open area near the summit, but the bare southeast spur crossed by Rainbow Trail is a better viewpoint. A bare rock peak, Mt. Hight (4,675 ft.), has the best views in the range. South Carter Mtn. (4,430 ft.) is wooded but has a partial view south. Middle Carter Mtn. (4,610 ft.) is wooded but has good outlooks from various points along its ridge crest, including an excellent view of the Presidentials 70 yd. north of the summit. North Carter Mtn. (4,530 ft.) has limited views from its summit and fine views from ledges along the ridge north and south of the summit; the best views are east to the Baldface Range. Imp Mtn. (3,730 ft.) is a rocky, trailless north spur of North Carter. The Imp Face (3,165 ft.) is an interesting cliff on a west spur of North Carter. The profile, which is named for its imagined resemblance to the grotesquely misshapen face of a part-human wood sprite, is best seen from Hayes Field in the WMNF Dolly Copp Campground. The top of the cliff affords an excellent view of the Presidentials.

From its ledgy summit block, Mt. Moriah (4,049 ft.) has fine views in most directions, and there are several excellent viewpoints along its ledgy southwest ridge. A northwest spur of Moriah, Mt. Surprise (2,194 ft.), offers partly restricted views. Shelburne Moriah Mtn. (3,735 ft.) offers magnificent views—surpassed in this range only by Mt. Hight—from acres of flat ledges at the summit and outlooks on its southwest and east ridges.

The Baldface–Royce Range extends southwest from Evans Notch, between the Wild River and the Cold River. The summits are relatively low, but so are the valleys; thus, the mountains rise impressively high above their bases. The highest peaks in the range are North Baldface (3,610 ft.) and South Baldface (3,570 ft.). Their upper slopes were swept by fire in 1903, and the resulting great expanses of open ledge make the circuit over these peaks one of the finest trips in the White Mtns. With Eagle Crag (3,030 ft.), a northeast buttress, these peaks enclose a cirquelike valley on their east. To the southwest are Sable Mtn. (3,519 ft.) and Chandler Mtn. (3,335 ft.), both wooded and trailless, and to the southeast is Eastman Mtn. (2,939 ft.), which affords good views from its ledgy summit.

A ridge descends northeast from Eagle Crag over Mt. Meader (2,782 ft.), which has ledgy outlooks, to the Basin Rim, where you find fine views from the brink of a cliff, then ascends to the Royces. West Royce Mtn. (3,210 ft.), with views to the east and southeast from ledges near the summit, is located in New Hampshire, and East Royce Mtn. (3,114 ft.), with good views in nearly all directions from various ledges, is in Maine; the state line crosses slightly to the east of the col between them. The Basin is an unusual low-elevation glacial cirque on the east side of the range between Mt. Meader and West Royce Mtn.; on its floor lies Basin Pond.

A number of lower mountains rise from the ridges that extend south from the main ranges. Spruce Mtn. (2,270 ft.), which is trailless, and Eagle Mtn. (1,613 ft.), which has a path and views from the summit, are small peaks on a south ridge of Wildcat Mtn. Black Mtn. (3,304 ft.)—which lies across broad, flat Perkins Notch (2,590 ft.) from Carter Dome—is a long ridge with a multitude of bumps, of which seven have traditionally been considered summits. The highest summit is wooded and trailless. Good views can be obtained from the southernmost summit, the Knoll (2,010 ft.), which is part of the Black Mtn. Ski Area, and restricted views from a knob (2,757 ft.) in the middle of the ridge that is reached by Black Mtn. Ski Trail. North Doublehead (3,053 ft.), with a cabin on the summit and good views east and west from outlooks near the summit, and South Doublehead (2,939 ft.), with good views from several ledges, form a small, sharp ridge southeast of Black Mtn. Southwest of Doublehead Mtn. is the low range composed of Thorn Mtn. (2,282 ft.) and Tin Mtn. (2,031 ft.). Tin Mtn. is said to have been the site of the first discovery of tin ore in the United States. Tin Mountain Conservation Center (TMCC) owns a 228-acre tract on the mountain, with a network of hiking and snowshoeing trails that provide access to the summit (where there is a partial view south), the tin mines, and a small pond. A signed trailhead parking area is on Rockwell Rd., just off Tin Mine Rd., 0.5 mi. from NH 16B in Jackson. A trail map is available at tinmountain.org/facilities-sanctuaries/tin-mountain-field-station-jackson-nh/. The former hiking trail on privately owned Thorn Mtn. is closed. East of Doublehead lie the valleys of the East Branch of the Saco River and Slippery Brook. In the valley of Slippery Brook is Mountain Pond, a large crescent-shaped body of water entirely surrounded by woods and overlooked by South Baldface, Walter, and Doublehead Mtns.

SEC
9

Mt. Kearsarge North (3,268 ft.), sometimes called Mt. Pequawket, rises prominently above the village of Intervale. The open ledgy summit bears an abandoned fire tower that is in good condition, and the views are magnificent in all directions, whether or not one ascends the tower; this is one of the finest viewpoints in the White Mountains. Bartlett Mtn. (2,661 ft.) is a shoulder extending westward toward Intervale; it has no official trails, but a number of ledges invite exploration. Tiny, boggy Shingle Pond is on the southeast side of Mt. Kearsarge North amid a tract of old-growth forest. A range of trailless hills extends northeast from Mt. Kearsarge North, including Rickers Knoll (2,477 ft.); the Twins, or Gemini (2,490 ft. and 2,519 ft.); Mt. Shaw (2,585 ft.); and Walter Mtn. (2,430 ft.). Province Pond lies at the eastern base of this range.

Running south from Mt. Kearsarge North are the Green Hills of Conway: Hurricane Mtn. (2,100 ft.), Black Cap (2,369 ft.), Peaked Mtn. (1,739 ft.), Middle Mtn. (1,857 ft.), Cranmore Mtn. (1,690 ft.), and Rattlesnake Mtn. (1,590 ft.). The summits of Black Cap, Peaked Mtn., Cranmore Mtn. (which has a ski area on its west slope), and Middle Mtn. afford excellent views and have several other good viewpoints. Except for Hurricane Mtn., these peaks are included within the Green Hills Preserve, a tract of more than 5,500 acres of hilly terrain with several streams and cascades and a beaver pond, as well as numerous rare and endangered plants and a beautiful high-elevation stand of red pine on Peaked Mtn. and Middle Mtn. This reservation is owned and managed by The Nature Conservancy (TNC), a private organization that maintains the preserve for the benefit of the public. Additional lands in the range are within Conway State Forest and the town of Conway's conservation land. All the major peaks except Rattlesnake Mtn. are reached by well-maintained paths. The trails in the Green Hills are shown on AMC's *White Mountains Trail Map 5: Carter Range–Evans Notch.* Visitors are requested to park their vehicles only at designated sites. To protect this resource for the enjoyment of all, removal of rocks, minerals, plants, or artifacts from the preserve is forbidden. Information and a Green Hills Preserve trail map can be obtained from the TNC website by visiting nature.org/newhampshire or by calling 603-356-8833; information is also posted at several kiosks along the trails, which have detailed maps on display and often have a supply of trail maps. Several of the hiking trails in the preserve are open to mountain biking, and there are frequent intersections with other mountain biking trails not described in this guide or shown on the AMC map; these are shown on the TNC map.

HUTS

Carter Notch Hut (AMC)

For more than 125 years, AMC's White Mountain hut system has offered hikers a bunk for the night in spectacular locations, with home-cooked dinners and breakfasts, cold running water, and composting or waterless toilets. AMC constructed this stone hut in 1914. It is located at an eleva-tion of 3,288 ft., about 60 yd. south of the smaller Carter Lake, at the southern terminus of Nineteen-Mile Brook Trail and the northern termi-nus of Wildcat River Trail. The hut, with two bunkhouses, accommodates 40 guests in rooms for four to six people. Pets are not permitted in the hut. The hut is open for full service with meals provided from June to mid-September, and is open on a caretaker basis the rest of the year. Lim-ited drinks, snacks, and gear are available for purchase by day visitors. For current information and schedule, contact AMC's Reservations Office (603-466-2727) or visit outdoors.org/lodging.

CAMPING
Wild River Wilderness
All shelters in the Wild River Wilderness have been removed and replaced with tentsites. In accordance with USFS Wilderness policy, hiking groups may not exceed ten people, and no more than ten people may occupy any designated or non-designated campsite. See p. xiii for more information about Wilderness Area regulations.

Forest Protection Areas
WMNF has established a number of FPAs, where camping and wood or charcoal fires are prohibited throughout the year. See p. xxiv for general FPA regulations. In the area covered by Section Nine, no camping is per-mitted within 0.25 mi. of Zeta Pass. No camping is permitted within 200 ft. of certain trails. In 2016 designated trails included the first mile of Wild River Trail south of Wild River Campground. No camping is per-mitted on WMNF land within 0.25 mi. of certain roads (camping on pri-vate roadside land is illegal except by permission of the landowner). In 2016 these roads included Wild River Rd. (FR 12) and NH 16. No wood or charcoal fires are permitted in Shingle Pond and Mountain Pond Candi-date Research Natural Areas.

Established Trailside Campsites
To reduce overcrowding during peak summer and fall periods, groups of six or more planning to use AMC-managed backcountry campsites are required to use AMC's group notification system. For more information, visit outdoors.org/group_notification.

Imp Campsite (AMC) is located on a spur path from Carter–Moriah Trail between Mt. Moriah and North Carter. The campsite has a shelter and five tent platforms. In summer, there is a caretaker and a fee is charged. Water (must be treated) is available in a nearby brook. In summer and fall, this

SEC
9

campsite fills up quickly; when capacity is reached, the caretaker will direct backpackers to a designated overflow area.

Rattle River Shelter (WMNF) is located next to Rattle River on Rattle River Trail, 1.7 mi. from US 2.

Spruce Brook Tentsite (WMNF), with three tent pads, is located on a spur path off Wild River Trail, 3.5 mi. from Wild River Campground, just north of the crossing of Spruce Brook. The former shelter at this site has been removed.

Perkins Notch Tentsite (WMNF), with three tent pads, is located on a spur path off Wild River Trail, just south of No-Ketchum Pond. The water source is 0.3 mi. east along the trail, at the uppermost crossing of Wild River. The former shelter at this site has been removed.

Blue Brook Tentsite (WMNF), with three tent pads, is located beside a brook on a spur path off Black Angel Trail 0.5 mi. west of Rim Junction. The former shelter at this site has been removed.

Baldface Shelter (WMNF) is located on Baldface Circle Trail, just below the ledges on South Baldface. The water source near the shelter is not reliable.

Province Pond Shelter (WMNF) is located on Province Brook Trail at Province Pond.

Mountain Pond Shelter (WMNF) is located on Mountain Pond Loop Trail at Mountain Pond.

Doublehead Cabin (WMNF) is located at the summit of North Doublehead, with bunks for eight. The cabin is kept locked, and reservations for its use must be made at recreation.gov or 877-444-6777. There is no water nearby.

Black Mtn. Cabin (WMNF) is located on Black Mtn. Ski Trail (which is also used for hiking) near the central summit of Black Mtn. The cabin has bunks for eight. The cabin is kept locked, and reservations for its use must be made at recreation.gov or 877-444-6777. A spring (unreliable water source in summer, usually frozen in winter) is located near the cabin.

SEC 9

SUGGESTED HIKES

■ Easy Hikes
LOST POND

		🔃	📈	⏱
RT via Lost Pond Trail		1.2 mi.	100 ft.	0:40

This pleasant spot—reachable by Lost Pond Trail, part of the AT—has excellent views across to the east face of Mt. Washington. See Lost Pond Trail, p. 427.

SQUARE LEDGE

	�룹	⤤	◔
RT via Lost Pond and Square Ledge trails	1.2 mi.	400 ft.	0:50

A fairly rugged but short trip leads to this spot with a fine view of Mt. Washington. See Lost Pond Trail, p. 427.

MOUNTAIN POND

	↺	⤤	◔
LP via Mountain Pond Loop Trail	2.7 mi.	50 ft.	1:25

A nearly level trail, rocky in places, circles this large, remote pond. See Mountain Pond Loop Trail, p. 454.

BLACK CAP MTN.

	↺	⤤	◔
RT via Black Cap Trail	2.2 mi.	650 ft.	1:25

An easy route connects steep Hurricane Mtn. Rd. to this excellent viewpoint in the Green Hills. See Black Cap Trail, p. 466.

■ Moderate Hikes
PEAKED AND MIDDLE MTNS.

	↺	⤤	◔
RT to Peaked Mtn. via Peaked Mtn. Trail	4.2 mi.	1,200 ft.	2:40
RT to Middle Mtn. via Middle Mtn. Trail	4.2 mi.	1,350 ft.	2:45
LP of Peaked and Middle mtns. via Peaked Mtn. Trail, Peaked Mtn.– Middle Mtn. Connector, and Middle Mtn. Trail	5.4 mi.	1,750 ft.	3:35

Pass beautiful red pines and open ledges en route to Peaked Mtn. (see Peaked Mtn. Trail, p. 469). Another option in the Green Hills is nearby Middle Mtn. (see Middle Mtn. Trail, p. 470) or a loop combining both summits (to begin, see Peaked Mtn. Trail).

IMP FACE

	↺	⤤	◔
RT via Imp Trail	4.4 mi.	1,850 ft.	3:10

The north half of Imp Trail provides the shortest access to this spectacular cliff-top perch in the northern part of the Carter Range. See Imp Trail, p. 434.

SEC 9

EAST ROYCE MTN.

	⤴⤵	↗	○
RT via East Royce Trail	2.6 mi.	1,650 ft.	2:10

A steep and rugged ascent leads to fine views of the Evans Notch area. See East Royce Trail, p. 447.

DOUBLEHEAD MTN.

	⤴⤵	↗	○
LP via Doublehead Ski Trail, Old Path, New Path, Old Path, and Doublehead Ski Trail	3.7 mi.	1,850 ft.	2:45

Complete the loop for views from both the south and north peaks of this mountain in Jackson. To begin, see Doublehead Ski Trail, p. 462.

BASIN RIM

	⤴⤵	↗	○
RT via Basin Trail (east half) and Basin Rim Trail	4.8 mi.	1,300 ft.	3:05

Hermit Falls and a striking view over the cirque known as the Basin provide this hike's dual highlights. See Basin Trail, p. 445.

MT. KEARSARGE NORTH

	⤴⤵	↗	○
RT via Mt. Kearsarge North Trail	6.2 mi.	2,600 ft.	4:25

A steady, moderate climb leads to one of the finest views in the White Mountains. See Mt. Kearsage North Trail, p. 464.

BASIN RIM AND WILD RIVER

	⤴⤵	↗	○
LP via Basin, Basin Rim, Black Angel, and Wild River trails	8.0 mi.	1,350 ft.	4:40

This scenic loop goes both high to a fine viewpoint and low along the river. To begin, see Basin Trail, p. 445.

CARTER NOTCH

	⤴⤵	↗	○
RT via Nineteen-Mile Brook Trail	7.6 mi.	2,000 ft.	4:50

The hike to this magnificent mountain pass features ponds, cliffs, and an AMC hut. See Nineteen-Mile Brook Trail, p. 433.

■ Strenuous Hikes
CARTER DOME

	⇅	⤢	◔
LP via Nineteen-Mile Brook, Carter-Moriah, and Carter Dome trails	10.2 mi.	3,600 ft.	6:55

An excellent loop over two high summits follows Nineteen-Mile Brook Trail to Carter Notch then Carter–Moriah Trail over Carter Dome and Mt. Hight (the best viewpoint on the Carter Range) before a relatively easy descent on Carter Dome Trail. To begin, see Nineteen-Mile Brook Trail, p. 433.

MT. MORIAH

	⇅	⤢	◔
RT via Stony Brook and Carter-Moriah trails	10.0 mi.	3,100 ft.	6:35

The ascent of this peak near Gorham is very scenic, affording excellent views both along the way and at the summit. See Stony Brook Trail, p. 435.

SHELBURNE MORIAH MTN.

	⇅	⤢	◔
RT via Rattle River and Kenduskeag trails	11.2 mi.	3,200 ft.	7:10

An ascent of this less-visited peak offers exceptional views from the ledges on the upper part of the ridge and at the summit. See Rattle River Trail, p. 437.

THE BALDFACES

	⇅	⤢	◔
LP via Baldface Circle Trail, Bicknell Ridge Trail, and Baldface Circle Trail	9.7 mi.	3,600 ft.	6:40
LP via Baldface Circle, Slippery Brook, Baldface Knob, Baldface Circle, Bicknell Ridge, and Baldface Circle trails	10.7 mi.	3,700 ft.	7:10

One of the finest ridge traverses of the White Mountains, with nearly 4 mi. of open ledge walking, includes South Baldface and North Baldface. South Baldface's steep ledges can be avoided by using the second route above. To begin, see Baldface Circle Trail, p. 450.

SEC 9

TRAIL DESCRIPTIONS

CARTER RANGE RIDGE AND WEST SLOPES

WILDCAT RIDGE TRAIL (AMC; MAP 5: G9–F10)

Cumulative from Glen Ellis Falls parking area (1,960 ft.) to:	↕	↗	⟳
E Peak summit (4,046 ft.)	1.9 mi.	2,200 ft. (rev. 100 ft.)	2:05
Wildcat Col (3,775 ft.)	2.5 mi.	2,300 ft. (rev. 400 ft.)	2:25
C Peak summit (4,298 ft.)	3.3 mi.	2,850 ft.	3:05
A Peak summit (4,422 ft.)	4.2 mi.	3,150 ft. (rev. 200 ft.)	3:40
Nineteen-Mile Brook Trail (3,388 ft.)	4.9 mi.	3,150 ft. (rev. 1,050 ft.)	4:00

This trail climbs up to and across the numerous summits on the long ridge of Wildcat Mtn. then descends to Nineteen-Mile Brook Trail 0.3 mi. north of Carter Notch Hut. The trail officially begins at the Glen Ellis Falls parking lot on NH 16, 0.8 mi. south of Pinkham Notch Visitor Center, but this end is more commonly reached by following Lost Pond Trail for 0.9 mi. from Pinkham Notch Visitor Center to avoid the often-difficult and sometimes-dangerous crossing of Ellis River. From Lost Pond Trail jct. to Carter Notch, Wildcat Ridge Trail is a part of the AT. The sections from Lost Pond Trail jct. to E Peak and from A Peak to Carter Notch are very steep and rough, and there are several ups and downs and other steep, rough sections along the rest of the trail that make it more difficult and time-consuming than one might infer from a casual glance at the map or the distance summary. (*Caution:* The section between NH 16 and E Peak may be dangerous when wet or icy, and hikers with heavy packs should allow substantial extra time.)

Wildcat Ridge Trail starts on the east side of NH 16 opposite the parking area for Glen Ellis Falls (a pedestrian underpass is provided for crossing the highway) and leads east across Ellis River (may be very difficult) to a trail marker. At 0.1 mi., Lost Pond Trail enters on the left, and the trail shortly begins the very steep climb up the end of the ridge (use care on all ledge areas). The first pitch up rock steps and a ladder leads to an outlook across Pinkham Notch. After a tricky traverse and a fairly difficult scramble up a rock chimney, the trail crosses a ledge with an excellent view of Mt. Washington. The trail climbs steeply past another good view of Mt. Washington, and at 0.9 mi., passes a level, open ledge with fine views south. The trail dips slightly, traverses a shoulder, then resumes the climb. At 1.2 mi., a side path leads left to a spring, and at 1.5 mi., the main trail climbs rock and wood steps to the top of a steep ledge with a superb view of the great ravines on the east side of Mt. Washington. The trail continues to climb over several knobs and passes 3 yd. left of the wooded summit of E Peak at 1.9 mi. then descends to the summit station of Wildcat Ski Area in the col at 2.1 mi.

An alternate route to this point, about 2.4 mi. long with 2,000-ft. elevation gain, follows Stray Cat, Middle Polecat, and Upper Polecat ski trails along the north edge of Wildcat Ski Area, from parking at the base lodge (1,950 ft.) off NH 16, 0.9 mi. north of the AMC's Pinkham Notch Visitor Center and 2.8 mi. south of the trailhead for Nineteen-Mile Brook Trail. Views are excellent from the ski trails. During the ski season, hikers using these ski trails must purchase a hiker's pass at the base lodge.

From the col, Wildcat Ridge Trail next climbs steeply to the summit of D Peak, which has a recently rebuilt observation tower with good views; an easier trail maintained by the ski area parallels this segment to the west. Wildcat Ridge Trail then descends fairly steeply into Wildcat Col, the deepest col on the main ridge, at 2.5 mi. Here, the trail passes over a small hogback and through a second sag then begins the climb to C Peak over several "steps"—fairly steep climbs interspersed with level sections, with occasional views, to the wooded summit of C Peak at 3.3 mi. The trail makes a significant descent into a col and a climb to B Peak then a descent to a shallower col and an easy climb to A Peak at 4.2 mi. As the trail turns left near this summit, a spur path leads right 20 yd. to a spectacular view into Carter Notch. The actual summit of Wildcat Mtn. is a rock in the scrub just off the spur path within a few yards of this outlook. The trail now descends by switchbacks, rather steeply at times, with many rock steps, to a sharp right turn. The trail continues down steeply, passing a spring and then crossing a landslide track (potentially dangerous if icy) that provides a view north, and about 0.2 mi. beyond the landslide meets Nineteen-Mile Brook Trail at the height-of-land in Carter Notch. For Carter Notch Hut, turn right (south) on Nineteen-Mile Brook Trail.

SEC 9

LOST POND TRAIL (AMC; MAP 1: F9–G9)

From NH 16 opposite Pinkham Notch Visitor Center (2,022 ft.) to:	⇅	↗	○
Wildcat Ridge Trail (1,980 ft.)	0.9 mi.	50 ft. (rev. 100 ft.)	0:30

This short link trail runs from Pinkham Notch Visitor Center to the lower end of Wildcat Ridge Trail, avoiding the difficult and sometimes dangerous crossing of Ellis River at the beginning of Wildcat Ridge Trail. Lost Pond Trail is part of the AT.

Lost Pond Trail leaves the east side of NH 16, 50 yd. south of the entrance to Pinkham Notch Visitor Center, crosses a bridge over Ellis

River in an area of beaver activity, and turns south at the end of the bridge, where Square Ledge Trail leaves on the left. Lost Pond Trail follows the east bank of Ellis River, which is soon joined from the opposite side by the larger Cutler River. The trail then leaves the riverbank and climbs at a moderate grade to Lost Pond at 0.5 mi. The trail follows the east shore with good views of Mt. Washington, descends slightly through a rocky area, and ends at Wildcat Ridge Trail.

SQUARE LEDGE TRAIL (AMC; MAP 1: F9–F10)

From Lost Pond Trail (2,020 ft.) to:	↥↧	↗	○
Square Ledge (2,419 ft.)	0.5 mi.	400 ft.	0:25

This short trail (with blue blazes) leads to an excellent outlook from a cliff-top ledge that rises from the floor of Pinkham Notch on the side of Wildcat Mtn. The trail diverges left where Lost Pond Trail turns south, 20 yd. beyond the east end of the footbridge across Ellis River. Square Ledge Trail climbs moderately, and after 80 yd., a spur path leads left 60 yd. to a ledge (sign: Ladies' Lookout), which offers a view of the east side of Mt. Washington. The trail bears right (east) and crosses Square Ledge Loop Ski Trail. Square Ledge Trail then rises moderately, passes Hangover Rock, and ascends to the base of Square Ledge. The trail swings around to the east side of the ledge then scrambles steeply up a ledgy V-slot (potentially dangerous if wet or icy) about 50 yd. to an outlook that offers excellent views of Pinkham Notch and Mt. Washington. Use caution on the ledge, as there is a sharp dropoff in front.

THOMPSON FALLS TRAIL (WMNF; MAP 5: F10)

From Wildcat Ski Area (1,930 ft.) to:	↥↧	↗	○
End of trail (2,140 ft.)	0.7 mi.	200 ft.	0:25

This trail runs from Wildcat Ski Area to Thompson Falls, a series of cascades on Thompson Brook flowing from Wildcat Mtn. Except in wet seasons, the brook is apt to be low.

From the Wildcat Ski Area parking lot, cross the bridge to the east side, turn left, and follow Way of the Wildcat nature trail north. (Here, you see signs for the nature trail and then for Thompson Falls Trail.) In a short distance, continue straight ahead as the nature trail makes a short loop to the right. Where the nature trail rejoins from the right, continue ahead on Thompson Falls Trail, which crosses a small stream and a maintenance road then leads up the south side of the brook to the foot of the first fall at 0.6 mi. The trail crosses to the north side above the fall, bears right, and continues up the brook for another 0.1 mi., with restricted views of Mt. Washington.

CARTER–MORIAH TRAIL (AMC; MAP 5: E10–F10)

Cumulative from Bangor St. (800 ft.) to:	⇅	↗	⟳
Mt. Moriah summit (4,049 ft.)	4.5 mi.	3,400 ft.	3:55
Moriah Brook and Stony Brook trails (3,127 ft.)	5.9 mi.	3,450 ft.	4:40
Imp Shelter spur trail (3,350 ft.)	6.6 mi.	3,750 ft.	5:10
North Carter Trail (4,470 ft.)	8.5 mi.	4,950 ft.	6:45
Middle Carter summit (4,610 ft.)	9.1 mi.	5,150 ft.	7:10
South Carter summit (4,430 ft.)	10.4 mi.	5,400 ft.	7:55
Zeta Pass (3,890 ft.)	11.2 mi.	5,400 ft.	8:20
Mt. Hight summit (4,675 ft.)	11.8 mi.	6,200 ft.	9:00
Black Angel Trail (4,600 ft.)	12.2 mi.	6,250 ft.	9:15
Carter Dome summit (4,832 ft.)	12.6 mi.	6,500 ft.	9:35
Nineteen-Mile Brook Trail (3,300 ft.)	13.8 mi.	6,500 ft.	10:10

CARTER–MORIAH TRAIL, IN REVERSE (AMC; MAP 5: F10–E10)

Cumulative from Nineteen-Mile Brook Trail (3,300 ft.) to:	⇅	↗	⟳
Carter Dome summit (4,832 ft.)	1.2 mi.	1,550 ft.	1:25
Black Angel Trail (4,600 ft.)	1.6 mi.	1,550 ft.	1:35
Mt. Hight summit (4,675 ft.)	2.0 mi.	1,700 ft.	1:50
Zeta Pass (3,890 ft.)	2.6 mi.	1,700 ft.	2:10
South Carter summit (4,430 ft.)	3.4 mi.	2,250 ft.	2:50
Middle Carter summit (4,610 ft.)	4.7 mi.	2,700 ft.	3:40
North Carter Trail (4,470 ft.)	5.3 mi.	2,750 ft.	4:00
Imp Shelter spur trail (3,350 ft.)	7.2 mi.	2,850 ft.	5:00
Moriah Brook and Stony Brook trails (3,127 ft.)	7.9 mi.	2,950 ft.	5:25
Mt. Moriah summit (4,049 ft.)	9.3 mi.	3,850 ft.	6:35
Bangor St. (800 ft.)	13.8 mi.	4,000 ft.	8:55

SEC 9

This trail runs 13.8 mi. from Gorham to Carter Notch, following the crest of the Carter–Moriah Range. To reach the trailhead at Gorham, follow US 2 east from its eastern jct. with NH 16 for 0.5 mi., turn sharply right onto Bangor St. just past the bridge and railroad track, and follow this paved road 0.5 mi. to the turnaround at its end. There is limited parking here; park only on the left (east) side of the road, opposite the homes, and away from the fire hydrant and a posted grassy area. Better parking is available at a power-line clearing 0.1 mi. back to the north, on the east side of Bangor St. (It is also possible to use public parking at the Libby Recreation Area in Gorham, located on Mill St. off the east side of NH 16, 0.4 mi. south of US 2. On foot, follow Mill St. north for 0.2 mi. and turn right onto a path that leads across Peabody River on a footbridge. Turn right here and follow the road to its end, where the trail enters the woods on the left. The distance from the recreation-area parking to the trailhead is 0.4 mi.)

From the Kenduskeag Trail jct. near the summit of Mt. Moriah to Carter Notch, Carter–Moriah Trail is part of the AT. Water is very scarce on many parts of this trail because it runs mostly on or near the crest of the ridge.

The following description of the path is in the southbound direction (from Gorham to Carter Notch). Distances, elevation gains, and times are also given for the reverse (northbound) direction.

Part I: Gorham to Mt. Moriah

From the end of Bangor St., blue-blazed Carter–Moriah Trail follows a logging road up a steep bank then eases after 50 yd. and winds moderately upward through second-growth woods, passing a path that joins on the left at 0.2 mi. The trail climbs more steeply, enters the WMNF at 1.1 mi., and continues up through open hardwoods. The grade eases on a spruce-wooded shoulder, and at 2.0 mi. a ledge 25 yd. down to the right affords good views.

The trail soon passes to the right of the insignificant summit of Mt. Surprise and its small flume. From here, the trail descends slightly, ascends gradually, and soon becomes steep as it climbs over a series of ledges that have partly restricted views west and north; the ledges are slippery when wet. A ledge at 2.5 mi. affords a more open view. The trail reenters the woods and climbs, steeply at times, staying near the ridge top but winding from side to side. It then slabs the west side of the ridge, passing to the left of a large boulder named Quimby's Pillow (after E.T. Quimby, a Dartmouth professor who led a survey party on Mt. Moriah in 1879) at 3.6 mi. The trail now traverses several ups and downs over small wooded humps, and at 4.2 mi. it begins the final steep climb of the summit cone. At 4.5 mi a spur path ascends right 50 yd. to the small rock knob summit of Mt. Moriah, which affords excellent views, especially to the south and east.

Part II: Mt. Moriah to North Carter

From the jct. with the Mt. Moriah summit spur path, Carter–Moriah Trail drops very steeply down the ledges of the Mt. Moriah summit block; this rock scramble is dangerous when icy (in which case it may be better to bushwhack down through the woods). In less than 100 yd., the trail reaches the jct. where Kenduskeag Trail turns left then shortly right, toward Shelburne Moriah Mtn. Here, Carter–Moriah Trail turns right (southwest). (In the reverse direction, Carter–Moriah Trail turns left to ascend the steep ledges.) From this jct. south, the trail is part of the AT and has white blazes. The trail follows the broad ridge crest south at easy grades with minor ups and downs, through woods then over an open knob at 4.7 mi. It drops to the left off a ledge, and in another 100 yd. it swings right across a ledge where there is a fine view east 20 yd. to the left.

The trail meanders southwest down through woods and over occasional ledges to an excellent outlook from the top of the south cliffs at 5.3 mi. In the next 0.2 mi., it passes several more outlooks then descends steadily through the woods. It passes two more outlooks shortly before reaching the deep col between Moriah and the Carters at 5.9 mi. Here Moriah Brook Trail enters left, and Carter–Moriah Trail turns right and follows a boardwalk. In 40 yd., Stony Brook Trail enters straight ahead, and Carter–Moriah Trail turns left. It skirts the northwest side of a hump with minor ups and downs, climbs to a ledgy area with interesting views, turns sharply right, and descends to a jct. at 6.6 mi. with a spur trail that descends right 0.2 mi. and 150 ft. to Imp Campsite, which has a shelter, tent platforms, and water.

The main trail crosses a small brook and passes through a wet area, ascending on the plateau south of Imp Mtn. and crossing a couple of minor knobs. After a slight dip, at 7.7 mi., the trail climbs steeply to a shoulder. It eases briefly then begins a steep and rough climb to North Carter Mtn., with several fairly difficult ledge scrambles and occasional good views north. The grade moderates near the top as the trail swings left (south), and at 8.2 mi., it reaches the partly open summit of North Carter, with limited views.

SEC 9

Part III: North Carter to Zeta Pass

Carter Moriah Trail continues south, passes a fine outlook east over Wild River valley, and winds along the crest of the ridge. At 8.5 mi., North Carter

Trail enters right, and the trail continues over a series of five ledgy humps, with boggy depressions between. Good views are available from ledges on the two southernmost knobs. Ascending from the col south of the last knob, the trail passes a good outlook west and north, and in another 70 yd., it reaches the level, wooded summit of Middle Carter Mtn., at 9.1 mi.

The trail descends easily and passes an open area with a fine view west at 9.3 mi then continues along the nearly level ridge with one climb up a short, steep ledge and occasional views. It then descends moderately to the col between Middle and South Carter at 10.0 mi. The trail ascends steadily to a point 10 yd. left (east) of the wooded summit of South Carter (reached by a side path) at 10.4 mi. A few steps farther along the main trail, another side path leads 15 yd. left to a view southeast. Carter-Moriah Trail now descends steeply at first then more gradually to Zeta Pass, where the trail makes a short ascent to the jct. with Carter Dome Trail on the right at 11.2 mi. Water may occasionally be available in a small stream (usually dry in midsummer) that can be reached from Carter Dome Trail, 80 yd. below this jct.

Part IV: Zeta Pass to Carter Notch

The two trails coincide and climb easily to the south for 0.2 mi. Carter Dome Trail continues ahead, and Carter Moriah Trail turns left before quickly swinging right and climbing steeply with rocky footing up to the summit of Mt. Hight at 11.8 mi. At this bare summit, which commands the best views in the range, the trail makes a very sharp right turn; great care must be exercised to stay on the trail if visibility is poor, particularly going north, because a beaten path that soon peters out continues north from the summit. (From the summit, the southbound trail heads southwest, and the northbound trail heads west-northwest.)

The trail passes through a shallow sag, and Carter Dome Trail reenters from the right at 12.2 mi. In another 25 yd., Black Angel Trail enters on the left, and Carter–Moriah Trail climbs steadily, passing a side path leading 10 yd. right to an excellent viewpoint at 12.5 mi. The trail reaches the partly open summit of Carter Dome at 12.6 mi., where Rainbow Trail enters on the left, near the southwest end of the summit clearing; the best views in the summit area are 25 yd. to the right (west) at the northeast end of the clearing. From the southwest end of the clearing, Carter–Moriah Trail descends moderately southwest, passing a side path at 13.1 mi. that leads 60 yd. right to a fine spring. At 13.5 mi., a side path leads 30 yd. left to an excellent outlook over Carter Notch and out to the south, with Pulpit Rock close by on the left. Soon Carter–Moriah Trail begins to descend very steeply to Carter Notch; use caution on one exposed spot with poor footing, just below the outlook. The trail continues down over rock steps, ending on Nineteen-Mile Brook Trail at the shore of the larger Carter Lake. Carter Notch Hut is 0.1 mi. to the left.

NINETEEN-MILE BROOK TRAIL (AMC; MAP 5: F10)

Cumulative from NH 16 (1,487 ft.) to:	↑↓	↗	↻
Carter Dome Trail (2,322 ft.)	1.9 mi.	850 ft.	1:25
Wildcat Ridge Trail (3,388 ft.)	3.6 mi.	1,900 ft.	2:45
Carter Notch Hut (3,288 ft.)	3.8 mi.	1,900 ft. (rev. 100 ft.)	2:50

This trail runs from a parking area on the east side of NH 16, 1.0 mi. north of Mt. Washington Auto Rd., to Carter Notch Hut and is the easiest route to the hut. (The parking area is a stop for the AMC Hiker Shuttle.) Sections of the trail close to the brook bank sometimes become dangerously icy in the cold seasons.

Leaving NH 16, the trail enters the woods to the left of a kiosk on a relocated section then rejoins the original route at 0.1 mi. and follows the northeast bank of Nineteen-Mile Brook on the remains of an old road. At 0.7 mi. the trail crosses an open bank above the brook and soon turns left up rock steps on another relocation, returning to the old route at 0.9 mi. At 1.1 mi. it crosses a major tributary on a large new bridge just downstream from the former crossing.

At 1.2 mi., the trail passes a dam in the brook and becomes somewhat rougher, with minor ups and downs, and at 1.9 mi., Carter Dome Trail diverges left for Zeta Pass. Here Nineteen-Mile Brook Trail crosses a tributary on a footbridge, and at 2.2 mi., the trail crosses another brook at a small cascade, also on a footbridge. At 3.1 mi., the trail crosses a small brook and begins to ascend more steeply to the height-of-land at 3.6 mi., where Wildcat Ridge Trail diverges right (west). Nineteen-Mile Brook Trail then drops steeply to the larger Carter Lake, passes Carter–Moriah Trail left at 3.8 mi., crosses between the lakes, and reaches Carter Notch Hut and the jct. with Wildcat River Trail.

CARTER DOME TRAIL (WMNF; MAP 5: F10)

Cumulative from Nineteen-Mile Brook Trail (2,322 ft.) to:	↑↓	↗	↻
Zeta Pass (3,890 ft.)	1.9 mi.	1,550 ft.	1:45
Carter Dome summit (4,832 ft.)	3.1 mi.	2,500 ft.	2:50

This trail runs from Nineteen-Mile Brook Trail 1.9 mi. from NH 16 to Zeta Pass and the summit of Carter Dome, following the route of an old

SEC 9

road that served the long-dismantled fire tower that once stood on Carter Dome. Grades are steady and moderate all the way.

Leaving Nineteen-Mile Brook Trail, Carter Dome Trail follows a tributary brook, crossing two branches of it at 0.5 mi. and recrossing it at 0.8 mi., at a small, attractive cascade; in this area, parts of the trail were damaged by the 2011 storm. Here, the trail swings left then in 50 yd. turns sharply right and ascends by a series of seven switchbacks, passing a good spring left at 1.1 mi., and reaching the jct. with Carter–Moriah Trail at Zeta Pass at 1.9 mi. Carter Dome Trail coincides with Carter–Moriah Trail to the right (south). Then at 2.1 mi., Carter–Moriah Trail, which offers excellent views but is steep and exposed to weather, turns left to climb to the bare summit of Mt. Hight, whereas Carter Dome Trail continues its steady, sheltered ascent along the east slope of Mt. Hight. At 2.7 mi., Carter–Moriah Trail reenters from the left; Black Angel Trail enters from the left in another 25 yd.; and Carter Dome and Carter–Moriah trails coincide, ascending through high scrub, passing a side path leading 10 yd. right to an excellent viewpoint at 3.0 mi., and continuing to the jct. with Rainbow Trail near the southwest end of the Carter Dome summit clearing.

IMP TRAIL (WMNF; MAP 5: F10)

Cumulative from northern terminus on NH 16 (1,270 ft.) to:	⇅	↗	⏱
Imp Face viewpoint (3,100 ft.)	2.2 mi.	1,850 ft.	2:00
North Carter Trail (3,220 ft.)	3.1 mi.	2,050 ft. (rev. 100 ft.)	2:35
Southern terminus on NH 16 (1,283 ft.)	6.3 mi.	2,050 ft. (rev. 1,950 ft.)	4:10

This trail makes a loop over the cliff that bears the Imp Face, providing fine views of the Presidential Range. The ends of the loop are 0.3 mi. apart on NH 16, with the north end 2.6 mi. north of the Mt. Washington Auto Rd. and 5.4 mi. south of Gorham; there is roadside parking at both trailheads.

The north branch of the trail heads east up the south side of Imp Brook valley, through a pleasant stand of hemlocks, then crosses the brook at 0.8 mi. (difficult at high water). The trail angles north up to a ridge and follows its crest, nearly level for some distance. The trail then angles more steeply up the north side of the ridge and continues nearly to the bottom of a ravine northeast of the Imp Face cliff, where the trail turns right and then climbs steeply, swinging to the left, to reach the Imp viewpoint at 2.2 mi.

From the cliff, the trail drops over a ledge, passes a viewpoint, and skirts the edge of Imp Brook ravine, crossing two small brooks and then a larger brook at 2.7 mi. Becoming gradual but somewhat rough, the trail continues generally south, ascending and then descending, and crosses another small brook then the head of Imp Brook shortly before reaching the jct. with North Carter Trail on the left at 3.1 mi. Imp Trail turns sharply right here and descends a rocky old logging road generally southwest; then, just before reaching Cowboy Brook, it turns northwest at 4.7 mi. At 5.2 mi., shortly after crossing a brook, the trail crosses a newer logging road. (To the left, this road runs 0.2 mi. to AMC's Camp Dodge Volunteer Center. From there, an access road runs another 0.2 mi., bearing left at a fork, to NH 16, 0.4 mi. north of the trailhead for Nineteen-Mile Brook Trail. Call AMC's Pinkham Notch Visitor Center to confirm this shortcut is open during Camp Dodge renovations, scheduled to begin in 2017: 603-466-2721.)

Imp Trail meanders across a flat area and follows an old logging road north downhill to cross a small brook then a larger brook immediately after. The trail turns sharply left, runs about level for 75 yd., and ends at NH 16.

NORTH CARTER TRAIL (WMNF; MAP 5: F10)

From Imp Trail (3,220 ft.) to:	↕	↗	↺
Carter–Moriah Trail (4,470 ft.)	1.2 mi.	1,250 ft.	1:15

This trail leaves the jct. at the upper end of the Imp Trail loop, 3.1 mi. from NH 16 via the north branch of Imp Trail or 3.2 mi. from NH 16 via the south branch. North Carter Trail follows an old logging road, and at 0.3 mi., turns to the right onto another old road. At 0.5 mi., the trail turns sharply left off the old road and climbs more steeply to Carter–Moriah Trail, 0.3 mi. south of the summit of North Carter.

STONY BROOK TRAIL (WMNF; MAP 5: E10–F11)

Cumulative from NH 16 (930 ft.) to:	↕	↗	↺
Carter–Moriah Trail (3,127 ft.)	3.6 mi.	2,200 ft.	2:55
Mt. Moriah (4,049 ft.) via Carter–Moriah Trail	5.0 mi.	3,100 ft.	4:05

This trail, with moderate grades and good footing until its upper 0.5 mi., begins at a parking area just off NH 16 on a paved road (Stony Brook Rd.) that leaves the east side of the highway just south of the bridge over Peabody River, 1.8 mi. south of the eastern jct. of NH 16 and US 2 in Gorham. The trail ends in the col between North Carter and Mt. Moriah and provides the best access to the beautiful south ledges of Mt. Moriah.

SEC 9

The trail leaves Stony Brook Rd. at a hiker sign, crosses Stony Brook on a footbridge, and then a smaller brook in a flume on another bridge. The trail follows Stony Brook upstream. Then, at 1.0 mi., the trail descends sharply to the right, recrosses the brook on rocks above an attractive pool, and turns left onto an old logging road. (Descending, be sure to turn right off this old road; ahead, it leads to a private housing development.) The trail ascends at easy to moderate grades, and at 2.3 mi., it crosses a branch of Stony Brook below a pleasant small cascade and pool and begins to climb more steeply. At 3.1 mi., the trail crosses a small brook under a mossy ledge and climbs steadily with fairly rough footing to the ridge and Carter–Moriah Trail; turn left for Mt. Moriah.

MORIAH GROUP RIDGE AND NORTH SLOPES

KENDUSKEAG TRAIL (WMNF; MAP 5: E11–E12)

Cumulative from Carter-Moriah Trail (3,980 ft.) to:	⇅	↗	↻
Rattle River Trail (3,350 ft.)	1.4 mi.	100 ft. (rev. 750 ft.)	0:45
Shelburne Moriah Mtn. summit (3,735 ft.)	2.7 mi.	600 ft. (rev. 100 ft.)	1:40
Shelburne Trail (2,750 ft.)	4.1 mi.	700 ft. (rev. 1,100 ft.)	2:25

This trail runs from Carter–Moriah Trail just east of the summit of Mt. Moriah to Shelburne Trail in the col between Shelburne Moriah Mtn. and Howe Peak. The ledges of Shelburne Moriah afford excellent views. The name of Kenduskeag Trail is derived from an Abenaki word meaning "a pleasant walk." From Mt. Moriah to Rattle River Trail jct., Kenduskeag Trail is part of the AT.

From the trail jct. below the summit ledges of Mt. Moriah, Kenduskeag Trail turns sharply right in 15 yd. and runs over a lesser summit with a restricted view then descends steeply past an outlook. The trail runs nearly level across a saddle, climbs along the south slope of Middle Moriah Mtn., then descends to the jct. with Rattle River Trail on the left at 1.4 mi. Kenduskeag Trail climbs (with several intervening descents) over a section of knobs and ledges (with many plank walkways over alpine bogs, some muddy sections, and fine views) to the flat, ledgy summit of Shelburne Moriah Mtn. at 2.7 mi. The upper part of this section of trail is very exposed to weather—more so than any other part of the Carter–Moriah Range. The trail runs across the summit plateau to an outlook east then descends steeply with rough footing to a sharp, narrow col at 3.3 mi. The trail then climbs over two knolls with views; on the second knoll, at

3.7 mi., one must scramble up a ledge on the right to obtain the fine view of Wild River valley. The trail then descends rather steeply, with one ledge scramble, passes under two cliff faces, and ends at Shelburne Trail.

RATTLE RIVER TRAIL (WMNF; MAP 5: E11)

Cumulative from US 2 (760 ft.) to:	⇅	↗	↻
Rattle River Shelter (1,250 ft.)	1.7 mi.	500 ft.	1:05
Kenduskeag Trail (3,350 ft.)	4.3 mi.	2,600 ft.	3:25

This trail runs from US 2 to Kenduskeag Trail in the Moriah–Shelburne Moriah col. The trailhead is on US 2 near the east end of the bridge over Rattle River, about 250 yd. east of the North Rd. intersection and 3.5 mi. east of the eastern jct. of US 2 and NH 16 in Gorham. Rattle River Trail is a part of the AT.

From the parking area off US 2, the trail leads generally south, following a logging road on the east side of the stream. A snowmobile trail enters on the right at 0.3 mi.; the trails enter the WMNF; and the snowmobile trail leaves on the left at 0.6 mi., just before Rattle River Trail crosses a tributary brook. At 1.7 mi., the trail passes WMNF Rattle River Shelter (left), where a side path descends right to attractive ledges and pools in the river. In another 0.1 mi. the trail crosses Rattle River (look carefully for markings; may be difficult at high water) then crosses back over its westerly branch. At 3.2 mi., the trail crosses an upper branch of the river and starts to climb steadily. The trail passes a small cascade to the left at 3.7 mi. and soon bears away from the brook and climbs steeply, with many rock steps, to the ridge top, where Rattle River Trail meets Kenduskeag Trail.

SHELBURNE TRAIL (WMNF; MAP 5: E12–F12)

Cumulative from gate on FR 95 (850 ft.) to:	⇅	↗	↻
Kenduskeag Trail (2,750 ft.)	4.0 mi.	1,900 ft.	2:55
Wild River Rd. (1,079 ft.)	7.2 mi.	1,900 ft. (rev. 1,700 ft.)	4:35

This trail begins on FR 95, 1.0 mi. from US 2 near the Maine–New Hampshire border, passes through the col between Shelburne Moriah Mtn. and Howe Peak, and descends to Wild River Rd. Most of the trail south of the ridgeline is within or adjacent to the Wild River Wilderness. For the north terminus, leave the south side of US 2 about 9 mi. east of Gorham, at the west end of an abandoned wayside area, 0.2 mi. west of the

Maine–New Hampshire border and just east of a sign for Old Man of the Valley (a boulder profile in the woods); the entrance is marked with a sign (Parking) and hiker symbol. At a fork in 0.1 mi. take FR 95 (a rough gravel road, closed in winter) right for 0.9 mi. to a gate. At the Wild River end, the trail leaves Wild River Rd. (FR 12) 0.6 mi. north of Wild River Campground and fords the river, which usually requires wading and can be difficult even at moderate water levels and dangerous in high water. (The removal of the Moriah Brook Trail bridge over the Wild River in 2016 due to flood damage has eliminated an alternative approach to Shelburne Trail that avoided a river crossing.)

Shelburne Trail follows the continuation of FR 95 past the gate, up a grassy logging road. The trail follows this road for 2.1 mi. then turns left off the main road (arrow and cairn) onto an older logging road and begins to climb moderately above East Brook. This turn may be difficult to discern; it is 0.2 mi. after a snowmobile trail diverges right in a clearing. At 3.1 mi., the trail makes the first of four crossings of the east branch of East Brook and reaches the height-of-land at 4.0 mi., where it meets the eastern terminus of Kenduskeag Trail. (For Shelburne Moriah Mtn., follow this trail to the right.) Shelburne Trail continues through a narrow col, entering the Wild River Wilderness, and descends steadily with fairly rough footing, crossing a small brook several times. After the last crossing, at 5.2 mi., the grade eases, and the footing improves on an old logging road. The trail then turns sharply left at 6.3 mi. onto an old railroad grade, which the trail follows east down the valley of Bull Brook, soon leaving the Wilderness and bearing left to cross a brook at a double blaze where a beaten path diverges right. At 7.0 mi., Highwater Trail (signs) enters from the right (southwest) and leaves on the left (northeast) 10 yd. farther on. Shelburne Trail continues straight, and for the next 0.1 mi. cairns must be followed carefully through a series of turns in a confusing area of brookbeds and dry channels. In 30 yd. from the second jct. with Highwater Trail, Shelburne Trail drops over a bank, angles left across a brook, and follows a dry stony brookbed another 30 yd. ahead. It then turns right and 30 yd. farther turns left, following a washout 20 yd. to another stream crossing. It angles left across this channel then enters the woods and runs 100 yd. to the west bank of the Wild River. The trail fords the river and continues 0.1 mi. through the woods to Wild River Rd. In the reverse direction, the trail fords the river directly across to a cairn in a sandy area on the west side.

WILD RIVER VALLEY

WILD RIVER TRAIL (WMNF; MAP 5: F12–G10)

Cumulative from Wild River Campground trailhead parking area (1,150 ft.) to:	⇅	↗	⟳
Moriah Brook Trail (1,170 ft.)	0.4 mi.	0 ft.	0:10
Black Angel Trail–Highwater Trail jct. (1,510 ft.)	2.8 mi.	350 ft.	1:35
Eagle Link (2,070 ft.)	4.9 mi.	900 ft.	2:55
East Branch Trail (2,400 ft.)	6.4 mi.	1,300 ft. (rev. 50 ft.)	3:50
No-Ketchum Pond (2,560 ft.)	7.0 mi.	1,450 ft.	4:15
Rainbow Trail (2,590 ft.)	7.9 mi.	1,550 ft. (rev. 50 ft.)	4:45
Bog Brook Trail (2,417 ft.)	8.6 mi.	1,550 ft. (rev. 150 ft.)	5:05
Wildcat River Trail (2,320 ft.)	9.7 mi.	1,650 ft. (rev. 200 ft.)	5:40

This trail begins at a parking area near the end of Wild River Rd. (FR 12) and just outside of Wild River Campground, a trailhead shared with Basin Trail. Wild River Trail runs along Wild River valley to Perkins Notch then descends to Wildcat River Trail between Carter Notch Rd. and Carter Notch. Wild River Rd. (gravel, closed in winter) leaves ME 113, 3.2 mi. south of US 2 and just south of the bridge over Evans Brook at Hastings, and runs 5.7 mi. southwest to the campground, where a parking area is on the left just before the campground entrance.

There is much damage from the 2011 storm in the first mile of the trail and occasional washouts beyond. All of the Wild River crossings and those of Spruce Brook and Red Brook may be difficult at moderate water levels and dangerous at high water. Between Eagle Link and Perkins Notch Tentsite, parts of the trail may be very muddy and at times obscured by luxuriant undergrowth. From a point just beyond its jct. with Moriah Brook Trail to its jct. with Rainbow Trail, Wild River Trail is within the Wild River Wilderness.

Leaving the west side of the parking area, the trail immediately crosses Wild River Rd. then two small streams and follows the bank of Wild River. At 0.2 mi., the trail turns right onto the old logging railroad grade that extends from the end of Wild River Rd. and runs southwest along the southeast bank of Wild River. At a washed-out spot at 0.4 mi., Moriah Brook Trail leaves on the right to cross the river. *Caution:* The bridge at this crossing was removed in 2016 due to flood damage; check with the Androscoggin Ranger District for the current status of this crossing, which is difficult at normal levels and dangerous in high water.

SEC
9

Following a gullied section of the railroad grade, Wild River Trail soon enters the Wild River Wilderness. At 0.6 mi. it makes a 50-yd. detour to the left around a pile of debris from the 2011 storm, crosses a brook bed, and rejoins the original route. The trail crosses a field, and at 1.1 mi. it bears left off the grade to traverse a steep, washed-out slope for 0.1 mi. on a narrow, rough footway. It rejoins the grade, passes through some stony sections, and crosses a sluggish brook at 1.8 mi.

The trail continues up the grade with improved footing, and at 2.8 mi., 70 yd. beyond the former crossing on Spider Bridge (which was washed away in 2005 and will not be replaced), Black Angel Trail enters from the left and coincides with Wild River Trail as both trails bear right and descend 50 yd. to a crossing of Wild River on rocks; this crossing may be very difficult and is dangerous in high water. From the west bank, the trails continue together for another 90 yd. to a four-way jct. Here Black Angel Trail continues directly across toward Carter Dome; Highwater Trail enters from the right; and Wild River Trail turns left onto the old railroad grade and leads southwest on a scenic section along the bank above the river, skirting a washout at 3.5 mi.

At 3.6 mi., the trail reaches Spruce Brook Tentsite, where a side path diverges right and ascends 0.1 mi. to three tent pads; the former shelter here has been removed. Here, also, another spur path descends 25 yd. left to a scenic spot on the river. Just beyond, the main trail turns right off the grade, crosses Spruce Brook 20 yd. upstream, then bears left back to the grade and continues up the valley, skirting another washout at 3.7 mi. At 4.5 mi., the trail crosses Red Brook near the top of a ledgy cascade then bears right off the railroad grade (avoid a beaten path ahead) and ascends moderately.

At 4.9 mi., Eagle Link diverges left for Eagle Crag. The trail climbs a spruce-covered knoll then descends to the bank of Wild River, turns right, and runs nearly level through a brushy area where the footway may be obscure. At 5.8 mi., the trail crosses to the south bank of Wild River and ascends gradually through a swampy area with rough, muddy footing. At 6.4 mi., East Branch Trail leaves on the left, and Wild River Trail crosses Wild River to the north bank then climbs over a knoll and recrosses for the last time at 6.8 mi.

The trail swings right and soon skirts the south side of No-Ketchum Pond (a small pool in an extensive boggy area), passing two side paths on the right that lead to views of Carter Dome from the edge of the bog, and at 7.1 mi. crosses the right side of a small grassy clearing, the former site of Perkins Notch Shelter. A side path diverges sharply left from the clearing and leads 70 yd. to Perkins Notch Tentsite, with three tent pads on a knoll above the trail. Wild River Trail soon swings left (south) for a short climb then bears right (west) on a gradual though rocky traverse through broad Perkins Notch. At 7.9 mi., after a brief descent (where the trail leaves the Wild River Wilderness), Rainbow Trail leaves right for Carter Dome, and at 8.6 mi., after a gradual descent with occasional minor ascents, Bog Brook Trail leaves left for Carter Notch Rd. From this jct., Wild River Trail ascends slightly then descends gradually and ends at Wildcat River Trail.

HIGHWATER TRAIL (WMNF; MAP 5: E13–F11)

Cumulative from Wild River Rd. (840 ft.) to:	⇅	↗	⟳
Site of former logging bridge (905 ft.)	2.3 mi.	150 ft. (rev. 100 ft.)	1:15
Shelburne Trail (1,090 ft.)	5.3 mi.	400 ft. (rev. 50 ft.)	2:50
Moriah Brook Trail, lower jct. (1,190 ft.)	6.7 mi.	500 ft.	3:35
Wild River Trail–Black Angel Trail jct. (1,510 ft.)	9.7 mi.	1,250 ft. (rev. 450 ft.)	5:30

Note: This trail was severely damaged by the 2011 storm. Multiple washouts occurred north of the Moriah Brook Trail jct., and the suspension bridge over the Wild River at the north end of the trail was washed away. Since then short trail relocations have been made around the washouts, and the suspension bridge has been replaced.

Highwater Trail starts at a parking lot near the jct. of Wild River Rd. (FR 12) and ME 113, crosses Wild River on a suspension bridge, and follows along the northwest side of the river to Wild River Trail at the west side of the latter trail's first river crossing. Highwater Trail's southern half makes various loop hikes possible. The crossings of Bull, Moriah, and Cypress brooks may be difficult in high water. Most of the way, Highwater Trail follows old logging roads with easy grades, close to the river with many views of it, although it has a number of ups and downs. The trail is poorly marked in places and requires care to follow. Beyond its jct. with Moriah Brook Trail, Highwater Trail is within the Wild River Wilderness.

From the parking lot on the north side of Wild River Rd. (the site of the deserted logging village of Hastings, Maine), Highwater Trail runs north for 100 yd. then turns left (west) and crosses Wild River on a new suspension bridge. On the far side, the trail turns left again (avoid an abandoned trail continuing straight ahead) and follows the river to the southwest, crossing a brook and skirting to the left of a beaver pond. At 0.7 mi., the trail bears right and climbs up away from the river then descends, crossing a brook, passing a beaver meadow on the left, and entering New Hampshire. At the bottom of the descent, the trail swings right and continues up the river.

SEC 9

At 2.3 mi., the trail passes the site of a logging bridge that formerly crossed Wild River to connect with Wild River Rd. The trail crosses another brook and continues along the river with minor ups and downs, skirting roughly below two small slides. The trail crosses Martins Brook at 4.0 mi. and, after a short up-and-down, crosses the outlet from a beaver pond. It continues along the river, following two relocations to the right; after the second relocation, at 5.0 mi., there is an especially fine view of the river. The trail then makes a short, steep climb and an easier descent. At 5.3 mi., the trail enters Shelburne Trail, turns right and follows it for 10 yd., turns left off it (signs), and soon crosses a dry brook bed and then Bull Brook. In 2016 the north side of the Bull Brook crossing was difficult due to flood debris.

About 40 yd. beyond Bull Brook, Highwater Trail ascends rock steps and swings left. It soon comes close to the river again and alternately runs along the riverbank and follows sections in the woods to the right. Use caution along the bank, which is undercut in some places. At 6.0 mi. it swings right, up onto a hardwood plateau, then returns to the riverbank again at 6.3 mi. After a short uphill pitch, it leads through spruces to a jct. with Moriah Brook Trail at 6.7 mi., 40 yd. above where Moriah Brook Trail crosses the Wild River and 0.4 mi. from Wild River Campground. (*Caution:* The bridge at this crossing was removed in 2016 due to flood damage; check with the Androscoggin Ranger District for the current status of this crossing, which is difficult at normal levels and dangerous in high water.)

Highwater Trail joins Moriah Brook Trail. The trails continue ahead (southwest) and soon descend a short, steep pitch to the left; in another 0.1 mi., they turn right. At 7.0 mi., Highwater Trail turns left off Moriah Brook Trail and descends to cross Moriah Brook (very difficult in high water). Highwater Trail climbs to the top of a steep bank and runs along its edge, with a descent and ascent to cross a brook and an occasional glimpse across the valley. The trail descends twice more to cross small brooks then climbs again before descending to cross Cypress Brook at 9.5 mi. The trail soon passes the former crossing of Wild River at Spider Bridge (which was washed away in 2005 and will not be replaced) and ends at a four-way jct. with Black Angel and Wild River trails.

BURNT MILL BROOK TRAIL (WMNF; MAP 5: F12)

From Wild River Rd. (990 ft.) to:	⇅	↗	○
Royce Trail (2,610 ft.)	2.0 mi.	1,600 ft.	1:50

This trail ascends from a parking area off Wild River Rd. (FR 12), 2.7 mi. south of ME 113, to Royce Trail in the col between East Royce Mtn. and

West Royce Mtn., passing several cascades on Burnt Mill Brook in its lower section. From Wild River Rd., Burnt Mill Brook Trail ascends south at easy grades on old logging roads, passing an especially fine cascade on the left at 0.6 mi. The trail crosses two small tributary brooks, and at 1.4 mi., the trail begins to climb more steeply. It crosses Burnt Mill Brook at 1.7 mi. and ascends to the col between the Royces, where it meets Royce Trail.

MORIAH BROOK TRAIL (WMNF; MAP 5: F12–F11)

Cumulative from Wild River Trail (1,170 ft.) to:	↥↧	↗	⟳
Moriah Gorge (1,521 ft.)	1.4 mi.	350 ft.	0:55
Carter-Moriah Trail (3,127 ft.)	5.5 mi.	1,950 ft.	3:45

This trail ascends to the col between Mt. Moriah and North Carter from Wild River Trail 0.4 mi. south of Wild River Campground. Moriah Brook Trail is an attractive trail, passing Moriah Gorge and several cascades and pools, traversing beautiful birch woods that have grown up after fires, and providing views up to the impressive south cliffs of Moriah. Nearly the entire trail is within the Wild River Wilderness.

The trail leaves to the right from Wild River Trail and in 75 yd. crosses Wild River. (*Caution:* The bridge at this crossing was removed in 2016 due to flood damage; check with the Androscoggin Ranger District for the current status of this crossing, which is difficult at normal levels and dangerous in high water.) On the far side, Highwater Trail joins on the right as Moriah Brook Trail swings left. The trails descend a short, steep pitch to the left and follow the washed-out riverbank about 0.1 mi. then turn right and generally follow the course of the former lumber railroad up the north bank of Moriah Brook. At 0.4 mi., Highwater Trail leaves left, as Moriah Brook Trail continues up the railroad grade with occasional rougher, washed-out sections.

At 1.4 mi., Moriah Brook Trail crosses Moriah Brook (may be difficult at high water); Moriah Gorge, just downstream from this crossing, merits exploration. The trail follows the south bank of the brook, crossing beaver dams at 1.8 mi., then recrosses the brook in an area of ledges and pools at 2.8 mi. In another 0.4 mi., the trail passes some attractive cascades and pools, crosses a ledge, then crosses a branch of Moriah Brook just above the confluence with the main brook. The trail continues past more cascades and through birch woods and crosses the main brook four more times; the last crossing is in a boulder area below a small cascade at 5.0 mi. The trail winds through almost pure stands of white birch below the impressive

SEC 9

south cliffs of Mt. Moriah, crosses a flat swampy spot where the trail may be overgrown and muddy, then climbs to the col and Carter–Moriah Trail.

BLACK ANGEL TRAIL (WMNF; MAP 5: F12–F10)

Cumulative from Rim Junction (1,950 ft.) to:	⇅	↗	⟳
Blue Brook Tentsite spur (1,780 ft.)	0.5 mi.	0 ft. (rev. 200 ft.)	0:15
Wild River Trail–Highwater Trail jct. (1,510 ft.)	2.8 mi.	600 ft. (rev. 850 ft.)	1:40
Carter–Moriah Trail (4,600 ft.)	7.7 mi.	3,700 ft.	5:40

This trail begins at the five-way Rim Junction—where Basin and Basin Rim trails cross—and descends to cross Wild River 70 yd. beyond the former crossing on Spider Bridge (which was washed away in 2005 and will not be replaced) along with Wild River Trail, then makes a long climb to Carter–Moriah Trail 0.4 mi. north of Carter Dome. Nearly the entire Black Angel Trail is within the Wild River Wilderness.

Leaving Rim Junction, the trail descends gradually southwest 0.5 mi. to a four-way jct., where Black Angel Trail turns left. Here a spur path leads ahead to Blue Brook Tentsite; in 75 yd. a path diverges right off this spur and leads to three tent pads (the former shelter has been removed). The spur descends ahead another 60 yd. to a ledgy area on Blue Brook. At the four-way jct., Blue Brook Connector (sign: Basin Trail 0.3) diverges sharply right (northeast), ascending gradually for 0.3 mi. to connect with Basin Trail 0.3 mi. west of Rim Junction. From the jct., Black Angel Trail rises gradually, crosses Blue Brook at 0.6 mi., then ascends steadily west and crosses a shoulder to the north of a col at 1.4 mi. It then descends to an old logging road and follows it generally west down the Cedar Brook valley, remaining well up on the north side of the stream and making several shortcuts at curves. The trail then leaves the logging road, turns more north, and joins Wild River Trail, turning left and in 50 yd. crossing Wild River on rocks; this crossing may be very difficult and is dangerous in high water. From the west bank, the trails continue together for another 90 yd. to a four-way jct. at 2.8 mi. Here, Highwater Trail enters from the right, Wild River Trail turns left, and Black Angel Trail continues directly ahead.

Black Angel Trail now rises slowly through open hardwoods. About 2 mi. up from Wild River, the grade becomes steeper. At 5.2 mi., the trail crosses a north branch of Spruce Brook and climbs steadily on a sidehill, entering conifer forest in another 0.5 mi. At 6.4 mi., the trail attains a shoulder, and the grade lessens. At 7.3 mi., the trail angles up across the steep southeast slope of Mt. Hight, with rough footing and several tricky rock scrambles, passing several restricted views over the valley. The trail swings southwest, leaves the Wild River Wilderness, and ends at Carter–Moriah Trail.

BASIN TRAIL (WMNF; MAP 5: F12)

Cumulative from Wild River Campground trailhead parking area (1,150 ft.) to:	⇅	↗	○
Rim Junction (1,950 ft.)	2.2 mi.	800 ft.	1:30
Hermit Falls Loop, lower jct. (750 ft.)	3.2 mi.	800 ft. (rev. 1,200 ft.)	2:00
Basin Pond parking area (680 ft.)	4.5 mi.	850 ft. (rev. 100 ft.)	2:40

This trail runs from the parking area just outside of Wild River Campground (also the trailhead for Wild River Trail) to the parking area at Basin Pond (0.7 mi. from NH 113, near Cold River Campground), crossing the ridge connecting Mt. Meader to West Royce Mtn. somewhat north of its lowest point and giving easy access to the magnificent views along the brink of the cliffs. Most of the trail west of the ridge crest is within the Wild River Wilderness.

Leaving the Wild River parking area, the trail leads south for 0.2 mi. and then turns left onto an old lumber road. At 0.4 mi., where the road swings right, the trail continues straight ahead on plank walkways through a wet area, enters the Wild River Wilderness, and crosses a tributary brook. The trail soon approaches the southwest bank of Blue Brook and follows it for about 0.8 mi. At 1.3 mi., the trail crosses the brook at the foot of a pretty cascade and then follows the east bank, passing opposite a striking cliff to the west of the brook.

The trail leaves Blue Brook, crosses another small brook, then climbs somewhat more steeply. At 2.0 mi., Blue Brook Connector branches right for 0.3 mi. and descends gently to Black Angel Trail, where a spur leads right to Blue Brook tentsite. (The former shelter has been removed.) At 2.2 mi., Basin Trail crosses Basin Rim Trail (running north-south) and meets Black Angel Trail (diverging sharply right, or southwest) at the five-way Rim Junction. The best viewpoint from the top of the cliff that overhangs the Basin is located 0.1 mi. south of this jct. on Basin Rim Trail. Continuing east-northeast, Basin Trail passes an outlook over the Basin on the right then descends very steeply with poor footing along the south side and foot of the great cliff. After crossing a brook, the trail swings right and descends moderately.

At 3.0 mi., the trail passes the upper end of Hermit Falls Loop (CTA), a loop path slightly longer than the main trail that descends steeply right 0.1 mi. to Hermit Falls and then returns to the main trail 0.2 mi. and

200 ft. below its point of departure. Basin Trail descends to an old logging road, turns right on it, follows segments of other old roads along the flat floor of the Basin, crosses two brooks (the second on a bridge), and at 4.0 mi. bears right on a relocation above a swampy area. The trail then skirts the shore of Basin Pond with minor ups and downs, crossing two brooks and passing several side paths leading left to the shore of the pond (good views) and right to Basin Campground, and ends at the parking area.

EAGLE LINK (AMC; MAP 5: F11–F12)

From Wild River Trail (2,070 ft.) to:	⥮	↗	◷
Baldface Circle Trail–Meader Ridge Trail (2,990 ft.)	2.7 mi.	1,100 ft. (rev. 200 ft.)	1:55

This trail runs from Wild River Trail 4.9 mi. southwest of Wild River Campground to the jct. with Baldface Circle and Meader Ridge trails 0.2 mi. south of Eagle Crag. Nearly the entire Eagle Link is within the Wild River Wilderness. The trail, which may be overgrown in places, leaves Wild River Trail and descends gradually for 0.2 mi. then crosses two branches of Wild River (may be difficult at high water). After the second crossing, Eagle Link bears sharply right on the far bank and ascends generally east at a moderate grade. (In the reverse direction, the trail turns sharply left off the brook bank and crosses the brook.) The trail crosses a small brook at 1.2 mi., angles up through a birch forest on the north slope of North Baldface, descends gradually for about 0.2 mi., crossing another brook, then climbs again and ends at the jct. with Baldface Circle and Meader Ridge trails.

SEC 9

BALDFACE–ROYCE RANGE, EAST SIDE

ROYCE TRAIL (AMC; MAP 5: F12)

Cumulative from ME 113 (600 ft.) to:	⥮	↗	◷
Mad River Falls (900 ft.)	1.6 mi.	300 ft.	0:55
Laughing Lion Trail (2,200 ft.)	2.7 mi.	1,600 ft.	2:10
Royce Connector Trail (2,650 ft.)	2.9 mi.	2,050 ft.	2:30
Burnt Mill Brook Trail (2,610 ft.)	3.6 mi.	2,150 ft. (rev. 150 ft.)	2:55
West Royce Mtn. summit (3,210 ft.)	4.3 mi.	2,750 ft.	3:30

This trail runs to the summit of West Royce Mtn. from the west side of ME 113, opposite the Brickett Place (a USFS information center) about 0.3 mi. north of the access road to the WMNF Cold River Campground. The first two crossings of the Cold River are difficult in high water. Leaving ME 113, the trail follows a narrow road for about 0.3 mi., bears right where another road joins from the left, crosses the Cold River, and bears off the road to the right onto a yellow-blazed footpath. The trail recrosses the river at 0.7 mi., crosses a tributary at 1.1 mi., and crosses the river again at 1.3 mi.

Then, after crossing the west branch of the Mad River, the trail rises more steeply and soon passes Mad River Falls, where a side path leads left 25 yd. to a viewpoint. The trail climbs moderately up the valley, passing several cascades as it comes back near the Mad River, then becomes rather rough and rises steeply under the imposing ledges for which East Royce Mtn. is famous. At 2.7 mi., Laughing Lion Trail enters right, and at a height-of-land at 2.9 mi., after a very steep and rough ascent, Royce Connector Trail branches right, leading to East Royce Trail for East Royce Mtn.

Royce Connector Trail (AMC). This short trail, 0.2 mi. long (10 min., ascent 50 ft., rev. 100 ft.), links Royce Trail and East Royce Trail, permitting the ascent of either summit of Royce from either trail, crossing some ledges with restricted views. **Royce Trail** bears left at this jct. and descends somewhat, crossing a small brook, then climbs to the height-of-land between the Royces at 3.6 mi., where Burnt Mill Brook Trail to Wild River Rd. diverges right. Here, Royce Trail turns abruptly left (west) and zigzags up the steep wall of the pass, turns sharply left (southeast), then swings more to the southwest. The trail climbs moderately up the ridge over ledges and through stunted spruce, crossing a ledge with a view east at 4.1 mi. It passes side paths to two more outlooks on the left shortly before reaching the summit area of West Royce Mtn., where the trail meets Basin Rim Trail.

EAST ROYCE TRAIL (AMC; MAP 5: F13–F12)

SEC 9

Cumulative from ME 113 (1,420 ft.) to:	⇅	↗	⏱
Royce Connector Trail (2,610 ft.)	1.0 mi.	1,200 ft.	1:05
Ledge at end of East Royce Trail (3, 070 ft.)	1.3 mi.	1,650 ft.	1:30

This trail climbs steeply to East Royce Mtn. from a parking area on the west side of ME 113, just north of the height-of-land in Evans Notch and 3.2 mi. north of the WMNF Cold River Campground. Leaving the parking area, the trail immediately crosses Evans Brook and ascends, soon swinging left to cross a brook on ledges at the top of a fine cascade. The trail continues up, steeply at times, crossing several other brooks in the first 0.5 mi. At the final brook crossing at 1.0 mi., Royce Connector Trail leaves on the left, leading in 0.2 mi. to Royce Trail for West Royce Mtn.

After ascending a steep and rough section with several scrambles, East Royce Trail emerges on open ledges at 1.1 mi.; here, you find a view east to Speckled Mtn. The trail soon reaches a subsidiary summit with views to the south, turns right, and climbs to a broad open ledge at 1.3 mi. with wide-ranging views, where the plainly marked trail ends. An unmaintained path continues north 0.2 mi. along the summit ridge, dropping off a ledge, crossing several ledgy knobs (including the true summit), and ending at a ledge with a Forest Service radio repeater and wide views west and north.

LAUGHING LION TRAIL (CTA; MAP 5: F13–F12)

From ME 113 (1,370 ft.) to:	⇅	↗	⟳
Royce Trail (2,200 ft.)	1.1 mi.	1,000 ft. (rev. 150 ft.)	1:05

This trail (sign) begins on the west side of ME 113, 100 yd. north of a roadside picnic area and about 2.3 mi. north of the road to the WMNF Cold River Campground, and ends on Royce Trail. Parking is available at a pull-off on the west side of the road, 40 yd. south of the trailhead. Laughing Lion Trail descends to and crosses the Cold River (here, a rather small brook) then ascends west to a ridge crest, which the trail follows north, with alternating moderate and steep sections, and passes two outlooks on the left looking down the valley. The trail then swings west and levels off just before ending at Royce Trail.

BASIN RIM TRAIL (AMC; MAP 5: F12)

Cumulative from Mt. Meader Trail–Meader Ridge Trail jct. (2,750 ft.) to:	⇅	↗	⟳
Rim Junction (1,950 ft.)	1.4 mi.	100 ft. (rev. 900 ft.)	0:45
West Royce Mtn. summit (3,210 ft.)	3.9 mi.	1,550 ft. (rev. 200 ft.)	2:45

This trail follows the ridge that runs north from Mt. Meader, starting from the east knob at the jct. with Mt. Meader and Meader Ridge trails and ending at the summit of West Royce Mtn., where the trail meets Royce Trail. Basin Rim Trail has fine views, particularly at the top of the cliff that forms the wall of the Basin.

The trail leaves the east knob of Mt. Meader, passing an outlook on the right, and descends easily north over ledges then more steeply through spruce woods. Just after crossing a small brook, the trail reaches a col then ascends slightly along the east side of a prominent hump called Ragged Jacket. The trail soon descends steeply down the north slope to the lowest point of the ridge (1,870 ft.) then rises gradually over ledges.

The trail passes two fine outlooks over the Basin on the right about 0.1 mi. before reaching five-way Rim Jct. at 1.4 mi., where Basin Trail crosses (running generally east-west), and Black Angel Trail enters from the left (southwest).

Basin Rim Trail continues northeast from the jct., and at 1.5 mi., a short spur leads right to Basin Outlook, a restricted viewpoint at the edge of the cliffs on the east. The trail climbs over a knob and at 1.8 mi. passes another good view east over the great cliff of the Basin Rim. Passing west of the prominent southeast knee of West Royce Mtn., the trail climbs, with short intervening descents; there is a tricky scramble up a ledge at 2.2 mi. At 2.6 mi., it climbs a very steep pitch then passes a small brook (unreliable) and ascends easily on a long spruce-wooded shoulder with occasional short descents. At 3.7 mi. the trail passes an outlook south to the Baldfaces on the right, dips to a col, and then ascends to the wooded summit of West Royce Mtn. Views to the southeast are available by continuing a short distance ahead on Royce Trail then descending a short distance on ledges to the right.

MT. MEADER TRAIL (AMC; MAP 5: G12–F12)

Cumulative from NH 113 (520 ft.) to:	⇅	↗	↻
Spur to Brickett Falls (840 ft.)	1.0 mi.	300 ft.	0:40
Meader Ridge Trail–Basin Rim Trail (2,750 ft.)	3.0 mi.	2,250 ft.	2:40

This trail runs from the west side of NH 113, 0.6 mi. north of the entrance to Baldface Circle Trail, to a jct. with Meader Ridge and Basin Rim trails on the ridge crest at an easterly knob of Mt. Meader. Limited roadside parking is available; do not block the entrance to the trail, which starts on a private logging road.

From NH 113, Mt. Meader Trail follows the logging road; in 70 yd., bear left at a fork. The trail follows the north side of Mill Brook, entering the WMNF at 0.7 mi. and crossing an overgrown skid road at 0.9 mi. At 1.0 mi., the trail passes a side path left (sign) that rises easily 0.1 mi. to Brickett Falls. The main trail crosses a small brook and soon turns left uphill, off the logging road. The trail crosses a brook above a small cascade, crosses another stream twice, and at 2.1 mi. turns right and begins a steep climb by switchbacks up the heel of the ridge. The trail turns sharply left at the top of the heel at 2.5 mi., passes an outlook south, and climbs through fine spruce woods. Coming out on open ledges with fine views at 2.9 mi., the trail soon reaches the east knob of Mt. Meader.

MEADER RIDGE TRAIL (AMC; MAP 5: F12)

From Mt. Meader Trail– Basin Rim Trail jct. (2,750 ft.) to:	⇅	↗	↻
Baldface Circle Trail–Eagle Link (2,990 ft.)	2.0 mi.	600 ft. (rev. 350 ft.)	1:20

This trail runs along the ridge crest from the jct. with Mt. Meader and Basin Rim trails on the east knob of Mt. Meader to the jct. with Baldface Circle Trail and Eagle Link, 0.2 mi. south of Eagle Crag.

From the east knob of Mt. Meader, Meader Ridge Trail descends slightly in a southwest direction, climbs out of a sag, and in 0.2 mi. passes just south of the true summit of Mt. Meader. Descending again, with a small intervening ascent, the trail passes two restricted views and then an excellent open view to the east. At 0.4 mi., just beyond the best eastern viewpoint, a side path (sign) leads right (west) 100 yd. up to a large open ledge with a somewhat restricted view of the Baldfaces and Carter Dome.

Meader Ridge Trail passes the deepest col of the ridge at 0.6 mi., where the trail crosses an unreliable small brook; sometimes water is also a short distance upstream in a swampy place called the Bear Traps. The trail then climbs to an intermediate peak at 1.2 mi. and descends to another col at 1.4 mi. Climbing again, the trail emerges from timberline at 1.9 mi., passes over the summit of Eagle Crag, and then descends slightly to meet Baldface Circle Trail (left) and Eagle Link (right). In the reverse (north) direction, descending from the ledges of Eagle Crag, the trail drops off to the right (northeast) into the woods.

BALDFACE CIRCLE TRAIL (AMC; MAP 5: G12)

Cumulative from NH 113 (520 ft.) to:	⇅	↗	↻
Circle Junction (720 ft.)	0.7 mi.	200 ft.	0:25
Slippery Brook Trail (775 ft.)	0.9 mi.	250 ft.	0:35
South Baldface Shelter (2,130 ft.)	2.5 mi.	1,600 ft.	2:05
Baldface Knob Trail (3,030 ft.)	3.2 mi.	2,500 ft.	2:50
South Baldface summit (3,570 ft.)	3.7 mi.	3,050 ft.	3:25
North Baldface summit (3,610 ft.)	4.9 mi.	3,500 ft. (rev. 400 ft.)	4:10
Bicknell Ridge Trail, upper jct. (3,050 ft.)	5.8 mi.	3,600 ft. (rev. 650 ft.)	4:40
Eagle Link–Meader Ridge Trail (2,990 ft.)	6.1 mi.	3,650 ft. (rev. 100 ft.)	4:55
Bicknell Ridge Trail, lower jct. (970 ft.)	8.4 mi.	3,650 ft. (rev. 2,000 ft.)	6:00
Circle Junction (720 ft.)	9.1 mi.	3,650 ft. (rev. 250 ft.)	6:25
NH 113 (520 ft.), for complete loop	9.8 mi.	3,650 ft. (rev. 200 ft.)	6:45

This trail makes a loop over North and South Baldface from NH 113 at a parking area on the east side of the road, 0.1 mi. north of the driveway to AMC's Cold River Camp. Baldface Circle Trail is one of the most attractive trips in the White Mountains, with about 4 mi. of open and semi-open ledge providing long stretches of unobstructed views but equally great exposure to storms. On the ledges, the trail, marked by cairns and blazes (often faded), should be followed with care. This is a strenuous trip that should not be underestimated.

Leaving the west side of NH 113 about 60 yd. north of the parking area, the trail runs at easy grades with fairly rocky footing to Circle Junction at 0.7 mi., where a side path leads right (north) 0.1 mi. to Emerald Pool, a popular swimming spot. From here, the trail is described in a clockwise direction: up South Baldface, over to North Baldface, and down from Eagle Crag, because the steep ledges on South Baldface are easier to ascend than descend.

From Circle Junction, the south branch follows an old road then turns left (south), crosses a brook bed, and climbs past the jct. with Slippery Brook Trail on the left at 0.9 mi. to an old logging road that the south branch follows west for almost a mile. At 1.2 mi., lightly used Chandler Gorge Loop (CTA), 0.4 mi. long, leads left to Chandler Gorge (a small flume with several pools and lesser cascades in a rocky bed) and rejoins the main trail 0.1 mi. and 125 ft. above its departure point; follow with care. Baldface Circle Trail swings around the south side of Spruce Knoll and, at 2.5 mi., leaves the old road in a rocky area and soon reaches Last Chance Spring (unreliable) and South Baldface Shelter (left).

In a short distance, the trail comes out on the ledges and makes a long, very steep climb in the open on rock slabs and shelves that are dangerous if wet or icy; this danger can be avoided by using Slippery Brook Trail and Baldface Knob Trail instead of this part of Baldface Circle Trail. At 3.0 mi., the trail reaches the crest of a rounded ridge and swings left, ascending near the crest toward a knob, becoming much less steep. On that knob, at 3.2 mi., Baldface Knob Trail enters on the left (south). Baldface Circle Trail then ascends steadily west over open ledges to the summit of South Baldface at 3.7 mi.

Bearing right (northwest) at the summit of South Baldface, the trail follows the broad ridge, descending into the shelter of mature conifers in a col at 4.0 mi. then coming out on a semi-open knob at 4.2 mi. From here to North Baldface, the trail runs mostly in the open, although some shelter could be obtained from several small cols in a storm. From the main col on the ridge, the trail climbs steeply to a shoulder, briefly eases, then at 4.9 mi. mounts the last steep and scrambly pitch to the summit of North Baldface, where the views are particularly fine over Wild River valley. The trail

SEC 9

descends steeply northeast on ledges then descends broad slabs with excellent views across to the Carter–Moriah Range. After minor ups and downs, it drops steeply, with several ledge scrambles, to a col. At 5.8 mi., after an easy ascent, Bicknell Ridge Trail leaves right, providing a scenic alternative route to NH 113.

Baldface Circle Trail descends to another col then ascends slightly and, at 6.1 mi., reaches a multiple jct. where Eagle Link leaves left (west) for Wild River valley; Meader Ridge Trail continues straight ahead (northeast) for Eagle Crag and Mt. Meader; and Baldface Circle Trail turns sharply right and descends on a steep and rough way over ledges for 0.2 mi., with two tricky scrambles. At the base of the ledges, the trail swings left and, after a short gradual section, descends moderately.

At 6.9 mi., the trail crosses a very small brook (unreliable) with a ledgy, mossy bed and becomes less steep; at 7.3 mi., the trail enters an old logging road and follows it to the right. At 7.7 mi., Eagle Cascade Link leaves on the right. Baldface Circle Trail continues to descend gradually, crossing a branch of Charles Brook, and at 8.4 mi. Bicknell Ridge Trail enters right just after crossing a branch of Charles Brook on flat ledges. Baldface Circle Trail now angles left away from the brook then returns to it and crosses it (may be difficult in high water) at 9.0 mi., just before reaching Circle Junction.

BICKNELL RIDGE TRAIL (CTA; MAP 5: G12)

Cumulative from Baldface Circle Trail, lower jct. (970 ft.) to:	⇅	↗	↺
Eagle Cascade Link (2,050 ft.)	1.4 mi.	1,100 ft.	1:15
Baldface Circle Trail, upper jct. (3,050 ft.)	2.5 mi.	2,100 ft.	2:20

SEC 9

This scenic trail begins on the north branch of Baldface Circle Trail, 1.4 mi. from NH 113 and ends on the same trail, 0.9 mi. north of North Baldface. Diverging from Baldface Circle Trail, Bicknell Ridge Trail immediately crosses a branch of Charles Brook and ascends gradually through hardwood forest, with good footing. After about 1.0 mi., the trail rises more rapidly along the south side of Bicknell Ridge, enters spruce forest and becomes rougher, and, just before the first ledges, crosses a brook bed where water can usually be found among the boulders. Soon the trail emerges on open ledges, with impressive views of South Baldface, and Eagle Cascade Link enters right. Above this jct., Bicknell Ridge Trail climbs, steeply at times, over broad, open ledges with excellent views south, east, and north, interspersed with patches of spruce woods; in places the trail requires care to follow. Reaching the open, flat ridge top, the trail swings left and rejoins Baldface Circle Trail.

EAGLE CASCADE LINK (CTA; MAP 5: G12)

From Baldface Circle Trail (1,440 ft.) to:	⥮	⌁	◷
Bicknell Ridge Trail (2,050 ft.)	0.7 mi.	600 ft.	0:40

This trail provides a link between the north branch of Baldface Circle Trail, 2.1 mi. from NH 113, to Bicknell Ridge Trail, 1.4 mi. above its lower jct. with the north branch of Baldface Circle Trail, where it first emerges on open ledges. Leaving Baldface Circle Trail, it traverses to a short side path (left) that provides a view of Eagle Cascade (impressive in high water), climbs steeply to cross the brook above the cascade (use caution) at 0.4 mi., and climbs steadily to Bicknell Ridge Trail.

BALDFACE KNOB TRAIL (CTA; MAP 5: G12)

From Slippery Brook Trail (2,625 ft.) to:	⥮	⌁	◷
Baldface Circle Trail (3,030 ft.)	0.7 mi.	450 ft. (rev. 50 ft.)	0:35

This trail, in combination with Slippery Brook Trail, provides an alternative route to South Baldface from NH 113 that avoids the steepest ledges on Baldface Circle Trail. Baldface Knob Trail begins at Slippery Brook Trail, just north of the col between Eastman Mtn. and South Baldface, opposite the beginning of Eastman Mtn. Trail. Baldface Knob Trail rises gradually and then climbs steeply, emerging on open ledges below the flat, open summit called Baldface Knob, an excellent viewpoint. The trail descends into a scrubby saddle and then climbs easily along the open ridge to Baldface Circle Trail on the shoulder below the summit of South Baldface.

EASTMAN MTN. TRAIL (CTA; MAP 5: G12)

From Slippery Brook Trail (2,625 ft.) to:	⥮	⌁	◷
Eastman Mtn. summit (2,939 ft.)	0.8 mi.	400 ft. (rev. 100 ft.)	0:35

This trail ascends Eastman Mtn. from Slippery Brook Trail just north of the col between Eastman Mtn. and South Baldface, opposite the lower terminus of Baldface Knob Trail. Eastman Mtn. Trail runs through a beautiful birch forest, first descending slightly then rising at a moderate grade onto the north ridge, where outlook points provide partial views of South Baldface and Sable Mtn. The trail continues generally southeast to the summit, where open areas provide good though somewhat restricted views in most directions.

SEC
9

SLIPPERY BROOK TRAIL (CTA/WMNF; MAP 5: G12)

Cumulative from Baldface Circle Trail (775 ft.) to:	↥↧	↗	⟳
Baldface Knob Trail–Eastman Mtn. Trail (2,625 ft.)	2.6 mi.	1,900 ft. (rev. 50 ft.)	2:15
Left turn onto logging road (1,950 ft.)	4.4 mi.	1,900 ft. (rev. 700 ft.)	3:10
Slippery Brook Rd. (1,610 ft.)	6.6 mi.	1,900 ft. (rev. 350 ft.)	4:15

This trail runs from the south branch of Baldface Circle Trail, 0.9 mi. from NH 113, through the col between South Baldface and Eastman Mtn. to the north end of Slippery Brook Rd. (FR 17, called Town Hall Rd. at its south end). To reach the south trailhead, leave NH 16/US 302 1.5 mi. south of the traffic lights in Glen and go north on Town Hall Rd. Bear left onto Slippery Brook Rd. at 2.5 mi. from NH 16/US 302, where the pavement ends, then bear right at 5.9 mi. (left at this fork is East Branch Rd., FR 38) and continue to a gate at 7.3 mi., where the south end of the trail begins.

Leaving Baldface Circle Trail, the north end of Slippery Brook Trail ascends a small ridge and then descends, crossing a branch of Chandler Brook and a tributary before joining an older route on an old logging road. The trail ascends generally southwest through woods, first easily then moderately, and swings left up through a beautiful birch grove to reach the height-of-land just north of the col between South Baldface and Eastman Mtn. at 2.6 mi. Here, Baldface Knob Trail leaves right (north) for South Baldface, and Eastman Mtn. Trail leaves left (south).

After a slight rise, Slippery Brook Trail begins a moderate descent southward toward Slippery Brook; this section may be overgrown and poorly marked, requiring some care to follow. The trail traverses the lower slopes of Eastman Mtn. well above Slippery Brook. At 4.4 mi., after a short descent, it turns left into a logging road (in the reverse direction, turn right off the road onto a woods path) then bears right at 4.6 mi. (in the reverse direction, bear left at an arrow). The trail continues at easy grades on this grass-grown road (FR 17) through several small clearings to the gate at the end of Slippery Brook Rd.

EAST BRANCH OF THE SACO RIVER

MOUNTAIN POND LOOP TRAIL (WMNF; MAP 5: G11–G12)

From Slippery Brook Rd. (1,483 ft.) for:	↥↧	↗	⟳
Complete loop around Mountain Pond (1,509 ft.)	2.7 mi.	50 ft.	1:25

This trail begins from a parking area off the east side of Slippery Brook Rd. (FR 17, called Town Hall Rd. at its southern end), 6.5 mi. from NH 16/ US 302. (See the Slippery Brook Trail description for directions. In winter, the road is plowed for about 3.5 mi., after which it receives heavy use by snowmobiles.) Mountain Pond Loop Trail is mostly level, but the footing is often rough, rocky, and slippery, and the footway may be obscured by undergrowth.

The trail runs 0.3 mi. from the road to a fork; bearing left, the trail reaches Mountain Pond Shelter at 1.0 mi. then continues around the pond with moderately rough footing. From points along the east and south shores, you have views of Doublehead Mtn. and South Baldface. Just before returning to the fork, the trail crosses the pond's outlet brook on slippery rocks, where at times of high water the crossing may be difficult and the trail hard to follow (but it may be possible to bushwhack along the south bank of the outlet brook, back to the road and parking area).

EAST BRANCH TRAIL (WMNF; MAP 5: G11)

Cumulative from end of East Branch Rd. (1,700 ft.) to:	⇅	↗	○
Shoulder of Black Mtn. (2,590 ft.)	3.7 mi.	900 ft.	2:20
Wild River Trail (2,400 ft.)	4.1 mi.	900 ft. (rev. 200 ft.)	2:30

This lightly used trail ascends along the East Branch of the Saco River from the end of gravel East Branch Rd. (FR 38, not plowed in winter) and crosses a height-of-land between Black Mtn. and the Baldface Range, ending on Wild River Trail at the foot of the hill east of Perkins Notch, 0.7 mi. east of Perkins Notch Tentsite. East Branch Trail is very muddy south of the height-of-land and is at times difficult to follow. The upper part of the trail is in the Wild River Wilderness. (*Note:* The former 3.5-mi. section of East Branch Trail south of the end of East Branch Rd. is no longer maintained by the WMNF.)

To reach the trailhead, leave NH 16/US 302, 1.5 mi. south of the traffic lights in Glen, and go north on Town Hall Rd. Bear left at 2.5 mi. from NH 16 onto Slippery Brook Rd. (FR 17), where the pavement ends, then bear left at a fork at 5.9 mi. onto East Branch Rd. and continue to a parking area at the end of the road at 9.1 mi., where the trail begins.

From the end of East Branch Rd., follow a path 60 yd. ahead, bearing right (northeast) to a T jct., where the trail turns left onto an old railroad bed. (To the right at this jct. is the abandoned lower section of the trail.) The trail crosses Gulf Brook at 0.2 mi., soon leaves the railroad bed, and follows old logging roads along the East Branch of the Saco River, crossing several small

SEC 9

brooks and a number of muddy stretches. At 1.4 mi. the trail crosses Black Brook, and in another 0.3 mi. it bears away from the river, leading north and then northwest. The trail then climbs by easy grades, crossing a logging road, and continues at moderate grades, with poor footing at times, to a flat shoulder of Black Mtn. at 3.7 mi. The trail then descends moderately on a narrow footway to its jct. with Wild River Trail on the south bank of Wild River. About 0.1 mi. before the jct., East Branch Trail crosses an open bog where the footway is muddy and obscure and must be followed with care.

BALD LAND TRAIL (WMNF; MAP 5: G11)

Cumulative from Black Mtn. Rd. (1,585 ft.) to:	↿⇂	↗	⟲
Scenic vista spur (2,080 ft.)	1.5 mi.	500 ft.	1:00
East Branch Rd. (1,740 ft.)	2.2 mi.	500 ft. (rev. 350 ft.)	1:20

This trail follows an old roadway from Black Mtn. Rd. to the East Branch of the Saco through the divide between Black Mtn. and North Doublehead. From its western trailhead to the height-of-land, Bald Land Trail is also a cross-country ski trail and intersects several other ski trails; Bald Land Trail is somewhat hard to follow, although most of the intersections are marked. The west trailhead is reached from NH 16 in Jackson by following NH 16A (Main St.) for 0.5 mi. from the covered bridge and turning right on Black Mtn. Rd. (NH 16B). At 1.6 mi. from the bridge, bear right on Black Mtn. Rd., continue past Black Mtn. Ski Area at 2.2 mi., then bear left uphill on Black Mtn. Rd. at 2.4 mi. and continue to a small parking area on the right at 3.0 mi., just before driveways diverge to the left and right. The east trailhead is 0.4 mi. before the end of East Branch Rd. (FR 38), a branch of Slippery Brook Rd. (FR 17); see the East Branch Trail description for driving directions.

Bald Land Trail (WMNF sign) coincides with East Pasture Trail (X-C ski) for the first 0.4 mi. It follows a gravel road for 0.1 mi. then continues ahead past a cable gate on a rougher road, where a driveway diverges left. The trail continues straight at a three-way intersection, and at 0.4 mi., it turns right onto a woods road (signs). (Here, East Pasture Trail continues ahead, leading 1.8 mi. to the upper end of Black Mtn. Ski Trail. There is a good view of Doublehead Mtn. from a field, 0.2 mi. up this trail.) Bald Land Trail crosses a branch of Great Brook on a bridge, enters the WMNF, and runs nearly level on the old road with a stone wall on the right.

The trail crosses a muddy area, turns right onto another old road at 0.8 mi., then bears left and ascends gradually. At 1.2 mi., the trail bears right at a fork (sign) and ascends to a T intersection at 1.5 mi. Here, a spur (sign: scenic vista) leads right to two former log landings where the views are now completely overgrown. At the intersection, the main trail turns left then in 100 yd. diverges right off the wide woods road onto a footpath. The trail descends moderately, swings left and crosses a logging road at 2.1 mi., crosses muddy areas and a small brook, and reaches East Branch Rd.

CARTER RANGE, SOUTHERN RIDGES

RAINBOW TRAIL (WMNF; MAP 5: G11–F10)

Cumulative from Wild River Trail (2,590 ft.) to:	⇅	↗	○
South knob (4,274 ft.)	1.5 mi.	1,700 ft.	1:35
Carter Dome summit (4,832 ft.)	2.5 mi.	2,300 ft. (rev. 50 ft.)	2:25

This trail climbs over an open knob with good views to the summit of Carter Dome from Wild River Trail in Perkins Notch, 0.8 mi. west of Perkins Notch Tentsite near No-Ketchum Pond. After leaving Wild River Trail, Rainbow Trail passes through a sag then ascends steadily through beautiful birch woods with luxuriant undergrowth on the southeast slope of Carter Dome. At 1.5 mi., the trail passes just east of the summit of a southerly knob and runs in the open with fine views, especially to the south and west. The trail returns into the woods at a sag then climbs moderately, with an occasional glimpse back to the knob, to Carter Moriah Trail at the summit of Carter Dome.

BOG BROOK TRAIL (WMNF; MAP 5: G10)

Cumulative from parking area on FR 233 (1,860 ft.) to:	⇅	↗	○
Wildcat River Trail (1,780 ft.)	0.7 mi.	0 ft. (rev. 100 ft.)	0:20
Wild River Trail (2,417 ft.)	2.8 mi.	650 ft.	1:45

This trail begins at a new parking area, before a gate near the start of FR 233, which diverges to the right from the end of Carter Notch Rd., 5.4 mi. from the jct. of NH 16B and NH 16A in Jackson by Wentworth Resort. (The upper section of this road is not plowed in winter; parking may be available 0.5 mi. below, just above Hutmen's Trail.) Bog Brook Trail ends on Wild River Trail 1.5 mi. west of Perkins Notch Tentsite. Bog Brook Trail is wet in places, and some brook crossings may be difficult at high water, but the first three can be avoided by following gravel FR 233 on foot past the gate to the point where Bog Brook Trail crosses the road; this route is 0.6 mi. longer.

Starting at a sign 25 yd. to the right of the parking area, a new section of Bog Brook Trail descends 150 yd. to meet the original route, where it turns left. Descending slightly, the trail crosses Wildcat Brook, then another brook, and then Wildcat River, the most difficult crossing on the trail. In 60 yd., at 0.7 mi., Wildcat River Trail continues straight ahead, and Bog Brook Trail diverges right. The trail now ascends moderately, at 1.0 mi. crossing the gravel logging road (FR 233) that leads back (to the left) 1.6 mi. to the trailhead.

The trail continues up at mostly easy grades with some muddy footing, passing through some swampy areas, and makes the first of five crossings of Bog Brook at 1.9 mi. It makes two more crossings in the next 0.2 mi. and a fourth at 2.5 mi. After a muddy section, the trail turns left (arrow) at 2.7 mi. and runs along a relocation (around beaver flooding) to the fifth crossing, below a beaver dam. On the far side of the crossing, the trail swings right, rejoins the original route, and soon ends at Wild River Trail.

WILDCAT RIVER TRAIL (AMC; MAP 5: G10–F10)

Cumulative from Bog Brook Trail (1,780 ft.) to:	⇅	↗	↺
Bog Brook crossing (2,050 ft.)	1.0 mi.	250 ft.	0:40
Wild River Trail (2,320 ft.)	1.9 mi.	550 ft.	1:15
Carter Notch Hut (3,288 ft.)	3.6 mi.	1,500 ft.	2:35

This pleasant yellow-blazed trail runs to Carter Notch Hut from Bog Brook Trail just east of the Wildcat River crossing, 0.7 mi. from FR 233. Brook crossings may be difficult at high water, but those on Bog Brook Trail can be avoided by following gravel FR 233 from the Bog Brook Trail parking area to the point where Wildcat River Trail crosses the road, just beyond the bridge over Wildcat River; this route is 0.3 mi. longer.

From the Bog Brook Trail jct., Wildcat River Trail follows the east bank of Wildcat River, at 0.3 mi. crossing gravel FR 233, which leads back (to the left) 1.3 mi. to the Bog Brook Trail trailhead. The trail climbs over a rise, descends to cross Bog Brook at 1.0 mi., and Wild River Trail enters right at 1.9 mi. Soon the trail crosses Wildcat River (may be difficult at high water), turns sharply right in 100 yd., and continues to ascend at a moderate grade through fine hardwood and birch forest. At 3.1 mi. Wildcat River Trail crosses the outwash from a 2011 slide and climbs more steeply through spruce forest toward Carter Notch, passes a side trail right that leads to the rocks of the Rampart, and soon reaches the Carter Notch Hut complex. It passes to the right of one bunkhouse and to the left of another then descends rock steps to meet Nineteen-Mile Brook Trail in front of the main hut building.

HUTMEN'S TRAIL (HA; MAP 5: G10)

From NH 16 (1,050 ft.) to:	⇅	↗	↻
Carter Notch Rd. (1,803 ft.)	3.1 mi.	950 ft. (rev. 200 ft.)	2:00

This trail crosses the flat ridge between Spruce Mtn. on the south and Wildcat Mtn. on the north, running from the east side of NH 16, 3.7 mi. north of the covered bridge in Jackson and 5.6 mi. south of Pinkham Notch Visitor Center, to Carter Notch Rd., 4.9 mi. north of the jct. of NH 16B and NH 16A in Jackson by Wentworth Resort and 0.5 mi. south of the end of Carter Notch Rd. Views are very limited. There is limited roadside parking available at the trailhead on NH 16 (do not block the driveway) and better parking at a pull-off on the west side of the road, 0.1 mi. to the north. There is a large parking area on the west side of Carter Notch Rd., just north of the eastern trailhead.

The western section follows its traditional route as a hiking trail, although the part near the trailhead on NH 16 may be disrupted by new housing construction. The middle and eastern sections follow logging roads of various ages that become cross-country ski trails during the winter. The ski-trail sections are grassy and wet in places, with little evident footway, and signs and other markings must be followed with care at several intersections with other ski trails.

Leaving NH 16, where there is a trail sign and hiker symbol to the left of a house, the trail follows a road for 50 yd., then bears right off the road (obscure turn), shortly swings right and left at small cairns, and enters the woods, where the footway becomes much clearer. The trail ascends rather steeply up the west slope of Spruce Mtn., following the left side of a small brook. After 0.4 mi., the grade decreases. The trail bears left away from the brook, turns more north, crosses a small brook, and runs nearly level through mixed softwoods. The trail enters the WMNF at 0.6 mi., passing through brushy areas. At 0.8 mi., Dana Place Trail (X-C ski) enters from the left and the trails coincide, passing an apple orchard on the left.

At 1.1 mi., Hutmen's Trail swings left and in 15 yd. left again onto a grassy logging road, still coinciding with Dana Place Trail, and follows the road generally northeast along the flat ridge crest, with wet footing in places. At 1.7 mi., Hutmen's Trail bears right onto a newer logging road; to the left, this road is UST Trail (X-C ski). Hutmen's Trail ascends and then descends gradually along this road. At 2.2 mi., the trail follows Quail Trail (X-C ski) straight ahead along the road, as Dana Place Trail branches left toward Hall's Ledge Trail. Soon Hutmen's Trail enters a clearing with a view of Wildcat Mtn. over the trees. Here the trail turns right into the woods and onto another logging road (Marsh Brook Trail [X-C ski]), crosses the brook, and leaves the WMNF. After a flat, wet section, the trail swings left, where an orange-blazed footpath diverges right, and descends past a dilapidated camp to Carter Notch Rd., where there is a sign for Hutmen's Trail.

HALL'S LEDGE TRAIL (HA; MAP 5: G10)

Cumulative from NH 16 (1,150 ft.) to:	↥	↗	○
South viewpoint (2,580 ft.)	1.9 mi.	1,450 ft.	1:40
Carter Notch Rd. (1,850 ft.)	3.3 mi.	1,500 ft. (rev. 800 ft.)	2:25

This trail starts on the east side of NH 16, just south of the bridge over Ellis River and 5.2 mi. north of the covered bridge in Jackson. The trail sign is on a bank behind a guardrail and is easily missed. Use the Rocky Branch Trail parking lot, on the west side of NH 16, 0.1 mi. north of the bridge. The trail ends at the upper end of Carter Notch Rd., 5.4 mi. from Jackson village. At this end, it is signed as both Wildcat Valley Trail (X-C ski) and Hall's Ledge Trail, and continues ahead (west) past a kiosk and gate at the end of Carter Notch Rd. Parking is available at the Bog Brook Trail/Hall's Ledge Trail trailhead, a short distance in on the right side of FR 233, which diverges right at the end of Carter Notch Rd. Hall's Ledge itself is completely overgrown, but you have a restricted vista of Mt. Washington from a small cleared area and a fine view south from a large clearing.

From NH 16, follow the river for 80 yd. then veer right uphill and in another 100 yd. bear right across a clearing. The trail runs through a brushy, swampy area then swings left uphill and ascends to a high bank overlooking a brook with a long cascade. The yellow-blazed trail soon bears away from the brook and climbs steeply through hardwood forest for about 0.3 mi. From the top of this rise, the trail runs generally north and northeast at an easier grade through an area where there has been much recent logging activity and where blazes and flagging must be followed with care. The trail then ascends moderately through spruce forest, levels, and, at 1.7 mi., reaches a small clearing on the left with a picnic table and a view of Mt. Washington and its eastern spurs and ravines.

From here, the trail follows wide, grassy Hall's Ledge Overlook Trail (X-C ski), rising easily for 0.2 mi. to a large clearing on the right with an excellent view south. Hall's Ledge Trail continues gradually up to a jct. with Wildcat Valley Trail (X-C ski) at 2.0 mi., where the trail turns sharply right and follows the latter trail east. The trail descends moderately through Jackson's Prospect Farm conservation area, passing a jct. with Beth Hendrick Trail (X-C ski) on the left then at 2.7 mi. in quick succession passing jcts. with Hub's Loop Trail (X-C ski) on the left, Orchard Trail (X-C ski) on the right, and a gravel spur road on the left. Hall's Ledge Trail continues down past jcts. with Dana Place and Quail trails (X-C ski), both on the right, and follows a gravel road to the gate at the end of Carter Notch Rd.

BLACK MTN. SKI TRAIL (WMNF; MAP 5: G10)

Cumulative from parking area on Melloon Rd. (1,260 ft.) to:	↥↧	↗	↻
Black Mtn. Cabin (2,450 ft.)	1.3 mi.	1,200 ft.	1:15
Summit of knob (2,757 ft.)	1.6 mi.	1,500 ft.	1:35

This trail leads to Black Mtn. Cabin and a nearby knob (2,757 ft.) on the ridge of Black Mtn. that provides restricted views of Carter Notch and the Baldfaces. To reach the trailhead, follow Carter Notch Rd. for 3.7 mi. from Wentworth Hall in Jackson then turn right onto Melloon Rd. at the jct. where the WMNF trail sign is located. Follow Melloon Rd. (gravel) across Wildcat River then bear left uphill, passing Wildcat Valley Trail (X-C ski; right). Continue to a parking area on the left, 0.3 mi. from Carter Notch Rd., just before a private driveway with a chain gate. The road is plowed to this point in winter. Black Mtn. Cabin is kept locked, and reservations for its use must be made at recreation.gov or 877-444-6777. A spring (unreliable water source) is located near the cabin, and the trail crosses several small streams (also unreliable).

Black Mtn. Ski Trail ascends the gravel driveway and turns to the right onto an old woods road (sign) just before reaching a brown house. The trail crosses several small brooks, enters the WMNF, then swings right and angles up the western slope of Black Mtn., ascending moderately at first and then more steeply. At 1.3 mi., the trail reaches Black Mtn. Cabin, where you have a view northwest toward Mt. Washington. The direct route to the restricted viewpoint on the nearby knob of Black Mtn. follows the main trail left (northeast), ascending steadily for 0.3 mi. to a spur path (sign: Summit) that leads 80 yd. left to the outlook.

SEC 9

To make a scenic loop back to the cabin that is only 0.3 mi. longer than the direct route, with a 50-ft. ascent, follow a connector to East Pasture Trail (X-C ski), which leads east downhill from the viewpoint spur path jct., for 0.1 mi. Turn right here onto Black Mtn. Cutoff (0.5-mi. long) and ascend, crossing the ridge crest in a beautiful softwood forest; then swing right and descend, emerging just to the south of the cabin on a path that leads to the left to a nearby spring.

EAGLE MTN. TRAIL (MAP 5: H10)

From NH 16B (1,000 ft.) to:	⇅	↗	○
Eagle Mtn. summit (1,613 ft.)	0.9 mi.	600 ft.	0:45

Eagle Mtn. is a small peak with an interesting view to Doublehead Mtn., Mt. Kearsarge North, and the Moat Range. The mountain can be climbed from NH 16B (Carter Notch Rd.), 0.8 mi. from Wentworth Hall in Jackson, by a path that starts in the upper parking lot directly behind the Eagle Mtn. House. The path is lightly used and marked, but its faded green blazes and cairns can be followed fairly easily by careful hikers. Eagle Mtn. Trail starts from the right (north) side of the parking lot (sign). It follows a woods road for 150 yd. and, just before reaching the crest of the ridge, turns right off the road (sign).

In another 150 yd., the trail bears to the left of a pump house, and at 0.3 mi. it passes a jct. where a snowshoe trail (Eagle Ridge Path) diverges left. Eagle Mtn. Trail then ascends to an open swampy area. Cairns mark the way along the right side of the swamp and into the woods, where the climbing becomes steeper. After passing a large boulder on the right, the trail turns left uphill and climbs a steep and rough section by switchbacks, aiming for a small gap at the top right edge of the rock face. At the top of the rock face, the trail turns left and climbs up the right side of a ledge then turns left toward a false summit. The trail then turns right to a cleared view to the south on the left, and the path ends in 90 yd. at a large cairn, near the true summit.

DOUBLEHEAD MTN.

DOUBLEHEAD SKI TRAIL (WMNF; MAP 5: H11–G11)

From Dundee Rd. (1,480 ft.) to:	⇅	↗	○
North Doublehead summit (3,053 ft.)	1.8 mi.	1,600 ft.	1:40

This trail ascends North Doublehead from a proposed new trailhead parking area on Dundee Rd., scheduled to open in 2017. From NH 16 at the

Jackson covered bridge, follow NH 16A (Main St.) then at 0.5 mi., turn right onto Black Mountain Rd. (NH 16B). Go up a long hill, bear right on Black Mountain Rd. at 1.6 mi., continue past Black Mtn. Ski Area at 2.2 mi., turn right onto Dundee Rd. at 2.4 mi., and continue to the new parking area on the east (left) side of the road 3.0 mi. from NH 16. The WMNF Doublehead Cabin, located on the summit, is kept locked, and reservations for its use must be made at recreation.gov or 877-444-6777.

From the parking area, the trail will follow a newly cut route, ascending generally northeast through the woods and joining the original route at 0.4 mi. (The original section of trail below this point will be decommissioned.) At 0.6 mi., the trail bears slightly left where Old Path leaves right. The wide, grassy ski trail ascends north up the west slope of North Doublehead then swings south and then southeast, climbing steadily on a zigzag route and terminating at Doublehead Cabin on the summit. The nearest water is alongside the trail about halfway down. Beyond the cabin, a path leads 30 yd. to a good view east, overlooking Mountain Pond, the Baldface Range, and the hills and lakes of western Maine.

OLD PATH (WMNF; MAP 5: H11–G11)

Cumulative from Doublehead Ski Trail (1,860 ft.) to:	⇅	↗	○
New Path (2,710 ft.)	0.6 mi.	850 ft.	0:45
North Doublehead summit (3,053 ft.)	0.9 mi.	1,200 ft.	1:05

This trail ascends to North Doublehead from Doublehead Ski Trail, 0.6 mi. from Dundee Rd. Old Path diverges right and passes a brook left in 50 yd., rises at a moderate grade for about 0.1 mi., then becomes steeper until the path reaches the height-of-land in the col between the peaks at 0.6 mi. Here, New Path enters right, and Old Path turns left and ascends moderately then more steeply, passing a side path that leads left somewhat downhill about 100 yd. to a splendid view west to Mt. Carrigain, Moat Mtn., and the Sandwich Range. In a short distance, Old Path reaches the summit of North Doublehead, the cabin (which is kept locked), and Doublehead Ski Trail. Beyond the cabin, a path leads 30 yd. to a good view east.

NEW PATH (WMNF; MAP 5: H11)

Cumulative from Dundee Rd. (1,590 ft.) to:	⇅	↗	○
South Doublehead summit (2,939 ft.)	1.2 mi.	1,350 ft.	1:15
Old Path (2,710 ft.)	1.4 mi.	1,350 ft. (rev. 250 ft.)	1:25

SEC 9

This trail ascends South Doublehead and continues to the col between South and North Doublehead, where New Path meets Old Path. New Path (sign) starts on Dundee Rd., 3.3 mi. from NH 16 at the Jackson covered bridge and 0.3 mi. beyond the new parking area for Doublehead Ski Trail. Limited roadside parking is available. New Path is marked with cairns, and its upper half is very steep with poor footing. The trail descends slightly as it leaves the road and, in 60 yd., bears right then left and follows a logging road at a slight upgrade. At 0.3 mi. from Dundee Rd., bear left and in about 100 yd. descend slightly and cross a small brook. Proceed uphill for 100 yd. and bear right at a cairn. About 0.2 mi. from this point, the trail crosses a small, almost flat ledge then crosses a smaller ledge a short distance beyond.

From here, the trail begins a steep climb through spruce forest to South Doublehead, approaching it from the southwest slope. The footing is poor in places, with loose rock and gravel. The trail meets the ridge crest between two knobs. To the right, a spur path, 0.1 mi. long, leads over two knobs with open ledges and partly restricted but interesting views; the first knob has views south and west, and the second knob has views north and east. New Path turns left and crosses the summit of South Doublehead; just before the trail starts to descend, it bears right, and a spur path leads to the left about 30 yd. to a superb outlook ranging from the Sandwich Range to Carter Notch. New Path then descends to meet Old Path in the col to the north.

MT. KEARSARGE NORTH REGION

MT. KEARSARGE NORTH TRAIL (WMNF; MAP 5: I11–H11)

Cumulative from Hurricane Mtn. Rd. (680 ft.) to:	⇅	↗	↺
Boulders (1,400 ft.)	1.1 mi.	700 ft.	0:55
Crest of ridge (2,750 ft.)	2.4 mi.	2,050 ft.	2:15
Kearsarge North summit (3,268 ft.)	3.1 mi.	2,600 ft.	2:50

This trail ascends Mt. Kearsarge North from a small parking area on the north side of Hurricane Mtn. Rd., 1.5 mi. east of NH 16 near the state highway rest area at Intervale. The trail is a very popular and moderate trail to the magnificent views of Kearsarge North, but inexperienced hikers should not underestimate the total climb of 2,600 ft., which is comparable to the ascent required for many much higher peaks.

Leaving the road, the trail runs level for a short distance then climbs easily past a summer residence on an old road, well up on the bank above a brook. The trail enters the WMNF at 0.7 mi. and begins to climb steadily through a fine hemlock forest. At 1.1 mi., the trail passes several boulders, and the old road starts to become rougher. At 1.8 mi., the trail enters a ledgy area with red pines, where you have restricted views to Mt. Chocorua and Moat Mtn. Continuing its steady climb, the trail reaches a ledge with an open view south. The trail crosses the crest of the ridge connecting Kearsarge North to Bartlett Mtn. at 2.4 mi. then swings right and ascends through spruce forest mostly along the north side of the ridge. At 2.9 mi., the trail makes a sharp right turn at a steep spot then angles upward, circling to the left around to the west edge of the summit ledges, and climbs to the tower.

WEEKS BROOK TRAIL (WMNF; MAP 5: H12–H11)

Cumulative from trailhead on FR 317 (550 ft.) to:	↕	↗	↻
Shingle Pond (1,710 ft.)	3.1 mi.	1,150 ft.	2:10
Kearsarge North summit (3,268 ft.)	5.1 mi.	2,700 ft.	3:55

This trail ascends Mt. Kearsarge North from the east, passing by Shingle Pond. This is a somewhat rough and sparsely marked route that, for experienced hikers, provides an attractive, lightly used alternative to the popular Mt. Kearsarge North Trail. An area of 1,100 acres adjacent to Shingle Pond that includes some old-growth forest has been designated as a Candidate Research Natural Area by the WMNF.

Weeks Brook Trail begins at a trailhead on Hardwood Hill Rd. (FR 317) 0.1 mi. from Green Hill Rd.; FR 317 leaves Green Hill Rd. 3.8 mi. north of NH 113 in East Conway and 0.4 mi. north of the east terminus of Hurricane Mtn. Rd. Following this trail may require considerable care, particularly in the part near the road and in the upper part. In fall of 2016, new logging activity had disrupted sections along the lower part of the trail; follow markings carefully in these areas. From the parking area, this trail follows FR 317 uphill and crosses a branch of Weeks Brook on a bridge at 0.4 mi. The trail soon bears left (south). At 0.6 mi., it turns right off FR 317 onto a gated USFS road then quickly bears left off the road into a hemlock forest, following old logging roads marked by yellow blazes.

In a brushy clearing at 1.5 mi., the trail turns left back onto the USFS road and follows it along the right edge of the clearing for about 100 yd. Here, the trail bears right into the woods on an old logging road (arrow); this turn is rather obscure. This road quickly becomes distinctly older and rougher, and begins to climb gradually then moderately, with some wet footing, to boggy Shingle Pond, where you find a view of Kearsarge North.

SEC
9

At 3.1 mi., the trail makes its closest approach to the pond, which has been visible for some time. At 3.5 mi., the trail reaches a branch of Middle Brook then soon crosses on a ledge and follows the north bank of the attractive brook, crossing and recrossing a branch several times.

The trail skirts an open boggy area in the sag between Kearsarge North and Rickers Knoll at 4.2 mi. and turns sharply left (west) at a sign. The trail makes a winding ascent through spruces (watch for arrows), first moderately then steeply, and enters low scrub and blueberries, passing a fine view east. Here, the trail turns sharply right and soon reaches a ledge with views south, from which the fire tower is visible. From here to the summit, the trail may be somewhat obscure, but the direction is obvious up the ledges. Descending from the tower, the trail leads east down over ledges then bears left into the scrub; follow with care.

PROVINCE BROOK TRAIL (WMNF; MAP 5: H12)

From north end of Peaked Hill Rd.
(950 ft.) to:

	⇅	↗	⟳
Province Pond Shelter (1,330 ft.)	1.6 mi.	400 ft.	1:00

This trail provides an easy hike to Province Pond, where a WMNF shelter is located. The trail begins at the north end of Peaked Hill Rd. (FR 450), 2.6 mi. from Green Hill Rd. Peaked Hill Rd. (closed in winter) leaves Green Hill Rd. 4.3 mi. north of NH 113 in East Conway and 0.9 mi. north of the east end of Hurricane Mtn. Rd.

The trail leaves the north end of Peaked Hill Rd. then in 30 yd. turns right onto a wide snowmobile trail and heads northwest parallel to, but well away from, Province Brook. The trail crosses two tributaries on snowmobile bridges then crosses Province Brook on another bridge shortly before reaching the boggy south end of Province Pond at 1.2 mi., where you have a view of Mt. Shaw. The trail leads north along the east shore then turns left off the wide snowmobile trail onto a yellow-blazed footpath; the turn is marked with an arrow, a cairn, and a blaze. The trail passes to the right of a prominent peaked rock then bears left well back from the north end of the pond, where the trail at times has been overgrown and difficult to follow, then swings left again and leads south to the shelter.

GREEN HILLS OF CONWAY

BLACK CAP TRAIL (TNC; MAP 5: I12)

From Hurricane Mtn. Rd.
(1,720 ft.) to:

	⇅	↗	⟳
Black Cap summit (2,369 ft.)	1.1 mi.	650 ft.	0:55

This path provides a relatively easy ascent to the bare summit of Black Cap, the highest peak in the Green Hills Preserve, which affords the best views in the Green Hills range. The trail begins on the south side of steep, winding Hurricane Mtn. Rd. (the upper part of which is closed to automobiles from November through mid-May) from a parking lot at the height-of-land, 3.8 mi. east of NH 16 at the Intervale scenic vista and rest area, and 2.5 mi. west of Green Hill Rd. in South Chatham. In winter, the trail is used by snowmobiles up to the Black Cap Connector jct.

The trail, marked with red blazes, runs almost level through spruce woods in Conway State Forest then ascends moderately through mixed hardwoods on Conway town land to a kiosk at 0.5 mi. At 0.7 mi., Cranmore Trail leaves right, and at 0.8 mi. Black Cap Connector diverges right to traverse the west side of Black Cap toward Peaked Mtn. Black Cap Trail enters the Green Hills Preserve and soon reaches ledges that become more open, with excellent views westward. Nearing the summit, a blue-and-salmon-blazed side path makes a short loop to the right, over a ledge with a view south and west, and rejoins the main trail 15 yd. from its starting point.

The summit, where the views are less open, is reached in another 90 yd. and is marked by a red dot. You have views in all directions (though not from any single spot); an obscure spur path marked by blue and yellow blazes leads left (east) 80 yd. to a very limited view east toward the hills of western Maine. From the summit, Black Cap Spur Trail, leading down cut granite steps and then many wooden retaining steps, descends to the right to meet Black Cap Connector in 0.2 mi. (150-ft. descent), which can be followed to the right, 0.4 mi. back to Black Cap Trail, making a short loop from the summit.

CRANMORE TRAIL (TNC; MAP 5: I12–I11)

From Black Cap Trail (2,020 ft.) to:	⇅	↗	↻
Cranmore Mtn. summit (1,690 ft.)	1.2 mi.	50 ft. (rev. 400 ft.)	0:40

This yellow-blazed path provides access to the summit of Cranmore Mtn. and the Cranmore Mtn. Ski Area from Hurricane Mtn. Rd. The trail is open to mountain bikes. Leaving Black Cap Trail at a sign 0.7 mi. from Hurricane Mtn. Rd., Cranmore Trail descends gradually, passing a jct. with Red Tail Trail (mountain bike) on the right at 0.2 mi. At 1.0 mi., Cranmore Trail climbs over a small but steep knob and resumes its descent to the main col at 1.1 mi. Here, the trail starts to ascend Cranmore Mtn., joining a service road coming up from the left after 30 yd. This service road climbs to the flat summit area, passing to the left of a radio tower and reaching the actual summit at the top of the chairlift. The Cranmore Ski Area base lodge can be reached in about 1.2 mi. with about 1,100 ft. of descent via ski trails.

BLACK CAP CONNECTOR (TNC; MAP 5: I11–I12)

Cumulative from Middle Mtn. Trail jct.

(730 ft.) to:	⇅	↗	↺
Mason Brook Snowmobile Trail (1,780 ft.)	2.1 mi.	1,100 ft. (rev. 50 ft.)	1:35
Black Cap Trail (2,070 ft.)	4.0 mi.	1,700 ft. (rev. 300 ft.)	2:50

This yellow-blazed trail traverses the west slope of the Green Hills, connecting Peaked Mtn. and Middle Mtn. with Black Cap and Cranmore Mtn. The trail begins where the coinciding Middle Mtn. and Peaked Mtn. trails diverge, 0.7 mi. from their Thompson Rd. trailhead, and ends on Black Cap Trail just south of its jct. with Cranmore Trail, 0.8 mi. from Hurricane Mtn. Rd. Black Cap Connector mostly follows old logging roads and is open to mountain bikes.

From the jct. where Middle Mtn. Trail diverges, Black Cap Connector coincides with Peaked Mtn. Trail on an old road ascending north for 0.5 mi., with minor ups and downs, to a kiosk, where Peaked Mtn. Trail turns uphill to the right toward Peaked Mtn., and a path (an old route of the trail) turns downhill to the left to return in 0.3 mi. to Thompson Rd., where parking is forbidden. Black Cap Connector continues straight from this jct. then swings right (east) and ascends the valley of Artist Brook between Peaked Mtn. and Cranmore Mtn. At 0.7 mi., the trail turns right onto a well-defined old logging road (descending, turn left here). At 0.9 mi., the trail passes a jct. on the right with Peaked Mtn. Connector, which climbs steeply 0.1 mi. and 100 ft. to Peaked Mtn. Trail at the lower ledges.

Black Cap Connector soon crosses a small brook and climbs, with eroded footing in places, for about a mile to a ridge crest, where the trail descends briefly and then climbs again to the jct. with Mason Brook Snowmobile Trail on the right at 2.1 mi. (From here on, Black Cap Connector is open to snowmobiles.) At a point 50 yd. above this jct., Black Cap Connector diverges right off the snowmobile trail onto a yellow-blazed footpath, climbs by switchbacks, then turns left at a ledge with a limited view and rejoins the snowmobile trail at 2.5 mi. Hikers may also follow the snowmobile trail to this jct.; the distance is about the same. Black Cap Connector ascends northward at easy grades by several switchbacks, occasionally descending into gullies. At 3.6 mi., Black Cap Spur diverges right and reaches Black Cap Trail at the summit of Black Cap in 0.2 mi. (150-ft.

ascent), and at 4.0 mi., after a gradual descent, Black Cap Connector ends at its jct. with Black Cap Trail.

PEAKED MTN. TRAIL (TNC; MAP 5: I11)

From Thompson Rd. parking area (530 ft.) to:	⇅	↗	⟳
Peaked Mtn. summit (1,739 ft.)	2.1 mi.	1,200 ft.	1:40

This trail offers an unusual variety of scenic vistas and natural features, including fine open stands of red and pitch pine, for relatively little effort. The sharp, rocky knoll of Peaked Mtn. affords excellent views toward Mt. Washington, the Saco Valley, and nearby mountains. From NH 16 in North Conway, take Artist's Falls Rd. (just south of the town center) east for 0.4 mi. then turn right and follow Thompson Rd. 0.3 mi. to the Pudding Pond Loop Trail parking area on the right, just before the power-line crossing.

Peaked Mtn. Trail, coinciding with Pudding Pond Loop and Middle Mtn. trails, follows a logging road parallel to the power lines for 0.2 mi. to a kiosk. Here Pudding Pond Loop Trail diverges right (west), and a mountain bike trail (sign: Sticks & Stones) continues ahead (south), whereas Peaked Mtn. and Middle Mtn. trails turn left (east) and cross under the power lines, with another mountain bike trail (sign: Pump Track) diverging right (southeast). Peaked Mtn. and Middle Mtn. trails enter the woods and ascend gradually on an old road. At 0.7 mi., at the boundary of the Green Hills Preserve, Middle Mtn. Trail continues straight uphill, and Peaked Mtn. Trail, now coinciding with Black Cap Connector, turns left onto another old road. Peaked Mtn. Trail ascends, with occasional dips, to a four-way jct. at another kiosk at 1.2 mi. (Here a blue-blazed path [Artist Falls Trail on the TNC map] descends 0.3 mi. and 200 ft. left to the end of Thompson Rd. near a small reservoir; parking is forbidden here. Just before reaching Thompson Rd., this old route turns right and makes a difficult crossing of Artist's Falls Brook at a small flume. From the end of Thompson Rd, one may follow the road 0.6 mi. on foot down the road to the official parking area.)

At the kiosk and four-way jct., Black Cap Connector (yellow blazes) continues straight ahead for Black Cap and Hurricane Mtn. Rd., whereas Peaked Mtn. Trail (blue blazes) turns right and ascends moderately to a ledge at 1.5 mi., where Peaked Mtn. Connector descends steeply left 0.1 mi. and 100 ft. to Black Cap Connector. Here, Peaked Mtn. Trail turns sharply right and ascends scattered ledges into stands of red pine with increasing views to the west and north. The trail passes an old route that

SEC 9

has been closed to permit the vegetation to recover (sign on right) then bears left and crosses a ledge that offers fine views of Kearsarge North and Mt. Washington. At 1.9 mi., Peaked Mtn.–Middle Mtn. Connector leaves on the right and descends 0.3 mi. and 250 ft. on several switchbacks to Middle Mtn. Trail. Peaked Mtn. Trail swings left and ascends the final ledges to the summit, a pointed, grassy knoll with views east, south, and west—particularly fine of the Ossipee Range and Mt. Chocorua.

MIDDLE MTN. TRAIL (TNC; MAP 5: I11)

From Thompson Rd. parking area (530 ft.) to:	⇅	↗	⏱
Middle Mtn. summit (1,857 ft.)	2.1 mi.	1,350 ft.	1:45

This red-blazed trail provides access to a fine southern outlook from Middle Mtn. and passes through a scenic hemlock ravine with several small cascades in its middle section that are interesting when there is a good flow of water. The trailhead is the same as for Peaked Mtn. Trail (see previous description).

Middle Mtn. Trail coincides with Peaked Mtn. and Pudding Pond Loop trails for 0.2 mi. to the kiosk then turns left (east) and continues along with Peaked Mtn. Trail, crossing straight under the power lines into the woods and ascending gradually on an old road to the Green Hills Preserve boundary at 0.7 mi. from the parking area. Here, the combined Peaked Mtn. Trail and Black Cap Connector leave on the left, whereas Middle Mtn. Trail continues to ascend straight ahead on the old road, immediately passing a jct. with a mountain bike trail on the right and reaching the cascades at 1.2 mi. After a short steep climb, the grade eases, and at 1.4 mi., Peaked Mtn.–Middle Mtn. Connector leaves on the left and ascends by switchbacks for 0.3 mi. and 250 ft. to Peaked Mtn. Trail, 0.2 mi. below the summit of Peaked Mtn.

Middle Mtn. Trail continues east up the valley for another 0.2 mi. then swings right (south), crosses the brook, and ascends moderately up the north ridge of Middle Mtn. The trail bears right (sign), ascends moderately to a small ridge crest, then descends slightly and swings left around a boulder before the final ascent to the pine grove at the summit. (On the descent, be sure to swing right around the boulder where a false path continues ahead.) The best view is obtained from a ledge about 40 yd. west of the highest point—a fine outlook to the Ossipee Range, Mt. Chocorua, Mt. Passaconaway, and the Moat Range.

PUDDING POND LOOP TRAIL (TNC/TOWN OF CONWAY; MAP 5: I11)

From Thompson Rd. parking area (530 ft.) for:	↥	↗	↻
Complete loop around Pudding Pond (530 ft.)	2.0 mi.	50 ft.	1:00

This trail provides an easy 2.0-mi. nature walk to a beaver pond and wetland in Town of Conway conservation land. Views of the pond itself are limited. The trailhead is the same as for Peaked Mtn. Trail (discussed earlier). Follow signs carefully, as a potentially confusing network of mountain-bike trails is in the area. Pudding Pond Loop Trail itself is open to mountain bikes.

The trail follows the logging road parallel to the power lines for 0.2 mi. to the kiosk, where Peaked Mtn. and Middle Mtn. trails diverge left and Sticks & Stones mountain bike trail continues ahead. Pudding Pond Loop Trail (sign) turns right (west) onto an old road and continues to the loop jct. at 0.4 mi. from the trailhead (sign for loop). The loop is described in a counterclockwise direction. Turn right at the loop jct. then turn sharply left at 0.5 mi. where a spur path diverges right, crosses a bridge over the outlet brook, and leads 250 yd. to a crossing of a railroad track and the North–South Rd. (use caution); on the far side of the road, a gravel path ascends to a small parking area at the end of Locust Lane. The main trail leads south along the east bank of the brook, and at 0.9 mi. it swings left and follows a relocation to the left of an abandoned section of trail. At 1.1 mi., the trail turns sharply left (northeast) away from the pond, coinciding with northbound Pillar to Pond mountain bike trail. At 1.4 mi., Pudding Pond Loop Trail turns left (northwest) onto a woods road and follows it downhill. (In the reverse direction, turn right off the woods road into the woods.) Pudding Pond Loop Trail returns to the loop jct. at 1.6 mi.; turn right to return to the kiosk and Thompson Rd. trailhead.

SEC
9

SECTION TEN
SPECKLED MTN. REGION

Map 5: Carter Range–Evans Notch

INTRODUCTION

This section covers the mountains and trails in the region east of Evans Notch, and the valleys of Evans Brook and the Cold River that lead up to Evans Notch from the north and south, respectively. The section is bounded on the west by NH/ME 113 (the highway that runs through Evans Notch from Chatham, New Hampshire, to Gilead, Maine) and on the north by US 2. Except for a sliver of land near North Chatham, New Hampshire, the entire section lies in Maine. Almost all of the land in this section is within the WMNF, and most of its central portion is included in the 11,236-acre Caribou–Speckled Mtn. Wilderness. In accordance with USFS Wilderness policy, the trails in the Caribou–Speckled Mtn. Wilderness are generally maintained to a lower standard than are non-Wilderness Area trails. Considerable care may be required to follow them. AMC's *White Mountains Trail Map 5: Carter Range–Evans Notch* covers the entire area. The CTA publishes a detailed map of the trail system in the Cold River valley.

The AT does not pass through this section.

ROAD ACCESS

Trails on the west side of the Speckled Mtn. region are reached from NH/ME 113, the road that leads through Evans Notch. In winter, this road is not plowed between the road to Basin Pond and a gate 1.8 mi. south of US 2. Stone House Rd. (private) leads 1.1 mi. east from NH 113 (1.3 mi. north of AMC's Cold River Camp) to a gate and parking area; the road is not plowed in winter. Deer Hill Rd. (FR 9, also known as Evergreen Valley Rd. and Shell Pond Rd. within Maine) runs between NH 113 in North Chatham, New Hampshire (0.7 mi. south of AMC's Cold River Camp), and Adams Rd. in Stoneham, Maine; Deer Hill Rd. is not plowed in winter. Other access roads are covered in individual trail descriptions.

GEOGRAPHY

The majority of this region is occupied by a jumbled mass of ridges with numerous ledges; although the peaks are not high, they offer a variety of fine walks. With the exception of a few trails off ME 113, this area probably receives less hiking traffic than any comparable section of the WMNF, allowing visitors to enjoy relative solitude on trails in an area that is quite rugged and scenic.

Speckled Mtn. (2,906 ft.) is the tallest peak in the region, one of at least three mountains in Maine that have been known by this name, and its open summit ledges have excellent views in nearly all directions. Blueberry

SEC 10

Ridge, ending in Blueberry Mtn. (1,781 ft.), is a long, flat spur running south from Speckled Mtn. The top is mostly one big open ledge, where mature trees are slowly reclaiming what was once a burned-over summit with only sparse and stunted trees. Numerous open spaces afford excellent views, especially from the southwest ledges on Blueberry Mtn.'s summit. In the valley between Blueberry Mtn. and the southwest ridge of Speckled Mtn., Bickford Brook passes the Bickford Slides, a series of beautiful flumes and waterfalls. The southeast ridge of Speckled Mtn. also bears many open ledges with fine views. A long ridge extends east from Speckled Mtn. to Miles Notch, running over Durgin Mtn. (2,404 ft.), Butters Mtn. (2,246 ft.), Red Rock Mtn. (2,141 ft.), and Miles Knob (2,090 ft.). Durgin Mtn. and Red Rock Mtn. offer interesting views from ledges near their summits, and the south cliff of Red Rock Mtn. is one of the most impressive features of the region. The wooded west ridge of Speckled Mtn., which descends toward ME 113, includes Ames Mtn. (2,686 ft.) and Spruce Hill (2,510 ft.).

To the north of Speckled Mtn. is Caribou Mtn. (2,850 ft.), the second-highest peak in the area. It also has a bare, ledgy summit that affords excellent views. South of Caribou Mtn. is Haystack Notch, with the cliffs of trailless Haystack Mtn. (2,205 ft.) rising on its north side. Peabody Mtn. (2,462 ft.) is a wooded mountain that rises to the north of Caribou Mtn. Located on the eastern edge of the WMNF, Albany Mtn. (1,930 ft.) has open ledges near its summit with excellent views in several directions. To the west of Albany Mtn. and Albany Notch are several small but interesting rugged mountains that have no trails but invite exploration, of which the most prominent is Farwell Mtn. (1,865 ft.). Round Pond is an interesting mountain pond that lies east of Albany Mtn. and is easily visited from Crocker Pond Campground.

Deer Hill (1,367 ft.), often called Big Deer Hill, is located south of Speckled Mtn. and east of the Cold River. The views from the east and south ledges are excellent. Little Deer Hill (1,090 ft.), a lower hill west of Deer Hill that rises only about 600 ft. above the valley, gives fine views of the valley and the Baldfaces from its summit ledges. Pine Hill (1,250 ft.) and Lord Hill (1,257 ft.) rise southeast of Deer Hill, with scattered open ledges that afford interesting views. Several short paths in the vicinity of AMC's Cold River Camp are not covered in this guide because they are not open to the public, although some are mentioned where they intersect other, more important trails. The Roost (1,374 ft.) is a low mountain near Hastings, Maine, with open ledges that afford fine views of the Wild River valley, the Evans Brook valley, and surrounding mountains.

CAMPING
Caribou–Speckled Mtn. Wilderness

In accordance with USFS Wilderness policy, hiking groups may not exceed ten people, and no more than ten people may occupy any designated or non-designated campsite. See p. xiv for more information about Wilderness Area regulations.

Forest Protection Areas

The WMNF has established a number of FPAs, where camping and wood or charcoal fires are prohibited throughout the year. See p. xxiv for general FPA regulations.

Established Trailside Campsites

No shelters or established trailside campsites are available in this section.

SUGGESTED HIKES

■ Easy Hikes
THE ROOST

	⮌	↗	⟳
RT via Roost Trail and spur trail	1.2 mi.	700 ft.	0:55

A short climb from this trail's northern end leads to a spur trail that descends to ledges with views of Evans Notch and the Wild River valley. See Roost Trail, p. 477.

ROUND POND

	⮌	↗	⟳
RT via Albany Brook Trail	2.0 mi.	250 ft.	1:10

An easy ramble leads to a pair of ponds. See Albany Brook Trail, p. 483.

DEER HILLS

	⮌	↗	⟳
RT to Little Deer Hill via Deer Hills Connector and Deer Hills Trail	2.6 mi.	700 ft.	1:40
LP to Little and Big Deer hills via Deer Hills Connector, Deer Hills Trail, and Deer Hills Bypass	4.3 mi.	1,250 ft.	2:45

These low hills provide good views of the Cold River valley and the Baldfaces. Options include a shorter out-and-back trip or a longer loop over Little and Big Deer hills. To begin, see Deer Hills Trail, p. 496.

SEC 10

■ Moderate Hikes
CARIBOU MTN.

		⇅	↗	↻
LP via Caribou and Mud Brook trails		6.9 mi.	1,950 ft.	4:25

A loop trip delivers extensive views from the bare summit. To begin, see Caribou Trail, p. 478.

ALBANY MTN.

		⇅	↗	↻
RT via Albany Mtn. Trail and Albany Mtn. spur		4.4 mi.	1,200 ft.	2:50

This small mountain offers good views over western Maine, the best of which are reached by a path to the southwest ledges (included above). See Albany Mtn. Trail, p. 481.

BLUEBERRY MTN.

		⇅	↗	↻
LP via Shell Pond Trail, White Cairn Trail, Blueberry Ridge Trail, Overlook Loop, and Stone House Trail		4.3 mi.	1,200 ft.	2:45

A visit to Blueberry includes many ledges with views, as well as a short side trip to beautiful Rattlesnake Pool. To begin, see Shell Pond Trail, p. 492.

■ Strenuous Hikes
BLUEBERRY AND SPECKLED MTNS.

		⇅	↗	↻
LP via Bickford Brook and Blueberry Ridge trails		8.6 mi.	2,500 ft.	5:35

Pairing these two open summits makes for a scenic circuit. To begin, see Bickford Brook Trail, p. 485.

RED ROCK MTN.

		⇅	↗	↻
LP via Miles Notch, Red Rock, and Great Brook trails		10.3 mi.	2,900 ft.	6:35

An interesting valley and ridge loop for experienced hikers passes through a wild, less-visited area, with fine views from Red Rock Mtn. To begin, see Miles Notch Trail, p. 484.

TRAIL DESCRIPTIONS
NORTH AND EAST OF SPECKLED MTN.

ROOST TRAIL (WMNF; MAP 5: E13)

Cumulative from ME 113, north trailhead (820 ft.), to:	⬆⬇	↗	⟳
The Roost (1,374 ft.)	0.5 mi.	550 ft.	0:30
ME 113, south trailhead (850 ft.)	1.2 mi.	550 ft. (rev. 500 ft.)	0:55

This trail ascends to the Roost, a small mountain with fine views of the Wild River and Evans Brook valleys, from two trailheads 0.8 mi. apart on the east side of ME 113. The north trailhead (sign; parking on shoulder) is 0.1 mi. north of a bridge over Evans Brook and 0.2 mi. north of the jct. of ME 113 with Wild River Rd. at Hastings, Maine. The south trailhead is just south of another bridge over Evans Brook; parking is available north of the bridge, on the west side of the road.

Leaving the north trailhead, the trail ascends a steep bank for 90 yd. then bears right (east) and ascends gradually along a wooded ridge, rejoining an older route of the trail at 0.1 mi. Roost Trail crosses a small brook at 0.3 mi. then rises somewhat more steeply, swings right, and emerges on a ledge at the summit (no views) at 0.5 mi. Here, a side trail descends steeply 0.1 mi. and 150 ft. right (southwest) through woods to spacious open ledges, where the views are excellent. The main trail descends generally southeast from the summit at a moderate grade and crosses a small brook then turns right (southwest) on an old road (no sign) and follows it past a cellar hole and a brushy area back to ME 113.

WHEELER BROOK TRAIL (WMNF; MAP 5: E13)

From US 2 (680 ft.) to:	⬆⬇	↗	⟳
Gate on Little Lary Brook Rd. (1,240 ft.)	3.5 mi.	1,350 ft. (rev. 800 ft.)	2:25

The two trailheads for this wooded, viewless trail are on the south side of US 2 (sign; limited roadside parking), 2.3 mi. east of the jct. of US 2 and ME 113, and at a locked gate on the gravel-surface Little Lary Brook Rd. (FR 8), 1.6 mi. from its jct. with ME 113, which is 7.0 mi. north of the road to the WMNF Cold River Campground and 3.8 mi. south of the jct. of US 2 and ME 113. The trail is lightly used and requires care to follow.

From US 2, the trail follows a gated, grassy logging road (FR 711) south, soon crossing an old road and then passing jcts. with another woods road

SEC 10

on the right and a snowmobile trail on the left. Wheeler Brook Trail enters the WMNF at 0.3 mi., bears left on a grassy road, and joins and follows Wheeler Brook, crossing it four times. The trail turns left (arrow) at a logging road fork at 0.9 mi., just before the third crossing of the brook. The trail rises steadily to its highest point, just over 2,000 ft., at the crest of the northwest ridge of Peabody Mtn. at 2.1 mi. (There is no trail to the wooded summit of Peabody Mtn.) The trail then descends generally southwest, merges onto a grassy old logging road (FR 8) that comes down from the left at 3.1 mi., and reaches Little Lary Brook Rd. Turn left onto Little Lary Brook Rd. and continue about 150 yd. to a locked gate near the bridge over Little Lary Brook, 1.6 mi. from ME 113.

In the reverse direction, proceed along Little Lary Brook Rd. about 150 yd. from the locked gate then turn right onto FR 8 at the jct. where FR 885 continues straight ahead. The trail (arrow) leaves the left side of the road in another 0.3 mi.

CARIBOU TRAIL (WMNF; MAP 5: E13–E14)

Cumulative from ME 113 (935 ft.) to:	⇅	↗	○
Mud Brook Trail (2,420 ft.)	3.0 mi.	1,550 ft. (rev. 50 ft.)	2:15
Bog Rd. (860 ft.)	5.5 mi.	1,550 ft. (rev. 1,550 ft.)	3:30
Caribou Mtn. summit (2,850 ft.) via Mud Brook Trail	3.5 mi.	1,950 ft.	2:45

This trail provides access (via Mud Brook Trail) to the attractive ledges of Caribou Mtn. The middle section of this trail is in the Caribou–Speckled Mtn. Wilderness. The west trailhead, which Caribou Trail shares with Mud Brook Trail, is located at a parking area on the east side of ME 113, 6.1 mi. north of the road to WMNF Cold River Campground and 4.6 mi. south of US 2. The east trailhead is on Bog Rd. (FR 6), which leaves the south side of US 2 1.3 mi. west of the West Bethel Post Office (a sign for Pooh Corner Farm and a road sign are at this jct.) and leads 2.8 mi. to the trailhead, where a gate ends public travel on the road.

From the parking area off ME 113, Caribou Trail runs north, ascending slightly and then descending. It crosses Morrison Brook at 0.4 mi. (no bridge) and turns east to follow the brook, crossing it five more times and entering the Wilderness Area. The third crossing, at 2.0 mi., is at the head of Kees Falls, a 25-ft. waterfall; a side path descends steeply on the north side of the brook to a good view of the falls. The trail climbs steadily then levels off at the height-of-land as it crosses the col between Gammon Mtn. and Caribou Mtn. at 2.9 mi.

Soon, Mud Brook Trail leaves right to return to ME 113 via the summit of Caribou Mtn. Caribou Trail continues ahead at the jct., descending steadily into a ravine and swinging left to cross a small brook. The trail leaves the Wilderness Area at 3.4 mi., continues down the valley of Bog Brook, and turns northeast, crossing Bog Brook at 4.3 mi. and a tributary in another 0.2 mi. The trail continues at easy grades, bears right across a brook, and at 5.2 mi., just after crossing another brook, turns left onto a logging road (FR 6). At 5.4 mi., the trail turns right at a jct. with another logging road and continues to the gate on Bog Rd. (Ascending, turn left at 0.1 mi. and bear right off the logging road at 0.3 mi.)

MUD BROOK TRAIL (WMNF; MAP 5: E13)

Cumulative from ME 113 (935 ft.) to:	⬇︎⬆︎	↗︎	⟳
Caribou Mtn. summit (2,850 ft.)	3.4 mi.	1,900 ft.	2:40
Caribou Trail (2,420 ft.)	3.9 mi.	1,900 ft. (rev. 450 ft.)	2:55
Loop over Caribou Mtn. (2,850 ft.) via Mud Brook Trail and Caribou Trail	6.9 mi.	1,950 ft.	4:25

This trail begins on ME 113 at the same parking area as Caribou Trail, 6.1 mi. north of the road to WMNF Cold River Campground, then passes over the summit of Caribou Mtn. and ends at Caribou Trail in the pass between Caribou Mtn. and Gammon Mtn. Despite the ominous name, the footing on Mud Brook Trail is generally dry and good. The eastern section of this trail is in the Caribou–Speckled Mtn. Wilderness.

From the parking area off ME 113, the trail runs generally south then turns east along the north side of Mud Brook, rising gradually. The trail crosses the brook at 1.5 mi. then recrosses it at 1.9 mi. and swings left (north) uphill, climbing more steeply. The trail crosses several smaller brooks and, at 3.0 mi., comes out on a small bare knob with excellent views east. The trail turns left into the woods and makes a short descent into a small ravine then emerges in the open, passing a short side path on the right leading to ledges with excellent views east.

The trail scrambles up to open ledges on the south summit knob, with views south and west (hikers should walk only on bare rock in the summit area to preserve fragile vegetation). The trail, which is poorly marked and requires care to follow, runs northeast across the broad, ledgy summit, descending slightly and generally keeping to the right (southeast) side of the crest. At 3.4 mi., the trail turns left up a short scramble then turns right (sign), with the open ledges of the north summit knob a few steps to the left. The trail enters the woods and descends north, passes Caribou Spring (unreliable) left at 3.6 mi., and meets Caribou Trail in the pass.

HAYSTACK NOTCH TRAIL (WMNF; MAP 5: F13–E14)

Cumulative from ME 113 (1,070 ft.) to:	⇅	⌁	⟳
Haystack Notch (1,810 ft.)	2.1 mi.	750 ft.	1:25
WMNF gate (900 ft.)	5.5 mi.	750 ft. (rev. 900 ft.)	3:05

This trail, with mostly easy grades but some potentially difficult brook crossings, runs through Haystack Notch, the pass between Haystack Mtn. and the Speckled Mtn. range. The trail is lightly used and in places requires care to follow. The middle section of this trail is in the Caribou–Speckled Mtn. Wilderness. The west trailhead is on the east side of ME 113, 4.8 mi. north of the road to WMNF Cold River Campground; roadside parking is available a short distance to the north or south.

The east trailhead is shared with the north trailhead for Miles Notch Trail. To reach this trailhead, follow Flat Rd. south from US 2 opposite the West Bethel Post Office, and at 3.2 mi., turn right (west) on Grover Hill Rd. Stay straight at 0.5 mi. from Flat Rd. on Tyler Rd. (FR 5). Paving ends at 1.0 mi., where the surface changes to a narrow but sound gravel road that was passable for most vehicles in 2016, with a rough spot at the very end that might prevent low-clearance vehicles from driving all the way to the trailhead. At 2.4 mi. the road rises steeply, bears right at a fork, descends to cross Miles Brook on a bridge, then rises again over a rough spot to a grassy clearing at 2.5 mi. with a signboard and arrow, where the road continues to the left (southwest) past a WMNF gate. (Alternative parking is available on the right side of Tyler Rd. at 2.0 mi. and 2.4 mi.) Park here and continue on foot up the road past the gate for 0.1 mi., where the road emerges in a large brushy clearing, with signs for Haystack Notch Trail and Miles Notch Trail on the right.

From the west trailhead on ME 113, the trail runs generally east along the east branch of Evans Brook, crossing the branch and its south fork then following its north fork, with three more crossings. The first crossing, in particular, may be difficult at high water. The trail enters the Wilderness Area at 1.3 mi. and climbs under the cliffs of Haystack Mtn. to the broad height-of-land in Haystack Notch at 2.1 mi. The trail then descends moderately through fine hardwood forest into the valley of the Pleasant River's West Branch, where the grade becomes easy. The trail leaves the Wilderness Area at 3.4 mi., and at 4.4 mi., after crossing a tributary brook, makes the first of three crossings of the West Branch in the next 0.4 mi., which may be difficult at high water.

Beyond the crossings, the trail rises slightly to an open brushy area at 5.2 mi. Here it makes a diagonal crossing of a small gravel road at a point where the road curves sharply. The trail is very obscure in the brush on the far side of the road; do not follow the road descending to the left. About 50 yd. after this crossing, the trail turns left onto a grassy old logging road and follows it east and then northeast along the north edge of the large clearing, with views south to Miles Notch. At 5.4 mi. it meets the northern end of Miles Notch Trail at the trail signs, 0.1 mi. southwest of the WMNF gate at the eastern trailhead. To reach the gate and trailhead, follow the logging road left (northeast).

In the reverse direction, from the trail signs in the brushy clearing, Haystack Notch Trail begins as a faint track leading to the right (west) along the north side of the clearing, to the right of the signs. Bear left at a fork 80 yd. west of the trail signs then bear right and downhill (small cairn, blaze) off the grassy logging road, 0.2 mi. from the trail signs. Cross the gravel road in 50 yd. and continue down into the woods.

ALBANY MTN. TRAIL (WMNF; MAP 5: F15–F14)

Cumulative from FR 18 (820 ft.) to:	⬆⬇	↗	◷
Spur trail to Albany Mtn. summit (1,740 ft.)	1.5 mi.	900 ft.	1:10
Albany Notch (1,500 ft.)	1.9 mi.	900 ft. (rev. 250 ft.)	1:25
Trailhead on Birch Ave. (750 ft.)	4.4 mi.	950 ft. (rev. 800 ft.)	2:40
To northeast outlook on Albany Mtn. (1,910 ft.) via Albany Mtn. Trail and Albany Mtn. Spur from:			
North trailhead (820 ft.)	1.9 mi.	1,100 ft.	1:30
South trailhead (750 ft.)	3.3 mi.	1,200 ft. (rev. 50 ft.)	2:15

This yellow-blazed trail provides access to ledges and views on Albany Mtn. from trailheads to the north and the south. Due to extensive beaver flooding north of Albany Notch, a 1.1-mi. section of Albany Notch Trail has been abandoned, and the remainder of that trail—0.6 mi. on the north end, 2.5 mi. on the south end, and a 0.4-mi. connecting path—has been combined with Albany Mtn. Trail into a single through route under the name of Albany Mtn. Trail, with Albany Mtn. Spur leading to the summit of Albany Mtn. (Trail signs for Albany Notch Trail may still be present until new signage is in place.)

The southern section, which is located partly on old, rather overgrown logging roads, is poorly marked, wet in places, and requires care to follow. Logging activity is planned for the near future, south of Albany Notch. Most use of this trail is on the northern end, which is well maintained, with many recent volunteer-built improvements, and provides the easiest access to Albany Mtn.

To reach the north trailhead, follow Flat Rd., which leads south from US 2 opposite the West Bethel Post Office and becomes FR 7 (gravel) when it enters the WMNF at 4.5 mi. At 5.8 mi., turn right on FR 18, following signs for Crocker Pond Campground. The trailhead parking lot and kiosk are on the right in another 0.6 mi. The trailhead can also be reached from ME 5, just south of Songo Pond, by turning west onto Patte Brook Rd., which becomes FR 7. At 2.8 mi., turn left onto FR 18 and follow it 0.6 mi. to the trailhead on the right. The last several miles of both of these approaches are not open to public vehicle travel in winter.

The south trailhead is reached by leaving ME 5 at the west end of Keewaydin Lake, 2.4 mi. west of the East Stoneham Post Office and 0.7 mi. east of the Lovell–Stoneham town line, and following Birch Ave. north. Bear right on Birch Ave. at 0.4 mi. from ME 5; the trail begins at a sign at 1.0 mi., where pavement ends and the road ahead becomes gravel, narrow, and rough. The beginning of the trail is in a residential area, but parking is available in a dirt lot on the right, by the end of pavement; parking is extremely limited beyond this point.

Leaving the parking lot for the north trailhead on FR 18, the trail follows an old logging road, with one relocation up to the left. At 0.4 mi. it turns left on another relocation then in 75 yd. turns right, crosses an old beaver dam, and reenters the woods. It swings left at 0.5 mi. and bears left again at 0.6 mi. toward Albany Mtn., where the abandoned section of Albany Notch Trail continues ahead. Albany Mtn. Trail now ascends moderately southwest, crosses a brook at 1.0 mi., swings left, and climbs through several turns to a signed jct. at 1.5 mi.

Here, **Albany Mtn. Spur** diverges left, soon crossing a ledge with a view of the Moriahs and Mt. Washington over the treetops. It winds upward at easy grades across ledges and through stands of red pine and reaches an open ledge with restricted northeast views near the summit of Albany Mtn. at 0.4 mi. from the main trail, where blazing ends. The best view here is found by descending 50 yd. east to ledges at the edge of the ridgecrest. The best views on the mountain are from the southwest ledges, reached by a well-defined path marked by cairns, easy to follow for experienced hikers. From the ledge where the blazed trail ends, this path leads south 100 yd.

across ledges to the true summit, marked by a larger cairn. Here the path turns right (west) and descends then swings back to the south and slabs along the west side of the ridge with minor ups and downs, crossing several ledges with views west. It ends at an open ledge with wide views south and west, 0.3 mi. from the end of the blazed trail.

At the jct. with Albany Mtn. Spur, **Albany Mtn. Trail** turns sharply right (west), rises slightly, then descends moderately for 0.4 mi. to the height-of-land in Albany Notch; partway down, the trail crosses a ledge with a view west. In the notch, the trail turns sharply left (south); in the reverse direction, be sure to make this right turn where the abandoned section of Albany Notch Trail continues ahead. Albany Mtn. Trail now descends moderately, with a steeper pitch just below the pass, and crosses two small brooks; this section may be overgrown. The trail then runs at easy grades until it reaches a logging road used as a snowmobile trail at 2.6 mi. and turns left on this road. (If ascending from the south, turn sharply right off the road onto a narrow footpath leading into the woods just before the road dips to cross a small brook; the arrow marking this turn is easily missed.)

This road is fairly easy to follow, but is very wet in places and overgrown with tall grasses and other vegetation that permit little evidence of a footway. At 3.0 mi., the trail bears right off the logging road onto an older road (arrow), which is also wet and overgrown. At 3.3 mi., the newer road rejoins from the left. The trail soon passes a WMNF gate and then merges with a gravel road that joins from the left. The trail passes a branch road on the right (in the reverse direction, bear right at this fork) and a camp on the left, crosses Meadow Brook at 3.8 mi., and climbs gradually past several private homes and camps to the trailhead on Birch Ave.

ALBANY BROOK TRAIL (WMNF; MAP 5: F15)

From Crocker Pond Campground (830 ft.) to:	⬆⬇	↗	⟳
Round Pond (790 ft.)	1.0 mi.	100 ft. (rev. 150 ft.)	0:35

This short, easy trail follows the shore of Crocker Pond and then leads to attractive, secluded Round Pond. In 2016 the WMNF began upgrading the first 0.2 mi. for universal accessibility. Logging activity is planned for the near future along parts of this trail. Albany Brook Trail begins at the turnaround at the end of FR 18, the main road at Crocker Pond Campground (do not enter the actual camping area), 0.9 mi. south of the north trailhead for Albany Mtn. Trail; see that trail description for driving directions. Leaving the west side of the turnaround, the trail descends around to the left and follows the west shore of Crocker Pond for 0.2 mi., makes a short and moderate ascent, then runs along the lower east slope of Albany Mtn. with minor ups and downs. It then descends, crosses an old logging road at 0.9 mi. with a clearing visible on the right, and soon reaches the north end of Round Pond.

SPECKLED MTN.

MILES NOTCH TRAIL (WMNF; MAP 5: F14–E14)

Cumulative from south terminus (490 ft.) to:	�199	↗	⟳
Red Rock Trail (1,740 ft.)	3.2 mi.	1,800 ft. (rev. 550 ft.)	2:30
WMNF gate (900 ft.)	5.5 mi.	1,800 ft. (rev. 850 ft.)	3:40

This yellow-blazed trail runs through Miles Notch, giving access to the east end of the long ridge that culminates in Speckled Mtn. The trail is lightly used and sparsely marked and in places requires care to follow. Future logging activity is planned on the southern 1.5 mi. To reach the trail's south terminus, leave ME 5 in North Lovell, Maine, 2.0 mi. south of Keewaydin Lake, on West Stoneham Rd. and follow that road northwest for 1.8 mi. then turn right onto Hut Rd. just before the bridge over Great Brook. Continue 1.5 mi. to the trailhead (sign), where parking is available on the left. For directions to the northern trailhead of Miles Notch Trail, see directions for the eastern trailhead of Haystack Notch Trail on p. 480.

From the south terminus, the trail climbs north on an old logging road, soon bearing left (sign: no ATVs) as a snowmobile trail bears right and downhill. At 0.3 mi., the trail bears left off the old road (arrow) then climbs over a small ridge and descends steadily northeast into the valley of Beaver Brook. At 1.2 mi., at the bottom of the descent, the trail turns left onto another old logging road and follows it 0.2 mi. then bears right off the road and soon crosses a branch of Beaver Brook. The trail climbs steadily, crosses Beaver Brook at 2.3 mi., and continues to ascend the east side of the valley through an ice-damaged area where undergrowth may obscure the footway.

The trail runs along the gully of a small brook then turns left away from the brook and reaches Miles Notch at 2.9 mi.; while ascending to the notch, you see the cliffs of Miles Knob up to the left. Just north of the notch, the trail enters the Caribou–Speckled Mtn. Wilderness. The trail now descends gradually along the east side of a ravine, and at 3.2 mi., Red Rock Trail leaves on the left for the summit of Speckled Mtn. Miles Notch Trail soon leaves the Wilderness Area and descends moderately, making six crossings of various branches of Miles Brook. The trail bears left onto a grassy logging road at 4.6 mi. (in the reverse direction, bear right off the road at an arrow) and swings left down through a clearing to cross Miles Brook at 5.0 mi. It ascends slightly across a drainage dip and past a road forking to the right then continues on the main road into the large brushy clearing (with a view of Caribou Mtn.), where the trail meets the eastern end of Haystack Notch Trail at the trail signs. Follow the logging road northeast for 0.1 mi. to reach the WMNF gate at the northern trailhead. In the reverse direction, from the trail signs in the brushy clearing 0.1 mi. southwest of the WMNF gate, Miles Notch Trail begins as a grassy, two-track road leading ahead (south) across the clearing.

BICKFORD BROOK TRAIL (CTA; MAP 5: F12–F13)

Cumulative from ME 113 (600 ft.) to:	↿⇂	↗	◔
Blueberry Ridge Trail, lower jct. (970 ft.)	0.7 mi.	350 ft.	0:30
Spruce Hill Trail (2,400 ft.)	3.1 mi.	1,800 ft.	2:25
Blueberry Ridge Trail, upper jct. (2,585 ft.)	3.8 mi.	2,000 ft.	2:55
Speckled Mtn. summit (2,906 ft.)	4.3 mi.	2,300 ft.	3:20

This trail ascends Speckled Mtn. from parking at Brickett Place (a historic brick building that serves as a WMNF visitor center during summer) on the east side of ME 113, 0.2 mi. north of the road to WMNF Cold River Campground. Most of this trail is in the Caribou–Speckled Mtn. Wilderness.

The trail enters the woods near the garage adjacent to Brickett Place. It climbs moderately then, at 0.3 mi., turns right onto an old WMNF service road built for access to the former fire tower on Speckled Mtn. and follows this road for the next 2.5 mi. The trail soon enters the Wilderness Area, and at 0.7 mi., Blueberry Ridge Trail leaves on the right (east) for the lower end of the Bickford Slides and Blueberry Mtn.; this trail rejoins Bickford Brook Trail 0.5 mi. below the summit of Speckled Mtn., affording the opportunity for a loop hike. At 1.1 mi., the upper end of Bickford Slides Loop enters on the right.

Bickford Brook Trail crosses a tributary at 1.5 mi., swings away from the main brook, and winds up a southwest spur to the crest of the main west ridge of the Speckled Mtn. range, where Spruce Hill Trail enters left at 3.1 mi. Bickford Brook Trail then passes west and north of the summit of Ames Mtn. into the col between Ames Mtn. and Speckled Mtn., where Blueberry Ridge Trail rejoins right at 3.8 mi. Bickford Brook Trail then climbs steadily to the open summit of Speckled Mtn. The trail continues 30 yd. beyond the summit to a signed jct. with Red Rock Trail (straight ahead, northeast) and Cold Brook Trail (on the right, southeast).

SEC
10

BLUEBERRY RIDGE TRAIL (CTA; MAP 5: F13)

Cumulative from Bickford Brook Trail, lower jct. (970 ft.) to:	⇅	↗	↺
Stone House Trail (1,780 ft.)	0.9 mi.	900 ft. (rev. 100 ft.)	0:55
Bickford Brook Trail, upper jct. (2,585 ft.)	3.1 mi.	1,850 ft. (rev. 150 ft.)	2:30

This trail begins and ends on Bickford Brook Trail, leaving at a sign 0.7 mi. from its trailhead at Brickett Place on ME 113 and rejoining 0.5 mi. below the summit of Speckled Mtn. (The upper part of Blueberry Ridge Trail may also be reached from Stone House Rd. via Stone House or White Cairn trails.) Blueberry Ridge Trail is in the Caribou–Speckled Mtn. Wilderness.

Leaving Bickford Brook Trail, Blueberry Ridge Trail descends toward Bickford Brook, and at 0.1 mi., a graded spur path descends 50 yd. to the right to a view of the Lower Slide from a high bank. In a short distance, the lower end of Bickford Slides Loop diverges left from the main trail, just before the latter crosses Bickford Brook. Care should be taken to avoid several unofficial side paths in this area.

Bickford Slides Loop (CTA). This side path, 0.5 mi. long, leaves Blueberry Ridge Trail on the left just before Blueberry Ridge Trail crosses Bickford Brook, 0.1 mi. from its lower jct. with Bickford Brook Trail. About 20 yd. from its beginning, Bickford Slides Loop crosses Bickford Brook (may be difficult at high water) and climbs northeast alongside it for 0.2 mi., with three minor stream crossings. The loop climbs steeply over a low rise and descends to a jct. at 0.3 mi., where a short side path descends steeply left to a pool at the base of the Middle Slide. (The former continuation of this branching path up the steep west wall of the ravine has been abandoned.) Bickford Slides Loop now climbs on a narrow, rough footway past the Middle and Upper slides then drops sharply to cross the brook above the Upper Slide. Here, the loop turns sharply left and climbs easily to Bickford Brook Trail, 0.4 mi. above that trail's lower jct. with Blueberry Ridge Trail (ascent 400 ft., rev. 50 ft., 25 min.).

From the jct. with the spur path to the Lower Slide and Bickford Slides Loop, **Blueberry Ridge Trail** crosses Bickford Brook (may be difficult at high water) and ascends steeply southeast past a good western outlook to an open area just over the crest of Blueberry Ridge, where White Cairn Trail enters right at 0.7 mi.

Overlook Loop (CTA), 0.4 mi. long, with excellent views to the south, leaves Blueberry Ridge Trail on the right shortly after this jct. It runs nearly level out to the south cliffs of Blueberry Mtn. then loops back to the north and rejoins Blueberry Ridge Trail just before the latter drops over a ledge to the jct. with Stone House Trail on the right, at 0.9 mi.

From the jct. with Stone House Trail, marked by signs and a large cairn, **Blueberry Ridge Trail** bears left and descends gradually to a col. Here it bears right and ascends northeast and then north up the long ridge at easy to moderate grades, alternating through patches of spruce woods and across ledges with fine views, where the trail is marked by cairns. The best viewpoints are passed at 1.5 mi., 1.8 mi., and 2.5 mi. After crossing one more ledgy area at 2.8 mi., the trail swings right into spruce woods, climbs slightly, then turns right and descends to meet Bickford Brook Trail in the shallow pass at the head of the Rattlesnake Brook ravine, 0.5 mi. below the summit of Speckled Mtn.

SPRUCE HILL TRAIL (WMNF/CTA; MAP 5: F13)

Cumulative from ME 113 (1,425 ft.) to:	⥮	↗	○
Bickford Brook Trail (2,400 ft.)	1.9 mi.	1,150 ft. (rev. 150 ft.)	1:30
Speckled Mtn. summit (2,906 ft.) via Bickford Brook Trail	3.1 mi.	1,650 ft.	2:25

This trail begins on the east side of ME 113, 3.2 mi. north of the road to WMNF Cold River Campground, opposite the start of East Royce Trail (where there is parking), and ascends to Bickford Brook Trail, with which Spruce Hill Trail forms the shortest route to the summit of Speckled Mtn. Most of Spruce Hill Trail is in the Caribou–Speckled Mtn. Wilderness. The trail ascends moderately through woods, passing the Wilderness boundary sign at 0.6 mi., to the wooded summit of Spruce Hill at 1.5 mi. The trail then descends into a sag and climbs to meet Bickford Brook Trail on the ridge crest west of Ames Mtn.

COLD BROOK TRAIL (WMNF; MAP 5: F14–F13)

Cumulative from Adams Rd. (485 ft.) to:	⥮	↗	○
Evergreen Link Trail (1,175 ft.)	2.7 mi.	800 ft. (rev. 100 ft.)	1:45
Speckled Mtn. summit (2,906 ft.)	4.9 mi.	2,500 ft.	3:40

SEC 10

This trail ascends Speckled Mtn. from the southeast and affords fine views from numerous open ledges in its upper part, which is in the Caribou–Speckled Mtn. Wilderness. Below the jct. with Evergreen Link Trail, Cold Brook Trail mostly follows logging roads on private land and is poorly marked. There has been extensive recent logging on parts of this section. Its trailhead is reached from ME 5 in North Lovell, Maine, 2.0 mi. south of Keewaydin Lake, by following West Stoneham Rd. for 1.9 mi. and turning right onto Adams Rd. (Evergreen Valley Inn sign), just after the bridge over

Great Brook, then continuing to the gravel-surface Enid Melrose Rd. on the right, 2.2 mi. from ME 5. The WMNF sign is on paved Adams Rd., where parking is very limited. It may be possible to drive 0.5 mi. on the rough Enid Melrose Rd. to a small parking spot on the right. The upper part of Cold Brook Trail can also be approached via Evergreen Link Trail, a shorter and much more attractive alternative to the lower section of Cold Brook Trail.

Beyond the parking area, from which hikers should proceed on foot, the road becomes rougher, and at 0.7 mi. from Adams Rd., Cold Brook Trail bears left past a gate. The next 1.0 mi. is on a road, muddy in places, that climbs then circles at a nearly level grade to a cabin (the Duncan McIntosh House). Continuing ahead on the road, take the left fork then the right. The trail descends to Cold Brook and crosses it at 1.9 mi. then crosses a logging yard, bearing right on the far side. The trail, which soon enters an area that has been extensively logged, may be difficult to follow due to diverging logging roads. It climbs moderately, crosses a branch brook, and passes west of Sugarloaf Mtn. The trail then climbs easily past the WMNF boundary at 2.5 mi. to a jct. left at 2.7 mi. with Evergreen Link Trail (sign) from Evergreen Valley.

Cold Brook Trail ascends moderately then swings left and climbs rather steeply up the southeast side of Speckled Mtn.'s south ridge. The grade eases as the trail swings more to the north and emerges on semi-open ledges at 3.5 mi.; follow cairns and blazes carefully as the trail winds over ledges and through patches of scrub. The trail crosses an open ledgy area with excellent views south, dips and passes a small pond on the left, then climbs to another open ledgy area. Above this fine viewpoint, the trail swings left across a ledgy shoulder and reenters the woods at 4.4 mi. The trail descends slightly then ascends through dense conifers. At 4.9 mi., the trail emerges on semi-open ledges again and soon reaches a signed jct. with Red Rock Trail on the right and Bickford Brook Trail on the left; the summit of Speckled Mtn. is 30 yd. left (southwest) on Bickford Brook Trail.

EVERGREEN LINK TRAIL (WMNF; MAP 5: F13)

Cumulative from upper end of gravel parking area (550 ft.) to:	⇅	↗	↻
Cold Brook Trail (1,175 ft.)	1.4 mi.	650 ft.	1:00
Speckled Mtn. summit (2,906 ft.) via Cold Brook Trail	3.6 mi.	2,350 ft.	3:00

This trail provides the easiest access to Speckled Mtn. via the scenic ledges on the upper Cold Brook Trail. Evergreen Link Trail is lightly used but easily followed by experienced hikers. To reach the trailhead, leave ME 5 in North Lovell, 2.0 mi. south of Keewaydin Lake, and follow West Stoneham Rd. northwest for 1.9 mi. Just beyond the bridge over Great Brook, turn right onto Adams Rd. (sign for Evergreen Valley) and follow it for 1.5 mi., passing the trailhead for Cold Brook Trail. Then turn right onto Mountain Rd. (sign for Evergreen Valley Inn); the trail begins as a gravel road diverging right 0.5 mi. from Adams Rd. Trailhead parking is available in a gravel parking area located a short distance along a side road to the left off Mountain Rd., 0.3 mi. from Adams Rd., or it may be possible to park at the inn (ask for permission) at 0.4 mi.

From either parking area (distances are given from the upper end of the gravel parking lot), follow paved Mtn. Rd. uphill on foot; where it bears left at 0.1 mi., take the gravel road (soon blocked by a cable) straight ahead and climb steeply. At 0.5 mi., turn left onto a grassy logging road (arrow and yellow blaze) then right onto yellow-blazed Evergreen Link Trail proper at 0.8 mi. (sign: Speckled Mtn. via Cold Brook Trail). The trail crosses a woods road at 1.1 mi. and reaches Cold Brook Trail at 1.4 mi. (sign here for Evergreen Link only); turn left for the ledges and Speckled Mtn.

RED ROCK TRAIL (WMNF; MAP 5: F14–F13)

Cumulative from Miles Notch Trail (1,740 ft.) to:	↥↧	↗	↻
Great Brook Trail (2,000 ft.)	3.4 mi.	1,100 ft. (rev. 850 ft.)	2:15
Speckled Mtn. summit (2,906 ft.)	5.6 mi.	2,200 ft. (rev. 200 ft.)	3:55

This trail ascends to Speckled Mtn. from Miles Notch Trail 0.3 mi. north of Miles Notch, 3.2 mi. from its southern trailhead and 2.3 mi. from its northern trailhead. Red Rock Trail traverses the long eastern ridge of the Speckled Mtn. range, affording fine views of the surrounding mountains. The trail is lightly used, sparsely marked, and in places requires great care to follow. This entire trail is in the Caribou–Speckled Mtn. Wilderness.

Red Rock Trail leaves Miles Notch Trail, descends to cross Miles Brook in its deep ravine, then angles up the north slope of Miles Knob and gains the ridge crest northwest of that summit. The trail descends to a col then ascends to the east knob of Red Rock Mtn., where it passes an obscure side path that leads left 50 yd. downhill to a spectacular ledge viewpoint (potentially dangerous if wet or icy) at the top of the sheer south cliff of Red Rock Mtn.; the side path leaves the trail 10 yd. east of a more obvious path that leads to a ledge with a limited view. The main trail continues to the ledgy true summit of Red Rock Mtn. at 1.2 mi., where you have a view to the north. A short distance beyond the summit, at a ledge with a view

SEC 10

southwest, the trail swings right and descends over more ledges to the Red Rock–Butters col. The trail crosses the col (avoid a beaten path leading to the right through the col) then ascends to the east knob of Butters Mtn. The trail follows the ridge, with several ups and downs, passing just south of the summit of Butters Mtn. at 2.5 mi. and then continuing on to the next sag to the west. Here, at 3.4 mi., Great Brook Trail diverges left (east) and descends southeast to its trailhead, which is very close to the southern trailhead of Miles Notch Trail. Red Rock Trail swings southwest and climbs to the summit of Durgin Mtn.—which is ledgy with some outlooks, the best located on an obscure side path to the right just before the high point—at 4.4 mi. The trail then descends easily to a notch, climbs sharply, then ascends generally southwest to the signed jct. with Cold Brook Trail (on the left) and Bickford Brook Trail (straight ahead); the latter trail leads 30 yd. southwest to the summit of Speckled Mtn. A spring is located near the trail about 0.1 mi. east of the summit.

GREAT BROOK TRAIL (WMNF; MAP 5: F14–F13)

Cumulative from trailhead on Hut Rd. (500 ft.) to:	⇅	↗	⟳
Red Rock Trail (2,000 ft.)	3.7 mi.	1,500 ft.	2:35
Speckled Mtn. summit (2,906 ft.) via Red Rock Trail	5.9 mi.	2,600 ft. (rev. 200 ft.)	4:15

This trail ascends to Red Rock Trail east of Speckled Mtn. The upper part of Great Brook Trail is in the Caribou–Speckled Mtn. Wilderness; this section is sparsely marked, requires care to follow, and has poor footing in places. To reach its trailhead, leave ME 5 in North Lovell, Maine, 2.0 mi. south of Keewaydin Lake, on West Stoneham Rd. and follow that road northwest for 1.8 mi. Turn right just before the bridge over Great Brook onto Hut Rd. (FR 4; paved then gravel) and continue 1.5 mi. to the trailhead, which is just before a gate, about 100 yd. past the southern trailhead for Miles Notch Trail. (*Note:* The WMNF plans to relocate this trailhead in the near future to the next gate on FR 4, 0.8 mi. north of the present trailhead.)

The trail follows the gravel road north past the gate, and at 0.8 mi. it passes a second gate (the location of the future trailhead, with parking available near a small cascade) and crosses Great Brook on a bridge. At times in the past, the first gate has been open, making it possible to drive to the second gate. About 80 yd. past the bridge, the trail turns right onto FR 823, an extension of FR 4. (Avoid an older road that diverges right just after the bridge and another road that continues ahead where the trail turns right.) At 1.6 mi., the older road rejoins from the right. (Bear right here on the descent.)

At a fork at 1.9 mi., the trail turns left onto a grassy older road and follows Great Brook, passing a stone wall, cellar hole, and gravesite marking the mid-1800s homestead of the Butters family on the left at 2.1 mi., just before crossing a tributary brook. The trail narrows to a footpath and, at 2.5 mi., crosses Great Brook, with some interesting cascades below and above the crossing. In another 0.1 mi. the trail enters the Wilderness Area then bears left (arrow) and climbs, steeply at times, keeping well above the brook. At the head of the valley, the trail crosses the brook twice and soon reaches the ridge crest, where Great Brook Trail meets Red Rock Trail in the col between Butters Mtn. and Durgin Mtn.

STONE HOUSE TRAIL (CTA; MAP 5: G13–F13)

From Stone House Rd.–Shell Pond Trail (615 ft.) to:	⇅	↗	↻
Blueberry Ridge Trail (1,780 ft.)	1.5 mi.	1,150 ft.	1:20

This trail ascends to the scenic ledges of Blueberry Mtn. from Stone House Rd. (formerly Shell Pond Rd.). The upper part of this trail is in the Caribou–Speckled Mtn. Wilderness. To reach the trailhead, leave NH 113 on the east side 1.3 mi. north of AMC's Cold River Camp and follow Stone House Rd. 1.1 mi. to a padlocked steel gate, where a parking area is on the right. The lower part of this trail, including Rattlesnake Flume and Rattlesnake Pool, is on private land, and hikers are requested to stay on the marked trails.

The trail leaves the road (which is also Shell Pond Trail here) on the left (north), 0.5 mi. beyond the gate, east of an open shed. Stone House Trail follows a logging road and approaches Rattlesnake Brook. At 0.2 mi. from Stone House Rd., the trail merges with a private road (descending, bear right at arrow) and immediately reaches the jct. with a spur path that leads right 30 yd. to a bridge overlooking Rattlesnake Flume, a small, attractive gorge. The main trail soon swings right (arrow), and at 0.5 mi., just after crossing a bridge over a small brook, another spur leads right 0.1 mi. to the exquisite Rattlesnake Pool, which lies at the foot of a small cascade. The main trail soon enters the WMNF, and at 1.2 mi., swings left and begins to climb rather steeply straight up the slope, running generally northwest to the top of the ridge, where the trail ends at Blueberry Ridge Trail only a few steps from the top of Blueberry Mtn. The eastern jct. with Overlook Loop is 30 yd. to the left up a ledge. For Speckled Mtn., turn right onto Blueberry Ridge Trail.

WHITE CAIRN TRAIL (CTA; MAP 5: F13)

From Stone House Rd.–Shell Pond Trail (600 ft.) to:	↻	↗	○
Blueberry Ridge Trail (1,750 ft.)	1.4 mi.	1,150 ft.	1:15

This trail, steep in places, provides access to the open ledges on Blueberry Mtn. and, with Stone House Trail, makes a rewarding half-day circuit. The upper part of White Cairn Trail is in the Caribou–Speckled Mtn. Wilderness. The trail begins on Stone House Rd. (formerly Shell Pond Rd.), which leaves NH 113 on the east side 1.3 mi. north of AMC's Cold River Camp and runs 1.1 mi. to a padlocked steel gate, where a parking area is available on the right.

The trail leaves Stone House Rd. (which is also Shell Pond Trail here) at a small clearing 0.3 mi. beyond the gate. White Cairn Trail follows an old logging road north across a flat area then ascends moderately, entering the WMNF at 0.3 mi. from Stone House Rd. At 0.8 mi., the trail climbs steeply up a well-constructed rock staircase then turns sharply left and begins to climb on ledges along the edge of the cliffs that are visible from the road. The grade moderates as the trail runs northwest along the crest of the cliffs, with excellent views to the south.

At 1.2 mi., the trail passes a spring then swings right (north) at easy grades; follow cairns carefully as the trail winds through ledgy areas. The trail passes another spring just before ending at the jct. with Blueberry Ridge Trail, 0.2 mi. west of the upper terminus of Stone House Trail. Overlook Loop, which leaves Blueberry Ridge Trail just east of its jct. with White Cairn Trail, provides a scenic alternate route, 0.4 mi. long, to Stone House Trail.

SOUTH OF SPECKLED MTN.

SHELL POND TRAIL (CTA; MAP 5: F13–G13)

From gate on Stone House Rd. (600 ft.) to:	↻	↗	○
Deer Hill Rd. (755 ft.)	1.8 mi.	150 ft.	1:00

This trail runs between Stone House Rd. (formerly Shell Pond Rd.), at the locked gate 1.1 mi. from NH 113, and Deer Hill Rd. (FR 9), 3.5 mi. from NH 113 (limited roadside parking nearby). Stone House Rd. leaves NH 113 on the east side, 1.3 mi. north of AMC's Cold River Camp. Much of this trail is on private property, and hikers are requested to stay on the marked trails, especially in the vicinity of the Stone House. The trail itself does not come within sight of the pond, but Shell Pond Loop provides access to a viewpoint on the shore.

From the gate on Stone House Rd., continue east on the road on foot. Shell Pond Loop leaves right at 0.2 mi., and in another 80 yd., White Cairn Trail leaves left. At 0.4 mi., the road emerges at the side of a large field and soon turns right onto a grassy airplane landing strip; here, at 0.5 mi., Stone House Trail diverges left, and the road ahead (not open to hikers) leads to a private house. Shell Pond Trail soon swings left and heads east across the field with good views of the surrounding mountains, passing to the right of the Stone House at 0.6 mi. The trail leaves the landing strip at 0.8 mi., entering a patch of woods to the left, and follows a grassy old road through an orchard. (The trail is not clearly marked in this area; in the reverse direction, bear left at a fork to reach the landing strip.) The trail crosses Rattlesnake Brook on a bridge at 1.1 mi., passes through a wet area, and turns left off the road at 1.2 mi., where Shell Pond Loop bears right. From here, Shell Pond Trail ascends gradually to Deer Hill Rd.

SHELL POND LOOP (CTA; MAP 5: F13–G13)

From western jct. with Shell Pond Trail (600 ft.) to:	⇅	↗	○
Eastern jct. with Shell Pond Trail (610 ft.)	1.9 mi	200 ft. (rev. 200 ft.)	1:05

This trail skirts the south side of Shell Pond, making possible a pleasant loop hike in combination with Shell Pond Trail. Shell Pond Loop is located almost entirely on private property and also serves as an ATV trail; hikers are requested to stay on the marked trail, which leaves the south side of Shell Pond Trail 0.2 mi. east of the gate on Stone House Rd. (formerly Shell Pond Rd.) and leads through woods near the edge of a field, making several turns marked by yellow blazes.

At 0.2 mi., Shell Pond Loop turns right onto a grassy road, crosses a bridge over Shell Pond Brook, and soon swings left (east) on a well-worn woods road. The trail traverses the slope well above the south shore of Shell Pond, with several minor ups and downs. At 1.3 mi., the trail turns left off the road and descends then meanders through the woods behind the east shore of the pond, crossing several small brooks. At 1.7 mi., a spur path leads 25 yd. left to a clearing and a bench with a fine view across the pond to the Baldfaces and Mt. Meader. Shell Pond Loop bears right here and continues at easy grades to Shell Pond Trail, 0.6 mi. west of the latter's eastern trailhead on Deer Hill Rd. and 1.2 mi. from the gate on Stone House Rd.

HORSESHOE POND TRAIL (CTA; MAP 5: G13)

From Deer Hill Rd. (700 ft.) to:	⇅	↗	◯
Conant Trail (1,115 ft.)	1.1 mi.	500 ft. (rev. 100 ft.)	0:50

This yellow-blazed trail starts from Deer Hill Rd. (FR 9), 4.7 mi. from NH 113 at a small pull-off at a curve in the road, and ends on Conant Trail, 0.2 mi. north of the ledges near the summit of Lord Hill. The former Horseshoe Pond Loop is now closed to public use, so there is no public trail access to the shore of this pond. From Deer Hill Rd., the trail descends moderately for 0.1 mi. past the Styles grave, which is on the right of the trail and is enclosed by a stone wall, then turns right onto a gravel logging road. The trail follows this road, keeping straight at a jct. in 100 yd. At 0.3 mi., the trail turns right onto a grassy road that leads up into a brushy area and ascends through a regenerating area. The trail continues ascending moderately to the southwest through woods to Conant Trail.

CONANT TRAIL (CTA; MAP 5: G13)

From trailhead off Deer Hill Rd. (550 ft.) for:	⇅	↗	◯
Complete loop over Pine Hill and Lord Hill on Conant Trail	5.2 mi.	1,050 ft.	3:10
Loop over Lord Hill via north branch of Conant Trail and Mine Loop	4.3 mi.	850 ft.	2:35

This loop path to Pine Hill and Lord Hill is an interesting and fairly easy walk with several good outlooks. Much of Conant Trail, especially the south loop, is on private land. This trail is frequently referred to (and may be signed as) Pine–Lord–Harndon Trail, although it does not go particularly close to the summit of Harndon Hill; this trail should not be confused with Conant Path, a short trail (not open to the public) near AMC's Cold River Camp. Conant Trail is reached by following Deer Hill Rd. (FR 9) from NH 113, 0.7 mi. south of AMC's Cold River Camp, and making a right turn onto FR 9A, 1.5 mi. from NH 113; best parking is at a four-way jct. about 100 yd. from Deer Hill Rd., where there is a sign for North Barbour Rd. There may be a trail sign here.

Continue on foot along the road that leads east (left at the four-way jct.), soon descending to the dike across swampy Colton Brook. Beyond the dike, the yellow-blazed trail continues on a gravel road to the loop jct. at 0.4 mi., where the path divides. From here, the trail is described in a counterclockwise direction. The south branch, also a snowmobile route, turns right and follows a logging road (Hemp Hill Rd.). At 0.7 mi., the trail reaches a road section that leads through an area of beaver activity that had been flooded but was once again dry and passable in 2016. Beyond, the road climbs to a level spot at 1.0 mi. near the old Johnson cellar hole. Here the trail turns left on a logging road then left again in a few steps.

Conant Trail swings right and then left again at 1.2 mi. and ascends Pine Hill, rather steeply at times, passing a ledge with a fine view west at 1.4 mi. Here the trail turns right and climbs to the west end of the summit ridge and continues to the most easterly knob, which has a good view north, at 2.0 mi. The trail swings left off the ledges and zigzags steeply down through hemlock forest. The trail crosses Bradley Brook at 2.3 mi. and then quickly crosses a logging road that can be followed 0.2 mi. left to Mine Loop Trail, 0.4 mi. below the mine on Lord Hill. Conant Trail then climbs moderately to an outlook over Horseshoe Pond. Here, the trail turns left and climbs ledges to a jct. near the summit of Lord Hill at 3.0 mi., where Mine Loop leaves on the left.

Mine Loop. This path is 1.0 mi. long, 0.1 mi. shorter than the section of Conant Trail it bypasses. Except for the one critical turn mentioned later, Mine Loop is fairly easy to follow. From the jct. with Conant Trail near the summit of Lord Hill, Mine Loop climbs briefly to the ledge at the top of the old mica mine, swings left and quickly right onto a woods road, descends for 40 yd., and turns left at 0.1 mi., where a spur path leads right 30 yd. to the mine. The trail soon swings right, and at 0.3 mi., turns sharply left on a clear logging road. At 0.5 mi., the trail reaches a fork and turns sharply right back onto a less-used branch road (sign)—a turn that is easily missed. (The main road, continuing straight at this fork, crosses Conant Trail between Pine Hill and Lord Hill in 0.2 mi. and continues south toward Kezar Lake.) Mine Loop descends to a flat area and climbs easily over a shoulder. At a clearing, the trail leaves the road on the right and descends 50 yd. to rejoin Conant Trail 1.1 mi. from its trailhead (ascent 100 ft., rev. 250 ft., 35 min.).

From Lord Hill, **Conant Trail** descends, with one tricky drop over a ledge, to the jct. with Horseshoe Pond Trail on the right at 3.2 mi. Here, the trail bears left then soon turns left again through a gap in a stone wall and runs at a fairly level grade, with minor ups and downs, along the south side of Harndon Hill. The trail passes a cellar hole, and Mine Loop rejoins on the left at 4.1 mi. At 4.5 mi., the road passes a gate, becomes wider (in the reverse direction, avoid logging roads branching to the right), passes a cemetery on the right, reaches the loop jct., and continues straight ahead across the dike to the trailhead.

SEC 10

DEER HILLS TRAIL (CTA; MAP 5: G12–G13)

Cumulative from ME 113 at
Baldface Circle Trail parking area (500 ft.)
via Deer Hills Connector to:

	⇅	↗	↺
Little Deer Hill summit (1,090 ft.)	1.3 mi.	650 ft. (rev. 50 ft.)	1:00
Big Deer Hill summit (1,367 ft.)	2.0 mi.	1,100 ft. (rev. 200 ft.)	1:35
Deer Hills Bypass, eastern jct. (1,025 ft.)	2.5 mi.	1,100 ft. (rev. 350 ft.)	1:50
Deer Hill Rd. (530 ft.)	3.3 mi.	1,100 ft. (rev. 500 ft.)	2:10

This trail ascends Little Deer Hill and Big Deer Hill, providing a relatively easy trip that offers interesting views. The trail runs from a jct. by the Cold River, near AMC's Cold River Camp, to Deer Hill Rd. (FR 9), 1.4 mi. from NH 113, where roadside parking is limited.

Deer Hills Connector. Access to the north end of the trail is from the Baldface Circle Trail (Section 9) trailhead parking area on the east side of NH 113 (0.1 mi. north of the entrance to Cold River Camp) via a yellow-blazed path called Deer Hills Connector.

Deer Hills Connector (yellow blaze, no sign in 2016) leaves the east side of the lot, runs level for 150 yd., then turns left down a short pitch and descends gradually on the south side of Charles Brook, in an area where the trail was eroded by the 2011 storm. Deer Hills Connector passes an unmarked private path on the right at 0.3 mi. and reaches a dam on the Cold River at 0.4 mi. Here, a trail from AMC's camp enters on the right (this trail is not open to the public). At this jct., Deer Hills Trail begins; distances given here include those traveled on Deer Hills Connector.

Deer Hills Trail crosses Cold River on the dam abutments (may be difficult in high water). (In the reverse direction, after crossing the dam, turn right onto Deer Hills Connector at the sign: Baldface Parking Lot.) The trail soon passes the jct. on the left with Leach Link Trail, crosses the state line into Maine, and quickly passes the jct. on the right with Deer Hills Bypass. Deer Hills Trail continues straight ahead and climbs moderately past an outlook west then bears left onto ledges and reaches the open summit of Little Deer Hill at 1.3 mi., where there is a fine view of the Baldfaces. Here, Frost Trail enters on the right, having ascended from Deer Hills Bypass.

Deer Hills Trail descends into a sag then climbs to a point near the summit of Big Deer Hill at 2.0 mi. Here, the trail turns right, descends 40 yd., and turns right again where there is a fine eastern outlook 20 yd. to the left. The trail then descends the south ridge, passing another outlook, and turns left at 2.5 mi., where Deer Hills Bypass leaves on the right. Soon Deer Hills Trail turns left again then turns right onto an old logging road at 2.7 mi. Here, a spur path (sign) follows the logging road left for 20 yd. then turns right and descends in 0.2 mi. and 150 ft. to Deer Hill Spring, a shallow pool with air bubbles rising through a small area of light-colored sand. The main trail descends south from the jct. to Deer Hill Rd.

DEER HILLS BYPASS (CTA; MAP 5: G12–G13)

From western jct. with Deer Hills Trail (460 ft.) to:	⇅	↗	↻
Eastern jct. with Deer Hills Trail (1,025 ft.)	1.4 mi.	650 ft. (rev 100 ft.)	1:00

This trail skirts the south slopes of the Deer Hills, making possible various loop hikes over the summits. The trail leaves Deer Hills Trail on the right (southeast) just east of Cold River Dam and follows a level grassy road along the river. At 0.4 mi., Deer Hills Bypass turns left off the road and soon ascends a steep ledge with a view west. The trail swings left, and at 0.6 mi., Ledges Trail leaves left, and Deer Hills Bypass climbs steadily alongside a stone wall. At 0.8 mi., Frost Trail leaves left, climbing 0.15 mi. and 150 ft. to the summit of Little Deer Hill, passing a jct. left with Ledges Trail 70 yd. before the summit. Deer Hills Bypass descends into a shallow ravine, crossing two small brooks, and ascends again. The trail soon turns left onto a woods road, follows it for 0.1 mi., then turns left off it (both turns are marked with signs and arrows). The trail then ascends easily to rejoin Deer Hills Trail on the south ridge of Big Deer Hill, 0.5 mi. below the summit.

LEDGES TRAIL (CTA; MAP 5: G12)

From Deer Hills Bypass (730 ft.) to:	⇅	↗	↻
Little Deer Hill summit (1,090 ft.)	0.3 mi.	350 ft.	0:20

This trail passes interesting ledges and a cave but is very steep and rough, dangerous in wet or icy conditions, lightly used, and not recommended for descent. The trail diverges left from Deer Hills Bypass, 0.6 mi. from the Cold River Dam, and climbs steeply with several outlooks. At 0.2 mi., Ledges Trail divides; the left branch (sign: Ledges Direct) ascends through a small cave, and the slightly longer right branch (sign: By-Pass) loops out through the woods then swings left across an excellent outlook ledge and rejoins the left branch in about 140 yd. About 40 yd. above the point where these branches rejoin, Ledges Trail meets Frost Trail, a connecting path from Deer Hills Bypass. The summit of Little Deer Hill is 70 yd. left on Frost Trail.

SEC 10

LEACH LINK TRAIL (CTA; MAP 5: F12–G12)

From Stone House Rd. (540 ft.) to:	↑↓	↗	↻
Deer Hills Trail (450 ft.)	1.2 mi.	0 ft. (rev. 100 ft.)	0:35

This trail gives access to Little Deer Hill and Big Deer Hill from Stone House Rd. (formerly Shell Pond Rd.), which leaves NH 113 on the east side, 1.3 mi. north of AMC's Cold River Camp. The trail starts at a gated road on the right side of Stone House Rd. 0.3 mi. from NH 113; roadside parking is available. The northern part of the trail uses the former Shell Pond Brook Trail.

Beyond the gate, Leach Link Trail follows a grassy road across a snowmobile bridge over Shell Pond Brook. At 0.2 mi., the trail turns right off the road (sign) then in another 50 yd. bears left and runs through hemlock woods along a bank high above the brook. The trail then descends, and at 0.5 mi., turns left where the former route of the trail came across the brook from the right. The trail continues south along the Cold River at easy grades and ends at Deer Hills Trail a few steps east of Cold River Dam. To ascend the Deer Hills, turn left onto Deer Hills Trail.

SECTION ELEVEN
MAHOOSUC RANGE AREA

Map 6: North Country–Mahoosuc Range

INTRODUCTION

This section includes the region along the Maine–New Hampshire border that lies east and north of the Androscoggin River, which runs south from Lake Umbagog near Errol to Gorham then swings east from Gorham to Bethel, Maine. The region is bounded by NH 16 on the west, by US 2 on the south, and by ME/NH 26 on the northeast. The backbone of the region is the Mahoosuc Range, which rises from the east bank of the river above Berlin and Gorham, runs east at first, then gradually swings toward the north as the range continues to its far end at Grafton Notch. This section covers the main Mahoosuc Range and all the trails on it. The most important peaks in the Mahoosuc Range (listed north to south) are Old Speck Mtn., Mahoosuc Arm, Fulling Mill Mtn., Goose Eye Mtn., Mt. Carlo, Mt. Success, Bald Cap Mtn., Cascade Mtn., and Mt. Hayes. The region is completely covered by AMC's *White Mountains Trail Map 6: North Country–Mahoosuc Range*.

The Mahoosuc Range has a mix of public and private land ownership. Some of the private timberland on the lower western and southern slopes of the range has been intensively managed for timber, and hikers can expect to see evidence of timber harvest along the trails in these areas. In 2010, as part of the Mahoosuc Initiative (in which AMC has been a partner since its inception in 2005), a 4,777-acre parcel of private timberland on the western slopes was acquired through the Forest Legacy program and is now part of the AT corridor, managed by the WMNF. This ensures continued access to several trails that lead onto the range. More recently 300 acres around Bald Cap Peak were added to the AT corridor. Additional lands on the southern slopes of the Mahoosucs are under conservation easement. The MBPL manages more than 19,000 acres in the Mahoosuc Public Reserved Lands on the Maine side of the range, including the 9,993-acre Carlo–Speck Ecological Reserve. The MBPL also holds easements on an additional 10,000 acres to the south and east. At the northeast end of the range is Maine's 3,191-acre Grafton Notch State Park, which includes the northern slopes of Old Speck Mtn.

In this section, the AT begins at the trailhead of Rattle River Trail (Section Nine) on US 2. The AT follows the highway west 0.2 mi. to North Rd., follows North Rd. for 0.5 mi. (crossing the Androscoggin River), and turns left onto Hogan Rd. for 0.2 mi. to Centennial Trail. The AT then follows Centennial Trail, Mahoosuc Trail, and Old Speck Trail to Grafton Notch, the eastern boundary of the area covered in this guide; Baldpate Mtn. Trail (see AMC's *Maine Mountain Guide*) continues the AT on the opposite side of Grafton Notch. In its course through the Mahoosucs, the AT crosses the summits of Cascade Mtn., Mt. Success, and

Mt. Carlo and passes near the summits of Mt. Hayes, Goose Eye Mtn., Fulling Mill Mtn., Mahoosuc Arm, and Old Speck Mtn.

ROAD ACCESS

Success Pond Rd. is a gravel main-haul logging road, sound but rough in places, that runs north from Hutchins St. on the east side of the Androscoggin River in Berlin, New Hampshire. In 5.4 mi., the road passes the first of four trailheads leading onto the Mahoosuc Range. The road bears right at a fork at 11.4 mi., passes the last trailhead at 12.2 mi. from Hutchins St., and continues to another road fork at 17.6 mi. The right fork, York Pond Rd., formerly continued to ME 26; however, this section of road is now permanently closed. Access to ME 26 is provided by the left fork, North Rd., which continues 4.0 mi. to reach ME 26, 4.9 mi. north of the Old Speck Trail trailhead.

To find Success Pond Rd., leave NH 16 just south of the city of Berlin, 4.5 mi. north of its eastern jct. with US 2 in Gorham, and follow Unity St. across the Androscoggin River on the Cleveland Bridge. At the east end of the bridge, Unity St. swings left and passes through a set of traffic lights in 0.7 mi. from NH 16. At 0.8 mi., the road bears right across railroad tracks, and at 0.9 mi., it bears left and becomes Hutchins St. It bears left again at 1.6 mi. and at 1.9 mi., where there are signs on the left reading, "Success Pond Rd." and "OHRV Parking 1 Mile," Success Pond Rd. begins on the right (east). The first part of the road may be difficult to distinguish from branch roads. At 0.5 mi. from Hutchins St., the road bears left under a power line, and at 1.0 mi., it passes parking for Success ATV Trail on the right.

Once past this area, the road is well defined, although it is often easy to take a dead-end branch road by mistake. (*Caution:* This road passes through an area of active logging, so drivers must be prepared to yield to large and fast-moving logging trucks; it is not always easy to find a place to get out of the way quickly.) The road is not generally open to public vehicular use in winter and early spring, and it can be very rough and muddy after heavy rains. Trailheads are marked only with small road signs and, in some cases, AMC's small standard trail signs, often at diverging logging roads with no well-defined parking area, so one must look for them carefully. The lower parts of the trails originating on this road have been disrupted frequently in the past by construction of new logging roads; great care is necessary to follow the blazes that mark the proper roads, ascending or descending.

North Rd. in Shelburne, New Hampshire (not to be confused with the North Rd. described earlier that runs from ME 26 to Success Pond Rd.), provides access to the trails on the south side of the Mahoosuc Range. This road leaves US 2, 3.4 mi. east of its easterly jct. with NH 16 in Gorham, and

SEC 11

crosses the Androscoggin River on the Lead Mine Bridge; the AT follows this part of the road. North Rd. then swings east and runs along the north side of the river to rejoin US 2 just north of Bethel, Maine. Bridges connect North Rd. with US 2 at the villages of Shelburne, New Hampshire, and Gilead, Maine.

Trails on the eastern side of the range are reached from ME 26 and, in the case of Wright Trail, via Sunday River Rd. and Bull Branch Rd. off US 2.

GEOGRAPHY

The southern part of the Mahoosuc Range is a broad, ledgy, lumpy ridge, with numerous spurs extending south toward the Androscoggin valley. The main peaks, from west to east, are Mt. Hayes (2,555 ft.), Cascade Mtn. (2,631 ft.), Bald Cap (3,065 ft.), and Bald Cap's two subsidiary peaks, Bald Cap Peak (2,795 ft.) and North Bald Cap (2,893 ft.); the summits of all three Bald Cap peaks are trailless, although the ledges of Bald Cap Peak are now accessed by a spur trail. The northern part of the range is taller and narrower, with a well-defined ridge crest and two long subsidiary ridges running southeast toward the Androscoggin and Bear rivers; the Sunday River flows between these subsidiary ridges. The main peaks, from southwest to northeast, are Mt. Success (3,565 ft.), Mt. Carlo (3,565 ft.), the three peaks of Goose Eye Mtn. (West Peak, the highest at 3,870 ft.; East Peak, 3,790 ft.; and North Peak, 3,675 ft.), Fulling Mill Mtn. (trailless North Peak, 3,450 ft., and South Peak, 3,395 ft.), trailless Mahoosuc Mtn. (3,470 ft.), Mahoosuc Arm (3,765 ft.), and Old Speck Mtn. (4,170 ft.). Old Speck is the third-highest mountain in Maine; its name distinguishes Old Speck from the several other Speckled mtns.—so called for their scattered open ledges—in the general area. Mt. Success is named for the unincorporated township in which it is located, and Mt. Carlo is named for a dog, the faithful companion of Eugene B. Cook. Cook was a pioneer White Mountains trail builder who made several early explorations of the Mahoosuc area, often accompanied by Lucia and Marian Pychowska; all three were prominent early members of AMC. The origin of Goose Eye Mtn.'s peculiar name is in doubt; the most plausible explanation maintains that Canada geese in their flight south from the Rangeley Lakes appear almost to graze its summit, and it is, therefore, "goose high."

The views from Goose Eye, a striking rock peak, are among the best in the White Mountains, and most of the other peaks have fine views, either from the summits or from the numerous open ledges scattered throughout the range. There are several fine mountain ponds, including Speck Pond (one of the highest ponds in Maine), Gentian Pond, Moss Pond, Dream Lake, and Page Pond. The most remarkable feature of the range is Mahoosuc Notch, where the trail winds around and under huge fragments of rock that have fallen from the cliffs of Mahoosuc Mtn. to the northwest; Fulling Mill Mtn. forms the southeast wall.

A range of peaks that extends southeast from Old Speck Mtn. is accessible by the western section of Grafton Loop Trail. The most prominent of these are wooded, trailless Slide Mtn. (3,250 ft.) and the spectacular open ledgy peak of Sunday River Whitecap (3,335 ft.), which is traversed by the trail. These two peaks are separated by Miles Notch. Extending southeast from Sunday River Whitecap are Stowe Mtn. (2,730 ft.) and Bald Mtn. (2,085 ft.); Grafton Loop Trail crosses both of these lower, mostly viewless peaks.

From the major peaks of the southern part of the range, ridges run toward the Androscoggin River, bearing interesting smaller peaks. Among these mountains are Middle Mtn. (2,010 ft.), Mt. Crag (1,412 ft.), Mt. Ingalls (2,242 ft.), Mt. Cabot (1,512 ft.), and Crow's Nest (1,287 ft.). All of these peaks are reached by trails; in recent years, the Shelburne Trails Club (STC) has been active in trail maintenance in this area, and members have restored several formerly abandoned routes and opened several new connecting paths. In 2016 STC published a map of these trails and others in the Shelburne area created by AMC cartographer Larry Garland. In addition to the trails described below, STC maintains Bill Hastings Memorial Trail, named for a longtime New Hampshire Fish and Game Conservation Officer, in Shelburne's William Hastings Memorial Forest. The trail starts at a sign on the north side of US 2, just west of the New Hampshire/Maine state line; parking is available at a road entrance across the highway. After crossing railroad tracks (use caution), the trail makes a loop along the bank of the Androsocggin River, returning though an unusual floodplain forest. The distance for the complete loop is 0.5 mi.

Two notable waterfalls are located on the south side of the range. Dryad Fall is reached by Dryad Fall Trail; the name was given by the pioneer explorer and path maker Eugene Cook, an incurable punster, referring to the fact that unless it has rained recently, the falls are fairly dry. Giant Falls is accessible by a spur path off Peabody Brook Trail. Lary Flume, located east of Austin Brook Trail, is a wild chasm that resembles the Ice Gulch and Devils Hopyard (Section Twelve), with many boulder caves and one fissure cave but no trail.

CAMPING

The WMNF manages the AT corridor along the New Hampshire section of the range and also manages a newly acquired parcel on the western slopes in New Hampshire. Along the New Hampshire section, camping is allowed within the AT corridor except within 0.25 mi. of shelters and designated campsites; fires are allowed only at shelters and at designated

SEC 11

campsites. Most of the Maine portion of the Mahoosuc Range (except for Old Speck Mtn., which is in Grafton Notch State Park), including the ridge crest, the upper part of the western slopes, and much of the land to the east, is within the state-owned Mahoosuc Public Reserved Lands. In this area, camping is not allowed above treeline, and fires are permitted only at shelters and designated sites (fires are not permitted at campsites located on private lands along Grafton Loop Trail). Below treeline, back-country camping is allowed, but fires are not. No camping is allowed in Grafton Notch State Park. Along Grafton Loop Trail, much of which is located on private land, camping is allowed only at designated sites. To reduce overcrowding, during peak summer and fall periods, groups of six or more planning to use AMC-managed backcountry campsites are required to use AMC's group notification system. For more information, visit outdoors.org/group_notification. In areas located on private land, camping is not allowed without advance permission from the landowner.

Trident Col Tentsite (AMC) is located on a side path from Mahoosuc Trail in Trident Col and has four tent pads. Water is available about 50 yd. below (west of) the site.

Gentian Pond Campsite (AMC) on Gentian Pond is located on Austin Brook Trail 0.1 mi. from Mahoosuc Trail and has a shelter and four tent platforms. Water is available from a small brook on the southbound Mahoosuc Trail, a short distance north of the jct. with Austin Brook Trail.

Carlo Col Campsite (AMC), consisting of a shelter and five tent platforms, is located on a spur trail from Carlo Col Trail, 0.2 mi. below Mahoosuc Trail at Carlo Col. Water is found in a small brook along the spur trail.

Full Goose Campsite (AMC), consisting of a shelter and four tent plat-forms, is located on Mahoosuc Trail between Fulling Mill Mtn. and Goose Eye Mtn. A spring is located 80 yd. east of the shelter.

Speck Pond Campsite (AMC), located at Speck Pond just off Mahoosuc Trail, includes a shelter (rebuilt in 2016–17) and six tent platforms. In summer, there is a caretaker, and a fee is charged. Water is available along a blue-blazed trail behind the caretaker's site.

Bald Mtn. Tentsite (AMC), with two tent platforms, is located on a short side path from Grafton Loop Trail on the east side of Bald Mtn. Water is found in a brook along the spur path to the tentsite.

Sargent Brook Tentsite (AMC), with three tent pads, is located on a side path from Grafton Loop Trail south of Sunday River Whitecap. Water is found in a brook along the side path.

Slide Mtn. Tentsite (AMC), with three tent pads, is located on a side path from Grafton Loop Trail on the west side of Slide Mtn. The water source is a brook on the main trail near the spur path jct.

Bull Run Tentsite (AMC), with two tent platforms, is located on a side path from Grafton Loop Trail southeast of Old Speck Mtn. Water is available from a brook along the side path.

SUGGESTED HIKES

■ Easy Hikes
MT. CRAG

RT via Austin Brook and Yellow trails	2.4 mi.	700 ft.	1:35

This small peak has excellent views over the Androscoggin valley. See Austin Brook Trail, p. 526.

GIANT FALLS

RT via Peabody Book Trail and spur path	3.0 mi.	950 ft.	2:00

This is an easy hike to a high waterfall. See Peabody Brook Trail, p. 525.

■ Moderate Hikes
EYEBROW LOOP

LP via Eyebrow and Old Speck trails	2.4 mi.	1,050 ft.	1:45

This loop features some steep climbing and fine views of Grafton Notch. See Eyebrow Trail, p. 519.

MIDDLE MTN.

RT via Gates Brook and Middle Mtn. trails	3.2 mi.	1,250 ft.	2:15

A pleasant climb from North Rd., fairly steep near the top, leads up a small mountain with interesting views. To begin, see Gates Brook Trail, p. 530.

MT. SUCCESS

RT via Success and Mahoosuc trails	6.2 mi.	1,950 ft.	4:05

A trip to this open summit must include the side loop to the beautiful, unusual outlook on the way up. See Success Trail, p. 514.

SEC 11

BALD CAP PEAK LEDGES

	⇅	↗	○
RT via Peabody Brook and Bald Cap Peak Ledges trails	6.2 mi.	2,150 ft.	4:10
RT via Peabody Brook and Bald Cap Peak Ledges trails and Giant Falls spur path	6.8 mi.	2,400 ft.	4:35

This spectacular viewpoint gets even better with the addition of a side trip to Giant Falls. To begin, see Peabody Brook Trail, p. 525.

MT. HAYES

	⇅	↗	○
RT via Centennial and Mahoosuc trails	7.2 mi.	2,200 ft.	4:40

This low, ledgy mountain provides wide views of the Gorham region and the Presidentials; use a short section of Mahoosuc Trail to reach the open ledges at the southwest end of the flat summit. See Centennial Trail, p. 524.

■ Strenuous Hikes

GOOSE EYE MTN.

	⇅	↗	○
LP via Goose Eye, Mahoosuc, and Carlo Col trails	7.6 mi.	2,750 ft.	5:10
RT via Wright and Mahoosuc trails	9.6 mi.	3,050 ft.	6:20

The first route, a rewarding loop over the two open peaks of Goose Eye Mtn. and Mt. Carlo, has some very steep spots (to begin, see Goose Eye Trail, p. 516). The second—and very scenic—route approaches Goose Eye Mtn. from the east (see Wright Trail, p. 523).

OLD SPECK MTN.

	⇅	↗	○
RT via Old Speck and Mahoosuc trails	7.6 mi.	3,000 ft.	5:20

A moderately steep route ascends to observation-tower views from Maine's third-highest peak. See Old Speck Trail, p. 518

SEC 11

MAHOOSUC PONDS

	⇅	↗	○
LP via Austin Brook, Dryad Fall, Peabody Brook, Mahoosuc, and Austin Brook trails	9.8 mi.	2,100 ft.	5:55
LP to Mahoosuc Ponds and Bald Cap Peak Ledges via trails named above plus Bald Cap Peak Ledges Trail	11.6 mi.	2,400 ft.	7:00

The first route visits Dryad Fall and three high-mountain ponds: Dream Lake, Moss Pond, and Gentian Pond. The second route adds the fine view ledges of Bald Cap Peak as an out-and-back side trip. To begin either, see Austin Brook Trail, p. 526.

TRAIL DESCRIPTIONS
MAHOOSUC RANGE CREST
MAHOOSUC TRAIL (AMC; MAP 6: E10–C13)

Cumulative from Hogan Rd. (820 ft.) to:	⮃	↗	⏱
Mt. Hayes summit (2,555 ft.)	2.5 mi.	1,750 ft.	2:10
Centennial Trail (2,550 ft.)	2.7 mi.	1,750 ft.	2:15
Cascade Mtn. summit (2,631 ft.)	4.5 mi.	2,450 ft.	3:30
Trident Col (2,030 ft.)	5.7 mi.	2,550 ft.	4:05
Page Pond (2,220 ft.)	6.7 mi.	2,950 ft.	4:50
Wocket Ledge viewpoint (2,700 ft.)	7.3 mi.	3,450 ft.	5:20
Dream Lake, inlet brook crossing (2,620 ft.)	8.4 mi.	3,750 ft.	6:05
Austin Brook Trail (2,160 ft.)	10.5 mi.	3,950 ft.	7:15
Mt. Success summit (3,565 ft.)	13.3 mi.	5,850 ft.	9:35
Success Trail (3,170 ft.)	13.9 mi.	5,850 ft.	9:55
Carlo Col Trail (3,170 ft.)	15.7 mi.	6,450 ft.	11:05
Mt. Carlo (3,565 ft.)	16.1 mi.	6,850 ft.	11:30
Goose Eye Trail (3,800 ft.)	17.5 mi.	7,550 ft.	12:30
Wright Trail (3,630 ft.)	17.8 mi.	7,550 ft.	12:40
Goose Eye Mtn., East Peak (3,790 ft.)	17.9 mi.	7,700 ft.	12:50
Goose Eye Mtn., North Peak (3,675 ft.)	19.1 mi.	8,000 ft.	13:35
Full Goose Campsite (2,950 ft.)	20.1 mi.	8,000 ft.	14:05
Notch Trail (2,460 ft.)	21.6 mi.	8,450 ft.	15:00
Foot of Mahoosuc Notch (2,150 ft.)	22.7 mi.	8,450 ft.	15:35
Mahoosuc Arm summit (3,770 ft.)	24.3 mi.	10,150 ft.	17:15
Speck Pond Campsite (3,400 ft.)	25.2 mi.	10,150 ft.	17:40
Old Speck Trail jct. (4,030 ft.)	26.3 mi.	11,000 ft.	18:40
Old Speck Mtn. summit (4,170 ft.)	26.6 mi.	11,150 ft.	18:55

SEC 11

MAHOOSUC TRAIL, IN REVERSE (AMC; MAP 6: E10–C13)

Cumulative from Old Speck Mtn. summit (4,170 ft.) to:	⇅	↗	○
Old Speck Trail jct. (4,030 ft.)	0.3 mi.	0 ft.	0:10
Speck Pond Campsite (3,400 ft.)	1.4 mi.	200 ft.	0:50
Mahoosuc Arm summit (3,770 ft.)	2.3 mi.	600 ft.	1:25
Foot of Mahoosuc Notch (2,150 ft.)	3.9 mi.	700 ft.	2:15
Notch Trail (2,460 ft.)	5.0 mi.	1,000 ft.	3:00
Full Goose Campsite (2,950 ft.)	6.5 mi.	1,950 ft.	4:15
Goose Eye Mtn., North Peak (3,675 ft.)	7.5 mi.	2,650 ft.	5:05
Goose Eye Mtn., East Peak (3,790 ft.)	8.7 mi.	3,050 ft.	5:55
Wright Trail (3,630 ft.)	8.8 mi.	3,050 ft.	5:55
Goose Eye Trail (3,800 ft.)	9.1 mi.	3,200 ft.	6:10
Mt. Carlo (3,565 ft.)	10.5 mi.	3,700 ft.	7:05
Carlo Col Trail (3,170 ft.)	10.9 mi.	3,700 ft.	7:20
Success Trail (3,170 ft.)	12.7 mi.	4,300 ft.	8:30
Mt. Success summit (3,565 ft.)	13.3 mi.	4,700 ft.	9:00
Austin Brook Trail (2,160 ft.)	16.1 mi.	5,200 ft.	10:40
Dream Lake, inlet brook crossing (2,620 ft.)	18.2 mi.	5,850 ft.	12:00
Wocket Ledge viewpoint (2,700 ft.)	19.3 mi.	6,250 ft.	12:45
Page Pond (2,220 ft.)	19.9 mi.	6,250 ft.	13:05
Trident Col (2,030 ft.)	20.9 mi.	6,450 ft.	13:40
Cascade Mtn. summit (2,631 ft.)	22.1 mi.	7,150 ft.	14:35
Centennial Trail (2,550 ft.)	23.9 mi.	7,800 ft.	15:50
Mt. Hayes summit (2,555 ft.)	24.1 mi.	7,800 ft.	15:55
Hogan Rd. (820 ft.)	26.6 mi.	7,800 ft.	17:10

This trail extends along the entire length of the Mahoosuc Range from Gorham, New Hampshire, to the summit of Old Speck. Beyond its jct. with Centennial Trail, Mahoosuc Trail is a link in the AT. (See above for camping options and p. xxii for trailside camping regulations.) Water is scarce, particularly in dry weather, and its purity is always in question. Do not be deceived by the relatively low elevations; this trail is among the most rugged of its kind in the White Mountains, a very strenuous trail—particularly for those with heavy packs—with numerous minor humps and cols, and many ledges, some of them quite steep, that are likely to be slippery when wet.

Many parts of the trail may require significantly more time than that provided by the formula, particularly for backpackers, and Mahoosuc Notch may require several extra hours, depending partly on how much time one spends enjoying the spectacular scenery. Mahoosuc Notch is regarded by many who have hiked the entire length of the AT as the trail's most difficult mile. (*Caution:* Mahoosuc Notch can be hazardous in wet or icy conditions and can remain impassable due to unmelted snowdrifts through the end of May and perhaps even longer. Some sections of the ridge, especially the one traversing Goose Eye Mtn., have significant weather exposure.)

Part I: Gorham to Centennial Trail

Mahoosuc Trail begins on the east side of Hogan Rd. in Gorham, 0.1 mi. north of a powerhouse and dam (sign: Gorham Hydro Station) on a canal next to the Androscoggin River. To reach this trailhead by car, follow North Rd. north from US 2 in Shelburne and in 0.5 mi., just north of the bridge over the Androscoggin River, turn left (west) onto Hogan Rd. This gravel road, very rough in places and slow going but sound, passes the trailhead for Centennial Trail at 0.2 mi. from North Rd. and follows the river southwest then west. Bear left at 1.3 mi. and again at 2.4 mi., beyond which the road narrows and becomes rougher. At 4.5 mi., after the road has swung to the northwest, park on the right, opposite the Gorham Hydro Station; do not park next to the station. Proceed north up the road on foot for 0.1 mi. to the start of the trail (sign) on the right; mileages are given from the parking area.

Note: The south end of Mahoosuc Trail can also be reached on foot across private land from a parking area on NH 16 in Gorham, thus avoiding the long and tedious drive up Hogan Rd. Follow signs carefully, as there is a network of potentially confusing Coos Cycling Club mountain bike trails in the area. From the western jct. of NH 16 and US 2 in Gorham, drive north on NH 16 for 0.3 mi. to a parking area on the right, on the north side of the old railroad bridge. Cross the Androscoggin River on the pedestrian walkway on the lower level of the bridge; watch for low head clearance on both ends of the bridge. On the east bank, turn sharply left (AMC trail sign) onto a dirt road and follow it northeast, bearing right at a fork to meet Presidential Rail Trail at 0.3 mi. from NH 16. Turn left onto the rail trail (AMC trail sign) and follow it across a bridge over the canal. On the far side of the bridge, just before a gate, turn right onto a trail (blue blaze and small sign: Mahoosuc Hiking Trail Detour) into the woods.

SEC 11

Ascend this trail past a jct. with Undermine mountain bike trail on the right to a dirt road (an extension of Hogan Rd.) at 0.6 mi. Turn right onto this road and follow it to the point where Mahoosuc Trail diverges sharply left from Hogan Rd. at 1.1 mi. from NH 16.

From Hogan Rd., Mahoosuc Trail enters the woods and climbs moderately, crosses a power-line clearing at 0.2 mi., then follows a brook for 100 yd. The trail ascends at only a slight grade to a side path at 0.5 mi. that leads right 0.2 mi. to Mascot Pond, which lies just below Leadmine Ledge, the cliffs seen prominently from Gorham. Mahoosuc Trail bears left and climbs moderately, crosses a gravel road at 1.0 mi., then ascends gradually along the valley of a small brook, which the trail crosses several times. It then swings right and ascends steadily, passing a short spur (sign) at 1.9 mi. that leads left to Popsy Spring. The trail climbs steeply and emerges on the southwest side of the flat, ledgy summit of Mt. Hayes at 2.2 mi. An unmarked spur leads a few yards right to the best viewpoint south over the valley. The trail climbs easily to the true summit of Mt. Hayes, marked by a cairn on the left, at 2.5 mi. The trail runs across open ledges with restricted views north to the jct. with Centennial Trail on the right at 2.7 mi.

Part II: Centennial Trail to Gentian Pond

From here north, Mahoosuc Trail is part of the AT, marked with white blazes. It bears left and descends steadily then gradually north to the col between Mt. Hayes and Cascade Mtn. at 3.5 mi., where you can sometimes find water. The trail then ascends Cascade Mtn. by a southwest ridge, climbing steeply over large, broken rock slabs and then ledges, emerging on a ledge with excellent views south at 3.9 mi. The trail crosses a shoulder and a minor col then ascends easily to the wooded summit of Cascade Mtn. at 4.5 mi. At a ledge, the trail turns back sharply left, descending gradually with occasional slight ascents to the east end of the mountain, passing an outlook south. The trail then enters a fine forest and descends rapidly beside cliffs and ledges to Trident Col at 5.7 mi., where a side path leads left 0.2 mi. to Trident Col Tentsite. Water is available about 50 yd. below (west of) the site. The bare ledges of the rocky cone to the east of Trident Col repay the effort required to scramble to its top; a route ascends between two large cairns where Mahoosuc Trail crosses open ledges with views south a short distance east of the tentsite side path.

The trail descends rather steeply to the east and runs along the side of the ridge at the base of the Trident, which is made up of the previously mentioned cone, the ledgy peak just west of Page Pond, and a somewhat less prominent peak between them. The trail crosses several small brooks, at least one of which usually has water. The trail follows an old logging road for 0.1 mi. then turns left off the road at a sign and ascends to Page Pond at 6.7 mi., where beaver activity may cause wet conditions. The trail passes the south end of the pond, crosses a beaver dam, and climbs gradually then steeply to a short spur path at 7.3 mi. that leads left to a fine outlook from ledges near the summit of Wocket Ledge, a shoulder of Bald Cap. The main trail crosses the height-of-land and descends east, crosses the upper (west) branch of Peabody Brook, then climbs around the nose of a small ridge and descends gradually to the head of Dream Lake. It crosses the inlet brook at 8.4 mi. and just beyond, Peabody Brook Trail leaves on the right.

From this jct., Mahoosuc Trail soon crosses an open bog on wooden walkways and runs generally northeast, with several minor ups and downs. It swings briefly southeast then resumes its northeast course and descends moderately to Moss (Upper Gentian) Pond. It makes a rough traverse above the north shore then dips to an open spot on the edge of the attractive pond at 9.9 mi. The trail descends along the outlet brook, first northeast with one steep, rough pitch and then south. It swings left across a flat area, crosses a swampy spot, and reaches a jct. near the northeast corner of Gentian Pond at 10.5 mi. Here, Austin Brook Trail diverges right and leads 0.1 mi. south to Gentian Pond Campsite (shelter and tentsites).

Part III: Gentian Pond to Carlo Col

From the jct. near Gentian Pond, Mahoosuc Trail turns left and runs east along a relocated section for 0.2 mi. then swings left onto the original route. The trail climbs to the top of the steep-sided hump whose ledges overlook the pond from the east then descends moderately to a sag. The trail then starts up the west end of Mt. Success, climbing rather steeply over a hump then moderately over another hump, and passes a small stream at 11.9 mi. in the col that lies under the main mass of Mt. Success. The trail now climbs steeply and roughly for about 0.5 mi., ascending 800 ft. to the relatively flat upper part of the mountain. The trail then ascends over open ledges with excellent views south and west, passes through a belt of high scrub, crosses an alpine meadow, and finally comes out on the open summit of Mt. Success at 13.3 mi.

The trail turns sharply left here and descends through scrub then forest, with one steep scramble up a ledge, to the sag between Mt. Success and a northern subpeak, where Success Trail enters left at 13.9 mi. The main trail climbs slightly then descends moderately, with a rougher boulder scramble at the bottom, to the main col between Mt. Success and Mt. Carlo at 14.6 mi. The trail then rises over a low hump and descends to a lesser col,

SEC 11

where the trail turns right then left, passes the Maine–New Hampshire border signs, and ascends moderately again. At 15.7 mi., the trail passes a fine outlook ledge on the left, and drops sharply over a difficult rocky pitch into the little box ravine called Carlo Col. Carlo Col Trail from Success Pond Rd. enters left here; Carlo Col Campsite is located on a spur trail 0.2 mi. down Carlo Col Trail, at the head of a small brook.

Part IV: Carlo Col to Mahoosuc Notch

From Carlo Col, Mahoosuc Trail climbs steadily to the bare southwest summit of Mt. Carlo at 16.1 mi., where you find views over the trees. The trail descends briefly and climbs over a lower knob to the northeast, crosses a mountain meadow with a fine view of Goose Eye ahead, then descends steeply over many slippery ledge slabs and reaches the col at 16.7 mi. From the col, the trail swings left and climbs moderately by switchbacks to a southern shoulder of Goose Eye, crosses an open meadow with excellent views, then climbs a short and steep pitch to an open ledgy knoll below the summit of Goose Eye. The trail then passes through a sag and climbs a very steep pitch (with two sets of iron rungs and a large wooden ladder on the steepest ledges) to the narrow ridge of the main peak of Goose Eye Mtn. at 17.5 mi. (Use care on this section.)

Here, at the ridge top, Goose Eye Trail branches sharply left, reaching the open summit and its spectacular views in 0.1 mi. and continuing to Success Pond Rd. From the ridge-top jct., Mahoosuc Trail turns sharply right (east) and follows the ridge crest down through mixed ledge and scrub to a col at 17.8 mi., where Wright Trail diverges right to Bull Branch Rd. in Ketchum, Maine. Mahoosuc Trail then climbs steeply for 0.1 mi. through woods and up open ledges to the bare summit of the East Peak of Goose Eye Mtn. Here the trail turns north and descends steeply, with one tricky ledge scramble, then makes a long switchback out to the east, heading downhill through scrub over plank walkways, passing the former jct. with the closed north branch of Wright Trail at 18.1 mi.

Mahoosuc Trail descends steeply again over ladders and ledges to a minor col then rises slightly and emerges in open subalpine meadows on the broad ridge. At 18.3 mi., it swings left on a relocation, passes a view over a valley from the western edge of the ridge, and swings right back to the original route in 0.1 mi. In another 0.1 mi., it drops to the bottom of a box ravine (possible but unreliable water), the true col between the East and North peaks. It climbs steeply out of the ravine and continues mostly in the open at easy grades for another 0.4 mi., nearly to the foot of the North Peak. It climbs moderately through woods and emerges in the open on the broad summit of the North Peak at 19.1 mi. Here it swings right (east) on a relocation that bypasses the high point, turning right back onto the original route in 70 yd. It then swings northeast down the steep slope with fine views, winding through several patches of scrub and dropping over several steep ledges.

At the foot of the steep slope, Mahoosuc Trail enters the woods, contours along the west side of a hump, then angles steeply down the west face of the ridge, with two sets of iron rungs, to the col at 20.1 mi. The trail ascends a ladder to Full Goose Campsite, located on a ledgy shelf near the col; a spring is located 80 yd. downhill to the right (east of the campsite). In front of the shelter, the trail turns sharply left, descends a ladder, ascends steeply then moderately, and comes into the open 0.1 mi. below the bare summit of the South Peak of Fulling Mill Mtn., which is reached at 20.6 mi. At the broad summit ledge, the trail turns sharply left and runs through a meadow. The trail descends northwest through woods, first gradually then steeply, with two more sets of iron rungs and many rock steps, to the head of Mahoosuc Notch at 21.6 mi. Here, Notch Trail to Success Pond Rd. diverges sharply left (southwest).

Part V: Mahoosuc Notch to Old Speck

From the head of Mahoosuc Notch, Mahoosuc Trail turns sharply right (northeast) and descends the length of the narrow notch along a rough footway with numerous rock scrambles, some of which are fairly difficult, and passes through a number of boulder caverns, some with narrow openings where progress will be slow and where ice remains into summer. The trail is blazed on the rocks with white paint. (*Caution:* Great care should be exercised in the notch due to the numerous slippery rocks and dangerous holes. Large packs will be a particular hindrance through this section. The traverse of the notch is not recommended for dogs. The notch may be impassable through early June due to snow, even with snowshoes. Heavy backpacks will impede progress considerably.)

At the lower end of the notch the trail skirts to the left of a small beaver pond. At 22.7 mi. it bears left and ascends, moderately but roughly at times, under the east end of Mahoosuc Mtn., along the valley that leads to Notch 2, before crossing to the north side of the brook at 23.2 mi. The trail then winds upward among rocks and ledges on the very steep wooded slope of Mahoosuc Arm with a steep, rough footway and many slabs that may be slippery when wet. A little more than halfway up, the trail passes the head of a little flume, in which there is sometimes water. Near the top of the climb, an open ledge a few yds. to the right of the trail affords an excellent view of Mahoosuc Notch and the Mahoosuc Range.

SEC
11

At 24.3 mi., a few yds. past the top of the flat ledges near the summit of Mahoosuc Arm (with a good view north from these ledges), May Cutoff diverges left and leads 0.3 mi. over the true summit to Speck Pond Trail. Mahoosuc Trail swings right (southeast) and wanders across the semi-open summit plateau, turns left twice and climbs slightly, then drops steeply to Speck Pond, one of the highest ponds in Maine, bordered with thick woods. The trail crosses the outlet brook and continues around the east side of the pond to a jct. a short distance east of Speck Pond Campsite at 25.2 mi. (In summer there is a caretaker and a fee for overnight camping.) Here Speck Pond Trail leads ahead 80 yd. to the shelter and continues to Success Pond Rd. At this jct. Mahoosuc Trail turns right (north) on a relocation and in 100 yd. turns right again to rejoin the original route.

Mahoosuc Trail then turns right again and climbs to the southeast end of the next hump on the ridge, passes over it, and runs across the east face of a second small hump. In the gully beyond, a few yards east of the trail is an unreliable spring. The trail climbs steeply up the west shoulder of Old Speck, reaching an open ledgy area with excellent views, where the footway is well defined on the crest. Near the top of the shoulder, the trail bears right, reenters the woods, descends slightly, then ascends along the wooded crest. At 26.3 mi., shortly after the trail enters Grafton Notch State Park, Old Speck Trail, which continues the AT north, diverges left to Grafton Notch. Here, Mahoosuc Trail runs straight ahead, ascending moderately southeast to the cleared summit of Old Speck (views northeast) and its observation tower, which offers fine views in all directions. Here, Grafton Loop Trail leads southeast to Sunday River Whitecap and ME 26.

SUCCESS POND RD. TO MAHOOSUC RANGE

SUCCESS TRAIL (AMC; MAP 6: D12)

Cumulative from Success Pond Rd.
(1,610 ft.) to:

	⇅	↗	↻
End of drivable logging road (1,710 ft.)	0.4 mi.	100 ft.	0:15
Outlook Loop, lower jct. (2,920 ft.)	1.6 mi.	1,300 ft.	1:25
Mahoosuc Trail (3,170 ft.)	2.4 mi.	1,550 ft.	2:00
Mt. Success summit (3,565 ft.) via Mahoosuc Trail	3.0 mi.	1,950 ft.	2:30

This trail ascends to Mahoosuc Trail 0.6 mi. north of Mt. Success, starting on a gravel logging road (sign: Success Trail Head) off Success Pond Rd., 5.4 mi. from Hutchins St. in Berlin. Parking is very limited on Success Pond Rd.; the best parking is along the road the trail follows in its lower part. The trail follows the logging road, bears right at a fork (sign) at 0.15 mi. (parking space on right), and continues on the road, which is now narrower and rougher (high clearance vehicle recommended), to a large grassy clearing at 0.4 mi., with ample parking space. The trail exits the upper right corner of the clearing as a footpath; a trail sign is located a short distance into the woods.

The trail ascends on an old woods road through regenerating forest, crosses a small brook twice, swings right (southeast) at 0.9 mi. from Success Pond Rd., then begins to climb at a moderate grade. At 1.4 mi., the trail swings right and ascends steeply along an eroded streambed, where care must be taken due to slippery slabs. At 1.6 mi., a loop path 0.3 mi. long with a 100-ft. ascent diverges right to a spectacular ledge known as the Outlook, with fine views of the Presidentials and the mountains of the North Country. In a little more than 100 yd., the upper end of the loop path rejoins, and the main trail ascends to a ridge crest, from which it descends to a brook (unreliable) at an old logging campsite. The trail soon enters a wet, boggy area, which has been improved with some bog bridges, climbs over a small ridge, passes through another short boggy area, and then makes a short, steep ascent to Mahoosuc Trail at the main ridge crest.

CARLO COL TRAIL (AMC; MAP 6: C12–D12)

Cumulative from Success Pond Rd. (1,630 ft.) to:	⇅	↗	⟳
Goose Eye Trail (1,660 ft.)	0.2 mi.	50 ft.	0:10
Spur to Carlo Col Campsite (2,960 ft.)	2.5 mi.	1,350 ft.	1:55
Mahoosuc Trail (3,170 ft.)	2.7 mi.	1,550 ft.	2:10

This trail ascends to Mahoosuc Trail at the small box ravine called Carlo Col and, in combination with Goose Eye Trail, makes possible a scenic loop over Mt. Carlo and Goose Eye Mtn. Carlo Col Trail leaves Success Pond Rd. on a gravel logging road (AMC trail sign and road sign for Carlo Col Trail Head) that begins 8.1 mi. from Hutchins St. Parking for several cars is available a few yds. up the road on the left.

From the parking area, the trail follows the road southeast, and in 0.2 mi. Goose Eye Trail (sign) diverges left down an embankment, and Carlo Col Trail continues straight ahead on the road, climbing easily through a logged area. At 0.7 mi., the trail takes the left-hand road at a fork, descends on it for 0.1 mi., then turns left (sign) onto a footpath into the woods and immediately crosses the brook that flows from Carlo Col (may be difficult at high water).

SEC 11

The trail ascends easily and, at 1.0 mi., turns right onto a relocated section where the older route climbed left into a brushy clear-cut. The trail runs through woods between the brook and the clear-cut, swings right to cross the brook at 1.3 mi., and recrosses it in another 100 yd. The trail then skirts the edge of the clear-cut, crosses the brook again, and climbs moderately, turning right onto the original route at 1.8 mi. At 2.2 mi., the trail bears right onto a newer relocation, climbs steadily by switchbacks with many log steps, and swings left to a jct. at 2.5 mi. (Here a spur trail, the former route of Carlo Col Trail, descends left to cross a small, mossy brook—the last water, perhaps for several miles—and then ascends to Carlo Col Campsite, about 60 yd. from the jct.) The main trail turns right at the jct. and climbs moderately to Mahoosuc Trail at Carlo Col. Mt. Carlo is 0.4 mi. to the left on this trail, and to the right a fine outlook ledge is reached in a short distance via a fairly difficult scramble.

GOOSE EYE TRAIL (AMC; MAP 6: C12–C13)

Cumulative from Carlo Col Trail (1,660 ft.) to:	⇅	↗	↻
Goose Eye Mtn. summit (3,870 ft.)	2.9 mi.	2,200 ft.	2:35
Mahoosuc Trail (3,800 ft.)	3.0 mi.	2,200 ft. (rev. 50 ft.)	2:40

This trail ascends Goose Eye Mtn. from Carlo Col Trail, 0.2 mi. from Success Pond Rd., ending at Mahoosuc Trail 0.1 mi. beyond the summit. The trail has easy to moderate grades for most of its length then climbs very steeply, with some ledge scrambling, to the scenic summit. The lower part of the trail must be followed with care through logged areas.

From the gravel logging road that Carlo Col Trail follows, Goose Eye Trail diverges left at a sign, drops down an embankment, follows a newer section of trail for 90 yd., and turns right onto the original route, an old logging road. Goose Eye Trail quickly crosses a brook, runs through a brushy and overgrown area, crosses another brook, and bears left onto a gravel road at 0.3 mi. from Carlo Col Trail (descending, bear right into the woods here at a sign). Goose Eye Trail follows this road for 0.1 mi. then diverges right (watch carefully for sign) and passes through a clear-cut area where the footway may be very obscure through tall grass. The trail swings to the right (southeast) across a wet spot at 0.6 mi. and climbs gradually through woods between logged areas, crossing an overgrown skid road at an angle.

At 1.2 mi., the trail reaches the Maine–New Hampshire state line and enters a fine hardwood forest. The trail swings right at 1.7 mi. and angles up the south side of a ridge at a moderate grade, climbs more steeply uphill, then becomes gradual at the crest of the ridge in dense conifers; at 2.4 mi., you have a glimpse of the peak of Goose Eye ahead. The trail ascends moderately along the north side of the ridge then climbs steeply, swinging left to bypass a very difficult ledge, then scrambling up a somewhat less difficult ledge. The trail soon comes out on the open ledges below the summit, to which it makes a steep, scrambly ascent. From the summit, which is reached at 2.9 mi. and has magnificent views in all directions, the trail descends gradually over ledges 0.1 mi. to Mahoosuc Trail, which turns right (southbound) and runs straight ahead at the jct. (northbound).

NOTCH TRAIL (AMC; MAP 6: C12–C13)

From parking area on Shelter Brook Rd. (1,650 ft.) to:	⥮	↗	↺
Mahoosuc Trail (2,460 ft.)	1.9 mi.	800 ft.	1:20

This trail ascends at easy grades to the southwest end of Mahoosuc Notch, providing the easiest access to that wild and beautiful place. The trail begins on Shelter Brook Rd. (sign: Notch Trail), a spur road that leaves Success Pond Rd. 10.9 mi. from Hutchins St. and runs 0.3 mi. to a jct., where limited parking is available on the left. Shelter Brook Rd. turns right here (the road ahead is blocked off) and crosses two bridges. At 0.6 mi. from Success Pond Rd., a parking area is on the right, and 50 yd. farther, the trail leaves the road on the left (sign).

The trail ascends easily, following old logging roads along Shelter Brook, crossing to its north side at 0.9 mi. then back to the south side at 1.1 mi. Here, the trail swings left (northeast), soon crosses the brook again, skirts to the left of an area of beaver activity, and continues with many bog bridges up to the height-of-land, where Notch Trail meets Mahoosuc Trail; turn left to traverse the notch. A short distance along Mahoosuc Trail, the valley, which has been an ordinary one, changes sharply to a chamber formation, and the high cliffs of the notch, which have not been visible at all on Notch Trail, come into sight.

SPECK POND TRAIL (AMC; MAP 6: C12–C13)

From Success Pond Rd. (1,730 ft.) to:	⥮	↗	↺
Mahoosuc Trail (3,400 ft.)	3.6 mi.	2,000 ft. (rev. 350 ft.)	2:50

This trail ascends to Speck Pond and its campsite from Success Pond Rd.; take the right fork of the road 11.4 mi. from Hutchins St. (marked by "SPECK MT. TRAIL, RT. 26" painted on a boulder) and continue 0.8 mi.

SEC 11

to the trailhead (sign). Parking is available on the left just beyond the trailhead, opposite the entrance to Speck Pond Rd.

The trail leaves Success Pond Rd., enters the woods, and in 100 yd. makes a crossing of Sucker Brook that may be difficult; in another 75 yd., the trail recrosses the brook. (In high-water conditions, it may be best to walk 200 yd. up Speck Pond Rd. and then bushwhack south to the trail, which runs a short distance away on the near side of the brook, parallel to the road and the brook.) The trail follows the north side of the brook at easy then moderate grades for 1.4 mi., passing through brushy logged areas (follow with care). It then turns left away from the brook and traverses northward across another area of recent logging, crossing several skid roads and the top of an open brushy area. Follow markings carefully here, especially where the trail bears right at a cairn as it leaves the open area.

The trail then swings right (east) and climbs moderately, crosses a relatively level section, then bears left and climbs rather steeply and roughly, with one wooden ladder up a wet ledge, to the jct. at 3.1 mi. with May Cutoff, which diverges right.

May Cutoff (AMC) runs from Speck Pond Trail to Mahoosuc Trail—0.3 mi., 50-ft. ascent, 10 min.—with only minor ups and downs, ascending across a scrubby hump that is probably the true summit of Mahoosuc Arm along the way.

Speck Pond Trail continues over a height-of-land, passes an outlook over the pond and up to Old Speck, then descends steeply to the pond. It skirts the west shore of the pond, swings right to Speck Pond Campsite, passes to the left of the shelter (where a closed former section of trail is on the left), and continues 80 yd. to a new jct. with Mahoosuc Trail, which goes ahead (southbound) and left (northbound, on a short relocation).

GRAFTON NOTCH TO OLD SPECK MTN.

OLD SPECK TRAIL (AMC; MAP 6: B13–C13)

Cumulative from ME 26 (1,500 ft.) to:	↧↥	↗	↻
Eyebrow Trail, upper jct. (2,480 ft.)	1.1 mi.	1,000 ft.	1:05
Mahoosuc Trail (4,030 ft.)	3.5 mi.	2,700 ft. (rev. 150 ft.)	3:05
Old Speck Mtn. summit (4,170 ft.) via Mahoosuc Trail	3.8 mi.	2,850 ft.	3:20

This trail, part of the AT, ascends Old Speck Mtn. from a well-signed parking area (small fee) on ME 26 at the height-of-land in Grafton Notch. From a kiosk on the north side of the parking lot, follow the trail leading to the left (the right-hand trail goes to Baldpate Mtn.). In 0.1 mi., Eyebrow Trail leaves right to circle over the top of an 800-ft. cliff shaped like an eyebrow before rejoining Old Speck Trail. The main trail crosses a brook and soon begins to climb, following a series of switchbacks with many rock steps to approach the falls on Cascade Brook. Above the falls, the trail, now heading in a more northerly direction, crosses the brook for the last time (last water), turns left at a ledge with a view up to Old Speck, and at 1.1 mi. passes the upper terminus of Eyebrow Trail on the right.

The main trail bears left and ascends gradually to the north ridge, where it swings more to the left and follows the ridge, with frequently ledgy footing and numerous short descents interspersed through the ascent. High up, the trail turns southeast toward the summit, and at 3.0 mi. there is an outlook east from the top of a ledgy hump. The trail descends again briefly then ascends steadily to the south, passing the abandoned and closed Link Trail on the left. Old Speck Trail climbs a fairly steep and rough pitch and passes an excellent north outlook just before its jct. with Mahoosuc Trail, where Old Speck Trail ends. The flat, wooded summit of Old Speck, where an observation tower (ascended by a vertical metal ladder) and the cleared summit plateau afford fine views, is 0.3 mi. left (southeast); Speck Pond Campsite is 1.1 mi. to the right.

EYEBROW TRAIL (MBPL/AMC; MAP 6: B13)

From Old Speck Trail, lower jct. (1,525 ft.) to:	⇅	↗	↺
Old Speck Trail, upper jct. (2,480 ft.)	1.2 mi.	1,050 ft. (rev. 100 ft.)	1:10

This trail provides a steep and rough alternative route to the lower part of Old Speck Trail, passing along the edge of the cliff called the Eyebrow that overlooks Grafton Notch. Eyebrow Trail is better suited for ascent than descent. The trail leaves Old Speck Trail on the right, 0.1 mi. from the parking area off ME 26. Eyebrow Trail climbs moderately northwest and north for 0.4 mi. then swings left and ascends more steeply with the aid of cable handrails. The trail turns right at the base of a rock face, crosses a rock slab where iron rungs and a small ladder have been placed to assist hikers (but is still potentially dangerous if icy), then turns sharply left and ascends steeply, bearing right where a side path leaves straight ahead for an outlook. Soon the trail runs at a moderate grade along the top of the cliff, with good views, then descends to an outlook and runs mostly level until it ends at Old Speck Trail.

SEC 11

GRAFTON LOOP TRAIL, WESTERN SECTION
(AMC; MAP 6: C13–C14, NGTI MAP)

Cumulative from Grafton Loop Trail (eastern section) trailhead parking area on ME 26 (730 ft.) to:	⇅	⌁	○
Start of western section via ME 26 (730 ft.)	0.6 mi.	0 ft.	0:20
Bald Mtn. Tentsite spur (1,370 ft.)	2.2 mi.	650 ft.	1:25
High point on Bald Mtn. (2,070 ft.)	3.2 mi.	1,350 ft.	2:15
Stowe Mtn. summit (2,730 ft.)	4.5 mi.	2,250 ft. (rev. 250 ft.)	3:25
Sargent Brook Tentsite spur (2,650 ft.)	6.0 mi.	2,500 ft. (rev. 350 ft.)	4:15
Sunday River Whitecap summit (3,335 ft.)	7.1 mi.	3,250 ft. (rev. 50 ft.)	5:10
Miles Notch (2,350 ft.)	8.3 mi.	3,250 ft. (rev. 1,000 ft.)	5:45
Slide Mtn. Tentsite spur (2,550 ft.)	10.4 mi.	3,850 ft. (rev. 400 ft.)	7:10
Bull Run Tentsite spur (2,700 ft.)	11.4 mi.	4,050 ft. (rev. 50 ft.)	7:45
Old Speck Mtn. summit (4,170 ft.)	13.3 mi.	5,500 ft.	9:25

This major trail was constructed by AMC and other members of the Grafton Loop Trail Coalition, including the MBPL, the Maine Appalachian Trail Club, the ATC, the Maine Conservation Corps, Hurricane Island Outward Bound School, several timber management companies, Sunday River Ski Resort, and other private landowners. The group's goal was to develop multiday hiking opportunities that offer alternatives to heavily used sections of the AT. This unique public-private partnership was the first major new AMC trail construction project in the White Mountains since Centennial Trail was opened in 1976. About 30 mi. of new trail were constructed on either side of Grafton Notch, which, along with an 8-mi. section of the AT between Old Speck Mtn. and Baldpate Mtn., created a 38-mi. loop that connects a series of scenic peaks and other natural features. The eastern section of Grafton Loop Trail is described in AMC's *Maine Mountain Guide.*

The western section of the trail, 12.7-mi. long, opened in 2007 and provides access to spectacular views from Sunday River Whitecap (although views from the rest of this section are limited). Grades are mostly easy to moderate with a few short, steep pitches. The first 7 mi. of this section passes through private land (some of which is under conservation easement), where landowners have generously granted public access. Camping in this section is allowed only at the four designated campsites, and fires are not permitted.

Parking for the south end of the western section of the trail is allowed only at the trailhead for the eastern section. This parking area is on the east side of ME 26, 4.9 mi. north of its jct. with US 2 at Newry and almost opposite Eddy Rd. To reach the western section trailhead, walk 0.6 mi. south on the shoulder of ME 26 to a sign for Grafton Loop Trail. By agreement with the landowner, parking is prohibited at the western section trailhead. Mileages are given from the eastern section trailhead parking and include the 0.6-mi. road walk to the western trailhead.

From ME 26, the trail follows a farm road along the left edge of a field for 90 yd. then bears left off the road (sign) and in another 125 yd. turns right to cross the Bear River on a snowmobile bridge. Marked with snowmobile arrows, the trail crosses two fields and enters the woods, following an old road south. At 1.2 mi., the road swings left, and in another 50 yd., the trail turns right (west) off the road (sign) onto a footpath. In 20 yd., the blue-blazed trail crosses a small brook and swings right to follow it, climbing at mostly easy grades and crossing the brook three more times in the next 0.4 mi.; between the second and third of these crossings, the trail passes a small flume.

The trail continues following the brook at moderate grades up the northeast slope of Bald Mtn., occasionally making use of old woods roads. The main trail crosses the brook twice more, and at 2.2 mi., just beyond the second of these crossings, a spur path leads 60 yd. left across the brook to Bald Mtn. Tentsite, with two tent platforms. At 2.4 mi., the main trail turns left, crosses the brook (or its dry bed) for the last time, and climbs steadily by switchbacks to the broad crest of Bald Mtn. The trail continues at easy grades across the plateau, crosses a small sag, and reaches its high point on Bald Mtn. at 3.2 mi. The trail then descends moderately to a flat saddle, where it runs nearly level to the right of a brushy logged area.

The trail soon begins the ascent of Stowe Mtn., first at easy grades then becoming steep with many rock steps as it enters spruce woods. At 4.3 mi., the trail ascends a series of wooden ladders. The grade eases as the trail crosses the flat, wooded crest of Stowe Mtn. at 4.5 mi. The trail then descends to a minor col at 4.8 mi., where it crosses a small brook, and ascends briefly to the semi-open, ledgy west knob of Stowe Mtn., where you have limited views. Marked by cairns, the trail runs across the ledges for 0.1 mi. then reenters the woods. The trail follows a winding course through dense growth then swings north and descends at mostly easy grades. The trail now traverses the southwestern slope of Sunday River Whitecap through open woods, with minor ups and downs, crossing several small, unreliable brooks.

SEC 11

At 6.0 mi., a spur path diverges left and descends 0.2 mi. to Sargent Brook Tentsite, crossing a small brook (reliable) in 50 yd. Three tent pads are located here. The main trail traverses to the west then turns right (north) at 6.2 mi. and ascends moderately along the west slope of Sunday River Whitecap, gaining the ridge crest in a small col at 6.7 mi. The trail follows the ridge over a hump, descends to another col, then climbs again, emerging on open ledges at 7.0 mi., where AMC trail crews have used innovative construction techniques—including scree walls and raised wooden walkways—to protect the fragile alpine vegetation. Hikers are urged to stay on the defined trail and outlook areas. At 7.1 mi., just before the summit is reached, a side path descends 25 yd. right to a designated viewing area looking east. In another 20 yd., a similar path leads 20 yd. left to a western outlook with a fine view of the northern Mahoosucs and the distant Presidentials.

The main trail crosses the summit and descends steeply north over open ledges then swings more to the northeast, winding down over ledges and through patches of scrub with excellent views of the peaks around Grafton Notch. The trail descends into a belt of woods then in 125 yd. swings left (west) and emerges on an open shoulder. At 7.6 mi., the trail enters the woods for good and descends steadily west then southwest through an area where some yellow blazes remain from a former unofficial trail.

The grade eases in open woods, and at 8.3 mi., the trail swings left (south) on the broad floor of Miles Notch, runs nearly level for 0.1 mi., then bears right (west) and ascends through partly logged areas onto the lower slope of Slide Mtn. The trail turns left (south) again and contours along the slope, with occasional rough footing, then descends through a boulder-strewn area to a low point at 9.1 mi. The trail soon swings west and ascends briefly then runs northwest at easy grades, with minor ups and downs, passing to the left of a large boulder at 9.5 mi. The trail runs at easy grades through fine hardwood forest for some distance along the base of Slide Mtn. then rises gradually into mixed woods.

At 10.4 mi., a spur on the right ascends 110 yd. to Slide Mtn. Tentsite, which has three tent pads. About 35 yd. past this jct., Grafton Loop Trail crosses a small brook (the water source for the campsite), runs west, then soon swings right and ascends through a hardwood glade. The trail then bears left and winds gradually up the east side of a valley. At 11.4 mi., a spur path leads 0.1 mi. left to Bull Run Tentsite (two tent platforms), crossing a brook that is the water source. The main trail enters conifers and climbs more steadily across the slope, gaining the crest of a southeastern spur of Old Speck Mtn. at 11.9 mi. Here, the trail swings left and ascends up the ridge crest then bears left again and climbs by easy switchbacks with good footing. At 12.2 mi., the trail climbs through a blowdown patch with restricted views south. The grade increases at 12.7 mi., and the footway becomes rough with rocks, roots, and holes as it angles across the south slope of Old Speck. At 13.0 mi., there is an outlook southeast toward Sunday River Whitecap and the Bear River valley.

The trail soon swings right and the footing improves. After one more steady climb, the trail levels, passes a trail sign, and 10 yd. farther emerges in the clearing at the summit of Old Speck Mtn. Here, you have fine views northeast, and a full panorama may be obtained from the observation tower, which is ascended by a vertical metal ladder. From the summit, Mahoosuc Trail leads 0.3 mi. northwest to Old Speck Trail.

KETCHUM TO GOOSE EYE MTN.

WRIGHT TRAIL (AMC; MAP 6: C13)

Cumulative from parking area on Bull Branch Rd. (1,240 ft.) to:	⇅	↗	↻
MBPL tentsite and former loop jct. (2,300 ft.)	2.5 mi.	1,150 ft. (rev. 100 ft.)	1:50
Mahoosuc Trail (3,630 ft.)	4.4 mi.	2,600 ft. (rev. 100 ft.)	3:30
West Peak of Goose Eye Mtn. (3,870 ft.) via Mahoosuc and Goose Eye trails	4.8 mi.	2,850 ft.	3:50
From parking area on Bull Branch Rd. (1,240 ft.) to:			
East Peak of Goose Eye Mtn. (3,790 ft.)	4.5 mi.	2,750 ft.	3:35

This trail, steep and rough in places, provides access to Goose Eye Mtn. and the Mahoosuc Range via a scenic route from the east that begins in a place known as Ketchum, located on a branch of the Sunday River. The upper part of the trail formerly had two separate branches, but the north branch, which ascended through a small glacial cirque, has been closed due to erosion and safety concerns. The south branch, which follows a ledgy ridge, is now the sole route up to the main ridge crest.

To reach the trailhead, leave US 2, 2.8 mi. north of Bethel, Maine, and follow Sunday River Rd. to the left (northwest). At a fork at 2.2 mi., bear right (signs: Jordan Bowl and covered bridge), and at 3.3 mi., bear right again (sign: covered bridge) and continue past Artist Covered Bridge (left) at 3.8 mi. from US 2. At 6.5 mi., the road becomes gravel. At 7.8 mi., turn left across two bridges then immediately take the first right, which is Bull Branch Rd. (Both of these turns may have signs: Frenchmans, Goose Eye. Frenchman's Hole is a popular swimming area on Bull Branch Rd.) At 9.3 mi., Goose Eye Brook is crossed on a bridge, and the trailhead is on the left at 9.5 mi. from US 2. The trail starts at a signboard with a small trail sign. Parking is available a short distance farther up the road.

Leaving Bull Branch Rd., the blue-blazed trail immediately splits into two branches, which rejoin in 0.5 mi. The left and more scenic branch descends toward Goose Eye Brook then follows the north bank upstream past several cascades and pools and a 30-ft. gorge. It then turns left on an old woods road, which the right branch has followed ahead from the trailhead. The single trail now follows this woods road for 0.2 mi. then makes a right turn onto an older road. At 0.9 mi., the trail bears left off the road and descends gradually 100 yd. to Goose Eye Brook at its confluence with a tributary, where the trail bears right and follows the tributary for 125 yd. then turns sharply left and crosses it. From this point, the trail roughly follows the north side of Goose Eye Brook, with minor ups and downs, crossing two small tributaries, until it reaches the former loop jct. at 2.5 mi. A designated MBPL tentsite is on the right just before the jct.

From the former loop jct., where the north branch (now closed) continued ahead across a tributary brook, the south branch of the trail immediately crosses Goose Eye Brook to the left and starts its climb, gradually at first and then moderately by switchbacks with rough sections and wooden steps, to the ridge crest at 3.1 mi. At 3.4 mi., after a rough ascent, the trail reaches an open spot then descends slightly back into the woods. The trail then resumes a steep, rough ascent on ledges to an open knob with beautiful views at 3.6 mi. The trail continues along the ridge with several open areas and occasional minor descents to cross small sags then finally climbs moderately to Mahoosuc Trail in the small gap between the East Peak and the West Peak (main summit) of Goose Eye Mtn. at 4.4 mi. The main summit can be reached in 0.4 mi. by following Mahoosuc Trail to the left (southbound) and then Goose Eye Trail. The ledgy East Peak is reached by climbing steeply for 0.1 mi. on Mahoosuc Trail to the right (northbound).

NORTH RD. TO MAHOOSUC RANGE

CENTENNIAL TRAIL (AMC; MAP 6: E11–D11)

From Hogan Rd. (750 ft.) to:	⇅	↗	↻
Mahoosuc Trail (2,550 ft.)	3.1 mi.	1,950 ft. (rev. 150 ft.)	2:30

This trail, a part of the AT, was constructed by AMC in 1976, the club's centennial year. The trail begins on Hogan Rd., a rough dirt road that diverges left (west) from North Rd. 0.5 mi. from US 2, a short distance north of North Rd.'s crossing of the Androscoggin River and just before

SEC 11

the road swings abruptly to the east; there is a trail sign here. Parking is permitted at a small area on the left, 0.2 mi. from North Rd., and at the jct. of North Rd. and Hogan Rd.; do not block the road.

Starting across from the parking area on Hogan Rd., Centennial Trail (sign) follows a woods road for 50 yd. then bears left off the road and up into the woods (white blazes), levels off, and reaches the first of many stone steps in 0.1 mi. The trail ascends rather steeply then more gradually. The trail turns left onto a woods road and follows it briefly then crosses a brook at 0.7 mi. (last water). The trail climbs steadily past several overgrown viewpoints, swings right and passes a restricted outlook on the right, then descends to a sag in a birch grove at 1.6 mi.

After a long, gradual climb angling up the side of the ridge, the trail turns sharply left and continues upward past ledges that provide limited views. At 2.8 mi., the trail reaches an easterly summit of Mt. Hayes, where you have a restricted view south. Here, the trail turns right and descends slightly then ascends across a series of ledges to end at Mahoosuc Trail at 3.1 mi. Here, the AT turns right (north) on Mahoosuc Trail. The summit of Mt. Hayes, with limited views, is 0.2 mi. to the left; the fine open ledges at the southwest end of the summit, with the best views on the mountain, are 0.3 mi. farther with an elevation loss of 100 ft.

PEABODY BROOK TRAIL (AMC; MAP 6: E11–D11)

Cumulative from North Rd. (750 ft.) to:	⇅	↗	○
Side path to Giant Falls (1,450 ft.)	1.2 mi.	700 ft.	0:55
Bald Cap Peak Ledges Trail (2,620 ft.)	2.6 mi.	1,850 ft.	2:15
Mahoosuc Trail (2,630 ft.)	3.1 mi.	1,900 ft.	2:30

This blue-blazed trail ascends to Mahoosuc Trail at Dream Lake from North Rd., 1.3 mi. east of its jct. with US 2. There is limited parking on the shoulder on the south side of the road; take care not to block driveways. Overnight parking is not permitted at the base of this trail, much of which is on private land.

The trail follows a logging road between two houses, passes a gate, bears right at a four-way intersection, and crosses Peabody Brook at 0.2 mi. on a new (2016) bridge. The trail follows a grassy logging road to the left up along the brook, skirts the left side of a brushy clearing at 0.4 mi., and continues up the road. At 0.8 mi., the trail bears left at a fork; the right fork is the west end of yellow-blazed Middle Mtn. Trail (sign). Peabody Brook Trail soon becomes a footpath and ascends moderately up the side of the

SEC 11

ravine. At 1.2 mi., a side path (sign) leaves left for Giant Falls, an impressive waterfall 0.3 mi. from the main trail (ascent 150 ft., rev. 100 ft.).

Peabody Brook Trail rises more steeply and crosses a slide at 1.5 mi. where caution is required at one tricky spot; here is a fine view of the Presidentials beyond the Androscoggin valley. The trail climbs a ladder (use caution) just beyond the slide. At 2.1 mi., the trail crosses the east branch of the brook then recrosses it at 2.4 mi. The trail climbs to a jct. at 2.6 mi. where Bald Cap Peak Ledges Trail (sign) diverges right, leading to excellent views. Peabody Brook Trail now runs nearly level through a wet area over many wooden walkways, and at 3.0 mi. it reaches Dream Lake and the jct. on the right with Dryad Fall Trail. Peabody Brook Trail continues along the southeast shore of the lake, passing a spot with a striking view across the water to mts. Washington and Adams, to Mahoosuc Trail.

BALD CAP PEAK LEDGES TRAIL (STC; MAP 6: D11)

From Peabody Brook Trail (2,620 ft.) to:	⇅	↗	○
Bald Cap Peak Ledges (2,530 ft.)	0.5 mi.	100 ft. (rev. 200 ft.)	0:20

This yellow-blazed spur trail, opened by STC in 2012, leads to open ledges with wide views on the south face of Bald Cap Peak. It partly follows the route of a long-abandoned trail originally cut by AMC members in 1877. It diverges right (southwest) from Peabody Brook Trail 2.6 mi. from North Rd. and ascends gradually through fern-filled woods. It swings left as it skirts the slope west of the summit of Bald Cap Peak with minor ups and downs, descends moderately then steeply through woods and over ledges, and crosses the yellow-blazed Appalachian Trail corridor boundary. At the bottom of the pitch, it swings right at a ledge with a view southeast and runs 70 yd. southwest to the main ledges, with wide views.

AUSTIN BROOK TRAIL (AMC; MAP 6: E12–D12)

Cumulative from North Rd. (730 ft.) to:	⇅	↗	○
Mill Brook Rd. (950 ft.)	1.3 mi.	200 ft.	0:45
Dryad Fall Trail (1,470 ft.)	2.5 mi.	750 ft.	1:40
Mahoosuc Trail (2,160 ft.)	3.6 mi.	1,450 ft.	2:30

This blue-blazed trail ascends to Mahoosuc Trail near Gentian Pond from North Rd., 0.6 mi. west of its jct. with Meadow Rd. (which runs from US 2 at Shelburne village across the Androscoggin River to North Rd.). Parking is available on the south side of the road. The trail passes through a turn-stile on private land and follows a woods road at easy grades along the west side of Austin Brook, crossing Yellow Trail at 0.4 mi. Austin Brook Trail turns left off the road at 0.6 mi. to skirt posted private property then rejoins the old road at 0.9 mi. At 1.1 mi., the trail continues ahead along the west side of Austin Brook on a relocated section where the trail formerly crossed the brook to the right. At 1.3 mi., the trail crosses a tributary brook and quickly reaches gravel Mill Brook Rd. (private) just beyond the point where a logging bridge over Austin Brook has been removed. (Austin Brook and Mill Brook are different names for the same stream.) In the reverse direction, turn right off the road into the woods to a sign for the trail.

Mill Brook Rd. leaves North Rd. 0.6 mi. east of the Austin Brook Trail trailhead and just west of the jct. with Meadow Rd. In the past, this road has been gated at times and open to public vehicular use at other times. In 2016, it was possible to drive on this road (rough near the end) for 1.6 mi. to the former bridge over Austin Brook and park; to join the trail from this point, one must ford the unbridged brook crossing. Logging operations could change this road access at any time, and drivers should heed any signs posted by the landowner.

After entering the road, Austin Brook Trail almost immediately bears right at a signed fork. (The left fork, a western branch of the road, is orange-blazed Gates Brook Trail.) Austin Brook Trail follows the grassy main road north, ascending gradually and passing clearings on the left with views of the ridges to the west at 1.4 mi. and 1.8 mi.. At 2.1 mi., shortly after crossing a brook to the left of old bridge abutments, the trail turns left into the woods on an older road (sign) and ascends moderately, passing a newer skid road on the right. At 2.5 mi., Dryad Fall Trail diverges left. Here, Austin Brook Trail turns right, and in another 0.1 mi. a steep, over-grown skid road joins from the right. The trail and skid road coincide for 100 yd. before Austin Brook Trail bears slightly right, and the former skid road swings left and uphill. The trail swings right at 2.7 mi., and at 2.9 mi. it makes a hairpin turn left and ascends gradually to a plateau.

At 3.1 mi., the trail crosses the brook that drains Gentian Pond and runs on bog bridges through an open area of beaver activity, with views of the surrounding ridges; the trail may occasionally be flooded in this area. The trail swings right along the yellow-blazed Appalachian Trail corridor boundary to the base of a steep slope then bears left and climbs steeply, bearing right near the top, and at 3.5 mi., the trail reaches Gentian Pond Shelter, where you have a view south. A path to the right of the shelter leads 70 yd. to four tent platforms. Austin Brook Trail continues to the left of the

SEC 11

shelter; here a side path descends 30 yd. left to the shore of Gentian Pond, where you find a fine view of cliffs on a spur of Bald Cap Mtn. Austin Brook Trail runs up and down above the east shore of the pond and ends at Mahoosuc Trail, near the northeast corner of the pond.

DRYAD FALL TRAIL (AMC; MAP 6: D12–D11)

Cumulative from Austin Brook Trail (1,470 ft.) to:	⇅	↗	○
Spur trail to Dryad Fall and view (1,790 ft.)	0.4 mi.	300 ft.	0:20
Peabody Brook Trail (2,630 ft.)	1.5 mi.	1,150 ft.	1:20

This yellow-blazed trail runs from Austin Brook Trail to Peabody Brook Trail near Dream Lake, passing Dryad Fall, one of the highest cascades in the mountains—particularly interesting for a few days after a rainstorm, when its several cascades fall at least 300 ft. over steep ledges.

The trail leaves Austin Brook Trail on the left 2.5 mi. from North Rd., where that trail turns right. Dryad Fall Trail immediately crosses a brook and follows an old woods road, climbing moderately across the slope. At 0.4 mi., a spur trail (sign) descends 60 yd. left to ledges near the top of the falls, where there is a fine view southeast. (*Caution:* Rocks in the vicinity of the falls are very slippery and hazardous.) The main trail climbs above the falls, passing interesting logging artifacts to the right of the trail, and at 0.6 mi., it turns left on an old road (descending, make sure to turn right here), crosses Dryad Brook, and in another 0.3 mi. turns sharply right. The trail climbs at mostly moderate grades to a height-of-land then descends slightly to Peabody Brook Trail near Dream Lake, 0.1 mi. southeast of Mahoosuc Trail.

SOUTHERN MINOR PEAKS

SCUDDER TRAIL (STC; MAP 6: E12–D12)

Cumulative from Mill Brook Rd. (770 ft.) to:	⇅	↗	○
Mt. Cabot Connector (1,330 ft.)	1.3 mi.	550 ft.	0:55
Mt. Ingalls summit (2,242 ft.)	2.7 mi.	1,500 ft. (rev. 50 ft.)	2:05
Ray's Pond (2,190 ft.)	2.8 mi.	1,500 ft. (rev. 50 ft.)	2:10

This trail, blazed in orange, provides access to the ledges and summit of Mt. Ingalls. Originally opened in the 1950s, the trail was reopened in 2010 by STC following a period of abandonment due to logging. The trail begins on Mill Brook Rd., a private gravel road that leaves North Rd. about 50 yd. west of Meadow Rd. (the road that crosses the Androscoggin River on a bridge from Shelburne village). Mill Brook Rd. was open and passable for passenger vehicles in 2016; Scudder Trail diverges right at a parking area and sign on the second road from the right, 0.5 mi. from North Rd.

The footway is obscure in places, so the blazes must be followed with care. The trail leads northeast through open logged areas, crossing Yellow Trail in 0.1 mi. Scudder Trail passes a clearing on the left, and at 0.4 mi., the trail swings right onto a very grassy skid road and climbs moderately to a four-way jct. just north of the Mt. Ingalls–Mt. Cabot col at 1.3 mi.

Here yellow-blazed **Mt. Cabot Connector** diverges right, descends 20 yd. to a jct. with Judson Pond Trail on the left, then climbs moderately to meet Red Trail at 0.2 mi. from Scudder Trail (ascent 150 ft.).

At the jct., **Scudder Trail** turns sharply left, and at 1.4 mi., it comes out on a ledge on the west side of the ridge, with views over the Androscoggin valley. The trail traverses west along a ledgy shelf, descending slightly, then turns right (northeast) and ascends, steeply at times, bearing left at 2.0 mi. as the trail gains the crest of the mountain's south ridge. The trail now ascends north at varying grades, winding back and forth across the ridge, passing an outlook southwest at 2.2 mi. and then an outlook east 20 yd. to the right of the trail. After a slight descent, the trail circles out to the left across ledges with partial views (follow with care), reenters the woods, then soon swings left to an extensive ledge with views southwest. The trail then climbs 150 yd. to the wooded summit of Mt. Ingalls (sign). From here, the blazed trail descends 0.1 mi. north to Ray's Pond, a scenic mountain tarn.

JUDSON POND TRAIL (STC; MAP 6: D12)

From Mt. Cabot Connector (1,330 ft.) to:	⇅	↗	⟳
Judson Pond (1,350 ft.)	0.4 mi.	100 ft. (rev. 100 ft.)	0:15

This former trail was reopened by STC in 2016; its yellow blazes must be followed carefully. It diverges northeast from Mt. Cabot Connector at a low spot 20 yd. south of Scudder Trail, descends to a wet area, crosses Ingalls Brook, and climbs steeply on and alongside a skid road through a logged area to the top of a minor ridge. It then descends easily through woods to the west shore of small, secluded Judson Pond.

MIDDLE MTN. TRAIL (STC; MAP 6: D12–D11)

Cumulative from Gates Brook Trail (1,220 ft.) to:	⇅	↗	⟳
Boulder near Middle Mtn. summit (2,000 ft.)	0.7 mi.	800 ft.	0:45
Peabody Brook Trail (1,060 ft.)	2.1 mi.	850 ft. (rev. 1,000 ft.)	1:25

SEC 11

This yellow-blazed trail traverses Middle Mtn., which affords interesting views from ledges around its summit. The trail runs from Gates Brook Trail, 0.9 mi. north of North Rd., to Peabody Brook Trail, 0.8 mi. north of North Rd. The trail diverges left (west) from Gates Brook Trail at a sign and ascends easily on an old woods road. At 0.2 mi., Middle Mtn. Trail swings left on the first of several turns, alternating between sections of footpath and old woods roads. At 0.4 mi., the trail turns right at a sign, climbs a very steep pitch, then soon swings left and ascends steadily through a ledgy oak forest. At 0.7 mi., the trail emerges on ledges with limited views, passing to the left of a boulder painted, "TOP."

Views are limited here, but a beaten path can be followed 90 yd. to the right (northeast) over ledges and through patches of scrub, passing a sign marking the summit, to open ledges with views east over the Androscoggin valley and eastern Mahoosucs, and north to the cliffs of Bald Cap Peak; please stay on the path to protect fragile lichens. From the boulder, the main trail—which from here on has received much less use and must be followed with great care—descends north over ledges past a sign for Peabody Brook Trail, continues down through spruces to a col at 0.9 mi, then ascends slightly and swings left twice. Middle Mtn. Trail then descends generally southwest, making use of a succession of old woods roads; several turns should be carefully watched for. At 1.8 mi., the trail descends along the right edge of a brushy opening and continues down a grassy skid road, crossing a red-blazed boundary and a small brook, to meet Peabody Brook Trail.

GATES BROOK TRAIL (STC; MAP 6: E12–D12)

Cumulative from North Rd. (750 ft.) to:	⇅	↗	↻
Yellow Trail (960 ft.)	0.4 mi.	200 ft.	0:20
Middle Mtn. Trail (1,220 ft.)	0.9 mi.	450 ft.	0:40
Austin Brook Trail (960 ft.)	1.9 mi.	500 ft. (rev. 300 ft.)	1:10

This orange-blazed trail leads from North Rd. to Austin Brook Trail and provides access to Mt. Crag and Middle Mtn. Gates Brook Trail starts as a woods road that leaves North Rd. on the north, just east of Gates Brook; this is 2.5 mi. east of the jct. of North Rd. and US 2 and 1.4 mi. west of Meadow Rd; there is a cable gate and a sign a short way up the trail. Parking is available at a pull-off on the south side of North Rd., 50 yd. east of the trail; the woods road directly across from the parking is not the trail.

From North Rd., Gates Brook Trail climbs moderately along Gates Brook, passing a jct. with Yellow Trail (leading to Mt. Crag) on the right at 0.4 mi. At 0.6 mi., the trail turns left onto another woods road, crosses a small brook, and ascends at an easier grade. At 0.9 mi., the trail bears right at a fork, as Middle Mtn. Trail diverges left. At 1.1 mi., Gates Brook Trail makes a short detour to the right around a slash pile and enters a large clearing. Here, the trail turns right and follows a gravel road—the western branch of Mill Brook Rd.—downhill to the east, soon making a steep crossing of a brook where a bridge has been removed. The trail continues down the brushy road, passing several small cascades on the brook to the right, and meets Austin Brook Trail where it first emerges on the main branch of Mill Brook Rd., 1.3 mi. from that trail's beginning on North Rd.

YELLOW TRAIL (STC; MAP 6: D12–E12)

Cumulative from Gates Brook Trail (960 ft.) to:	↕	↗	↻
Mt. Crag (1,412 ft.)	0.3 mi.	450 ft.	0:25
Austin Brook Trail (800 ft.)	1.1 mi.	450 ft. (rev. 600 ft.)	0:45
North end of Philbrook Farm Inn access road (750 ft.)	2.1 mi.	450 ft. (rev. 50 ft.)	1:15

This trail provides convenient access to Mt. Crag, which is easily climbed and offers an excellent view up and down the Androscoggin valley, and connects with trails in the Philbrook Farm Inn area. At its west end, Yellow Trail leaves Gates Brook Trail 0.4 mi. from North Rd. and climbs steeply to the open ledge at the summit of Mt. Crag at 0.3 mi. Yellow Trail descends easily northeast then swings right and descends steadily. The grade then eases, and Austin Brook Trail is crossed at 1.1 mi. In another 0.1 mi. Yellow Trail crosses Austin Brook (may be difficult at high water) and then Mill Brook Rd. (In high water, hikers may use a cable car installed by STC for crossing the brook; it is reached by a yellow-blazed path, 0.1-mi. long, that diverges left 90 yd. before the trail crossing. On the far side, follow Mill Brook Rd. 100 yd. right to rejoin the trail. Use of the cable car requires arm strength and caution.)

Beyond Mill Brook Rd., Yellow Trail bears right and runs southeast at a nearly level grade through logged areas, crossing Scudder Trail at 1.5 mi. At 1.7 mi., an unmarked connecting path diverges left, leading 0.2 mi. to Red Trail. Yellow Trail continues ahead on a grassy logging road, and at 2.0 mi., the trail turns left onto a footpath descending into the woods and crosses a small brook and a gravel road. After a short ascent, Red Trail joins as a woods road from the left, and the two trails coincide for 90 yd. to the north end of the access road (on the right, 0.4-mi. long) behind the

SEC
11

cottages connected with Philbrook Farm Inn; here Blue Trail diverges left, and Wiggins Rock Trail leads ahead.

Mt. Cabot and Crow's Nest

This subsection of the southern minor peaks runs south and southeast from Mt. Ingalls. Several trails, distinguished by color, start from an access road on North Rd., in Shelburne, at the historic Philbrook Farm Inn, which has welcomed hikers since the 1860s. The inn is located on the north side of the road, 0.5 mi. east of Meadow Rd. Hikers are allowed to park in an area with a cement pad just southwest of the main inn building but are asked to speak with inn management before leaving their vehicles. From the parking area, an access road leads 0.4 mi. west then north past three cottages to the jct. of the Blue, Red, Yellow, and Wiggins Rock trails. The Blue and Red trails both lead to the summit of Mt. Cabot, which has two viewpoints, making a loop trip possible. The path farthest to the east, White Trail, leads to Crow's Nest, which has limited views. Yellow Trail, described earlier, runs northwest to Mt. Crag.

BLUE TRAIL (STC; MAP 6: E12–D12)

From north end of Philbrook Farm Inn access road (750 ft.) to:	⇅	↗	○
Mt. Cabot (1,512 ft.)	1.3 mi.	750 ft.	1:00

This trail starts from the north end of the Philbrook Farm Inn access road, described above. Here, Blue Trail continues straight ahead on a woods road; the coinciding Red and Yellow trails lead to the left; and Wiggins Rock Trail leads to the right. At 0.1 mi., Blue Trail passes another woods road diverging left. The trail continues ahead on an older road for 60 yd. then diverges right onto another old road and in 50 yd. bears left on yet another road and climbs moderately. The trail turns left at 0.6 mi. and meanders across a plateau with several more turns; follow the blue blazes carefully.

At 1.0 mi. it reaches a yellow-and-orange blazed boundary, climbs briefly along the left edge of a clearcut, climbs steeply along a boundary profusely blazed in yellow, and reaches a side path on the right (sign: View) at 1.3 mi. that leads 50 yd. to a view northeast. The main trail reaches the wooded summit of Mt. Cabot in another 35 yd., where it meets Red Trail by an old foundation. Here a loop path (sign: View Loop) diverges left and descends 75 yd. by a switchback to a ledge with a fine view across the Androscoggin valley to the Moriahs and the Presidential Range. The view loop turns right at the back of the ledge and climbs 50 yd. to meet Red Trail, 30 yd. west of the summit.

RED TRAIL (STC; MAP 6: E12–D12)

From north end of Philbrook Farm Inn access road (750 ft.) to:	⤴	↗	⏱
Mt. Cabot (1,512 ft.)	1.2 mi.	750 ft.	1:00
From hiker parking at Philbrook Farm Inn (700 ft.) for:			
Loop over Mt. Cabot (1,512 ft.) via access road, Blue Trail, and Red Trail	3.3 mi.	800 ft.	2:05

This trail diverges left (west) from the multitrail jct. at the north end of the access road west of the Philbrook Farm Inn, coinciding for 90 yd. with Yellow Trail, which then diverges left. Following a woods road north, Red Trail crosses a gravel road and a small brook, and at 0.2 mi., the trail turns right onto another old road (sign); the road continuing ahead leads 0.2 mi. to Yellow Trail. Red Trail ascends moderately, and at 0.5 mi., a side path (sign) leads right up a bank and continues 75 yd. to Mary's Aerie, a very limited viewpoint. In another 30 yd., the main trail turns left off the road onto a footpath, soon crossing a small brook. The trail swings right and climbs moderately, turns left onto an old woods road at 0.7 mi., then turns right off it in 30 yd. The grade is easier for a while, until the trail climbs steeply to approach Mt. Cabot from the northwest, passing a jct. on the left with yellow-blazed Mt. Cabot Connector, which descends 0.2 mi. and 150 ft. to Judson Pond and Scudder trails. Red Trail swings right, passes the west end of a view loop (sign) on the right in 70 yd., and in another 30 yd., at 1.2 mi., reaches the summit and the upper jct. with Blue Trail. (See Blue Trail for description of views.)

WHITE TRAIL (STC; MAP 6: E12)

From access road (750 ft.) to:	⤴	↗	⏱
Crow's Nest (1,287 ft.)	1.3 mi.	550 ft.	0:55

This trail is best approached from the access road that leaves the north side of North Rd., 0.15 mi. east of the hiker parking area at Philbrook Farm Inn; alternate parking is 100 yd. east of the access road at a pull-off on the south side of North Rd. Follow the access road for 0.1 mi. to a point beside the first cottage, where White Trail diverges right on a footpath (white blaze on tree). In 75 yd., the trail bears left onto a woods road, and at

0.1 mi. from the access road, Wiggins Rock Trail leaves left at a cairn, whereas White Trail bears right and ascends along a succession of old and newer logging roads through brushy logged areas, crossing several intersecting logging roads; follow the white blazes carefully. At 1.2 mi., the trail turns right off the last logging road and makes a short, steep ascent to the wooded summit of Crow's Nest at 1.3 mi. The trail ends a few yards farther at a limited viewpoint to the northeast.

WIGGINS ROCK TRAIL (STC; MAP 6: E12)

From White Trail (820 ft.) to:	↕	↗	↻
Access road and jct. with Blue, Yellow, and Red trails (750 ft.)	0.4 mi.	100 ft. (rev. 150 ft.)	0:15

This orange-blazed trail begins at a jct. with White Trail (cairn), 0.1 mi. from that trail's beginning. Wiggins Rock Trail climbs north for 0.2 mi. then turns left onto an old logging road. In 5 yd., a side path diverges right and continues another 60 yd. up then slightly down to Wiggin Rock, a small ledge with a very limited view across the Androscoggin valley. From the jct., Wiggins Rock Trail descends 0.2 mi. to the north end of the access road where the Red, Yellow, and Blue trails begin.

SECTION TWELVE
NORTHERN NEW HAMPSHIRE

Map 2: Franconia–Pemigewasset
Map 6: North Country–Mahoosuc Range

INTRODUCTION

This section covers the part of New Hampshire that lies west of NH 16 and north of US 2. South of NH 110, a fairly extensive network of trails is on or adjacent to lands of the WMNF. North of NH 110 lies the North Country proper, a sparsely populated region with extensive woodlands owned mostly by corporations and managed for lumber and pulpwood production. In this area, there are only a few trails to widely scattered natural features, and the region is far better known for hunting, fishing, and snowmobiling than for hiking, although hiking opportunities have increased significantly in recent years.

We cover four relatively distinct ranges and trail networks in this region, treated in separate subsections: the Cherry–Dartmouth Range, along with the nearby Pondicherry National Wildlife Refuge; the Crescent Range; the Pliny and Pilot ranges; and the North Country proper, which in this guidebook is further divided into three subsections (Nash Stream Forest, Dixville Notch Region, and Connecticut Lakes Region). The Cherry–Dartmouth Range is completely covered by AMC's *White Mountains Trail Map 2: Franconia–Pemigewasset;* the Crescent Range and the Pliny and Pilot ranges (except for the trails on Mt. Prospect) are completely covered by AMC's *White Mountains Trail Map 6: North Country–Mahoosuc Range;* and the North Country requires USGS maps or other maps as indicated for each objective.

ROAD ACCESS

Road access for Northern New Hampshire is addressed within each of the four subsections: the Cherry–Dartmouth Range, the Crescent Range, the Pliny and Pilot ranges, and the North Country proper.

COHOS TRAIL

Traversing northern New Hampshire from south to north is the Cohos Trail, a challenging 170-mi. route that runs the length of Coos County, from Crawford Notch to the Canadian border. As of 2016, The Cohos Trail Association (TCTA) had opened the entire length of the trail, using a combination of existing hiking trails (including about 60 mi. through the WMNF, where it is not marked as the Cohos Trail), snowmobile and cross-country ski trails, logging and skid roads, old railroad grades, paved and gravel roads, and many newly cut sections of foot trail. The trail is blazed in yellow, although the markings may vary within the WMNF and in some other locations. Some sections of the Cohos Trail have changed significantly since it was first developed in 2000, especially in the

Connecticut Lakes Region. New routes that would move the trail off roads and ATV trails have been proposed for several sections between Coleman State Park and the Cohos Trail's northern terminus.

Space does not allow a complete description of the trail in this guide; however, several particularly interesting segments suitable for day hikes have been included here in the Nash Stream Forest, Dixville Notch Region, and Connecticut Lakes Region subsections, and complete coverage is given to the trail network around the Percy Peaks. TCTA has several relevant publications: a guidebook, *The Cohos Trail* (Fourth Edition, 2017), by Kim Nilsen; *The Cohos Trail Databook* (2017), with trail mileages and brief summaries, available in both northbound and southbound versions; and a set of four maps by the AMC cartographer Larry Garland (2017). These may be ordered from TCTA. Additional day hikes are described in *50 Hikes North of the White Mountains* (Countryman Press, 2012), also by Kim Nilsen.

Hikers should be aware that some sections of the Cohos Trail are poorly defined, overgrown, wet, and muddy, although TCTA has performed much work to improve blazing, signage, drainage, and footing in problem areas. Parts of the trail (such as in the remote country at the north end of Nash Stream Forest) have little or no evident footway, and numerous intersecting logging roads and snowmobile trails can cause considerable confusion. Hikers who venture into these areas should have adequate supplies and be proficient with a map and compass. As such, this area offers backpackers a wilder and more primitive experience, far from the crowds, compared with the heavily used AT.

A designated campsite is located beside Percy Loop and Trio Trails in Nash Stream Forest, and as of 2016 there were three backcountry shelters: Old Hermit Shelter and Baldhead Lean-to in the Nash Stream Forest, and Panorama Shelter north of Dixville Notch. Fires are not permitted at any of these sites. As of 2016, these are the only permitted backcountry camping sites on the Cohos Trail north of the WMNF, much of which crosses private timberlands. Several additional shelters and campsites are planned by TCTA in the near future, including the Neil Tillotson Shelter in Pittsburg in 2017. State of New Hampshire campgrounds are available along the trail at Coleman State Park, Lake Francis State Park, and Deer Mountain Campground. Hikers interested in the Cohos Trail can obtain guidebooks, maps, trail updates, and much other information at TCTA's website, cohostrail.org.

CAMPING

Substantial portions of the territory covered in the Cherry–Dartmouth Range and the Pliny and Pilot ranges subsections are included in the WMNF, and normal WMNF camping regulations apply in such areas.

SEC 12

Most of the remaining forested areas in these subsections and all of the territory covered by the North Country subsection are private commercial woodlands, New Hampshire state parks or state forests, or town forests. On state lands, camping is usually restricted to official campgrounds, and on private lands, camping requires the permission of the landowner, which often isn't given due to owners' justifiable unwillingness to risk forest fire. See information above about camping along the Cohos Trail.

Forest Protection Areas

The WMNF has established a number of FPAs, where camping and wood or charcoal fires are prohibited throughout the year. See p. xxiv for general FPA regulations. No camping is permitted within 0.25 mi. of any trailhead, picnic area, or any facility for overnight accommodation, such as a hut, cabin, shelter, tentsite, or campground, except as designated at the facility itself, or at Unknown Pond except at the designated sites. In this section, camping is also forbidden at South Pond Recreation Area. No camping is permitted on WMNF land within 0.25 mi. of certain roads (camping on private roadside land is illegal except by permission of the landowner). In 2016, these roads included Old Cherry Mountain Rd. (FR 14).

Established Trailside Campsites

Cabot Firewarden's Cabin (WMNF) is located on Kilkenny Ridge Trail just south of the partly open south summit of Mt. Cabot, where the fire tower used to stand. The cabin has bunks for about eight people. The nearest reliable water source is the brook followed by Bunnell Notch Trail on the east side of Bunnell Notch. An unreliable spring is located on a steep, obscure side path off Kilkenny Ridge Trail 0.2 mi. north of the cabin.

Unknown Pond Tentsite (WMNF) is a designated campsite with five tent pads and an outhouse located on a spur path off Unknown Pond Trail near the southeast corner of Unknown Pond. Water is available from the pond or its outlet brook. Camping is prohibited within 0.25 mi. of Unknown Pond except at the designated sites.

Rogers Ledge Tentsite (WMNF) is a designated campsite with four tent pads and an outhouse located on a spur path off Kilkenny Ridge Trail 0.5 mi. south of Rogers Ledge. Water is available from a small brook 0.1 mi. south on Kilkenny Ridge Trail.

Percy Loop Tentsite (TCTA) is a designated campsite with a tent platform and outhouse located on Trio Trail near its jct. with Percy Loop Trail in Nash Stream Forest. Fires are not permitted. Water is available from a nearby brook. TCTA also maintains Old Hermit Shelter and Baldhead Lean-to in Nash Stream Forest, and Panorama Shelter north of Dixville

Notch, although the trail sections that lead to those shelters are not described in this guide.

SUGGESTED HIKES

■ Easy Hikes

DIXVILLE NOTCH

🏃🤸🥾   ↕️   ↗️   ⏱️

RT to Table Rock via Table Rock Trail (western section)	1.6 mi.	750 ft.	1:10
RT to Table Rock via Huntington Cascade and Three Brothers trails	3.2 mi.	1,300 ft.	2:15
RT to Sanguinary Ridge via Sanguinary Ridge Trail	0.6 mi.	350 ft.	0:30

On one side of Dixville Notch is the spectacular perch known as Table Rock; choose between a shorter approach from the west (see Table Rock Trail, p. 592) or a longer, more scenic approach from the east, including a side trip to another outlook (see Huntington Cascade Trail, p. 593). Across the notch, a short, steep hike leads to open ledges on Sanguinary Ridge (see Sanguinary Ridge Trail, p. 594).

MAGALLOWAY MTN.

🎿🚶🐕🍃   ↕️   ↗️   ⏱️

LP to Magalloway Mtn. via Coot, Bobcat, and Overlook trails	2.2 mi.	900 ft.	1:35
LP to Garfield Falls via Garfield Falls Path	1.0 mi.	200 ft.	0:35

This remote peak overlooks an extensive uninhabited region, with sweeping views from a fire tower and a superb viewpoint at the top of the east cliff. Coot and Bobcat trails make a convenient loop, along with the side trip to the east cliff viewpoint (to begin, see Coot Trail, p. 598). If in the area, the easy loop to Garfield Falls is worthwhile (see Garfield Falls Path, p. 599).

LOOKOUT LEDGE

🚶🐕📷🍃   ↕️   ↗️   ⏱️

RT via Ledge Trail	2.6 mi.	950 ft.	1:45

A fairly steep climb is rewarded with this excellent overlook of the northern Presidentials. See Ledge Trail, p. 556.

SEC 12

FALLS IN THE RIVER

	〽	📈	⏱
RT via Falls in the River Trail	2.8 mi.	100 ft.	1:25

Starting at Second Connecticut Lake dam, a mostly easy walk along the Connecticut River leads to this scenic cascade and gorge. See Falls in the River Trail, p. 600.

DEVIL'S HOPYARD

	〽	📈	⏱
RT via Kilkenny Ridge and Devil's Hopyard trails	2.6 mi.	200 ft.	1:25

Start from South Pond off NH 110 to reach this miniature version of the more spectacular—but more difficult—gorges at the Ice Gulch and Mahoosuc Notch. Use care on the slippery rocks. To begin, see Kilkenny Ridge Trail, p. 571.

CHERRY PONDS

	〽	📈	⏱
RT via Pondicherry Rail Trail, spur trail to viewing platform, Waumbek Link, Shore Path, Rampart Path, and Little Cherry Pond Loop Trail	5.1 mi.	150 ft.	2:30

A nearly level walk leads to Cherry Pond and Little Cherry Pond for wildlife viewing platforms, interesting flora, and excellent mountain vistas. To begin, see Pondicherry Rail Trail, p. 546.

■ Moderate Hikes

DIAMOND PEAKS

	〽	📈	⏱
RT via Dead Diamond Rd. and Diamond Peaks Trail	6.6 mi.	800 ft.	3:40

The hike to this scenic small ridge with good views in the Dartmouth Second College Grant starts with an interesting stroll along the Diamond River. See Diamond Peaks Trail, p. 595.

MT. CRESCENT

	〽	📈	⏱
RT via Peek Path and Mt. Crescent Trail	2.8 mi.	1,300 ft.	2:05

Some fairly steep climbing leads to good Presidential Range views and an unusual vista of the Pliny and Pilot ranges. Longer loop hikes are possible using Crescent Ridge Trail and others trails in the extensive network on the Crescent Range. To begin, see Peek Path, p. 557.

NORTH PERCY PEAK

		⇅	↗	○
RT via Percy Peaks Trail		4.4 mi.	2,200 ft.	3:20
LP via Percy Peaks Trail, Percy Loop Trail, and Nash Stream Rd.		6.0 mi.	2,200 ft.	4:05

A fairly rugged climb up this ledgy mountain delivers excellent views over Nash Stream Forest. A loop option varies the descent. To begin, see Percy Peaks Trail, p. 582.

SUGARLOAF MTN.

	⇅	↗	○
RT via Sugarloaf Mtn. Trail	4.2 mi.	2,200 ft.	3:10

A steady ascent leads to a partly open peak in the upper Nash Stream valley. See Sugarloaf Mtn. Trail, p. 589.

OWL'S HEAD

		⇅	↗	○
RT via Owl's Head Trail		4.8 mi.	2,000 ft.	3:25
RT including Cherry Mtn. via Owl's Head Trail and Martha's Mile		6.4 mi.	2,550 ft.	4:30

A steady climb leads to this ledgy knob and its fine view of the Presidentials. For a longer hike, Martha's Mile continues to the summit of Cherry Mtn. and more views. To begin, see Owl's Head Trail, p. 544.

■ Strenuous Hikes
ROGERS LEDGE

		⇅	↗	○
RT from York Pond Rd. via Mill Brook and Kilkenny Ridge trails		8.4 mi.	1,600 ft.	5:00
RT from South Pond via Kilkenny Ridge Trail		8.2 mi.	1,850 ft.	5:00

This spectacular, remote, and seldom-visited viewpoint can be reached via two routes: From York Pond Rd., see Mill Brook Trail, p. 578; and, if the gate is open, from South Pond, see Kilkenny Ridge Trail, p. 571.

**SEC
12**

MT. WAUMBEK

	⇅	↗	↻
RT via Starr King and Kilkenny Ridge trails	7.2 mi.	2,800 ft.	5:00

A moderate climb through fine woods reaches Mt. Starr King and Presidential Range views, with even better views from an opening just past the summit of Mt. Waumbek. See Starr King Trail, p. 574.

MT. CABOT

	⇅	↗	↻
RT via York Pond, Bunnell Notch, and Kilkenny Ridge trails	9.6 mi.	3,000 ft.	6:20
LP including the Horn and Unknown Pond via York Pond, Bunnell Notch, and Kilkenny Ridge trails, Horn side path, and Unknown Pond Trail (south section)	11.6 mi.	3,350 ft.	7:30
RT to Unknown Pond and the Horn via Unknown Pond (north section) and Kilkenny Ridge trails and Horn side path	8.4 mi.	2,350 ft.	5:25
RT to Unknown Pond, the Horn, and Mt. Cabot via Unknown Pond (north section) and Kilkenny Ridge trails and Horn side path	10.6 mi.	3,350 ft.	7:00

With Mt. Cabot Trail closed, the first route, above, is the shortest to New Hampshire's northernmost 4,000-footer, with two good viewpoints along the way. The second route adds the magnificent views from the Horn and beautiful Unknown Pond via a longer loop hike. To begin either of the first two routes, see York Pond Trail, p. 576. The third route, from Mill Brook Rd. (FR 11) off NH 110, is an alternative approach to Unknown Pond and the Horn. The fourth option adds Mt. Cabot. To begin the latter two routes, see Unknown Pond Trail, p. 577.

TRAIL DESCRIPTIONS

CHERRY–DARTMOUTH RANGE

Cherry Mtn. is a prominent mountain ridge located in the town of Carroll, west of the Presidential Range. The highest peak on its long ridge is Mt. Martha (3,573 ft.), which has three outlooks from the summit area at the site of a former fire tower. A northern spur, Owl's Head (3,258 ft.), has a spectacular view from fine ledges just south of the wooded summit. The Dartmouth Range is a ridge with numerous humps running southwest to northeast between Cherry Mtn. and the Presidentials. The range is completely trailless; Mt. Dartmouth (3,727 ft.) and Mt. Deception (3,671 ft.) are the most important summits. Cherry Mountain Rd. (FR 14), 6.9-mi. long, runs from US 302 0.9 mi. west of the Cog Railway Base Rd. to the jct. of NH 115 and NH 115A, passing through the high notch that separates the two mountain masses. This area is covered by AMC's *White Mountains Trail Map 2: Franconia–Pemigewasset.*

Pondicherry National Wildlife Refuge (a division of the Silvio O. Conte National Fish & Wildlife Refuge) is a fine 6,400-acre tract of forest with several ponds and extensive wetlands located in Jefferson and Whitefield. Its prominent features include Cherry Pond (about 100 acres) and Little Cherry Pond (about 20 acres). As "Great Ponds," these are in the custody of the state. Surrounding each are bands of open bog and bog-swamp forest belonging to New Hampshire Audubon. To the north of the Cherry ponds is tiny Mud Pond. All three of these ponds can now be reached by easy-graded trails.

Refuge trails are maintained by the Friends of Pondicherry (FOP). Pondicherry is the old name for Cherry Pond and nearby Cherry Mtn. The refuge is managed jointly by the U.S. Fish and Wildlife Service, New Hampshire Fish and Game Department, New Hampshire Trails Bureau, and NHA. At least 230 species of birds, including uncommon land and water species, have been seen here. Pondicherry is also interesting for its variety of vegetation (including several "champion trees" of various species) and its spectacular views of the Presidential Range. Its importance has been recognized by its designation as a National Natural Landmark and an Important Bird Area. The refuge is open from half an hour before sunrise to half an hour after sunset. Camping and fires are not allowed.

At the southern base of Cherry Mtn. are the Lower Falls of the Ammonoosuc River, easily reached by a trail that starts at the east end of the large parking area on the north side of US 302, 0.3 mi. east of the junction with Zealand Rd. The trail (sign: Lower Falls) follows a grassy roadbed (a former route of US 302) 0.5 mi. at easy grades to ledges beside the falls.

CHERRY MTN. TRAIL (WMNF; MAP 2: F6–F7)

Cumulative from parking area off NH 115 (1,650 ft.) to:	⇵	↗	⟳
Mt. Martha summit spur trail (3,370 ft.)	1.7 mi.	1,700 ft.	1:40
Mt. Martha summit (3,573 ft.) via spur trail	1.9 mi.	1,900 ft.	1:55
Cherry Mtn. Rd. (2,190 ft.)	5.3 mi.	1,800 ft. (rev. 1,300 ft.)	3:35

SEC 12

This trail runs across the ridge of Cherry Mtn. just south of the summit of Mt. Martha (which is reached by a spur path). The west trailhead is at a parking area opposite Lennon Rd. on NH 115, 1.9 mi. north of its jct. with US 3; the east trailhead, which is far less frequently used, is on Cherry Mtn. Rd. (FR 14, which is narrow; use care), just north of its height-of-land, 3.2 mi. from US 302 and 3.7 mi. from NH 115. The eastern part of the trail is heavily used by snowmobiles in winter; parts of it are grassy and brushy in summer.

Leaving the parking area off NH 115, the trail ascends at easy to moderate grades through young growth on an old logging road, paralleling Carter Brook, which is in a small ravine to the right. At 0.6 mi. it skirts the edge of a large clearcut on the left. At 0.7 mi., the trail becomes a footpath and ascends more steeply through mature woods on an old roadbed, climbing higher above the brook, and passes a spring on the left at 1.3 mi. At 1.7 mi., the trail reaches the ridge crest (signs), and a spur path turns left and climbs 0.2 mi. to the partly open summit of Mt. Martha, swinging left at the top to reach the small summit clearing from the north. Here the trail meets Martha's Mile (sign), which diverges sharply right (north); in 2016 there was no sign for Cherry Mtn. Trail at the summit. To the left of where the trail emerges is a view east to the Presidentials. A beaten path continues ahead (southwest) a few steps to the brushy firetower site, where there are old supports and a restricted view north, then descends 40 yd. to a good view west and southwest.

From the jct. with the summit spur, Cherry Mtn. Trail turns right (south) and descends at mostly easy grades with occasional minor ascents on an old road with good footing in the upper part. At 3.1 mi., the trail turns left (east) and soon begins a steady descent. After passing through a long switchback, the trail runs at an easier grade on the north side of a minor knob, becoming muddy at times, and continues down the old road to its terminus on Cherry Mtn. Rd.

OWL'S HEAD TRAIL (RMC; MAP 2: E7)

From NH 115 (1,250 ft.) to:	⇅	↗	○
Owl's Head summit (3,258 ft.)	2.4 mi.	2,000 ft.	2:10

This trail ascends to the fine outlook on Owl's Head. The trail begins on the south side of NH 115 at a parking lot with the Cherry Mtn. Slide historical marker, 5.9 mi. from the jct. with US 3 and 0.8 mi. from the jct.

SEC 12

with NH 115A. The lower half is on private land, where logging operations have taken place in recent years. Parts of the trail in the lower section were relocated in 2000 and 2010; the yellow blazes and other markings should be followed carefully.

From the parking area, the trail crosses a small stream, turns right onto an old road, then in 50 yd. bears left off the road at sign (Path). The trail leads east and then northeast through young growth, descending slightly with fairly rough footing, then turns right (south) at 0.3 mi. and ascends easily. In another 0.2 mi., the trail bears right and soon swings to the west, running nearly level, then at 0.6 mi. bears left (south) toward the mountain. The trail rises at easy grades, dips to cross Stanley Slide Brook at 1.1 mi., then climbs steeply up the far bank and turns sharply left at the WMNF boundary. After crossing an old logging road, the trail climbs steadily through hardwoods. At 1.9 mi., it turns right off an old route of the trail and angles west across a rocky slope.

The trail climbs steeply past a WMNF boundary marker and turns sharply left at 2.1 mi., gaining the crest of a northwest ridge. The grade is easy at first then steep as the trail zigzags up the cone, passing two restricted outlooks. The trail meets Martha's Mile on a wooded ledge at the summit, which has a partial view to the north. To reach the main outlook ledges, descend a short distance south on Martha's Mile.

MARTHA'S MILE (WMNF; MAP 2: E7–F7)

From Owl's Head (3,258 ft.) to:	⇅	⬈	⟲
Mt. Martha summit (3,573 ft.)	0.8 mi.	450 ft. (rev. 100 ft.)	0:40

Martha's Mile is a link trail between the summits of Mt. Martha and Owl's Head. From the wooded ledge at the summit of Owl's Head, the trail descends a short distance south to the main outlook ledges, which have a magnificent view of the Presidential Range. The trail turns right (west), where a spur leads a few steps left to the view ledges, then quickly right again (north) along the edge of a dropoff (use caution). It then descends a short, very steep pitch and turns sharply left. The trail continues steeply for a short distance before descending easily to a col and climbing moderately then gradually through attractive woods, with good footing, to the summit of Mt. Martha.

SEC 12

PONDICHERRY RAIL TRAIL (FOP/NHDP; MAP 2: E6)

Cumulative from parking area off Airport Rd. (1,130 ft.) to:	↕	↗	○
Viewing platform at Cherry Pond via spur trail (1,110 ft.)	1.5 mi.	50 ft. (rev. 50 ft.)	0:45
Little Cherry Pond Loop Trail (1,130 ft.) via trails below	1.9 mi.	50 ft.	0:55
Colonel Whipple Trail jct. (1,110 ft.) via trails below	2.2 mi.	50 ft.	1:10

This trail, which follows an abandoned Maine Central Railroad right of way to Cherry Pond, is the main access route to Pondicherry National Wildlife Refuge. From NH 115, 4.4 mi north of its jct. with US 3 in Carroll, turn left (west) on Hazen Rd. (also signed as Airport Rd. in some locations). At 1.4 mi from NH 115, turn right into a parking area (sign: Presidential Recreational Trail). Pondicherry Rail Trail begins beyond a kiosk and gate and follows the railroad grade generally northeast through woods and brush, crossing under a power line at 0.8 mi. From the power line on, the trail is mostly in the open and can be a hot walk in the summer sun.

At 1.4 mi., a spur trail (sign: Observation Deck) diverges right and follows a connecting section of railroad grade for 0.1 mi. then crosses another abandoned railroad grade. (To the right, this railroad grade is Presidential Rail Trail, which leads 19 mi. east to Gorham; in 0.2 mi. this trail enters Moorhen Marsh, an extensive wetland with fine views and excellent opportunities for birding and wildlife viewing. For 1.9 mi., this trail is also the route of the Cohos Trail. To the left, this railroad grade [sign: Waumbek Link] leads 0.1 mi. to the main Pondicherry Rail Trail.) After crossing this railroad grade, the spur trail follows an elevated walkway for 40 yd. to a viewing platform (dedicated to the New Hampshire ornithologist and refuge founder Tudor Richards) on the southwest shore of Cherry Pond, where you have magnificent views of the Pliny, Crescent, and Presidential ranges.

From the jct. with the spur trail, Pondicherry Rail Trail continues ahead, and at 1.5 mi., it meets Waumbek Link at a location known as Waumbek Junction, where there is a large sign. The main route to the Cherry ponds continues straight ahead (northeast) beyond the jct., crossing the Johns River on a railroad bridge where an occasionally active track joins from the left; hikers should exercise caution here. Walk along the right edge of the tracks past a swamp. At 1.6 mi., Shore Path (sign) diverges right into the woods, reaching the shore of Cherry Pond and a view of the Presidential Range in 100 yd.; here a spur path leads 70 yd. right to another viewpoint. At this jct. Shore Path turns left, passing more vistas, a bench and a National Natural Landmark plaque, and loops back to rejoin the railroad track 0.1 mi. from its start. By continuing north along the tracks, you can reach three more trails.

About 150 yd. beyond the north end of Shore Path, Rampart Path (sign) leads right 80 yd. to an opening on the shore of Cherry Pond, with a sweeping view of the Pliny, Crescent, Presidential, and Dartmouth ranges and Cherry Mtn. Rampart Path, then runs north on a natural upthrust known as an ice push rampart. At 0.1 mi. from its start (1.9 mi. from the trailhead), the path reaches a jct. where a connecting path (sign: Little Cherry Pond Trail) leads left 40 yd. to the railroad tracks across from the start of Little Cherry Pond Loop Trail.

Rampart Path (sign) continues ahead (north) along the ice push rampart, following a narrow and somewhat rough footpath through dense growth behind the edge of the bog on the north side of Cherry Pond, with occasional views. At 0.3 mi. from the jct. it reaches a bench with an extensive view across the bog to the Presidential Range and Cherry Mtn. It soon swings left into the woods and reaches a jct. with Colonel Whipple Trail (sign) at 100 yd. from the bench, in an area with many large black cherry trees. Colonel Whipple Trail—brushy and very wet in places, although recently placed bog bridges have improved the footing—continues ahead, carrying the Cohos Trail 2.2 mi. north to Whipple Rd. in Jefferson.

LITTLE CHERRY POND LOOP TRAIL (FOP; MAP 2: E6)

From railroad tracks opposite connector with Rampart Path (1,130 ft.) to:	↕	↗	○
Little Cherry Pond (1,100 ft.) via east loop	0.6 mi.	0 ft. (rev. 50 ft.)	0:20
Little Cherry Pond (1,100 ft.) via west loop	0.7 mi.	0 ft. (rev. 50 ft.)	0:20
Complete loop	1.3 mi.	50 ft.	0:40

Little Cherry Pond Loop Trail, which was designated in 2006 as a National Recreation Trail, leaves the west side of the railroad tracks (sign) opposite a short connecting path from Rampart Path and runs nearly level through conifers, reaching the first loop jct. in 0.2 mi. Here, the east loop continues straight ahead, and the west loop turns sharply left (arrow). The east loop passes over wooden walkways through an attractive black spruce forest, passes a jct. with Mooseway X-C ski and snowshoe trail (winter use only) on the right in 0.1 mi., and descends slightly to rejoin the west loop at 0.3 mi. from the first loop jct., near the edge of the bog surrounding Little Cherry Pond. From the first loop jct., the west loop runs west then swings gradually north to meet the east loop in 0.4 mi. From the second loop jct.,

SEC 12

the trail descends gently to the bog, traverses wooden walkways for 100 yd., and ends at an observation platform on the shore of Little Cherry Pond.

MUD POND TRAIL (FOP; MAP 6: E6)

From parking area off NH 116 (1,200 ft.) to:	⇅	↗	⟳
Mud Pond (1,130 ft.)	0.6 mi.	0 ft. (rev. 70 ft.)	0:20

This trail provides universal access to a viewing platform on the shore of Mud Pond, a small and secluded pond surrounded by an extensive wetland. The trail begins at a parking area off NH 116 (sign) between Whitefield and Jefferson, 1.0 mi. east of the Whitefield–Jefferson town line and 0.8 mi. west of the jct. with Whipple Rd. From NH 116, drive 0.1 mi. south on a gravel road to the trailhead. The trail begins to the right of a kiosk and follows a graded, gravel-surface path gently downhill with several short switchbacks. At 0.5 mi., the trail enters a raised wooden boardwalk and follows it 0.1 mi. to the viewing platform overlooking Mud Pond.

CRESCENT RANGE

The Crescent Range lies north of US 2 and west of NH 16 in the towns of Jefferson, Randolph, and Berlin. This area is covered by AMC's *White Mountains Trail Map 6: North Country–Mahoosuc Range*. The chief summits, from southwest to northeast, are Mt. Randolph, Mt. Crescent, Black Crescent Mtn., Mt. Jericho, and Mt. Forist. Mt. Crescent (3,251 ft.) offers good views south and north; this peak is ascended by Mt. Crescent and Crescent Ridge trails. The heavily wooded peak at the southern end of the Crescent Range, Mt. Randolph (3,081 ft.), is reached by Crescent Ridge Trail. Black Crescent Mtn. (3,264 ft.) lies to the north across the deep notch called Hunter's Pass. It is the highest peak in the range but has no trails to the summit; a prominent rockslide, once called the Crescent Scar, is on its southwest face. Lookout Ledge (2,260 ft.) is a granite cliff on a knob of the southeast ridge of Mt. Randolph that affords an excellent view of King Ravine, with moderate effort. The ledge is reached by several trails. The ledge is on private property, and no fires are permitted. Boy (Bois) Mtn. (2,234 ft.) is a small peak on private land at the west edge of the Crescent Range that offers an interesting view.

At the northeast end of the Crescent Range, located on private land just west of the city of Berlin, are Mt. Jericho (2,487 ft.), with a number of ledges on its south face that were bared in an early-1900s forest fire, and Mt. Forist (2,068 ft.), with an impressive east cliff that rises from the edge of the city. Both of these mountains have been heavily logged in recent years, with logging roads and snowmobile trails running practically to their summits, and there are now several wind turbines on Mt. Jericho. Mt. Jasper (1,584 ft.) is a small, isolated mountain just north of Mt. Forist, across NH 110 and the Dead River. It has great historical interest, as Abenaki natives mined rhyolite from its ledges to use for weapons and tools. Its summit ledges offer excellent views south, east, and west, and a recently constructed trail provides easy access from Berlin High School.

The Ice Gulch, one of the wildest and most beautiful places in the White Mountains, is a deep cut on the southeast slope of the Crescent Range, between Mt. Crescent and Black Crescent Mtn. The bed of the gulch is strewn with great boulders that lie in picturesque confusion, similar in many respects to those scattered over the floor of King Ravine. Among the boulders are many caves, some with perpetual ice. Springs and the melting ice form the headwaters of Moose Brook. Two paths lead to the gulch: Cook Path to the head, and Ice Gulch Path to the foot and from there up through the gulch. A short trail, Peboamauk Loop, follows Moose Brook below the Ice Gulch, past Peboamauk Fall and several fine springs back to Ice Gulch Path. The walk along the gulch itself is very strenuous with constant scrambling over wet, slippery rocks, requiring great care. This trip is not appropriate for dogs.

Pond of Safety is an attractive pond that lies within the WMNF, just north of the Crescent Range and east of the Pliny Range in the town of Randolph. Pond of Safety derived its name from an incident that occurred during the American Revolution. Four local men who had joined the Continental army were captured by the British and paroled on condition that they not participate further in the conflict. The Continental authorities felt the men's parole papers were spurious and insisted the men return to their units. Because the men feared severe punishment if they were recaptured by the British, they retired to this isolated region to hunt and fish, remaining out of reach until there was no danger they might be apprehended as deserters. Many years after the end of the war, having become respected citizens in the region, they were exonerated of the desertion charges and placed on the pension rolls. The pond has continued to be a place of refuge from the woes of civilization for those who love fishing, hunting, hiking, cross-country skiing, and snowmobiling. The pond may be reached by car from Jefferson by turning north off US 2, 0.4 mi. west of its jct. with NH 115, onto Ingerson Rd. then in 1.0 mi. turning right on Pond of Safety Rd. (FR 250; rough but usually passable for most vehicles with careful driving, though seasonally gated). Bear left at 1.4 mi. from Ingerson Rd., right at 2.1 mi., left at 2.4 mi., and left at a T jct. at 3.1 mi. At 3.7 mi. a spur road (FR 250B) on the left leads 0.2 mi. to a parking area above the pond. From here a universally accessible gravel path, built in 2015 by RMC and WMNF, leads 125 yd. to a perched beach and boat launch on the south shore. Pond of Safety may also be reached from Randolph by two RMC footpaths, Four Soldiers Path and Underhill Path.

Most of the paths in this region are part of the RMC trail system and are blazed primarily in orange. The town of Randolph consists of two sections: The lower section lies along Durand Rd. (the former US 2), in the Moose River valley, and the upper section is situated on Randolph Hill, a plateau extending southeast from the foot of Mt. Crescent that is reached by Randolph Hill Rd. (also known as Mt. Crescent Rd.). Lowe's Store and the Ravine House site are located in the lower section, and the trailheads for paths on the higher summits of the Crescent Range are in the upper section. On the south slope of the hill, connecting the two sections of the town and providing access from various points to major mountain trails, is a well-developed network of paths maintained by RMC. Several of these paths also provide access to Mossy Glen, a small gorge on Carlton Brook. In addition to the coverage in this guide, these local paths are described in detail in the RMC guidebook *Randolph Paths* (9th ed., 2016). They also are shown in detail on the RMC trail map titled *Randolph Valley and the Northern Peaks of the Presidential Range.*

Many of the trails on the Crescent Range are partly or wholly within the 10,000-acre Randolph Community Forest (RCF). For more information, visit randolphforest.org. On the northeast side of the Crescent Range is the town of Gorham's 4,000-acre Paul Doherty Memorial Forest, named for a longtime Gorham resident and New Hampshire Fish and Game official; the Ice Gulch is included within this tract. Bordering this forest on the southeast is Moose Brook State Park, which has a small network of multi-use trails that are shown on AMC's *White Mountains Trail Map 6: North Country–Mahoosuc Range* but are not described in this guide. For more information, visit nhstateparks.org/visit/state-parks/Moose-Brook-State-Park.aspx. North of Paul Doherty Memorial Forest and west of Jericho Mtn. is Jericho Mtn. State Park, with an extensive trail system that is primarily designed for ATV use.

Active lumbering and residential developments on the south slopes outside the Randolph Community Forest may intrude on some of the following trails, many of which are partly or wholly on private land; watch carefully for markers and signs.

Road Access

Most of the trails in the Crescent Range are reached from either of two roads north of US 2. Durand Rd. runs through the Moose River valley parallel to US 2 for 3.2 mi., from Lowe's Store on the west to Broadacres

Farm on the east, with short spurs connecting to US 2 at both ends. Randolph Hill Rd. leaves US 2 at the top of Gorham Hill, the high point of the highway between Randolph and Gorham, and runs for 2.2 mi. to Randolph Hill at the southern base of the Crescent Range. It is paved for 1.6 mi. then becomes gravel.

In 2014 a new Community Forest Trailhead loop parking area was opened on town land at the end of Randolph Hill Rd., 0.4 mi. northwest of the older, very small Mt. Crescent Trail parking area opposite Grassy Lane. Hikers are requested to use the new parking area, which can accommodate numerous vehicles, as the principal access point for hikes off Randolph Hill Rd. From this trailhead, recently constructed Peek Path provides access to Mt. Crescent Trail and Cook Path. Another new trail, Community Forest Interpretive Trail, makes a 0.8-mi. loop from the trailhead using short segments of Jimtown Logging Rd., Castleview Loop, and Carlton Notch Trail, with connecting sections along logging roads and through fields. There are eight signed interpretive stops keyed to an informational brochure that is usually available at the trailhead kiosk. The Community Forest Trailhead parking area is plowed in winter.

BOY MTN. PATH (MAP 6: E8)

From US 2 (1,575 ft.) to:	⇅	↗	⟳
Boy Mtn. summit (2,234 ft.)	0.7 mi.	650 ft.	0:40

This path ascends Boy (Bois) Mtn., a small mountain located east of Jefferson Highlands, with an open ledge near the summit that provides a fine view of the Presidential Range and Dartmouth Range. The path is on private land and is maintained by the Carter-Bridgman family. There is no trail sign where the path leaves US 2, 1.1 mi. east of the jct. of US 2 and NH 115. Park on an elevated grassy shoulder on the south side of the highway, just west of Carter Cut Rd.; do not park at the spring on the north side of the highway or in the driveway to the Carter estate.

Go up the first driveway to the west, which runs along the edge of a field, bear right at a fork, and pass between the house and barn to the base of a grassy slope. Walk up the slope past a small shed with a sign (Bois Mt. Trail) to the point where the trail, marked by a sign (Trail), enters the woods to the right and ascends. At 0.2 mi. from the parking area, turn left (arrow) across a traversing woods road and onto an old logging road that climbs up the slope. At 0.4 mi., turn right (east) onto a path (descending, bear left here). The path climbs moderately past a cement marker and bears right to the ledge near the summit.

SEC 12

CRYSTAL MINE TRAIL (RMC; MAP 6: E8)

From parking off US 2 (1,525 ft.) to:	⇅	↗	⟳
Crystal Mine site (2,135 ft.)	2.0 mi.	650 ft. (rev. 50 ft.)	1:20

Opened in 2016, this new trail in the Randolph Community Forest (RCF) leads to the site of a mine that was used by General Electric Co. during World War II to provide quartz crystals for radio sets. It begins at a two-story house and garage on a property that is now part of the RCF, located on the north side of US 2, 0.8 mi. west of Bowman (Castle Trail trailhead) and 0.2 mi. east of the jct. with Valley Rd. There is ample parking in front of the building.

The orange-blazed trail leaves from the right side of the building at a sign. It dips into the woods and ascends easily to the north along old woods roads and connecting sections of rocky footpath. After crossing two traversing woods roads, at 0.6 mi. Crystal Mine Trail turns left onto a major woods road (arrow). It descends gently along this road then ascends and turns right (arrow) onto a grassy spur road at a jct. at 1.0 mi. It follows this road uphill, with one minor descent, to a grassy clearing at 1.5 mi. where logging roads lead ahead, left, and right. The trail turns left into the woods on a footpath (sign: Path) just before this road jct. and winds northward through an open sugar maple forest. At 1.7 mi. it turns left onto an older woods road, ascends gently for 0.2 mi., then diverges left off the road and descends gradually 0.1 mi. to the mine site, where there are three small shaft openings (use caution) and numerous quartz pieces scattered on the ground. Hobby collecting with hand tools is allowed at the site.

BEE LINE (RMC; MAP 6: E9)

From US 2 (1,306 ft.) to:	⇅	↗	⟳
Pasture Path (1,760 ft.)	1.5 mi.	500 ft. (rev. 50 ft.)	1:00

This path is an important connecting link between the Appalachia parking area, the Ravine House site, and the trails on Randolph Hill. Beginning on US 2 directly opposite the Appalachia parking area, the trail descends through an opening in the chain-link fence. The trail swings left then right, running around the grassy west and northwest shores of Durand Lake, with fine views. The trail turns left and descends slightly to cross Moose River on Baldwin Bridge then at 0.3 mi. climbs briefly to Durand Rd. just east of the Ravine House site, following the road 40 yd. to the right. The trail then turns left off Durand Rd., ascends 20 yd. on a driveway, bears right into the woods (sign: Path), ascends across an excellent spring, then crosses a woods road diagonally and reaches a jct. on the right with Diagonal at 0.8 mi. From here, Mossy Glen can be reached in a short distance by following Diagonal and then Glenside downhill.

Bee Line bears left and crosses Carlton Brook on the Peeko Folsom Memorial Bridge, passes a jct. on the right with Burnbrae Path, and turns right onto an old logging road. It ascends north by easy to moderate grades for 0.5 mi. then bears left onto a driveway. In 30 yd. it reaches Glover Spring Rd. (which at this point is followed by Pasture Path) at its jct. with High Acres Rd. (In the reverse direction, follow the driveway south down from Glover Spring Rd. past a branching driveway on the right and the sign for Bee Line; the path enters the woods on the right a few steps beyond the sign.) To follow Pasture Path west toward Lookout Ledge, turn left here on High Acres Rd.; to follow Pasture Path east, turn right on Glover Spring Rd. For trails to the Crescent Range, follow High Acres Rd. straight ahead for 0.2 mi. to Randolph Hill Rd.; the new Community Forest Trailhead is 0.6 mi. to the left (west) along Randolph Hill Rd., and Ice Gulch Path begins 0.5 mi. to the right (east) along Randolph Hill Rd.

SHORT PATHS IN RANDOLPH VILLAGE AREA (MAP 6: E9)

	⇅	↗	↻
Diagonal, from Bee Line to Pasture Path	1.3 mi.	300 ft. (rev. 50 ft.)	0:50
Burnbrae Path, from Durand Rd. to Bee Line	0.5 mi.	250 ft.	0:25
Glenside, from Burnbrae Path to Diagonal	0.2 mi.	50 ft.	0:05
Wood Path, from the east end of Durand Rd. to Pasture Path	0.9 mi.	500 ft.	0:40
EZ Way, from Durand Rd. to Randolph Hill Rd.	1.0 mi.	550 ft.	0:45
Groveway, from Durand Rd. to Glenside	0.2 mi.	125 ft.	0:10
Bluffway, from Groveway to Glenside	<0.1 mi.	20 ft.	0:05
Church Path, from Randolph Church to Randolph Hill Rd.	0.5 mi.	50 ft. (rev. 30 ft.)	0:15
Short Circuit, from Pasture Path Rd. to Randolph Hill Rd.	0.1 mi.	60 ft.	0:05

Diagonal (RMC). This path begins on Bee Line 0.5 mi. from the Ravine House site on Durand Rd. and runs northeast uphill, linking many of the paths on the lower part of Randolph Hill. From Bee Line, Diagonal descends gradually to a jct. with Glenside, which continues straight ahead. Diagonal turns sharply left (northeast) here, crosses Carlton Brook, and

SEC 12

begins a gentle to moderate ascent. The trail crosses Burnbrae Path, soon bears left, and ascends moderately. At 0.5 mi., the trail crosses EZ Way and becomes level through a wet area with many bog bridges and rock steps. Diagonal crosses Wood Path at 0.9 mi., turns sharply left at 1.1 mi., and climbs to its end at Pasture Path, reaching the latter a short distance west of Pasture Path Rd. Randolph Hill Rd. is 0.1 mi. north via Short Circuit, which begins a short distance to the right (east) near the end of Pasture Path Rd.

Burnbrae Path (RMC). This path begins on Durand Rd. just east of Carlton Brook and the former Randolph Public Library. The path crosses a field, ascends through woods, crosses a driveway, passes a jct. on the left with Glenside at 0.2 mi., and then crosses Diagonal at 0.3 mi. Burnbrae Path ends at Bee Line, just above Bee Line's crossing of Carlton Brook.

Glenside (RMC). This scenic short path leaves Burnbrae Path 0.2 mi. north of Durand Rd. and follows Carlton Brook up through beautiful Mossy Glen. Shortly after passing a jct. with Groveway on the left, Glenside turns left and crosses to the west side of the brook, bears right as Bluffway enters left, and ends at Diagonal, 140 yd. east of the jct. of Diagonal and Bee Line.

Wood Path (RMC). This path connects the east end of Durand Rd. with Pasture Path. From the dead-end eastern section of the road, 0.1 mi. east of its connecting link with US 2, Wood Path climbs moderately through a field and then through woods, joins a woods road, and crosses Diagonal at 0.6 mi. Wood Path then climbs easily to end at Pasture Path, 0.3 mi. west of Pasture Path Rd.

EZ Way (RMC). This path leads from Durand Rd., near its east end, to Randolph Hill Rd., east of the Mt. Crescent House site. The path leaves Durand Rd. just east of a cemetery and just west of the connecting link with US 2, runs along the edge of a field, and enters the woods. The path climbs easily then more steadily, crossing Diagonal at 0.5 mi. EZ Way ascends at an easier grade through wet areas, crosses Pasture Path at 0.9 mi., and ends at Randolph Hill Rd.

Groveway (RMC). This path climbs from Durand Rd. just west of the former town library to Glenside at Mossy Glen. The path starts up a driveway then continues ahead, ascending through woods and passing a staircase that leads down to the right to a natural amphitheater in Mossy Glen. The path passes a jct. left with Bluffway, crosses the Nepalese Bridge over Carlton Brook, and ends at Glenside.

Bluffway (RMC). This short trail, less than 0.1 mi. long, runs along the west side of Mossy Glen between Groveway and Glenside.

Church Path (RMC). This path runs from behind the Randolph Church on US 2 to Randolph Hill Rd. across from Boothman Lane. Church Path starts behind the church, crosses a new cemetery with a view south, enters the woods, and runs at easy grades to a dirt road, where the path turns left (sign in reverse direction: Path) and leads 100 yd. to Randolph Hill Rd.

Short Circuit (RMC). This path leads from the west end of Pasture Path Rd. (which is also the eastern terminus of Pasture Path) north to Randolph Hill Rd., 0.4 mi. west of that road's 90-degree turn. From Pasture Path Rd., Short Circuit follows the edge of a field then runs along a stone wall and through a strip of woods between two houses to Randolph Hill Rd.

VYRON D. LOWE TRAIL (RMC; MAP 6: E9)

Cumulative from Durand Rd. (1,400 ft.) to:	⇅	↗	⏱
Crescent Ridge Trail (2,340 ft.)	1.6 mi.	950 ft.	1:15
Lookout Ledge (2,260 ft.)	1.7 mi.	950 ft. (rev. 100 ft.)	1:20

This orange-blazed path ascends from Durand Rd. to Crescent Ridge Trail near Lookout Ledge. Vyron D. Lowe Trail starts at the parking area for Randolph Spring on the north side of the road, 0.3 mi. east of Lowe's Store. The trail is lightly used, and the blazes should be followed with care. It enters the woods behind the spring (sign) and climbs moderately north and northeast, crossing two small brooks and entering the RCF (blue boundary blazes) at 0.4 mi. The trail crosses an overgrown logging road, climbs by switchbacks, and crosses another old road at 0.8 mi. The trail swings right through a cluster of boulders at 1.3 mi. then climbs easily through an open area of forest and berry bushes. At 1.5 mi., the trail bears right onto an old road and continues 0.1 mi. to Crescent Ridge Trail. For Lookout Ledge, follow Crescent Ridge Trail ahead (east) 0.1 mi.

SARGENT PATH (RMC; MAP 6: E9)

From Durand Rd. (1,310 ft.) to:	⇅	↗	⏱
Lookout Ledge (2,260 ft.)	0.8 mi.	950 ft.	0:55

This is the most direct route to Lookout Ledge, as well as the steepest. The trail is little used but well blazed, and with care, it can be readily followed. Leave Durand Rd. opposite a dark-red cottage 0.8 mi. west of the Ravine House site and 1.0 mi. east of Randolph Spring. Limited parking is available on the south side of the road; do not park next to the signpost. The path enters the woods and immediately bears left at a fork. The path rises steadily, eases briefly on a plateau at 0.3 mi., then climbs steeply, bearing right near the top to the ledge, where the path meets Ledge and Crescent Ridge trails.

LEDGE TRAIL (RMC; MAP 6: E9)

From Ravine House site (1,300 ft.) to:	⇅	⬈	↻
Lookout Ledge (2,260 ft.)	1.3 mi.	950 ft.	1:10

Leading from Durand Rd. at the Ravine House site to Lookout Ledge, this trail forms a steep but direct route to the outlook. Park at a small trailhead just west of the former hotel site, a long field with benches and an historic marker, 2.1 mi. east of Lowe's Store. The trail (signs) starts up into the woods between two driveways and climbs steadily northwest to a minor notch at 0.6 mi., where Notchway diverges right for Randolph Hill. Ledge Trail turns sharply left here, enters the RCF, becomes steeper, and follows an old logging road through second growth. The trail then bears right off the road and shortly intersects Pasture Path on the right at 1.1 mi. Ledge Trail turns left here, climbs steeply over some rocks then descends slightly, passing the Eyrie (a small outlook) and continuing a few yd. more to its end at Crescent Ridge Trail. Just below to the left are Lookout Ledge and the upper end of Sargent Path.

PASTURE PATH (RMC; MAP 6: E9)

Cumulative from end of Pasture Path Rd. (1,680 ft.) to:	⇅	⬈	↻
Ledge Trail (2,160 ft.)	2.3 mi.	550 ft. (rev. 50 ft.)	1:25
Lookout Ledge (2,260 ft.) via Ledge Trail	2.5 mi.	650 ft.	1:35

This orange-blazed trail leads from Pasture Path Rd. to Ledge Trail near Lookout Ledge. Pasture Path begins at the end of Pasture Path Rd., 0.4 mi. west of Randolph Hill Rd., and runs west through old pastures and woods, passing jcts. with several local paths: Diagonal (in 70 yd.), Wood Path (at 0.25 mi.), and EZ Way (at 0.6 mi.). Shortly after passing EZ Way, Pasture Path briefly coincides with Glover Spring Rd. and then High Acres Rd.; follow signs carefully. Where these two roads intersect at

0.7 mi., Bee Line enters from the left; to the right (north) High Acres Rd. leads 0.2 mi. to Randolph Hill Rd. Pasture Path continues ahead (west) on High Acres Rd., and at 0.8 mi., the path turns right off the road.

Grassy Lane (RMC), which follows a path and then a driveway, diverges right from Pasture Path at 1.0 mi., providing a shortcut 0.1-mi. long (60-ft. ascent) to Randolph Hill Rd. opposite the start of Mt. Crescent Trail. (Grassy Lane affords the most direct route from Randolph Hill Rd. to Lookout Ledge via the upper part of Pasture Path.)

Pasture Path traverses a level swampy area with bog bridges and stepping-stones and turns left onto a logging road at 1.5 mi., passing a jct. with Four Soldiers Path on the right. Pasture Path descends briefly then turns right (west) off the road where Notchway continues straight ahead. Pasture Path runs across three branches of Carlton Brook, skirts the edge of a clearcut at 1.9 mi., then ascends to meet Ledge Trail 0.2 mi. below Lookout Ledge; turn right to reach the ledge.

NOTCHWAY (RMC; MAP 6: E9)

From Ledge Trail (1,825 ft.) to:	⥮	↗	○
Pasture Path (1,805 ft.)	0.5 mi.	100 ft. (rev. 100 ft.)	0:20

This is a connecting path from Ledge Trail, 0.6 mi. from Durand Rd., to Pasture Path, 1.6 mi. from Pasture Path Rd. Notchway leaves Ledge Trail at a minor notch and ascends slightly then descends across two logging roads. Notchway crosses two branches of Carlton Brook, turns right and then left, and climbs to Pasture Path 0.9 mi. below Lookout Ledge.

PEEK PATH (RMC; MAP 6: E9)

Cumulative from Community Forest Trailhead (1,950 ft.) to:	⥮	↗	○
Mt. Crescent Trail (2,200 ft.)	0.3 mi.	250 ft.	0:15
Cook Path (2,120 ft.)	0.7 mi.	250 ft. (rev. 100 ft.)	0:30

This new trail, opened in 2014, provides access to Mt. Crescent Trail and Cook Path from the new Community Forest Trailhead at the end of Randolph Hill Rd. Blazed in orange, it leaves the west end of the parking area to the right of a kiosk, immediately crosses Jimtown Logging Rd., and climbs steadily northwest with rocky footing. It swings right (northeast), crosses Mt. Crescent Trail at 0.3 mi., then runs at easy grades with minor up and downs, crossing an overgrown logging road and passing a view of

SEC 12

the Carter Range from the top of a logging cut. It descends moderately with rocky footing and ends at Cook Path.

MT. CRESCENT TRAIL (RMC; MAP 6: E9)

Cumulative from trailhead on Randolph Hill Rd. opposite Grassy Lane (1,850 ft.) to:	⇅	↗	○
Crescent Ridge Trail, lower jct. (2,700 ft.)	1.1 mi.	850 ft.	1:00
Crescent Ridge Trail, upper jct. (3,230 ft.)	1.7 mi.	1,400 ft.	1:35
From Community Forest Trailhead (1,925 ft.) to:			
Crescent Ridge Trail, upper jct. (3,230 ft.) via Peek Path and Mt. Crescent Trail	1.4 mi.	1,300 ft.	1:20

Mt. Crescent Trail provides a relatively short but steep route to the two fine viewpoints near the summit of Mt. Crescent. It is best accessed via Peek Path or Jimtown Logging Rd. from the new Community Forest Trailhead at the end of Randolph Hill Rd., located 0.4 mi. northwest of the trail's original trailhead on Randolph Hill Rd., which is opposite Grassy Lane and has parking for only one car (just east of the trail on the north side of the road).

From the trailhead opposite Grassy Lane, orange-blazed Mt. Crescent Trail enters the woods to the right of a residence, and at 0.1 mi. Cook Path diverges right. Mt. Crescent Trail soon bears right at a fork, and at 0.3 mi. it crosses Jimtown Logging Rd. (This road, not open to vehicles, leads 0.1 mi. left to Community Forest Trailhead.) In another 30 yd. Boothman Spring Cutoff diverges sharply right. Mt. Crescent Trail now climbs more steadily, and at 0.6 mi. it crosses Peek Path (which has ascended 0.3 mi. from Community Forest Trailhead). At 0.7 mi. Castleview Loop diverges left.

Mt. Crescent Trail continues up at an easy to moderate grade with good footing, and at 1.1 mi., Crescent Ridge Trail, an alternate route that rejoins Mt. Crescent Trail at the north summit of Mt. Crescent, branches right. Mt. Crescent Trail now climbs steeply northwest with rougher footing. A fairly difficult ledge scramble leads to the south viewpoint at 1.5 mi., where you have an excellent view of the Northern Presidentials. The trail then runs northeast across the wooded south summit of Mt. Crescent, passes through a shallow col, and ascends slightly to its upper jct. with Crescent Ridge Trail at 1.7 mi. near the north summit, also wooded. A few steps ahead from this jct. is a fine north outlook from which the Pliny and Pilot ranges can be seen across the broad valley of the Upper Ammonoosuc.

CRESCENT RIDGE TRAIL (RMC; MAP 6: E9)

Cumulative from Mt. Crescent Trail, lower jct. (2,700 ft.) to:	↥↧	↗	↻
Mt. Crescent, north outlook (3,230 ft.)	0.6 mi.	650 ft. (rev. 100 ft.)	0:40
Carlton Notch Trail (2,825 ft.)	1.6 mi.	700 ft. (rev. 450 ft.)	1:00
Lafayette View (3,025 ft.)	2.3 mi.	950 ft. (rev. 50 ft.)	1:40
Mt. Randolph summit (3,081 ft.)	2.9 mi.	1,250 ft. (rev. 250 ft.)	2:05
Four Soldiers Path (2,550 ft.)	3.4 mi.	1,250 ft. (rev. 550 ft.)	2:20
Lookout Ledge (2,260 ft.)	3.8 mi.	1,250 ft. (rev. 300 ft.)	2:30

This trail links Mt. Crescent, Mt. Randolph, and Lookout Ledge, making various loop hikes possible over the crest of the Crescent Range. Crescent Ridge Trail branches right from Mt. Crescent Trail 1.1 mi. from Randolph Hill Rd. (0.8 mi. from Community Forest Trailhead via Peek Path) and crosses the east flank of the mountain, ascending then descending. From there, Crescent Ridge Trail turns north and then west and climbs steeply to the fine north outlook where the trail again meets Mt. Crescent Trail, joining from the left at 0.6 mi. Continuing southwest, Crescent Ridge Trail descends at easy to moderate grades, first through fine fir woods then passing through brushy old logging cuts where markings should be followed carefully. At 1.3 mi., the trail crosses Carlton Brook, rises slightly, then continues down to Carlton Notch, where Crescent Ridge Trail passes jcts. on the left with Carlton Notch Trail at 1.6 mi. and on the right with Underhill Path at 1.8 mi.

Crescent Ridge Trail then ascends the ridge that rises west from Carlton Notch, with occasional minor descents, and passes Lafayette View, an outlook with a restricted view of the Northern Presidentials. The trail then descends rather steeply to the east side of the col between Mt. Randolph and the slightly higher unnamed peak north of it, crosses the headwaters of a branch of Carlton Brook, and climbs to the wooded summit of Mt. Randolph at 2.9 mi. At the south end of the flat summit, the trail swings left to descend, soon passing a ledge on the right with a view of the Northern Presidentials. From here, the trail descends steeply, crosses Four Soldiers Path at 3.4 mi. and then a logging road, then turns left (east) on an old logging road where Vyron D. Lowe Trail joins on the right, and continues for 0.1 mi. to meet Ledge Trail just above Lookout Ledge.

CARLTON NOTCH TRAIL (RMC; MAP 6: E9)

From Randolph Hill Rd. (1,900 ft.) to:	⇅	↗	↻
Crescent Ridge Trail (2,825 ft.)	1.6 mi.	950 ft.	1:15

Carlton Notch Trail leads from Randolph Hill Rd., 0.1 mi. south of the new Community Forest Trailhead at the end of the road (where parking is available), to Crescent Ridge Trail in Carlton Notch, the pass between Mt. Randolph and Mt. Crescent. Carlton Notch Trail leads west from Randolph Hill Rd., ascending gradually, and at 0.2 mi. Community Forest Interpretive Trail joins from a wildlife meadow on the right. The two trails coincide, reaching Jimtown Logging Rd. in another 0.1 mi., turning left and following the road for 35 yd., then turning right off the road into the woods. At 0.4 mi., Castleview Loop diverges right, just before the Mt. Crescent Water Co. reservoir, which is also on the right; Community Forest Interpretive Trail follows Castleview Loop. Carlton Notch Trail continues ahead on an old road, crosses Carlton Brook at 0.8 mi., soon crosses a branch brook, and ascends moderately with several switchbacks to Carlton Notch, where Carlton Notch Trail ends at Crescent Ridge Trail.

CASTLEVIEW LOOP (RMC; MAP 6: E9)

From Carlton Notch Trail (2,080 ft.) to:	⇅	↗	↻
Mt. Crescent Trail (2,260 ft.)	0.4 mi.	200 ft.	0:20

This short trail ascends from Carlton Notch Trail to Mt. Crescent Trail, passing one open view and two limited viewpoints and making a short loop hike possible. Castleview Loop diverges right from Carlton Notch Trail 0.4 mi. from that trail's lower terminus on Randolph Hill Rd. Coinciding with Community Forest Interpretive Trail, it leads 70 yd. through woods to the top edge of a large meadow, where there is a view of the Carter–Moriah Range. Here Community Forest Interpretive Trail diverges right (east) across the meadow, while Castleview Loop runs ahead (north) along the top edge of the meadow and enters the woods. Castleview Loop climbs gradually then steadily, passing Castleview Ledge, which has a restricted view of mts. Madison and Adams, at 0.3 mi. The loop continues up to a rough side trail on the right that descends 35 yd. to Castleview Rock, an interesting boulder; a scramble to the top provides a restricted view of Mt. Adams. The main trail continues a short distance farther to meet Mt. Crescent Trail, 0.4 mi. above Community Forest Trailhead at the end of Randolph Hill Rd., via Peek Path.

FOUR SOLDIERS PATH (RMC; MAP 6: E8–E9)

Cumulative from Pasture Path (1,820 ft.) to:	⇅	↗	⟳
Crescent Ridge Trail (2,550 ft.)	1.4 mi.	750 ft.	1:05
Eye of the Needle (2,800 ft.)	2.0 mi.	1,000 ft.	1:30
Underhill Path (2,280 ft.)	3.3 mi.	1,000 ft. (rev. 500 ft.)	2:10
Pond of Safety (2,190 ft.) via FR 250 and FR 250B	4.1 mi.	1,000 ft. (rev. 100 ft.)	2:35

This lightly used trail through Randolph Community Forest leads from Pasture Path, 1.5 mi. west of its trailhead on Pasture Path Rd., over the Crescent Range to Pond of Safety Rd. (FR 250), 0.3 mi. from the pond. Four Soldiers Path is well blazed in yellow, although it requires care in places to follow. In combination with Underhill Path and other trails on the Crescent Range, Four Soldiers Path makes possible various loop hikes from Randolph to Pond of Safety. The trail is named for the quartet of American soldiers who, during the Revolutionary War, were unjustly accused of desertion and sought refuge at the pond (see p. 549 for more history about Pond of Safety). RMC has posted an article titled "Guide to the Cultural and Natural History of the Four Soliders Path" on its website.

Four Soldiers Path leaves Pasture Path on the right (west) 10 yd. beyond a sharp left turn. Four Soldiers Path soon crosses Carlton Brook and ascends west through hardwoods at easy grades, crossing an old logging road, an abandoned snowmobile trail, and several small branches of Carlton Brook. Swinging to the south, the path then ascends moderately along the southeast slope of Mt. Randolph, crossing the snowmobile trail twice more. At 1.3 mi., the path levels where a boulder on the left provides a framed view of Mt. Adams. In 130 yd., the path crosses Crescent Ridge Trail, and in another 20 yd., Four Soldiers Path turns right and climbs gradually northwest, passing along the upper edge of several old logging cuts. The trail reenters deeper woods and at 1.9 mi. swings right where a spur path leads 50 yd. left to a ledge with a view of the Northern Presidentials.

The main trail climbs easily for 0.1 mi. to the height-of-land and the Eye of the Needle (sign), a spot where there was once a unique perspective on Mt. Washington through Edmands Col; the view is now completely overgrown. The trail descends gradually, swinging more to the north and passing through occasional small, brushy, logged patches. At 2.5 mi., Four Soldiers Path enters an extensive semi-open logged area with dense brush that obscures the trail, which must be followed with great care. In 0.2 mi.

SEC 12

the trail reenters deeper woods and descends easily, crossing a gravel road at 3.3 mi.; Underhill Path begins 25 yd. right (east) along this road.

Four Soldiers Path meanders down to the northwest then crosses a series of bog bridges in a dense, wet conifer grove. The trail crosses two branches of the outlet brook from Pond of Safety, and at 3.8 mi., Four Soldiers Path ends at the gravel-surface Pond of Safety Rd. (also a snowmobile trail). To reach the pond, follow the road left 0.1 mi. then a spur road (FR 250B) right 0.2 mi. before descending a graded gravel path 125 yd. to the shore.

UNDERHILL PATH (RMC; MAP 6: E9)

From Four Soldiers Path (2,280 ft.) to:	↥↧	↗	↻
Crescent Ridge Trail (2,850 ft.)	1.4 mi.	750 ft. (rev. 150 ft.)	1:05

This yellow-blazed trail leads from Four Soldiers Path, 0.8 mi. south of Pond of Safety, to Crescent Ridge Trail, 0.2 mi. west of Carlton Notch Trail. Underhill Path is named for Miriam Underhill, a pioneer in women's mountaineering and, with her husband, Robert, a longtime resident of Randolph. The trail is lightly used, and in places the footway requires care to follow. It begins at a sign (Path) on a gravel logging road 25 yd. east of the point where Four Soldiers Path crosses the road and climbs gradually southeast through hardwoods, crossing some wet areas on plank walkways where undergrowth may obscure the trail. At 0.7 mi., Underhill Path turns right and climbs through a series of switchbacks, with fairly rough footing, in a beautiful forest of fir and birch. The trail crosses a height-of-land at 1.1 mi. and descends, soon turning to the left (east). The trail then swings briefly to the south and ends at Crescent Ridge Trail.

BOOTHMAN SPRING CUTOFF (RMC; MAP 6: E9)

From Randolph Hill Rd. at Mt. Crescent House site (1,800 ft.) to:	↥↧	↗	↻
Mt. Crescent Trail (1,950 ft.)	0.5 mi.	150 ft.	0:20

This short path, with mostly easy grades, provides access to Cook Path and Mt. Crescent Trail from the Mt. Crescent House site on Randolph Hill Rd., just east of the jct. with High Acres Rd. and 0.4 mi. west of the southern terminus of Ice Gulch Path. Parking is very limited; take care not to block the driveway. It starts up a driveway (sign on right) at the west end of the Mt. Crescent House site, passes left of a barn, bears left at a fork, and in another 35 yd. continues straight along the right edge of a field as the driveway bears left. It enters the woods at 0.1 mi. and runs northwest. It then swings west, passing Boothman Spring (sign) at 0.3 mi., and ascends moderately to cross Cook Path at 0.5 mi. In another 90 yd. it crosses Jim-town Logging Rd., making a jog 10 yd. to the left, and soon ends at Mt. Crescent Trail.

COOK PATH (RMC; MAP 6: E9–D9)

From Mt. Crescent trailhead on Randolph Hill Rd. (1,850 ft.) to:	⇅	↗	↺
Ice Gulch Path (2,460 ft.)	2.5 mi.	900 ft. (rev. 300 ft.)	1:45
From Community Forest Trailhead (1,925 ft.) via Peek Path and Cook Path to:			
Ice Gulch Path (2,460 ft.)	2.4 mi.	950 ft. (rev. 400 ft.)	1:40

This orange-blazed path provides access to the top of the Ice Gulch from the trailhead for Mt. Crescent Trail, where parking is very limited, or from the Community Forest Trailhead (ample parking) via Peek Path or Jim-town Logging Rd. It diverges right from Mt. Crescent Trail 0.1 mi. from Randolph Hill Rd. At 0.3 mi. from Randolph Hill Rd. it crosses Booth-man Spring Cutoff and then in a short distance it crosses Jimtown Log-ging Rd. (This road, not open to vehicles, leads 0.1 mi. left to Community Forest Trailhead.) Cook Path enters the RCF and climbs moderately. The jct. with Peek Path is at 0.8 mi. on the left. Cook Path now makes a long, angling, moderate ascent to the north, up the east slope of Mt. Crescent (with some rocky footing), and crosses several small streams. It then runs across two level shoulders of Mt. Crescent, with a slight dip between, pass-ing through a brushy logged area (watch carefully for blazes and signs) and crossing some wet areas and a stream. The path then descends moderately to the head of the Ice Gulch, where Cook Path meets Ice Gulch Path.

ICE GULCH PATH (RMC; MAP 6: E9–D9)

Cumulative from Randolph Hill Rd. (1,780 ft.) to:	⇅	↗	↺
Peboamauk Loop, lower jct. (1,780 ft.)	2.0 mi.	200 ft. (rev. 200 ft.)	1:05
Cook Path (2,460 ft.)	3.4 mi.	950 ft. (rev. 50 ft.)	2:10
Complete loop via Ice Gulch and Cook paths, Boothman Spring Cutoff, and Randolph Hill Rd.	6.5 mi.	1,250 ft.	4:55

This path gives access to the wild, beautiful Ice Gulch from Randolph Hill Rd., starting at an old farm with a red barn and prominent sign (Sky Meadows) located 0.6 mi. west of the 90-degree turn in Randolph Hill Rd. and 1.0 mi. east of the new Community Forest Trailhead at the end of Randolph Hill Rd. Please park cars off the south side of the road,

SEC
12

opposite the start of Ice Gulch Path. The trail runs to the bottom of the Ice Gulch and then up through it. Many hikers will feel more comfortable ascending, rather than descending, the slippery rocks in the gulch. Thus, although the route has traditionally been described for the descent through the gulch, it is described here in the ascending direction. From the top of the gulch, one can then return to Randolph Hill Rd. via Cook Path and Boothman Spring Cutoff.

Caution: The trip through the gulch itself is one of the most difficult and strenuous trail segments in the White Mountains, involving nearly constant scrambling over wet, slippery rocks, with deep holes between them, and it may take much more time than the standard formula allows. There is no way to exit from the ravine in the mile between Fairy Spring and the Vestibule; hikers must either retrace their steps to the end they started from or continue to the other end, and should keep this in mind when considering the suitability of this trip for their party or estimating the amount of time they should allow for it. The trail is emphatically not suitable for dogs.

From Randolph Hill Rd., Ice Gulch Path follows a driveway to the left of the red barn and continues across a small field, entering the woods at a sign (Path) and descending gradually. The trail passes the blue-blazed RCF boundary and crosses a brook then ascends through brushy woods and crosses Jimtown Logging Rd. at 0.6 mi. The trail runs at easy grades, crosses another brook, and continues north across the slope with several ups and downs, passing into Paul Doherty Memorial Forest and crossing several more brooks. The trail then descends to the "Marked Birch" (sign) at 2.0 mi., where Peboamauk Loop diverges right. Here Ice Gulch Path turns left, ascends through some wet areas, and passes through an area disrupted by logging for about 100 yd., where it must be followed with care; keep to the right. It then swings right and descends steeply to a jct. at 2.5 mi., where Peboamauk Loop rejoins from the right.

Ice Gulch Path descends to the south bank of Moose Brook and follows it upstream to Fairy Spring then crosses the small brook and begins the ascent of the rock-strewn gulch, heading northwest and passing along the base of a large talus slope on the right. You have views back toward Gorham and down the gulch. Farther up in the gulch, the trail climbs over a low wall dividing two "chambers." The scrambling becomes more strenuous and difficult, and the walls close in. Near the top of the gulch, the trail passes through a narrow gorge called the Vestibule, which has an excellent spring. Ice Gulch Path then climbs very steeply for 0.1 mi. to meet Cook Path at the head of the gulch.

PEBOAMAUK LOOP (RMC; MAP 6: E9)

From Ice Gulch Path, lower jct. (1,780 ft.) to:	⮃	↗	⏱
Ice Gulch Path, upper jct. (1,950 ft.)	0.5 mi.	250 ft. (rev. 100 ft.)	0:25

This path is an alternate route to the main Ice Gulch Path at the lower end of the gulch, more strenuous but more rewarding than the main route. Peboamauk Loop passes Peboamauk Fall, a fine cascade fed by the slowly melting ice in the gulch (Peboamauk means "winter's home"), and travels along a pleasant stream. The trail leaves Ice Gulch Path by the Marked Birch, 2.0 mi. from Randolph Hill Rd., and descends a steep, rough pitch to Moose Brook, swinging left to the base of Peboamauk Fall. Peboamauk Loop climbs steeply to the left of the fall, passing a view over the top of the fall, then climbs moderately with rough footing along the brook for 0.4 mi., crossing it four times, and rejoins Ice Gulch Path at the foot of the gulch, just below Fairy Spring.

MT. JASPER TRAIL (BERLIN HIGH SCHOOL/AMC; MAP 6: D10)

From Berlin High School parking lot (1,070 ft.) to:	⮃	↗	⏱
Mt. Jasper summit (1,584 ft.)	0.7 mi.	500 ft.	0:35

This trail to the open ledges of Mt. Jasper was built in 2011 as a cooperative effort by the Berlin High School Jobs for America's Graduates (JAG) program and AMC Trails. There are several interpretive signs detailing local human and natural history. The trail begins from a parking area at Berlin High School. From the stoplight at the jct. of NH 110 and the southbound side of NH 16 in downtown Berlin, follow NH 110 west 0.3 mi. and turn right on Hillside Ave. At 0.5 mi. from NH 16, turn left on Madison Ave. and follow it through several crossing streets. At 1.0 mi. bear left onto a one-way loop driveway and continue ahead to the northernmost parking area, to the right of a track-and-field facility. The trail begins as a gravel snowmobile trail to the right of a fence. In 70 yd., just past a metal gate, the trail turns right into the woods, between a kiosk and a historical map, and blue blazes begin.

Mt. Jasper Trail ascends moderately through a pine forest then swings left and crosses a snowmobile trail at 0.3 mi. and a branching woods road just beyond. It swings right up a rock staircase, turns left onto a steep woods road and follows it for 20 yd., then turns right off it and ascends a steep pitch to a T jct. with an orange-blazed trail at 0.4 mi. It turns left here and runs generally west, climbing easily then steadily, and swings left where yellow-blazed Cates Hill Trail, ascending 1.1 mi. from Cates

Hill Rd., joins from the right. In another 125 yd. the trail emerges on the summit ledge with partly restricted views. For the best views, follow a well-beaten path that descends 100 yd. southwest to open ledges at the edge of the south cliff, with excellent views of the Mahoosuc Range, the city of Berlin, and the Pliny and Pilot ranges.

PLINY AND PILOT RANGES

These two ranges are essentially one mountain mass, extending north and south between the Israel and Upper Ammonoosuc rivers, east of Lancaster. The Pliny Range forms the semicircular southern end of this mass; its chief summits are Mt. Starr King, Mt. Waumbek, and the three peaks of Mt. Weeks. Across Willard Notch from Mt. Weeks, the Pilot Range begins, including Terrace Mtn., Mt. Cabot, the Bulge, the Horn, and Hutchins Mtn. Farther northeast is a group of smaller peaks, the most prominent of which is Rogers Ledge. The region that includes the Pliny and Pilot ranges, along with the wide valley to the east drained by the headwaters of the Upper Ammonoosuc River, has been traditionally known to local residents as the Kilkenny. The name comes from the uninhabited township in which many of the peaks are located. In addition to Kilkenny township, this region includes parts of Berlin, Randolph, Milan, Stark, Lancaster, and Jefferson.

Rising at the west end of the Pliny Range is Mt. Starr King (3,907 ft.), named for Thomas Starr King, a minister in Boston and San Francisco who was the author of *The White Hills*—one of the most important and influential books ever written about the White Mountains. King Ravine on Mt. Adams and a peak in the Sierra Nevada of California are also named for him. New Hampshire's Mt. Starr King is located northeast of Jefferson village, from which the mountain is reached by Starr King Trail. The summit is wooded, with restricted views west and south from a cleared area.

Immediately east of Mt. Starr King is Mt. Waumbek (4,006 ft.), which is also reached by Starr King Trail and is the southern terminus of Kilkenny Ridge Trail. Formerly called Pliny Major, Mt. Waumbek is the highest point of the Pliny Range; just east of the summit is a view of the Presidentials from a blowdown opening. Located northeast of Mt. Waumbek, Mt. Weeks has three distinct peaks—North Peak (3,901 ft.), Middle Peak (3,684 ft.), and South Peak (3,885 ft.)—all of which are wooded, with no significant views, and are traversed by Kilkenny Ridge Trail. Formerly known as Round Mtn., it was renamed to honor John W. Weeks, who was the sponsor and chief proponent of the Weeks Act (1911), the federal legislation that authorized the purchase of lands for national forests and thereby made possible the establishment of the WMNF. On their north and west sides, respectively, Mt. Waumbek and Mt. Weeks enclose Willard Basin, a broad valley drained by Great Brook and Garland Brook.

The Pilot Range begins on the north side of Willard Notch and Willard Basin with Terrace Mtn., a narrow ridge with several summits, named for its appearance when seen from the west. Both its South Peak (3,655 ft.) and North Peak (3,638 ft.) are traversed by Kilkenny Ridge Trail. An opening just below the summit of South Peak affords an interesting view southeast; there are no views from wooded North Peak. The tallest peak of the North Country, Mt. Cabot (4,170 ft.), is located north of Terrace Mtn. across Bunnell Notch. Mt. Cabot's true summit is wooded. Partly restricted outlooks east and west are available at the site of a former fire tower, 0.4 mi. southeast of the true summit, and Bunnell Rock, a ledge above Bunnell Notch, provides an excellent vista.

The Bulge (3,950 ft.) and the Horn (3,905 ft.) lie just northeast of Mt. Cabot; both peaks are reached via Kilkenny Ridge Trail. The Bulge is a wooded hump with no views. The Horn, accessed by a spur path, is a fine sharp peak composed of a jumble of bare rocks that afford views in most directions. A long arm of the Pilot Range extends northwest from the Bulge over Mt. Mary (3,570 ft.) and several unnamed peaks to Hutchins Mtn. (3,730 ft.), sometimes also called Mt. Pilot, which was named for Alpheus Hutchins, an early settler. Ledges near the summit provide interesting views, but there are no trails. See the USGS Stark quad.

On a high plateau at the northeast base of the Horn lies Unknown Pond, which is reached by Kilkenny Ridge Trail or Unknown Pond Trail. The pond is one of the jewels of the White Mountains: a beautiful mountain tarn in a birch forest carpeted with dense ferns, offering a picturesque view up to the Horn from its shore. To the east of the pond is a prominent but officially nameless ridge, sometimes called Unknown Pond Peak (3,510 ft.). Northeast of this ridge is a high tableland with several wetlands, including small Kilback Pond.

Farther east is a cluster of smaller peaks at the northeast end of the Pilot Range: Rogers Ledge (2,965 ft.), Square Mtn. (2,735 ft.), Green's Ledge (2,492 ft.), Deer Ridge (2,808 ft.), Deer Mtn. (2,785 ft.), and Round Mtn. (2,150 ft.). Rogers Ledge, Square Mtn., and Green's Ledge all bear impressive cliffs on their south faces, and Round Mtn. and Deer Mtn. have ledges with views, but only Rogers Ledge can be reached by trail. This interesting peak was named in honor of Major Robert Rogers, leader of Rogers's Rangers in the French and Indian War. The view from the top includes the Kilkenny area, the Mahoosucs, the Carter–Moriah Range, and the Presidential Range. Rogers Ledge may be reached from South

Pond by Kilkenny Ridge Trail, or from Berlin Fish Hatchery by Mill Brook Trail and Kilkenny Ridge Trail.

To the north of Rogers Ledge is South Pond, where the WMNF operates the South Pond Recreation Area, a picnic and swimming spot south of NH 110 in Stark; camping is not permitted here. This is the northern terminus of Kilkenny Ridge Trail. The Devil's Hopyard is a picturesque gorge on a brook that empties into South Pond. The gorge resembles the Ice Gulch in Randolph but is shorter and narrower; it is reached by Devil's Hopyard Trail.

The flat, densely forested valley east of the Pliny and Pilot ranges is drained by the Upper Ammonoosuc River. This area is better known by loggers and those who love to hunt and fish than by hikers. There is currently only one maintained (and little used) trail in this area. Historically this region has been a major timber harvest area, and many of the features of interest reflect past and present logging activity.

Two fire towers that can be reached by driving provide excellent views that may be helpful to hikers planning trips in this region. Mt. Prospect (2,077 ft.) is located in Weeks State Park, the former estate of John W. Weeks, reached by a paved road that leaves US 3 at its high point between Whitefield and Lancaster; see Mt. Prospect Auto Road, p. 569. A small trail network is also located on this mountain. Milan Hill (1,737 ft.) is located in Milan Hill State Park (campground) on NH 110B west of Milan village; its fire tower offers a panoramic view that includes the Mahoosucs and the mountains north of NH 110, as well as the region covered in this subsection.

This entire subsection (except for the trails in Weeks State Park) is covered by AMC's *White Mountains Trail Map 6: North Country–Mahoosuc Range;* the USGS Jefferson, Mt. Crescent, West Milan, and Stark quads may also be useful.

ROAD ACCESS

The eastern side of the Pilot Range can be reached by York Pond Rd. (FR 13) to the Berlin Fish Hatchery at York Pond, which leaves NH 110 7.4 mi. northwest of its beginning at NH 16 in Berlin and extends 7.1 mi. to the trailhead for York Pond Trail. At 5.0 mi. from NH 110, a gate at the hatchery is closed from 4 P.M. to 8 A.M., although it may remain closed but unlocked until later in the evening. Hikers who plan to leave cars at the trailheads west of this gate and exit after 4 P.M. should make prior arrangements in person or by phone with the hatchery (603-449-3412). Foot travel past the gate is unrestricted. This road has been open, ungated, and plowed in recent winters, with a plowed parking area at the Unknown Pond Trail trailhead or the York Pond Trail trailhead.

Bog Dam Rd. (FR 15; not open in winter) makes a 15.5-mi. loop south of York Pond; Bog Dam Rd. has two jcts. with York Pond Rd., the first at 1.6 mi. from NH 110 and the second at 4.0 mi. Bog Dam Rd. follows in part a long-abandoned trail route and an old logging-road network, passing the sites of several former logging camps and providing access to Landing Camp Trail.

South Pond Rd., the 1.8-mi. access road to South Pond Recreation Area and the northern terminus of Kilkenny Ridge Trail, leaves NH 110 14.4 mi. west of NH 16 in Berlin and 10 mi. east of US 3 in Groveton. Bear right at a fork 0.7 mi. from NH 110; just beyond this fork is a WMNF gate, which is locked from 8 P.M. to 10 A.M. during the summer/fall season when the beach and picnic area are open. A fee is charged for day use, although in the past there has been no charge for parking of hikers' vehicles with a WMNF parking pass. Hikers should park in one of the first two lots on the left past the gatehouse. When the beach and picnic area are not open, the gate is usually locked, necessitating a 1.1-mi. walk to the trailhead. Foot travel is always permitted. Check with the Androscoggin Ranger District office of the WMNF for details. Mill Brook Rd. (FR 11) runs 4.5 mi. south from NH 110, 0.5 mi. east of Stark village, and provides access to the north end of Unknown Pond Trail; Mill Brook Rd. is not maintained for winter travel.

MT. PROSPECT AUTO ROAD (WSPA/NHDP; NHDP MAP)

From US 3 (1,430 ft.) to:	⬍	↗	↻
Mt. Prospect summit (2,077 ft.)	1.6 mi.	650 ft.	1:10

This road runs from US 3 at the crest of a hill between Lancaster and Whitefield to the summit of Mt. Prospect in Weeks State Park, where the picturesque fieldstone tower and surrounding grounds provide excellent views. The road has been open to vehicles on weekends in spring and fall, and Wednesday to Sunday from mid-June to Labor Day. At other times, the road is gated and open to pedestrian use (and to skiers and snowshoers in winter) only. When the gate is closed, parking is available at a lot on the right side of the summit auto road, just off US 3 and before the gate. Information and a Weeks State Park trail map are available at nhstate-parks.org/visit/state-parks/weeks-state-park.aspx.

Leaving US 3 at the top of the hill between Whitefield and Lancaster, the road ascends in a counterclockwise direction, crossing Around the Mountain Trail in 0.1 mi. At 0.6 mi., Davidge Path diverges right and descends 0.2 mi. through brushy logged areas to Around the Mountain Trail. At

SEC 12

0.7 mi., the road passes a restricted southwest viewpoint, and at 1.1 mi., Mt. Prospect Auto Road passes an excellent outlook to the Presidentials with a mountain identification sign. At 1.3 mi., at a hairpin turn to the left, Old Carriage Path diverges right and descends along the north slope of the mountain, crossing Around the Mountain Trail in 0.4 mi. and reaching Reed Rd. in 0.7 mi. The Auto Rd. continues to the summit and its buildings. At the summit, Ken Jordan Nature Trail provides a 0.2-mi. loop walk, starting at the summit lodge, looping around the fire tower, and ending at the Carriage House parking lot. Behind the summit lodge, a path (sign: North Overlook) descends 0.1 mi. to a wooden platform with a view north.

AROUND THE MOUNTAIN TRAIL (WSPA/NHDP; NHDP MAP)

From Mt. Prospect Ski Area (1,410 ft.) for:	⇅	↗	↻
Complete loop	3.0 mi.	350 ft.	1:40

This trail runs completely around the lower slopes of Mt. Prospect, providing a pleasant 3-mi. loop on interconnecting woods roads. The trail begins at the parking area for Mt. Prospect Ski Area on US 3, 0.2 mi. north of the lower end of the Mt. Prospect Auto Rd., where ample parking is available; the trail is described here in the counterclockwise direction. Parking is also available at the bottom of the Mt. Prospect Auto Rd., just below the gate and 0.1 mi. below the trail's crossing of the road.

From the south end of the ski area parking lot, walk 20 yd. up a gated road and turn right onto an old grassy road leading southward, marked by yellow blazes as part of New Hampshire Heritage Trail. Around the Mountain Trail ascends gradually, and at 0.3 mi., it crosses Mt. Prospect Auto Rd. At 0.4 mi., New Hampshire Heritage Trail diverges right, whereas Around the Mountain Trail swings left and eastward through a brushy logged area, where the trail must be followed with care. At 1.2 mi., the trail crosses an opening above a log yard with a view south; here, Davidge Path (leading through a brushy logged area) diverges left, ascending 0.2 mi. and 150 ft. to the Auto Rd. Around the Mountain Trail then turns left (north) onto an old woods road bordered with stone walls. The trail bears left off the road and ascends to a semi-open outlook to the east near a stone wall.

The trail continues to climb across a small stream and reaches its high point at 1.8 mi. then descends left (west). The trail crosses over several small streams and under maple-sugaring sap lines then swings left past old building foundations (right) and crosses Old Carriage Path at 2.6 mi. (The summit of Mt. Prospect is 0.7 mi. to the left, with 500 ft. of ascent, via Old Carriage Path and the Auto Rd.) New Hampshire Heritage Trail, which has followed Old Carriage Path 0.3 mi. up from Reed Rd., now coincides with Around the Mountain Trail for the rest of its distance. Soon, Around the Mountain Trail swings left (south) and descends gradually to the starting point at the ski area.

KILKENNY RIDGE TRAIL (WMNF; MAP 6: B8–D7)

Cumulative from South Pond Recreation Area (1,120 ft.) to:	⇅	↗	○
Rogers Ledge (2,965 ft.)	4.1 mi.	1,850 ft.	3:00
Mill Brook Trail (2,400 ft.)	4.7 mi.	1,850 ft. (rev. 550 ft.)	3:15
Unknown Pond Trail (3,190 ft.)	6.8 mi.	2,800 ft. (rev. 150 ft.)	4:50
Side trail to the Horn (3,650 ft.)	8.5 mi.	3,350 ft. (rev. 100 ft.)	5:55
Mt. Cabot summit (4,170 ft.)	9.6 mi.	4,100 ft. (rev. 250 ft.)	6:50
Bunnell Notch Trail (3,040 ft.)	11.4 mi.	4,250 ft. (rev. 1,300 ft.)	7:50
Terrace Mtn. summit spur (3,590 ft.)	13.3 mi.	5,100 ft. (rev. 300 ft.)	9:10
York Pond Trail, western jct. (2,720 ft.)	14.4 mi.	5,100 ft. (rev. 850 ft.)	9:45
North Weeks summit (3,901 ft.)	15.7 mi.	6,300 ft.	11:00
South Weeks summit (3,885 ft.)	18.1 mi.	7,100 ft. (rev. 800 ft.)	12:35
Mt. Waumbek summit (4,006 ft.)	20.6 mi.	7,700 ft. (rev. 500 ft.)	14:10

Kilkenny Ridge Trail is a ridge-crest trail that runs across the Pilot and Pliny ranges from South Pond Recreation Area off NH 110 to the summit of Mt. Waumbek. This trail, opened in the 1980s, was designed primarily to provide an extended route for backpackers interested in avoiding crowds of day-hikers. Except for the section south of the summit of Mt. Cabot, use of the trail is generally light. The trail has mostly easy to moderate grades and reaches several fine viewpoints—notably the Horn and Rogers Ledge—but has long stretches of woods walking that are pleasant but lacking in significant views. The trail is blazed in yellow, but many of the blazes may be faded; in recent years yellow plastic blazes have been placed along parts of the trail. In summer some sections may be obscured by ferns and other undergrowth.

For directions to the northern trailhead at South Pond Recreation Area, see "Road Access" on p. 568. From the South Pond parking lot, go right (south) toward the west shore to the sign for Kilkenny Ridge Trail. The trail follows the shore for 0.4 mi. (for the first 0.2 mi. on a graded, universally accessible surface), with several views across the water to Location Hill, then bears right away from the pond. At 0.7 mi., shortly after the trail crosses Devil's Hopyard Stream on a two-log bridge, Devil's Hopyard Trail diverges right (west), and Kilkenny Ridge Trail continues straight ahead. It crosses Cold Stream on rocks at 0.9 mi. and ascends southeast and south at a moderate grade through hardwood forest, following old logging roads with good footing.

After crossing another brook the footing gets rockier, and at 2.5 mi., the trail bears sharply right (west) then soon resumes its generally southerly course, entering a spruce forest. It swings right again at 3.0 mi. and crosses the town boundary between Stark and Kilkenny, marked by a wooden post, at 3.3 mi. Soon the trail climbs more steeply for a short distance then bears left along the crest of a narrowing ridge. After an easier section through an area of birch glades, the trail ascends moderately, bearing left several times, to a sharp left turn at 4.1 mi., with the summit of Rogers Ledge (with a benchmark and view) 20 yd. ahead on a side path. The edge of the cliff is reached by any of several short spurs on the right just before this turn. The large, flat, south-facing ledge provides wide views.

The trail descends steeply from the left turn near the summit of Rogers Ledge, curving to the east around the foot of the ledge, then descends moderately to the south. At 4.6 mi., the trail passes a side path left that leads 50 yd. to Rogers Ledge Tentsite then continues to its jct. on the left with Mill Brook Trail at 4.7 mi. Kilkenny Ridge Trail crosses a small brook, climbs to a plateau, and swings west through a muddy section to Kilback Pond at 5.3 mi. The trail crosses the pond outlet on bog bridges (views) then crosses a beaver-flooded area on more bog bridges. The trail climbs steeply over a minor ridge, crosses a level shoulder, then at 6.0 mi. begins a steady ascent through an extensive birch forest to the ridge east of Unknown Pond, reaching the crest at 6.4 mi. The trail descends to the pond at 6.8 mi., where it meets Unknown Pond Trail. (For Unknown Pond Tentsite, follow Unknown Pond Trail 75 yd. left to a spur path on the left; other than at the campsite, camping is not allowed within 0.25 mi. of the pond.)

Kilkenny Ridge Trail follows Unknown Pond Trail to the right for 100 yd. (avoid marked revegetation areas along the shore), soon passing a side path that descends 20 yd. left to a beautiful view of the Horn from the shore of the pond, then turns left off Unknown Pond Trail and runs around the north shore of the pond, passing another side path on the left. Kilkenny Ridge Trail descends to a wet sag, ascends moderately, then swings west and then south around the end of the ridge. At this point, it begins the climb up the northwest slope of the Horn, with rocky footing, to the sag between the Bulge and the Horn at 8.5 mi. Here, a side trail climbs to the left (east) 0.3 mi. and 250 ft. to the open rocks of the Horn, from which you have magnificent views. The upper part of the side trail has several ledge scrambles, including a fairly difficult one to reach the summit ledge;

an easier route leads left around to the back side of the ledge. Kilkenny Ridge Trail bears right (southwest) and ascends to the wooded summit of the Bulge, drops to the saddle, and makes a fairly steep and rough climb to a point near the true summit of Mt. Cabot at 9.6 mi. (The high point is on a side path 30 yd. to the right.)

Kilkenny Ridge Trail turns left (southeast), immediately passing a summit sign and then a side path that leads 30 yd. right to a restricted view west. The main trail descends past an obscure side trail on the left (cairn) that drops steeply for 250 yd. to an unreliable spring. At 10.0 mi., Kilkenny Ridge Trail crosses the viewpoint at the lower but more open summit of Mt. Cabot (with views northeast and southwest) and passes the cabin on the right just below the viewpoint, which has views west. (In the near future, WMNF plans to construct a wooden helipad platform at the viewpoint to service a radio repeater on the true summit.) The trail descends moderately by switchbacks and passes the fine outlook from Bunnell Rock on the left (sign: View) at 10.6 mi. as it makes a great curving 180-degree turn to the right. The trail then turns sharply left and, at 11.0 mi., turns left again where the unmaintained Mt. Cabot Trail (closed by a landowner in the trail's lower section) continues ahead.

Kilkenny Ridge Trail runs southeast, descending slightly then ascending gradually, and at 11.3 mi., it turns left and ascends another 0.1 mi. to a jct. with Bunnell Notch Trail, which continues ahead towards York Pond Rd. Here, Kilkenny Ridge Trail turns right to begin the ascent of Terrace Mtn., climbing easily at first then moderately to the densely wooded North Peak of Terrace Mtn. (sign). Kilkenny Ridge Trail then continues along the ridge with a significant climb and descent over a middle peak. At 13.3 mi., a spur path continues straight 0.1 mi. to the restricted southeast outlook at the South Peak of Terrace Mtn. (A more open view can be obtained from a fern-filled clearing just below the summit on the southeast side, reached by an obscure path that leaves the summit spur on the right just before the high point.)

From the jct. with the summit spur, the main trail turns sharply left and drops off the ridge then begins a long circling descent through an attractive birch forest, with rather rough footing. Crossing a small brook at its low point in Willard Notch, which has a trailside campsite, the trail ascends slightly to the west end of York Pond Trail at 14.4 mi., follows that trail left (east) for 100 yd., then leaves it on the right. Here, Kilkenny Ridge Trail begins a rather long and winding ascent of North Weeks, reaching the broad, wooded summit at 15.7 mi. Kilkenny Ridge Trail descends at easy to moderate grades on a long switchback past a small spring (unreliable) at 16.0 mi., to a potential campsite in the main col at 16.5 mi.

Ascending again, the trail passes over Middle Weeks at 17.1 mi., crosses through a much shallower col, and climbs to South Weeks at 18.1 mi. Here a short spur continues straight to the wooded summit, and the main trail turns left and descends to the col between Weeks and Waumbek at 18.7 mi. From here, the trail climbs steadily to a shoulder then swings to the west and ascends along the long east ridge of Waumbek, slowly gaining elevation despite occasional losses. It crosses the interesting, steep-sided east knob of Waumbek, where you have a restricted view north, and continues another 0.2 mi. to the true summit, where the trail meets Starr King Trail. About 50 yd. before the summit, a short side path leads left to a view of the Presidentials from a blowdown area.

DEVIL'S HOPYARD TRAIL (WMNF; MAP 6: B8)

From Kilkenny Ridge Trail (1,160 ft.) to:	⇅	↗	○
End of trail (1,300 ft.)	0.6 mi.	150 ft.	0:35

This trail leaves Kilkenny Ridge Trail on the right (west) 0.7 mi. from South Pond Recreation Area off NH 110 and provides access to the wild and beautiful Devil's Hopyard, a small gorge with steep walls and a boulder-strewn floor. The section in the Hopyard is very rough, leading through a jumble of mossy, slippery boulders with awkward footing; use caution and allow extra time. Leaving Kilkenny Ridge Trail, Devil's Hopyard Trail runs at easy grades along the south side of Devil's Hopyard Stream, crosses to the north side of the brook on a two-log bridge at 0.1 mi., and at 0.2 mi. becomes rough and rocky as it enters the Hopyard. For the most part, the small stream that drains the gorge is completely out of sight as it gurgles beneath moss-covered boulders, and high ledges overhang the path in several places. Near the upper end, the trail leaves the WMNF, and in another 150 yd. it ends beneath a high rock wall, beyond which is a sign (End of Trail).

STARR KING TRAIL (RMC; MAP 6: D7)

Cumulative from trailhead parking area (1,580 ft.) to:	⇅	↗	○
Beginning of traverse (2,900 ft.)	1.4 mi.	1,300 ft.	1:20
Mt. Starr King summit (3,907 ft.)	2.6 mi.	2,300 ft.	2:25
Mt. Waumbek summit (4,006 ft.)	3.6 mi.	2,600 ft. (rev. 200 ft.)	3:05

This trail begins on Starr King Rd., a gravel road to several houses that leaves the north side of US 2 (trail sign) 0.2 mi. east of its jct. with NH 115A. Go up the road, always bearing left to avoid driveways on the right, then bear right into a small parking lot (improved by the WMNF in 2016) at 0.25 mi. If the parking lot cannot be reached by car (as when the access road is unplowed in winter), park in the plowed lot across US 2 and just west of Starr King Rd. and walk up the road; do not obstruct the road or driveways by parking cars on them. (Additional parking may be found 0.1 mi. farther west on US 2, also on the south side.) The trail is generally fairly easy all the way up, with moderate grades and good footing.

From the parking area, ascend gradually on a logging road for 100 yd. then turn left (arrow) and ascend another 100 yd. to meet the old route of the trail, an old logging road on which the trail turns uphill to the right and soon passes the stone foundations of a springhouse (right). At 0.7 mi., the trail bears right and ascends the broad southwest ridge of the mountain through a beautiful hardwood forest. At 1.4 mi., the trail angles left into conifers and runs north on a long traverse of the west flank of the mountain, passing a spring (sign) on the left (downhill side) of the trail at 2.1 mi.

Swinging right and leaving the traverse at 2.5 mi., the trail climbs steadily to the wooded summit of Mt. Starr King at 2.6 mi. The trail continues another 40 yd. to a ledge with a limited view west then turns left and descends 20 yd. to a clearing at the site of a former shelter, where there is a partly cleared view of the Presidential Range. The trail enters the woods to the right of the remains of the old cabin's fireplace, descends briefly northeast, then swings right (east) and follows close to the crest of the ridge or slightly below it on one side or the other. The trail dips just below the col on the south and then rises moderately to the summit of Mt. Waumbek, where it meets the south end of Kilkenny Ridge Trail. About 50 yd. ahead on Kilkenny Ridge Trail, a short side path leads right to a view of the Presidentials from a blowdown patch.

MT. CABOT TRAIL (WMNF)

Note: The lower section of this trail was closed by the landowner in 2000, and the section on WMNF land below its jct. with Kilkenny Ridge Trail is no longer maintained. Therefore, no legal access is available to Mt. Cabot from the west side. Hikers wishing to climb Mt. Cabot should use one of the routes from York Pond Rd. (York Pond Trail, Bunnell Notch Trail, and Kilkenny Ridge Trail or the south end of Unknown Pond Trail and Kilkenny Ridge Trail) or the route from Mill Brook Rd. (north end of Unknown Pond Trail and Kilkenny Ridge Trail).

YORK POND TRAIL (WMNF; MAP 6: D8)

From York Pond Rd. trailhead (1,670 ft.) to:	⇅	↗	↻
Kilkenny Ridge Trail, western jct. (2,720 ft.)	2.5 mi.	1,100 ft. (rev. 50 ft.)	1:50

Note: The lower west section of this trail was closed by the landowner in 2000, and the section on WMNF land west of its western jct. with Kilkenny Ridge Trail is no longer maintained. Therefore, no legal access to this trail is available from the west side.

This yellow-blazed trail leaves York Pond Rd. (FR 13) near the latter's west end and follows old logging roads with generally good footing to Willard Notch and two jcts. with Kilkenny Ridge Trail, providing access to Mt. Weeks and Terrace Mtn. From the fish hatchery gate at York Pond (see the warning under "Road Access" on p. 568 concerning the gate at the fish hatchery, closed 4 P.M. to 8 A.M.), continue west 2.1 mi. on York Pond Rd. to a fenced raceway. The trailhead (sign) is at a gated logging road on the left, with room for several cars to park. York Pond Trail follows the logging road beyond the gate for 0.2 mi., across a bridge over a brook and into an overgrown clearing, then bears left (arrow) where Bunnell Notch Trail diverges right toward Mt. Cabot.

In 100 yd., York Pond Trail crosses a small concrete dam then continues up the south side of the brook at easy grades, crossing two branches 75 yd. apart. After a swampy area with wooden walkways, the trail begins to swing up a hardwood ridge at 0.9 mi., following a well-defined old logging road. At 1.8 mi., the trail swings right and ascends into birch glades. Soon the grade eases. At 2.4 mi., the trail reaches its highest point, just east of Willard Notch on a minor ridge from North Weeks. Descending slightly, the trail passes two jcts. with Kilkenny Ridge Trail 100 yd. apart; at the first, Kilkenny Ridge Trail leads left (south) to Mt. Weeks and Mt. Waumbek, and at the second, the trail leads right (north) to Terrace Mtn. Beyond this second jct., York Pond Trail is no longer maintained.

BUNNELL NOTCH TRAIL (WMNF; MAP 6: D8)

From York Pond Trail (1,690 ft.) to:	⇅	↗	↻
Kilkenny Ridge Trail (3,040 ft.)	2.8 mi.	1,450 ft. (rev. 100 ft.)	2:10
From York Pond Rd. trailhead (1,670 ft.) to:			
Mt. Cabot summit (4,170 ft.) via York Pond, Bunnell Notch, and Kilkenny Ridge trails	4.8 mi.	2,750 ft. (rev. 250 ft.)	3:45

SEC 12

This trail connects York Pond Trail with Kilkenny Ridge Trail in Bunnell Notch. In recent years, Bunnell Notch Trail has seen a considerable increase in usage as an alternative route to Mt. Cabot because the standard western route to that peak has been closed to the public since 2000; this also makes possible a rather long but very attractive loop trip to Unknown Pond, the Horn, and Mt. Cabot. Although still wet in places, the trail is better maintained and easier to follow than it has been in the past.

Leaving York Pond Trail on the right in an overgrown clearing 0.2 mi. from York Pond Rd., Bunnell Notch Trail follows a grassy logging road, bearing right at a fork in another clearing at 0.3 mi. from York Pond Trail. The trail descends gradually, crossing several small streams and the larger stream that flows down from Bunnell Notch at 0.7 mi. At 0.9 mi., the trail turns left (sign) off the logging road. At 1.1 mi., the trail swings right to climb to a high bank then descends slightly to the edge of the brook flowing down from the notch. The trail follows the north side of the brook up the valley, alternately close beside the stream and higher up on the slope. At 2.4 mi., the trail bears right at an arrow and climbs into Bunnell Notch, reaching the height-of-land at 2.8 mi. After a slight dip, Kilkenny Ridge Trail leaves on the left (south) for Terrace Mtn. and continues ahead (west) for Mt. Cabot.

UNKNOWN POND TRAIL (WMNF; MAP 6: D8–C8)

Cumulative from York Pond Rd. trailhead (1,640 ft.) to:	⇅	↗	⟳
Unknown Pond Campsite (3,190 ft.)	3.3 mi.	1,550 ft.	2:25
Mill Brook Rd. (1,750 ft.)	5.5 mi.	1,550 ft. (rev. 1,450 ft.)	3:30

This trail connects York Pond Rd. with Mill Brook Rd. near the village of Stark, passing beautiful Unknown Pond and crossing Kilkenny Ridge Trail. The south terminus is on York Pond Rd., 2.0 mi. west of the fish hatchery gate (sign) at a parking area on the right just beyond a small pond (see the warning under "Road Access" on p. 568 concerning the gate at the fish hatchery, closed 4 P.M. to 8 A.M.). The north terminus is on gravel Mill Brook Rd. (FR 11) 4.5 mi. south of NH 110. There is a sign (hiker symbol) on NH 110 at the beginning of Mill Brook Rd., which is 0.5 mi. east of Stark village, and a trail sign at the trailhead, which is just east of a bridge across Mill Brook. Limited parking is available beyond the bridge on the right.

Leaving the parking area on York Pond Rd., the trail reaches an old railroad grade at 0.1 mi. and turns left onto it. At 0.4 mi., the trail turns right off the grade and climbs northwest up the valley of the brook that

SEC 12

drains Unknown Pond, with several muddy sections. At 1.9 mi., the trail crosses the main brook then a tributary and recrosses the main brook at 2.1 mi. At about 2.5 mi., the trail begins a steeper ascent to Unknown Pond, passing through birch woods with luxuriant undergrowth (where the trail may be difficult to follow) and becoming rocky at times. Near the top of the climb, the trail passes a meadowlike area with restricted views. At 3.3 mi., near the southeast corner of Unknown Pond, a side trail on the right leads to Unknown Pond Tentsite; other than the five tentsites, camping is not allowed within 0.25 mi. of the pond.

In another 75 yd., Kilkenny Ridge Trail enters from the right (east) and coincides with Unknown Pond Trail for 100 yd. A few steps beyond this jct. a side path descends 20 yd. left to a beautiful view of the Horn rising above the pond; avoid the marked revegetation areas between the trail and the pond. The coinciding trails swing west around the pond, and at the northwest corner of the pond, Kilkenny Ridge Trail leaves left (west) toward the Horn and Mt. Cabot. Unknown Pond Trail goes northwest toward Mill Brook Rd. in Stark, rising slightly and crossing a moist area then descending moderately in beautiful birch woods for a mile. The trail then becomes more gradual, soon crossing the Kilkenny–Stark town line. The trail traverses the slope east of Mill Brook and ends at Mill Brook Rd. at 5.5 mi.

MILL BROOK TRAIL (WMNF; MAP 6: C8)

From end of spur road off York Pond Rd. (1,520 ft.) to:	⇅	↗	⟳
Kilkenny Ridge Trail (2,400 ft.)	3.6 mi.	1,050 ft. (rev. 150 ft.)	2:20

Formerly a through route from Stark village to York Pond, the north section of this trail, from the jct. with Kilkenny Ridge Trail at the height-of-land to Stark, was abandoned many years ago, and beaver activity and logging have obliterated the old footway. The remaining part of the trail, which actually follows Cold Brook, provides the most convenient route from the south to the spectacular views from Rogers Ledge. Mill Brook Trail begins near the main building of the Berlin Fish Hatchery at the end of a 0.2-mi. spur road off York Pond Rd. (FR 13); this road diverges right (north) 0.2 mi. west of the hatchery gate at a trail sign. (See the warning under "Road Access" on p. 568 concerning the gate at the fish hatchery, closed 4 P.M. to 8 A.M.) Parking is available to the left of the hatchery building, where there is another trail sign. (The lower part of the trail may be difficult to follow; if so, ask at the hatchery for directions.)

From the parking area, walk up a grassy road to the left of the hatchery building for 150 yd. then turn sharply right (sign), and in another 50 yd., turn sharply left onto the well-worn trail. (Avoid an old road to the right of the trail.) The trail follows an old woods road, bearing left at a fork, then narrows to a footpath, ascending along Cold Brook. At 1.0 mi., the trail climbs away from the brook then returns to the stream and follows it through several wet areas with luxuriant undergrowth that sometimes obscures the trail. At 2.2 mi., the trail swings right and climbs away from the brook to a plateau, runs nearly level through birch forest, then descends west from the height-of-land and ends at Kilkenny Ridge Trail. To the right (north), it is 0.6 mi. to Rogers Ledge; to the left (south), it is 2.1 mi. to Unknown Pond.

LANDING CAMP TRAIL (WMNF; MAP 6: D9)

From Bog Dam Rd. (1,820 ft.) to:	⇅	↗	↻
Jct. with abandoned Upper Ammonoosuc Trail (1,600 ft.)	1.9 mi.	50 ft. (rev. 250 ft.)	1:00

This yellow-blazed trail is the remnant of an old trail that once connected Bog Dam (built to provide a water head for spring logging drives on the Upper Ammonoosuc River and later used as a town water supply) with Randolph through Hunter's Pass. The trail is lightly used, minimally maintained, and very wet in places, and some sections may be obscured by annual growth; the trail must be followed with great care. WMNF may decommission it in the future. This trail does provide an interesting route through a low-lying area with extensive wetlands. It leaves the west side of the east leg of Bog Dam Rd. at a sign (easily missed), 6.3 mi. south of its jct. with York Pond Rd. (which is 1.6 mi. south of NH 110); parking is available 40 yd. north of the trail entrance.

The trail descends gradually to the site of the old logging camp 18 at 0.4 mi. and bears right through the brushy clearing. Landing Camp Trail crosses the first of several wet areas and a small stream, bears left, right, and left again, and crosses two more brooks, the second of which may require a detour to the right. The trail leads through an overgrown brushy area then follows an old road through a very swampy section. The trail crosses another brook, bears left at a fork, soon swings right and climbs over a knoll, and descends to another fork at 1.7 mi. Here, an unofficial path bears left, and Landing Camp Trail turns right, passes through a brushy area and a spruce grove, bears right again, and in 120 yd. ends at a T jct. with the abandoned Upper Ammonoosuc Trail. To the right, the abandoned footway leads 70 yd. to a large meadow on the bank of the Upper Ammonoosuc River, where you have a view of Mt. Weeks.

SEC 12

NORTH COUNTRY

The North Country proper is about 30 mi. long from north to south and varies in width from 20 mi. at the southern end to less than 15 mi. at Pittsburg. Its natural boundaries are the Upper Ammonoosuc, Androscoggin, and Magalloway rivers on the south and east and the Connecticut River on the west. The mountains here are lower than are those to the south—only ten or so exceed 3,500 ft.—and most have wooded summits. In much of the North Country, the appearance of wilderness masks the active presence of logging operations, and there is an extensive network of gravel roads. There are only a few marked hiking trails, even on mountains over 3,000 ft.

Many experienced hikers will find pleasure in the area's remoteness, but those who expect to find their trails groomed and manicured are doomed to disappointment—and possibly to the inconvenience of getting lost. The scarcity of settlements and the confusing river drainages make inappropriate the usual advice about following a stream when lost; one must have a map and compass, know how to use them, and be prepared to traverse considerable distances on a compass course to the nearest road, possibly obstructed by swamps or logged areas with slash piles and dense second growth. In general, camping and fires are prohibited throughout the region.

Road Access

Only three main highways cut through this northern section. Following the Connecticut Valley to its uppermost headwaters on the Canadian border beyond the Connecticut Lakes is US 3; NH 145 is an alternate road between the towns of Colebrook and Pittsburg. On the east side of the state, NH 16, which continues as ME 16, accompanies the Androscoggin and Magalloway rivers north to the outlet of Lake Aziscohos then swings east to the Rangeley Lakes. The only east–west paved road north of NH 110 is NH 26, which crosses from Errol to Colebrook through Dixville Notch. Even public secondary roads are few and short, although the timber companies have constructed an intricate system of gravel roads. Many of these have gates or are restricted, and heavy log trucks have the right of way on all of them. These roads are not always signed, and the lack of striking landmarks makes travel on them confusing for the inexperienced.

Because this northern section is managed for the continuous production of timber, roads and trails may change from one year to the next. For current conditions, official resources include the New Hampshire Fish and Game Department in Concord (wildlife.state.nh.us; 603-271-3211) or the Region 1 Office in Lancaster (reg1@wildlife.nh.gov; 603-788-3164); the New Hampshire Division of Forests and Lands (nhdfl.org; 603-271-2214; North

Region Office, 603-788-4157); and the New Hampshire Division of Parks and Recreation (nhparks@dred.nh.gov; nhstateparks.org; 603-271-3556; Great North Woods Region, 603-538-6707).

Nash Stream Forest

In the valley of Nash Stream, north of NH 110 between Groveton and Stark, a tract of nearly 40,000 acres is managed by the New Hampshire Division of Forests and Lands as Nash Stream Forest. It is approached via the gravel-surface Nash Stream Rd., about 11-mi. long. To access Nash Stream Rd., take NH 110 east from US 3 in Groveton for 2.6 mi. and turn left (north) onto Emerson Rd. At 1.4 mi. from NH 110, bear right onto Northside Rd. At 2.1 mi. Nash Stream Rd. diverges sharply left, as Northside Rd. bears right. Nash Stream Rd. is not plowed in winter beyond a gate at 0.5 mi. from Northside Rd., at which time it is heavily used for snowmobiling.

Included in this tract are the Percy Peaks and their trails, and most of the trail to Sugarloaf Mtn. but not its summit. The twin domes of the Percy Peaks, located northeast of Groveton, are the most conspicuous mountains in the northern view from Mt. Washington. The summit of North Percy (3,430 ft., with trail approaches from several directions) is bare ledge, except for low scrub; that of South Percy (3,234 ft.) is wooded and has no maintained trail but several good viewpoints. Sugarloaf Mtn. (3,710 ft.) rises east of North Stratford at the head of Nash Stream, and its rocky peak, reachable by trail, commands an extensive view, particularly of the Percy Peaks. Long Mtn. (3,661 ft.) is a broad, trailless wooded ridge just to the northeast of the Percy Peaks; in the saddle between its two principal summits is Long Mtn. Pond, one of the highest water bodies in the state. Victor Head (2,265 ft.) is a low peak south of Long Mtn. with interesting views near its summit; it is easily reached by a side path from the Cohos Trail. Just east of Victor Head is ledgy Bald Mtn. (2,378 ft.), which has no maintained trail to its summit.

Bunnell Mtn. (3,730 ft.), formerly called Blue Mtn., is a trailless peak in the same mountain mass as Sugarloaf Mtn. and is the highest peak in New Hampshire outside the WMNF; Bunnell Mtn. is located in the Nature Conservancy's 10,330-acre Vickie Bunnell Preserve, which borders Nash Stream Forest on the northwest. The mountain and preserve, as well as an adjacent tract of working forest, are named for Vicki Bunnell, a local lawyer and judge who was murdered in 1997. No maintained trails are in the preserve, which includes several other peaks over 3,000 ft. Eastward across the valley of Nash Stream are trailless Mt. Muise (3,615 ft.) and Whitcomb Mtn. (3,354 ft.). Pond Brook Falls, an attractive series of cascades where Pond Brook, an eastern tributary of Nash Stream, slides over broad ledges, can be easily accessed by Pond Brook Falls Trail.

SEC 12

Other interesting features of Nash Stream Forest include the Devil's Jacuzzi, an unusual formation in Nash Stream forming a natural bathtub, and Nash Stream Bog, a 200-acre wetland created when the dam holding back Nash Bog Pond gave way in 1969. Both of these can be visited by following East Side Trail, an attractive section of the Cohos Trail, north from East Side Trail's southern trailhead, starting at a sign on the east side of Nash Stream Rd., 8.2 mi. north of Northside Rd. and just south of the bridge over Nash Stream. See Sugarloaf Mtn. Trail description for parking directions and refer to the Cohos Trail map. Side paths descend left to Devil's Jacuzzi at 0.6 mi. and a viewpoint over Nash Stream Bog at 1.5 mi. (250 ft., rev. 200 ft., 55 min.). Nash Stream Forest also contains several attractive high mountain ponds, including Whitcomb Pond, which can be reached on foot via a 0.7-mi. walk up woods roads from the end of Trio Ponds Rd., which leaves the east side of Nash Stream Rd. 5.1 mi. from Northside Rd. and is rough but usually drivable for 3.0 mi. to the outlet of Little Bog Pond.

Located south of Nash Stream Forest, Devil's Slide (1,590 ft.) is a small mountain with a sheer cliff that rises 600 ft. on the north edge of Stark village; most of the mountain's summit and slopes are in the SPNHF Kauffmann Forest, and portions of the lower slopes are within Devil's Slide State Forest or private ownership. The top of the cliff can be reached by a rough, yellow-blazed trail, 0.8-mi. long (very steep near the top), with a 650-ft. ascent. From the top of the trail, the best views are found by carefully descending a beaten path 50 yd. downhill to the right. The trail leaves Northside Rd. at a grassy pull-off on the right, 0.8 mi. west of the jct. with Percy Rd. by the Stark covered bridge; the start of the trail is marked only by a yellow blaze on a tree. The parking and first 0.2 mi. of this trail are on private land; please stay on the trail. This trail may be closed during the peregrine falcon nesting season (April 1 to August 1). For more information, go to forestsociety.org/property/kauffmann-forest.

PERCY PEAKS TRAIL (NHDP; MAP 6: B7)

Cumulative from Nash Stream Rd. (1,242 ft.) to:	⇅	↗	○
Old Summer Club Trail (2,930 ft.)	1.7 mi.	1,700 ft.	1:40
North Percy summit (3,430 ft.)	2.2 mi.	2,200 ft.	2:10

This orange-blazed trail ascends North Percy Peak from Nash Stream Rd., climbing over spectacular open slabs (potentially hazardous if wet or icy) in its upper section. Relocations and rock-step construction by the North Woods Stewardship Council have alleviated serious erosion problems on the middle section of this trail. The trailhead is on the gravel-surface Nash

Stream Rd. (see access directions above), 2.7 mi. north of Northside Rd. There is a small area with angled parking (sign) on the right (east) side of the road; the trail (sign) begins 50 yd. farther up, just beyond the bridge over Slide Brook, also on the east side of the road. The trails on the Percy Peaks are shown on AMC's *White Mountains Trail Map 6: North Country–Mahoosuc Range*.

Leaving Nash Stream Rd., Percy Peaks Trail ascends moderately for 0.3 mi. then bears right, crosses a small stream, and follows old logging roads and relocated sections at easy to moderate grades, generally parallel to and north of Slide Brook. At 1.0 mi., the trail turns left at a large boulder, swings out to the left and then back to the right on a relocation, and rejoins the older route. The trail becomes steeper and rougher and soon reaches the base of the lower slabs at 1.2 mi. The slabs to the left of the trail in this area are mossy and extremely slippery and dangerous when wet; the trail stays to the right (south) of the slabs, climbing steeply with one tricky scramble.

The trail traverses several side-sloping ledges on the south flank of North Percy then continues up through the woods, drops off a ledge, turns left, and winds up at easier grades to a jct. at 1.7 mi., where yellow-blazed Old Summer Club Trail (the southbound Cohos Trail) enters on the right. Orange-blazed Percy Peaks Trail soon swings left (northeast) and, in 100 yd., bears left again, as red-and-yellow-blazed Percy Loop Trail (the northbound Cohos Trail) diverges right. At 1.9 mi., after a scramble up an eroded spot, Percy Peaks Trail emerges at the base of open slabs, turns left, and ascends steeply up the ledges with wide views south. Although the ledges offer good traction, they are potentially dangerous if wet or icy. The trail continues climbing generally northwest over ledges and through scrub, making several turns; look carefully for cairns and blazes. The grade eases on the approach to the flat summit, where good views can be seen in all directions around the rim. Descending, the trail heads south at first then veers left (southeast) in the direction of Christine Lake.

PERCY LOOP TRAIL (TCTA; MAP 6: A7–B7)

Cumulative from Nash Stream Rd. (1,360 ft.) to:	⬆⬇	↗	⟳
Trio Trail and Percy Loop Campsite (2,310 ft.)	1.6 mi.	950 ft.	1:15
Percy Peaks Trail (2,950 ft.)	2.3 mi.	1,600 ft.	1:55
North Percy summit (3,430 ft.) via Percy Peaks Trail	2.7 mi.	2,050 ft.	2:25

SEC 12

This trail provides a pleasant northern approach to the Percy Peaks from Nash Stream Rd., 1.1 mi. north of the Percy Peaks Trail trailhead. Its lower section, up to its jct. with Trio Trail, is blazed in red. Above this jct. it is a link in the Cohos Trail and is blazed in both red and yellow. Percy Loop Trail can be combined with Percy Peaks Trail and a road walk to create a 6.0-mi. loop over North Percy. Percy Loop Trail, marked by a trail sign and red blazes, leaves the right (east) side of Nash Stream Rd. 3.8 mi. from Northside Rd., just before the crossing of Long Mtn. Brook. Parking is possible on the east side of the road, south of the bridge. Additional parking is available on the west side just north of the bridge, at a grassy spot beside the driveway to a private camp; do not block access to the driveway.

The trail climbs moderately on an old logging road on the south side of Long Mtn. Brook, with good footing. At 0.3 mi., the trail bears left onto another old road and climbs up the side of Boman Valley through hardwood forest, well above the brook. At 0.8 mi., the trail descends slightly and swings right; the grade is mostly easy until the trail turns sharply right (south) off the road at 1.5 mi. The trail soon reaches a jct. on the left with Trio Trail (a new section of the Cohos Trail opened in 2016), which crosses a small brook and leads 100 yd. to Percy Loop Tentsite (tent platform and privy, no fires allowed) in a birch glade, then continues 3.1 mi. north to Trio Ponds Rd. and the upper end of Pond Brook Falls Trail.

From the jct., Percy Loop Trail climbs steadily on a winding course up the northeast slope of North Percy. Higher up are some rough sections with slippery rocks and roots. At 2.2 mi., the grade eases and the footing improves; after a slight descent, the trail swings right (southwest) and contours around the side of North Percy to meet Percy Peaks Trail, 0.4 mi. below the summit of North Percy. Turn right for the summit.

POND BROOK FALLS TRAIL (TCTA; COHOS TRAIL MAP)

From Nash Stream Rd. (1,387 ft.) to:	⇅	↗	↻
Trio Ponds Rd. and Trio Trail (1,630 ft.)	0.7 mi.	250 ft.	0:30

This trail, completed in 2016, provides easy access to attractive Pond Brook Falls and is a link in the Cohos Trail north of the Percy Peaks, providing the first part of a longer northern approach to the fine views on North Percy. It starts at a signed grassy parking area on the east side of Nash Stream Rd., 5.6 mi. from Northside Rd. and just north of the culvert over Pond Brook. It follows an older route along the north side of the brook at easy grades then turns left onto the new route at 0.1 mi., as the older route continues ahead and uphill as a spur path, which reaches the broad ledges of the falls in 35 yd. Use caution, as the ledges are slippery when wet. The main trail quickly swings right and climbs steadily, keeping well back from the brook, then eases and crosses the brook on rocks at 0.6 mi.; this crossing is difficult and potentially dangerous in high water. In another 0.1 mi. it ends at the gravel-surface Trio Ponds Rd. To continue towards North Percy, turn right on the road and in 30 yd. turn left onto Trio Trail.

TRIO TRAIL (TCTA; COHOS TRAIL MAP)

From Trio Ponds Rd. (1,630 ft.) to:	⇅	↗	⏱
Percy Loop Trail (2,310 ft.)	3.2 mi.	1,050 ft. (rev. 350 ft.)	2:10

This new section of the Cohos Trail, completed in 2016, connects Pond Brook Falls Trail with Percy Loop Trail at Percy Loop Campsite, skirting around the lower western slope of Long Mtn. It follows older and newer logging roads and many newly cut sections of footpath. Footing is mostly good, although there are occasional rougher sections. In combination with Pond Brook Falls Trail, Percy Loop Trail, and Percy Peaks Trail, it makes possible an attractive longer northern approach to North Percy.

At its northern end, it begins at a small grassy clearing with a signpost (CT) and arrow on the south side of Trio Ponds Rd., 0.9 mi. east of Nash Stream Rd. and 30 yd. west of the southern terminus of Pond Brook Falls Trail. It runs 20 yd. south on a grassy road then turns right into the woods at a trail sign and arrow. At 0.1 mi is a view left across a beaver meadow to a spur of Whitcomb Mtn. The trail continues south at easy grades then bears right and descends slightly. At 0.5 mi. it begins a moderate ascent and soon runs along the left side of a logging cut. At 0.7 mi. it swings right, passing a vista northwest to Sugarloaf Mtn., and climbs steadily along the left side of several more logging cuts. It swings right at 1.0 mi. and runs at easy grades across more logged openings with limited vistas.

At 1.3 mi. the trail enters mature hardwoods and makes a gradual descent then follows a long curve south and southeast around the lower slope of Long Mtn., mostly on contour or climbing gradually but with numerous minor descents, and crosses several small brooks. At 2.8 mi. it swings left onto an old logging road and ascends along it for 0.1 mi. then turns right off it and runs south, crossing Long Mtn. Brook at 3.0 mi. It then makes a winding ascent to Percy Loop Tentsite, passes by the tent platform and kiosk, and reaches Percy Loop Trail just after crossing a small brook.

OLD SUMMER CLUB TRAIL (TCTA; MAP 6: B8–B7)

Cumulative from Christine Lake parking area (1,210 ft.) to:	⇅	↗	○
Victor Head side trail (1,775 ft.)	2.0 mi.	550 ft.	1:15
Percy Peaks Trail (2,930 ft.)	3.8 mi.	1,750 ft. (rev. 50 ft.)	2:45
North Percy Peak (3,430 ft.) via Percy Peaks Trail	4.3 mi.	2,250 ft.	3:15
From Old Summer Club Trail (1,775 ft.) to:			
Victor Head (2,265 ft.)	0.4 mi.	500 ft.	0:25

This trail, a section of the Cohos Trail, partly follows a restored portion of an old trail to the Percy Peaks from the Percy Summer Club on Christine Lake. In combination with a route on unmarked woods roads from a public parking lot on Christine Lake, Old Summer Club Trail provides hikers with a southeastern approach to the Percy Peaks and offers access via a side trail to interesting views from the cliffs of Victor Head. The lower part of this route is on private conservation land, including the SPNHF Kauffmann Forest.

To reach the trailhead, turn north off NH 110 in the village of Stark, 7.0 mi. east of US 3 in Groveton. Drive through the covered bridge, turn right (east) on Percy Rd. and follow it for 2.2 mi., turn left (north) on Christine Lake Rd. (paved but rough), and in 0.4 mi. bear left at a fork into the parking area at the east end of the lake, where you find a beach with a fine view across the water to Victor Head and South Percy. Walk 100 yd. back to the fork just east of the parking area and turn left onto the gated, gravel-surface Summer Club Rd. (No Trespassing signs here do not apply to hikers who stay on the trails.) In 0.1 mi., where the road curves left, bear right (ahead) onto an older woods road, soon passing a metal gate, where a snowmobile trail joins from the left. (Descending, bear left here.)

At 0.4 mi. from the parking area, bear left in a grassy clearing where a snowmobile trail diverges right. At 0.5 mi., turn sharply left (west) onto another woods road lined with birches; this jct. is marked only by a large snowmobile arrow. (The continuation of the road ahead ascends 1.1 mi. and 600 ft. to meet Bald Mtn. Notch Trail and Rowell Link, both of which are parts of the Cohos Trail, at a three-way jct.) Follow the left-branching road at easy grades, crossing Rowell Brook on a bridge at 1.0 mi. The road climbs more steadily, passing the blue-blazed boundary of Nash Stream Forest at 1.3 mi., and reaches a T jct. with a wide, grassy logging road (Jimmy Cole Brook Rd.) at 1.7 mi.; to the right, this road is Rowell Link, the southbound Cohos Trail. Old Summer Club Trail (the northbound Cohos Trail, leading to Percy Peaks) enters the woods across the road and slightly to the left (yellow blazes and "CT" on rocks).

The trail passes a large boulder on the left and ascends moderately on an old logging road. At 2.0 mi., the unblazed side trail to Victor Head leaves right (sign).

The well-worn **Victor Head Side Trail** climbs steadily, and at times steeply, to the northeast, swinging right into a deep spruce forest on the northwest side of the peak. The trail bears right again and climbs a short, steep, and rough section through wooded ledges then levels and reaches a point near the wooded summit where one spur path leads 20 yd. right to a cleared outlook toward the Percy Peaks. Another spur path descends 50 yd. left to a ledge, with partly restricted views east to the Mahoosucs and south over Christine Lake to the Pilot Range. Use caution descending to the ledge.

Old Summer Club Trail continues up the old road then turns sharply right off it onto a footpath at 2.3 mi. At 2.5 mi., the trail turns left onto another old road, follows it for 140 yd., and turns sharply right into the woods. At 2.7 mi., the trail turns left onto another road then turns right off it in 40 yd. (All the turns are well blazed.) At 2.8 mi., the trail crosses a branch of Jimmy Cole Brook and, in 100 yd., crosses another branch. The trail now climbs moderately up the east slope of South Percy, crossing an overgrown road at 3.2 mi., following several twists and turns, then traversing a rough section with rocks and holes. After passing a small cave on the right, the trail becomes steep and rough in a rocky area. The trail follows the edge of a ledge shelf then drops to the col between the Percy Peaks at 3.7 mi., where it turns sharply right; here, a rough, unmaintained path diverges left at a sign and climbs steeply in 0.3 mi. (350 ft.) to the summit of South Percy. From this jct., Old Summer Club Trail rises easily to meet Percy Peaks Trail; to reach the summit of North Percy, in 0.5 mi., turn right.

BALD MTN. NOTCH TRAIL (TCTA; MAP 6: B8)

Cumulative from Percy Rd. (990 ft.) to:	⬆⬇	↗	⟳
Bald Mtn. Notch (1,950 ft.)	2.3 mi.	950 ft.	1:35
Rowell Link/connecting path to Christine Lake jct. (1,850 ft.)	2.9 mi.	950 ft. (rev. 100 ft.)	1:55

This pleasant yellow-blazed trail, a section of the Cohos Trail, leads from Percy Rd. in Stark through the small, sharp pass of Bald Mtn. Notch on the north side of Bald Mtn. then descends to a three-way jct. on the west side of Bald Mtn. To reach the trailhead, take NH 110 east for 3.1 mi. from Stark village and turn left (north) onto Bell Hill Rd., crossing the Upper Ammonoosuc River; this turn is 0.3 mi. west of the jct. of NH 110 and the access road to South Pond. In 0.2 mi., turn left (west) on Percy Rd. and continue another 0.3 mi. to the trailhead (sign) at an orange gate on the right; limited roadside parking is available by the entrance; do not block the gate. Better parking is available a short distance east on the south side of the road, by the old Stark landfill.

The trail follows a grass-grown woods road at easy grades; there is little evident footway but the footing is good. The trail crosses a power-line swath at 0.2 mi. and curves left at a small clearing at 0.5 mi., where blue-blazed Pike Pond Trail, an alternate access from parking on Pike Pond Rd., joins from the right. The trail continues ahead at 0.8 mi. and 1.2 mi., where other woods roads diverge right. At 1.3 mi., it crosses a rickety bridge over a brook, and in another 0.1 mi. it turns right onto a footpath and ascends northwest at a moderate grade toward Bald Mtn. Notch. The trail reaches its high point in the notch at 2.3 mi., traverses a wet area, then descends gradually through birch woods, passing through an old logging camp clearing just before meeting Rowell Link (ahead, continuing the north-bound Cohos Trail) and an unmarked connecting path from Christine Lake (left). The connecting path descends 1.1 mi. and 600 ft. to meet a woods road, which leads right to Old Summer Club Trail and ahead another 0.5 mi. to the parking area at Christine Lake.

ROWELL LINK (TCTA; MAP 6: B8)

From jct. of Bald Mtn. Notch Trail and Christine Lake connecting path (1,850 ft.) to:	⇅	↗	↻
Old Summer Club Trail (1,590 ft.)	1.3 mi.	100 ft. (rev. 350 ft.)	0:40

This trail continues the northbound Cohos Trail from Bald Mtn. Notch Trail to the jct. with Old Summer Club Trail. Rowell Link (no sign, yellow blazes) starts at the jct. of Bald Mtn. Notch Trail with a connecting path to Christine Lake and descends west on a short, steep pitch then turns left onto an old logging road and descends along Rowell Brook. At 0.1 mi., Rowell Link turns right to cross the brook on a bridge, follows the brook briefly, then bears right away from it and meanders through conifer forest, with minor ups and downs, on a rough footway that must be followed with care. At 0.5 mi., the trail turns right onto an old woods road and ascends for 0.2 mi. to a jct. with a newer logging road (Jimmy Cole Brook Rd.) at a gravelly spot. The trail turns left here (in the reverse direction, watch carefully for the right turn off this major road), descends steadily for a short distance, then swings right and meanders gently downhill on the wide, grassy road. At 1.3 mi., Rowell Link ends at a four-way jct. where an unmarked woods road coming from the Christine Lake trailhead joins from the left, and Old Summer Club Trail (the northbound Cohos Trail, marked by yellow blazes) diverges right off the major road.

SUGARLOAF MTN. TRAIL (NHDP/NWSC; USGS PERCY PEAKS QUAD, COHOS TRAIL MAP)

Cumulative from Nash Stream Rd. (1,530 ft.) to:	⇅	↗	⟳
Warden's cabins site (3,220 ft.)	1.6 mi.	1,700 ft.	1:40
Sugarloaf Mtn. summit (3,710 ft.)	2.1 mi.	2,200 ft.	2:10

This trail provides access to the rocky, partly open summit of Sugarloaf Mtn., which commands good views of the Nash Stream valley and surrounding areas. The trail ascends the east side of the mountain by a direct route, following a logging road that was the fire warden's trail to the former fire tower. Sugarloaf Mtn. Trail starts on the left (west) side of Nash Stream Rd., 8.2 mi. north of Northside Rd., 70 yd. beyond its bridge over Nash Stream. The trail begins on the left as the driveway to a private camp. In 2016 the entrance was marked with a yellow blaze on a post but no sign. Park in a grassy area on the left, near the driveway entrance, taking care not to block the driveway, or on the right (east) side of the road just south of the bridge. Refer to the USGS Percy Peaks quad or the Cohos Trail map.

The trail follows the grassy driveway to the left of a camp, crosses a bridge over a small brook, goes around a gate and through a brushy clearing, and enters the woods. At 0.1 mi., the trail bears right at a fork where the yellow-blazed southbound Cohos Trail (here signed as Sugarloaf Arm Trail) goes left; there is a sign for Sugarloaf Mtn. Trail here. Sugarloaf Mtn. Trail ascends generally northwest at a moderate grade on the wide, old road, passing a jct. with a snowmobile trail on the left at 0.4 mi. Sugarloaf Mtn. Trail continues ahead here (cairn), and the grade soon steepens, with eroded rocky footing at times; the ascent is steady to a clearing where the remains of the fire warden's cabins are on the right at 1.6 mi. A few steps farther, the trail bears right at a fork (the left branch is a short spur to a spring) and leads through a brushy area. Sugarloaf Mtn. Trail climbs rather steeply to the ridge north of the summit, turns left (south), and ascends gradually along the ridgeline to the summit ledges.

Dixville Notch Region

Dixville Notch, the most spectacular spot in the North Country, lies between Sanguinary Mtn. (north) and Mt. Gloriette (south). With the Mohawk River flowing west and Clear Stream flowing east, the notch itself is less than 2 mi. in length with a steep grade on each side and is wide enough only to admit the highway. The cliff formations, composed of vertical strata, are impressively jagged. The heart of the notch is included within 127-acre Dixville Notch State Park.

Just west of the notch is the Balsams, a hotel and resort complex that includes most of the land west of the notch on both sides of NH 26. The resort, along with its accompanying Wilderness Ski Area on the northwest slopes of Dixville Peak, has been closed since 2011; there are plans to renovate and reopen the hotel and to greatly expand the ski area. The resort maintained many miles of summer and winter trails in this area and published a trail map that is no longer available. The trails were identified by numbers that were posted at jcts.; many of the number signs remain in place. In general, signage is inconsistent in this area, so care is required to follow the trails, especially at jcts. Only the trails immediately on either side of Dixville Notch, maintained by NHDP and TCTA, are covered in this guide. The Cohos Trail passes through this region, skirting the side of Dixville Peak and descending over Table Rock to the notch then continuing up onto Sanguinary Mtn. Although the scale is small, most of the trails in Dixville Notch described below are shown on the Cohos Trail map; some are shown on the USGS Dixville Notch quad.

The mountains in the vicinity of Dixville Notch are relatively low and have no open summits. The south side of the notch is Mt. Gloriette (2,630 ft.), which bears the rock formations Table Rock, Old King, Third Cliff, and Profile Cliff. There were once paths to all of them, but only that to Table Rock is now maintained and signed; hiking to the others is not encouraged because the terrain is very rough and it is easy to stray into dangerous areas. Table Rock (2,510 ft.) is a cliff that juts out from the north side of Mt. Gloriette, south of the highway. Formed of vertical slabs, Table Rock is less than 10 ft. wide at its narrowest point and extends more than 100 ft. from the shoulder of the mountain. The view is spectacular and extensive. Table Rock can be climbed by a trail that begins and ends at points 0.7 mi. apart on NH 26 in the heart of the notch. The rock formation known as the Profile can be seen high on the cliffs by looking south from the high point in the notch. On the north side of the road just west of the high point is Lake Gloriette (1,846 ft.), an artificial lake on the grounds of the Balsams, formed from the headwaters of the Mohawk River.

Dixville Peak (3,490 ft.) is the highest mountain in the vicinity of Dixville Notch, but the peak is wooded except for the cleared summit. Due to wind-tower construction, the summit is no longer accessible to the public; the Cohos Trail has been rerouted around the west slope. Sanguinary Mtn. (2,710 ft.) forms the north wall of Dixville Notch and is named for the color of its cliffs at sunset. Sanguinary Ridge Trail, which does not go to the summit, traverses the cliffs north of the notch. On the southwest side of the notch, and reachable by trail, are the Huntington Cascades. From the cascades, Three Brothers Trail runs to Table Rock, passing an excellent outlook and the Ice Cave along the way. There are no maintained trails to Cave Mtn. (3,191 ft.), which rises northeast of the notch. To the west of Dixville Notch, in the town of Colebrook, is Beaver Brook Falls, a beautiful waterfall located in a small state-managed Scenic Area on the east side of NH 145, 2.4 mi. north of its jct. with US 3. Paths lead about 80 yd. from the parking and picnic area to either side at the base of the falls.

Also included in this subsection is a region of rivers and lakes north of Berlin and east of Dixville Notch and the mountains to its north. Only a handful of hiking opportunities exist among these waterways, which include Umbagog Lake and the Androscoggin, Magalloway, and Diamond rivers. More than 25,000 acres of land around Umbagog Lake are within Umbagog National Wildlife Refuge, and the states of Maine and New Hampshire each own an additional 1,000 acres. Excellent paddling and camping opportunities can be found at Umbagog Lake, but at present, there is only one small network of short, level walking paths designated as Magalloway River Trail. The main path (Orange Trail) is a graded, universally accessible trail 0.4-mi. long leading east then north to a covered viewing platform overlooking a backwater of the Magalloway River. It is shown on the *AMC Mahoosucs Map & Guide*. From this trunk path, Blue Trail makes a 0.7-mi. loop to the right, rejoining at a left turn, and Green Trail makes a 0.2-mi. loop to the left, rejoining at the viewing platform. The main path begins (sign) at a parking area on the east side of NH 16, 7.3 mi. north of its jct. with NH 26 in Errol and 1.6 mi. north of the refuge headquarters. (This is 1.4 mi. south of the jct. with Dead Diamond Rd., the access road into Dartmouth's Second College Grant.) For information on the refuge, visit www.fws.gov/refuge/umbagog/ or call 603-482-3415.

Much of the rest of the land in this region is in private hands, with gates on the access roads. The chief landowners are Dartmouth College and woods products corporations. Both are hospitable to hikers but do not usually permit vehicular traffic over their roads, which limits access to the region due to the considerable distances that are frequently involved. Thirteen Mile Woods, along the Androscoggin River between the New Hampshire towns of Milan and Errol, is managed by a consortium of landowners and state agencies. This provides a scenic drive along the river, access to fishing and canoeing, and a public campground at Mollidgewock State Park.

Above the headwaters of the Androscoggin River lies the Second College Grant, given to Dartmouth College by the state in 1807 "for the assistance of indigent students." On this grant, between Errol, New Hampshire,

SEC
12

and Wilsons Mills, Maine, the Swift Diamond River and the Dead Diamond River come together to form the Diamond River, which then enters the Magalloway River from the west. This in turn joins the Androscoggin River at Umbagog Lake. Branches of the Dead Diamond extend well up into the Connecticut Lakes region. (Refer to the USGS Wilsons Mills quad.) The Diamond Peaks are three small peaks (West Peak, 2,010 ft.; East Peak, 2,050 ft.; and South Peak, 1,994 ft.) capping a nearly semicircular ridge that rises between the Dead Diamond and Magalloway rivers; they can be reached by trail and offer fine views.

Immediately below the confluence of its two branches, the Diamond River has carved a wild and beautiful gorge between the Diamond Peaks on the north and Mt. Dustan (2,878 ft.) on the south. This valley is served by Dead Diamond Rd., Dartmouth's private gravel road, open to pedestrians but not to vehicles without a permit. In the village of Wentworth Location, New Hampshire, 8.7 mi. north of Errol or 0.3 mi. west of the Maine–New Hampshire state line, this gravel road leaves NH 16 on the west near a small cemetery. Hikers may leave their cars in a parking area on the right, just before the gate 0.2 mi. from NH 16; public travel beyond this gate is on foot only. Gate Camp is reached in 0.7 mi. from the gate, where the road soon crosses Diamond River on a bridge and proceeds up through the gorge.

The best outlook into the gorge is reached at about 1.6 mi. and the Dartmouth Management Center at 2.2 mi. Hellgate, another scenic gorge named for the trouble river drivers had getting their logs through its narrow channel without jamming, is 12.5 mi. from the gate. For hikers, the principal feature of interest is the path that runs from the Dartmouth Management Center to the fine ledges on the Diamond Peaks. Other short paths to points of interest have been opened. For further information, contact the Dartmouth Outdoor Programs Office (603-646-2428). The office publishes a topographic map of the Second College Grant, showing roads, trails, and points of interest, as well as the *Dartmouth Outing Guide* (5th edition, 2004), which has an extensive section on the grant.

TABLE ROCK TRAIL (NHDP; USGS DIXVILLE NOTCH QUAD, COHOS TRAIL MAP)

To Table Rock (2,510 ft.) from:	⇅	↗	↻
East trailhead (1,930 ft.)	0.3 mi.	600 ft.	0:25
West trailhead (1,870 ft.)	0.8 mi.	700 ft. (rev. 50 ft.)	0:45

This short, rough loop path begins and ends on the south side of NH 26 and gives access to the spectacular, airy viewpoint at Table Rock, 'consisting of a narrow ledge rising several hundred feet over a cliff face. The east trailhead, which gives access to the much steeper section of the loop (sign: 57, Table Rock Climbing Trail) is in a roadside parking area 0.1 mi. east of the main entrance to the Balsams (Cold Spring Rd.). The west trailhead (sign: 50, Table Rock Trail; roadside parking) is 0.6 mi. west of the main entrance to the Balsams. From the east trailhead, the trail climbs extremely steeply (not recommended for descent) with rough and often slippery footing, rising 600 ft. in 0.3 mi. It emerges just behind Table Rock (no sign); turn right and scramble up a few yards to the open ledge.

From the west trailhead, the trail (recommended for the average hiker) follows a cross-country ski trail (sign: 5) for 25 yd. then diverges left on another trail (sign: 50) and climbs steadily, with some loose rock underfoot, easing as the trail approaches the height-of-land. At 0.7 mi., the trail bears left where yet another trail (sign: 9; the southbound Cohos Trail) diverges right for the top of Wilderness Ski Area. Table Rock Trail descends 50 yd. to a jct. where Three Brothers Trail (sign: 59; also the northbound Cohos Trail) diverges right. Here, the trail (sign: To View) turns left and descends steeply for 25 yd., meets the east branch of Table Rock Trail on the right—which virtually plunges down to NH 26—and bears left and ascends briefly to Table Rock.

HUNTINGTON CASCADE TRAIL (NHDP; USGS DIXVILLE NOTCH QUAD, COHOS TRAIL MAP)

From Cascade Brook Picnic Area (1,510 ft.) to:	⇅	↗	↻
Three Brothers Trail (1,870 ft.)	0.5 mi.	350 ft.	0:25

This short trail begins on the southwest side of NH 26 at the Cascade Brook picnic area by the eastern entrance to Dixville Notch State Park, 1.3 mi. east of the Balsams main entrance. This is a link in the Cohos Trail. Drive into the wayside area, and in 0.1 mi. bear left into the picnic area. The trail (sign: Huntington Falls) begins at the far side of a cul-de-sac at the end of this somewhat rough road. Leaving the picnic area, the trail meanders through hardwoods for 0.1 mi. then turns right where a spur path leads ahead to the edge of the brook. The trail crosses Cascade Brook on a bridge to sign (59) on the far side, where an unmarked side trail diverges left and leads about 0.5 mi. southeast to a wildlife viewing area just off NH 26. The main trail climbs steeply up the south bank, passing an overlook of the mossy lower Huntington Cascade. The trail continues to ascend steeply high above the brook through spruces, where other beaten paths parallel the trail; the one on the right provides a restricted view of upper Huntington Cascade in a

SEC 12

deep canyon. Use caution in this area, as dangerous dropoffs are close to the trail, and the trail is poorly marked. Higher up, the grade moderates, and at 0.5 mi. the trail turns right and descends, crosses Cascade Brook, and meets Three Brothers Trail (sign) on the north bank.

THREE BROTHERS TRAIL (NHDP; USGS DIXVILLE NOTCH QUAD, COHOS TRAIL MAP)

From Huntington Cascade Trail (1,870 ft.) to:	⇅	↗	↻
Table Rock (2,510 ft.)	1.0 mi.	750 ft. (rev. 100 ft.)	0:55

This trail, part of the Cohos Trail, links the top of Huntington Cascade Trail with Table Rock. From the jct. with Huntington Cascade Trail, Three Brothers Trail (also signed 59) climbs the east ridge of Mt. Gloriette at a moderate grade through hardwoods. At 0.5 mi., the trail crosses a blue-blazed state park boundary line and stays near it for some distance. The grade becomes easy on a shoulder, and after a slight dip, the trail climbs to a spur trail (sign) right at 0.8 mi. leading to Middle Brother Outlook. This spur, 0.1-mi. long, descends 75 ft. then swings right to a clifftop outlook with a spectacular view of Table Rock and the Balsams resort. The main trail climbs to a high point, passes another view of Table Rock on the right, then turns right and descends to the Ice Cave, an interesting chasm in a ledge on the left. Here, Three Brothers Trail turns left and meets Table Rock Trail just behind Table Rock. To reach Table Rock, bear right and descend steeply for 25 yd. to a jct. where the east branch of Table Rock Trail descends very steeply to the right; bear left and ascend a short distance to the ledge.

SANGUINARY RIDGE TRAIL (NHDP; USGS DIXVILLE NOTCH QUAD, COHOS TRAIL MAP)

Cumulative from Flume Brook picnic area (1,570 ft.) to:	⇅	↗	↻
Jct. at height-of-land (2,500 ft.)	1.2 mi.	950 ft.	1:05
Balsams entrance road (1,870 ft.)	1.7 mi.	950 ft. (rev. 650 ft.)	1:20

This trail provides access to the spectacular views from the open rocks and clifftops of Sanguinary Ridge on the north side of Dixville Notch. It begins and ends on NH 26; the yellow-blazed eastern section is also part of the Cohos Trail. The western trailhead (sign: Sanguinary Ridge Trail) is at the main entrance to the Balsams resort (Cold Spring Rd., at the east end of Lake Gloriette; parking at west side of entrance). The eastern trailhead is 1.0 mi. to the east, at the Flume Brook picnic area of Dixville Notch State Wayside, a rest area on the northeast side of NH 26.

Note: From the southeast side of the Flume Brook picnic area, Flume Brook Trail (trail 60), marked with a CT sign and yellow blazes, descends south along Flume Brook then swings right to cross NH 26 at 0.25 mi. The trail runs through woods to the Cascade Brook wayside, passing a grave site, and then follows the road into the picnic area, reaching the start of Huntington Cascade Trail at 0.4 mi., thus making possible a loop hike around both sides of Dixville Notch; Flume Brook Trail is a link in the Cohos Trail.

Leaving the northeast corner of the wayside area to the right of an interpretive sign (sign: CT; yellow blazes), Sanguinary Ridge Trail (trail 58) climbs alongside Flume Brook, passing a small flume on the right in 50 yd. The trail soon turns sharply left away from the brook (sign: Sanguinary Ridge Trail), crosses an old road at 0.1 mi., and in another 100 yd. passes a spur trail left leading to the west end of the wayside. The trail begins climbing a scenic ridge at easy to moderate grades, passing the first outlook on the left at 0.4 mi. (In this section, the trail parallels a yellow-blazed property line.) Three more outlooks are passed in the next 0.3 mi., with good views of Table Rock and Old King cliffs and also east down the valley toward the Mahoosuc Range.

At 0.8 mi., Sanguinary Ridge Trail turns right and ascends more steeply through hardwoods, reaching its high point on the ridge at 1.2 mi. Here Sanguinary Summit Trail (trail 64, also the northbound Cohos Trail) diverges right, leading about 2.7 mi. along the ridge to the TCTA Panorama lean-to. There is a restricted view west 50 yd. up this trail. Sanguinary Ridge Trail bears left at the jct. and switchbacks down to two spectacular rocky viewpoints overlooking Lake Gloriette and the Balsams resort at 1.4 mi. Here, the trail turns left and soon emerges on an open slope of gravel and loose rock, where rock steps constructed by the North Woods Stewardship Center have greatly improved the footing; use caution descending this section. The trail descends to the right past needlelike Index Rock, with good views up to the cliffs across the notch, reenters the woods, and switchbacks down a very steep slope, negotiating one tricky scramble with a dropoff on the left, to the Balsams entrance.

DIAMOND PEAKS TRAIL (DOC; USGS WILSONS MILLS QUAD, SECOND COLLEGE GRANT MAP)

Cumulative from gate on Dead Diamond Rd. (1,250 ft.) to:	⇅	↗	⏱
Diamond Peaks Trail (1,350 ft.)	2.2 mi.	150 ft. (rev. 50 ft.)	1:10
Diamond Peaks, East Peak (2,050 ft.)	3.3 mi.	900 ft. (rev. 50 ft.)	2:05

The most rewarding hiking opportunity in Dartmouth's Second College Grant is the trail to the Diamond Peaks in the John Sloan Dickey Natural Area. The most attractive feature of the Diamond Peaks is a high cliff on the concave side of the ridge, facing south, with a number of good viewpoints. The trail to the summit is short but has a number of fairly steep, rough sections. The trail may be closed during the peregrine falcon nesting season (April 1 to August 1). Refer to the USGS Wilsons Mills quad and the Second College Grant map.

The trail is approached via a 2.2-mi. walk up Dead Diamond Rd., starting at the gate 0.2 mi. from NH 16; see the introduction to the Dixville Notch Region for driving directions. The road walk is interesting, offering views of Mt. Dustan across a wetland, vistas of the Diamond River and adjacent meadows, and a down-look into a scenic gorge on the river. The yellow-blazed trail begins at a sign for Alice Ledge, Linda Ledge, and Diamond Peaks, on the north side of the clearing across the road from the Dartmouth Management Center, 2.2 mi. from the gate. The trail crosses a wet, mossy area on plank bridges then ascends fairly steeply to a ridge crest at 2.5 mi. from the gate. Here, a side trail (not well cleared but fairly easy to follow) leads left 100 yd. to the summit of a small crag then down slightly another 20 yd. to Alice Ledge, with a view across and down the Diamond River valley.

The main trail turns sharply right and climbs, reaching at 2.7 mi. the first of several fine cliff outlooks on the side of Linda Ledge (use caution here in wet or icy conditions). The trail continues to climb, rather steeply at times, then makes a short, steep descent to a fork at 3.1 mi. Here, Diamond Back Trail (sign), used as a winter bypass of the lower ledges, enters on the left; the lower part is not marked or cleared for non-winter use. The main trail, which is less obvious at this point, bears to the right, crosses a ledgy area near the ridge crest, and reaches a fine outlook ledge in 50 yd. The trail continues, first descending slightly then climbing, and passes a short distance to the right of the highest point of the mountain. The trail then descends a short distance over a broken ledge to another viewpoint, which offers a particularly fine vista of the meandering Magalloway River.

Connecticut Lakes Region

Some 10 mi. above Colebrook, New Hampshire, the Connecticut River valley bends northeast and, just beyond the village of Beecher Falls, Vermont, comes wholly within New Hampshire. Between its source near the Canadian line and the village of Pittsburg, New Hampshire, the river passes through a chain of lakes of increasing size, numbered first to fourth in upstream order from the south. A high dam at Pittsburg created Lake

Francis—the lowest lake in the series, below First Lake—and dams are responsible for the present size of both First and Second Connecticut Lakes. US 3, the only major highway in the region, passes close to all of the lakes except Fourth Connecticut Lake, crossing the river from west to east between Second Connecticut Lake and Third Connecticut Lake, and eventually entering Canada. Refer to USGS Second Connecticut Lake, Indian Stream, and Moose Bog quads.

A majority of the land in this region is within the 171,500-acre Connecticut Lakes Headwaters Working Forest (CLHWF), a public-private partnership between the state of New Hampshire and the Connecticut Lakes Timber Company (CLTC). The state owns 25,000 acres, which are reserved as three Natural Areas, and CLTC practices sustainable forestry on 146,400 acres, under the terms of a conservation easement held by the state. Under the public access, recreation, and road management plan that has been developed for the CLHWF, many of the hundreds of miles of gravel logging roads are open to public vehicular use, though subject to closure during timber harvests. Overnight camping and open fires are prohibited on the CLHWF. For more information on the CLHWF, see nhstateparks.org/visit/state-parks/connecticut-lakes-headwaters-working-forest.aspx.

Other conservation lands in this area include the 1,548-acre Connecticut Lakes State Forest along US 3 and several parcels owned by private conservation organizations. Many natural features in this region, particularly ponds, are reached by gravel roads, by woods roads passable to four-wheel-drive vehicles, or by snowmobile trails, with limited appeal to pedestrian users, but many others, including most mountain summits, are simply pathless; to reach them requires fairly sophisticated navigational skills.

Magalloway Mtn. (3,383 ft.), located east of First Connecticut Lake, overlooks the Middle Branch of Dead Diamond River and is reached by two hiking trails, described below. A fire tower affords excellent views; there are also good views from a ledge near the summit, at the top of the mountain's east cliff, with an impressive talus slope below. Garfield Falls is a remote and picturesque waterfall on the East Branch of the Dead Diamond River that can be reached by two short paths, described below. In 2016 a short trail to the remote Little Hellgate Falls (Hellgate Brook Falls) on the southwest side of Magalloway Mtn. was improved and expanded into a loop. This leaves the east side of gravel Cedar Stream Rd. at a snowmobile kiosk about 8.8 mi. from US 3 (via Magalloway Rd. and Buckhorn Rd.). Also maintained is a short path to Indian Stream Canyon, a small gorge on Indian Stream located about 16 mi. up Indian Stream Rd.

Falls in the River is an attractive cascade and gorge on a remote section of the Connecticut River south of Second Connecticut Lake that is easily

**SEC
12**

reached via a section of the Cohos Trail, described below. TCTA has been actively opening other trail segments in the Connecticut Lakes region in recent years, including sections leading over Prospect Mtn. (2,204 ft.) and Covell Mtn. (2,410 ft.), small mountains on the west side of US 3, both of which provide views over First Connecticut Lake; the view from the cleared summit of Prospect is especially expansive. TCTA, with assistance from North Woods Stewardship Center, has also reopened a trail to the north peak of Deer Mtn. (2,997 ft.), which is located west of the Connecticut River between Second and Third Connecticut lakes and formerly offered extensive views from a now-abandoned and partially dismantled fire tower (unsafe to climb). Along the way, the trail passes cascades and an interesting high-elevation bog.

From the west side of US 3, 0.1 mi. south of the entrance to Deer Mtn. Campground, the route follows Sophie's Lane, a rough logging road (a section of the Cohos Trail) for 0.6 mi. then turns left on a 0.15-mi. spur road to a cul-de-sac (parking for high-clearance vehicles) and left again on Deer Mountain Trail (blue blazes). The distance from US 3 is about 2.8 mi. with 1,050-ft. ascent (rev. 50 ft.). Fourth Connecticut Lake (2,670 ft.), a little mountain tarn northwest of Third Connecticut Lake and just south of the Canadian border, is the ultimate source of the Connecticut River. The lake is located in a 78-acre reservation owned by The Nature Conservancy (TNC) and can be reached from US 3 by a maintained trail, described below. The trails to Falls in the River, Prospect Mtn., Covell Mtn., Deer Mtn., and Fourth Connecticut Lake are shown on the Cohos Trail map and are described in the Cohos Trail guidebook. All of the hikes mentioned above are fully described in *50 Hikes North of the White Mountains*, by Kim Nilsen.

COOT TRAIL (NHDP; USGS MAGALLOWAY MTN. QUAD)

From end of gravel road (2,580 ft.) to:	⇅	↗	○
Magalloway Mtn. summit and fire tower (3,383 ft.)	0.8 mi.	800 ft.	0:50

This trail follows the old fire warden's Jeep road to the fire tower on the summit of Magalloway Mtn. Refer to the USGS Magalloway Mtn. quad. From US 3, 4.7 mi. north of the dam on First Connecticut Lake, take gravel Magalloway Rd. (sign: lookout tower) to the southeast. This is a wide, well-graded, main-haul private logging road, usually gated in winter. Drivers must always be prepared to yield to large and fast-moving logging trucks; it is not always easy to find a place to get out of the way quickly. At

1.2 mi., cross the Connecticut River on a bridge and continue straight. Bear left at 2.3 mi. and again at 2.9 mi. At 5.3 mi., turn sharply right onto a branch road (Tower Rd.) that is narrower and rougher (with several culverts that require careful driving) and bear right again at 6.3 mi. The road ends in a turnaround at 8.4 mi., where hikers should park.

Coot Trail (sign) starts on the right across from a privy and follows the rough, eroded Jeep road, passing a cabin and spring at 0.1 mi. The trail ascends steadily with occasional short bypasses and a few relatively steep grades. At 0.6 mi., Coot Trail passes the jct. with the upper end of Bobcat Trail on the right; here, you have a view back over First Connecticut Lake. Coot Trail soon swings left at an easy grade and reaches the grassy summit clearing and the fire tower at 0.8 mi. The extensive views from the tower include portions of New Hampshire, Vermont, Maine, and Quebec. From the clearing, an unmarked side path descends right rather steeply for 0.1 mi. to a spring, and a spur path (sign: Overlook Trail) diverges left (north), passes to the right of the warden's cabins, and descends easily for 0.2 mi. (losing 100 ft. elev.) to an excellent viewpoint at the top of the mountain's east cliff.

BOBCAT TRAIL (NHDP; USGS MAGALLOWAY MTN. QUAD)

From gravel road (2,580 ft.) to:	⇅	⌵⌃	⟳
Coot Trail (3,320 ft.)	0.8 mi.	750 ft.	0:45

This trail, in combination with Coot Trail, makes possible a loop hike on Magalloway Mtn. Its footing is generally better than that on the old Jeep road. Bobcat Trail leaves the gravel road (sign) 60 yd. to the right (west) of Coot Trail. Bobcat Trail crosses a log bridge, climbs a brushy bank, and enters the woods. The grade is fairly easy with some muddy footing for 0.2 mi. before swinging left and climbing steadily, with an occasional short breather. At 0.6 mi., a good viewpoint overlooking Second Connecticut Lake can be found 10 yd. to the left. The trail ends at Coot Trail at the top of a steep pitch, 0.2 mi. below the summit. Descending, Bobcat Trail diverges left from Coot Trail at a sign.

GARFIELD FALLS PATH (NHDP; USGS BOSEBUCK MTN. QUAD)

From northern trailhead (1,862 ft.) for:	⇅	⌵⌃	⟳
Complete loop to Garfield Falls (1,710 ft.) via woods road and Garfield Falls Path	1.0 mi.	200 ft.	0:35

SEC 12

Garfield Falls is a remote waterfall on the East Branch of the Dead Diamond River, accessed by a short trail after a long drive on gravel roads. From US 3, 4.7 mi. north of the dam on First Connecticut Lake, follow Magalloway Rd. as described earlier for Coot Trail. At 5.3 mi., where the route to Magalloway Mtn. turns right, continue ahead on the main haul road. At 6.4 mi., a fine view of Magalloway Mtn. is found to the right. Bear left with the main road at 8.4 mi., and at 10.7 mi., stay straight at a major intersection on the road (signs: 112-S and Garfield Falls). The main (northern) trailhead for the falls is at a kiosk (sign: Welcome to Garfield Falls) with parking area on the left at 12.0 mi.

From this trailhead, the hike to the falls is described as a loop, including a short road walk to an alternate southern trailhead. Walk a short distance south on the gravel road then turn left at a fork and descend 0.4 mi. along a woods road to its end. Here the trail (no sign) enters the woods to the left (avoid a beaten path leading ahead, down to the stream) and in 35 yd. bears left at a fork onto a newer route. The trail rises gently along the East Branch with one brief descent and reaches a pool below the falls at 0.4 mi. Here, the trail turns left and climbs wooden steps to a bluff with an excellent view of the falls, which drop 40 ft. amid pools and steep ledges. The trail climbs well above the falls, swings right, and ascends easily then bears left to the kiosk at the northern trailhead.

FALLS IN THE RIVER TRAIL (TCTA; COHOS TRAIL MAP, USGS SECOND CONNECTICUT LAKE QUAD)

Cumulative from parking area on US 3 by Second Connecticut Lake dam (1,874 ft.) to:	⇅	↗	⟳
Falls in the River (1,760 ft.)	1.4 mi.	0 ft. (rev. 100 ft.)	0:40
Moose Alley Trail (1,730 ft.)	2.1 mi.	100 ft. (rev. 150 ft.)	1:05
US 3 (1,740 ft.) via spur trail	2.2 mi.	100 ft.	1:10

This section of the Cohos Trail delivers a scenic walk along the Connecticut River and provides access to a rocky cascade and gorge known as Falls in the River. Falls in the River Trail (sign) begins at the south side of the parking area by the Second Connecticut Lake dam, on the east side of US 3, 2.2 mi. north of the jct. with Magalloway Rd. and 9.0 mi. south of the customs station at the U.S.–Canada border.

The trail, well blazed in yellow, enters the woods and descends along the west side of the Connecticut River, rather steeply at first, then at easy to moderate grades. At 0.4 mi., a spur leads 10 yd. left, to the edge of the river. The main trail follows the river at easy grades then bears away from the river, traverses a swampy area on wooden walkways, passes red boundary blazes, and crosses a path in a clearing. The trail swings left back to the river at 0.9 mi. and runs along a scenic stretch where the wide, slow-moving river is bordered by meadows. The trail swings right away from the river, ascends slightly, turns left onto an old logging road for 30 yd., then turns left off it.

After running along a bank high above the river, the trail descends through spruces, and at 1.4 mi., it passes ledges down to the left overlooking Falls in the River (sign). Here, the trail turns sharply right, climbs briefly, runs along a high bank, then descends moderately back to the river and swings right to follow it at 1.8 mi. The trail again bears right, away from the river, crosses a bridge over Big Brook, and ascends gradually to meet Moose Alley Trail at 2.1 mi. To the right, a spur leads 0.1 mi. to a trailhead on US 3 (sign: Moose Alley Trail), 1.5 mi. south of the Second Connecticut Lake dam. To the left, Moose Alley Trail, part of the Cohos Trail, leads 1.6 mi. to Magalloway Rd.

FOURTH CONNECTICUT LAKE TRAIL (TNC; COHOS TRAIL MAP, USGS SECOND CONNECTICUT LAKE AND PROSPECT HILL QUADS)

From U.S. Customs station (2,360 ft.) for:	⇅	↗	↺
Complete loop around Fourth Connecticut Lake (2,670 ft.)	2.0 mi.	400 ft.	1:10

This trail, the northernmost section of the Cohos Trail, begins at the U.S. Customs station at the Canadian border on US 3. Parking is available in a designated area (sign) on the east side of the road. The trail begins at a TNC signboard on a grassy bank on the west side of the road, just north of the customs building. (Hikers do not need to check in with customs officials.) Follow a worn footway along the international boundary uphill to the left (west). The boundary is a wide, brushy swath cut through the forest and marked at irregular intervals by brass disks set in concrete. The trail climbs steeply with rough footing, swings left (southwest) at 0.1 mi. and eases, then resumes the climb, with occasional views of the border mountains to the northeast. The trail levels again, and at 0.5 mi., it continues ahead into the woods (sign) as the boundary swath swings to the right. The trail descends gradually through dense woods to a loop jct. at 0.7 mi. From here, the trail makes a 0.6-mi. loop around the small, boggy lake, with minor ups and downs; for the best view of the lake, follow the loop 10 yd. to the right and then follow a short side path left to the shore. On the southeast side of the pond, the loop crosses two small outlet streams that form the initial flow of the Connecticut River.

SEC 12

APPENDIX A

HELPFUL INFORMATION AND CONTACTS

Organization	Office	Phone number
Appalachian Mountain Club (AMC)	Main Office	617-523-0636 (membership, headquarters)
	Pinkham Notch Visitor Center	603-466-2727 (reservations)
AMC Four Thousand Footer Club		
Appalachian Trail Conservancy (ATC)	Main Office	304-535-6331
	New England Regional Office	413-528-8002
Chatham Trails Association (CTA)		
Chocorua Mountain Club (CMC)		
Cohos Trail Association (TCTA)		
Dartmouth Outdoor Programs Office		603-646-2428
Dartmouth Outing Club (DOC), Director of Trails and Shelters		603-646-2429
Friends of Pondicherry National Wildlife Refuge		
Lakes Region Conservation Trust (LRCT)	Main Office	603-253-3301
Leave No Trace	Main Office	800-332-4100
Maine Appalachian Trail Club (MATC)		
Maine Bureau of Parks and Lands (MBPL)	Western Public Lands Office	207-778-8231
Mount Washington Observatory	Mount Washington	603-356-2137 (weather phone: ext. 1)
National Weather Service	Gray Weather Forecast Office	207-688-3216 (office), 603-225-5191 (forecast)
The Nature Conservancy (TNC), Green Hills Preserve		603-356-8833

Address or Location	Website, Email
10 City Square, Boston, MA 02129	outdoors.org
PO Box 298, 361 Route 16, Gorham, NH 03581	
PO Box 444, Exeter, NH 03833	amc4000footer.org
PO Box 807, Harpers Ferry, WV 25425	appalachiantrail.org,
PO Box 264/62 Undermountain Rd., South Egremont, MA 01258	info@appalachiantrail.org
2062 Main Rd., Chatham, NH 03813	chathamtrails.org, president@chathamtrails.org
Chocorua Mountain Club, Chocorua, NH 03817	chocorualakeconservancy.org/ mt-chocorua/cmc/
PO Box 82, Lancaster, NH 03584	cohostrail.org, cohos@cohostrail.org
Dartmouth College, PO Box 9, Hanover, NH 03755	outdoors.dartmouth.edu/opo
Dartmouth College, PO Box 9, Hanover, NH 03755	outdoors.dartmouth.edu
	friendsofpondicherry.org
PO Box 766, Center Harbor, NH 03226	lrct.org, lrct@lrct.org
PO Box 997, Boulder, CO 80306	lnt.org
PO Box 283, Augusta, ME 04332	matc.org, info@matc.org
PO Box 327, Farmington, ME 04938	maine.gov/dacf/parks
PO Box 2310, North Conway, NH 03860	mountwashington.org
PO Box 1208, 1 Weather Lane, Route 231, Gray, ME 04039	weather.gov/gyx
PO Box 310, North Conway, NH 03860	nature.org

Organization	Office	Phone number
New Hampshire Department of Resources and Economic Development, Division of Parks and Recreation (NHDP)		603-271-3556
NHDP Camping Reservations		1-877-647-2757
New Hampshire State Police		800-525-5555 (emergency in NH only) Emergency cell phone in NH, ME, MA: *77
Randolph Mountain Club (RMC)		
Rivendell Trails Association (RTA)		
Shelburne Trails Club		
Society for the Protection of New Hampshire Forests (SPNHF)		603-224-9945
Squam Lakes Association		603-968-7336
Upper Valley Land Trust		603-643-6626
WMNF Camping Information	Campground Reservations	877-444-6777
WMNF Offices and Ranger Districts (RDs)	Androscoggin Ranger District	603-466-2713, TTY 603-466-2856
	Forest Supervisor	603-536-6100, TTY 603-536-3665
	White Mountain Visitor Center	603-745-3816
	Lincoln Woods Visitor Center	603-630-5190
	Pemigewasset Ranger District	603-536-6100, TTY 603-536-3665
	Saco Ranger District	603-447-5448, TTY 603-447-3121
Waterville Valley Athletic & Improvement Association (WVAIA)		
Wonalancet Outdoor Club (WODC)		

Address or Location	Website, Email
172 Pembroke Rd., PO Box 1856, Concord, NH 03302-1856	nhstateparks.org, nhparks@dred.nh.gov
Camping Reservations, Division of Parks and Recreation, PO Box 1856, Concord, NH 03302-1856	newhampshirestateparks .reserveamerica.com
	nh.gov/safety/divisions/nhsp/
PO Box 279, Gorham, NH 03581	randolphmountainclub.org, info@randolphmountainclub.org
PO Box 202, Fairlee, VT 05045	crossrivendelltrail.org, rivendelltrail@rivendellstudent.org
	facebook.com/ ShelburneTrailsClub/, shelburnetrails@gmail.com
54 Portsmouth St., Concord, NH 03301	forestsociety.org, info@forestsociety.org
PO Box 204, Holderness, NH 03245	squamlakes.org, info@squamlakes.org
19 Buck Road, Hanover, NH 03755	uvlt.org
PO Box 1354, Campton, NH 03223	icampnh.com, recreation.gov
300 Glen Rd., Gorham, NH 03581 (at south end of town along NH 16)	www.fs.usda.gov/whitemountain
71 White Mountain Drive, Campton, NH 03223 (west side of I-93 at Exit 27)	
Exit 32 off I-93	
On NH 112 at Exit 32 off I-93, Lincoln Woods Trail trailhead on Kancamagus Highway	
71 White Mountain Drive, Campton, NH 03223 (west side of I-93 at Exit 27)	
RFD 1, Box 94, Conway, NH 03818 (at 33 Kancamagus Highway, just west of NH 16)	
PO Box 412, Waterville Valley, NH 03215	wvaia.org, wvaiatrails@gmail.com
HCR 64, PO Box 248, Wonalancet, NH 03897	wodc.org, trails@wodc.org

APPENDIX B

4,000-FOOTERS

AMC's Four Thousand Footer Club was formed in 1957 to bring together hikers who had traveled to some of the less frequently visited sections of the White Mountains. The Four Thousand Footer Committee recognizes three lists of peaks: the White Mountain 4,000-footers, the New England 4,000-footers, and the New England Hundred Highest. Applicants for the White Mountain Four Thousand Footer Club must climb all 48 peaks in New Hampshire. To qualify for membership, a hiker must climb on foot to and from each summit on the list. The official lists of the 4,000-footers, in New Hampshire, Maine, and Vermont are included at the end of this appendix. Criteria for mountains on the official list are (1) each peak must be 4,000 ft. high, and (2) each peak must rise 200 ft. above the low point of its connecting ridge with a higher neighbor. All 67 4,000-footers, are reached by well-defined trails, although the paths to Owl's Head and Mt. Redington, as well as some short spur trails to other summits, are not officially maintained. Applicants for the New England Four Thousand Footer Club must also climb the 14 peaks in Maine and the five in Vermont. Separate awards are given to those who climb all peaks on a list in winter; to qualify as a winter ascent, the hike must not begin before the hour and minute of the beginning of winter (winter solstice) or end after the hour and minute of the end of winter (spring equinox).

If you are interested in becoming a member of one or more of the clubs, please visit amc4000footer.org or send a self-addressed, stamped envelope to the Four Thousand Footer Committee, Appalachian Mountain Club, PO Box 444, Exeter, NH 03833, and an information packet, including application forms, will be sent to you. If you are interested in the New England Four Thousand Footer Club or the New England Hundred Highest Club, please specify this in your letter, as these lists are not routinely included in the basic information packet. After climbing each peak, please record the date of the ascent, companions, if any, and other remarks.

On the following lists, elevations have been obtained from the latest USGS maps, some of which are now metric, requiring conversion from meters to feet. Where no exact elevation is given on the map, the elevation has been estimated by adding half the contour interval to the highest contour shown on the map; elevations so obtained are marked on the list with an asterisk (*). The elevations given here for several peaks in the Presidential region differ from those given elsewhere in this book because the Four Thousand Footer Committee uses the USGS maps as the authority for all elevations, whereas in the rest of the book, the Bradford Washburn map of the Presidential Range supersedes the USGS maps in the area it covers.

4,000-FOOTERS IN NEW HAMPSHIRE

| | Elevation | | |
Mountain	(feet)	(meters)	Date Climbed
1. Washington	6,288	1,916.6	
2. Adams	5,774	1,760	
3. Jefferson	5,712	1,741	
4. Monroe	5,384*	1,641*	
5. Madison	5,367	1,636	
6. Lafayette	5,260*	1,603*	
7. Lincoln	5,089	1,551	
8. South Twin	4,902	1,494	
9. Carter Dome	4,832	1,473	
10. Moosilauke	4,802	1,464	
11. Eisenhower	4,780*	1,457*	
12. North Twin	4,761	1,451	
13. Carrigain	4,700*	1,433*	
14. Bond	4,698	1,432	
15. Middle Carter	4,610*	1,405*	
16. West Bond	4,540*	1,384*	
17. Garfield	4,500*	1,372*	
18. Liberty	4,459	1,359	

| | | Elevation | |
Mountain	(feet)	(meters)	Date Climbed
19. South Carter	4,430*	1,350*	
20. Wildcat	4,422	1,348	
21. Hancock	4,420*	1,347*	
22. South Kinsman	4,358	1,328	
23. Field	4,340*	1,323*	
24. Osceola	4,340*	1,323*	
25. Flume	4,328	1,319	
26. South Hancock	4,319	1,316	
27. Pierce (Clinton)	4,310	1,314	
28. North Kinsman	4,293	1,309	
29. Willey	4,285	1,306	
30. Bondcliff	4,265	1,300	
31. Zealand	4,260*	1,298*	
32. North Tripyramid	4,180*	1,274*	
33. Cabot	4,170*	1,271*	
34. East Osceola	4,156	1,267	
35. Middle Tripyramid	4,140*	1,262*	
36. Cannon	4,100*	1,250*	
37. Hale	4,054	1,236	
38. Jackson	4,052	1,235	
39. Tom	4,051	1,235	
40. Wildcat D	4,050*	1,234*	
41. Moriah	4,049	1,234	
42. Passaconaway	4,043	1,232	
43. Owl's Head	4,025	1,227	
44. Galehead	4,024	1,227	
45. Whiteface	4,020*	1,225*	
46. Waumbek	4,006	1,221	
47. Isolation	4,004	1,220	
48. Tecumseh	4,003	1,220	

4,000-FOOTERS IN MAINE

Mountain	Elevation (feet)	(meters)	Date Climbed
1. Katahdin, Baxter Peak	5,268	1,606	
2. Katahdin, Hamlin Peak	4,756	1,450	
3. Sugarloaf	4,250*	1,295*	
4. Crocker	4,228	1,289	
5. Old Speck	4,170*	1,271*	
6. North Brother	4,151	1,265	
7. Bigelow, West Peak	4,145	1,263	
8. Saddleback	4,120	1,256	
9. Bigelow, Avery Peak	4,090*	1,247*	
10. Abraham	4,050*	1,234*	
11. South Crocker	4,050*	1,234*	
12. Saddleback, the Horn	4,041	1,232	
13. Redington	4,010*	1,222*	
14. Spaulding	4,010*	1,222*	

4,000-FOOTERS IN VERMONT

Mountain	Elevation (feet)	(meters)	Date Climbed
1. Mansfield	4,393	1,339	
2. Killington	4,235	1,291	
3. Camel's Hump	4,083	1,244	
4. Ellen	4,083	1,244	
5. Abraham	4,006	1,221	

*No exact elevation is given on the map; therefore, elevation has been estimated by adding half the contour interval to the highest contour shown on the map.

INDEX

Trail names in **bold type** indicate a detailed description found in the text.

Where multiple page references appear, bold numbering indicates the main entry or entries for the trail.

[Bracketed information] indicates which of the six maps displays the feature and where, by map section letter and number.

AMC Books

White Mountain National Forest Trail Map Set
AMC Books

Have you loved your White Mountain trail maps to death? Upgrade to this durable, lightweight set printed on waterproof Tyvek, featuring the same comprehensive coverage of the White Mountain National Forest across six full-color, GPS-rendered, AMC-tested maps.

$29.95 · 978-1-62842-077-7

WMNF Map & Guide, 3rd Edition
AMC Books

If you have only one trail map of the White Mountains, make it this one, featuring the entire national forest. Waterproof and tear-resistant, this newly revised third edition is larger scale and easier to read, with updated safety, planning, and packing tips; plus, a 4,000-footer checklist and 24 recommended hikes for all skill levels.

$9.95 · 978-1-62842-093-7

AMC's Best Day Hikes in the White Mountains, 3rd Edition
Robert N. Buchsbaum

Now in its third edition and available for the first time in full color, this trusted resource takes you to 60 of the most unforgettable day hikes in New Hampshire and Maine's White Mountain National Forest.

$19.95 · 978-1-62842-028-9

Southern New Hampshire Trail Guide, 4th Edition
Steven D. Smith

This trusted companion to AMC's *White Mountain Guide* covers trails south of the White Mountain National Forest, including Pisgah State Park, the Lakes Region, and the seacoast. With full-color, GPS-rendered, AMC-tested maps, it's a must-have for every New England hiker.

$23.95 · 978-1-934028-96-4

Find these and other AMC titles, as well as ebooks, through ebook stores, booksellers, and outdoor retailers. Or order directly from AMC at amcstore/outdoors.org or call 800-262-4455.